BRITISH MILITARY AIRCRAFT SERIALS

1911-1979

BRITISH MILITARY AIRCRAFT SERIALS

1911-1979

Bruce Robertson

PSL Patrick Stephens, Cambridge

First published in 1964 by Ian Allan
Fourth revised edition 1971
This revised edition published by Patrick Stephens Ltd 1979

British Library Cataloguing in Publication Data

Robertson, Bruce
British military aircraft serials, 1911-1979.
— 5th revised ed.
1. Airplanes, Military — Identification marks
2. Great Britain. Royal Air Force
I. Title
358.4/18/3 UG1245.G7

ISBN 0 85059 360 3

Printed in Great Britain on Opaque MF 72 gsm by
The Garden City Press Limited, Letchworth,
and bound by J. M. Dent & Sons (Letchworth) Limited,
for the publishers Patrick Stephens Limited,
Bar Hill, Cambridge, CB3 8EL, England

CONTENTS

FOREWORD

THIS BOOK is a compilation of all aircraft known to have been ordered, acquired or impressed for British military service. The British Services concerned are the Royal Flying Corps, Royal Naval Air Service, Royal Air Force, Fleet Air Arm, Army Air Corps and Air Training Corps. Also included are service aircraft held on charge by Ministries that have acted as agencies for the Services, *viz.*, the past Ministry of Munitions, Ministry of Supply, Ministry of Aviation, Ministry of Technology and the recent Ministry of Aviation Supplies.

The compilation is by the official service serial numbers, in sequence, with the aircraft type details appropriate to each number or range of numbers. Allocations are given from the inauguration of numbering to the present day. The term "aircraft" is taken to include aeroplanes, seaplanes, airships, blimps, helicopters and gliders.

In general the simple numbered series, followed by alphabetical prefix letters, is in chronological sequence, although some exceptions do occur. They are recorded here in number/letter sequence for ease of reference.

Throughout the book the use of hyphens between numbers may be taken as "to" and a stroke as "and": *e.g.*, AA100-149 would be AA100 to AA149 inclusive, and remarks such as "K5066 & K5069 became G-AHVO/RZ" may be taken to mean that the two serials gave way to G-AHVO and G-AHRZ respectively. Where aircraft were constructed other than by the designing firm this has been indicated in the remarks column.

There have in the past been many popular misconceptions concerning serial numbers. In some service log books the prefix number to the serial has not been given and in some cases the unit number, not the serial number, is given. Even in many official documents the aircraft's identity letter has been given as a prefix letter in lieu of the current serial prefix.

Late allocations to operational aircraft have not been included for obvious reasons of security.

In recording aircraft names and designations, the official service name and designation at the time of service is given. Thus a Tempest V converted as a target tug in 1950 after the mark number system had changed from Roman to Arabic, becomes T.T.5 *not* T.T.V.

The remarks column is intended to include reference to all changes to the standard form given in the Aircraft Type column. Where space permits further detail has been included such as disposal to other air forces.

I give my grateful thanks to J. M. Bruce, M.A. and Michael J. F. Bowyer who read portions of the original MSS, and the late Peter W. Moss for information on impressed aircraft. My thanks are also due to Miss Rose Coombs of the Imperial War Museum and F. G. Swanborough who put me in touch with valuable sources of information. In particular, I am indebted to Ray Sturtivant who has made valuable contributions from the first edition. Others to whom I give my grateful thanks for additions over the years are: R. C. B. Ashworth, P. H. Butler, Robert J. Carter, J. M. Cheers, E. F. Cheesman, R. W. Deacon, H. J. Fairhead, M. P. Fillmore, Michael H. Goodhall, Donald H. Hannah, Terry Hobbs, Philip Jarrett, G. A. Jenks, Stuart Leslie, Roger Levy, Keith Mann, Tim Mason, D. E. Monk, E. B. Morgan, James D. Oughton, Arthur Pearcy, Jnr., Stephen Ransom, Alex Revell, Douglas Rough, the late H. H. Russell, Gerard Terry, J. D. Thomas, Lt. Col. J. D. Thompson, U.S.A.F., Norbert F. Yaggi and Frank Yeoman.

APRIL 1979 BRUCE ROBERTSON

LIGHTER-THAN-AIR CRAFT

THE Army acquired its first airship in 1907; this and all subsequent were given names. The Navy acquired its first airship in 1911 and adopted a simple numbering system starting at No. 1; but to distinguish rigid airships (i.e. with gas envelopes contained within a metal or wood frame) from non-rigid airships (i.e. the gas-filled envelope conditioning shape as with a balloon), an ' R ' prefix was added to the number allotted to rigid types.

The Naval Wing of the Royal Flying Corps, which in July 1914 became officially the Royal Naval Air Service, took control of all military airships from July 1st 1914 and the former named Army airships were renumbered in the naval series as Nos 17-22 and are thereby out of chronological sequence as regards their date of building.

BRITISH MILITARY AIRSHIPS— Original Series and ' R ' Series

Type, Name or Number	*Remarks on Class, Builder and Power Units*
Nulli Secundus	Built at the Balloon Factory, Farnborough, this was the first military airship constructed in Britain. Of 50,000 cub. ft. it first flew in September 1907 powered by an Antoinette engine of 40 h.p. driving two metal-bladed propellers. Rebuilt as Nulli Secundus II.
Nulli Secundus II	Nulli Secundus rebuilt with Lebaudy-type car in 1908.
Baby	Built 1908-1909 at the Balloon Factory of 21,000 cub. ft. powered by 2 Buchet engines later replaced by an R.E.P. engine.
Clement Bayard	Built by Clement Bayard and delivered from Paris October 16th 1910 under *Daily Mail* reader presentation arrangements. Taken over by Army but owing to 13,000 cub. ft. of gas being necessary daily was deflated and stored at Farnborough.
Lebaudy	Built by Lebaudy Freres of 350,000 cub. ft. under subscription arrangements by *Morning Post* readers. Powered by two 150 h.p. engines was flown to Farnborough October 26th, 1910, but was damaged entering shed which was too small. After repair was wrecked on trial flight, May 1911.
Naval Airship No. 1 (*Mayfly*)	First British naval airship. Built by Vickers of rigid type of 660,000 cub. ft. powered by two 200 h.p. Wolseley engines. Broke back on initial trials in September 1911.
Naval Airship No. 2 (ex-Willows No. 4)	Small non-rigid of 24,000 cub. ft. for training purposes designed by T. E. Willows and built in France and Spain; powered by 35 h.p. Anzani engine. Envelope used for the blimp S.S.1.
Naval Aircraft No. 3 (Astra Torres)	Non-rigid of 229,450 cub. ft., powered by two 210 h.p. engines, ordered from France in 1912. Delivered 1913 and was equipped with Hotchkiss machine-gun. Deleted May 1916.
Naval Airship No. 4 (Parseval PL18)	Non-rigid of 330,000 cub. ft. ordered from Germany in 1912. Powered by two 170 h.p. Maybach engines. Deleted July 1917.
Nos. 5-7 (Parseval PL19-21)	Ordered from Germany as same class as No. 4, but were held by Germany when war was declared. Substitute airships were ordered from Vickers powered by two 200 h.p. Renault engines.
No. 8 (Astra Torres)	Delivered from France. Deleted May 1916.

Type, Name or Number	*Remarks on Class, Builder and Power Units*
R9 (Modified Z.4)	Built by Vickers at Barrow. Powered by two 180 h.p. and one 250 h.p. Maybach engines. Was first airship to bear the ' R ' for rigid prefix marking. Trials from November 27th 1916. To station at Howden April 4th 1917.
No. 10 (Astra Torres)	French-built. Envelope used for blimp C.1.
Nos. 11-13 (Forlanini)	Ordered July 1913 from Italy but not delivered.
R14-15 (R9 Type)	Order cancelled.
No. 16 (Astra Torres)	French-built. Deleted May 1916.
No. 17 *Beta* rebuilt as *Beta II*	Completed in May 1910 at the Balloon Factory for the Army, powered by a 35 h.p. Green engine driving two propellers. Was of non-rigid type of 35,000 cub. ft. Rebuilt with 45 h.p. Clerget engine in 1912. Transferred to Navy January 1914. Deleted May 1916.
No. 18 *Gamma*	Designed at Farnborough, but envelope of 75,000 cub. ft. made by Astra of Paris. Car and carrying frame made in England. Delivered to Army powered by an 80 h.p. Green engine driving swivelling propellers for which gearing and shafting was made by Rolls Royce. In 1911 two 45 h.p. Iris engines substituted. In 1912 re-rigged with envelope of 101,000 cub. ft. Transferred to Navy January 1914. Deleted May 1916.
No. 19 *Delta*	Building at the Balloon Factory started in 1911, but due to alterations completion delayed until August 1912. Was of non-rigid type similar to Parseval, powered by two White & Poppe engines. Transferred to Navy January 1914. Deleted May 1916.
No. 20 *Eta*	Built at the Royal Aircraft Factory for Army and completed August 1913, powered by two 80 h.p. Canton Unné engines, it was of 118,000 cub. ft. Transferred to Navy January 1914. Deleted May 1916.
Nos. 21-22 *Epsilon I & II*	Ordered for Army. Building when Navy took over airships. Erected at Kingsnorth but found unsatisfactory in view of standardised blimps becoming available.
R23 (R23 Class Ship)	Built by Vickers at Barrow, powered by three Rolls Royce Eagle IIIs and an Eagle VI. Delivered to Pulham September 15th 1917. Deleted September 1919.
R24 (R23 Class)	Built by Beardmore at Inchinnin, powered by four Rolls-Royce Eagle IIIs. Delivered to East Fortune October 28th 1917, later to Pulham station.
R25 (R23 Class)	Built by Armstrong Whitworth at Selby, powered as R24. Delivered to Howden October 15th 1917, later on Cranwell station. Scrapped September 1919.
R26 (R23 Class)	Built by Vickers at Barrow, powered by four Rolls-Royce Eagles. Stationed at Pulham. Scrapped March 1919.
R27 (R23X Class)	Built by Beardmore at Inchinnin. Powered by four Rolls-Royce Eagle IIs. Commissioned June 29th 1918, Deleted August 16th 1919.
R28 (R23X Class)	Ordered from Beardmore & Vickers, but cancelled before completion.
R29 (R23X Class)	Built by Armstrong Whitworth in 1918. Powered as R26. Stationed East Fortune 1918-19. Deleted October 24th 1919.
R30 (R23X Class)	Ordered from Armstrong Whitworth, but cancelled before completion.
R31 (R31 Class Ship)	Built by Shorts at Bedford on Schutte Lanz principles, powered by five Rolls-Royce Eagles. Deleted at Howden July, 1919.

Type, Name or Number	*Remarks on Class, Builder and Power Units*
R32 (R31 Class)	Built by Shorts at Bedford. Power as R31. Scrapped 1921.
R33 (R33 Class Ship)	Built by Armstrong Whitworth at Barlow. Powered by five 270 h.p. Sunbeam Maoris. Stationed at Pulham, East Fortune and Howden. Became G-FAAG. Scrapped 1927.
R34 (R33 Class)	Built by Beardmore at Inchinnin. Powered as R33. Made Atlantic crossings.
R35 (R33 Class)	Ordered from Armstrong Whitworth at Barlow but cancelled before completion.
R36 (Large R33 Class)	Built by Beardmore at Inchinnin. Powered by four 350 h.p. Sunbeam engines. Became G-FAAF. Scrapped.
R37 (Large R33 Class)	Ordered from Shorts at Bedford. Cancelled before completion.
R38 (Large R33 Class)	Built by Shorts at Bedford. Sold to U.S.A. as ZR-2. Crashed in Humber on trials August 24th 1921.
R39	Ordered from Armstrong Whitworth at Barlow, but cancelled before completion.
R40-41	Ordered from Beardmore and Vickers, but cancelled before completion.
R80 (Small R33)	Ordered from Vickers at Barrow with four 250 h.p. Wolseley-Maybachs, delivered to Cardington but not used.

N.B.—The R100 and R101 were purely civil airships.

NAVAL BLIMPS

THE naval blimps were non-rigid airships of several types. They were numbered in separate series, starting at No. 1 for each type, prefixed with significant letters according to that type. Each one built is listed below in alphabetical/numerical sequence. Except for a few retained for coastal mine-watching, all were scrapped during 1919 and where individual craft were deleted before the end of the war their fate is given in the Remarks column. Locations given relate to the normal station for the particular craft. Airships rebuilt or replaced were given an ' A ' suffix to their number to denote that the craft was not as originally built.

Coastal Type

These blimps initially fitted with 150 h.p. Sunbeams were variously fitted with different engines so that, where known, the actual power units fitted are given in the remarks. Where engines of different power were fitted in the one craft, the higher-powered engine was normally at the rear and the other at the front of the car which was constructed from joining two Avro 510 fuselages together. C1 was of 190 feet long with an envelope of 140,000 cub. ft. capacity, but all others were 200 feet long with envelopes of 170,000 cub. ft. capacity.

No.	*Remarks*
C1	2×150 h.p. Sunbeam. First flew 9.6.15. Experimental work at Kingsnorth.
C2	110 h.p. Berliet & 220 h.p. Renault. Mullion & Howden.
C3	150 h.p. Sunbeam & 220 h.p. Renault. Pembroke & East Fortune.
C4	110 h.p. Berliet & 220 h.p. Renault. Howden & Longside.

No.	*Remarks*
C5	2 × 150 h.p. Sunbeam. Longside. Replaced 30.1.17 as C5A. 160 h.p. Sunbeam & 220 h.p. Renault. Pembroke, Longside & Howden.
C6	2 × 150 h.p. Sunbeam. Lost at sea from Pembroke 24.3.17.
C7	150 h.p. Sunbeam and 220 h.p. Renault. East Fortune and Longside.
C8	2 × 150 h.p. Sunbeam. Crashed into sea from Kingsnorth 9.6.16.
C9	110 h.p. Berliet and 220 h.p. Renault. Mullion and Howden.
C10	2 × 150 h.p. Sunbeam. Mullion. Replaced as C10A 10.10.16. 150 h.p. Sunbeam and 220 h.p. Renault. Longside.
C11	Rebuilt at Kingsnorth after hitting hill flying from Howden 23.4.17. Power units not known.
C12	Presumed utilised for prototype of C Star series as C*1.
C13	Number apparently not used.
C14	150 h.p. and 160 h.p. Sunbeam. Longside. Replaced as C14A. 110 h.p. Berliet and 220 h.p. Renault. Used for experiments at Pulham.
C15	Rebuilt at Kingsnorth. Further detail not known.
C16	2 × 150 h.p. Sunbeam. East Fortune. Deleted 14.9.16.
C17	2 × 150 h.p. Sunbeam. Shot down in flames off North Foreland 21.4.17.
C18	2 × 150 h.p. Sunbeam. Longside.
C19	100 h.p. Green and 220 h.p. Renault. Howden and Capel.
C20	2 × 150 h.p. Sunbeam presumed. East Fortune. Deleted 22.12.17.
C21	100 h.p. Green and 220 h.p. Renault. Howden.
C22	2 × 150 h.p. Sunbeam. Mullion. Lost at sea 21.3.17.
C23	2 × 150 h.p. Sunbeam presumed. Replaced by C23A. 150 h.p. Sunbeam and 220 h.p. Renault. Mullion.
C24	2 × 150 h.p. Sunbeam. Rebuilding at Kingsnorth 1918.
C25	100 h.p. Green and 240 h.p. Renault. East Fortune, Mullion and Longside.
C26	2 × 150 h.p. Sunbeam presumed. Pulham. Blown over Holland and interned 13.12.17.
C27	2 × 150 h.p. Sunbeam presumed. Shot down in flames over North Sea by Brandenburg W.12 floatplanes.

In addition Ca, Cb, Cc & Cd were produced for Russia and Ce for France.

Improved Coastal Type —C Star

The improved Coastal blimps, numbered in a separate series with a 'star' between the 'C' prefix letter and the number, were of 210 feet in length and had an envelope of 210,000 cub. ft. C1 had a 110 h.p. Berliet replaced later by a 240 h.p. Fiat, and a 220 h.p. Renault, but all others had a 110 h.p. Berliet and a 240 h.p. Fiat as standard power units. Since all survived the war and were scrapped 1919-1920, and power units were standardised, remarks are confined to stations.

C*1	East Fortune	C*6	Mullion & Howden
C*2	Howden	C*7	East Fortune & Howden
C*3	East Fortune	C*8	Cranwell & East Fortune
C*4	Howden, E. Fortune & Longside	C*9	Howden
C*5	Longside	C*10	Pulham & Howden

North Sea Type

The North Sea (NS) Type were larger craft of 262 feet in length and with a capacity of 360,000 cub. ft. Precise allocation of engine types to individual craft is not known, but the policy effected was original powering with two 250 h.p. Rolls-Royce engines which, by the end of the war, were replaced by two Fiats of 240 h.p. up to and including NS11 and of 300 h.p. for NS12-18.

No.	*Remarks*
NS1	Trials from 2.2.17. Replaced at Kingsnorth 22.2.18.
NS2	Wrecked at Stonehaven near Stowmarket 27.6.17.
NS3	East Fortune. Wrecked off Dunbar in gale during 1918.
NS4	East Fortune and Longside.
NS5	Longside. Force landed at Agton 22.2.18.
NS6	Longside.
NS7	East Fortune. Instructional craft for U.S. Navy 1919.
NS8	East Fortune. Did War Loans flight tour.
NS9	
NS10	
NS11	Longside. Lost at sea in mine-search off N.E. coast, 15.7.19.
NS12	Longside.
NS13	Believed number not used.
NS14	Built for U.S. Government; transferred 8.11.18.
NS15	Held in reserve at Kingsnorth.
NS16	Held in reserve at Wormwood Scrubs.
NS17	Held in reserve at Kingsnorth.
NS18	Still under construction when war ended.

K1 a proposed Improved North Sea blimp was cancelled before construction was completed.

Submarine Scout Type

The Submarine Scouts (SS) were relatively small airships of 145 feet in length and of 70,000 cub. ft., built with three different types of cars as follows: SS1-26 B.E.2c fuselage type car with 70 or 75 h.p. Renault engines in general, but SS23-25 had 75 h.p. Rolls-Royce Hawks; SS27-39 had Maurice Farman nacelle type cars with Hawk engines, but known exceptions are notified in remarks column; SS40-49 had Armstrong Whitworth FK3 fuselage type cars with 100 h.p. Green engines.

SS1	Used envelope of Airship No. 2. Burnt landing at Capel 7.5.15.
SS2	Unsatisfactory and not accepted from makers.
SS3	Shipped out to Mudros. Presumed deleted in 1918.
SS4-6	Transferred to Italian Government.
SS7-8	Shipped out to Kassandra 1916. Presumed deleted 1918.
SS9	Replaced at Polegate 13.9.16. SS9A used at Polegate for mooring experiments.
SS10	Replaced at Capel after a crash into the Channel 10.9.15 as 10A which was replaced 2.6.16 by SS10B which was transferred to the Italian Government.
SS11	Transferred to the Italian Government.
SS12	Replaced at Capel 14.3.17.

No.	*Remarks*
SS13	Number presumed not used.
SS14	Rebuilt at Kingsnorth as SS14A with Hawk engine. Pembroke and Pulham.
SS15	Pembroke. Wrecked off Lundy Island 18.1.17.
SS16	Polegate. Rebuilding at Wormwood Scrubs early 1918 and believed deleted later that year.
SS17	Shipped to Kassandra.
SS18	Anglesey. Lost at sea 9.11.16.
SS19	Shipped to Mudros.
SS20	Luce Bay and Wormwood Scrubs. Deleted during 1918.
SS21-22	Transferred to French and Italian Governments respectively.
SS23	Luce Bay. Deleted during 1918.
SS24	Anglesey and Wormwood Scrubs. Deleted during 1918.
SS25	Anglesey. Deleted during 1918.
SS26	Transferred to French Government.
SS27	Deleted at Marquise 5.8.15.
SS28	Rebuilt at Cranwell as SS28A early in 1918.
SS29	Training craft at Cranwell.
SS30	Wrecked and rebuilt as SS30A. Cranwell.
SS31	Known as " Flying Bedstead " at Kingsnorth. Rebuilt as SS31A as training craft at Cranwell.
SS32	Replaced at Folkestone 10.10.16 as SS32A. When repaired at Barrow early in 1918 was reported to have 75 h.p. Renault.
SS33	Rebuilt early in 1918 at Wormwood Scrubs, but deleted same year.
SS34	Experimental fitting of Nieuport seaplane floats. Believed deleted in 1917.
SS35	Luce Bay, then used for experimental work at Pulham.
SS36	Non-standard with 75 h.p. Renault. Pulham.
SS37	Pembroke. Rebuilt as SS37A with 110 h.p. Berliet. Cranwell.
SS38	Luce Bay. Lost at Sea 25.2.17.
SS39	Used at Cranwell for training. Rebuilt as SS39A with 110 h.p. Berliet.
SS40	Rebuilt early 1918 at Wormwood Scrubs and shipped to Kassandra.
SS41	Caldale. Deleted in 1918.
SS42	Pembroke. Crashed 15.9.16. Replaced as SS42A 4.10.16 and believed deleted 1917.
SS43	Replaced at Pembroke 4.10.16 and shipped to Kassandra. Returned to U.K. in 1917.
SS44-47	Transferred to Italian Government.
SS48-49	Transferred to French Government.

Submarine Scout Experimentals

The experimental batch of Submarine Scout blimps (SSE) built at R.N.A.S. Depots were an attempt to increase the power of the SS Type and were powered by two 75 h.p. Rolls Royce Hawk engines.

SSE1	Built at Wormwood Scrubs and sent to Pulham. Proved unsatisfactory.
SSE2	Known as " Mullion Twin " at Mullion. Also used at Pulham.
SSE3	Trials at Kingsnorth.

Submarine Scout Patrol Type

The Submarine Scout Patrol (SSP) craft were modified SS Type initially fitted with 100 h.p. Green engines and the three surviving the war of the six built were re-engined with 110 h.p. Berliets.

No.	*Remarks*
SSP1	Operational at Anglesey, training craft at Cranwell.
SSP2	Cardale. Lost at sea 26.11.17.
SSP3	Wrecked at Faversham 21.3.17.
SSP4	Cardale. Lost at sea 22.12.17.
SSP5	Operational at Anglesey, training craft at Cranwell.
SSP6	Operational at Anglesey, experimental at Pulham, trainer at Cranwell.

Submarine Scout Twin Type

The twin-engined SS Types were known as SSTs and were in production when the war ended.

SST1-12	Sent to service with 2×75 h.p. Rolls-Royce Hawk engines: SST1 Capel, SST2 Polegate and Mullion, SST3-5 Howden, SST6 believed deleted in 1918, SST7 Howden, SST8 Capel, SST9-12 Howden.
SST13-29	Under construction at Wormwood Scrubs. 2×110 h.p. Berliets originally specified, but changed to 100 h.p. Sunbeam Dyaks. Not completed.
SST30-68	Ordered from Wormwood Scrubs with 2×75 h.p. Rolls-Royce Hawks and cancelled.
SST69-90	Under construction at Kingsnorth with 2×110 h.p. Berliets when war ended. Not completed.
SST91-115	Ordered from Kingsnorth with 2×75 h.p. Rolls-Royce Hawk engines. Order cancelled.

Submarine Scout Zero Type

Zero Type was the name given to the Standard version of patrol blimps put into large-scale production, with the short title SSZ. 75 h.p. Rolls-Royce Hawk engines were standard fitting.

SSZ1	Built at, and ran trials from, Capel.
SSZ2	No record.
SSZ3	Pulham and East Fortune.
SSZ4-5	Capel including Godmersham Park sub-station.
SSZ6	Polegate including Slindon and Upton sub-stations.
SSZ7	Polegate. Collided with SSZ10 landing at Jevington, 20.12.17. Caught fire and bomb exploded wrecking craft.
SSZ8-9	Polegate including Slindon and Upton sub-stations.
SSZ10	Polegate. Burnt at Jevington. See SSZ7.
SSZ11-13	Luce Bay.
SSZ14-15	Mullion. SSZ14 force landed at Crasvily 7.9.17 and was refitted at Brest.
SSZ16	Pembroke including sub-station at Wexford.
SSZ17	Pembroke. Destroyed by fire 22.1.18.
SSZ18-20	Capel, Polegate and Luce Bay respectively.
SSZ21-22	Transferred to French Government.

Nos	*Remarks*
SSZ23-24	Transferred to United States Government.
SSZ25	Mullion and Wormwood Scrubs.
SSZ26	Capel including Godmersham Park sub-station.
SSZ27	Polegate and Mullion.
SSZ28-30	Polegate, Capel and Polegate respectively.
SSZ31	Anglesey and Howden.
SSZ32	Howden including Lowthorpe and Kirkleatham sub-stations.
SSZ33	Howden and Anglesey.
SSZ34-35	Anglesey. SSZ35 deleted October 1918.
SSZ36-37	Capel and Pembroke respectively.
SSZ38	Howden. Wrecked in gale at Lowthorpe 11.5.18.
SSZ39-45	Polegate (39, 41, 43, 44) and Mullion (40, 42, 45).
SSZ46-49	Capel, Mullion, Polegate and Mullion respectively.
SSZ50-51	Anglesey including Malahide sub-station.
SSZ52-53	Pembroke including Wexford sub-station.
SSZ54	Howden. Wrecked hitting trees at Lowthorpe 1918.
SSZ55-56	Howden and Pembroke respectively.
SSZ57-58	Longside including Auldbar sub-station.
SSZ59-60	East Fortune including Chathill sub-station.
SSZ61	Used for training at Cranwell.
SSZ62-64	Howden including sub-stations at Lowthorpe and Kirkleatham.
SSZ65-66	Longside including Auldbar sub-station.
SSZ67	Pembroke including Wexford sub-station.
SSZ68	Shipped from Wormwood Scrubs to Kassandra 24.8.18.
SSZ69	Capel including Godmersham Park sub-station.
SSZ70	Shipped from Wormwood Scrubs to Kassandra 24.8.18.
SSZ71	Used for experimental work at Pulham.
SSZ72-73	Anglesey including Malahide sub-station.
SSZ74-76	Capel, Mullion and Pembroke respectively.
SSZ77	Held in reserve at Kingsnorth.
SSZ78-93	Construction cancelled.

Semi-Rigid SR1

In addition to the blimps and airships numbered in the R series, a semi-rigid was acquired from Italy and was flown to England 28.10.18. Numbered SR1 for Semi-Rigid No. 1, it was powered by 2×220 h.p. Itala D.2s and a 200 h.p. S.P.A.6a.

THE PRE-SERIALING SYSTEM FOR AEROPLANES

BEFORE a continuous serialling system was initiated in 1912, the few aeroplanes acquired by the Army were numbered in two series prefixed by 'B' and 'F'; and the Royal Aircraft Factory designations B.E. for Bleriot Experimental and S.E. for Santos Experimental, both being rather misleading as after the initial aircraft in the series they had no real relevance. Aircraft on Army strength during 1911 were:

No.	*Aircraft Type*	*Remarks*
B1	Voisin rebuilt as B.E.1 (60 h.p. Wolseley)	Became numbered B.E.1
B2	Blériot Monoplane (70 h.p. Gnôme)	Later serialled 251
B3	Breguet Biplane (60 h.p.Renault)	Later serialled 202
B4	Nieuport Monoplane (50 h.p. Gnôme)	Later serialled 253
B5	Deperdussin (60 h.p. Anzani)	Later serialled 252
B6	Bristol Prier (50 h.p. Gnôme)	Later serialled 256
B7	Bristol Boxkite (60 h.p. Renault)	Non-standard, believed scrapped
BE1	B.E.1 (60 h.p. Renault)	Later serialled 201
BE2	S.E.2 reconstructed to B.E.2	Later serialled 202
BE3	B.E.3 (70 h.p. Gnôme)	Later serialled 203
BE4	B.E.4 (80 h.p. Gnôme)	Later serialled 204
BE5	B.E.2 (60 h.p. E.N.V.)	Later serialled 205
BE6	B.E.2 (60 h.p. Renault)	Ex-F3, later No. 206
F1	Henri Farman Biplane (50 h.p. Gnôme)	Scrapped before serialling started
F2	Paulham Biplane (50 h.p. Gnôme)	Scrapped before serialling started
F3	Howard Wright Biplane (60 h.p. E.N.V.)	B.E.6 reconstructed
F4	Flanders Monoplane No. 3	Scrapped before serialling started
F5-9	Bristol Boxkite (50 h.p. Gnôme)	F7-8 became 408 and 407
FE1	D.H. Farman type (45 h.p. D.H. Iris)	Acquired 14.1.11
FE2	F.E.2 (50 h.p. Gnôme)	Later serialled 604
RE1	R.E.1 (70 h.p. Renault)	Later serialled 607 & 608
RE2	R.E.2 (70 h.p. Renault)	Later serialled 17
SE1	S.E.1 (60 h.p. E.N.V.)	Crashed 18.8.11

The first aeroplanes to be used by the Admiralty had been two machines lent by a patriot, Mr. Francis K. McClean (later Sir Francis); their availability to naval officers was promulgated in General Fleet Orders of 6th December, 1910. The marking of aeroplanes loaned to the Admiralty by Mr. McClean was complicated by his own private numbering system. Short Nos. 27 and 39 were McClean Nos. 11 and 10 respectively. In the year following, the first naval officers received official flying training, and by agreement with the Royal Aero Club a further two aircraft were taken on loan; and gradually, by loan, presentation and purchase, the Admiralty obtained further aircraft.

At the time of the July 1912 Naval Review a simple identification system was in use, consisting of a letter for the type, followed by a number. Type letters were "H" for "Hydro-aeroplane" (this term was used up to 17th July, 1913, when Winston Churchill announced in the Commons that the term would be superseded by "Seaplane"), "M" for "Monoplane" and "T" for "Tractor" Known examples are:

H1	Short S.41 Tractor Biplane	Later serialled 10
H5	Short S.43 Biplane	Later serialled 401
M1	Deperdussin Monoplane (70 h.p. Gnôme)	Later serialled 7
M2	Short S.37 Tractor Monoplane	Later serialled 14
T1	Short S.34 "Long Range" Biplane	Later serialled 1
T2	Short S.38 Tractor Biplane	Later serialled 2
T3	Short S.39 Triple-Twin	Later serialled 3
T4	Short S.47 Triple Tractor	Later serialled 4
T5	Short S.45 Tractor Biplane (50 h.p. Gnôme)	Later serialled 5

A NUMBERING SYSTEM IS INAUGURATED

THE Air Committee, newly formed as a permanent body under the Committee of Imperial Defence, advocated in mid-1912 a standard marking and identification numbering system for all military aeroplanes; this coincided with a decision already made by the Admiralty and War Office to standardise on numbering. Elements of the Royal Flying Corps and the Naval Wing between them formed the Central Flying School, and in the summer of 1912 Naval aircraft had participated in Army manoeuvres inland, from which both Services had encountered difficulties due to their dual numbering systems. A straightforward system embracing both Services was therefore agreed.

In the early days the Services did not have a nomenclature for aircraft types. Manufacturers' names and engine horse-power were often the terms used to identify a particular type, together with descriptive words such as "tractor biplane"; in consequence a nickname often became an officially accepted abbreviation. These early aircraft were individually identified by their constructors' serial number, but since the Services were but one customer among many, including foreign governments, flying schools and private owners, the constructors' numbers on military aircraft were not necessarily consecutive.

THE ROYAL NAVY

1–200

THE Admiralty, representing the Senior Service, were allotted the first allocation of numbers from 1 to 200 and these were applied retrospectively to aircraft already in service.

When the numbering system took effect in November 1912 (coinciding with the setting up of an Air Department in the Admiralty), the Naval Wing had on strength 16 aircraft, consisting of 8 biplanes, 5 monoplanes and 3 seaplanes. These were re-numbered into the system and the allocation of numbers was taken up in numerical/chronological sequence as aircraft were ordered but, since some orders took longer than others to fulfil, deliveries were not necessarily in the same sequence. The first 200 were as follows:—

1–17

No.	*Aircraft Type and Remarks*
1-5	Short Biplanes. No. 1 S.34, pusher, No. 2 Short S.38, No. 3 S.39 "Triple Twin", No. 4 S.47 'Triple Tractor', No. 5 S.45.
6	Breguet Biplane with 80 h.p. Chenu (later 110 h.p. Canton Unné) engine. Bought from France, August 1912.
7	Deperdussin Monoplane, 70 h.p. Gnôme. Acquired from the Army 24.7.12 and was for a time fitted with floats.
8	Short S.38 Biplane, 50 h.p. (later 80 h.p.) Gnôme.
9	Etrich Monoplane, 65 h.p. Austro-Daimler. Purchased from Germany.
10	Short S.41, 100 h.p. Gnôme (later 140 h.p. engine). At Dardanelles in 1915.
11	Henry Farman, 70 h.p. Built by the Aircraft Manufacturing Co. Ltd. Hendon.
12	Short S.46 'Tandem Twin' monoplane. 70 h.p. Gnôme. Believed never flown.
13	*Not allotted—official superstition?*
14	Short S.37 single-seat monoplane, ex-M.2. 60 h.p. Gnôme.
15	Bristol T.B.8H. Bristol No. 205. Stationed at Calshot, January 1914.
16	Avro 503 seaplane converted to landplane. 100 h.p. Gnôme. Eastchurch 1916.
17	H.R.E.2 (Hydro Reconnaissance Experimental No. 2). Originally built as R.E.2 with 70 h.p. Renault engine; later a seaplane with a 100 h.p. Renault.

18	Donnet-Levêque Flying Boat, 80 h.p. Gnôme. Purchased from France. Delivered to Sheerness 20.10.12.
19	Short Biplane S.38. Used by Sir Winston Churchill, 15.5.15.
20-21	Short S.41, 100 h.p. Gnôme. No. 20 used in Gregory-Riley-White wheel/float experiments.
22	Deperdussin Monoplane, 80 h.p. Anzani. Stationed at Eastchurch.
23	Maurice Farman S.7 Longhorn, built by the Aircraft Manufacturing Co. Ltd., Hendon.
24	Bristol Boxkite, 50 h.p. Gnôme. Stationed at Eastchurch. Bristol No. 99.
25	Astra, 100 h.p. Renault.
26	R.E.5, 120 h.p. Austro-Daimler. Built by the Royal Aircraft Factory. Acquired from War Office.
27	Sopwith Tractor Biplane, 80 h.p. Gnôme. Used for machine gun practice at Eastchurch early in 1914.
28	Short Biplane S.38, 80 h.p. Gnôme. Still in service in 1916 at Eastchurch.
29	Maurice Farman S.11 Shorthorn seaplane, 70 h.p. Renault. Allotted to Yarmouth from June 1913 but was rarely flown.
30	Deperdussin Monoplane, 80 h.p. Anzani.
31	Henry Farman Biplane, 70/80 h.p. Gnôme. Built by the Aircraft Manufacturing Co. Ltd., Hendon.
32	Vickers F.B.5 " Gunbus ", 100 h.p. Gnôme Monosoupape. Eastchurch 1914-15 on " Zeppelin standby ".
33	Sopwith Tractor Biplane, 80 h.p. Gnôme. Stationed at Eastchurch.
34	Short S.38, 50 h.p. (later 80 h.p.) Gnôme. Used at Eastchurch for armament practice.
35	Bristol Boxkite, 70 h.p. Gnôme. Bristol No. 139.
36	Deperdussin Monoplane, 80 h.p. Anzani. Stationed at Eastchurch.
37	Borel Seaplane. Purchased from France. Crashed in River Swale.
38	Sopwith Bat Boat No. 1, 100 h.p. Green engine.
39	Blériot Monoplane Type XI, 80 h.p. Le Rhône. Stationed at Eastchurch; Went to France in 1914.
40	Caudron G.III, 80 h.p. Gnôme. Built by W. H. Ewen & Co.
41	Avro 500, 50 h.p. Gnôme. Stationed at Eastchurch late 1914.
42	Short Seaplane, 80 h.p. Gnôme. Converted to landplane. Wrecked at Morbecque, France in September 1914.
43	Bristol T.B.8. Wrecked at Leigh, Essex, 1914. Rebuilt. In service at Eastchurch in 1916.
44	Deperdussin Monoplane.
45	Caudron G.III, 50 h.p. (later 70 h.p.) Gnôme. To Chingford in May 1915.
46-47	B.E.2a. Built by the Royal Aircraft Factory. No. 46 stationed at Eastchurch; No. 47 at Chingford in 1916.
48	Borel Seaplane. Wrecked by heavy seas aboard H.M.S. *Hermes* during fleet manoeuvres 23.7.13.
49-50	B.E.2a, 70 h.p. Renault. Built by Hewlett & Blondeau Ltd. for War Office and transferred to the Royal Navy. No. 50 was used in France, Belgium and Gallipoli.
51-53	Avro 500. No. 51 written off at Hendon 11.8.15; No. 52 lost at Hendon 1916; No. 53 was at Eastchurch in 1916.
54	Coventry Ordnance Works, 160 h.p. Gnôme.
55-57	Caudron Seaplane 80/100 h.p. Gnôme. No. 55 was fitted for amphibious use.
58-60	Sopwith Seaplane, 100 h.p. Anzani. No. 59 at Cromarty 1913; No. 60 at Yarmouth 1914.
61	Sopwith, 120 h.p. Austro-Daimler.
62-65	Short Biplane S.38. No. 62 at Eastchurch January 1916; No. 65 was converted to take a wheel/float undercarriage.
66	Short S.28. Eastchurch " Gun Machine ". Used for machine gun and bomb-dropping experiments.

No.	*Aircaft Type and Remarks*
67-73	Maurice Farman S.7 Longhorn. Built by the Aircraft Manufacturing Co. Ltd., Hendon. No. 67, 70 h.p. Renault; No. 68, 100 h.p. Renault, was converted to a seaplane; Nos. 69-70, 70 h.p. Renault of which No. 70 had a 120 h.p. Renault engine; No. 72 was written off at Dover 23.5.14. Nos. 70-73 believed seaplane versions.
74-80	Short Seaplane Type 74. Initially 100 h.p. Gnôme.
81-82	Short Folder Seaplane, 160 h.p. Gnôme.
83-88	Borel Seaplane, 80 h.p. Gnôme. Built by Delacombe & Marechal.
89-90	Short Folder Seaplanes, 160 h.p. Gnôme.
91-92	Maurice Farman. Built by the Aircraft Manufacturing Co. Ltd., Hendon.
93	Sopwith Pusher Seaplane " Gunbus ", 120 h.p. Austro-Daimler.
94	Avro 500, 50 h.p. Gnôme.
95-96	Maurice Farman Seaplane, 130 h.p. Canton Unné.
97-100	Henry Farman, 80 h.p. Gnôme. Built by the Aircraft Manufacturing Co. Ltd., Hendon. No. 97 fitted with a 100 h.p. Gnôme was used as a seaplane with sprung floats at Kirkwall.
101	Believed B.E.2a.
102	Henry Farman. Built by the Aircraft Manufacturing Co. Ltd., Hendon.
103-104	Sopwith Tractor Biplane, 80 h.p. Gnôme. No. 104 " anti-Zeppelin standby " January 1915 at Eastchurch.
105	Hamble, Luke & Co. Floatplane, 150 h.p. N.A.G.
106-107	Astra CM, 70 h.p. Renault.
108-110	Farman. No. 108 Henry Farman; No. 109 Maurice Farman; No. 110 Henry Farman Seaplane.
111-112	Breguet " Tinwhistle ".
113-117	Farman. No. 113 Maurice Farman Seaplane; No. 114-116 Henry Farman Seaplane; No. 115 Farman, 100 h.p. Renault; No. 117 Maurice Farman Seaplane, 120 h.p. Renault.
118	Sopwith Bat Boat, 90 h.p. Austro-Daimler. At Scapa Flow early 1915.
119-122	Short Folder Seaplane, 160 h.p. Gnôme. During October 1914 No. 119 was on board H.M.S. *Hermes* and Nos. 120-122 were on board H.M.S. *Engadine*.
123-124	Sopwith Tabloid, 80 h.p. Gnôme. Both at Isle of Grain, October 1914.
125	Farman. Built by the Aircraft Manufacturing Co., Ltd., Hendon.
126	Short S.81 Gun-carrier, 160 h.p. Gnôme. 1½ pdr. quick firing gun mounted.
127	Sopwith, 200 h.p. Canton Unné.
128-129	Wight Pusher Seaplane, 135 h.p. Canton Unné.
130-134	Avro 510 Seaplane, 150 h.p. Sunbeam. All but No. 131 at Supermarine Aviation in June 1916 for rebuilding.
135-136	Short Admiralty Type 135. No. 135 with 135 h.p. Canton Unné; No. 136, 200 h.p. Canton Unné, H.M.S. *Riviera* October 1914, Dardanelles 1915.
137-138	Sopwith Seaplanes. No. 137 120 h.p. Austro-Daimler, No. 138 200 h.p. Canton Unné. Both at Calshot in 1914.
139-144	Henry Farman. Nos. 139 and 142-144 were floatplanes. No. 140 was also reported as a Short Folder with 135 h.p. Canton Unné.
145	Short, 65 h.p. Austro-Daimler.
146	Maurice Farman S.7 Longhorn, 70 h.p. Renault. French built. Stationed Hendon and Chingford.
147-148	Bristol 200 h.p. Canton Unné Seaplane. Order cancelled.
149	Sopwith " Churchill ", 100 h.p. Gnôme. Side-by-side seater suggested by Winston Churchill.
150	Avro 500, 50 h.p. Gnôme. Stationed at Eastchurch 1914.
151	Sopwith Seaplane, 100 h.p. Green.
152	Short Biplane, 80 h.p. Gnôme. Dual control. Yarmouth 1914, Eastchurch 1916.
153	Bristol T.B.8, 80 h.p. Gnôme. Ostend Sept. 1914, Eastchurch Oct. 1914.

154	D.F.W. Arrow biplane ex-Beardmore. 100 h.p. Mercedes. Stationed at Immingham October 1914. Grounded for identification reasons.
155	Wight Pusher Seaplane, 200 h.p. Canton Unné. W/T fitted. Fort George October 1914.
156	Henry Farman Seaplane, 80 h.p. Gnôme. Built by A.M.C., Hendon.
157-159	Sopwith Floatplanes. 200 h.p. Canton Unné.
160	Sopwith biplane. 80 h.p. Gnôme.
161-166	Short Admiralty Type 166 Seaplane. 200 h.p. Canton Unné. All allotted to H.M.S. *Ark Royal*. 163 and 166 converted to landplanes in Aegean.
167-169	Sopwith Tabloid 80 h.p. Gnôme. No. 169 was Tabloid prototype.
170	Sopwith Tractor Biplane, 100 h.p. Green engine. At Calshot 1914.
171-176	Wight Type AI Improved Navyplane. 200 h.p. Canton Unné.
177	Wight Type AII Improved Navyplane.
178	Short Type B. 200 h.p. Le Rhône planned. Order cancelled.
179	Avro 504, 80 h.p. Gnôme. To France November 1914 for Friedrichshafen raid. Eastchurch 1916.
180-183	Short Type 74. Nos. 180, 182, 183 had 100 h.p. Gnôme engines; No. 181, 80 h.p. Gnôme engine.
184-185	Short Admiralty Type 184 Seaplane prototypes.
186	Short Folder Type Seaplane, 160 h.p. Gnôme.
187	Wight Twin Seaplane, two 200 h.p. Canton Unné engines.
188	Henry Farman Landplane. At Eastchurch 1914.
189	Henry Farman Floatplane.
190-199	Short Type B. 200 h.p. Canton Unné. No. 190 only delivered. Reserved for Royal Aircraft Factory seaplane.
200	Henry Farman. At Hendon October 1914.

THE ARMY'S AEROPLANES

201—800 THE Army, following on from the Navy's allocation of Nos. 1-200, used the numbers 201-800, but in blocks as follows: 201-300, aircraft taken on charge at Farnborough; 301-400, aircraft orders resulting from 1912 Military Trials (although allotted for this reason, the allocation was used for general acquisitions after No. 301); 401-500, aircraft taken on charge by Central Flying School; 501-600, aircraft of French design taken on charge; 601-800, originally reserved for Royal Aircraft Factory prototypes and used later for general acquisitions. Some re-numbering took place on re-allocation 1912-14.

Serial Nos.	*Qty.*	*Aircraft Types*
201	1	B.E.1
202	1	Breguet Biplane (Ex-B.3)
203	1	B.E.3 "The Goldfish"
204-206	3	B.E.4, 5, 6 (Ex-B.E.4-6)
207	1	M.F.S.7
208-209	2	H.F. (70 h.p. Gnôme)
210-211	2	Breguet G.3
212-213	2	Breguet L.2
214-216	3	M.F.S.7 (70 h.p. Renault)
217-218	2	B.E.2a (Bristol-built 70 h.p. Renault fitted)
219	1	Blériot XI (1912)
220	1	B.E.2 (70 h.p. Renault)
221	1	Blériot Tandem
222	1	B.E.2 (Vickers-built)
223-224	2	M.F.S.7 (Renault)
225	1	B.E.2 (70 h.p. Renault)
226	1	B.E.2a (Bristol-built)
227-242	16	B.E.2 (All 70 h.p. Renault. 226, 231-233, 240, 242 by Bristol, 236 by Vickers, 235 by C.O.W. 228 D.C.)
243	1	Sopwith RG

Serial Nos.	Qty.	Aircraft Types	Serial Nos.	Qty.	Aircraft Types
244	1	H.F. (80 h.p. Gnôme)	312	1	Breguet (85 h.p.)
245	1	B.E.2 (Bristol-built)	313	1	Dunne (?)
246-247	2	Sopwith RG	314	1	B.E.2a (Vickers)
248	1	B.E.2a	315	1	Sopwith R.G.
249	1	B.E.2a (Bristol-built)	316-317	2	B.E.2a (Vickers)
250	1	B.E.2	318	1	B.E.2a (C.O.W.)
251	1	Blériot XXII (ex-B2 re-built)	319	1	Sopwith R.G.
			320	1	B.E.2a (Vickers)
252	1	Deperdussin (Ex-B5)	321	1	B.E.2a (C.O.W.)
253-255	3	Nieuport Monoplane (50, 70, 100 h.p. Gnômes)	322	1	M.F. S.7 (70 h.p. Renault)
			323	1	Blériot XI
256	1	Bristol Prier (Ex-B6)	324-325	2	Sopwith RG
257-259	3	Deperdussin Monoplane	326	1	Sopwith Tabloid
			327-329	3	B.E.2a (70 h.p. Renault)
260	1	Blériot XI (80 h.p. Gnôme)	330	1	H.F. (80 h.p. Gnôme)
261	1	Bristol Prier 2-seater	331-332	2	B.E.2a/B.E.2
			333	1	Sopwith RG
262-263	2	Bristol Coanda	334-335	2	R.E.5 (120 h.p. AD)
264	1	Nieuport Monoplane	336	1	B.E.2 (Vickers)
265	1	Flanders F.4	337-338	2	M.F. S.7
266	1	M.F. S.7 (later 472)	339-341	3	H.F. (80 h.p. Gnôme)
267	1	B.E.2a	342-345	4	M.F. S.11
268	1	Henri Farman	346	1	H.F. (80 h.p. Gnôme)
269-270	2	M.F. S.7	347-348	2	B.E.2 (C.O.W.)
271	1	B.E.2	349	1	B.E.2 (70 h.p. Renault)
272-273	2	B.E.2 (273 Bristol)			
274-277	4	H.F. (275-6 by G.W.)	350-353	4	H.F. (Some F.20)
278	1	Martinsyde IVB	354	1	G.W. Popular
279-280	2	Deperdussin	355-360	6	M.F. S.7 (70 h.p.)
281	1	Flanders F.4	361	1	R.E.5
282	1	Nieuport Monoplane	362	1	R.E.1 No. 2
283	1	G.W. Biplane	363-364	2	H.F. (80 h.p. Gnôme)
284	1	H.F. (80 h.p. Gnôme)	365	1	B.E.8 (Bristol)
285	1	Avro 500	366	1	Dunne biplane
286	1	H.F. (80 h.p. Gnôme)	367	1	H.F. (80 h.p. Gnôme)
287	1	G.W. Biplane	368	1	B.E.2
288-291	4	Avro 500	369-371	3	M.F. S.11
292-293	2	Blériot XI*bis*	372	1	B.E.2A (Vickers)
294-295	2	H.F. (80 h.p. Gnôme)	373	1	B.E.8 (Bristol)
296-298	3	Blériot (50 h.p. Gnôme)	374-375	2	Blériot (80 h.p.)
			376	1	Avro 504
299	1	B.E.2a (G.W. built)	377	1	B.E.8 (Vickers)
300	1	Sopwith RG	378	1	Sopwith Tabloid
301	1	Cody Military	379	1	M.F. S.7
302	1	M.F. S.7 (70 h.p. Renault)	380	1	R.E.5 (1-seater)
			381	1	Sopwith Tabloid
303	1	B.E.4 (50 h.p. Gnôme)	382	1	R.E.5
			383-385	3	B.E.2 (A.W. except 384 C.O.W.)
304	1	Cody Military			
305-307	3	M.F. S.7	386-387	2	Sopwith Tabloid
308	1	Caudron G.II	388-389	2	Blériot (80 h.p.)
309	1	H.F. (by G.W.)	390	1	Avro 504
310	1	Breguet (110 h.p.)	391	1	B.E.8
311	1	Caudron G.II	392	1	Sopwith Tabloid

393	1	H.F. (80 h.p. Gnôme)	474	1	B.E.2. (C.O.W.).
394-395	2	Sopwith Tabloid	475	1	B.E.2. (Vickers).
396	1	B.E.2b (Bristol)	476-478	3	Maurice Farman S.7.
397-398	2	Avro 504	479	1	B.E.8.
399	1	B.E.8	480-481	2	Maurice Farman.
401-402	2	Short Nos. 43-44	482	1	Morane-Saulnier Type G.
403	1	M.F. S.7 (70 h.p.)			
404-406	3	Avro 500	483-488	6	B.E.2a/b.
407-408	2	Ex-F.8 & F.7	489	1	B.E.2.
409	1	Nieuport Monoplane	490	1	Maurice Farman S.7.
410-411	2	M.F. S.7	491	1	Avro 500.
412	1	H.F. Ex-208	492-493	2	B.E.2b.
413	1	Short No. 48	494, 496, 498-500	5	Maurice Farman S.7. Longhorn.
415	1	M.F. S.7 (A.M.C.).			
416-417	2	B.E.3. (50 h.p. Gnôme).	502-513	12	Henry Farman.
			514-545	32	Maurice Farman S.11.
418	1	M.F. S.7 (70 h.p.).	546-557	12	Maurice Farman S.7.
419	1	Deperdussin.	558-566	9	Henry Farman.
420	1	H.F. (80 h.p. Gnôme).	570-586	17	Blériot Parasol.
421	1	Deperdussin.	587-598	12	Morane (G.W.).
422	1	Flanders F.4.	599	1	Martinsyde S.1.
423-424	2	Short Nos. 49-50 to R.N.A.S. Nos. 1268/79.	601-602	2	B.E.2.
			604-605	2	F.E.2/F.E.3.
			606	1	Blériot Parasol.
423-424	2	B.E.8. (80 h.p.).	607-608	2	R.E.1 Nos. 1 & 2.
425	1	H.F. (80 h.p. Gnôme).	609	1	S.E.2a.
426-429	4	M.F. S.7 (70 h.p.).	610	1	Bristol G.B.75.
430	1	Avro 500 (50 h.p.).	612-613	2	B.E./R.E.5.
431	1	M.F. S.7 (70 h.p.).	614-615	2	Bristol TB8, see 948.
432-433	2	Avro 500.	616	1	Blériot Parasol.
434-435	2	H.F. (434 G.W.).	617	1	R.E.5.
436-437	2	Deperdussin Monoplanes.	618-619	2	Blériot.
			620	1	Bristol T.B.8, see 917.
438	1	B.E.7. (140 h.p. Gnôme).	621	1	Blériot.
			622	1	B.E.
439	1	Flanders F.4.	623	1	Morane Biplane.
440	1	H.F. (80 h.p. Gnôme).	624-625	2	B.E.8.
441-442	2	B.E.2a. (Vickers).	626	1	Blériot Monoplane.
444-445	2	H.F. (80 h.p. Gnôme).	627	1	Morane Biplane.
446	1	Short No. 62.	628	1	S.E.4.
447	1	B.E.2a. (Vickers).	629	1	M.S. Type H (G.W.).
448	1	Avro 500.	630	1	Blériot Monoplane.
449	1	B.E.2a (oleo u/c).	631-632	2	R.E.5/B.E.8.
450-451	2	M.F. S.7 (70 h.p.).	633-634	2	Bristol Scout B.
452-454	3	B.E.2a. (Vickers).	635-636	2	B.E.2/B.E.8.
455-456	2	H.F. (80 h.p. Gnôme).	637-638	2	Avro 504.
457	1	B.E.2a.	639	1	Vickers Boxkite.
458-459	2	M.F. S.7 (70 h.p.).	640-641	2	Bristol Boxkite.
460	1	B.E.2. (H.P.).	642	1	Vickers Boxkite.
461-462	2	H.F. (80 h.p. Gnôme.)	643-645	2	B.E.8.
464	1	M.F. S.7. Ex-343.	644	1	Bristol Scout.
465	1	Maurice Farman S.11.	646	1	B.E.2b.
466	1	B.E.2a.	647	1	Blériot R.1.
467	1	H.F. (80 h.p. Gnôme).	648	1	Bristol Scout B.
468-471	4	B.E.2. (C.O.W., Saunders, R.A.F., C.O.W.).	649	1	Vickers Scout.
			650/651	2	B.E.2b/R.E.5.
			652/653	2	Avro 504/H.F.
472	1	Maurice Farman S.7.	654	1	Sopwith Tabloid.
473	1	Blériot.	655	1	Maurice Farman.

Serial Nos.	Qty.	Aircraft Type
656/658	2	B.E.8.
657	1	Bristol Boxkite.
659-660	2	R.E.5.
661	1	Maurice Farman S.7 Longhorn.
662-663	2	Blériot/B.E.8.
664	1	Vickers F.B. 4/5.
665	1	Avro (50 h.p. Gnôme.)
666-668	3	B.E.2a/2b/2.
669/670	2	Henry Farman/B.E.8.
671-673	3	Blériot.
674 & 676	2	R.E.5/B.E.
677-678	2	R.E.5.
679-680	2	Morane-Saulnier S.7/ Henry Farman.
681	1	Blériot.
682	1	Vickers Gunbus.
683	1	Avro 504.
687-688	2	B.E.2b/R.E.5.
689	1	Henry Farman.
691-702	12	See 1216-1227.
693	1	B.E.8.
694	1	Blériot Monoplane.
696	1	Blériot XI.
702	1	Martinsyde S.1.
705	1	B.E.2b (70 h.p. Renault).
706	1	Blériot Monoplane.
708	1	Henry Farman F.20.
709	1	B.E.2b.
710	1	Martinsyde S.1.
711	1	Blériot XI.
712-713	2	Maurice Farman S.7 Longhorn.
715	1	Avro 504.
720	1	Henry Farman.
722	1	B.E.
724	1	Martinsyde S.1.
725, 727, 729	3	B.E.8.
733	1	B.E.2a or B.E.2b.
734	1	Martinsyde S.1.
735	1	Maurice Farman S.7 Longhorn.
736	1	B.E.8.
737	1	R.E.5.
740	1	B.E.8.
741	1	Martinsyde S.1.
742	1	Maurice Farman S.11 Shorthorn.
743	1	Martinsyde S.1.
744	1	Maurice Farman (70 h.p. Renault).
745	1	R.E.5.
746	1	B.E.2b.
747	1	Vickers.
748-749	2	Martinsyde S.1.
750-793	44	Avro 504 (80 h.p. Gnôme except 769 and 777, fitted with 80 h.p. Le Rhône and Clerget respectively).
794-799	6	Avro 504D.

THE SECOND NAVAL ALLOCATION

801—1600

THE initial allocation to the Royal Navy of 1-200 was taken up in full by midsummer 1914, and a further allocation of 801-1600 was allotted. At this time the Air Department followed the peculiar practice of designating certain new aircraft by using the serial number of a representative aircraft as a type number. Impressed aircraft, commencing with No. 881, mark the outbreak of the 1914-1918 War and the 24 Bristol Scouts numbered 1243-1266 mark the last Admiralty contract for aeroplanes in 1914; thus, aircraft from 1267 onwards are from contracts placed in 1915.

Serial Nos.	Qty.	Aircraft Type	Remarks
801-806	6	Sopwith 806	Sopwith "Gunbus" No. 2, Admiralty Type 806. 150 h.p. Sunbeam.
807-810	4	Sopwith 807	Sopwith Folder Seaplane, Admiralty Type 807. 100 h.p. Gnôme.
811-818	8	Short Type 74	811 and 818 fitted with Rouzet W/T on H.M.S. *Riviera*, 1914.

819-821	3	Short 830 Seaplane	135 h.p. Canton Unné engines fitted.
822-827	6	Short 827 Seaplane	150 h.p. Sunbeam Nubian engine fitted.
828-830	3	Short 830 Seaplane	135 h.p. Canton Unné engine fitted.
831-834	4	Wight 177.	J. Samuel White & Co. built.
835-840	6	Wight 840.	J. Samuel White & Co. built.
841-850	10	Short 184 (225 h.p. Sunbeam).	No. 843 was partly rebuilt by Parnall, November 1916.
851-860	10	Sopwith 157 (225 h.p. Sunbeam).	Also known as Type 860.
861-872	12	Vickers 32 "Gunbus".	865-872 to R.F.C. with 100 h.p. Gnômes.
873-878	6	Avro 504 (80 h.p. Gnôme).	873-875 participated in the famous Friedrichshafen raid.
879	1	Sopwith Batboat.	225 h.p. Sunbeam fitted.
880	1	Sopwith Floatplane.	100 h.p. Gnôme fitted.
881	1	Avro 510 (150 h.p. Sunbeam).	Impressed civil aircraft.
882-883	2	White & Thompson No. 2 (Curtiss Batboat).	Also known as "Small America" type. Austro-Daimler engines fitted.
884	1	Wight No. 2 Navyplane Improved.	Impressed at Calshot 1914. 160 h.p. Gnôme.
885	1	Deperdussin Monoplane.	Impressed civil aircraft. 100 h.p. Anzani engine.
886-887	2	Henry Farman Seaplane.	886, A.M.C. built; 887 French built.
888	1	Maurice Farman Seaplane.	120 h.p. Sunbeam.
889	1	Avro (80 h.p. Gnôme).	Impressed civil aircraft.
890	1	Albatros B.II Biplane (100 h.p. Mercedes).	Impressed. Bought pre-war in Germany.
891	1	D.F.W. Biplane (100 h.p. Mercedes).	Impressed. Originally bought by Beardmore.
892	1	Handley Page H.P.7 Type G/100.	Impressed. 100 h.p. Anzani. Used at Chingford.
893-895	3	Wight 1914 Navyplane Pusher Seaplane.	Ex-German contract. 200 h.p. Canton-Unné.
896-901	6	Sopwith 880 (100 h.p. Gnôme).	896, 900-901 Landplanes; 897-899 Floatplanes ex-Greek contract.
902-903	2	Blériot Parasol (50 & 70 h.p. Gnômes).	No. 903 presented by Miss Trehawke Davies.
904	1	Short S.32 (70 h.p.)	Presented by Sir Francis McClean.
905	1	Short S.80 Nile Seaplane (160 h.p. Gnôme).	Presented by Sir Francis McClean.
906	1	Sopwith 3-Seat Tractor Biplane.	80 h.p. Gnôme. Eastchurch and France 1914.
907-908	2	Blériot Parasol.	French-built. 80 h.p. At Eastchurch, October 1914.
909-914	6	Maurice Farman S.7 Longhorn.	A.M.C. built. 70 h.p. Renault. 910-914 transferred to R.F.C.
915	1	Henry Farman Seaplane (80 h.p.).	A.M.C. built.
916-917	2	Bristol T.B.8.	917 ex-R.F.C. 620.

Serial Nos.	Qty.	Aircraft Type	Remarks
918	1	Flanders B.2	70 h.p. Gnôme. Civil aircraft impressed, Yarmouth 1914.
919-926	8	Sopwith 807 Seaplane	920 and 921 were shipped to East Africa.
927-938	12	Sopwith 860 Seaplane	933-934, 936-937, cancelled.
939	1	Avro 500	50 h.p. Gnôme. At Hendon October, 1914. Impressed.
940	1	Henry Farman	Built by the Aircraft Manufacturing Co. Ltd. at Hendon.
941	1	Morane	French-built. Stationed at Eastchurch, December 1914.
942-947	6	Bristol Boxkite	50 h.p. Gnôme. 943 and 945 used at Chingford.
948	1	Bristol T.B.8	Was R.F.C. No. 614.
949	1	Maurice Farman	Built by the Aircraft Manufacturing Co. Ltd. 100 h.p. Gnôme.
950-951	2	Curtiss H.4 " Small America "	Curtiss-built in U.S.A. 950 had two 125 h.p. Anzanis fitted and was modified at Felixstowe to become the Porte-Curtiss H.4. 951 had 100 h.p. Anzani engines fitted.
952-963	12	B.E.2c (70 h.p. Renault)	Built by Vickers Ltd. All transferred to R.F.C.
964-975	12	B.E.2c (70 h.p. Renault)	Built by Blackburn Aeroplane & Motor Co. 968-969 shipped to South Africa.
976-987	12	B.E.2c (70 h.p. Renault)	Built by Hewlett & Blondeau Ltd. at Clapham.
988-999	12	B.E.2c (70 h.p. Renault)	Built by Martinsyde Ltd., Brooklands, Byfleet, Surrey.
1000	1	White A.D.1000	Damaged beyond repair at Calshot, 18.12.17.
1001-1050	50	Avro 504B (80 h.p. Gnome).	1014 was shipped to the U.S.A. for exhibition. 1005-1008 and 1020-1025 transferred to R.F.C. 1019 h.p. Le Rhone.
1051-1074	24	Sopwith Two-seat Scout	Known as " Spinning Jenny ". 80 h.p. Gnôme.
1075-1098	24	B.E.2c (70 h.p. Renault)	Built by Vickers Ltd.
1099-1122	24	B.E.2c (70 h.p. Renault)	Built by William Beardmore & Co. Ltd., Dalmuir.
1123-1126	4	B.E.2c (70 h.p. Renault)	Built by Blackburn Aeroplane & Motor Co. Ltd., Leeds.
1127	1	B.E.2c/Maurice Farman	Blackburn-built B.E.2c exchanged with Belgium for a steel-framed Maurice Farman.
1128-1146	19	B.E.2c (70 h.p. Renault)	Built by Blackburn Aeroplane & Motor Co. Ltd., Leeds.
1147-1170	24	B.E.2c (70 h.p. Renault)	Built by Grahame-White Aviation Co. Ltd., Hendon.
1171-1182	12	White & Thompson Biplane ' Bognor Bloater '	70 h.p. Renault engine fitted. 1180-1182 built for spares only and were not assembled.

1183-1188	6	B.E.2c (75 h.p. Renault)	Built by Eastbourne Aviation Co. Ltd., Eastbourne.
1189-1194	6	B.E.2c (75 h.p. Renault)	Built by Hewlett & Blondeau Ltd., Clapham.
1195-1200	6	White & Thompson No. 3 Flying Boat	1195, 1197 & 1199 to Dover; 1196 to Fort George and 1198 to Dundee.
1201-1213	13	Sopwith Tabloid	1201-1202 aboard H.M.S. *Ark Royal* in 1914.
1214-1215	2	Sopwith Gordon Bennett	Racing models acquired by Admiralty.
1216-1227	12	Bristol T.B.8	Originally ordered by R.F.C. and transferred to R.N.A.S.
1228-1231	4	Curtiss H.4	Built by Aircraft Manufacturing Co. and Saunders. 1230 used in hull shape experiments.
1232-1239	8	Curtiss H.4	Built by Curtiss, U.S.A. Engines installed as follows: 1232-1235 had 90 h.p. Curtiss engines supplied but two 100 h.p. Anzanis were fitted; 1236-1237, two 90 h.p. Curtiss; 1238, two 150 h.p. Sunbeams; 1239, two 100 h.p. Anzanis.
1240	1	Maurice Farman	Built under licence by Aircraft Manufacturing Co. Interned in Holland 15.12.14.
1241	1	Maurice Farman F.27	Origin unknown. 100 h.p. Canton Unné.
1242	1	Morane-Saulnier G	Built by the Grahame-White Aviation Co. Ltd., Hendon.
1243-1266	24	Bristol Scout " C "	1247 was presented to the French Government.
1267	1	Pemberton-Billing (P.B.IX?)	Type unknown. Built by Supermarine. 80 h.p. Gnôme.
1268	1	Short S.45 Tractor	Ex-No. 423, 100 h.p. Clerget.
1269-1278	10	—	Cancelled order.
1279	1	Short S.45 Tractor	Ex-No. 424, 100 h.p. Clerget.
1280-1299	20	White & Thompson	Contract cancelled.
1300-1319	20	Wight	No record of delivery except for No. 1306.
1320	1	Caudron G.II or G.III	Built by British Caudron Co. 60 h.p. Anzani.
1321	1	Henry Farman	Built by Grahame-White Aviation Co. Ltd., 70 h.p. Gnôme.
1322	1	Perry Tractor	Believed impressed Perry-Beadle aircraft.
1323-1334	12	Curtiss B.2	Cancelled. Ordered from Curtiss, U.S.A. with 160 h.p. Curtiss engines.
1335-1346	12	Short 830	135 h.p. Canton Unné. Delivered from May 1915.
1347-1350	4	—	Order cancelled.
1351-1354	4	Wight 840	Delivered from November 1915 by J. S. White & Co.
1355-1361	7	Admiralty A.D.1000	Ordered from J. S. White & Co. 1355 and 1358 only built.

Serial Nos.	*Qty.*	*Aircraft Type*	*Remarks*
1362-1367	6	Curtiss JN-3	Delivered from Curtiss, U.S.A., in March 1915.
1368	1	Henry Farman	Built by the Aircraft Manufacturing Co. Ltd., Hendon.
1369-1371	3	Maurice Farman	Built by the Aircraft Manufacturing Co. Ltd., Hendon.
1372	1	Caudron G.III	Built by British Caudron Co. 50 h.p. Gnôme.
1373	1	Wright (35 h.p. Wright)	Civil aircraft purchased by R.N.A.S. at Eastchurch.
1374	1	Pemberton-Billing " Boxkite "	50 h.p. Gnôme. Also reported as 1908 Type Henry Farman at Hendon.
1375	1	—	Cancelled.
1376-1379	4	Deperdussin Monoplane	100 h.p. Gnôme Monosoupape. 1378-1379 used at Chingford.
1380-1387	8	Maurice Farman	French-built. 100 h.p. Renault. 1380-1381 to Gallipoli.
1388-1389	2	Supermarine Night Hawk	Pemberton Billing Type 29. Two 125 h.p. Anzani engines fitted.
1390-1394	5	Breguet de Chasse	1390, 135 h.p. Canton Unné; 1391, 200 h.p. Canton Unné; 1392, 225 h.p. Sunbeam; 1393, 200 h.p. Canton Unné; 1394, 220 h.p. Renault.
1395-1397	3	Nieuport Twin	Cancelled. Project with two 110 h.p. Clerget engines.
1398-1399	2	Breguet Concours	French built. 1398, 250 h.p. Rolls Royce; 1399, 225 h.p. Sunbeam.
1400-1411	12	Wight 840	Built by William Beardmore & Co. Ltd., Dalmuir.
1412-1413	2	A.D. Flying Boat	Built by the Supermarine Aviation Works, Woolston.
1414	1	—	Cancelled order.
1415-1416	2	Blackburn G.P./S.P.	1415 (G.P.), 150 h.p. Sunbeams; 1416 (S.P.), 190 h.p. Falcons.
1417-1423	—	—	Not allotted.
1424-1435	12	B.E.2c (75 or 100 h.p.)	Cancelled. Ordered from South Coast Aviation Co.
1436-1447	12	Sopwith Schneider	1445 was lost in wreck of s.s. *Junga*.
1448-1449	—	—	Not allotted.
1450-1451	2	Wight Twin Seaplane	Apart from trials both served only at Felixstowe.
1452-1453	2	A.D. Scout	Built by Hewlett & Blondeau. 100 h.p. Gnôme.
1454	1	Henry Farman	Built by Aircraft Manufacturing Co. Ltd.
1455-1466	12	Handley Page O/100	1455 was prototype Handley Page Bomber.
1467-1496	30	Avro 504C	Built by Brush Electrical Engineering Co. Ltd., Loughborough. Known as Avro Scout. 1491 to French.

1497-1508	12	White & Thompson	Cancelled order for Seaplanes.
1509-1517	9	Blackburn T.B. Twin	140 h.p. Smith engines planned; 1509-1510 had Gnômes, and 1517 Clergets, fitted.
1518-1533	16	Henry Farman F.22	French built. 1518, 80 h.p. Gnôme. 1531-1533 scrapped for spares.
1534-1535	2	Vickers "Gunbus"	Admiralty Type 32 with 140 h.p. Smith engine.
1536-1537	2	A.D. Scout	Blackburn built. 100 h.p. Gnôme. Tested at Chingford.
1538-1549	12	Blériot Parasol	French built. 80 h.p. Gnôme. All used at Eastchurch 1916.
1550-1555	6	Henry Farman (Steel)	Cancelled. Ordered from Brush with Canton Unné engines.
1556-1579	24	Sopwith Schneider	1560-1561 served aboard H.M.S. *Ben-my-Chree.*
1580-1591	12	Short S.38	Built by Supermarine Aviation. 80 h.p. Gnôme.
1592-1597	6	Caudron G.III (100 h.p.)	Built in France.
1598	1	Dyott Monoplane	Built by Hewlett & Blondeau at Clapham. 50 h.p. Gnôme.
1599	1	Henry Farman	Built by South Coast Aviation Works. 80 h.p. Gnome.
1600	1	Grahame-White 1600	Grahame-White Type XV prototype for R.N.A.S.

THE SECOND ALLOCATION TO THE ARMY

1601–3000

HAVING completed the allocation 201-800, and with 800-1600 reserved for the Royal Navy, the Army took up a further allocation of 1601-3000 in November 1914.

1601	1	Martinsyde Scout	Type not known.
1602-1613	12	Bristol Scout "C"	Ordered November 1914; delivered the following March.
1614-1615	2	Avro 519/522	Prototypes ordered 1914 but did not evolve until 1916.
1616-1647	32	Vickers F.B.5 "Gunbus"	1636 stored for preservation but later destroyed.
1648-1651	4	Vickers F.B.5 "Gunbus"	Numbers originally allotted to B.E.10 under Bristol order.
1652-1747	96	B.E.2c	Built by British and Colonial Aeroplane Co. 70 h.p. Renault engines fitted in early production models and 90 h.p. R.A.F. engines in late production models. 1697 became B.E.12 prototype, 1700 B.E.9, 1738 transferred to R.N.A.S.
1748-1779	32	B.E.2c	Built by Vickers, 1760-1779 at Weybridge.
1780-1800	21	B.E.2c	Built by Sir W. G. Armstrong Whitworth & Co. Ltd.

Serial Nos.	*Qty.*	*Aircraft Type*	*Remarks*
1801-1999	199	(Allotted for purchases by General Headquarters, Royal Flying Corps, British Expeditionary Force in France)	1801-1806, H.F.; 1807, B.E.2c; 1808-1812, Blériot Monoplane; 1813-1814, H.F.; 1815-1816, Blériot Monoplane; 1817-1818, H.F.; 1819-1820, Blériot Monoplane; 1821-1824, H.F.; 1825, Blériot Monoplane; 1827, M.F.S.7 Longhorn; 1828, 1829, Blériot Monoplane; 1830 M.F.S.7 Longhorn; 1832, 1834, 1836-1838, Blériot Monoplane; 1839-1841, M.F. S.11 Shorthorn; 1843, Morane; 1844 M.F. S.11 Shorthorn; 1845 Morane Parasol became Dutch LA35; 1846, M.F.; 1847, Blériot Monoplane; 1848-1849, Morane; 1850, Blériot Monoplane; 1851-1854, M.F.; 1855, Morane; 1856, Voisin (130 h.p. Canton Unné); 1857, M.F. (70 h.p. Renault); 1858, Voisin; 1859, Morane; 1860, Voisin; 1861-1863, Morane; 1864-1865, Voisin; 1866, Morane; 1867-1868, Voisin; 1869, M.F.; 1870-1876, Morane; 1877, Voisin; 1878, Morane; 1879, Voisin; 1880-1882, Morane; 1883, Voisin; 1884-1887, Caudron; 1888, Morane; 1890, Voisin; 1891, Caudron; 1892, Morane; 1893, M.F. (80 h.p. Renault); 1894, Morane; 1895, Caudron; 1896-1897, Morane; 1898-1899, Voisin; 1900, Caudron.
2000-2029	30	B.E.2c (90 h.p. R.A.F.)	Built by Armstrong Whitworth. 2029 became B.E.2e.
2030-2129	100	B.E.2c (90 h.p. R.A.F.)	Built by Daimler.
2130	1	B.E.8	Built by Vickers.
2131-2132	2	B.E.8	Built by C.O.W.
2133-2154	22	B.E.8a	Built by Vickers.
2155-2174	20	B.E.8a	Built by C.O.W.
2175-2180	6	B.E.2b	Built by Jonques.
2181-2184	4	B.E.8	Built by Bristol.
2185-2234	50	R.E.7	Built by C.O.W. 2191 and 2201 to R.N.A.S.
2235-2236	2	R.E.7	Constructor not known.
2237-2266	30	R.E.7	Built by Austin. 2241-2242 and 2260 to R.N.A.S.
2267-2286	20	—	Details not known.
2287-2336	50	R.E.7	Built by D. Napier & Sons. 2299 was converted to a three-seater with a 190 h.p. Rolls-

			Royce engine installed; 2322 had an R.A.F. 3a engine.
2337	1	Kennedy Giant	Components made by The Gramophone Co. Ltd. and Fairey Aviation. Erected at Northolt.
2338	1	Bleriot Monoplane	80 h.p. French-built.
2339	1	Curtiss	Used at Central Flying School.
2340-2347	8	Vickers F.B.5/5a "Gunbus"	Ex-R.N.A.S. Nos. 865-872.
2348-2447	100	R.E.7	Built by the Siddeley-Deasy Motor Co. Ltd. 2348 was flown as a two-seater with an R.A.F. 4a engine and as a three-seater with a Beardmore engine. 2362 was transferred to the R.N.A.S.
2448-2455	8	Martinsyde S.1	2449 served with No. 4 Squadron, April 1915.
2456-2459	4	R.E.5	Royal Aircraft Factory built.
2460	1	Maurice Farman	For Indian Government.
2461	1	R.E.5	Royal Aircraft Factory built.
2462-2468	7	Vickers "Gunbus"	French-built.
2469	—	—	Number not used.
2470-2569	100	B.E.2c/d/e	Built by Wolseley Motors Ltd. Early production mainly as B.E.2c. 2564 to R.N.A.S.
2570-2669	100	B.E.2c (90 h.p. R.A.F.)	Built by Daimler. 2578, 2590 and 2636 long range version for No. 9 Squadron.
2670-2769	100	B.E.2c (90 h.p. R.A.F.)	Built by Ruston, Proctor & Co. Ltd. 2735 and 2737 transferred to R.N.A.S.
2770-2819	50	B.E.2b/c/e	Built by Jonques. Ordered as B.E.2b but main delivery as B.E.2c.
2820-2831	12	Martinsyde S.1	Built by Martinsyde Ltd., Brooklands, Byfleet, Surrey.
2832	1	Henry Farman	80 h.p. Gnôme.
2838	1	Henry Farman F.22	Built by A.M.C.
2844 & 2851	2	Henry Farman	Used by Reserve Squadrons.
2852-2854	3	Blériot Monoplane	French-built.
2855-2856	2	Maurice Farman	From New Zealand.
2857-2860	4	Avro 504	Believed ex-R.N.A.S.
2861-2862	2	Blériot Parasol	French-built.
2863	1	Caudron	French-built C109.
2864	1	F.E.2a	Built by Royal Aircraft Factory, Farnborough.
2865-2868	4	Vickers F.B.5 "Gunbus"	Built by Vickers Ltd., Fulham.
2869	1	Blériot	French-built. Returned by B.E.F. and reconditioned by Vickers.
2870-2883	14	Vickers F.B. 5/5A "Gunbus"	Built by Vickers Ltd. at Bexley and Crayford.
2884-2889	6	B.E.2b	Built by Whitehead Aircraft Ltd., Richmond, Surrey.
2890-2939	50	Avro 504A	Built by S. E. Saunders Ltd.; 2929, 2930 & 2933-2934 were transferred to the R.N.A.S.

Serial Nos.	Qty.	Aircraft Type	Remarks
2940-2959	20	Maurice Farman S.11 Shorthorn	Constructor not known.
2960-3000	41	Maurice Farman S.7 Longhorn	Built by Aircraft Manufacturing Co. 2973, 2982 and 2984 were transferred to the R.N.A.S.

THE THIRD NAVAL ALLOCATION

3001–4000

WITH orders mounting in 1915 and Purchasing Commissions set up in France and America, the Admiralty took up a further allocation of one thousand numbers.

3001-3012	12	Maurice Farman	Built by Brush Electrical Engineering Co. Ltd.
3013-3062	50	Bristol Scout " C "	Built by British & Colonial Aeroplane Co. 3028 used in composite experiment with Porte Baby flying boat.
3063-3072	10	Short 827	150 h.p. Sunbeam.
3073-3092	20	Curtiss Triplane	3073 only built in U.S.A. and fitted with four 240 h.p. Renault engines in England. Known as Wanamaker-Curtiss. 3074-3092 cancelled.
3093-3112	20	Short 827 Seaplane	3093-3095 transferred to Belgian Government for use in African colonies.
3113-3114	2	Franco-British Aviation Flying Boat	French-built. 100 h.p. Gnôme Monosoupape engines fitted.
3115-3142	28	Handley Page O/100	Rolls-Royce Eagle engines fitted except for 3117 experimentally fitted with Hispano and Sunbeam engines. 3138 became the prototype of the H.P. O/400.
3143-3148	6	Short S.38	Built by White & Thompson. 80 h.p. Gnôme.
3149	1	Nieuport Scout	Purchased in France with 100 h.p. Gnôme.
3150	1	Henry Farman	Purchased in France with 125 h.p. Anzani engine.
3151-3162	12	Grahame-White G.W.XV	First production batch. 3151-3152 to Chingford.
3163-3186	24	Nieuport Type 10 or 12	French-built. 80 h.p. Le Rhône. 3168-3175 and 3179 shipped to Mudros 1915. Some converted to single-seat.
3187-3198	12	Nieuport Seaplane	French-built. 3194 and 3197 used by Northern Aircraft Co.
3199-3208	10	Franco-British Aviation Flying Boat	French-built. 3206 reconstructed by Norman Thompson Co.
3209-3213	5	Breguet de Chasse	Purchased in France.

3214-3238	25	Blériot Type XI Series II	Purchased in France.
3239-3263	25	Morane " L " Parasol	French-built. 3257-3262 shipped to Mudros.
3264-3288	25	Caudron G.III	French-built. 3268 used in East Africa.
3289-3300	12	Caudron G.IV	French-built.
3301-3320	20	Avro 504C	Built by The Brush Electrical Engineering Co. Ltd.
3321-3332	12	Short 827	Built by The Brush Electrical Engineering Co. Ltd.
3333-3344	12	Caudron G.IV	Built by the British Caudron Co. 3335-3336 to French Government.
3345-3423	79	Curtiss JN-3	American-built. 3345 to French Government. 3384, 3386, 3393 were rebuilt by Fairey Aviation.
3424-3444	21	Curtiss JN-4	American-built. 3425, 3432, 3434, 3436, 3438, 3440, 3442, 3444 fitted with dual control.
3445-3544	100	Curtiss R-2	American-built. 85 delivered. 160 h.p. Curtiss engines supplied were replaced by 200 h.p. Sunbeam engines. 3510 used for W/T experiments.
3545-3594	50	Curtiss H-4	American-built. Assembled at Felixstowe. 3580 became F.1 (Porte 1).
3595-3606	12	Vickers F.B.5 " Gunbus "	Built by Darracq. 3599-3600, 3602-3603 and 3605 transferred, less engines, to R.F.C.
3607-3616	10	Grahame-White G.W.XV	Various engines fitted according to availability.
3617-3636	20	Henry Farman	French-built. 3618-3619 served in East Africa.
3637-3656	20	Franco-British Aviation Flying Boat	French-built. 3648 and 3650 used by Northern Aircraft Company.
3657-3681	25	Burgess " Gunbus "	American-built. Not used apart from test. Placed in store.
3682	1	Henry Farman	Purchased in France.
3683	1	Morane Type BB	Purchased in France.
3684-3685	2	Armstrong Whitworth Triplane	Cancelled project. 250 h.p. Rolls-Royce Eagle engine planned.
3686	1	Sopwith A.1	Sopwith 1½-Strutter prototype.
3687-3688	2	Dyott Fighter	Built by Hewlett & Blondeau. 3687 to Hendon 17.8.16. 3688 to Dunkirk for trials.
3689-3690	2	F.E.8 (100 h.p. Gnôme)	Allocation cancelled.
3691	1	Sopwith Pup	Prototype. Exhibited in U.S.A., December 1917.
3692-3693	2	Bristol S.2A	110 h.p. Clerget. Re-allotted to R.F.C.
3694-3695	2	Avro 529/529A	Both crashed on test at Martlesham Heath.
3696-3697	2	Airco D.H.4	Prototypes. Record of 3696 only which became B394.

Serial Nos.	*Qty.*	*Aircraft Type*	*Remarks*
3698-3699	—	—	Not allotted.
3700	1	Curtiss Twin Canada	Curtiss (Canada)-built. Accepted at Hendon 11.11.16.
3701	1	Sloane-Day H.1 Biplane	American-built. Scrapped at Fairey works 26.2.17.
3702-3703	2	Fairey A.D. Tractor	Cancelled. Fairey F.1. Two 200 h.p. Brotherhood engines planned.
3704-3705	2	Fairey A.D. Pusher	Fairey F.2. Two 190 h.p. Rolls-Royce. 3704 only completed but as a Tractor.
3706	1	Short Bomber	Prototype. Wings extended after test.
3707-3806	100	Sopwith Schneider	Airframes of 3707, 3709, 3765 and 3806 transferred to Canadian Government. 3742 became P.V.1.
3807-3808	2	White & Thompson No. 3 Flying Boat	120 h.p. Beardmore. No. 3808 fitted with dual control.
3809-3820	12	Thomas T.2	American-built. 90 h.p. Curtiss. Not issued to squadrons.
3821-3832	12	Voisin	French built. 140 h.p. Canton Unné engines. 3825 transferred to No. 3 Squadron, R.F.C.
3833-3862	30	Sopwith 806	Built by Robey & Co. Ltd., Lincoln. 150 h.p. Sunbeam engines. 3850-3862 delivered for spares only.
3863-3882	20	Caudron G.III	Purchased in France.
3883-3887	5	Breguet de Chasse	Purchased in France.
3888	1	Breguet de Bombe	Purchased in France.
3889	—	—	Not allotted.
3890-3893	4	Blériot Tractor	Purchased in France.
3894-3899	6	Caudron G.IV	Purchased in France. 3896 returned to French.
3900-3919	20	Henry Farman	Purchased in France. 150 h.p. Canton Unné engines.
3920-3931	12	Nieuport 12	Purchased in France. Known as Nieuport 2-seater in R.N.A.S. 110 h.p. Clerget engines.
3932-3939	8	Maurice Farman S.7 Longhorn	3932 only purchased in France. 3933-3939 cancelled.
3940-3945	6	Nieuport Twin	Cancelled. Nieuport project with two 110 h.p. engines.
3946	1	Breguet Concours	Purchased in France. 250 h.p. Rolls-Royce engine fitted.
3947-3952	6	Blériot Tractor	Purchased in France.
3953	1	Nieuport Twin	Cancelled. Nieuport project with two 110 h.p. engines.
3954-3955	2	Maurice Farman S.7 Longhorn	Purchased in France.
3956-3958	3	Nieuport Scout	Purchased in France with 80 h.p. Le Rhône engines.
3959-3961	—	—	Reserved for purchases in France.

3962-3973	12	Nieuport 10	Purchased in France with 80 h.p. Le Rhône engines. Some converted to single.seat.
3974	1	Nieuport 11	Purchased in France.
3975-3994	20	Nieuport Scout	Purchased in France with 80 h.p. Le Rhône engines. 3978 transferred to Rumania.
3995-3997	3	Nieuport Twin	Cancelled Nieuport project with two 110 h.p. engines.
3998	1	Henry Farman	Purchased in France with 140 h.p. Canton Unné engine.
3999	1	B.E.2c (80 h.p. Renault)	Special aircraft for wireless telegraphy experiments built by Blackburn.
4000	1	Sloane Tractor	160 h.p. Sloane-Daniel.

THE ARMY'S THIRD ALLOCATION

4001–8000

WITH up to 4000 allocated to the Royal Naval Air Service, the Army took up a following range of four thousand numbers. Some 80 per cent of all aircraft acquired have been documented, but record cannot be traced of certain batches, which may have been numbers not taken up, cancelled orders, or due only to the lack of surviving records.

4001-4019	19	*See Remarks*	The identity of all 19 cannot be ascertained but the following have been noted: 4005, Maurice Farman S.7 Long-horn of No. 4 Reserve Squadron; 4010, Maurice Farman of No. 2 Reserve Squadron; 4016, B.E.2c; 4019, B.E. (2c?).
4020-4069	50	Avro 504A	4043-4044 were transferred to the R.N.A.S.
4070-4219	150	B.E.2c (90 h.p. R.A.F.)	Bristol Nos. 621-770. 4099, 4201 and 4205 were of the armoured version. 4111 and 4120 were converted to B.E.2c.
4220	1	D.H. Fighter	A.M.C. built.
4221-4225	5	Avro 504	Transferred from R.N.A.S.
4226	1	Caudron	French-built.
4227-4228	2	F.E.2a	Built by the Royal Aircraft Factory, Farnborough.
4229-4252	24	Martinsyde S.1	Mainly shipped for Middle East service.
4253	1	F.E.2a	Built by the Royal Aircraft Factory, Farnborough.
4254	1	Caudron	French-built.
4255	1	Avro 504	Transferred from R.N.A.S.

Serial Nos.	*Qty.*	*Aircraft Type*	*Remarks*
4256-4292	37	F.E.2b	Built by G. & J. Weir, Ltd. Beardmore engines fitted except for 4270 with 140 h.p. R.A.F. engine.
4293	1	Caudron	C567 from France.
4294	1	Maurice Farman	From overseas.
4295	1	F.E.2a	Built by the Royal Aircraft Factory. 120 h.p. Beardmore No. 135.
4296	1	Blériot Monoplane	French-built.
4297-4298	2	Maurice Farman	From France.
4299	1	Caudron	French-built C1887.
4300-4599	300	B.E.2c (90 h.p. R.A.F.)	Group-built under G. & J. Weir. 4524-4526 and 4570-4572 to R.N.A.S., of which 4571 was fitted with dual control. 4336-4337 and 4426 to R.N.A.S. with 90 h.p. Curtiss engines.
4600-4648	49	D.H.1/D.H.1A	Built by Savages, Kings Lynn.
4649	1	Nieuport Biplane	Built by Nieuport & General.
4650-4661	12	Blériot Tractor	French-built. 50 h.p. Gnôme engine.
4662-4699	38	Bristol Scout " C "	4663-4664 wrecked on delivery flight to France.
4700-4709	10	B.E.2c	Special single-seat version.
4710-4725	16	B.E.2c	Built by Vickers (Crayford).
4726-4731	6	Maurice Farman	French-built.
4732	1	D.H.2	Prototype.
4733-4734	2	Caudron	French-built C910/C902.
4735	1	Martinsyde Elephant	Type G.100 prototype. Crashed after 43½ hours flying.
4736	1	Vickers F.B.5 " Gunbus "	Built by Vickers Ltd. at Crayford.
4737-4786	50	Avro 504a	4784-4785 used in fabric tests at Air Depot, Egypt, 1916.
4787-4836	50	Voisin	Built under licence by Savages Ltd., Kings Lynn.
4837	1	Caudron	French-built C577.
4838-4900	63	F.E.2b	Built by G. & J. Weir. Beardmore or R.A.F.5 engines.
4901-5000	100	F.E.2b	Maker not confirmed.
5001-5200	200	(Purchased by General Headquarters, Royal Flying Corps, British Expeditionary Force.)	Details, as far as can be ascertained are as follows:—5001, Voisin; 5002, Morane; 5003, Caudron; 5004, M.F.; 5005-5007, Morane; 5008-5009, M.F.; 5010, Voisin; 5012, Morane; 5013-5014, Voisin; 5015, Maurice Farman (80 h.p. Renault); 5016, Caudron; 5017, Voisin; 5018-5019, Maurice Farman; 5020, Caudron (80 h.p. Gnôme); 5021-5023, Morane; 5024, Caudron; 5025-5026, Voisin; 5027, Maurice Farman; 5028, Voi-

sin; 5029, Morane; 5030, Maurice Farman (80 h.p. Renault); 5031, Morane; 5032, Caudron; 5033-5034, Morane; 5035, Caudron; 5036, Maurice Farman (80 h.p. Renault); 5037, Maurice Farman; 5038, Caudron; 5039, Morane (ex-MS424); 5040, Caudron (ex-C902); 5041, Morane; 5042-5043, Caudron (ex-C907/C922); 5044, Morane (ex-MS426); 5045-5048, Morane; 5049-5050, Caudron (ex-C566/C927); 5051-5052, Morane; 5053, Caudron (ex-C597); 5054, Maurice Farman (ex-MF618) (80 h.p. Renault); 5055-5058, Morane; 5059, Maurice Farman (ex-MF620); 5060-5061, Morane; 5062-5064, Caudron (ex-C612/616/592); 5065, Morane (ex-M476); 5066, Voisin (ex-V546); 5067, Caudron (ex-C594); 5068-5070, Morane; 5071, Maurice Farman (ex-MF608) (80 h.p. Renault); 5072-5073, Morane; 5074-5075, Vickers F.B.5 (Darracq-built); 5076-5077, Morane (ex-M478/M482); 5078-5079, Vickers F.B.5 (Darracq-built); 5080-5082, Morane; 5083-5084, Vickers F.B.5 (Darracq-built); 5085-5094 and 5096, Morane; 5097, Voisin; 5098, Morane Parasol; 5099-5103, Morane; 5104, Morane Biplane (110 h.p.); 5105-5126, Moranes (of which 5122 and 5126 are confirmed as biplanes and 5109, 5111, 5114, 5119, 5120, 5121 and 5125 as Parasols); 5127, Vickers Scout (*sic*) 5128, Morane Biplane; 5129, Morane (ex-M495); 5130, Morane Biplane; 5131, Morane; 5132-5133, Morane Parasol; 5134-5135, Morane; 5136-5137, Morane Biplane; 5139, 5141, 5143, 5150-5153, 5155, Morane Parasol; 5156, 5158, 5161, 5162, 5164, 5164, 5167, 5168, 5170, Morane Biplane; 5172-5173, Nieuport Scout; 5174, Morane Parasol; 5176-5177, Morane Biplane; 5179, Mor-

Serial Nos.	*Qty.*	*Aircraft Type*	*Remarks*
			ane Parasol; 5180, Morane; 5181-5185, Morane Biplane; 5187-5188, Morane Parasol; 5190, 5191, 5193, Morane Biplane; 5194-5195, Morane; 5196, Nieuport Scout; 5198-5199, Morane Parasol; 5200, Morane Biplane.
5201-5250	50	F.E.2b	Built by Boulton & Paul Ltd, Norwich.
5251-5270	20	Caudron G.III	From France.
5271-5290	2	Vickers F.B.9	Built by Vickers Ltd. at Crayford.
5291-5327	37	Bristol Scout "D"	Bristol Nos. 784-820.
5328-5334	7	Armstrong Whitworth F.K.3	5332 tested at Upavon 31.8.15 with oleo undercarriage.
5335-5383	49	D.H.1	Cancelled order.
5384-5403	20	B.E.2c (70 h.p. Renault)	Built by Wolseley Motors Ltd. Full range not confirmed.
5404-5412	9	Curtiss JN-?	Transferred from the R.N.A.S.
5413-5441	29	B.E.2c	Built by Vickers Ltd.
5442-5453	12	Martinsyde S.1	Built by Martinsyde Ltd., Brooklands, Byfleet, Surrey.
5454-5503	50	Vickers F.B.5 "Gunbus"	Built in France by Darracq. Delivered late 1915.
5504-5553	50	Armstrong Whitworth F.K.3	5504, 5505 and 5508 to Middle East.
5554-5603	50	Bristol Scout "D"	Bristol Nos. 1044-1093. 5554-5556 and 5564-5565 transferred to R.N.A.S. 5570 became G-EAGR.
5604-5605	2	Blériot Monoplane	Found in an aircraft park.
5606-5608	3	Curtiss JN	Presumed ex-R.N.A.S.
5609	1	S.E.4a	Royal Aircraft Factory built.
5610-5612	3	—	Not known.
5613	1	Caudron	French-built C921.
5614	1	A.W. F.K.3	Presumed prototype.
5615	1	Caudron	French-built C599.
5616	1	—	Not known.
5617	1	M.F. S.7 Longhorn	Built up from parts of 2976 and 2980 at No. 9 Reserve Squadron.
5618-5623	6	Vickers F.B.5	Known as "Gunbus" in R.N.A.S. service.
5624-5641	18	Curtiss JN-3/4	Transferred from R.N.A.S. orders.
5642-5648	7	F.E.2a	Delivered in autumn of 1915.
5649-5692	44	Vickers F.B.5	Known as "Gunbus" in R.N.A.S. service.
5693-5716	24	Morane Monoplanes	Ordered from Grahame-White.
5717	1	Vickers F.B.7/7a	F.B.7 modified to F.B.7a. First flew August 1915.
5718	1	Maurice Farman S.11 Shorthorn	Built up from spares at No. 2 Reserve Squadron.
5719-5721	3	Sopwith 1½-Strutter	Ex-9386, 9387, 9389 for No. 70 Squadron.
5722-5724	3	Curtiss JN-3/4	Ex-R.N.A.S. order.

5727	1	Curtiss Twin	Canadian-built.
5729	1	Vickers F.B.5	Believed transferred from R.N.A.S.
5730-5879	150	B.E.2d/e	Bristol Nos. 894-1043. No. 5844 converted to single-seater.
5880-5909	30	Maurice Farman S.11 Shorthorn	Contract awarded to Aircraft Manufacturing Company.
5910-5912	3	Curtiss JN-3/4	Ex-R.N.A.S.
5913-5915	3	Caudron	French-built. C544/473/598.
5916-6015	100	D.H.2	Built by Aircraft Manufacturing Company Ltd., Hendon.
6016-6115	100	R.E.7	Cancelled order with Austin.
6116-6135	20	Curtiss JN-3/4	Ex-R.N.A.S. 6121-6124 only confirmed.
6136-6185	50	B.E.12	Built by The Standard Motor Co. Ltd., Coventry.
6186-6227	42	Armstrong Whitworth F.K.3	Training aircraft, but 6213, 6221 & 6226 used operationally with No. 47 Squadron.
6228-6327	100	B.E.2d/e	Built by Ruston, Proctor & Co. Ltd. 6324-6327 transferred to R.N.A.S. less engines. 6228-6258 B.E.2d, rest B.E.2e.
6328-6377	50	F.E.2b	Built by the Royal Aircraft Factory. 6370 became F.E.2c.
6378-6477	100	F.E.8	Built by Darracq Motor Engineering Co. Ltd., Fulham, London.
6478-6677	200	B.E.12	Built by The Daimler Co., Ltd., Coventry. 6511 became B.E.12a.
6678-6727	50	Maurice Farman	Type S.7 Longhorn.
6728-6827	100	B.E.2d/e	Built by The Vulcan Motor & Engineering Co. Ltd. Initial production B.E.2d; late production B.E.2e.
6828-6927	100	R.E.7	Cancelled order G. &. J. Weir.
6928-7027	100	F.E.2b	Built by Boulton & Paul, Ltd., Norwich.
7028-7057	30	Bristol Scout " D "	Bristol-built Nos. 1094-1123.
7058-7257	200	B.E.2d/e	Bristol-built Nos. 1174-1373. Main deliveries as B.E.2e.
7258-7307	50	Martinsyde Elephant	Type G.100. Lewis gun on top wing tested on 7298.
7308-7311	4	Curtiss JN-3/4	Ex-R.N.A.S.
7312-7320	9	Caudron	French-built.
7321-7345	25	B.E.2c	Vickers-built.
7346-7395	50	Maurice Farman S.11	A.M.C.-built. 7385 (80 h.p. Renault) transferred to R.N.A.S. and returned to R.F.C.
7396-7445	50	Henry Farman	Constructor not known. 80 h.p. Gnôme. Used by Reserve Squadrons for training.
7446-7455	10	Avro 504A	Probably ex-R.N.A.S.
7456-7457	2	F.E.8	Prototypes. Built by the Royal Aircraft Factory.
7458	1	Voisin	French-built.

Serial Nos.	*Qty.*	*Aircraft Type*	*Remarks*
7459-7508	50	Martinsyde Elephant	Type G.100. Several despatched to Middle East.
7509	1	Vickers E.S.1	Experimental Scout No. 1. Known as " Barnwell Bullet."
7510-7519	10	Vickers F.B.5	Built by Darracq.
7520-7544	25	Avro 521	Unsatisfactory type. No record of delivery.
7545-7594	50	R.E.7	Cancelled order. Napier & Sons.
7595-7644	50	F.E.8	Built by Vickers Ltd. at Weybridge.
7645-7664	20	Blériot Type XI	7659-7664 not confirmed.
7665	1	Vickers	Type not confirmed.
7666-7715	50	F.E.2b	Built by Boulton & Paul Ltd., Norwich. 7700 used in No. 11 Squadron for message pick-up experiments.
7716-7740	25	Avro 504A	Ordered 19.1.16.
7741-7743	3	Caudron	French-built.
7744-7745	2	Airco D.H.3/3A	7744 D.H.3 modified to D.H.3A. No record of 7745 being built.
7746-7749	4	Henry Farman	From France to A.M.C. for engine fitting.
7750-7751	2	Bristol (Type 6) T.T.A.	T.T.=Twin Tractor. 7750 was tested in May, 1916.
7752-7755	4	Henry Farman	From France to A.M.C. for engine fitting.
7756-7758	3	Vickers Scout	Type not known. 7756 to No. 11 Squadron for report, but wrecked January 1917.
7759-7760	2	Vickers E.S.2	7759 flown in September 1915. Exhibited to King George V.
7761	1	Caudron	French-built.
7762-7811	50	Sopwith 1½-Strutter	Built by Ruston, Proctor & Co. Ltd., 7811 on Fleet charge in October 1918.
7812-7835	24	Vickers F.B.9	7816, 7820, 7826-7929 confirmed. Built by Darracq.
7836-7837	2	Bristol S.2A	Bristol Nos. 1377-1378. Built May-June 1916.
7838-7841	4	Armstrong Whitworth F.K.12	7838 built and modified. No record of delivery for 7839-7841.
7842-7941	100	Airco D.H.2	Built by the Aircraft Manufacturing Co. Ltd., Hendon.
7942	1	Sopwith 1½-Strutter	Transferred from R.N.A.S. Used by Nos. 52 and 70 Squadrons in turn. Ex-9381.
7943-7992	50	Avro 504A	Deliveries from June to September 1916.
7993-7994	2	F.E.4	Built by the Royal Aircraft Factory, Farnborough, in 1916.
7995	1	F.E.2d	Built by the Royal Aircraft Factory, Farnborough, 1916.

7996-7997	2	R.E.8	Built by the Royal Aircraft Factory, Farnborough, in 1916.
7998-8000	3	Sopwith 1½-Strutter	Ex-R.N.A.S. 7998 served with No. 70 Squadron.

THE FOURTH NAVAL ALLOCATION

8001–10000 FOLLOWING on from the 4000 numbers allocated to the Royal Flying Corps, the R.N.A.S. followed on with the allocation 8001-10000 in 1916 and had used it up within the year.

8001-8030	30	Short 184	Built by S. E. Saunders Ltd., East Cowes. 225 h.p. Sunbeam engines initially fitted, but 8014, 8019 and 8022 had 240 h.p. Sunbeams installed in service.
8031-8105	75	Short 184	Built by Short Bros., Rochester. 225 h.p. Sunbeam engines initially fitted, but many were fitted later with more powerful Sunbeams. 8053 was fitted with dual control. 8083-8084 transferred to the French, 8057 to Japan.
8106-8117	12	Maurice Farman S.11 Shorthorn	French-built. 8112-8117 transferred to R.F.C. with 70 h.p. Renault engines.
8118-8217	100	Sopwith Baby	Various engines fitted; the first five and last 31 had 100 h.p. Gnôme Monosoupapes and the others had 110 h.p. Clergets which weie replaced later by 130 h.p. Clergets. Transfers to other Governments were: 8128-8129 (110 h.p. Clergets) and 8185 (less engine) to France; 8125, 8197, 8204, 8209 (less engines) to Canada; 8201 to Japan.
8218-8229	12	Short 827	Built by Parnall & Sons Ltd., Bristol. 8226-8229 fitted with dual control.
8230-8237	8	Short 827	Built by The Brush Electrical Engineering Co., Ltd.
8238-8249	12	Henry Farman F.27	8238 and 8243 transferred to R.F.C.
8250-8257	8	Short 827	Built by Parnall & Sons Ltd., Eastville, Bristol.
8258-8268	11	Burgess " Gunbus "	Purchased in America. Placed in store.
8269-8280	12	Thomas T.2	Purchased in America. Placed in store.

Serial Nos.	*Qty.*	*Aircraft Type*	*Remarks*
8281-8292	12	Wight 840	Built by Portholme Aerodrome, Ltd., Huntingdon. 8281-8283 only assembled; remainder delivered as spares.
8293-8304	12	B.E.2c (90 h.p. R.A.F.)	Built by The Grahame-White Aviation Co. Ltd., Hendon.
8305-8316	12	G.W.1600 (G.W.XV)	Built by The Grahame-White Aviation Co. Ltd., Hendon.
8317-8318	2	Short 310 (Type A)	Fitted for launching 18 in. torpedos.
8319-8320	2	Short 320 (310 Type B) North Sea	Prototype reconnaissance and Zepp. attack seaplanes.
8321-8322	2	Wight Trainer Seaplane	Built by J. Samuel White & Co., East Cowes, I.O.W.
8323-8325	—	—	Numbers not allotted.
8326-8337	12	B.E.2c (90 h.p. R.A.F.)	Built by William Beardmore & Co. Ltd., Dalmuir.
8338-8343	6	Norman Thompson N.T.4 " Small America "	Built by the Norman Thompson Flight Co. Ltd., Bognor.
8344-8355	12	Short 184	Built by Mann Egerton & Co. Ltd., Norwich. Delivered from December 1915. Fitted for carriage of 14 in. torpedos.
8356-8367	12	Short 184	Built by Westland Aircraft Works, Yeovil. Delivered from January 1916. 8357 fitted with experimental 200 h.p. Mercedes engine.
8368-8379	12	Short 184	Built by The Phoenix Dynamo Manufacturing Co., Ltd., Bradford. Delivered from February 1916.
8380-8391	12	Short 184	Built by Frederick Sage & Co. Ltd., Peterborough. Delivered from November 1915.
8392-8403	12	Curtiss JN-3	Built by Canadian Curtiss, Toronto. 8403 transferred to French Government.
8404-8409	6	B.E.2c	Built by the Eastbourne Aviation Co. Ltd., Eastbourne.
8410-8433	24	B.E.2c (90 h.p. R.A.F.)	Built by Hewlett & Blondeau Ltd. 8424, 8425, 8427 and 8428 transferred to R.F.C.
8434-8439	6	Short S.38 (80 h.p. Gnôme)	Built by the Norman Thompson Flight Co. Ltd., Bognor.
8440-8441	2	Avro 519 Bomber	Experimental aircraft for evaluation.
8442-8453	12	Bristol T.B.8	Bristol Nos. 870-881.
8454-8465	12	R.E.P. Parasol	French (Robert Esnault-Pelterie)-built. Le Rhône engines fitted.
8466-8473	8	Maurice Farman S.11 Shorthorn	Built in France. Transferred from R.F.C. with 75 h.p. Renault engines.
8474	1	Maurice Farman S.7 Longhorn	Built in France.

8475-8486	12	Nieuport Twin	Cancelled. Nieuport project with two 110 h.p. engines.
8487	1	Pemberton-Billing School	Built by Supermarine Ltd., Woolston. 80 h.p. Le Rhône engine fitted.
8488-8500	13	B.E.2c (R.A.F.)	Built by Wm. Beardmore & Co. Ltd., at Dalmuir.
8501-8509	9	Voisin	8501-8504, 140 h.p. Canton-Unné, 8505-8509, 150 h.p.; 8506 to R.F.C.
8510-8515	6	Nieuport Type 12	Nieuport 2-seater. Built in France. 110 h.p. Clerget engines.
8516-8517	2	Nieuport Scout	Built in France.
8518-8523	6	Voisin	French-built. 150 h.p. Canton-Unné. 8518 & 8523 to R.F.C.
8524-8529	6	Nieuport Type 12	French-built. 110 h.p. Clerget. 8524-8525 to the Rumanian Government.
8530-8541	12	Short S.38	Built by White & Thompson, Ltd., Bognor, Sussex. 80 h.p. Gnôme.
8542-8549	8	Wight 840	Built by Portholme Aerodrome Ltd., Huntingdon; delivered unassembled for spares.
8550-8561	12	Short 827	Built by Fairey Aviation as their Nos. F4-15. 8560 transferred to R.F.C.
8562-8573	12	Bristol T.B.8	Bristol Nos. 882-893.
8574-8603	30	Avro 504C	Known as Avro Scout. 8603 became Avro 504F.
8604-8605	2	Maurice Farman S.7 Longhorn	Built by Aircraft Manufacturing Co. Ltd., Hendon. Most probably built up from salvaged parts.
8606-8629	24	B.E.2c (90 h.p. R.A.F.)	Built by The Blackburn Aeroplane & Motor Co. Ltd., Leeds.
8630-8649	20	Short 827	Built by The Sunbeam Motor Car Co. Ltd., Wolverhampton.
8650-8699	50	Curtiss H.12	Built by Curtiss, U.S.A. 160 h.p. Curtiss engines supplied, but were replaced by Rolls-Royce Eagle engines. 8691 had telescopic mast fitted. 8650 used for development work.
8700-8707	8	Voisin	French-built. 150 h.p. Canton-Unné. Known in R.N.A.S. as Voisin New Type.
8708-8713	6	Nieuport Type 12	French-built. 110 h.p. Clerget engines fitted.
8714-8724	11	B.E.2c (90 h.p. R.A.F.)	Built by Wm. Beardmore & Co. Ltd., Dalmuir. 8716 transferred to R.F.C.
8725	1	Airco D.H.2	Prototype. Transferred to R.F.C.

Serial Nos.	*Qty.*	*Aircraft Type*	*Remarks*
8726-8744	19	Nieuport Type 12	Purchased in France. 110 h.p. Clerget engine. 8731 to Rumanian Government. Some converted to single-seat.
8745-8751	7	Nieuport Scout	Purchased in France. 80 h.p. Le Rhône.
8752-8801	50	G.W.1600 (G.W.XV)	8752-8753 to Australian Government with 60 h.p. Le Rhônes.
8802-8901	100	Curtiss JN-4	Built by Curtiss, U.S.A. 8881-8900 not delivered. 8901 transferred to R.F.C. 8852, 8856 and 8858 handed over to French.
8902-8920	19	Nieuport Type 12	French-built. 110 h.p. Clerget engines.
8921-8940	20	Maurice Farman S.7 Longhorn	Built by The Brush Electrical Engineering Co. Ltd., Loughborough.
8941-8950	10	Caudron G.III	French-built. Known as Caudron School.
8951-9000	50	Bristol Scout " D "	Bristol Nos. 1124-1173. 8976 to Australian Government. 8981-9000 allocated to R.F.C. but were returned to Admiralty.
9001-9020	20	P.B.25 Scout	Built by Pemberton-Billing.
9021-9040	20	Wight 840	Built by William Beardmore & Co. Ltd., Dalmuir; 9029-9040 delivered as spare parts.
9041-9060	20	Short 184	Built by Robey & Co., Ltd., Lincoln, from June 1916.
9061-9064	4	Norman Thompson N.T.4A " Small America "	160 h.p. Green engines planned. 140 h.p. Hispano engines fitted.
9065-9084	20	Short 184	Built by Frederick Sage & Co. Ltd., Peterborough.
9085-9094	10	Short 184 modified	Built by Mann, Egerton & Co. Ltd., as their Type B seaplane.
9095-9096	2	Admiralty A.D. Naviplane	9095 built by Supermarine Aviation; 9096 cancelled.
9097-9098	2	Wight Baby Seaplane	Built by J. Samuel White & Co., East Cowes, I.O.W.
9099	1	Henry Farman	French-built. 160 h.p. Canton Unné. Transferred to R.F.C.
9100	1	Wight Baby	Built by J. Samuel White & Co., East Cowes, I.O.W.
9101-9131	31	Caudron G.IV	French-built. Known as Caudron Twin. 9101 & 9104-9106 transferred to R.F.C.
9132	1	—	Cancelled order.
9133	1	Maurice Farman F.37	French-built. 110 h.p. Renault.
9134-9153	20	Henry Farman F.27	French-built. 160 h.p. Canton Unné. 9152 transferred to R.F.C.
9154	1	Voisin Canon	French-built. 150 h.p. Canton Unné.

9155-9174	20	Farman F.40	French-built. 150 h.p. Renault.
9175-9200	26	Breguet Concours	French-built. 225 h.p. Renault.
9201-9250	50	Nieuport Type 12	Built by William Beardmore & Co. Ltd.; 9213-9232 and 9235 transferred to R.F.C.
9251-9260	10	Henry Farman Astral	Ordered from Brush Electrical Engineering Co., Ltd., Loughborough. 9251 only delivered, 12.3.17.
9261-9275	15	Henry Farman Astral	Order cancelled.
9276-9285	10	Avro 504E	Built by A. V. Roe. Dua control fitted.
9286-9305	20	Caudron G.IV	Cancelled. Caudron Twin with two 100 h.p. Anzani engines.
9306-9355	50	Short Bomber	35 built by Short Bros., Rochester. 9341-9355 cancelled. 9311 presented to French Government. 9315, 9319, 9320, 9325 transferred to R.F.C.
9356-9375	20	Short Bomber	15 built by The Sunbeam Motor Car Co. Ltd., 9371-9375 cancelled.
9376-9425	50	Sopwith 1½-Strutter	Initial production by Sopwith. 110 or 130 h.p. Clerget engines. 9396 and 9420 were interned in Holland.
9426-9455	30	Breguet Concours (G.W. Type XIX)	10 built by Grahame-White Aviation. 250 h.p. Rolls-Royce. 9436-9455 cancelled.
9456-9475	20	B.E.2c	Transferred from R.F.C. without engines. Re-engined as follows: 9456-9457, 90 h.p. Curtiss; 9458, 75 h.p. Rolls-Royce Hawk; 9459-9461, 90 h.p. R.A.F.; 9462-9469, 90 h.p. Curtiss; 9470, 90 h.p. R.A.F.; 9471-9475, 90 h.p. Curtiss.
9476-9495	20	Short Bomber	Built by Mann, Egerton & Co. Ltd., Norwich. 9476-9479, 9482-9485 and 9487-9488 transferred to R.F.C.
9496-9497	2	Sopwith Pup	Prototypes. Admiralty Type 9901. 80 h.p. Clerget.
9498-9499	2	Robey-Peters	Davis gun machine. 1 built.
9500-9600	101	Curtiss Twin Canada	Cancelled. Ordered from Curtiss, Canada.
9601-9610	10	Franco-British Aviation Flying Boat	French-built. 100 h.p. Gnôme Monosoupape.
9611-9612	2	SPAD S.7	French-built pattern aircraft for Mann, Egerton production. 9611 to R.F.C. as B388, 9612 compromised number below.
9612-9635	24	Franco-British Aviation Flying Boat	French-built. 9615, 9622 & 9623 transferred to R.F.C. as B3984-3986.
9636-9650	—	—	Reserved numbers for purchases in France.

Serial Nos.	Qty.	Aircraft Type	Remarks
9651-9750	100	Sopwith 1½-Strutter (Admiralty Type 9400 two-seater and Type 9700 single-seat)	Type 9400 except for 35 Type 9700 (single-seat) as follows: 9651-9652, 9655, 9657, 9660-9661, 9664, 9666-9673, 9700, 9704, 9707, 9711, 9714-9715, 9718, 9720, 9723-9724, 9727, 9729, 9732-9733, 9736, 9738, 9741-9742, 9745 and 9747. Several were transferred to R.F.C. and renumbered (*see* A888-891). 110 h.p. Clerget engines were standard fit, but a few had 130 h.p. Clergets.
9751-9770	20	Short 166 Seaplane	Built by Westland Aircraft Works, Yeovil, and delivered from July 1916. 9754 converted for use as a landplane in Aegean theatre.
9771-9780	10	Short Bomber	6 built by Parnall & Sons. 9777-9780 cancelled.
9781-9790	10	Short 830 Seaplane.	Short Nos. S.301-310. 140 h.p. Canton Unné.
9791-9799	9	—	Not allotted.
9800-9820	21	Porte Baby	Hulls constructed by May, Harden and May, Southampton Water. 9800-9811 only erected at Felixstowe.
9821-9830	10	Avro 504B	Built by A. V. Roe in 1916.
9831-9840	10	Short Bomber	6 built by The Phoenix Dynamo Co. 9837-9840 cancelled. 9832-9833 transferred to R.F.C.
9841-9860	20	Wight Seaplane	Built by J. S. White & Co., East Cowes. 9841-9850 built as landplanes, 9851-9860 completed as seaplanes.
9861-9890	30	Avro 504B	Built by Parnall & Sons Ltd. Planned armament of four 16 lb. bombs. 9890 fitted with gun interrupter gear.
9891	1	Sopwith 1½-Strutter	80 h.p. Gnôme. Prototype.
9892-9897	6	Sopwith 1½-Strutter	Admiralty Type 9400 (two-seat). 9892 transferred to R.F.C.
9898-9900	3	Sopwith Pup	Admiralty Type 9901. 80 h.p. Clerget.
9901-9950	50	Sopwith Pup	Built by Beardmore. Admiralty Type 9901. 80 h.p. Clerget initially fitted up to 9911, and 80 h.p. Le Rhône on all subsequent. From 9909 aircraft were fitted alternately with machine gun/rocket armament. 9950 was modified to become the Beardmore W.B.III.
9951-10000	50	B.E.2c (90 h.p. R.A.F.)	Built by the Blackburn Aeroplane & Motor Co. Ltd., Leeds.

PREFIXES INTRODUCED

A1—9999 FROM 1916 the character of serialling changed: numbers allotted were prefixed by a letter, without exception. It was the start of the sequence that is still being carried on today. It was considered impracticable to go into five-digit numbers, and after the allocation of the first 10,000 numbers in batches between the R.N.A.S. and the R.F.C. the numbering system began again with a special "N" series for the Navy. (This is dealt with in alphabetical sequence, rather than chronological order, to facilitate ease of reference and commences on page 136.) The R.F.C. series started at A1.

A1-40	40	F.E.2d	Built by the Royal Aircraft Factory.
A41-65	25	F.E.8	Built by The Darracq Motor Engineering Co. Ltd., Fulham. Originally ordered from the Royal Aircraft Factory.
A66-115	50	R.E.8	45 built by the Royal Aircraft Factory, A110-115 not completed. A95 became an R.E.8a.
A116-315	200	(Purchases by General Headquarters, Royal Flying Corps, British Expeditionary Force in France) Note M.S. for Morane-Saulnier. Type BB also known as Morane Biplane, Type L and LA known as Morane Parasol. Type N also known as Morane Scout or Bullet. Nieuports 11 & 12 were two-seaters and 16 & 17 single-seaters.	The full account of the purchases in France cannot be ascertained; from various records, combat reports, log-books, photographs, etc., the following are recorded: A116-118, Nieuport Scout; A119, Morane Biplane; A120, Morane Parasol; A121, Nieuport 16; A122, M.S. N; A123-124, M.S. L; A125, Nieuport 16; A126; Nieuport 11; A127-128, M.S. L; A130-131, Nieuport 16; 132 M.S. Biplane; A133-136, Nieuport 16; A137, 139, M.S. BB; A140, M.S.; A142-144, M.S. L; A147, M.S. BB; A148, M.S. N; A149, 151, M.S. BB; A152-153, M.S. L; A154, Nieuport 12; A155, M.S. BB; A156, Nieuport 12; A157, 159, M.S. L; A160, M.S. N; A161, M.S. BB; A164-165, Nieuport 16; A166-167, M.S. N; A168, M.S. L; A170, M.S.; A171-179, M.S. N; A180-181, M.S. L; A184, Nieuport 16; A186, M.S. N; A187, Nieuport 16; A188, Nieuport; A189-190, M.S. BB; A193, M.S. L; A194, M.S. N; A195, M.S. BB; A196, M.S. N; A197, M.S. L; A198-199, M.S. N; A200-201, Nieuport 17; A202, M.S. V; A203, Nieuport 17; A204, M.S. V; A205, M.S. L; A206-207, M.S. V; A208, Nieuport 16; A209, M.S. V; A210-211,

Serial Nos.	Qty.	Aircraft Type	Remarks
			Nieuport 16; A212-213, Nieuport 17; A214, Nieuport 16; A215, Nieuport 17; A216, Nieuport 16; A219, M.S. V; A220, M.S. BB; A221-222, M.S.; A223-225, Nieuport 16; A227, M.S. BB; A228-229, Nieuport 12; A234, M.S.; A236-237, M.S. V; A239, M.S. L; A242, M.S. BB; A245-246, M.S. V; A250, M.S. L; A251, M.S. BB; A252, M.S. V; A253, Spad S.7; A254, M.S. V; A255, M.S. L; A256, Spad S.7; A258, Nieuport 12; A259, Nieuport; A261, M.S. L; A262-263, Spad S.7; A264, M.S. L; A265, M.S.; A266, 268, M.S. L; A271-276, 278-279, 281, Nieuport 17; A283, M.S. BB; A285, Nieuport 12; A287, M.S. BB; A291, Nieuport; A292, Nieuport 12; A294, M.S. BB; A297, M.S. L; A301, M.S. BB; A305-307, Nieuport 17; A309, Nieuport 12; A310 Spad S.7; A311, Nieuport 17; A312, Spad S.7; A313-314, Nieuport.
A316-317	2	Avro (528?)	Numbers allotted to A.V. Roe.
A318-323	6	Martinsyde Trainer.	Experimental aircraft allotment.
A324-373	50	Maurice Farman S.11 Shorthorn	A.M.C. built. 80 h.p. Renault, A324, 334, 354 to R.N.A.S.
A374-375	2	Albatros	Captured.
A376	1	B.E.2c	Built up from spares.
A377-386	10	Sopwith 1½-Strutter	Ex-R.N.A.S. contract.
A387-410	24	Henry Farman	All-steel overseas version.
A411	1	A.W. F.K.8	Prototype.
A412-461	50	Avro 504A	Built by S. E. Saunders Ltd., East Cowes, Isle of Wight.
A462-511	50	Avro 504A	Built by the Blériot and SPAD aircraft works.
A512-561	50	Avro 504A	Built by A. V. Roe & Co. Ltd.
A562-611	50	B.E.12A	Built by Coventry Ordnance Works.
A612-613	2	Bristol F.3A	Bristol Type 7. 3-seat escort fighter project. Not built.
A614-625	12	Curtiss JN-3/4	Transferred to R.F.C. from R.N.A.S. orders.
A626-675	50	Sopwith Pup	Built by the Standard Motor Co. Ltd., Coventry.
A676-727	52	Vickers F.B.14	Fifty built and mainly delivered as airframes less engines. Held in store at Islington until scrapped.

A728	1	M.F. S.11 Shorthorn	Used by No. 2 R.S.
A729-777	49	A.W. Biplane	Cancelled order.
A778-877	100	F.E.2b	Built by G. & J. Weir, Cathcart. A826 transferred to the R.N.A.S. A838 had a searchlight installed August 1917.
A878-897	20	Sopwith 1½-Strutter	R.N.A.S. aircraft renumbered on transfer, *e.g.* A888-891 = ex-9675, 9676, 9678, 9681, and A896 = ex-9679.
A898-903	6	Curtiss JN-3/4	Transferred from R.N.A.S.
A904-953	50	Maurice Farman S.11 Shorthorn	Built by the Aircraft Manufacturing Co. Ltd., Hendon. 80 h.p. Renault.
A954-1053	100	Sopwith 1½-Strutter	Built by Fairey Aviation. Fairey Nos. F.27-126.
A1054-1153	100	Sopwith 1½-Strutter	Built by Vickers Ltd. at their Crayford factory.
A1154-1253	100	Henry Farman	Built by the Grahame-White Aviation Co. Ltd., Hendon.
A1254-1260	7	Curtiss JN-3/4	Ex-R.N.A.S. A1258-1260 to No. 6 Reserve Squadron, Beverley, 1916.
A1261-1310	50	B.E.2c/e	Built by Barclay, Curle & Co. Ltd., Whiteinch, Glasgow. A1284-1287 were transferred to the R.N.A.S. A1298 became G-EAJA.
A1311-1360	50	B.E.2c/e	Built by Napier & Miller Ltd., Old Kilpatrick. A1326-1329 transferred to the R.N.A.S. less engines.
A1361-1410	50	B.E.2c/e	Built by Wm. Denny & Bros., Dumbarton. A1382-1385 transferred to the R.N.A.S. A1404 & A1410 became G-EAJN and G-EAJV.
A1411-1460	50	Vickers F.B.9	Built by Vickers Ltd. at their Weybridge factory.
A1461-1510	50	Armstrong Whitworth F.K.3	Built by Hewlett & Blondeau Ltd., Leagrave, Luton. A1462, 1467, 1468, 1470 used operationally by No. 47 Squadron.
A1511-1560	50	Sopwith 1½-Strutter	Built by Hooper Ltd.
A1561-1610	50	Martinsyde Elephant	Type G.102. 160 h.p. Beardmore.
A1611-1660	50	Airco D.H.1/D.H.1A	Sub-let to Savages Ltd., Kings Lynn. A1631, 1635, 1638, 1643 were D.H.1As.
A1661-1710	50	Grahame-White Type XV	Built by the Grahame-White Aviation Co. Ltd., Hendon.
A1711	1	M.F. S.11 Shorthorn	Built up from spares at No. 2 R.S.
A1712-1741	30	Henry Farman	Built by the Aircraft Manufacturing Co. Ltd., Hendon.
A1742-1791	50	Bristol Scout " D "	A1769-1772 and 1790-1791 were transferred to the R.N.A.S.

Serial Nos.	*Qty.*	*Aircraft Type*	*Remarks*
A1792-1891	100	B.E.2d/e (90 h.p. R.A.F.)	Built by The Vulcan Motor & Engineering Co. Ltd., Crossens, Southport. A1829, 1833, 1835 transferred to the R.N.A.S. less engines.
A1892-1901	10	Caudron G.III	Built by British Caudron Co. Ltd., Cricklewood.
A1902-1931	30	Sopwith 1½-Strutter	Transferred from the R.N.A.S.
A1932-1966	35	F.E.2d	Built by the Royal Aircraft Factory, Farnborough.
A1967	1	A.W. Biplane	70 h.p. Renault.
A1968-1969	2	Vickers F.B.19 Mk. I	Prototypes.
A1970-2019	50	Avro 504A	Built by the Blériot & SPAD aircraft works, Addlestone.
A2020-2119	100	F.E.4	Cancelled order.
A2120-2121	2	Vickers F.B.15	Ordered from the Vickers factory at Bexley, but later cancelled.
A2122	1	Vickers F.B.19	Built at Vickers (Weybridge).
A2123-2124	2	Caudron	Built by the British Caudron Co. Ltd., Cricklewood. Type not ascertained.
A2125-2174	50	Airco D.H.4	Built by the Aircraft Manufacturing Co. Ltd., Hendon. B.H.P. or Rolls-Royce Eagle engines fitted in general; but A2168 had an R.A.F. engine and A2148 had the experimental installation of a Renault 12Fe engine.
A2175	1	Maurice Farman S.11 Shorthorn	Erected at Brooklands from spare parts, July 1916.
A2176-2275	100	Maurice Farman S.11 Shorthorn	Built by Whitehead Aircraft Ltd., Richmond. 80 h.p. Renault.
A2276-2375	100	Henry Farman	Ordered from the Grahame-White Aviation Co. Ltd., Hendon. No delivery record.
A2376-2380	5	Bristol Scout " D "	Transferred from the R.N.A.S. Ex-8981-8985.
A2381-2430	50	Sopwith 1½-Strutter	Built by Ruston, Proctor & Co. Ltd., Lincoln.
A2431-2432	2	Sopwith 1½-Strutter	Transferred from the R.N.A.S. A2431 was incorrectly numbered A3431.
A2433-2532	100	Maurice Farman S.11 Shorthorn	Built by the Aircraft Manufacturing Co. 70 h.p. Renault.
A2533-2632	100	Airco D.H.2	Built by the Aircraft Manufacturing Co. Ltd., Hendon.
A2633-2682	50	Avro 504A	Built by A. V. Roe & Co. Ltd., Manchester.
A2683-2732	50	Armstrong Whitworth F.K.8	A2696 was experimentally fitted with 150 h.p. Lorraine-Dietrich engine.
A2733-2982	250	B.E.2e	Built by the British & Colonial Aeroplane Co. Ltd., Filton.

A2983-2991	9	Sopwith 1½-Strutter	Transferred from R.N.A.S. contract direct from Sopwith Works, Aug. 1916.
A2992	1	Vickers F.B.19 Mk. 1	Prototype.
A2993-3005	13	Caudron G.III	Built by the British Caudron Co. Ltd., Cricklewood.
A3006-3020	15	Bristol Scout " D "	Transferred from the R.N.A.S. (ex-8986-9000).
A3021	1	Fokker	Captured. Used at C.F.S.
A3022	1	Curtiss JN	Used at C.F.S.
A3022	1	Henry Farman	Used at C.F.S.
A3024-3048	25	Caudron G.III	Built by British Caudron Co. Ltd., Cricklewood.
A3049-3168	120	B.E.2c/e	Built by Wolseley Motors Ltd., Birmingham.
A3169-3268	100	R.E.8	Built by The Austin Motor Co. Ltd., Birmingham.
A3269	1	B.E.2c	2076 rebuilt by 19th Wing.
A3270-3275	6	Nieuport Type 12	Ex-R.N.A.S. 9214-9219. Issued to equip No. 46 Squadron, R.F.C.
A3276-3280	5	Curtiss JN-4	Transferred from the Royal Naval Air Service.
A3281-3294	14	Nieuport Type 12	Ex-R.N.A.S. 9219-9232. Issued to equip No. 46 Squadron, R.F.C.
A3295-3302	8	Maurice Farman	Type S.11 mounted on floats.
A3303-3304	2	Bristol F.2A Fighter	Prototypes. A3303, 190 h.p. Rolls-Royce Falcon; A3304, 150 h.p. Hispano.
A3305-3354	50	Bristol F.2A Fighter	Rolls-Royce Falcon engines standard.
A3355-3404	50	Avro 504A	Built by S. E. Saunders Ltd., East Cowes, I.O.W.
A3405-3504	100	R.E.8	Built by The Siddeley-Deasy Motor Car Co., Ltd., Coventry.
A3431	1	Sopwith 1½-Strutter	Number incorrectly borne by A2431 (*q.v.*).
A3505	1	Vickers F.B.14	Vickers experimental aircraft. 160 h.p. Beardmore engine.
A3506-3530	25	R.E.8	Ordered from the Royal Aircraft Factory, Farnborough.
A3531-3680	150	R.E.8	Built by The Daimler Co. Ltd. A3542 & A3561 converted to R.E.9 with Sunbeam Maori engine.
A3681-3830	150	R.E.8	Built by The Siddeley-Deasy Motor Car Co. Ltd.
A3831	1	Curtiss	Ex-R.N.A.S.
A3832-3931	100	R.E.8	Built by D. Napier & Sons Ltd., Acton. A3902 had increased fin area of late production type. A3909-3912 were converted to R.E.9.
A3932	1	Short Bomber	Transferred from the Royal Naval Air Service. Ex-9833.
A3933-3934	2	Martinsyde F.1	Contract for two experimental aircraft.

Serial Nos.	*Qty.*	*Aircraft Type*	*Remarks*
A3935-4004	70	Martinsyde Elephant	A3997 had trials in June 1917 with radiator from a German aeroplane.
A4005	1	Short Bomber	Ex-R.N.A.S. 9325.
A4006-4055	50	B.E.12a	Built by The Daimler Co. Ltd., Coventry.
A4056-4060	5	Curtiss JN-4A	Transferred from the Royal Naval Air Service. Curtiss Nos. 147, 157, 163, 169, 172.
A4061-4160	100	Maurice Farman S.11 Shorthorn	Built by the Aircraft Manufacturing Co. Ltd., Hendon. A4144-4146 to the R.N.A.S., less engines.
A4161-4260	100	R.E.8	Built by The Daimler Co. Ltd., Coventry.
A4261-4410	150	R.E.8	Built by The Austin Motor Co. Ltd., Birmingham.
A4411-4560	150	R.E.8	Built by The Standard Motor Co. Ltd., Coventry.
A4561-4563	3	S.E.5	Prototypes built by the Royal Aircraft Factory. A4563 became the prototype S.E.5a.
A4564-4663	100	R.E.8	Built by The Standard Motor Co. Ltd., Coventry. A4600 and A4609 converted to R.E.9.
A4664-4763	100	R.E.8	Built by Coventry Ordnance Works Ltd., Coventry.
A4764-4813	50	Airco D.H.2	Built by the Aircraft Manufacturing Co. Ltd., Hendon.
A4814-4815	2	Vickers F.B.11	Experimental long range escort fighter by Vickers (Bexley).
A4816-4817	2	B.E.2c	Built up from spares at 2 and 18 R.Ss.
A4818-4844	27	F.E.9	Built by the Royal Aircraft Factory in 1917. Nacelles built complete but only eight aircraft completed.
A4845-4868	24	S.E.5	Built by the Royal Aircraft Factory, Farnborough. A4846 became S.E.5A.
A4869-4987	119	F.E.8	Built by The Darracq Motor Engineering Co. Ltd., Fulham.
A4988-5087	100	Airco D.H.2	Built by the Aircraft Manufacturing Co. Ltd., Hendon.
A5088-5137	50	Airco D.H.3	Cancelled order with the Aircraft Manufacturing Co.
A5138-5142	5	Bristol Monoplane	A5138, Type M.1A; A5139-5142, Type M.1B.
A5143-5152	10	F.E.2d	Built by the Royal Aircraft Factory, Farnborough, 1917.
A5153-5155	3	Short Bomber	Ex-R.N.A.S. 9484, 9483, 9319.
A5156	1	R.E.7	Built up from spares.
A5157-5159	3	Short Bomber	Ex-R.N.A.S. 9316, 9480, 9481.
A5160-5168	9	Curtiss JN-3/4	Transferred from the R.N.A.S.
A5169	1	Voisin	Original model for British production.
A5170-5171	2	Short Bomber	Ex-R.N.A.S. 9478 and 9772.

A5172	1	Airco D.H.5	Prototype built by A.M.C.
A5173	1	Short Bomber	Ex-R.N.A.S. 9485.
A5174	1	Vickers F.B.19 Mk.II	Prototype.
A5175-5176	2	Airco D.H.6	Prototypes built by A.M.C.
A5177-5178	2	Bristol M.R.1	Experimental all-metal aircraft, but A5177 was delivered with wooden wings. A5177 bore the number A58623.
A5179-5182	4	Short Bomber	Transferred from R.N.A.S. ex-9482, 9477, 9488, 9476.
A5183-5202	20	Nieuport Type 12	Ex-Beardmore-built 9213-9232 transferred from R.N.A.S.
A5203	1	Short Bomber	Ex-R.N.A.S. 9315.
A5204	1	Martinsyde	Built from spares by S.A.D.
A5205-5206	2	Curtiss Twin	Ex-R.N.A.S.
A5207-5208	2	B.E.2c	Built by No. 18 R.S.
A5209	1	Bristol Scout	Built by No. 18 R.S.
A5210	1	Vickers	Pusher type built from spares.
A5211	1	D.H.	Built by No. 19 R.S. from spares.
A5212-5213	2	A.W./F.K.10	Experimental Quadruplane.
A5214	1	Short Bomber	Ex-R.N.A.S. 9320.
A5215-5224	10	Curtiss Twin	Transferred from R.N.A.S.
A5225-5236	12	Vickers F.B.19 Mk.II	Built by Vickers (Weybridge).
A5237	1	—	Reservation.
A5238-5337	100	Sopwith 1½-Strutter	Built by Wells Aviation. Not all completed. Deliveries to foreign governments: A5234, Belgian, A5246-5251, Russian; A5254, Japanese.
A5338-5437	100	F.E.2b	Wells Aviation cancelled order.
A5438-5487	50	F.E.2b	Boulton & Paul-built.
A5488	1	B.E.2c	Built up from spares.
A5489-5490	2	Short Bomber	Ex-R.N.A.S. 9479 & 9487.
A5491	1	F.E.8	Built by Darracq, Fulham.
A5492-5496	5	Curtiss JN-3/4	Ex-R.N.A.S.
A5497-5499	3	B.E.2c	Built by No. 18 R.S. from spares.
A5500-5649	150	F.E.2b	Built by G. & J. Weir Ltd.
A5650-5799	150	F.E.2b	Group-built in Scotland. A5650 to U.S. Government. A5784 conv. to single-seater.
A5800-5899	100	Avro 504A	Cancelled order.
A5900-5949	50	Avro 504A	Avro (Manchester) built.
A5950-6149	200	Sopwith 1½-Strutter	Built by Morgan & Co. A5951, 5952, 5982-6000, 6006, 6010, 6019 conv. to Ship Strutter. Bomber version exports: A5973-5976, 6011, 6015, 6017, to Russia; A5977-5981, 6001-6002, 6012-6013, 6018, 6020, to Japan. No delivery record after A6050.
A6150-6249	100	Sopwith Pup	Built by Whitehead Aircraft.
A6250-6299	50	Martinsyde Elephant	A6299 experimentally fitted with Eeman gun gear.
A6300	1	Short Bomber	Ex-R.N.A.S. 9832.

Serial Nos.	*Qty.*	*Aircraft Type*	*Remarks*
A6301-6350	50	B.E.12	Daimler-built. Conv. to B.E. 12A included A6303, 6306, 6309, 6311-6313, 6315-6316, 6321-6323, 6326, 6337, 6339.
A6351-6600	250	F.E.2d/b	Erected by Boulton & Paul Ltd., nacelles built by Garrett. A6351-6570 (220) F.E.2d. A6571-6600 (30) F.E.2b. A6545 converted to F.E.2h with 200 h.p. B.H.P. A6460 shipped to U.S.A.
A6601-6800	200	(Allotted to General Headquarters, Royal Flying Corps, British Expeditionary Force, for purchases in France. Note M.S. L for Morane Saulnier Type L Parasol)	A6602, Nieuport 12; A6603-6605, Nieuport 17; A6607, M.S. LA Parasol; A6609-6611, 6613-6619, 6622-6624, Nieuport Scout; A6627, 6633-6634, Spad S.7; A6635-6638, M.S. L Parasol; A6640-6642, Spad S.7; A6643, M.S. L: A6644-6647, Nieuport 17; A6649, Spad S.7; A6650, 6652, M.S. L Parasol; A6654, Spad S.7; A6658, Nieuport; A6659, M.S. L Parasol; A6661-6663, Spad S.7; A6664, Nieuport 17; A6665, Nieuport 23; A6667-6678, Nieuport; A6679, M.S. L; A6680, Nieuport Scout; A6681-6682, Spad S.7; A6684, Nieuport 17; A6685, Spad S.7; A6686, Nieuport Triplane; A6687, Spad S.7; A6689, Nieuport 17; A6690, Spad S.7; A6692-6694, Nieuport; A6695, Spad S.7; A6700, M.S. L; A6701, Nieuport 17;A6706, Spad S.7; A6707, Nieuport 12; A6708, M.S. L: A6709-6714, Spad S.7; A6718, Nieuport 17; A6720-6721, Nieuport 23; A6725, M.S. L; A6726 Nieuport; A6730, M.S. L; A6731, Nieuport 20; A6732, Spad S.7; A6733 Nieuport 17; A6734, Nieuport; A6735, Nieuport 20; A6736, Nieuport 13; A6738-6739, Nieuport 17; A6740, Nieuport 12; A6741-6742, Nieuport 20; A6743, Spad S.7; A6744-6745, Nieuport; A6746-6749, Spad S.7; A6751, Nieuport 17; A6753, Spad S.7; A6754-6756, Nieuport; A6760, M.S. L; A6761, Nieuport; A6763-6766, Nieuport 23; A6768-6797, Nieuport.

A6801-7000	200	R.E.8	Cancelled. To have been built by the British & Colonial Aeroplane Co. Numbers reallotted as below.
A6801-6900	100	Maurice Farman S.11 Shorthorn	Built by the Aircraft Manufacturing Co. Ltd., Hendon.
A6901-7000	100	Sopwith 1½-Strutter	Built by Hooper & Co. Ltd., Chelsea, in the main as two-seaters. Single-seat versions were: A6901, 6906, 6914, 6943, 6993. Transfers to the Royal Navy and conversions to Ship Strutter were: A6905, 6911, 6913, 6917, 6919-6922, 6952, 6966-6968, 6971-6972, 6980-6981, 6985-6990.
A7001-7100	100	Maurice Farman S.11 Shorthorn	Built by the Aircraft Manufacturing Co. Ltd., Hendon. 70 h.p. Renault. A7043-7050 transferred to the R.N.A.S.
A7101-7300	200	Bristol F.2B Series I & II	Bristol Nos. 2069-2268. A7101-7176 and A7178-7250, Series I with Rolls-Royce Falcon I engines. A7177 and A7251-7300, Series II with Rolls-Royce Falcon II engines.
A7301-7350	50	Sopwith Pup	Built by The Standard Motor Co. Ltd., Coventry.
A7351-7400	50	Vickers F.B.12C	Ordered from Vickers' Weybridge factory. First 18 only built by Wells Aviation.
A7401-8089	689	Airco D.H.4	Built by the Aircraft Manufacturing Co. Ltd. Main production with Rolls-Royce Eagle or R.A.F. engines, A7559 became prototype D.H.9, A7988 became G-EAXH. Since D.H.4s had various power units, known details have been recorded as follows: A7401, Rolls-Royce Eagle VI No. 209/W.D.16083; A7436, R.A.F.3a; A7457, with R.A.F.3a, was fitted with hydrovane and flotation gear after transfer to the R.N.A.S.; A7451, transferred to R.N.-A.S. with R.A.F.3a; A7483, Rolls-Royce Eagle; A7488, B.H.P.; A7499, 7502, 7511, R.A.F.3a; A7532, Fiat; A7550, R.A.F.3a; A7620 and A7632, to R.N.A.S. without engines; A7665, Rolls-Royce Eagle; A7671, B.H.P. used for K.L.G. Type F.5.2B plugs test; A7726 and A7751, to R.N.A.S. without engines; A7760, 7764, 7772, 7773, to

Serial Nos.	*Qty.*	*Aircraft Type*	*Remarks*
			R.N.A.S. with Rolls-Royce Eagle VIII engines; A7819, Rolls-Royce Eagle; A7840, B.H.P.; A7864, experimental fitting of R.A.F.4d; A7893, 7929, 7937, 7993, Rolls-Royce Eagle VIII; A8006 to R.N.A.S. with Rolls-Royce Eagle; A8034, R.A.F.3a; A8059, 8063, 8065-8067, 8079, transferred to R.N.A.S.; A8083, to R.N.A.S. without engine and was fitted with Sunbeam Matabele.
A8090	1	Airco D.H.4	Believed re-built from spares.
A8091-8140	50	Armstrong Whitworth F.K.3	Built by Hewlett & Blondeau Ltd., Leagrave, Luton.
A8141-8340	200	Sopwith 1½-Strutter	Built by Ruston, Proctor & Co. Ltd., Lincoln. A8255, 8300 and 8317 modified to Ship Strutter and transferred to Royal Navy.
A8341-8490	150	Vickers F.B.14	First 51 only built at Vickers' Weybridge factory and held in store at Islington, except for A8391 which became the F.B.14F.
A8491-8500	10	—	Not allotted.
A8501-8600	100	Avro 504A	Built by A. V. Roe & Co. Ltd., Manchester.
A8601-8625	25	Vickers F.B.9	Built by Vickers Ltd. at their Weybridge factory.
A8626-8725	100	B.E.2e	Bristol Nos. 1737-1836. A8693-8699 transferred to the R.N.A.S. less engines.
A8726-8743	18	—	Cancelled order.
A8744-8793	50	Sopwith 1½-Strutter	Built by Vickers Ltd. at their Crayford factory. A8779 went to Royal Navy.
A8794-8893	100	SPAD S.7	Built by the Air Navigation Co. Ltd., Addlestone.
A8894	1	F.E.8	Built by Southern Aircraft Depot, Farnborough, Nos. 005-008.
A8895	1	F.E.2b	
A8896-8897	2	B.E.2c	
A8898-8947	50	S.E.5	Built by the Royal Aircraft Factory, Farnborough. A8901 became S.E.5a and A8947 became S.E.5b.
A8948-8949	2	B.E.2c	Built up from salvage at No. 18 R.S., Montrose.
A8950-8999	50	A.W. Quad	Order cancelled. Numbers re-allotted.
A8950	1	F.E.2b	Built by the Royal Aircraft Factory, Farnborough.
A8951-8956	6	T.E.1	Allotted to the Royal Aircraft Factory.
A8957-8962	6	Aerial Target	Allotted for radio-controlled aircraft.

A8963	1	Vickers F.B.16A/D	Built as F.B.16A at Vickers' Bexley factory and modified to F.B.16D.
A8964	1	Grahame-White M.1	Known as "Twin Airscrew Experimental Project". Not built.
A8965	1	SPAD S.7	S1321 from French Government.
A8966	1	Avro 504	Built up from spares at 21st Wing.
A8967	1	Nieuport 12	Sample from French Government to Beardmore's, purchased by R.F.C.
A8968-8969	2	Henry Farman	Ex-R.N.A.S. N3035 and N3029.
A8970-8973	4	Sopwith Scout	Type not confirmed. Warping Wings.
A8974-8998	25	Henry Farman	Ex-R.N.A.S. 9099, 9153, N3025-3028, N3030-3031, N3022-3024, N3036-49.
A8999	1	Aviatik (200 h.p. Benz)	Ex-German trainer.
A9000-9099	100	Sopwith Triplane	Sopwith-built. Transferred to the R.N.A.S.
A9100-9161	62	SPAD S.7	Built by Mann, Egerton & Co. Ltd., Norwich. Transferred from R.N.A.S.
A9162	1	Maurice Farman	Built from spares at No. 5 R.S.
A9163-9362	200	Airco D.H.5	Built by the Aircraft Manufacturing Co. Ltd., Hendon. A9362 was cancelled as the prototype A5172 was included in the contract for 200.
A9363-9562	200	Airco D.H.5	Built by the Darracq Motor Engineering Co. Ltd., Fulham.
A9563-9762	200	Airco D.H.6	Built by the Grahame-White Aviation Co. Ltd., Hendon.
A9763-9812	50	Avro 504A/J	Built by S. E. Saunders Ltd., East Cowes, I.O.W.
A9813-9918	106	Sopwith Triplane	Clayton & Shuttleworth contract, transferred to R.N.A.S. Allocation cancelled.
A9919	1	D.H. Fighter	Presumed D.H.1 or 2 built from spares.
A9920	1	Short 827	120 h.p. Sunbeam. At Bogton Oct. 18.
A9921	1	Maurice Farman S.11 Shorthorn	Built up from spares at No. 2 R.S., Brooklands.
A9922-9971	50	Avro 504A	Ordered from the Blériot & SPAD works. Cancelled.
A9972	1	A.W. F.K.3 (90 h.p. R.A.F.)	Used by No. 58 Squadron, Cromlington.
A9973-9974	2	B.E.2c	Built at Montrose.
A9975-9977	3	Avro 504	Ex-Admiralty, Parnall-built.
A9978-9979	2	Maurice Farman S.7 Longhorn	Ex-N5010-5011.
A9980-9999	20	Armstrong Whitworth F.K.8	Built by Sir W. G. Armstrong Whitworth & Co. Ltd., Gosforth.

BRITISH PRODUCTION, FRENCH PURCHASES AND RE-BUILT AIRCRAFT

B1–9999

THE "B"-prefixed series for the R.F.C., following the "A"-series from late 1916 included aircraft rebuilt from salvaged remains and issued with a new number, a range being reserved for each particular Aircraft Repair Depot. Final allocations for the purchase of French aircraft by G.H.Q., B.E.F., in 1917 appear on this page.

Serial Nos.	*Qty.*	*Aircraft Type*	*Remarks*
B1-200	200	S.E.5a	Built by Air Navigation Co., Addlestone, B18 conv. 2-seater.
B201-330	130	A.W. F.K.8	B214-215 R.A.F.4a engines.
B331-380	50	Airco D.H.5	Built by British Caudron Co.
B381	1	Sopwith Scout	Ex-R.N.A.S. Presumed Pup.
B382-385	4	Avro 504B	Ex-R.N.A.S. N6018-6021.
B386-387	2	B.E.2c (ex-spares)	Built at No. 18 R.S., Montrose.
B388	1	Spad S.7	Ex-R.N.A.S. 9611.
B389-392	4	Avro 504B	Ex-R.N.A.S. N6022-6025.
B393	1	M.F. S.7 Longhorn	Ex-R.N.A.S. N5012.
B394	1	D.H.4	Ex-R.N.A.S. 3696 prototype.
B395-396	2	Avro 504B	Ex-R.N.A.S. N6026-6027.
B397-400	4	M.F. S.7 Longhorn	Ex-N5016, 5014, 5013, 5015.
B401-500	100	F.E.2b/c	Built by Ransomes, Sims & Jeffries, Ipswich.
B501-700	200	S.E.5a	Vickers (Weybridge) built.
B701-900	200	(Various types rebuilt by No. 1 (Southern) Aircraft Repair Depot, South Farnborough)	B701, B.E.12; B702, B.E.2c; B704, F.E. 2b; B705, 707, 708, B.E.2d; B712, B.E. 2e; B714, 715, 1½-Strutter; B719, 722, 723, B.E.2e; B724, 725, 728, B.E.2c/e; B730 A.W.F.K.8; B733, S.E.5a; B734, R.E.8; B735, Pup; B736-739, 742, R.E.8; B744, Ship Strutter; B746, 748, B.E.2e; B750, 753, 759, 760, R.E.8; B762, 1½-Strutter (Single-seater); B763, Bristol Scout D; B764, 765, R.E.8; B771, B.E.2c; B774, D.H.4; B778, Camel; B780-781, 783, 787, R.E.8; B790, B.E.2c; B791, R.E.8; B792, B.E.2c; B793, 798, R.E.8; B799, 1½-Strutter; B803-805, Pup; B813, Bristol Scout D; B814, R.E.8; B817, Bristol F.2B; B821, 822, 824, 825, R.E.8; B828 Nieuport Scout; B832-833, 836, 841-846, R.E. 8; B847, Camel; B848, S.E.5a; B849, Pup; B851-852, Elephant; B853, R.E.8; B856, A.W.F.K.8; B860, 864-865, Elephant; B870-871, A.W.

			F.K.8; B872-873, Bristol F.2B; B875, S.E.5a; B876, R.E.8; B883, Bristol F.2B; B884, D.H.4; B885, Camel; B887, Bristol F.2B; B891, S.E.5a; B893, 898, 900, Camel.
B901-1000	100	Avro 504 A/J	Avro built.
B1001-1100	100	S.E.5a	Cancelled Whitehead order.
B1101-1350	250	Bristol F.2B (Rolls-Royce Falcon III engines fitted in general)	Bristol Nos. 2269-2518. B1200, Wolseley Viper; B1201 R.A.F. 4d later 200 h.p. Hispano, also had experimental 3-bay wings; B1204 Sunbeam Arab; B1206, Siddeley Puma.
B1351-1388	38	Spad S.7	Built by Mann, Egerton & Co. Ltd., Norwich. B1352-1354, 1356-1363, 1372, 1374-1376, 1384, 1386 went to U.S.A.
B1389	1	D.H. Scout (D.H.1 or 2)	Experimental order.
B1390-1394	5	Avro 504B	Ex-N6028-6029, 6650-6652.
B1395-1396	2	Morane Monocoque AC	Received via Paris. Incorrectly marked C1395.
B1397-1398	2	Avro 504B	Ex-R.N.A.S. N6653-6654.
B1399-1400	2	—	No record.
B1401-1481	81	Henry Farman	Cancelled A.M.C. order.
B1482	1	Airco D.H.4	Built by A.M.C., Hendon.
B1483	1	Maurice Farman	Built up by No. 2 R.S.
B1484-1489	6	Vickers F.B.26 Vampire I/II	B1484, 1486, Mk. I. B1485 conv. Mk. II. Rest cancelled.
B1490-1495	6	Martinsyde F.3	Protos. B1493-1494 cancelled.
B1496	1	Sopwith B.1/B.2	Experimental bomber.
B1497	1	A.W. (Beardmore)	Built by 18th Wing.
B1498	1	R.E.8	Built by 21st Wing.
B1499	1	Sopwith Scout (Pup?)	Built by 7th Wing.
B1500	1	B.E.12	Built by No. 37 Sqn.
B1501-1700	200	(Allotted for purchases of French aircraft by General Headquarters, British Expeditionary Force, France, mainly for Nieuport Types 17 & 23 to equip and maintain Nos 40 & 60 Sqns and Spad S.7s to equip and maintain Nos 19 & 23 Sqns)	B1501-1509, 1511-1520, Nieuport; B1521, Morane Parasol; B1522-1523 Nieuport; B1524-1531, 1535-1537, Spad S.7; B1539-1552, Nieuport; B1553, Spad S.7; B1554-1559, Nieuport; B1560-1565, Spad S.7; B1566-1572, Nieuport; B1573, Spad S.7; B1575-1579, Nieuport; B1580-1581 Spad S.7; B1582-1583, 1585, Nieuport; B1587-1589, Spad S.7; B1590, Nieuport; B1592-1593, Spad S.7; B1595, Nieuport; B1596, M.S. LA; B1597-1598, 1600-1602, Nieuport; B1604, M.S. LA; B1605-1608, 1610, Nieuport; B1611, M.S. LA; B1613, Nieuport; B1614-1615, M.S. LA; B1617-1619, Nieuport; B1620, Spad S.7; B1621, M.S. LA; 1622-1623, Spad S.7;

Serial Nos.	*Qty.*	*Aircraft Type*	*Remarks*
			B1624-1626, Nieuport; B1627-1628, Spad S.7; B1629-1631, 1633-1646, 1649-1650, 1652, Nieuport; B1653, Spad S.7; B1654-1656, 1658, Nieuport; B1660-1661, Spad S.7; B1662, Nieuport; B1663, Spad S.7; B1665-1667, Nieuport; B1668, M.S. LA; B1669 reported Spad and Nieuport; B1670, 1672, 1674-1675, 1677-1686, 1688-1694, Nieuport; B1695-1698, Spad S.7; B1700, Nieuport.
B1701-1850	150	Sopwith Pup	Standard Motor Co. built. B1816-1821 to R.N.A.S. B1807 became G-EAVX.
B1851-1900	50	F.E.2b	Built by Boulton & Paul Ltd.
B1901-1950	50	Curtiss JN-4/4A	Admiralty contract. To R.F.C.
B1951-2050	100	Maurice Farman S.11 Shorthorn	Built by A.M.C., Hendon. B2011-2012 to Australia.
B2051-2150	100	Airco D.H.4	Built by F.W. Berwick & Co. Ltd., London N.W.10.
B2151-2250	100	Sopwith Pup	Built by Whitehead Aircraft Co. Ltd., Richmond, Surrey.
B2251-2300	50	R.E.8	Built by D. Napier & Son Ltd.
B2301-2550	250	Sopwith 1F.1 Camel	Ruston, Proctor & Co. built. First Camel sub-contract. B2541 fitted with a 150 h.p. Gnôme Monosoupape engine. B2438, 2504 conv. to 2-seaters. B2543 to Greek Government.
B2551-2600	50	Sopwith 1½-Strutter (2-seater type)	Ruston, Proctor & Co. built. B2551 to R.N.A.S. less engine. B2566 conv. to Ship Strutter. B2568, 2575, 2580, 2584 to Belgian Government.
B2601-3100	500	Airco D.H.6	Built by A.M.C. B2801-2804 shipped to Australia. B2661 to Greek Government. 20 to Civil Register.
B3101-3250	150	Avro 504J	A.V. Roe (Hamble) built. B3104, 3106, 3157 conv. to 504K.
B3251-3300	50	Avro 504A	Built by The Humber Motor Co. Ltd., Coventry.
B3301-3400	100	Armstrong Whitworth F.K.8	B3316 used in doping and camouflage experiments.
B3401-3450	50	R.E.8	Built by The Daimler Co. Ltd.
B3451-3650	200	(Allotted for purchases of French aircraft by General Headquarters, British Expeditionary Force, France)	Purchases in the main for Nieuport Types 17, 23 & 27 to maintain Nos. 1, 29, 40 & 60 Sqns and Spad S.7 & 13 to maintain Nos. 19 & 23 Sqns of the R.F.C.; B3451, M.S. LA; B3452-3453, Nieuport;

			B3457, Spad S.7; B3458-3459, Nieuport; B3460, Spad; B3461-3473, Nieuport; B3464, Spad S.7; B3465-3466, 3470, Nieuport; B3471, Spad; B3473-3474, Nieuport; B3475, Spad S.7; B3476, M.S. LA; B3478, Spad S.7; B3479 the first Spad S.13 to R.F.C.; B3481-3483, 3485, 3486, Nieuport; B3488, 3490, Spad; B3491, Nieuport; B3492, Spad; B3494-3496, Nieuport; B3498-3499, Spad; B3500, Nieuport; B3502-3506, 3508-3510, 3515-3516, 3519-3520, 3524-3526, 3528, 3531-3535, 3538, Spad; B3540-3541, 3544, 3550, Nieuport; B3551, 3553, Spad; B3554-3555, Nieuport; B3556-3557, Spad; B3558, Nieuport; B3559-3560, 3562-3571, 3573, 3576, Spad; B3577-3578, 3582, 3584, 3586-3587, 3591, 3593, 3595, 3597-3598, 3600-3605, 3607-3608, 3611-3614, Nieuport; B3615-3616, Spad; B3617, Nieuport; B3618-3620, Spad; B3621-3635, 3637, Nieuport 27; B3638, 3640, Spad; B3641, 3643-3644, Nieuport; B3645, 3646, Spad; B3647-3650, Nieuport 27.
B3651-3750	100	B.E.2c/e	Built by The Vulcan Motor & Engineering Co. Ltd., Southport.
B3751-3950	200	Sopwith 1F.1 Camel (130 h.p. Clerget engines fitted in general)	Sopwith-built. B3773, 3785, 3794, 3808, 3817, 3835, 3853, 3885, 3888, 3936, etc. fitted B.R.1 engines. B3769 to Greek Government. B3772 to Canada. B3891 to French Government. B3801 conv. to 2-seater, 110 h.p. Le Rhône fitted. B3891 had 150 h.p. Gnôme fitted.
B3951	1	B.E.2c	Built up from spares.
B3952-3953	2	Avro 530	Recorded as Avro Fighter.
B3954	1	B.E.2d (ex-spares)	Built at 25th Wing.
B3955-3968	14	Airco D.H.4	Ex-R.N.A.S. N5970, 5980, 5986, 5987, 5990, 5991, 5994, 5995, 5998, 5999, 6002, 6003, 6006, 6007.
B3969	1	D.H.1 (ex-spares)	Built at No. 19 T.S.
B3970	1	B.E.2e (ex-spares)	Built at Netheravon with parts salvaged from 7189.
B3971-3976	6	N.E.1 (Night Experimental No. 1)	Royal Aircraft Factory built, 4 in 1917, 2 in 1918.

Serial Nos.	*Qty.*	*Aircraft Type*	*Remarks*
B3977	1	Sopwith 1F.1 Camel	N6338 to R.F.C. from Sopwith factory.
B3978-3979	2	B.E.2c	Built by 20th Wing.
B3980	1	Sopwith 1F.1 Camel	Repaired and taken on charge.
B3981	1	M.F. S.11 Shorthorn	Built from spares by No. 5 T.S.
B3982	1	M.F. S.7 Longhorn	Built from spares by No. 5 T.S.
B3983	1	B.E.2c (ex-spares)	Built from spares, Montrose.
B3984-3986	3	Franco-British Aviation Flying Boat	Ex-R.N.A.S. 9615, 9622 and 9623.
B3987	1	Airco D.H.4 (R.A.F. 3A)	Ex-R.N.A.S. N6380.
B3988	1	M.F. S.11 Shorthorn	Built from spares by 4 T.S.
B3989-3994	6	Bristol F/F.1 (Types 21/21A allotted retrospectively)	B3989-3990 F, B3991 F conv. to F.1. B3992 not completed. B3993-3994 not built.
B3995	1	B.E.2c	Built from spares by 18 T.S.
B3996-4000	5	Armstrong Whitworth F.K.10 Quadruplane	Ordered from Angus Sanderson. Allotted for target use.
B4001-4200	200	(Various types built by by No. 2 (Northern) Aircraft Repair Depot, Coal Ashton Sheffield including A.W. F.K.8, D.H.9, Sopwith Pup, Sopwith Ship Strutter)	B4009, B.E.2e; B4017-4018, F.K.8; B4029, 4036, 4038, 4040, R.E.8 (D.H.9 duplicated B4040); B4044, Ship Strutter; B4048, R.E.8; B4049, F.K.8; B4050-4051, 4059, R.E.8; B4061, F.K.8; B4069, 4086, 4089, 4093, 4094, 4097, 4105, R.E.8; 4108, 4120, F.K.8; B4124, 4128, Pup; B4134-4135, R.E.8; B4136, 4141, Pup; B4145, 4147, 4150, F.K.8; B4158, Pup; B4165-4166, 4170, 4174-4177, 4179, 4187, 4194, F.K.8; B4195, Pup; B4198, 4200, F.K.8.
B4201-4400	200	Avro 504J/A	Avro-built. B4201-4300, 504J (100 h.p. Monosoupape); B4301-4400 504A (80 h.p. Gnôme). B4221, 4242, 4265 conv. to 504K. B4305, 4306 to Norwegian Army. B4309-4317 to R.N.A.S.
B4401-4600	200	B.E.2e	Built by British & Colonial Aeroplane Co. Ltd., Filton. B4555 to R.N.A.S. B4562 conv. to B.E.2c.
B4601-4650	50	Sopwith 1F.1 Camel	Built by the Portholme Aerodrome Ltd. B4622 to Belgian Flying Corps.
B4651-4850	200	Maurice Farman S.11 Shorthorn (80 h.p.)	A.M.C. built. 80 h.p. engines. 25 transferred to R.N.A.S. B4674 became G-EAAZ.
B4851-4900	50	S.E.5a	Built by the Royal Aircraft Factory, Farnborough.
B4901-5000	100	Airco D.H.5	Ordered from March, Jones & Cribb Ltd., Leeds and up B4938 confirmed built.
B5001-5150	150	R.E.8	Built by The Daimler Co. Ltd.

B5151-5250	100	Sopwith 1F.1 Camel	Built by Boulton & Paul Ltd. B5228, 5242, 5248 to Belgian Flying Corps.
B5251-5400	150	Sopwith Pup	Built by Whitehead Aircraft.
B5401-5450	50	Sopwith 1F.1 Camel	Built by Hooper & Co. Ltd. B5428 used by 17th Aero Squadron, U.S.A.S.
B5451-5550	100	Airco D.H.4	Built by The Vulcan Motor and Engineering Co. Ltd. B5526 to 188th Sqn, U.S.A.S.
B5551-5650	100	Sopwith 1F.1 Camel	Built by Ruston, Proctor & Co. Ltd. B5605, 5607 to Belgian Flying Corps.
B5651-5750	100	Sopwith 1F.1 Camel	Built by Clayton & Shuttleworth for R.N.A.S. B5710, 5711, 5745, 5747, 5748 to Belgian Flying Corps. B5657, 5682, 5726 to Greek Government. B5679, 5680, 5727 to White Russian Forces. B5713 conv. 2-seater.
B5751-5850	100	A.W. F.K.8	A.W. built at Gosforth. B5795 wireless experimental aircraft.
B5851-5900	50	R.E.8	Built by Austin Motor Co.
B5901-6150	250	Sopwith Pup	Built by Standard Motors.
B6151-6200	50	B.E.2c/e	Built by British Caudron Co., at Alloa. B6183 became CFS18 in Australia.
B6201-6450	250	Sopwith 1F.1 Camel (Mainly 130 h.p. Clerget engines fitted)	Sopwith-built. B6318 conv. to 2-seater. B6329 had a 150 h.p. Gnôme Monosoupape. B6255, 6338, 6360, 6367, to Greek Government.
B6451-6630	180	R.E.8/R.T.1	Built by Siddeley-Deasy. B6625-6630 were R.T.1.
B6631-6730	100	R.E.8	Built by C.O.W.
B6731-7130	400	(Allotted for purchases of French aircraft by General Headquarters and British Expeditionary Force, but full allocation of numbers not used)	B6731-6739 Spad 13; B6751-6756, Nieuport 27; B6762, Spad S.7; B6765-6770, Nieuport 27; B6772-6773, Spad; B6774, Nieuport 27; B6775-6777, Spad; B6778-6779, Nieuport 27; B6780, Spad; B6784-6786, 6788-6793, Nieuport 27; B6794-6795, Spad; B6797-6798, Nieuport 27; B6799, Nieuport 23 *bis*; B6800, Nieuport 27; B6802, Spad; B6803-6804, Nieuport 27; B6805, Spad; B6807, Nieuport 27; B6808, Spad; B6809-6810, 6812-6815, Nieuport 27; B6816, Spad; B6818-6832, Nieuport 27; B6835, Spad 13; B6836-6837, Nieuport 27; B6838-6840, 6842-6862, 6864-6867, Spad 13; B6868-6871, Spad S.7; B6872-

Serial Nos.	*Qty.*	*Aircraft Type*	*Remarks*
			6875, Spad 13; B6877, Spad 12; B6878-6886, Spad 13.
B7131-7180	50	Sopwith 1F.1 Camel	Built by Portholme. B7147 to Belgium. B7150 to U.S.A.
B7181-7280	100	Sopwith 1F.1 Camel. (Mainly 130 h.p. Clerget and B.R.1 engines fitted, for R.F.C. and R.N.A.S. deliveries)	Clayton & Shuttleworth-built. B7181 to White Russians. B7182, 7207, 7209, 7211, 7270 to Greek Forces. B7235-7237 to Belgian F.C. B7219, 7244 conv. 2-seaters.
B7281-7480	200	Sopwith 1F.1 Camel	Ruston, Proctor built. B7289, 7323, 7371, 7464 to 2-seaters.
B7481-7580	100	Sopwith Pup	Built by Whitehead Aircraft.
B7581-7680	100	Airco D.H.9	Westland-built. B7664 conv. D.H.9A. B7620, 7623 became Dutch 433, 438.
B7681-7730	50	R.E.8	Built by Siddeley Deasy.
B7731-8230	500	(Various types re-built by No. 1 (Southern) Aircraft Repair Depot, South Farnborough. Note Camel, Dolphin, 1½-Strutter are all Sopwith aircraft types; Eagle engines fitted to D.H.4s, except B7910 Adriatic. Bristol F.2b Fighter recorded as just F.2b)	B7733, 7735, 7737, S.E.5A; B7739-7740, R.E.8; B7742, D.H.9; B7743, 7745-7746, Camel; B7747, D.H.4; B7749, D.H.9; B7756, Camel; B7760, Pup; B7764, D.H.4; B7765, S.E.5a; B7770-7771, S.E.5A; B7772, Camel; B7775, D.H.5; B7779, 7782, F.E.2b; B7786-7787, S.E.5a; B7789-7791, Camel; B7794-7795, F.E.2b; B7796, S.E.5a; B7700, F.E.2b; B7804, R.E.8; B7808, F.E.2b; B7812, D.H.4; B7814-7816, F.E.2b; B7821-7822, Camel; B7824, 7830-7833, S.E.5A; B7835, Camel; B7836, 7838-7839, 7843, 7848, F.E.2b; B7849, Dolphin; B7850, S.E.5A; B7855, Dolphin; B7856, 7858, F.E.2b; B7859-7860, Camel; B7866, D.H.4; B7867-7869, Camel; B7870, S.E.5a; B7872, F.E.2b; B7874, Camel; B7877, D.H.9; B7881-7882, S.E.5A; B7886, D.H.9; B7887, R.E.8; B7890, S.E.5a; B7893, R.E.8; B7896; Camel, B7899, 7901, S.E.5a; B7903 1½-Strutter; B7905; Camel; B7910, D.H.4; B7913, S.E.5a; B7914 - 7916, 1½ - Strutter; B7917, R.E.8; B7920, S.E.5a; B7925, D.H.4; B7927-7928, Dolphin; B7933, D.H.4; B7935-7937, Dolphin; B7938, 7940, 7941, D.H.4; B7947 F.2b; B7949, S.E.5a; B7950, 7951, 7962, 7964, 7969, D.H.4; B7978, Dolphin; B7979, 7986-

			7987, 7991-7993, 8004, 8013, 8016, D.H.4 mainly to S.A.A.F.; B8025, 8155, 8187, Camel; B8189, Dolphin.
B8231-8580	350	S.E.5a	Austin-built, B8305, 8309 to White Russian Forces. B8567 to R.A.A.F.
B8581-8780	200	Avro 504A/J/K	Parnall-built. B8758, 8774, became G-EABH/EB.
B8781-8830	50	Avro 504J	Cancelled. Nos. re-allotted.
B8781-8783	3	A.E.3 "Ram"	Royal Aircraft Factory built.
B8784-8786	3	Sopwith Pup	Built by 6th Wing, A.R.S.
B8787	1	B.E.2c	Built by 7th Wing, A.R.S.
B8788	1	M.F. S.11 Shorthorn	Built by 27th Wing, A.R.S.
B8789-8790	2	D.H.6	Built by 35th & 27th Wings.
B8791	1	S.E.5a	Built by 18th Wing, A.R.S.
B8792	1	Avro 504 (Mono)	Built by 23rd Wing, A.R.S.
B8793	1	M.F. S.11 Shorthorn	Built by No. 47 T.S.
B8794	1	B.E.2c	Built by 26th Wing, A.R.S.
B8795	1	Sopwith Pup	Built by 26th Wing, A.R.S.
B8796-8797	2	Avro 504 (Mono)	Built by 26th Wing, A.R.S.
B8798	1	R.E.8	Built by 26th Wing, A.R.S.
B8799-8800	2	D.H.6	Built up from spares, 1 T.D.S.
B8801	1	Sopwith Pup	Built by 7th Wing, A.R.S.
B8802-8813	12	Handley Page 0/400 (Eagle engines)	Royal Aircraft Factory-built. B8806 fitted as mail carrier.
B8814	1	Avro 504 (Mono)	Built from spares, 23rd Wing.
B8815	1	M.F. S.11 Shorthorn	Built from spares, 2 T.S.
B8816-8817	2	B.E.2e	Built by 18th Wing.
B8818-8819	2	Avro 504 (Mono)	18th Wing & 6 T.D.S. built.
B8820	1	B.E.2e	Built by 18th Wing, A.R.S.
B8821	1	Sopwith Pup (Gnôme)	Built by 26th Wing, A.R.S.
B8822-8823	2	Caudron R.11 Twin	French-built. C4962 & C4964.
B8824	1	Airco D.H.2	Built at Fighting School, Ayr.
B8825	1	B.E.2d	Built by 6th Wing.
B8826	1	B.E.12	Built by 19th Wing, Catterick.
B8827	1	A.W.F.K.3 (90 h.p.)	Built by 7th Wing, Norwich.
B8828	1	B.E.2e	Built by 7th Wing, Norwich.
B8829	1	Sopwith Pup	Built by 7th Wing, Norwich.
B8830	1	Sopwith Camel	Built by 6th Wing, Dover.
B8833-8836	3	B.E.2e	B8833-3834, 3836 from spares.
B8837-8840	4	Blackburn Kangaroo	B8837, 8839, 8840 became G-EBMD/OM/PK.
B8841-9030	190	(Various types rebuilt by No. 3 (Western) Aircraft Repair Depot, Yale, Bristol. Note F.2B is Bristol F.2B Fighter. Camel and 1½-Strutter are Sopwith types)	B8850-8854, B.E.2e; B8864, B.E.2c; B8874, 8876-8878, 8880-8881, 8883-8887, 8889, 8894-8896, R.E.8; B8899, B.E.2e; B8900, 8907, 8909, R.E.8; B8911-8912 1½-Strutter; B8914-8915, 8928, F.2B; B8932, S.E.5a; B8937, 8941, 8943, 8947, F.2B; B8997, Avro A/J or K.
B9031-9130	100	Airco D.H.6	A.M.C. order. Cancelled.
B9131-9330	200	Sopwith 1F.1 Camel	Built by Boulton & Paul Ltd. B9276 became Scooter later Swallow. B9140 conv. to 2-seater. B9278 became T.F.1.

Serial Nos.	Qty.	Aircraft Type	Remarks
B9331-9430	100	Airco D.H.9	Built by The Vulcan Motor & Engineering Co. Ltd. B9386-9393 shipped to Near East.
B9431-9432	2	Avro	Reported as experimental 2-seat fighter 3.8.17.
B9433	1	Maurice Farman S.11 Shorthorn	Built by Repair Section at Turnhouse.
B9434-9439	6	Airco D.H.4	Ex-N6382-6387. R.A.F. 3a engines fitted.
B9440	1	Sopwith Pup	Built by No. 63 T.S.
B9441-9443	3	Maurice Farman S.11 Shorthorn	Built by No. 25 T.S., 26th Wing and No. 2 T.S.
B9444	1	B.E.2c	Built by 26th Wing.
B9445	1	SPAD S.7	French-built. Received from Air Navigation Co. Works.
B9446-9451	6	Handley Page O/400	Handley Page-built. 320 h.p. Sunbeam Cossack engines.
B9452	1	Avro 504A	Built at 19th Wing.
B9453-9454	2	B.E.2c	Built at 19th Wing.
B9455	1	Sopwith Pup	Built by 6th Wing.
B9456	1	Airco D.H.4 (B.H.P.)	Ex-N6393.
B9457	1	B.E.2e	Built up from salvage.
B9458	1	Airco D.H.4 (B.H.P.)	Ex-N6397.
B9459	1	B.E.2c	Built by 30th Wing.
B9460-9461	1	Airco D.H.4 (B.H.P.)	Ex-N6401 and N6405.
B9462	1	B.E.12	Built by No. 75 Sqn.
B9463-9465	3	Handley Page V/1500	Prototypes built by Handley Page Ltd.
B9466	1	Maurice Farman S.11 Shorthorn	Built from spares by 27th Wing.
B9467	1	Competition Bomb Dropper	Title given to Beardmore for Contract AS7123.
B9468	1	D.H.5	Built at Dover.
B9469	1	B.E.2e	Built by No. 19 T.S.
B9470	1	D.H.4 (B.H.P.)	Ex-R.N.A.S.
B9471	1	D.H.4 (B.H.P.)	Built by 7th Wing.
B9472	1	D.H.6	Built by 26th Wing.
B9473	1	R.E.8	Built by 26th Wing.
B9474	1	B.E.2e	Built by 26th Wing.
B9475	1	Maurice Farman S.11 Shorthorn	Built by 27th Wing.
B9476-9500	25	Airco D.H.4	Built by Westland Aircraft Works. 200 h.p. B.H.P. engines.
B9501-9800	300	Armstrong Whitworth F.K.3	Built by Hewlett & Blondeau Ltd. B9518, 9603, 9612, 9629 became G-EABZ/LK/EU/BY.
B9801-9908	108	—	Cancelled orders.
B9909	1	Austin Ball AFB1	Built by Austin's to Captain Ball's spec.
B9910	1	Sopwith Bomber	Presumed 1½ Strutter, single-seat bomber. Built by 6th Wing.
B9911-9930	20	SPAD S.7	Built by Mann, Egerton & Co. B9911, 9913, 9914, 9916, 9917, 9920, 9924 to the U.S.A.

B9931	1	Sopwith Scout	Believed Pup built by 6th Wing.
B9933-9937	5	Morane Parasol	Acquired 14 Oct. 17.
B9938-9943	6	—	Not known.
B9944-9949	6	B.A.T. Bat/Bantam F.K.22, F.K.22/1, F.K.22/2 and F.K.23	B9944 (F.K.22) Bat fitted with 120 h.p. A.B.C. Mosquito which was found unsatisfactory and airframe was cannibalised. B9945 (F.K.22/1) Bantam flew first with 120 h.p. A.B.C. engine then with 170 h.p. A.B.C. and finally became an F.K.22/2 with a 100 h.p. Gnôme Monosoupape; then, with a 110 h.p. Le Rhône engine, it was redesignated F.K.23 Bantam Mk. II. B9946 was not completed. B9947 became an F.K.23. B9948-9949 were not completed.
B9950-9951	2	—	Reservation.
B9952-9954	3	Vickers F.B.27 Vimy	Built by Vickers Ltd. at Bexley. Hispano, Maori and Salmson engines respectively.
B9955-9961	7	—	Reservation.
B9962-9967	6	Sopwith 7F.1 Snipe	Snipe prototypes. Sopwith built. Various engines installed.
B9968-9969	2	—	Reservation.
B9970-9989	20	Blackburn Kangaroo	N1720-1739 re-numbered in R.F.C. series. 8 to civil register.
B9990	1	Sopwith 1F.1 Camel	R.N.A.S. N6344 as R.F.C. sample to Boulton & Paul.
B9991	1	Maurice Farman S.11 Shorthorn.	Built from spares.
B9992	1	D.H.6	Built by 7th Wing.
B9993	1	B.E.2c	Built by No. 19 T.S.
B9994	1	D.H.4	Built by 6th Wing.
B9995	1	Avro 504	Built by 7th Wing.
B9996	1	Maurice Farman S.11 Shorthorn	Built by No. 2 T.S.
B9997	1	R.E.8	Built by 26th Wing.
B9998	1	B.E.2c	Built by a T.S.
B9999	1	Maurice Farman	Built at Beverley.

BRITISH PRODUCTION AIRCRAFT

C1–9999

THE "C" series allocations reflect the increasing size in orders placed by the Air Board in 1917, including a contract to Daimler for 850 R.E.8s which was the largest single order for aircraft placed that year. This series is practically uncomplicated, being straightforward production aircraft for the Royal Flying Corps, except for small batches reserved for experimental aircraft. This allocation was fully subscribed by August 1917.

Serial Nos.	*Qty.*	*Aircraft Type*	*Remarks*
C1-200	200	Sopwith 1F.1 Camel	Built by the Nieuport & General Aircraft Co. Ltd. C19, 42, 57 were converted to 2-seaters.
C201-550	350	Sopwith Pup	Built by The Standard Motor Co. Ltd., 1917-18. Late deliveries went straight to store. C521-528 and C530-532 became A4-1 to -11 of the Royal Australian Air Force.
C551-750	200	504A/J/K	Built by The Humber Motor Co. Ltd. C723, 724, 747-749 became G-EABN/AY/BW/BF /BG on the Civil Register.
C751-1050	300	Bristol F.2B	Built by The British & Colonial Aeroplane Co. Ltd. with Falcon III engines, except for C1025 (Sunbeam Arab).
C1051-1150	100	S.E.5a	Built by the Royal Aircraft Factory, Farnborough. C1115 and 1121 delivered to the United States Air Service.
C1151-1450	300	Airco D.H.9	Built by G. & J. Weir Ltd., Cathcart, Glasgow.
C1451-1550	100	Sopwith Pup	Built by Whitehead Aircraft Ltd., Richmond. C1502-1503, 1508, 1516-1518, 1523, 1532, 1533, 1535, 1537, 1541 to the Royal Navy with 80 h.p. Le Rhône engines.
C1551-1600	50	Sopwith 1F.1 Camel	Built by Hooper & Co. Ltd., London. Le Rhône or Clerget engines fitted in general but C1588 had a special B.R.1 engine.
C1601-1700	100	Sopwith 1F.1 Camel	Built by Boulton & Paul Ltd., Norwich.
C1701-1750	50	B.E.2e	Cancelled. Ordered from British & Colonial Aeroplane Co. Ltd.
C1751-1950	200	S.E.5a	Built by The Air Navigation Co. Ltd., Addlestone.
C1951-2150	200	Airco D.H.6	Built by The Grahame-White Aviation Co. Ltd., Hendon. C1972, 2101, 2136 became G-AUDO/EAGG/G-EAQQ.
C2151-2230	80	Airco D.H.9	Built by F. W. Berwick & Co. Ltd., London. C2207 had a special high compression Puma engine fitted.
C2231-3080	850	R.E.8	Built by The Daimler Company Ltd., Coventry. Last 50 cancelled.
C3081-3280	200	B.E.12/12a/12b	Built by The Daimler Company Ltd., Coventry. B.E.1 contract modified to include B.E.12a/b.

C3281-3380	100	Sopwith 1F.1 Camel	Built by Boulton & Paul Ltd., Norwich. Even numbers C3326-3342 were shipped to the Mediterranean Area.
C3381-3480	100	Handley Page O/400	Built by Handley Page at Cricklewood. Eagle, Maori or Liberty engines specified.
C3481-3483	3	Grahame-White E.IV Ganymede	Experimental aircraft by the Grahame-White Aviation Co. Ltd., of which only C3481 was built. This eventually became G-EAMW.
C3484-3486	3	Nieuport B.N.1	British Nieuport-built. C3484 caught fire in the air over Suttons Farm, 10th March, 1918 on test and of the remaining two under construction one was static tested and the other not completed.
C3487-3498	12	Handley Page O/400	Built by the Royal Aircraft Factory, Farnborough in 1918, with Rolls-Royce Eagle engines installed.
C3499	1	Maurice Farman	Built by No. 2 T.S.
C3500-3503	4	Sopwith Pup	Built by 6th Wing.
C3504	1	—	Not known.
C3505	1	Avro 504	Built by 6th Wing.
C3506	1	D.H.6	Built by No. 2 T.D.S.
C3507-3706	200	Armstrong Whitworth F.K.8	Built by Angus Sanderson & Co., Newcastle-upon-Tyne.
C3707-3776	70	Sopwith Pup	Ordered from the Whitehead Aircraft Co. Ltd., Richmond, Surrey as spares.
C3777-4276	500	Sopwith 5F.1 Dolphin	Largest order placed with Sopwith to date.
C4277	1	Curtiss	Presumed ex-R.N.A.S.
C4278	1	Maurice Farman	Built by No. 12 T.S.
C4279	1	Maurice Farman	Built from spares by Brush with 90 h.p. Curtiss.
C4280	1	—	Reserved for captured German aircraft.
C4281	1	D.H.6	Built by No. 1 T.D.S.
C4282	1	R.E.8	Built by 7th Wing.
C4283	1	Airco D.H.10	Prototype (two 200 h.p. B.H.P. engines) built by the Aircraft Manufacturing Company. Later modified to D.H.10C with Liberty engines. Also given as F.E.2b.
C4284-4289	6	Sopwith 8F.1 Snail I/II	C4285 and C4289 Mk. I, remainder built as Mk. II.
C4290	1	Avro 504 (Mono)	Built by 7th Wing.
C4291-4293	3	Westland Wagtail	Experimental aircraft built by the Westland Aircraft Works. Originally named Hornet.
C4294	1	R.E.8	Built by 26th Wing.
C4295	1	Sopwith Pup	Built by 30th Wing.
C4296-4298	3	Bristol Types 24/25/26 Braemar	C4296 Braemar 1, C4297 Braemar II, C4298 Pullman G-EASP.

Serial Nos.	Qty.	Aircraft Type	Remarks
C4299	1	Avro 504 (Mono)	Built by 7th Wing.
C4300	1	Sopwith Bomber	Built by 26th Wing. Presumed to be 1½ Strutter Bomber version.
C4301-4500	200	Avro 504J	Built by A. V. Roe & Co. Ltd., Manchester.
C4501-4540	40	Airco D.H.4	Built by the Aircraft Manufacturing Co. Ltd., Hendon.
C4541-4546	6	Siddeley S.R.2 Siskin	Experimental fighter by The Siddeley-Deasy Motor Car Co. Ltd. of which the first was ready in May 1918, but tests were suspended until 1919 due to engine troubles. C4544-4546 cancelled.
C4547	1	Vickers F.B.14D	Experimental aircraft by Vickers, first flown in March 1917.
C4548	1	Bristol Fighter	Built by 18th Wing.
C4549	1	Avro 504	Built by 18th Wing.
C4550	1	A.W. F.K.8	Built by 18th Wing.
C4551-4600	50	R.E.8	Built by D. Napier & Sons Ltd., Acton.
C4601-4900	300	Bristol F.2B Fighter	Built by The British & Colonial Aeroplane Co. Ltd. Rolls-Royce Falcon engines were a general fit, but C4654-4655 were fitted with Siddeley Pumas.
C4901-5025	125	Bristol M.1C Monoplane	Built by The British & Colonial Aeroplane Co. Ltd., Bristol. Type 20 retrospectively allotted. C4964 became G-EAER.
C5026-5125	100	R.E.8	Built by the Coventry Ordnance Works Ltd., Coventry.
C5126-5275	150	Airco D.H.6	Built by The Kingsbury Aviation Co., Kingsbury. C5220, 5224, 5230 became G-EAGF/GE/NU on the Civil Register.
C5276-5300	25	Caudron	Built in France. Possibly Type G.III.
C5301-5450	150	S.E.5a	Built by Vickers Ltd. at Crayford.
C5451-5750	300	Airco D.H.6	Built by Harland & Wolff Ltd., Belfast. C5527, C5533 and C5547 became G-EARA-C on the Civil Register
C5751-6050	300	Avro 504J	Built by Harland & Wolff Ltd., Belfast. Some converted to 504K.
C6051-6350	300	Airco D.H.9	Built by the Aircraft Manufacturing Co. Ltd., Hendon. C6122 and C6350 were modified by the Westland Aircraft Works to become the prototype D.H.9As. C6054 became the first aircraft on the Civil Register as G-EAAA. B.H.P.

			engines were standard but C6052 had a Fiat A-12 fitted and C6078 a Napier Lion.
C6351-6500	150	S.E.5a	Built by Wolseley Motors Ltd., Birmingham.
C6501-6700	200	Airco D.H.6	Built by Morgan & Co., Leighton Buzzard.
C6701-6800	100	Sopwith 1F.1 Camel	Built by the British Caudron Co. Ltd. at Alloa.
C6801-6900	100	Airco D.H.6	Built by Savages Ltd., Kings Lynn. C6889 became G-EAHI.
C6901-7000	100	B.E.2e	Built by William Denny & Bros., Dumbarton. C6980 (140 h.p. R.A.F.) was fitted with metal planes in October 1919. C6953, 6964, 6968, 6986 became G-EARW/TW/TT and VH-UBF.
C7001-7100	100	B.E.2e	Built by Barclay, Curle & Co. Ltd., Whiteinch, Glasgow.
C7101-7200	100	B.E.2e	Built by Napier & Miller Ltd. C7101, 7175, 7178, 7179, 7185 became G-EAGH/CY/VA/VS/NW and C7198 VH-UBB.
C7201-7600	400	Airco D.H.6	Built by Ransome, Sims & Jeffries, Ipswich. C7434 and C7436 became G-EAOT and G-EAQC on the Civil Register.
C7601-7900	300	Airco D.H.6	Built by the Grahame-White Aviation Co. Ltd., Hendon. C7763 became G-EAUS on the Civil Register.
C7901-8000	100	Sopwith T.1 Cuckoo	Renumbered N7000-7099.
C8001-8200	200	Sopwith 5F.1 Dolphin	Built by The Darracq Motor Engineering Co. Ltd., Fulham. C8022 converted to 2-seater.
C8201-8300	100	Sopwith 1F.1 Camel	Built by Ruston, Proctor & Co. Ltd., Lincoln.
C8301-8400	100	Sopwith 1F.1 Camel	Built by March, Jones & Cribb Ltd., Leeds.
C8401-8650	250	Armstrong Whitworth F.K.8	Built by Sir W. G. Armstrong Whitworth & Co. Ltd., Gosforth.
C8651	1	—	Reservation.
C8652-8654	3	Boulton & Paul P.5	Named Hawk. Not built. Numbers re-allotted.
C8652	1	Avro 504	Built by 18th Wing.
C8653-8654	2	Sopwith Pup	Built by 7th Wing.
C8655-8657	3	Boulton & Paul P.3	Named Boblink, later Bobolink. Record of C8655 only delivered.
C8658-8660	3	Airco D.H.10 Amiens	Built by the Aircraft Manufacturing Co. Ltd., Hendon. Produced as Mks. I, II, III respectively.
C8661-9310	650	S.E.5a	Built by The Austin Motor Company, Birmingham.

Serial Nos.	*Qty.*	*Aircraft Type*	*Remarks*
			C8738, 8740, 8743, 8745-8747, 8749, 8750, 8752-8754, 9073-9074, 9076-9078, 9080-9086, 9088-9090, to the United States Air Service.
C9311-9335	25	Maurice Farman S.7 Longhorn	Built by The Brush Electrical Engineering Co. Ltd., Loughborough, from spares held by Robey and Phoenix. 90 h.p. Curtiss engines installed.
C9336-9485	150	Airco D.H.6	Built by The Gloucestershire Aircraft Co. Ltd., Cheltenham. C9374 and C9436 became G-AUBW and -EAUT on the Civil Registers.
C9486-9635	150	S.E.5a	Built by Vickers Ltd. at Weybridge.
C9636-9785	150	Handley Page O/400	Eagle, Maori or Liberty engines specified. C9699 and C9731 became G-EASL/M.
C9786-9835	50	F.E.2b	Ordered from Ransome, Sims & Jeffries, Ipswich.
C9836-9985	150	Bristol F.2B	Built by The Gloucestershire Aircraft Co. Ltd., Cheltenham. Sunbeam Arab engines planned.
C9986	1	Avro 504	Built by No. 7 T.D.S.
C9987	1	B.E.2e	Built by No. 7 T.D.S.
C9988-9989	2	B.E.2d	Built by 6th Wing.
C9990-9991	2	Sopwith Pup	Built by No. 7 T.D.S.
C9992	1	B.E.12b	Built by No. 50 Sqn.
C9993	1	Sopwith Pup	Built by 26th Wing.
C9994	1	D.H.6	Built by 27th Wing.
C9995	1	B.E.2d	Built by 7th Wing.
C9996	1	B.E.2e	Built by 18th Wing.
C9997	1	A.W. F.K.8	Built by 24th Wing.
C9998-9999	2	Avro 504	Built by 39th Wing.

R.F.C./R.A.F. CANADA

C101–2500

IN 1917, training squadrons were set up by the Royal Flying Corps in Canada, and since the training aircraft used were almost exclusively those of Canadian Aeroplanes Ltd. of Toronto they were numbered in a separate series, starting at No. 101, with the prefix "C" for Canada. It is known that Canadian Aeroplanes built 2,291 aircraft, but 680 of these were to JN-4D standard for the U.S. Army. One D.H.6 is believed to have been built and a JN-4 has been noted with the number C2290, but from individual loggings, in the absence of official documentation, the allocation pattern appears as follows:—

C101-500	400	Curtiss JN-4 (CAN)	C197, 247, 254, 282, 333, 375 presented by Canadian organisations.
C501-1450	950	Curtiss JN-4 (CAN) and JN-4A (CAN)	C501-650 and C1015-1051, JN-4A; remainder JN-4 except C1060-1260 and C1401-1451, believed not built or allotted to JN-4Ds for U.S. Army and re-numbered.
C1451-1500	50	Curtiss JN-4 (CAN)	C1451-1456 only confirmed. All built as ambulances.
C1501-2000	500	Avro 504 (CAN)	C1501-1504 only confirmed as built. Armistice halted production.

FINAL R.F.C. ALLOCATIONS

D1–9999

LIKE the preceding " C " series, the " D " series, resulting from orders placed late 1917/early 1918, was a straightforward allocation of numbers mainly for production aircraft.

D1-200	200	Avro 504J/K	A. V. Roe-built.
D201-300	100	S.E.5a	Built by Vickers Ltd. at Weybridge. D203 was non-standard with Dolphin-type rudder and narrow chord ailerons.
D301-450	150	S.E.5a	Built by Vickers Ltd. at Crayford. D340-343 to U.S.A.
D451-950	500	Airco D.H.9	Built by Cubitt Ltd., Croydon. Full delivery not confirmed.
D951-1000	50	Airco D.H.6	Built by the Grahame-White Aviation Co. Ltd., Hendon.
D1001-1500	500	Airco D.H.9	Ordered from National Aircraft Factory No. 2, Heaton Chapel. Less than 326 actually built.
D1501-1600	100	R.E.8	Ordered from The Standard Motor Car Co. Ltd., Coventry.
D1601-1650	50	Avro 504A	Eastbourne Aviation Co. Ltd., Nos. 201-250.
D1651-1750	100	Airco D.H.9	Built by Mann, Egerton & Co. Ltd., Norwich.
D1751-1775	25	Airco D.H.4	Built by Westland Aircraft Works. 200 h.p. B.H.P. D1769 *et seq* had high type undercarriage. D1769 was fitted with paravanes.
D1776-1975	200	Sopwith 1F.1 Camel	Built by Ruston, Proctor & Co. Ltd., Lincoln.
D1976-2125	150	Avro 504K	Built by Frederick Sage & Co. Ltd. D2035 became G-EAWJ.
D2126-2625	500	Bristol F.2B	Built by National Aircraft Factory No. 3, Aintree. Rolls-Royce Falcon engines

Serial Nos.	Qty.	Aircraft Type	Remarks
			fitted except for D2132 (Sunbeam Arab). 126 only completed.
D2626-2775	150	Bristol F.2B	Built by Marshall & Sons, Gainsborough. Sunbeam Arab engines fitted.
D2776-2875	100	Airco D.H.9	Built by Short Bros, Rochester. 250 h.p. Fiat engines specified. Fiats, Pumas and B.H.Ps. fitted.
D2876-3275	400	Airco D.H.9	Built by the Aircraft Manufacturing Co. Ltd., Hendon. D3117 modified to ambulance. D3017, 3187, 3189, 3191, 3207, 3220 became A6-11, 14, 9, 16, 20, 21 of the Royal Australian Air Force.
D3276-3325	50	Sopwith T.1 Cuckoo	Renumbered N6900-6949.
D3326-3425	100	Sopwith 1F.1 Camel	Built by Clayton & Shuttleworth Ltd., Lincoln.
D3426-3575	150	S.E.5a	Built by Vickers Ltd. at Weybridge.
D3576-3775	200	Sopwith 5F.1 Dolphin	Built by the Sopwith Aviation Co. Ltd., Kingston-upon-Thames.
D3776-3835	60	F.E.2b	Built by Garrett & Sons, Leiston. D3832 became G-EAHC.
D3836-3910	75	R.E.8	Cancelled. Ordered from D. Napier & Son Ltd., Acton.
D3911-4010	100	S.E.5a	Built by Martinsyde Ltd., Brooklands, Byfleet, Surrey.
D4011-4210	200	Sopwith Pup	Delivered by Whitehead Aircraft as spares.
D4211-4360	150	Martinsyde F.4 Buzzard	Built but did not enter service. D4274, 4281, 4285, 4298 became 4, 2, 1, 3 of the Irish Air Corps.
D4361-4560	200	Avro 504J/K	Built by The Sunbeam Motor Car Co. Ltd., Wolverhampton.
D4561-4660	100	Handley Page O/400	Built by The Metropolitan Wagon Co., Birmingham. Eagle or Liberty engines specified. Eight went later to the Civil Register.
D4661-4810	150	R.E.8	Built by The Standard Motor Co. Ltd., Coventry.
D4811-4960	150	R.E.8	Built by D. Napier & Son, Acton. First 75 had Eagle engines specified.
D4961-5000	40	(Allotted to No. 3 (Western) Aircraft Repair Depot for rebuilt aircraft)	D4980 and D4998 taken up by R.E.8s.
D5001-5200	200	Armstrong Whitworth F.K.8	Built by Angus Sanderson Ltd., Newcastle-upon-Tyne. D5150 became G-EAET.

D5201-5400	200	Sopwith F5.1 Dolphin	Built by Hooper & Co. Ltd. D5369 became G-EATC.
D5401-5450	50	Handley Page O/400	Built by the Birmingham Carriage Co. D5444 became G-EASO.
D5451-5550	100	Avro 504J/K	Built by A. V. Roe & Co. Ltd., Manchester. Delivered as spares for erection in Egypt.
D5551-5850	300	Airco D.H.9	Built by Waring and Gillow Ltd., Hammersmith. D5748 had a Fiat A-12 engine experimentally installed.
D5851-5950	100	Avro 504J/K	Built by The Henderson Scottish Aviation Factory. D5858 became G-EASF.
D5951-6200	250	S.E.5a	Built by Vickers Ltd. at Weybridge. D6101-3, 6105, 6107, 6109-6112 to the United States Air Service.
D6201-6250	50	Avro 504A/J/K	Built by The Humber Motor Co. Ltd. D6205 and D6230 became G-EAAX/DX.
D6251-6400	150	Avro 504A/J/K	Built by The Brush Electrical Engineering Co. Ltd., Loughborough. D6382 was converted to a 504N post-war.
D6401-6700	300	Sopwith 1F.1 Camel	Built by Boulton & Paul Ltd., Norwich.
D6701-6850	150	R.E.8	Built by the Coventry Ordnance Works Ltd., Coventry.
D6851-7000	150	S.E.5a	Built by Wolseley Motors Ltd., Birmingham.
D7001-7050	50	S.E.5a	Built by the Royal Aircraft Factory, Farnborough.
D7051-7200	150	Avro 504J/K	Built by Hewlett & Blondeau Ltd., Leagrave, Luton.
D7201-7300	100	Airco D.H.9	Built by the Westland Aircraft Works, Yeovil. D7215-7216 were cancelled.
D7301-7400	100	Airco D.H.9	Built by F. W. Berwick & Co. Ltd., Park Royal, London, and delivered as spares.
D7401-7500	100	Avro 504	Contract cancelled.
D7501-7800	300	Avro 504J/K	Built by A. V. Roe & Co. Ltd. D7588, 7619, 7648 became G-EADQ/JK/FE on the Civil Register.
D7801-8100	300	Bristol F.2B	Built by the British & Colonial Aeroplane Co. Ltd. Rolls-Royce Falcon III engines fitted in general with the following exceptions: D7860, R.A.F.4d engine; D7965, ungeared Sunbeam Arab; D7968, sub-contract built Arab; and D7971, normal Arab engine.
D8101-8250	150	Sopwith 1F.1 Camel	Built by Ruston, Proctor & Co. Ltd., Lincoln.

Serial Nos.	*Qty.*	*Aircraft Type*	*Remarks*
D8251-8300	50	Avro 504K	Built by The Humber Motor Co. Ltd. D8287 became G-EABK.
D8301-8350	50	Handley Page O/400	Built by the British Caudron Co. Ltd. Eagle, Maori or Liberty engines specified.
D8351-8430	80	Airco D.H.4	Built by the Aircraft Manufacturing Co. Ltd. Mainly Rolls-Royce Eagle IV engines fitted.
D8431-8580	150	S.E.5a	Built by Vickers Ltd. at Crayford. D8476 and D8490 went to the Royal Australian Air Force as A2-13 and A2-19.
D8581-8780	200	Airco D.H.6	Built by the Aircraft Manufacturing Co. Ltd., Hendon.
D8781-9080	300	Avro 504K	Built by the Grahame-White Aviation Co. Ltd., Hendon.
D9081-9230	150	F.E.2b	Built by Alex Stephen & Sons, Glasgow.
D9231-9280	50	Airco D.H.4	Built by the Aircraft Manufacturing Co. Ltd., Hendon.
D9281-9380	100	Avro 504K	Built by Parnall & Sons. D9303, 9329, 9341 became G-EAIB/DU/CS on the Civil Register.
D9381-9530	150	Sopwith 1F.1 Camel	Built by Boulton & Paul Ltd., Norwich. In the main, 110 h.p. Clerget (Long Stroke) engines were fitted.
D9531-9580	50	Sopwith 1F.1 Camel	Built by Portholme Aerodrome Ltd., Huntingdon. In the main, 130 h.p. Clerget engines were fitted.
D9581-9680	100	Sopwith 1F.1 Camel	Built by Clayton & Shuttleworth Ltd., Lincoln.
D9681-9730	50	Handley Page O/400	Built by Clayton & Shuttleworth Ltd., Lincoln. Rolls-Royce Eagle engines specified. Full delivery not confirmed.
D9731-9736	6	B.A.T. F.K.24 Baboon	Experimental advanced trainers built by The British Aerial Transport Co. Ltd., Willesden. First three only built; D9731 became K124/G-EACO.
D9737-9739	3	R.E.8	Built by No. 3 A.R.D.
D9740-9789	40	F.E.2b	Constructor not known.
D9790-9799	10	R.E.8	Built by No. 3 A.R.D.
D9800-9899	100	Airco D.H.9	Ordered from G. & J. Weir. No record of delivery.
D9900-9999	100	F.E.2b	Built by Ransome, Sims & Jeffries, Ipswich.

THE FIRST ROYAL AIR FORCE ORDERS

E1–9999

WHEN the Royal Naval Air Service and the Royal Flying Corps merged on 1st April, 1918, no change in serialling resulted, since the function of the Ministry of Munitions remained unchanged and that Ministry acted as an agency for the aircraft of the Services. The "E" series was subscribed in early- to mid-1918, and on the day of the merger of the two flying services, allocations for the R.F.C. had reached E1600.

E1-300	300	R.E.8	Built by The Siddeley-Deasy Motor Co. Ltd., Coventry.
E301-600	300	Avro 504K	Built by Harland & Wolff Ltd., Belfast. E444 conv. 504N. E449 rebuilt as first Avro 548A, G-EBKN.
E601-700	100	Airco D.H.9	Built by Whitehead Aircraft Ltd., Richmond, Surrey.
E701-1100	400	Airco D.H.9A	Built by Whitehead Aircraft Ltd., Richmond, Surrey. E752, 753, 754, 756, 757 became G-EAOG-K on the Civil Register. E746, 748-750, 752-757, 775 had Napier Lion engines installed.
E1101-1150	50	R.E.8	Built by D. Napier & Son Ltd., Acton.
E1151-1250	100	R.E.8	Built by The Siddeley-Deasy Motor Co. Ltd., Coventry.
E1251-1400	150	S.E.5a	Built by Vickers Ltd. from June 1918.
E1401-1600	200	Sopwith 1F.1 Camel	Built by Ruston, Proctor & Co. Ltd., Lincoln. Fitted with 130 h.p. Clerget engines.
E1601-1900	300	Avro 504J/K	A. V. Roe-built. E1611, 1640, 1644, 1660, 1665, became G-EAHO/LA/VI/FC/DD on the Civil Register.
E1901-2150	250	Bristol F.2B	Built by Sir W. G. Armstrong Whitworth & Co. Ltd., Gosforth, with Sunbeam Arabs. E2058 became G-EBCU.
E2151-2650	500	Bristol F.2B	Built by the British & Colonial Aeroplane Co. Ltd. Rolls-Royce Falcon III engines fitted in general, except for E2400 with 300 h.p. Hispano.
E2651-2900	250	Bristol F.2B	Built by Angus Sanderson & Co., Newcastle-on-Tyne.
E2901-3050	150	Avro 504K	Built by Morgan & Co.
E3051-3150	100	Avro 504K	Built by Savages Ltd.
E3151-3153	3	F.E.2h	Ordered from Ransomes, Sims & Jeffries.
E3154-3253	100	S.E.5a	Built by Martinsyde Ltd., Brooklands, Byfleet. E3169 went to the R.A.A.F. as A2-6.
E3254-3403	150	Avro 504K	Built by Parnall & Son. E3292, 3293, 3358, 3363, 3364, 3399 became G-EADI/DW/NT/FP/

Serial Nos.	*Qty.*	*Aircraft Type*	*Remarks*
			HW/MI and E3387 became Type 548 G-EBPO. E3390-3397 (100 h.p. Gnôme Monosoupape) were allotted to the Grand Fleet.
E3404-3903	500	Avro 504K	Built by A. V. Roe. E3797 converted to 504L at Hamble. E3480, 3481, 3501, 3502, 3671, 3672, 3724 became G-EABA/BP/EC/DH/WK/WI/MZ. E3742-3746, 3749-3750, became A3-27 to -33 of the R.A.A.F. E3432 became VH-UCJ ex-G-AUCJ.
E3904-4103	200	S.E.5a	Built by Vickers Ltd. at Weybridge.
E4104-4303	200	Avro 504K	Built by The Humber Motor Co. Ltd., Coventry. E4154 became Avro 548 G-EAAL.
E4304-4323	20	Handley Page V/1500	Erected by Handley Page Ltd., Cricklewood, London.
E4324-4373	50	Avro 504K	Built by The Eastbourne Aviation Co. Ltd. (Nos. 324-373). E4348 had Cosmos Lucifer engine fitted.
E4374-4423	50	Sopwith 1F.1 Camel	Built by Clayton & Shuttleworth Ltd., Lincoln. E4408 and E4412-4417 allotted to the Royal Navy with Bentley B.R.1 engines.
E4424-4623	200	Sopwith 5F.1 Dolphin	Built by Sopwith Aviation.
E4624-4628	5	Airco D.H.4	Built by A.M.C.
E4629-5128	500	Sopwith 5F.1 Dolphin	Built by Sopwith Aviation. E4642, 4643, 4646, 4647, 4650 to U.S.A.
E5129-5178	50	Sopwith 1F.1 Camel	Built by Portholme Aerodrome Ltd., Huntingdon.
E5179-5252	74	Bristol F.2B	Built by The Standard Motor Co. Ltd., with Sunbeam engines fitted. E5219 became G-EBDB.
E5253-5258	6	Bristol F.2B	Ordered from The Standard Motor Co. Ltd., but airframes were transferred to The British & Colonial Aeroplane Co. for the fitting of Siddeley Puma engines.
E5259-5308	50	Bristol F.2B	Ordered from the Standard Motor Co. Ltd., but order was transferred to the British & Colonial Aeroplane Co. Ltd., who fitted Sunbeam Arab engines.
E5309-5428	120	Bristol F.2B	Cancelled. Original order placed with The Standard Motor Co. Ltd.

E5429-5434	6	Sopwith T.F.2 Salamander	Order for 6 experimental aircraft from Sopwith Aviation which flew from 27.4.18 onwards.
E5435-5436	2	Airco D.H.9	Built by A.M.C. to replace C6350 and C6122.
E5437-5636	200	Airco D.H.10	Built by the Aircraft Manufacturing Co. Ltd., Hendon.
E5637-5936	300	S.E.5a	Built by The Austin Motor Co. Ltd. E5696 had a modified fuselage for parachute storage.
E5937-6036	100	S.E.5a	Built by The Air Navigation Co. Ltd., Addlestone.
E6037-6136	100	Airco D.H.10	Built by The Birmingham Carriage Co. E6042 was experimentally fitted with twin fins and rudders.
E6137-6536	400	Sopwith 7F.1 Snipe	Built by Boulton & Paul Ltd., Norwich.
E6537-6686	150	Sopwith 7F.1 Snipe	Built by the Coventry Ordnance Works Ltd., Coventry.
E6687-6736	50	F.E.2b	Cancelled order with Garrett.
E6737-6786	50	Avro 504K	Built by Morgan & Co., Leighton Buzzard.
E6787-6936	150	Sopwith 7F.1 Snipe	Built by D. Napier & Son Ltd.
E6937-7036	100	Sopwith 7F.1 Snipe	Built by Nieuport & General Co. Ltd. E6938 was rebuilt in the U.S.A. in recent years.
E7037-7136	100	F.E.2b	Built by Ransomes, Sims & Jeffries. E7100, 7102, 7110 to U.S.A.
E7137-7336	200	Sopwith 1F.1 Camel	Built by Ruston, Proctor Ltd., Lincoln from 2.7.18.
E7337-7836	500	Sopwith 7F.1 Snipe	Built by Ruston, Proctor Ltd., Lincoln but E7798, 7802-7832 and 7834 were completed by Portholme.
E7837-7986	150	Airco D.H.10	Ordered from The Siddeley-Deasy Motor Car Co. Ltd., Coventry. Full delivery not confirmed.
E7987-8286	300	Sopwith 7F.1 Snipe	Built by Sopwith. E7990 became a Dragon.
E8287-8306	20	Handley Page V/1500	Built by Wm. Beardmore & Co. Ltd., Dalmuir.
E8307-8406	100	Sopwith 7F.1 Snipe	Built by Portholme Aerodrome Ltd., Huntingdon.
E8407-8806	400	Airco D.H.9A	Built by the Aircraft Manufacturing Co. Ltd. E8781, 8788, 8791 became G-EBLC, G-EBAC & G-EAXC. E8458-8459, 8489-8492, 8510, 8512-8516 were allotted to the Royal Navy. E8449 was despatched to the U.S.A. as a pattern. E8522 was reconstructed as J6585. E8465-8467, 8469, 8472, 8475-8478,

Serial Nos.	*Qty.*	*Aircraft Type*	*Remarks*
			8480, 8501-8502, 8504, 8506-8507, 8538-8542 to U.S.M.C. E8616 to R.A.A.F.
E8807-8856	50	A.W.F.K.8	Armstrong-Whitworth-built.
E8857-9056	200	Airco D.H.9	Built by the Aircraft Manufacturing Co. Ltd., Hendon. Many shipped to Mudros late 1918.
E9057-9206	150	Airco D.H.10	Ordered from the Daimler Co. Ltd., Coventry. Full delivery not confirmed.
E9207-9506	300	Avro 504K	Built by The Grahame-White Aviation Co. Ltd. Some later became 504N, *e.g.* E9261, 9265, 9266, E9268. E9337 became Avro 548 G-EBPJ.
E9507-9656	150	Bristol F.2B	Built by The Gloucestershire Aircraft Co. Ltd. Sunbeam Arab engines fitted.
E9657-9756	100	Airco D.H.9A	Built by Mann, Egerton & Co. Ltd., Norwich. E9689 was used in flotation tests, August, 1920.
E9757-9856	100	Vickers F.B.27 Vimy	Cancelled order placed with Metropolitan Carriage Co.
E9857-9956	100	Airco D.H.9A	Built by The Vulcan Motor & Engineering Co. Ltd., Southport. E9895 had an experimental Vickers long-stroke oleo undercarriage fitted.
E9957-9963	7	R.E.8	Built by No. 3 A.R.D.
E9964-9983	20	Sopwith 1F.1 Camel	Built by No. 3 A.R.D. under April 1918 emergency arrangements. E9968 converted to 2-seater.
E9984	1	Avro 504 (Mono)	Built by 23rd Wing.
E9985	1	B.E.2e	Built at Hounslow.
E9986-9988	3	Maurice Farman	Built by 29th Wing.
E9989-9990	2	Avro 504 (Mono)	Built by 6th Wing.
E9991-9994	4	Avro 504 (Mono)	Built from spares.
E9995	1	Avro 504K	Built from spares.
E9996	1	Sopwith Pup	(80 h.p. Gnôme).
E9997	1	Sopwith 5F.1 Dolphin	Sopwith-built.
E9998	1	Maurice Farman	Built by No. 2 T.S.
E9999	1	Avro 504 (Mono)	Built by 23rd Wing.

ROYAL AIR FORCE REQUIREMENTS, 1918

F1–9999

PLACED in 1918, contracts for aircraft allotted numbers in the "F" series were of two main types, production aircraft intended for the battles that year and next, and experimental aircraft as prototypes for production envisaged in 1919. In the event, the Armistice came in November 1918 and production orders were cut; a few were completed, others partly completed and in some cases completed and delivered direct to storage. Most of the experimental aircraft were completed, but there was no longer the urgency to conduct their testing, which in some cases was delayed until 1920. A number of blanks in the ranges of numbers occur in this series due to cancelled orders for which details cannot be ascertained.

F1-300	300	Airco D.H.9	Ordered from National Aircraft Factory No. 1, Waddon. F1-142 only built.
F301-320	20	Handley Page O/400	Built by The Birmingham Carriage Company. F303, 308, 310, 312 became G-EATJ/SX/SZ/TL on the Civil Register.
F321-350	30	—	Reservation for No. 2 A.R.D.
F351-550	200	Airco D.H.10	Ordered from National Aircraft Factory No. 2, Heaton Chapel.
F551-615	65	S.E.5a	Built by Vickers Ltd. at their Crayford factory.
F616-700	40	—	Allotted to No. 2 A.R.D. F618 A.W. F.K.8 specially fitted for meteorological work. F685, R.E.8.
F701-850	150	Vickers F.B.27 Vimy	12 only completed by Vickers Ltd. at Crayford. B.H.P. or Fiat engines specified in the contract.
F851-950	100	S.E.5a	Built by Wolseley Motors Ltd., Birmingham.
F951-1100	150	Airco D.H.9A	Built by the Westland Aircraft Works, Yeovil. F963 became F9515.
F1101-F1300	200	Airco D.H.9	Built by Waring and Gillow Ltd., Hammersmith, London. F1238 and F1295 became A6-6 and -8 of the Royal Australian Air Force.
F1301-1550	250	Sopwith 1F.1 Camel	Built by Boulton & Paul Ltd., Norwich. Various engines fitted, *e.g.* F1303 and F1305, 110 h.p. Le Rhône; F1336, 150 h.p. Gnôme Monosoupape. F1344, 1451 to U.S.A.
F1551-1552	2	Airco D.H.4	A.M.C.-built to replace D8408 and D9231.
F1553-1602	50	R.E.8	Built by The Siddeley-Deasy Motor Co. Ltd., Coventry.
F1603-1652	50	D.H.9A	Built by the Westland Aircraft Works, Yeovil. The fuselage of F1632 was used for the H.P.20 research monoplane.
F1653-1664	12	B.A.T. F.K.23 Bantam	Built by the British Aerial Transport Co. Ltd., Willesden. Nos. 14-25. F1654-1657 became K-123, K-154, K-125, K-155 on the 1919 Civil Register. One went to the United States Air Service as A.S.94111/P-167. F1662-1664 were not completed.

Serial Nos.	Qty.	Aircraft Type	Remarks
F1665-1764	100	R.E.8	Ordered from The Standard Motor Co. Ltd., Coventry. Full delivery not confirmed.
F1765-1766	2	Tarrant Tabor	F1765 only completed by W. G. Tarrant Ltd., Byfleet, but crashed on first take-off.
F1767-1866	100	Airco D.H.9	Ordered from the Westland Aircraft Works, but full contract not completed due to Armistice.
F1867-1882	16	Airco D.H.10/10A	Built by the Aircraft Manufacturing Co. Ltd., Hendon.
F1883-1957	75	Sopwith 1F.1 Camel	Built by Boulton & Paul Ltd., Norwich.
F1958-2007	50	Sopwith 1F.1 Camel	Built by Portholme Aerodrome Ltd., Huntingdon.
F2008-2082	75	Sopwith 1F.1 Camel	Built by Ruston, Proctor and Co. Ltd., Lincoln.
F2083-2182	100	Sopwith 1F.1 Camel	Built by Hooper & Co. Ltd., London.
F2183-2185	3	Maurice Farman	Built by 29th Wing.
F2186-2187	2	—	Not known.
F2188	1	Avro 504 (Mono)	Built from spares.
F2189-2208	20	Sopwith 1F.1 Camel	Built by No. 3 A.R.D.
F2209	1	Avro 504	Erected from salvage at Aircraft Repair Section, 23rd Wing, South Carlton in June 1918. 80 h.p. Le Rhône.
F2210-2229	20	Sopwith Ship Strutter	Ex-French 1½-Strutters. 130 h.p. Clerget.
F2230	1	Maurice Farman S.11 Shorthorn	Built by No. 132 Sqn.
F2231-2232	2	Avro 504	Built at Hounslow and Dover.
F2233-2332	100	Avro 504K	Built by The Brush Electrical Engineering Co. Ltd. F2309-2310 allotted to the Royal Navy with 100 h.p. Gnôme Monosoupape engines fitted.
F2333-2532	200	Sopwith 7F.1 Snipe	Sopwith-built. F2408 converted to a 2-seater. F2340 had a 200 h.p. Clerget.
F2533-2632	100	Avro 504K	Ordered from The Sunbeam Motor Car Co. Ltd., Wolverhampton. F2533 became FR2533.
F2633-2732	100	Airco D.H.4	Built by Glendower less mainplanes and ailerons. F2663, 2664, 2665, 2694, 2681, 2699, 2702, 2704 converted to D.H.4A.
F2733-2902	170	Airco D.H.9A	Built by Berwick. F2867, 2868, 2872 became G-EBAN/CG/GX and F2776, 2779 became A1-16 and A1-17 of the Royal Australian Air Force.

F2903-2905	3	Boulton & Paul P.7. Bourges Mk. I/IA/II	F2903 (Mk. I) became K-129/ G-EACE. F2904 (Mk. IA) became P.8 Atlantic project. F2905 (Mk. II) later G-EAWS.
F2906-2908	3	B.A.T. F.K.25 Basilisk	British Aerial Transport Co.
F2909-2911	3	Nieuport Nighthawk	Built by The Nieuport & General Aircraft Co. Ltd.
F2912-2914	3	Westland Weasel (engines as given)	F2912 Dragonfly, F2913 Jupiter, F2914 Jaguar.
F2915-2944	30	Vickers Vimy. (Fiat engines)	Ordered from Royal Aircraft Factory. Up to F2920 built. F2916, 2919-2920 became H652, 656-657.
F2945-2994	50	F.E.2b	Ordered from Barclay Curle to erect with material from Alex Stephens. Cancelled.
F2995	1	Beardmore W.B.II	Experimental.
F2996-3095	100	Vickers Vimy (B.H.P.)	Ordered from Clayton & Shuttleworth Ltd. 3 delivered.
F3096-3145	50	Sopwith 1F.1 Camel. (Mainly B.R.1 engines)	Built by Clayton & Shuttleworth Ltd., Lincoln, 1918-19.
F3146-3195	50	Vickers Vimy	Built by Morgan & Co. Deliveries only up to F3185.
F3196-3245	50	Sopwith 1F.1 Camel. (Mainly B.R.1 engines)	Built by The Nieuport & General Aircraft Co. Ltd.
F3246-3345	100	R.E.8	Ordered from Siddeley-Deasy Motor Car Co. Not built.
F3346-3445	100	Airco D.H.6	A.M.C.-built. F3386 mod. wings. 6 to civil use.
F3446-3491	46	A.W.F.K.8	Built by Angus Sanderson.
F3492-3494	3	Avro 533 Manchester Mk. I/II/III	F3492, Mk. II; F3493, Mk. I; F3494 planned as Mk. III, completed as Mk. I.
F3495-3497	3	Bristol Badger. (Type 23)	Built by the British & Colonial Aeroplane Co. Ltd.
F3498-3547	50	F.E.2b	Cancelled Barclay Curle order.
F3548-3747	200	R.E.8	Daimler-built. F3663, 3680-3682, 3684-3685 to White Russia.
F3748-3767	20	Handley Page 0/400	11 (Cricklewood) built.
F3768-3917	150	F.E.2b	Cancelled order with Ransome, Sims & Jeffries, Ipswich.
F3918-3967	50	Sopwith 1F.1 Camel. (Mainly B.R.1 engines)	Built by the Nieuport & General Aircraft Co. Ltd.
F3968-4067	100	Sopwith 1F.1 Camel	Built by Ruston, Proctor & Co. Ltd. F4019 conv. 2-seater.
F4068-4070	3	Sopwith Snark	To Spec. R.A.F. Type 1.
F4071-4170	100	F.E.2b	Cancelled order placed with Alex Stephens.
F4171-4174	4	Avro 504	Built at A.R.S. Dover, Chattis Hill, Hounslow and Dover.
F4175	1	Sopwith 1F.1 Camel	Built by No. 112 Sqn.
F4176	1	S.E.5a	Built from salvage, Salonika.
F4177-4216	40	Sopwith 1F.1 Camel	Built by No. 3 (W) A.R.D.
F4217	1	Avro 504	No. 207 T.D.S. Chingford built.
F4218	1	B.E.2d	Built by No. 191 Sqn.
F4219	1	A.W.F.K.3	Built by No. 26 T.S.
F4220	1	Sopwith Pup	Built at Salisbury.

Serial Nos.	*Qty.*	*Aircraft Type*	*Remarks*
F4221-4270	50	A.W.F.K.8	A.W. built. F4231 became G-AUDE.
F4271-4970	700	Bristol F.2B Fighter. (Rolls-Royce Falcon III engines in general)	Built by British & Colonial Aeroplane Co. Ltd. F4631 200 h.p. Arab, F4360 single-bay and F4728 3-bay wings. F4336 gift to Canada.
F4971-4973	3	A.W. Ara	Experimental aircraft.
F4974-5073	100	Sopwith 1F.1 Camel. (Mainly B.R.1 engines)	Built by Clayton & Shuttleworth Ltd. Delivery to F5025.
F5074-5173	100	Bristol F.2B Fighter	Built by Harris & Sheldon.
F5174-5248	75	Sopwith 1F.1 Camel	March, Jones and Cribb built.
F5249-5348	100	S.E.5A	Built by Martinsyde Ltd.
F5349-5448	100	Handley Page 0/400. (Liberty 12N engines)	National Aircraft Factory No. 1 built. F5349 erected at Ford Junction. Next 69 erected by H.P. 30 cancelled.
F5449-5698	250	S.E.5a	Vickers (Weybridge) built.
F5699-5798	100	Airco D.H.4	Palladium Autocars built. F5764 conv. D.H.4A.
F5799-5800	2	Avro 504J	Built up by 23rd Wing.
F5801-6300	500	(Re - built aircraft. A.W.F.K.8, Bristol F.2B Fighter, Airco D.H.4 and D.H.9, Sopwith 1F.1 Camel and 5F.1 Dolphin; Royal Aircraft Factory F.E.2b, R.E.8 and S.E.5a. Series over-ran its allocation by F6301-6308 for re-built Camels ex-D8616, D1808, B2371, D6628, B6635, D8511, C1584, D8385.)	F5801, 5803, 5805, 5807, F.K.8; F5809, D.H.4; F5810-5815, 5817, 5819-5824, F.2B; F5825-5833, 5835, 5837-5840, 5844, D.H.4/9; F5845-5850, D.H.9; F5852-5854, 5856, 5858-5859, 5861-5862, F.E.2b; F5864, D.H.9; F5671-5872, 5874, 5876-5877, 5879-5883, 5895, 5909, R.E.8; F5910, 5912, S.E.5a; F5914-5916, 5918-5955, 5957-5960, Camel; F5961-5962, Dolphin; F5964-5965, 5967-5968, Camel; F5969, S.E.5a; F5970, 5972, Camel; F5973-5974, 5976-5980, R.E.8; F5981-5982, 5985, 5990-5994, Camel; F5997-5999, F.2B; F6001-6003, D.H.4; F6005, 6007, 6009-6019, R.E.8; F6020, Dolphin; F6022-6039 Camel; F6040-6043, F.2B; F6044-6050, R.E.8; F6052-6053, Camel; F6055, D.H.9; F6056, Camel; F6057, D.H.9; F6058, 6063-6064, Camel; F6066, 6070, 6072-6073, D.H.9; F6075, 6077, 6080-6081, F.E.2b; F6083-6084, Camel; F6085, R.E.8; F6087-6090; Camel; F6091-6092, R.E.8; F6093, F.2B; F6096, D.H.4; F6097, R.E.8; F6098, D.H.9; F6099, D.H.4; F6100-6102,

			Camel; F6103-6104, D.H.4; F6105, 6107, 6110-6111, Camel, F6112-6113, D.H.9; F6114-6115, D.H.4; F6116, F.2B; F6117, Camel; F6119-6120, D.H.4; F6122-6123, Camel; F6124, F.K.8; F6125, D.H.9; F6126-6127, Camel; F6128, F.E.2b; F6129, Camel; F6131, F.2B; F6132, Camel; F6133, D.H.4; F6134, R.E.8; F6135, Camel; F6137, F.K.8; F6138, Camel; F6139, D.H.4; F6140, Camel; F6141, D.H.9; F6142, F.2B; F6143, R.E.8; F6144-6146, Dolphin; F6149-6153, 6155, 6156, Camel; F6158, F.2B; F6159, 6163, F.K.8; F6164-6168, D.H.4; F6169, Camel; F6172, D.H.9; F6173-6174, F.E.2b; F6175-6177, Camel; F6178, R.E.8; F6180, 6182-6185, Camel; F6187, D.H.4; F6188-6194, Camel; F6195, F.2B; F6196, D.H.9; F6197-6201, Camel; F6203-6204, R.E.8; F6205, D.H.9; F6206, F.2B; F6207, D.H.4; F6208, F.2B; F6209, D.H.4; F6210-6211, Camel; F6212, D.H.4; F6213, D.H.9; F6214-6215, D.H.4; F6216, Camel; F6217, F.2B; F6218, R.E.8; F6219-6221, Camel; F6222, D.H.4; F6223, Camel; F6224, D.H.4; F6226, Camel; F6227, D.H.4; F6228; 6230, Camel; F6234, D.H.4; F6235, F.2B; F6238, 6240, 6244-6245, 6249-6251, Camel; F6253, D.H.4; F6254, R.E.8; F6257-6259, 6264, Camel; F6270, R.E.8; F6271, Camel; F6273, R.E.8; F6276, S.E.5a; F6277, 6279, R.E.8; F6294-6295, Camel; F6299, R.E.8.
F6301-6500	200	Sopwith 1F.1 Camel (130 h.p. Clerget engines initially)	Boulton & Paul-built. F6394 6398, 180 h.p. Le Rhône. F6317, 6319 to Belgium.
F6501-7000	500	Sopwith T.F.2 Salamander	Sopwith (Ham) built. Up to F6602 delivered. F6533 went to U.S.A.
F7001-7030	30	Sopwith 7F.1 Snipe/ Dragon	Snipes ordered from Ham factory with Dragon engines.
F7031-7033	3	Sopwith Snapper	Experimental (Kingston built).
F7034-7133	100	Sopwith 5F.1 Dolphin	Built Darracq, Fulham, F7046 to French Government. F7128 free issue to Polish Air Force.

Serial Nos.	*Qty.*	*Aircraft Type*	*Remarks*
F7134-7143	10	Handley Page V/1500	Ordered from Alliance. Completed by H.P.
F7144-7146	3	Sopwith 1F.1 Camel	Cancelled order for special experimental aircraft.
F7147-7346	200	Airco D.H.10	Ordered from the Alliance Aeroplane Co. Ltd. No record of deliveries.
F7347-7546	200	Armstrong Whitworth F.K.8	Built by Angus Sanderson & Co., Newcastle - on - Tyne. F7384 and 7484 became G-EATO/LW.
F7547-7596	50	Sopwith Ship Strutter (130 h.p. Clerget)	French-built 1½ Strutters of single and two-seat types acquired in late 1918 for conversion for naval use. F7590 to Japanese Government.
F7597-7598	2	Airco D.H.4	Replacements.
F7601-7750	150	Sopwith T.F.2 Salamander	Cancelled order placed with Wolseley Motors.
F7751-7800	50	S.E.5a	Built by Wolseley Motors. F7773-7779, 7781-7785, 7787, 7792-7793, 7796-7797, 7799-7800 (with E3167) were S.E.5a Imperial Gift to S.A.A.F.
F7801-7950	150	Sopwith T.F.2 Salamander	Cancelled order with Air Navigation Co.
F7951-8200	250	S.E.5a	Built by the Austin Motor Co. F7960, 7976, 7978, 7991, 7997 became G-EBGL/GM/FI/DX/DV. F8001-8200 to U.S. Air Service.
F8201-8230	30	Handley Page V/1500	Ordered from Beardmore. 10 reported delivered.
F8231-8280	50	Sopwith T.1 Cuckoo	Cancelled order placed with Blackburn.
F8281-8320	20	Handley Page V/1500	Ordered from Handley Page. 10 reported delivered.
F8321-8420	100	S.E.5a	Ordered from Martinsyde. No record of delivery.
F8421-8495	75	Airco D.H.10A	Built by Mann, Egerton & Co. Up to F8441, built as a D.H.10C confirmed as delivered.
F8496-8595	100	Sopwith 1F.1 Camel (B.R.1 engines)	Built by The Nieuport & General Aviation Co. Ltd., Cricklewood. Delivered to Hendon Aircraft Acceptance Park late 1918. To F8553 confirmed as delivered.
F8596-8645	50	Vickers Vimy. (Mainly Rolls-Royce Eagle VIII engines)	Built by Vickers Ltd. at Weybridge. F8625 and F8630 became G-EAOL/U.
F8646-8695	50	Sopwith 1F.1 Camel	Built by Portholme Aerodrome. Up to F8689 confirmed as delivered to Norwich Aircraft Acceptance Park.

F8696-8945	250	Avro 504K	Built by Parnall & Sons. F8812 and F8834 converted to 504N.
F8946-9145	200	S.E.5a	Built by Vickers Ltd. Ordered 19.7.18, delivered same year.
F9146-9295	150	Vickers Vimy	50 only delivered. F9186 ditching trials 1920.
F9296-9395	100	F.E.2h	Cancelled order placed with Richard Garrett & Sons.
F9396-9445	50	—	Reservation for machines built by 45th Wing.
F9446-9495	50	—	Cancelled order placed with British Caudron Co.
F9496-9695	200	Sopwith 1F.1 Camel	Cancelled order placed with Boulton & Paul. Numbers re-allotted.
F9496-9545	50	—	Allocation for aircraft rebuilt by No. 5 (Eastern) Aircraft Repair Depot which included F9506 Avro 504 and F9515 D.H.9A ex-F963.
F9546-9547	2	Avro 504 (130 h.p. Clerget)	Built up from salvage.
F9548	1	Sopwith 1F.1 Camel	Built by No. 207 T.D.S.
F9549	1	Bristol F.2B Fighter (Arab -engined)	Built by Marshall & Sons.
F9550	1	F.E.2b	160 h.p. Origin not known.
F9551-9565	15	—	Not known.
F9566	1	F.E.2b	Built by 4th Wing.
F9567	1	B.E.2d	Built by No. 5 T.D.S.
F9568	1	S.E.5A	Built by No. 30 T.D.S.
F9569-9570	2	Vickers Vimy	Replacements for B9952 and B9954.
F9571	1	B.E.2d	Built by No. 16 T.D.S.
F9572	1	Avro 504A	A8591 taken back on charge after being sent to the Scottish Aircraft Factory as pattern.
F9573-9622	50	—	Reservation for No. 3 A.R.D.
F9623-9624	2	Sopwith 1F.1	Built by 6th Wing.
F9625	1	Avro 504	Built by 6th Wing.
F9626	1	Bristol Scout	Built by No. 2 School of Aerial Navigation.
F9627	1	B.E.2c	Origin not known.
F9628-9630	3	Sopwith IF.1 Camel	Built by No. 3 T.D.S.
F9631-9632	2	Sopwith 1F.1 Camel	Built by No. 43 T.D.S.
F9633	1	Avro 504 (Le Rhône)	Origin not known.
F9634	1	Sopwith 1F.1 Camel	Built by No. 29 T.D.S.
F9635	1	Sopwith 1F.1 Camel	Built by C.F.S.
F9636	1	Avro 504	Built by 58th Wing.
F9637	1	Sopwith 1F.1 Camel	Built by No. 42 T.S.
F9638	1	Bristol F.2B Fighter	Believed built at Farnborough.
F9639-9694	56	—	Reservation to No. 2 A.R.D.
F9695	1	Sopwith 1F.1 Camel	Built at Upavon.
F9696-9745	50	Avro 504K	Built by Eastbourne Aviation Co.
F9746-9845	100	Avro 504K	Built by Hewlett and Blondeau Ltd.

Serial Nos.	Qty.	Aircraft Type	Remarks
F9846-9995	150	Sopwith 7F1 Snipe	Cancelled order placed with Coventry Ordnance Works, Ltd.
F9996-9999	4	—	Reservation for No. 2 A.R.D.

CAPTURED ENEMY AIRCRAFT

"G" and "AG" series

"G" did not follow "F" as a prefix letter in the general numbering series, because it could easily be confused with "C", but it was used as a prefix in a special series for the identification of enemy aircraft falling into British hands on the Western Front as it was an appropriately significant letter for "German". The numbers were not allocated for aircraft taken on charge by units as in the general series, but as a reference number, chiefly for intelligence purposes. In fact, in a number of cases, the "G" number denoted merely a heap of wreckage.

Strewn wreckage or wreckage under fire was not always salvaged, but in most cases it was taken to a depot for examination by intelligence officers in France. Usually the engine was in one piece and it was normal to despatch this to England where it was stored at the Agricultural Hall, Islington, for technical survey or awaiting allocation.

Ex-enemy aircraft that were airworthy, were flown to England on the normal ferry route to Lympne from where they were collected for store at Islington or held pending allocation to experimental establishments or Fighting Schools. Other aircraft, reasonably intact but not flyable, were shipped and transported to Islington. It was these two classes of relatively intact machines that actually bore their 'G' numbers in a manner similar to normal British service aircraft. The majority were scrapped after a survey in February 1919. G1 to G9 was apparently not allotted.

Serial No.	Aircraft Type and Number (if known)	Date acquired	Remarks on circumstances of acquisition
G10	Albatros DIII D1990/16	13. 2.17	Shot down nr. Sailly-Saillisel.
G11	Albatros	15. 2.17	Fell in lines nr. Vlamertinge.
G12	Halberstadt DV	15. 3.17	Hit by A.A. fire. Sent to U.K.
G13	D.F.W.		Wreckage found.
G14	Albatros Scout	4. 3.17	Shot down by No. 29 Sqn.
G15	(Unidentified)	25. 3.17	Shot down by Lt. Binnie, No. 60 Sqn.
G16	(Unidentified)	25. 3.17	Shot down by Lt. Binnie, No. 60 Sqn.
G17	Albatros DI D210/16	21. 3.17	Prince Charles Frederick of Prussia forced down by S.E.5A of No. 32 Sqn.
G18	Albatros D2012/16	1. 4.17	Shot down.
G19	Albatros CVII C2217/16	2. 4.17	Brought down by A.A. Crew captured.

G20	Albatros Scout D1942/16	5. 4.17	Forced down nr. Neuve Eglise.
G21	Albatros Scout D2234/16	8. 4.17	Shot down in British lines by French fighter.
G22	Albatros	21. 4.17	Shot down by R.N.A.S. pilots.
G23	Gotha GIV G610/16	23. 4.17	Shot down by R.N.A.S. pilot nr. Vron.
G24	D.F.W. CV C5927/16	24. 4.17	Forced down nr. Havrincourt.
G25	Aviatik	24. 4.17	Shot down.
G26	Albatros Scout	25. 4.17	Wreck under shell-fire not salvaged.
G27	D.F.W.	30. 4.17	Completely wrecked.
G28	Albatros 2-seater	30. 4.17	Brought down by ground fire. Crew P.O.Ws.
G29	D.F.W. CV C4909/16	1. 5.17	Brought down by A.A. fire nr. Arras.
G30	Albatros Scout D771/17	1. 5.17	Shot down by No. 1 Sqn nr. Elverdinghe.
G31	D.F.W.	2. 5.17	Brought down by fire from trenches.
G32	Albatros	3. 5.17	Landed undamaged. Flown to U.K.
G33	Albatros	5. 5.17	Conflicting reports of salvage.
G34	Albatros Scout	5. 5.17	Wreckage completely burned.
G35	Albatros Scout	6. 5.17	Shot down by F.Es. Not salvaged.
G36	(Unidentified)	7. 5.17	Not salvaged.
G37	Albatros CV C1394/17	12. 5.17	Shot down by A.A. fire nr. Armentieres.
G38	D.F.W.	18. 5.17	Shot down by m.g. fire from trenches.
G39	Albatros Scout D796/17	19. 5.17	By S.E.5A nr. St. Pol. Pilot P.O.W.
G40	D.F.W. C5872/16	20. 5.17	By No. 3 Sqn over Havrincourt Wood.
G41	(Unidentified)	21. 5.17	A.A. fire. Found to have fallen in German lines when investigated.
G42	Albatros DIII D2015/16	4. 6.17	Forced down by No. 29 Sqn. Flown in England with engine from G39.
G43	Albatros DIII	5. 6.17	By No. 60 Sqn. Crashed nr. front.
G44	D.F.W. C9045/16	12. 5.17	By No. 8(N) Sqn. nr. Arras.
G45	D.F.W.	13. 5.17	Wrecked.
G46	(Unidentified)	—	False report of wreckage in lines.
G47	D.F.W. CV C5046	16. 6.17	By 2 pilots of No. 8(N) Sqn.
G48	Rumpler	23. 6.15	By A.A. fire at Steenwich.
G49	Albatros	23. 6.17	By A.A. fire nr. Ypres.
G50	Albatros	2. 7.17	By fire from No. 12 Kite Balloon Sect.
G51	Albatros CVII C9289/16	12.17.17	By No. 70 Sqn over Bellevue.
G52	D.F.W.	12. 7.17	Mannock shot down S. of Lens.
G53	D.F.W. CV C799/17	12. 7.17	By No. 56 Sqn nr. Armentieres.
G54	(See remarks)	—	False report.
G55	D.F.W.	13. 7.17	By A.A. fire S.E. of Arras.
G56	Albatros DV D2129/17	15. 7.17	Forced down intact. To U.K.

Serial Nos.	*Aircraft Type and number (if known)*	*Date captured*	*Remarks on circumstances of acquision*
G57	Ago CIV C8964/16	29. 7.17	By 32 Sqn. Crashed in U.K.
G58	D.F.W. CV C776/17	5. 8.17	By No. 5 Sqn. 1 survivor.
G59	D.F.W.	10. 8.17	Shot down. Nothing salvaged.
G60	Albatros DIII	12. 8.17	By Mannock over Farbus.
G61	Albatros DIII	12. 8.17	By No. 7 Sqn.
G62	Rumpler CIV	19. 8.17	By A.A. fire N.W. of Ypres.
G63	Rumpler CIV	20. 8.17	By No. 66 Sqn. nr. Ypres.
G64	(Unidentified)	21. 8.17	Found to be in enemy lines.
G65	(Unidentified)	22. 8.17	Found to be in enemy lines.
G66	Rumpler CIV C1898/16	31. 8.17	Landed nr. Elverdinghe.
G67	A.E.G. GIV G166/16	3/4.9.17	By A.A. fire. 2 prisoners.
G68	(Unidentified)	4. 9.17	Completely burned.
G69	Rumpler CIV C8483/16	3. 9.17	Believed force landed.
G70	(Unidentified)	14. 9.17	No. 48 Sqn. Salvaged by Belgians.
G71	(Unidentified)	16. 9.17	Landed in No Man's Land.
G72	Fokker DrI F103/17	23. 9.17	Voss shot down nr. St. Julien.
G73	(Unidentified)	27. 9.17	Wreckage. Shot down in flames.
G74	Gotha GIV	25. 9.17	By A.A. fire at Oost Dunkerke.
G75	Albatros DV D2284/17	27. 9.17	Forced down jointly by R.F.C./R.N.A.S.
G76	(Unidentified)	28. 9.17	Completely destroyed.
G77	(Unidentified)	28. 9.17	Wreckage not salvaged.
G78	(Unidentified)	1.10.17	Wreckage at Hooge.
G79	(Unidentified)	14.10.17	Wreckage at Poelcapelle.
G80	(Unidentified)	17.10.17	By No. 22 Sqn east of Ypres.
G81	L.V.G.	17.10.17	By Capt. McCudden nr. Dickebusch.
G82	(Unidentified)	17.10.17	Wreckage in Polygon Wood.
G83	(Unidentified)	18.10.17	Wreckage in Polygon Wood.
G84	Rumpler C8431	21.10.17	Shot down by Capt. McCudden.
G85	Rumpler	22.10.17	Shot down by No. 11 Sqn.
G86	(Unidentified)	5.11.17	Shot down by infantry.
G87	(Unidentified)	5.11.17	Shot down by infantry.
G88	(Unidentified)	8.11.17	Nothing salvaged.
G89	Albatros DIII	13.11.17	Shot down by No. 24 Sqn.
G90	Albatros DV D5253/17	14.11.17	By A.A. in Third Army area.
G91	D.F.W. CV C4977/16	22.11.17	Forced down intact by Capt. Childs, No. 84 Sqn., nr. Bourlon Wood.
G92	(Unidentified)	29.11.17	Nothing salvaged. Near Passchendaele.
G93	Pfalz DIIIa D1116/17	30.11.17	Shot down by Capt. G. E. Thompson, No. 46 Sqn, nr. Flesquieres.
G94	L.V.G. CV C4958/17	30.11.17	Wreckage at Havrincourt, by A.A. fire.
G95	Rumpler	5.12.17	Wreckage nr. Hermies.
G96	(Unidentified)	5.12.17	Wreckage nr. Hermies.
G97	Albatros DV D4545/17	5.12.17	Down nr. Bethune. To U.K.
G98	Albatros DV	12.12.17	Total wreck. Second Army area.
G99	(Unidentified)	12.12.17	By A.A. of Second Army.
G100	Albatros DV D2356	17.12.17	Shot down north of Ypres.

G101	Albatros DVa D5390/17	17.12.17	Forced down by No. 3 Sqn,. A.F.C. Flown to U.K. Shipped to Australia.
G102	(Unidentified)	10.12.17	Presumed false report of wreck.
G103	(Unidentified)	18.12.17	Wreckage reported not located.
G104	D.F.W.	22.12.17	Shot down by Capt. J. B. McCudden.
G105	A.E.G. CIV G1125/16	23.12.17	A.A. at Achiet-le-Grand. Intact.
G106	Rumpler	23.12.17	Shot down by Capt. J. B. McCudden.
G107	Rumpler	23.12.17	By Capt. McCudden nr. Gontescourt.
G108	L.V.G.	23.12.17	By Capt. McCudden nr. Metz.
G109	(Unidentified)	23.12.17	Found to be in enemy lines.
G110	Pfalz DIII D1370/17	27.12.17	Landed intact. No. 35 Sqn. took over.
G111	Rumpler	28.12.17	Capt. McCudden shot down nr. Velu Wood.
G112	Rumpler	28.12.17	Capt. McCudden shot down nr. Flers.
G113	L.V.G.	28.12.17	Capt. McCudden shot down. Wreckage spread in Havrincourt Wood.
G114	(Unidentified)	28.12.17	By 46 Sqn over Gouzeacourt.
G115	(Unidentified)	28.12.17	By A.A. fire at Saillisel.
G116	Pfalz DIII	28.12.17	By A.A. fire nr. Le Transloy.
G117	Rumpler CV C8500/16	28.12.17	Forced down by A.A. at Monchy. Flown to U.K. Crashed at Grain on trials.
G118	L.V.G.	29.12.17	By Capt. McCudden nr. Havrincourt.
G119	L.V.G.	29.12.17	By Capt. McCudden nr. Epehy.
G120	Rumpler CIV	1. 1.18	By A.A. nr. Peronne.
G121	(Unidentified)	1. 1.18	By Capt. Mannock over Fampoux.
G122	(Unidentified 2-seater)	3. 1.18	Wreckage found to be in German lines.
G123	Albatros Scout	6. 1.18	By No. 13 Sqn. Nothing salved as wreckage could only be viewed at distance on enemy's trench wire.
G124	(Unidentified 2-seater)	13. 1.18	Wreckage.
G125	Fokker DrI Dr144/17	13. 1.18	Lt. Stapenhorst after shooting down British balloon was brought down by A.A. Shipped to U.K.
G126	A.E.G.	26.12.17	Brought down in Italy.
G127	—	—	False report of wreckage.
G128	D.F.W.	26.12.17	Brought down in Italy.
G129	(Unidentified)	29. 1.18	Brought down in French lines.
G130	L.V.G. C9725/17	2. 2.18	Brought down by Capt. McCudden.
G131	Albatros Scout	4. 2.18	Shot down by No. 60 Sqn. pilots.
G132	L.V.G. CV C9658/17	18. 1.18	By A.A. fire near Lens.
G133	Friedrichshafen GIII G283/17	15. 2.18	Landed in Third Army area.

Serial No.	*Aircraft Type and Number (if known)*	*Date acquired*	*Remarks on circumstances of aquisition*
G134	Albatros DV D4422/17	16. 2.18	Intact, but turned over in ploughed field when forced down by No. 1 Sqn.
G135	L.V.G. CV	16. 2.18	Landed intact nr. Catigny.
G136	Friedrichshafen GIII G326/17	16. 2.18	Forced down by A.A. fire nr. Isbergues. Crew of 4 prisoners.
G137	Rumpler CIV	16. 2.18	By Capt. McCudden nr. Lagnicourt.
G138	Albatros Scout D4495	19. 2.18	By No. 60 Sqn nr. Hollebeke.
G139	Halberstadt	—	Crashed in British lines.
G140	(Unidentified 2-seater)	21. 2.18	By No. 29 Sqn. Crashed in front line.
G141	Pfalz DIII 4184/17	26. 2.18	By No. 24 Sqn. Landed intact on British aerodrome. Flown to U.K. 6.3.18.
G142	Rumpler	—	Wreckage found.
G143	D.F.W. CV	1. 3.18	Believed by naval pilot.
G144	Albatros DV D2356	6. 3.18	By No. 13 Sqn nr. Arras. Flown to U.K.
G145	Albatros	6. 3.18	Wrecked
G146	(Unidentified)	6. 3.18	Fell in front line trenches.
G147	Friedrichshafen GIII G199/17	11. 3.18	Landed and destroyed by crew.
G148	(Unidentified)	12. 3.18	By No. 56 Sqn over Ribecourt.
G149	Albatros two-seater	12. 3.18	By No. 11 Sqn nr. Doignies.
G150	(Unidentified)	15. 3.18	By No. 84 Sqn S. of Villeret.
G151	Albatros DV	18. 3.18	Forced down nr. Essigny-le-Grand.
G152	(Unidentified)	22. 3.18	Down in flames. Not salved.
G153	Albatros Scout	22. 3.18	Brought down by infantry fire.
G154	Albatros Scout	22. 3.18	Brought down by infantry fire.
G155	Albatros Scout	22. 3.18	Brought down by infantry fire.
G156	Hannover CLII CL13199/17	29. 3.18	Brought down by A.A. fire. Flown to U.K. 26.4.18.
G157	Pfalz DIII D8078/17	—	Engine and guns to U.K.
G158	Fokker DrI	22. 3.18	Shipped to U.K.
G159	Albatros DV D5734/17	1. 4.18	Flown to U.K. 21.4.18.
G160	D.F.W.	1. 4.18	Shot down by No. 3 Sqn, A.F.C.
G161	(Unidentified 2-seater)	10. 4.18	Not salvaged.
G162	(Unidentified 2-seater)	10. 4.18	Not salvaged.
G163	(Unidentified)	10. 4.18	Not salvaged.
G164	—	10. 4.18	Report not substantiated.
G165	Hannover CL13135/17	9. 4.18	Engine only salvaged.
G166	L.V.G.	9. 4.18	Engine only salvaged.
G167	L.V.G.	11. 4.18	Engine only salvaged.

XG series

THE 'G' series had been started early in 1917, and once functioning as the standard register for captured aircraft, it was appreciated that earlier enemy aircraft captured had not been similarly registered. A register of these was therefore compiled in retrospect in a numbered series starting at No. 1 prefixed by 'XG' to denote the 'Extra G-series'.

Serial Nos.	Aircraft Type and number (if known)	Remarks on acquisition and disposal
XG1	Albatros A375	Believed arrived in U.K. 20.4.16.
XG2	Albatros A374	Farnborough 22.9.15. Given to Cambridge University.
XG3	L.V.G. C2234	From France 25.5.16. To London University.
XG4	Fokker 509	To Science Museum.
XG5	Fokker	Was A3021. To U.S.A. 11.12.17.
XG6	Albatros DI 391/16	Captured 1.12.16.
XG7	L.V.G. 1594	Farnborough from 14.6.17.
XG8	Albatros 2-seater	Arrived at Farnborough 5.7.18.
XG9	Halberstadt	Wreckage held at Islington.
XG10	C1788/16	Exhibited February 1917.
XG11	L.V.G. C4238	Allotted to H.Q. Honorable Artillery Coy.
XG12	Friedrichshafen GIII 168/17	Wreckage salved from sea by French after machine hit cliffs at Cape Blanchey 4/5.11.17.
XG13	CV4686/17	R.N.A.S. capture. Believed sent to Canada.
XG14		Wreckage held at Islington.

AB series

DURING 1917 the Germans intensified raids over Britain by aeroplanes and the occasional one was shot down. In the same way that H.Q., R.F.C. in the Field allotted serials in the 'G' series, so at Home, the R.F.C. registered the wrecks in this country in a series prefixed by the letters 'AB'.

Serial Nos.	Aircraft Type and number (if known)	Date captured	Remarks on location and how acquired
AB1	—	—	No details known.
AB2	Gotha	5/6.12.17	Hit by A.A. over Canvey Island was forced to land at Rochford. Burnt out after landing.
AB3	Gotha	5/6.12.17	Brought down near Canterbury. Crew set it on fire before capture.
AB4	Gotha	22.12.17	Landed in field at Margate and set on fire by crew before capture.
AB5	Gotha 938/16	28.12.17	Brought down in flames at Wichford.
AB6	Gotha GV 978/16	19. 5.18	Shot down by Bristol Fighter. Wreckage fell at East Ham, London.
AB7	Gotha GV 925/16	19. 5.18	Shot down by coastal A.A. at St. Osyth.
AB8	Gotha GV 979/16	19. 5.18	After aerial combat crashed at Frinstead.
AB9	Gotha	19. 5.18	Shot down by Sopwith Camel at Shellness, Isle of Sheppey.

AG series

IN November 1917 two R.F.C. Wings were sent to assist Italian Forces. Initially their intelligence reports were submitted through G.H.Q. in France and the first wreckage recordings were in the 'G' series. From December 1917 R.F.C., H.Q. Italy (VIIth Brigade R.F.C.) compiled its own register of enemy aircraft or their remains examined in a numbered series prefixed 'AG' to denote Austro-Hungarian and German series.

Serial Nos.	*Aircraft Type*	*Remarks*
AG1	D.F.W.	Totally wrecked at Povegliano, Dec. 1917.
AG2	A.E.G. G(?)	Brought down by A.A. fire at Biadene.
AG3	Albatros D.V D.4879/17	Shot down December 1917.
AG4	A.E.G. G.IV	Brought down by A.A. fire at Castelfranco.
AG5	Albatros D.III	Brought down February 1918.
AG6	Aviatik-Berg D.I	Austrian No. 138.27 crashed in British lines.
AG7	A.E.G. G.IV G.180	Landed with engine trouble, night of 18/19.2.18.
AG8	A.E.G.	Shot down in flames night of 20/21.2.18.

G/HQ & G/Bde series

THE general 'G' series lapsed in March 1918 in favour of General Headquarters and each R.F.C. Brigade in the Field (which became R.A.F. Brigades on April 1st 1918) with responsibility for sectors of the Front reporting enemy aircraft down in their area and reporting them separately. The approved form was in the styling G/1Bde/1 for the first registered by I Brigade, but the actual marking varied from G-1-1 to G/1BDE/1; for presentation here the approved form is used.

Serial No.	*Aircraft Type and Number (if known)*	*Date captured*	*Remarks on acquisition, condition and disposal*
G/HQ/1	Rumpler CVII 6460/17	16. 5.18	Landed fuel shortage at Cappelle.
G/HQ/2	Friedrichshafen GIII 402/17	19. 5.18	By A.A. fire nr. Calot'eries.
G/HQ/3	Gotha	22. 5.18	Crew burnt aircraft before capture.
G/HQ/4	D.F.W. CV	31. 5.18	Forced down. To U.K. 5.6.18.
G/HQ/5	(2-seater)	1. 7.18	Wreckage found on dump.
G/HQ/6	Pfalz DXII 2486/18	15. 9.18	By Nos. 1 and 62 Sqns.
G/1Bde/1	D.F.W. CV 7823/17	29. 4.18	Shot down by No. 40 Sqn.
G/1Bde/2	Pfalz DIIIa 8151/17	3. 5.18	Landed Gonnelieu, engine trouble.
G/1Bde/3	D.F.W. CV	3. 5.18	Brought down by A.A. fire.
G/1Bde/4	D.F.W. CV 938/18	8. 5.18	Brought down by small arms fire.
G/1Bde/5	D.F.W.	7. 5.18	Shot down by No. 46 Sqn.
G/1Bde/6	Rumpler CIV 1469/17	16. 5.18	Forced down.
G/1Bde/7	A.E.G. JI 209/17	16. 5.18	Brought down nr. Hianges by crew of R.E.8 B6568. To U.K.
G/1Bde/8	(Twin-engined)	1. 6.18	Wrecked.
G/1Bde/9	L.V.G.	7. 7.18	Shot down by No. 40 Sqn.
G/1Bde/10	Albatros DIII	9. 7.18	Total wreck near Steenwerck.
G/1Bde/11	D.F.W.	3. 8.18	Wreck not salvaged.
G/1Bde/12	Gotha GVb	10. 8.18	Forced down near Caucourt.
G/1Bde/13	Friedrichshafen	21. 8.18	By No. 151 Sqn near Arras.

G/1Bde/14	Gotha GVb	24. 8.18	By No. 151 Sqn nr. Haute-Avesnes.
G/1Bde/15	Halberstadt (2-seat)	—	Wreckage found. Salvaged 31.8.18.
G/1Bde/16	Fokker DVII	15. 9.18	Details not known.
G/1Bde/17	Fokker DVII	—	Flown to U.K. 6.11.18.
G/2Bde/1	D.F.W. CV 7877/17	21. 4.18	Brought down by A.A. fire at Westoutre. To Islington 6.5.18.
G/2Bde/2	Albatros DV	21. 4.18	Not salvaged.
G/2Bde/3	Rumpler	23. 4.18	Salvaged by French.
G/2Bde/4	Albatros DV	22. 4.18	Salvaged by French.
G/2Bde/5	Halberstadt	26. 4.18	Not salvaged.
G/2Bde/6	Halberstadt	30. 4.18	Destroyed on ground by shells.
G/2Bde/7	L.V.G.	3. 5.18	By No. 32 Sqn.
G/2Bde/8	Albatros	14. 5.18	Completely wrecked. Unsalvageable.
G/2Bde/9	Albatros DIII	14. 5.18	Details not known.
G/2Bde/10	Fokker DrI	19. 5.18	Engine only salvaged.
G/2Bde/11	Halberstadt CLII	22. 5.18	Hit by m.g. fire, Poperinghe.
G/2Bde/12	Albatros Scout	29. 5.18	Wreckage.
G/2Bde/13	Albatros Scout	31. 5.18	Unsalvageable.
G/2Bde/14	Fokker DVII FN1450/18	6. 6.18	Shot down near Hazebrouck by S.E.5A D5969. Shipped to U.K.
G/2Bde/15	Fokker DrI 517/17	9. 6.18	Shot down near Dickenbusch. Engine and parachute to U.K.
G/2Bde/16	Pfalz DIII	19. 6.18	Shot down near Bailleul.
G/2Bde/17	Rumpler	30. 6.18	Shot down by No. 74 Sqn.
G/2Bde/18	Friedrichshafen GIII 507/18	1/2.7.18	Forced down.
G/2Bde/19	Friedrichshafen GIII 555/17	1/2.7.18	Brought down by A.A. fire at Fanquernbergues. Fired by crew.
G/2Bde/20	L.V.G.	27. 7.18	Shot down and burned.
G/2Bde/21	L.V.G. CVI	2. 8.18	By S.E.5As C6468 and D3438 nr. P.oven.
G/2Bde/22	Fokker DVII	17. 9.18	Shot down.
G/2Bde/23	D.F.W.	17. 9.18	Complete wreck sent for scrap.
G/2Bde/24	Albatros	?	Engine salvaged from wreckage.
G/2Bde/25	Rumpler	?	Engine to Islington, Nov. 1918.
G/2Bde/26	—	—	No record.
G/2Bde/27	Fokker DVII	28.10.18	Shot down.
G/2Bde/28	Fokker DVII	28.10.18	Engine salvaged.
G/2Bde/29	Friedrichshafen	?	Believed by A.A. fire.
G/2Bde/30	L.V.G.	—	Shipped to U.K.
G/2Bde/31	—	—	No record.
G/2Bde/32	—	—	No record.
G/2Bde/33	Fokker DVII	—	No further detail.
G/3Bde/1	(Unidentified)	11. 4.18	Not salvaged.
G/3Bde/2	Hannover CI 13103/17	16. 4.18	Force-landed. Flown to U.K.
G/3Bde/3	D.F.W. CV 7787/17	22. 4.18	By A.A. fire. To U.K. 13.5.18.
G/3Bde/4	Pfalz DIII 8282/1724	24. 4.18	By small arms fire. To U.K.
G/3Bde/5	L.V.G. CV 9746/17	29. 4.18	Forced down. Sent to U.K.
G/3Bde/6	Gotha GV 969/17	21. 5.18	Shot down by A.A. To U.K.
G/3Bde/7	Albatros DV 7221/17	25. 5.18	Engine salvaged for U.K.
G/3Bde/8	Halberstadt CLII 1231/18	29. 6.18	Crashed nr. Fillieres.

Serial Nos.	*Aircraft Type and number (if known)*	*Date captured*	*Remarks on acquisition, condition and disposal*
G/3Bde/9	Friedrichshafen	17. 7.18	Completely burnt. Engines to U.K.
G/3Bde/10	Staaken RXIV R43	10. 8.18	By Camel, No. 151 Sqn. nr. Amiens.
G/3Bde/11	Gotha GV 922	22. 8.18	Shot down by Camel, No. 151 Sqn.
G/3Bde/12	Fokker DVII	21. 8.18	Shot down by No. 3 Sqn pilot.
G/3Bde/13	Fokker DVII	23. 8.18	By No. 12 Sqn R.E.8 crew.
G/3Bde/14	Pfalz DIII	27. 8.18	Details not known.
G/3Bde/15	L.V.G.	29. 8.18	Found during an advance.
G/3Bde/16	Halberstadt	3. 9.18	Located on ground at Biefvillers les Bapaume. Sent to U.K.
G/3Bde/17	Fokker DVII	5. 9.18	Date is day of location.
G/3Bde/18	Albatros	5. 9.18	Date is day of location.
G/3Bde/19	Fokker DVII	4. 9.18	Shot down by Camel F1972.
G/3Bde/20	(Unidentified)	3. 9.18	Not salvaged.
G/3Bde/21	Friedrichshafen or Gotha	13. 9.18	Shot down by No. 151 Sqn Camel. An engine sent to Wolseley Motors.
G/3Bde/22	Friedrichshafen	17. 9.18	By 151 Sqn Camel. Parts to U.K.
G/3Bde/23	Friedrichshafen	17. 9.18	By 151 Sqn Camel.
G/3Bde/24	Staaken RVI	15. 9.18	Badly burnt.
G/3Bde/25	(Twin-engined)	21. 9.18	Badly burnt.
G/3Bde/26	L.V.G.	27. 9.18	Date as day located.
G/3Bde/27	Friedrichshafen	28. 9.18	Date as day wreckage located.
G/3Bde/28	Hannover	26.10.18	Engine to U.K.
G/3Bde/29	Hannover	26.10.18	Engine to U.K.
G/3Bde/30	—	18	No detail.
G/3Bde/31	Junkers JI	11.18	Salvaged near La Vacquerie.
G/3Bde/32	L.V.G.	18	No further detail.
G/3Bde/33	—	18	Presume wreck found during advance.
G/3Bde/34	—	18	Presume wreck found.
G/3Bde/35	—	18	Presume wreck found.
G/3Bde/36	—	18	Presume wreck found.
G/3Bde/37	Halberstadt CLII	1.11.18	Wreck found.
G/5Bde/1	Rumpler	12. 4.18	Complete wreck but engine to U.K.
G/5Bde/2	Fokker Dr1 425/17	21. 4.18	von Richthofen brought down near Corbie.
G/5Bde/3	(Two-seater)	22. 4.18	Shot down nr. Somme-Aure.
G/5Bde/4	Albatros	25. 4.18	Shot down nr. Viller-Bretonneux.
G/5Bde/5	(Unidentified)	25. 4.18	Believed shot down by A.A. fire.
G/5Bde/6	Hannover CLII 13282/17	3. 5.18	Brought down by joint efforts of A.A. and aircraft.
G/5Bde/7	L.V.G.	4. 5.18	Brought down by A.A. nr. Arras.
G/5Bde/8	Fokker DrI	16. 5.18	Shot down by Camel B7199.
G/5Bde/9	A.E.G. GIV 588/17	16. 5.18	Hit by A.A. Landed nr. Villers-Bretonneux.
G/5Bde/10	Albatros Scout	17. 5.18	Unsalvageable.
G/5Bde/11	L.V.G.	27. 5.18	Completely burnt.

G/5Bde/12	Pfalz DIII 8284/17	30. 5.18	Landed short of fuel. Flown to U.K. 21.6.18.
G/5Bde/14	Rumpler	31. 5.18	Total wreck.
G/5Bde/15	Rumpler	1. 6.18	Badly burnt.
G/5Bde/16	Halberstadt CLII 1534/17	9. 6.18	Forced down by R.E.8 crew nr. Villers Bocage. Flown to U.K.
G/5Bde/17	Fokker DVII	17. 6.18	Shot down by S.E.5As.
G/5Bde/18	L.V.G. CV	17. 6.18	Shot down nr. Ailly sur Noye.
G/5Bde/19	D.F.W. C342/18	26. 7.18	Shot down.
G/5Bde/20	Fokker DVII	12. 8.18	By Camel. Sent to U.K.
G/5Bde/21	A.E.G. GIV 875/17	15. 8.18	Brought down by A.A. fire.
G/5Bde/22	Halberstadt CLIV	23. 8.18	Landed at Chipilly.
G/5Bde/23	A.E.G. JII 202/18	24. 8.18	Found near Morcourt.
G/5Bde/24	Fokker DVII	12. 8.18	Shot down.
G/5Bde/25	Friedrichshafen	7. 9.18	Believed force landed.
G/5Bde/26	Fokker DVII	10. 9.18	Salvage sent to U.K.
G/5Bde/27	A.E.G. GV	17. 9.18	Shot down by Camel.
G/5Bde/28	(Twin-engined)	13. 9.18	Believed not salvaged.
G/5Bde/29	Hannover	24. 9.18	Brought down nr. St. Quentin.
G/5Bde/30	Albatros JII 1566/1830	30.10.18	Found crashed nr. Montbrehain.
G/5Bde/31	A.E.G.	?	Two engines sent to U.K.
G/10Bde/1	Friedrichshafen GIVa	24. 7.18	Engines sent to U.K.
G/10Bde/2	D.F.W. CV 2238/18	10. 8.18	Wrecked near Hinges.
G/10Bde/3	A.E.G.	8.18	Wreck found. Parts to U.K.
G/10Bde/4	—	5. 9.18	Wreckage found.
G/10Bde/5	Fokker DVII	16. 9.18	Shot down. Engine salvaged.
G/10Bde/6	D.F.W.	16. 9.18	Date of location of wreck.
G/10Bde/7	Pfalz	17. 9.18	Complete wreck found.
G/10Bde/8	Pfalz DXII 2600/18	9.10.18	Driven down by Camels E7190 and E7241. Flown to U.K. Shipped to Australia.

END-OF-WAR ORDERS

H1–9999

THE " H " series, following directly on from the " F " series in late 1918, consists largely of orders that were cut or cancelled within a few months of being placed, due to the cessation of hostilities.

Serial Nos.	*Qty.*	*Aircraft Type*	*Remarks*
H1-200	200	Airco D.H.9A	Built by A.M.C. H93 rebuilt as HR93.
H201-350	150	Avro 504K	Built by the Scottish Aircraft Company. Up to H257 only confirmed delivered. H244 became HR244 on re-building.
H351-650	300	Sopwith Snipe	Built by Ruston, Proctor & Co. Ltd., Lincoln, except H408-418 completed by Portholme. H376-378, 382, 386-403, 419-450 not completed. H451-556 cancelled.

Serial Nos.	Qty.	Aircraft Type	Remarks
H651-670	20	Vickers Vimy	Ordered from the Royal Aircraft Establishment. First ten confirmed as delivered.
H671-673	3	Sopwith Cobham	Experimental bomber built by Sopwith Aviation; H671 with Puma and H672 and H673 with Dragonfly engines. H673 was grounded after test.
H674-733	60	S.E.5a	Built by the Air Navigation Co. Deliveries to service confirmed up to H710.
H734-833	100	Sopwith 1F.1 Camel	Built by Hooper Ltd. Deliveries confirmed up to H830. Fitted for night-fighting
H834-1083	250	Bristol F.2B	Built by the Gloucestershire Aviation Co. Ltd. H926, 927, 951 became G-EBEE/EBDN/EAWA on the Civil Register. H834-925 and H1061-1083 cancelled.
H1084-1239	156	Martinsyde F.4 Buzzard	Cancelled order. Duplicated D4211-4360 (150) and B1490-1495 (6).
H1240-1739	500	Bristol F.2B Fighter	Built by the British & Colonial Aeroplane Co. Ltd. H1240, 1242, 1244, 1245, 1258, 1281, 1291, 1292, 1389 to the Belgian Air Force; 5 to Civil Register and 2 (H1251 and H1485) to Irish Air Corps as II and III. H1420 became Mk. III prototype, H1460 conv. to Bristol Coupé H1690-1707, powered by Siddeley Pumas, did not enter service. H1708-1739 were not completed.
H1740-1745	6	Nieuport London	H1740 first flew 13.4.20 at Acton. H1741 first flew July 1920. H1742-1745 cancelled before construction.
H1746-1895	150	Bristol F.2B Fighter	Re-allocation of D2626-2775.
H1896-2145	250	Avro 504K	Built by The Sunbeam Motor Car Co. Ltd.
H2146-2645	500	Avro 504K	Built by A. V. Roe Ltd. H2308, 2581, 2582, 2590 converted to 504L. H2171-2179 to R.A.A.F. as A3-1 to -9. H2401 fitted with 100 h.p. Mono and metal propeller, 1920. H2402 became HR2402 504N with special enlarged rudder. H2432, 2618 became 504N.
H2646-2745	100	Sopwith 1F.1 Camel	Built by Boulton & Paul. H2700 became G-EAWN.

H2746-2945	200	Airco D.H.10	Ordered from the Aircraft Manufacturing Co. Ltd., Hendon. No record of delivery.
H2946-3195	250	Avro 504K	Built by The Brush Electrical Engineering Co. Ltd., Loughborough. H2968 was modified to 504R and H2990 to 504L. H3033-3034, 3036-3038, 3040-3043 became A3-16, -46, -17, -18, -19, -21, -22, -47, -23 of R.A.A.F.
H3196-3395	200	D.H.9	Cancelled order with National Aircraft Factory No. 2.
H3396-3545	150	Airco D.H.9A	Built by the Westland Aircraft Works, Yeovil. H3511-3513, 3515, 3518, 3529, 3530, 3534, 3536, 3539, 3540, 3543 converted to 3-seaters for maritime patrol.
H3546-3795	250	Airco D.H.9A	Built by the Vulcan Motor & Engineering Co. Up to H3659 confirmed delivered.
H3796-3995	200	Bristol F.2B Fighter	Cancelled order placed with Armstrong Whitworth.
H3996-4045	50	Sopwith 1F.1 Camel	Cancelled order with the British Caudron Co.
H4046-4195	150	Vickers F.B.27a Vimy	Ordered from Boulton & Paul Ltd., 30.8.18. Cancelled.
H4196-4215	20	Vickers Vimy	Cancelled order with Kingsbury Aviation Co.
H4216-4315	100	Airco D.H.9/9A	Ordered from A.M.C.
H4316	1	—	Cancelled order.
H4317-4319	3	Austin Greyhound	Experimental aircraft built by The Austin Motor Co. Ltd. H4317 delivered to Martlesham by air 15.5.19.
H4320-4369	50	D.H.9	Cancelled order placed with Berwick & Co.
H4370-4419	50	Handley Page 0/400	Numbers allotted to D8301-8350.
H4420-4421	2	Sopwith 3F.2 Hippo	Re-numbered from X-series of experimental aircraft.
H4422-4423	2	Sopwith 2FR.2 Bulldog	X3 and X4 re-numbered.
H4424	1	Sunbeam Bomber	Presumed ex-N515.
H4425-4724	300	Armstrong Whitworth F.K.8	Built by Angus Sanderson Ltd., Newcastle-upon-Tyne. Up to H4612 confirmed delivered. Several to Civil Register.
H4725-4824	100	Vickers F.B.27a Vimy	Cancelled order placed with Metropolitan Wagon Co.
H4825-4864	40	Handley Page V/1500	Cancelled order placed with Grahame-White Aviation Co.
H4865-5064	200	Sopwith Snipe	Sopwith Aviation-built. Delivery up to H4896 only confirmed.
H5065-5139	75	Vickers F.B.27a Vimy	25 only built by Westland Aircraft Works. Liberty engines planned but Rolls-Royce fitted. H5089 rebuilt.

Serial Nos.	*Qty.*	*Aircraft Type*	*Remarks*
H5140-5239	100	Avro 504K	London Aircraft Co. built. H5185, 5196, 5199 conv. 504N.
H5240-5289	50	Avro 504K	Eastbourne Aviation built.
H5290	1	D.H.4	Glendower Aircraft built.
H5291-5540	250	S.E.5a	Cancelled order with Austin.
H5541-5890	350	Airco D.H.9	Alliance Aeroplane Co. built. Deliveries from store to S.A.A.F., Belgium, Chilean, Irish, New Zealand and Polish air arms.
H5891-5893	3	Airco D.H.11 Oxford	A.M.C. built. H5892-5893 cancelled.
H5892-5893	2	Sopwith Buffalo	Experimental aircraft. Compromised numbers above.
H5894-5939	46	Airco D.H.4	Built by Palladium Autocars. H5894, 5905, 5928, 5929, 5934, 5939, conv. to D.H.4A.
H5940-6539	600	Bristol F.2B Fighter (Siddeley Puma engines)	Austin-built. H6055, 6058 only confirmed delivered.
H6540-6542	3	Martinsyde F.4 Buzzard 1A	Experimental long-range aircraft.
H6543-6842	300	Avro 504K	Humber Motors built, H6601, 6605, 6611, 6653, 6656 to Belgium. H6603 to Argentine. H6598, 6599 conv. to 3-seaters. Not all completed.
H6843-7342	—	Allocation for re-built aircraft: Bristol F.2B Fighter, D.H.4, D.H.9, D.H.9A, Sopwith 1F.1 Camel, Sopwith 5F.1 Dolphin, R.E.8 & S.E.5a.	H6843, R.E.8; H6847, 6855, 6860, Camel; H6934, Dolphin; H6997, Camel; H7000, 7003, 7007, 7012, Camel; H7018, 7022-7027, 7033, 7038, 7040, 7042, 7046-7048, 7055, 7057, R.E.8; H7061-7065, F.2B; H7072-7074, S.E.5a; H7089-7092, 7098, 7104 Camel; H7107 D.H.9A; H7118, 7123, D.H.4; H7139, R.E.8; H7147-7148, D.H.4; H7160, Camel; H7161-7166, S.E.5a; H7176, D.H.9; H7181, S.E.5a; H7239, Camel; H7245, Dolphin; H7247-7254, 7256-7261, S.E.5a; H7262, 7265, R.E.8; H7272, . 7279, 7281, 7283, 7288, Camel; H7292, F.2B; H7340, R.E.8.
H7343-7412	70	Sopwith 1F.1 Camel	Hooper-built up to H7391.

H7413-7562	150	Avro 504K	Built by Hewlett & Blondeau. H7534 converted to 504N.
H7563-7612	50	Airco D.H.9	Cancelled order placed with G. & J. Weir Ltd.
H7613-7912	300	Martinsyde F.4 Buzzard	Full delivery not completed. H7786 converted to F.4A.
H7913-8112	200	Airco D.H.9	Ordered from Crossley Motors Ltd., 25.9.18. (No. 4 N.A.F.)
H8113-8252	140	—	Reserved allocation for No. 2 A.R.D.
H8253	1	Sopwith 1F.1 Camel	Built by No. 42 T.S.
H8254-8255	2	Avro 504 (Clerget)	Built by 58th Wing.
H8256	1	B.E.2d	Built by No. 77 Sqn at Penstone.
H8257	1	Avro 504 (Clerget)	Built by No. 42 T.S.
H8258-8259	2	Sopwith 1F.1 Camel	Built as two-seaters from salvage at No. 43 T.D.S.
H8260-8262	3	Sopwith 1F.1 Camel	Built at No. 43 T.D.S.
H8263	1	Airco D.H.4	Built by Palladium Autocar Co. Converted to D.H.4.A
H8264	1	Sopwith 1F.1 Camel	Built by C.F.S.
H8265-8288	24	Caudron	Origin not known.
H8289-8290	2	Avro 504	Built by No. 7 T.D.S.
H8291-8292	2	Sopwith 1F.1 Camel	Built by C.F.S.
H8293-8412	120	—	Allocation not known.
H8413-8512	100	Martinsyde F.4 Buzzard.	Ordered from Martinsyde and cancelled.
H8513-8662	150	Nieuport Nighthawk	Originally ordered as Sopwith Snipes from the Nieuport & General Aircraft Co. Up to H8553 confirmed as built. Conversions were: H8535-8536 to Nightjar, H8539 to Mars X, H8544 to Mars VI.
H8663-8762	100	Sopwith 7F.1 Snipe	Order placed with Portholme Aerodrome Ltd.
H8763-9112	350	Martinsyde F.4 Buzzard	Cancelled order placed with Boulton & Paul Ltd.
H9113-9412	300	Airco D.H.9	Built by the Aircraft Manufacturing Co. Ltd., Hendon. H9140 became the Handley Page H.P.17.
H9413-9512	100	Vickers F.B.27a Vimy	Cancelled order placed with Ransome, Sims & Jeffries.
H9513-9812	300	Avro 504K	Built by the Grahame-White Aviation Co. Ltd.
H9813-9912	100	Avro 504K	Built by Frederick Sage & Co. Ltd. Up to H9870 confirmed delivered. Several converted to 504N. H9835-9840 became A3-36 to 41 of the R.A.A.F.
H9913-9962	50	F.E.2b/c	Cancelled order placed with Ransome, Sims & Jeffries. H9913-9924 F.E.2c, H9925-9962 F.E.2b.
H9963	1	Vickers F.B.27a Vimy	Ordered from Vickers.
H9964-9966	3	Sopwith 7F.1 Snipe	Cancelled orders for experimental escort fighters.
H9967-9999	33	—	Reservation, not used.

FINAL 1914-1918 WAR ALLOCATIONS

J1–6576 ONLY a few of the aircraft ordered in this series, started in October 1918, actually materialised. " I " was not used lest it be confused with " 1 " and therefore J1 followed straight on from H9999. An interposed 'R' indicated a re-built aircraft.

Serial Nos.	*Qty.*	*Aircraft Type*	*Remarks*
J1-150	150	Sopwith 5F.1 Dolphin	Built by Hooper Ltd. Up to J39 only confirmed delivered.
J151-250	100	Sopwith 5F.1 Dolphin	Built by Darracq. Up to J181 confirmed delivered.
J251-300	50	Vickers Vimy	Cancelled order placed with Clayton & Shuttleworth Ltd.
J301-400	100	Sopwith 7F.1 Snipe	Built by March, Jones & Cribb.
J401-450	50	Airco D.H.9A	Cancelled order placed with Westland Aircraft Works.
J451-550	100	Sopwith 7F.1 Snipe	Built by Boulton & Paul Ltd., Norwich. J453, 455, 459, 461, 465 became G-EAUV/AUW/AUU/BBE/ATF on the Civil Register. Up to J465 only confirmed delivered.
J551-600	50	Airco D.H.9A	Built by Mann, Egerton & Co. Ltd., Norwich. Up to J597 confirmed delivered.
J601-650	50	F.E.2b	Cancelled order placed with Barclay, Curle & Co.
J651-680	30	Sopwith 7F.1 Snipe	Cancelled order placed with The British Caudron Co.
J681-730	50	Sopwith 7F.1 Snipe	Cancelled order placed with March, Jones & Cribb.
J731-1230	500	Avro 504K	Ordered from A. V. Roe. Delivery to J803 only confirmed. J733 had a Lucifer engine fitted. J743 became Type 548 G-EALF; several to the Civil Register.
J1231-1730	500	Bristol F.2B	Cancelled.
J1731-1930	200	Bristol F.2B	Cancelled order placed with The Standard Motor Co. Ltd.
J1931-1933	3	Bristol	Allocation for an experimental two-seater.
J1934-1936	3	Handley Page O/400 & V/1500	Built by Harland and Wolff. J1934 O/400 converted to H.P.12. J1935-1936 V/1500.
J1936-1937	2	D.H.15 Gazelle	J1937 only completed. J1936 duplicated serial.
J1938-1940	3	D.H.14 Okapi	De Havilland Nos. E44-46. J1938-1939 D.H.14; J1940 D.H.14A, became G-EAPY.
J1941-1990	50	Vickers F.B.27a Vimy	Cancelled order placed with Morgan & Co.
J1991	1	Bristol	Allotted to experimental Bristol aircraft.
J1992-2141	150	Martinsyde F.4 Buzzard	Cancelled order placed with Boulton & Paul.

J2142-2241	100	Avro 504K	Cancelled order placed with Scottish Aviation.
J2242-2291	50	Handley Page O/400	Built by The Birmingham Carriage Co. Ltd. 9 went to the Civil Register. Up to J2275 confirmed delivered.
J2292-2391	100	Bristol F.2B Fighter	Cancelled order placed with Marshall & Son.
J2392-3341	950	Sopwith 7F.1 Snipe	Cancelled orders placed with British Caudron (150), Grahame-White (500) and Gloucester Aircraft (300).
J2403-2417	15	Nieuport Nighthawk	Numbers re-allotted. J2416 became Mars VI.
J3342-3541	200	Martinsyde F.4 Buzzard	Cancelled order placed with Hooper & Co.
J3542-3616	75	Handley Page O/400	Cancelled order placed with the Metropolitan Wagon Co.
J3617-3916	300	Sopwith Dragon	J3628, J3704, J3726 and J3809 only, confirmed as delivered from Sopwiths. Order was originally placed for Snipes.
J3917-3991	75	Sopwith 7F.1 Snipe	Cancelled order placed with Barclay, Curle & Co.
J3992-4091	100	Avro 504K	Cancelled order placed with Hewlett & Blondeau.
J4092-4591	500	Sopwith Snipe	Cancelled order placed with National Aircraft Factory No. 3.
J4592-5091	500	—	Reserved for aircraft rebuilt by Repair Depots in France.
J5092-5191	100	Avro 504K	Built by Frederick Sage & Co. J5185, 5187 produced as 504N.
J5192-5491	300	Airco D.H.9A	Cancelled order placed with the Aircraft Manufacturing Co. Ltd.
J5492-5591	100	Avro 504K	Built by Savages Ltd. Up to J5512 confirmed delivered.
J5592-5891	300	Martinsyde F.4 Buzzard	Cancelled order placed with The Standard Motor Co. Ltd.
J5892-6491	600	Sopwith Salamander	Orders placed with Glendower Aircraft (100), Palladium Autocars (100), National Aircraft Factory No. 3 (400) of which up to J5913 were built.
J6492	1	Bristol Badger II	4th prototype, but 3rd built.
J6493-6522	30	Sopwith 7F.1 Snipe	Built by Kingsbury Aviation.
J6523-6572	50	Handley Page V/1500	Cancelled order.
J6573	1	Handley Page V/1500	Replacement aircraft for F7140. Napier Lion engines fitted.
J6574-6576	3	Handley Page O/400	Replacement for F5414, 5417, 5418 to Civil Register.

THE "Js" CARRY OVER FROM WAR TO PEACE

J6577–9999

AT this point the character of serialling changes. The immediate change is apparent, small quantities and even single orders from 1919 onwards, differing vastly from the orders of the previous year; but more important is the change in the system itself. Hitherto the range of numbers had been from No. 1 to 9999, but when J9999 was reached the following 'K' series started at K1000. Thus *all* serials now had a 5 letter/digit combination. The alphabetical series continued, and for the next twenty years J to Z were allotted in sequence (with certain exceptions, as explained later) to a 1000-9999 range of numbers. The end of the war made no immediate change to the system of allocation, but the rate of allocation was greatly affected: whereas J1 to J6848 had been taken up in a matter of two months, it was several years, from 1919 to 1928 in fact, before J9999 was reached.

Serial Nos.	*Qty.*	*Aircraft Type*	*Remarks*
J6577	1	Westland Weasel	Experimental aircraft ordered 29.8.19.
J6578	1	Handley Page O/400	Replacement for D8350 cancelled 15.10.19.
J6579-6580	2	British Aerial Transport F.K.23 Bantam	F1653-1654 bought back, held up for Wasp Mk. II engines.
J6581-6582	2	Westland Wagtail	Experimental models for conversion to Wasp II engines.
J6583	1	Armstrong Siddeley Siskin	First steel Siskin, ordered 31.5.20.
J6584	1	Boulton & Paul P.15 Bolton	Development of Bourges with all-metal construction.
J6585	1	Armstrong Whitworth Tadpole	Prototype. Built from D.H.9A E8522 at Farnborough.
J6586-6800	215	Bristol F.2B Mk. II	First post-war production order. Several re-built, including J6788 as a single-seater. J6790 became G-ACCG.
J6801-6848	48	Nieuport Nighthawk	Ordered from British Caudron Co. and the Royal Aircraft Establishment.
J6849-6850	2	D.H.29 Doncaster	De Havilland Nos. 7-8. J6850 became G-EAYO on completion, September 1921.
J6851	1	Westland Limousine III	G-EAWF, ordered for Air Council 11.11.20.
J6852-6853	2	Avro Aldershot I/II	J6852, Avro 549 (Mk. I), modified to Avro 549A (Mk. II). J6853, Mk.1.
J6854	1	Short Silver Streak	G-EARQ, aquired 23.12.20.
J6855	1	Vickers Vernon	Ambulance version.
J6856-6857	2	Vickers Virginia I/III	Prototypes to Air Ministry Specification 1/21:J6858 later fitted with "fighting tops" to Mk. VII, then Mk. VIII standard and then rebuilt as Mk. X. J6857 later became Virginia Mk. VII and then Mk. X.
J6858-6859	2	Siddeley Sinai	J6858, Mk. I; J6859, planned as Mk. II/III, was not built.

J6860-6861	2	Vickers Victoria I/II	Prototypes to Air Ministry Specification 5/20.
J6862-6863	2	Parnall Possum	Prototype postal aircraft.
J6864-6993	30	Vickers Vernon	Ordered as Vickers Commercial. Prototype J6864 believed ex-Vimy Commercial G-EAUY.
J6894-6895	2	D.H.27 Derby	De Havilland Nos. 9-10. Experimental bomber with rearward folding wings to Air Ministry Specification 2/20.
J6896	1	Avro 504	Built up from spares at Halton.
J6897-6898	2	Armstrong Whitworth Awana	Experimental transports ordered from Armstrong Whitworth Aircraft.
J6899-6900	2	D.H.18A	G-EARO and G-EAUF, purchased 9.7.21.
J6901-6903	3	Bristol Bullfinch	Bristol Nos. 6125-6127. J6901-6902, Type 52 Monoplane; J6903, Type 53 Biplane.
J6904-6905	2	Vickers Vernon	Ambulance versions. J6904 rebuilt as JR6904.
J6906	1	D.H.9A/H.P.17	Variable incidence wing experimental aircraft ex-F1632.
J6907-6909	3	Fairey Fawn I/II	Fairey Nos. F403-405. To Air Ministry Specification 5/21. J6907, Mk. I; J6908-6909, Mk. II.
J6910-6911	2	Boulton & Paul Bodmin	Postal Biplane to Air Ministry Specification 11/20.
J6912-6913	2	Bristol Tramp	Bristol Nos. 5871-5872. Type 37. J6912 only built, but was not flown.
J6914	1	Handley Page H.P. 20	H.P. X.4B experimental monoplane. Fuselage of F1632 used.
J6915-6917	3	D.H.30 Denbigh	Experimental project by de Havilland.
J6918-6920	3	Hawker Duiker	1 built of 3 ordered to Air Ministry Specification 7/22. Variously modified.
J6921-6923	3	Armstrong Whitworth Wolf	J6921 became G-EBHJ.
J6924	1	Vickers Vanguard	Vickers Type 62, modified to Type 103 as G-EBCP.
J6925-6941	17	Nieuport Nighthawk	Built by Gloucester Aircraft except for J6928-6929 at the Royal Aircraft Establishment. Conversions were J6925-6927 to Mars VI, J6930 to Mars X. J6931-6941 converted to Nightjars.
J6942-6956	15	Avro Aldershot III	J6943-6953 to No. 99 Squadron from April 1924.
J6957-6968	12	D.H.9A	First six built by the Westland Aircraft Works, remainder by Handley Page. J6957-6962 fitted with Napier Lion engines, remainder with Liberty engines.

Serial Nos.	*Qty.*	*Aircraft Type*	*Remarks*
J6969-6971	3	Nieuport Nighthawk	Ordered from Gloucester Aircraft as Nighthawk (thick-winged). J6969 produced as Grebe prototype.
J6972	1	Nieuport Nightjar	Ordered from Gloucester Aircraft to replace J6930.
J6973	1	English Electric Wren	Ultra-light 'powered glider'.
J6974-6975	2	Short S.3 Springbok I	To Air Ministry Specification 19/21 for "Bristol Fighter replacement".
J6976-6980	5	Vickers Vernon	Built for Middle East service.
J6981-6983	3	Armstrong Whitworth Siskin III	J6981, the first Siskin III for service, flew 24.3.24.
J6984-6985	2	Boulton & Paul P.25 Bugle I	Bomber to Air Ministry Specification 30/22. Jupiter II/III engines.
J6986	1	Westland Dreadnought Postal Monoplane	Crashed on first flight, May 1923.
J6987-6988	2	Hawker Woodcock I/II	Prototypes to Air Ministry Specification 25/22. Mks. I & II respectively.
J6989	1	Hawker Heron	First Hawker metal aircraft. Became G-EBYC in 1928.
J6990-6991	2	Fairey Fawn	Fairey Nos. F.415-416. 4th and 5th Fawn prototypes.
J6992-6993	2	Vickers Virginia III	J6992 conv. Mk. VII then X. J6993 became Mk. VII prototype then Mk. IX.
J6994	1	Handley Page H.P.24 Hyderabad	Prototype to Air Ministry Specification 31/22. First flew in October 1923.
J6995-6996	2	Hawker Duiker	Not completed.
J6997	1	Bristol Brandon	Bristol Type 79. No. 6146. Ambulance.
J6998-7003	6	Armstrong Whitworth Siskin III	J7000 was Siskin dual-control prototype.
J7004	1	Bristol Seely	Bristol Type 36 No. 5870. G-EAUE modified as Type 85 for R.A.F.
J7005	1	D.H.42 Dormouse	De Havilland No. 84. To Air Ministry Specification 22/22.
J7006	1	D.H.42A Dingo I	De Havilland No. 85. To Air Ministry Specification 8/24.
J7007	1	D.H.42B Dingo II	De Havilland No. 115. Metal version of Dingo I.
J7008-7127	120	D.H.9A	Stored fuselages re-conditioned by: De Havilland (10), Handley Page (15), Westland (40), Gloucester (15), Hawker (15), R.A.F. Ascot (25). Some were converted to D.H.9J Stag standard.
J7128	1	Peyret Glider	Peyret Tandem Monoplane Glider, built by Morane-Saulnier at Puteaux.

J7129-7132	4	Vickers Virginia III	J7129 conv. to Mk. VII then X, J7130-7172 conv. to Mk. VII, then IX and finally X.
J7133-7142	10	Vickers Vernon	All to No. 45 Squadron.
J7143-7144	2	Vickers Vernon	Ordered as Vimy Ambulances.
J7145-7181	37	Armstrong Whitworth Siskin III	J7161 had experimental cockpit heating. J7160, 7162, 7178, 7180 and 7181 were built as 2-seaters.
J7182-7231	50	Fairey Fawn I/II	To Air Ministry Specification 20/23. J7182-7183 Mk. I, remainder Mk. II.
J7232	1	Junkers	Acquired for evaluation.
J7233	1	Handley Page H.P. 22	Ordered August 1923.
J7234	1	Gloster Bamel I	G-EAXZ to R.A.F. December 1923. Later became a floatplane for Schneider Trophy training.
J7235	1	Boulton & Paul P.25 Bugle I	Jupiter IV engines. Trials with No. 58 Squadron, 1925.
J7236-7237	2	Bristol Bloodhound	Types 84A and 84B. Nos. 6710-6711. Wooden wings.
J7238-7247	10	Vickers Vimy IV	Interim replacement aircraft.
J7248	1	Bristol Bloodhound	Type 84. No. 6709. Metal construction.
J7249-7258	10	D.H.9A	Built by Gloucester Aircraft.
J7259-7260	2	Boulton & Paul P.25 Bugle	Ordered in January 1924.
J7261-7264	4	Avro 561 Andover	J7261 became Type 563 as G-EBKW.
J7265	1	Handley Page H.P.22/23	Light plane for evaluation.
J7266-7267	2	Boulton & Paul P.25A Bugle II	Lion engines. Improved version with faired-in bomb racks.
J7268-7273	6	D.H.53 Humming Bird	De Havilland Nos. 107-112. Became G-EBRW/RJ/RA/XN/TT/RK.
J7274-7275	2	Vickers Virginia IV	J7274 conv. Mk. VII, then X; J7275 conv. Mk. VII and then used in flight-refuelling experiments as Mk. X.
J7276	1	Dornier Komet	Acquired for evaluation from Handley Page.
J7277-7282	6	Vickers 94 Venture	J7280 crashed 31.10.35.
J7283-7294	12	Gloster Grebe II	First Grebe production batch. To No. 25 Squadron.
J7295-7300	6	Short S.3a Springbok II-V	J7295 first flew 25.3.25 and was converted in 1927 to S.3b Chamois. No delivery record for J7298-7300.
J7301	1	Avro 504N	Ordered in 1924.
J7302-7321	20	D.H.9A	Re-built 1918 airframes by de Havilland (8) & Hawker (12).
J7322	1	Avro 560	Light monoplane with a Blackburn engine.
J7323-7324	2	Parnall Pixie II/III	For 1923 Lympne Trials. J7323 was G-EBKM.
J7325-7326	2	D.H.53 Humming Bird	D.H. Nos. 113-114. J7325-6 became G-EBXM and EBQP.

Serial Nos.	*Qty.*	*Aircraft Type*	*Remarks*
J7327-7356	30	D.H.9A	Rebuilt aircraft by Westland (20) and Gloucester (10).
J7357-7402	46	Gloster Grebe II	J7381, J7394 and J7400 to R.N.Z.A.F.
J7403-7405	3	Bristol Berkeley	Bristol Type 90, Nos. 6718-6720. To A.M.Spec. 26/23.
J7406-7417	12	Gloster Grebe	Standard service fighter.
J7418-7439	22	Vickers Virginia V	Converted to varying standards: J7418, Mk. VI; J7419, Mk. VIII-X; J7420-7421, Mk. VII-X; J7422, Mk. VI-VII-X; J7423, Mk. VI-IX; J7424, Mk. VII-X; J7425-7426, Mk. VII; J7427, Mk. VII-X; J7428, Mk. VII-IX-X; J7429-7430, Mk. VII-X; J7431-7432, VII; J7433-7434, Mk. VII-X; J7435, Mk. VII-IX; J7436, Mk. VII-IX-X; J7437, Mk. VI-IX-X; J7438, Mk. VI-VII-IX-X; J7439, Mk. VI- VII-X.
J7440-7454	15	Vickers Vimy IV	Ordered in June 1924.
J7455-7496	42	Fairey Flycatcher	Re-numbered N9854-9895.
J7497	1	Gloster Gamecock	Prototype. Grebe development to A.M.Spec. 37/23.
J7498-7500	3	Handley Page H.P.28 Handcross	Experimental day bomber to A.M.Spec. 26/23.
J7501-7503	3	Gloster G.16/16A Gorcock	Napier engines fitted as follows: J7501 (wooden wings), Lion IV; J7502 (metal wings), Lion VIII; J7503 (all-metal), Lion IV. J7502 was modified to become the Guan.
J7504-7505	2	Gloster II	Prototypes to Air Ministry Specification 37/23.
J7506	1	A.N.E.C.1	G-EBIL built by the Air Navigation & Engineering Co., acquired in 1921.
J7507	1	Breguet 19	Acquired for evaluation at the Royal Aircraft Establishment.
J7508-7510	3	Westland Yeovil	Experimental day bomber to A.M.Spec. 26/23, J7508-7509, Mk. I composite, J7510, Mk. II all-metal.
J7511	1	Hawker Horsley	Originally known as the Kingston. To A.M.Spec. 26/23.
J7512-7517	6	Hawker Woodcock II	J7515 as G-EBMA was entered in King's Cup Race, 1925.
J7518	1	Raynham Light Plane	Purchased from owner.
J7519-7538	20	Gloster Grebe III	J7520 won the 1929 Kings Cup Air Race.
J7539-7548	10	Vickers Vernon	Ordered 10.11.24.
J7549-7554	6	Armstrong Whitworth Siskin III	Two-seat version. Ordered in December 1924.
J7555-7556	2	Avro 504	Built to U.S. standards.

J7557	1	Beardmore Inflexible	Was constructed as G-EBNG. First flew 5.3.28.
J7558-7567	10	Vickers Virginia VI	Variously converted: J7558, Mk. IX; J7559, Mk. VII-X; J7560, Mk. VII to X; J7561, Mk. IX-X; J7562-7563, Mk. IX-X; J7564, Mk. IX; J7565, Mk. VII-X; J7566, Mk. VII to X; J7567, Mk. IX-X.
J7570	1	Bristol F.2B Fighter Mk. II	Served at School of Photography. Number duplicated.
J7568-7603	36	Gloster Grebe	J7570 above, compromised.
J7592-7595	4	Hawker Woodcock II	Equipped with night-flying equipment. Believed incorrectly numbered.
J7604-7615	12	D.H.9A	Rebuilt aircraft by Hawker.
J7616-7699	84	Bristol F.2B	Bristol Nos. 6721-6804.
J7700	1	D.H.9A	Ordered in 1924.
J7701-7705	5	Vickers Vimy IV	Ordered in March 1925.
J7706-7720	15	Vickers Virginia VI	Variously converted: J7706, Mk. VII to X; J7707, Mk. IX; J7708, Mk. IX to X; J7709, Mk. VII to IX; J7710, Mk. VII-X; J7711, Mk. VII-IX-X; J7712-7713, Mk. VII; J7715, Mk. IX-X; J7716, Mk. IX; J7717, Mk. X; J7718-7719, Mk. IX-X; J7720, Mk. IX.
J7721	1	Hawker Horsley	Second prototype.
J7722-7723	2	Gloster Guan	J7722, 450 h.p. Napier Lion (geared); J7723, 525 h.p. Napier Lion (direct drive).
J7724-7737	14	Hawker Woodcock II	To Nos. 3 and 17 Squadrons.
J7738-7752	15	Handley Page H.P.24 Hyderabad	J7745 became prototype H.P.33 Hinaidi; J7741 modified to Hinaidi.
J7753-7755	3	Armstrong Whitworth Ape	J7753 A.S. Jaguar, J7754 A.S. Lynx. J7755 not built.
J7756-7757	2	Gloster Gamecock	J7756 Bristol Jupiter IV, J7757 Bristol Jupiter VI.
J7758-7764	7	Armstrong Whitworth Siskin III	J7759 acquired by the Royal Canadian Air Force as No. 10.
J7765-7766	2	Westland Westbury	To A.M. Spec. 4/24. J7765 wooden wings, J7766 composite wood/metal wings.
J7767	1	Bristol Bagshot	Type 95. No. 7018. Originally named Bludgeon.
J7768-7779	12	Fairey Fawn III	Fairey Nos. F.783-794. Production to A.M.Spec 1/25. Supercharged Napier Lion engines.
J7780-7781	2	D.H.56 Hyena	De Havilland Nos. 182 and 195. To A.M.Spec. 33/26.
J7782	1	Hawker Hornbill	Variously modified. Flew 1,080 hrs before scrapping.
J7783	1	Hawker Woodcock	Served with No. 3 Squadron.
J7784-7786	3	Gloster Grebe	Ordered in 1924.

Serial Nos.	Qty.	Aircraft Type	Remarks
J7787-7819	33	D.H.9A	Ordered November 1925 from D.H. (12) and Westland (21).
J7820-7822	3	Armstrong Whitworth Siskin III	Replacement aircraft order.
J7823-7890	68	D.H.9A	Ordered in 1925 from Short Bros. (12), Hawker (20), Westland(12), Hawker (10), de Havilland (7), Short Bros. (7).
J7891-7920	30	Gloster Gamecock I	Production to Air Ministry Specification 18/25.
J7921-7935	15	Vickers Victoria III	J7921 converted to Valentia.
J7936-7937	2	Boulton & Paul P.31 Bittern	Twin-engined fighter to Air Ministry Specification 27/24. J7936 had engines placed centrally in wings, J7937 had engines underslung from the wings.
J7938-7939	2	Boulton & Paul P.29 Sidestrand	Medium bomber to Air Ministry Specification 9/24. J7938, Bristol Jupiter VI and VIII engines; J7939, Bristol Jupiter VI and VIF engines.
J7940	1	Gloster G.23 Goldfinch	Metal version of Gamecock to A.M.Spec. F.9/26 ordered January 1926.
J7941-7958	18	Fairey Fox I/IA	To Air Ministry Specification 21/25 for No. 12 Squadron. J7950 became G-ACXO. J7947-7949 Mk. IA with Rolls-Royce Kestrel engines, remainder Curtiss engines.
J7959	1	Gloster Gamecock	All-metal aircraft project by Boulton & Paul.
J7960-7977	18	Hawker Woodcock	Includes six aircraft rebuilt and possibly re-numbered.
J7978-7985	8	Fairey Fawn III	Fairey Nos. F.865-872. Ordered in March 1926.
J7986	1	Fokker F.VII/3M	For evaluation at Royal Aircraft Establishment, April 1927. Monospar S.T.2 wing fitted.
J7987-8026	40	Hawker Horsley	Ordered March 1926. J8003 had Rolls-Royce Condor IIIB.
J8027-8028	2	Armstrong Whitworth 14 Starling I/II	To Air Ministry Specification 9/26. J8027 (A.W. No. 277) became G-AAHC.
J8029	1	Avro 504K	Ex-F9723.
J8030-8032	3	D.H.60A Cirrus Moth	J8030 (D.H. No. 233) had slotted wings; J8031 (D.H. No. 247) was ex-G-EBVD; J8032 was D.H. No. 248.
J8033-8047	15	Gloster Gamecock I	J8047 was rebuilt with lengthened fuselage and later became G-ADIN.
J8048-8060	13	Armstrong Whitworth Siskin IIIA	Ordered in June 1926.
J8061-8066	6	Vickers Victoria III	Ordered May 1926. J8062-8065 converted to Mk. V. Later J8062, 8063 and 8065 converted to Valentias.

J8067	1	Westland Pterodactyl Mk. IA	34 h.p. Bristol Cherub engine.
J8068	1	Cierva C.6C/Avro 574	Design sponsored by Air Ministry. Avro-built Cierva C.6C, later C.8LI.
J8069-8095	27	Gloster Gamecock	J8075 tested with Bristol Mercury IIA engine.
J8096-8225	130	D.H.9A	Re-built aircraft by Westland (33), de Havilland (25), Short Bros. (18), Parnall (18), Saunders (18), Blackburn (18).
J8226-8235	10	Vickers Victoria III	J8230-8232 converted to Valentias.
J8236-8241	6	Vickers Virginia VII	J8236 converted Mk. IX and temporarily fitted with French-built Jupiter engines. J8237-8238, 8240-8241 conv. to Mk. X.
J8242-8291	50	Bristol Fighter Mk. III	Type 96 Army Co-op. type. Three to Civil Register.
J8292-8316	25	Hawker Woodcock II	Ordered September 1926.
J8317-8324	8	Handley Page H.P.24 Hyderabad	Ordered September 1926.
J8325	1	Hawker Harrier I	To A.M. Spec. 23/25. Ordered February 1927.
J8326-8330	5	Vickers Virginia VII	J8326, 8328-8330 conv. Mk. X.
J8331-8380	50	Avro 504K	J8333, 8342, 8343, 8371, 8379 became G-ABLL/BHI/BHJ/BHP/AFT.
J8381-8404	24	Armstrong Whitworth Siskin IIIA	J8390 used in catapult trials from H.M.S. *Repulse* in 1928.
J8405-8422	18	Gloster Gamecock	Service in Nos. 23 and 43 Squadrons.
J8423-8427	5	Fairey Fox I	Fairey Nos. F.875-879. J8424 became G-ACXX. J8427 had experimental towing gear.
J8428	1	Armstrong Whitworth Siskin IIIA	Tested at Farnborough, 1933 with experimental wing.
J8429-8458	30	Bristol F.2B Fighter III (DC)	Type 96 Trainers. Seven to Civil Register. Final F.2B production.
J8459	1	Boulton & Paul P.33 Partridge	To Air Ministry Specification F.9/26. Designed for Bristol Mercury, but Bristol Jupiter engine fitted.
J8460-8494	35	D.H.9A (D.C.)	Ordered January 1927 from Westland (23) and Parnall (12).
J8495	1	Westland Wapiti	Prototype.
J8496-8595	100	Avro 504N	First 504N production. J8571 rebuilt as JR8571.
J8596	1	Westland Witch	Originally to Spec. 23/25. Later used as parachute trainer.
J8597-8621	25	Hawker Horsley II	J8607-8608, special long range versions; J8611, Rolls-Royce Merlin engine test-bed; J8620, test-bed for Armstrong Siddeley Leopard and Junkers Jumo engines.

Serial Nos.	*Qty.*	*Aircraft Type*	*Remarks*
J8622	1	Handley Page H.P.34 Hare	To Air Ministry Specification 23/25. Became G-ACEL for long-range project.
J8623-8672	50	Armstrong Whitworth Siskin IIIA	J8628 used for wireless experiments. J8627 used at Royal Aircraft Establishment for experiments as IIIB.
J8673	1	Gloster G.22 Goral	Experimental design to use D.H.9A mainplanes. Jupiter or Jaguar engines.
J8674	1	Gloster G.25 Goring	Modified as a floatplane in 1931 with Bristol Jupiter VIII engine in place of Jupiter VI.
J8675	1	Armstrong Whitworth Atlas	Prototype. First flew 10.5.25. Fitted with horn-balanced ailerons, 1932.
J8676-8775	100	Avro 504N	J8695 and J8720 rebuilt as JR8695 and JR8720.
J8776	1	Hawker Hawfinch	G-AAKH with increased airfoil camber for Royal Aircraft Establishment tests, 1935.
J8777-8801	25	Armstrong Whitworth Atlas I	Production version to Air Ministry Specification 33/26. J8777, 2nd prototype; J8792, trainer version prototype; J8799, floatplane. J8793-8801 delivered as airframes for store.
J8802-8803	2	Armstrong Whitworth Ajax	Ordered in 1927.
J8804	1	Gloster Gamecock II	General purpose version ordered January 1928. Gamecock with narrow-chord ailerons, revised fin and rudder.
J8805-8815	11	Handley Page H.P.24 Hyderabad	Ordered August 1927. Used by No. 99 Squadron. J8809 converted to Hinaidi.
J8816-8821	6	D.H.60X Genet Moth	For Central Flying School. J8818 used by Director of Civil Aviation as G-EDCA.
J8822-8905	84	Armstrong Whitworth Siskin IIIA	J8822-8863, Bristol Nos. 7179-7220; J8864-8905 built by Blackburn.
J8906	1	Vickers 134 Vellore I	To Air Ministry Specification 34/24. Became G-EBYX Type 166 Vellore II. Crashed on Australian flight.
J8907-8914	8	Vickers Virginia IX	J8907-8908, 8910, 8912-8914 conv. Mk. X.
J8915-8929	15	Vickers Victoria III	Some converted to Mk. V and VI. J8916, 8919, 8921 became Valentias.
J8930-8931	2	Cierva C.8/C.9	Built by A. V. Roe. J8930, C.8; J8931, C.9.
J8932	1	Hawker Horsley	Prototype of all-metal version.
J8933-8974	42	Armstrong Whitworth Siskin IIIA	Built by Gloster Aircraft. J8971 had a Jaguar IV engine.

J8975-9024	50	Avro 504N	Ordered March 1927. J8976 became JR8976.
J9025-9028	4	Fairey Fox I/IA	Fairey Nos. F.952-955. J9027 sold back to firm 1930 for steam-cooling experiments.
J9029	1	Wibault 122c2	Bought from Vickers for service evaluation.
J9030	1	Handley Page Hinaidi	Troop-carrier trials.
J9031-9036	6	Handley Page H.P.23 Hinaidi	Ordered as Hyderabads in January 1928.
J9037	1	Armstrong Whitworth 17 Aries	Prototype to Air Ministry Specification 20/25.
J9038	1	Parnall Gyroplane	Parnall-built Cierva C.10 autogyro.
J9039-9050	12	Armstrong Whitworth Atlas I	Production batch for No. 26 Squadron.
J9051	1	Bristol Bullpup	Bristol No. 7178. Jupiter VIA, Mercury IIA and Aquila engines in succession.
J9052	1	Hawker Hart	Prototype to A.M. Spec. 12/26 for "High Performance Bomber". Became Osprey prototype.
J9053-9077	25	Fairey IIIF Mk. IVM	J9062, 9067, 9073 rebuilt as Gordon; J9061, communications version.
J9078-9102	25	Westland Wapiti I	First production Wapitis. J9084 used as floatplane. J9082-9083 fitted with dual control. J9095 Mk. 1A with special rear cockpit for Prince of Wales.
J9103-9121	19	D.H.60X Cirrus Moth	De Havilland Nos. 510-528.
J9122	1	Vickers 151 Jockey	To F.20/27 delivered 11.3.29, conv. to Vickers 171, 1932.
J9123	1	Hawker Interceptor	To Air Ministry Specification F.20/27. Initial Bristol Jupiter VII engine was replaced by Bristol Mercury II engine.
J9124	1	Westland F.20/27	Experimental high altitude, defensive patrol fighter.
J9125	1	Gloster S.S.18/19/19B	Experimental fighter to A.M. Spec. F.9/26 and F.10/27. Various designations due to engine changes: Mercury IIA, Jupiter III, Mercury IV.
J9126	1	Handley Page H.P.35 Clive III	Originally named Chitral. To Air Ministry Specification C.20/27. Became G-ABYX.
J9127	1	D.H.65 Hound	De Havilland No. 250, G-EBNJ, transferred to R.A.F. in January 1928.
J9128	1	Armstrong Whitworth Ajax	To Air Ministry Specification 20/25 for an easily maintained Army Co-operation aircraft.
J9129	1	Armstrong Whitworth Atlas	General purpose version Atlas, ordered in January 1928.
J9130	1	Handley Page H.P.38 Heyford	Prototype to Air Ministry Specification B.19/27. First flew in June 1930.

Serial Nos.	*Qty.*	*Aircraft Type*	*Remarks*
J9131	1	Vickers 150 Vannock I	Prototype to Air Ministry Specification B.19/27. Rebuilt as Vickers 195 Vannock II, reconstructed as Vickers 255 Vanox.
J9132-9174	43	Fairey IIIF Mk. IV (G.P.)	J9132-9156 had wooden wings and J9157-9174 all-metal wings. J9136, 9138, 9154, 9156, 9161, 9167, 9171, 9172 were converted to Gordon. Special engine installations were: J9150, Jupiter VIII; J9154, Jaguar VI; J9173-9174, Kestrel II.
J9175	1	Avro 504R Gosport	Mongoose engine. Ordered January 1928.
J9176-9181	6	Boulton & Paul P.29 Sidestrand III	Built as Mk. II. Produced to equip No. 101 Squadron. Conv. to Mk. III.
J9182	1	Avro 594 Avian IIIA	Avro No. 125. Ordered December 1927.
J9183	1	Avro 583 Antelope	To Air Ministry Specification 12/26 for a high performance bomber.
J9184	1	D.H.72 Canberra	De Havilland No. 392. Experimental all-metal night bomber.
J9185-9189	5	Boulton & Paul P.29 Sidestrand III	J9185-9186 were converted to Overstrands; J9186 had experimental modifications.
J9190-9236	47	Armstrong Whitworth Siskin IIIA (D.C.)	Two-seat version.
J9237-9247	11	Westland Wapiti II	J9237-9246, Mk. II; J9247, built as Mk. IIA.
J9248	1	Gloster Gamecock	Project for evaluation of G-EBOE with Bristol Orion engine.
J9249	1	Avro B.19/27 (project)	Experimental light bomber.
J9250	1	Vickers 145 Victoria VI	Crashed and written off 29.3.31.
J9251	1	Westland Pterodactyl Mk. IA/IB	—
J9252	1	Westland Wizard I-II	Original aircraft crashed and was rebuilt as Mk. I, then modified to Mk. II standard.
J9253-9292	40	Avro 504N	Ordered June 1928.
J9293-9303	11	Handley Page H.P.24 Hyderabad	J9298-9303 completed as Hinaidis. Service in Nos. 10 and 99 Squadrons.
J9304-9379	76	Armstrong Whitworth Siskin IIIA	J9304-9330, Bristol Nos. 7274-7300. J9331-9352 built by Gloster and J9353-9379 by Vickers.
J9380-9414	35	Westland Wapiti IIA	Composite wood/metal version. Majority shipped overseas.
J9415-9434	20	Avro 504N	Main deliveries to No. 5 Flying Training School.
J9435-9477	43	Armstrong Whitworth Atlas (D.C.)	Ordered August 1928.

J9478	1	Handley Page H.P.36 Hinaidi II	First Mk. II Hinaidi (all-metal).
J9479	1	Fairey Long Range Monoplane	Fairey No. F.1131. First flew in November 1928. Crashed in Tunisia.
J9480	1	Bristol Bulldog II	Prototype II, Bristol No. 7235. First flew 17.5.27.
J9481-9514	34	Westland Wapiti IIA	J9497-9498 used as floatplanes. Produced for squadrons based in India.
J9515	1	Fairey Fox	Used for steam cooling experiments with Rolls-Royce F.XIB engine.
J9516-9564	49	Armstrong Whitworth Atlas I	Engines fitted with Townsend rings. Service mainly in Nos. 4, 13 and 26 Squadrons.
J9565	1	Westland C.O.W. Fighter	To Air Ministry Specification F.29/27 with Coventry Ordnance Works 37 mm. gun. Became 738M.
J9566	1	Vickers 161	To Air Ministry Specification F.29/27 with Coventry Ordnance Works 37 mm. gun.
J9567-9590	24	Bristol Bulldog II	Bristol Nos. 7322-7330, 7332-7340, 7342-7347.
J9591	1	Bristol Bulldog III	G-AATR to R.A.F. December 1930.
J9592-9636	45	Westland Wapiti IIA	J9605 became Wallace K3677. J9612 and 9617 went to the R.C.A.F.
J9637-9681	45	Fairey IIIF Mk. IV(m)	Ordered July 1928. J9642, 9643, 9647, 9648, 9651, 9655, 9656, 9660, 9663, 9670, 9674, 9681 were converted to Gordon. J9651 sold to Egypt in April 1939.
J9682	1	Hawker Hornet	Fury prototype to Air Ministry Specification F.20/27.
J9683-9707	25	Avro 504N	Ordered March 1929.
J9708-9759	52	Westland Wapiti IIA/V	To J9724, Mk. IIA; from J9725, Mk. V.
J9760-9766	7	Vickers Victoria V	J9762 converted to Victoria VI. J9764-9766 converted to Valentia.
J9767-9770	4	Boulton & Paul P.29 Sidestrand III	J9770 was modified to become Sidestrand V and was renamed Overstrand.
J9771	1	D.H.77 Interceptor	De Havilland No. 391. Prototype to Air Ministry Specification F.20/27.
J9772-9782	11	Hawker Tomtit	J9781 became G-AEXC; J9782 became G-AEVP and later G-AFFL.
J9783	1	Avro Avian IVM	Acquired for evaluation.
J9784-9831	48	Fairey IIIF Mk. IV (G.P.)	J9784, 9785-9788, 9790, 9794, 9795, 9798, 9799, 9801, 9803, 9804-9806, 9808, 9811, 9813, 9819, 9821, 9822, 9826, 9829 converted to Gordon.

Serial Nos.	Qty.	Aircraft Type	Remarks
J9832	1	Gloster G.33 Goshawk	Prototype troop-transport/bomber.
J9833	1	H.P.43/H.P.51	To Air Ministry Specifications C.10/28 and C.26/31.
J9834	1	Fairey Fox IIM	Fairey No. F.1138. All-metal prototype to Air Ministry Specification 12/26. Later registered G-ABFG.
J9835-9871	37	Westland Wapiti IIA	J9864 rebuilt as Wallace K3676. J9868-9871 to Royal Canadian Air Force.
J9872-9921	50	Armstrong Whitworth Siskin IIIA/B	J9897-9911 (Bristol Nos. 7404-7418), IIIB; J9872-9896 (built by Vickers) and J9912-9921 (built by Gloster), IIIA.
J9922-9932	11	D.H.60 Gipsy Moth	J9922-9930, D.H.60G; J9931-9932, D.H.60M.
J9933-9947	15	Hawker Hart	To Air Ministry Specification 9/29 for No. 33 Squadron. J9933 was the prototype Demon.
J9948-9949	2	Handley Page H.P.35 Clive II	Metal version of Chitral (J9126) (*q.v.*).
J9950	1	Boulton & Paul P.32	To Air Ministry Specification B.22/27. Originally Jupiter XF, later XFBM engines.
J9951-9999	49	Armstrong Whitworth Atlas I	J9998 used as floatplane; J9971 rebuilt as JR9971; J9951 sold to Royal Egyptian Air Force in 1939.

BETWEEN THE WARS

K1000–9999

FOR the first time a series started at No. 1000 instead of at No. 1; and, also for the first time, a batch was carried over from one series to another, for the order for 87 Atlases were numbered J9951-K1037 (i.e. J9951-9999 and K1000-1037). During the British aircraft industry's lean years of the early 'thirties, work was shared to keep the industry alive and the remarks column again shows the constructor where this was other than the design firm. With the Rearmament Programme of 1935, larger orders were placed and new factories opened, making a further qualification necessary, in some cases, to show at which plant the aircraft were produced. The period covered by this allocation is from August 1929 to July 1936.

K1000-1037	38	Armstrong Whitworth Atlas	Continuation of a batch of 87 started in the "J" series (*q.v.*).
K1038-1062	25	Avro 504N	Deliveries mainly to Nos. 3 & 5 Flying Training Schools.
K1063-1078	16	Handley Page H.P.36 Hinaidi	Deliveries mainly to No. 99 Squadron.

K1079-1101	23	Bristol Bulldog II	Bristol Nos. 7364-7386. Deliveries from 6.3.30 to 7.6.30.
K1102	1	Hawker Hart I	Acquired to test experimental Rolls-Royce Kestrel V engine with steam cooling. Cockpit enclosed.
K1103-1112	10	D.H. 60M Gipsy Moth	De Havilland Nos. 1450-1459. Ordered in December 1929.
K1113-1114	2	Armstrong Whitworth Atlas	Replacement aircraft.
K1115-1121	7	Fairey IIIF Mk. IV M/A	K1120 converted to Gordon at Henlow in January 1933.
K1122-1157	36	Westland Wapiti IIA	K1139, 1143, 1146, 1148, 1149, 1152 renumbered in the Royal Canadian Air Force.
K1158-1170	13	Fairey IIIF Mk. IV M/A (G.P.)	Fairey Nos. F.1302-1314. K1159, 1160-1165, 1167-1170 were converted to Gordons. K1161 sold to New Zealand, K1162 converted for target towing.
K1171	1	Isacco Heliogyre	In use 6.1.30 to 30.12.31.
K1172-1197	26	Armstrong Whitworth Atlas (D.C.)	K1175 converted to a single-seater. Main deliveries to Nos. 3 & 5 Flying Training Schools.
K1198-1227	30	D.H. 60M Gipsy Moth	De Havilland Nos. 1510-29, 1500-9. K1213-1217 specially rigged for Central Flying School aerobatic team.
K1228-1229	2	Parnall Parasol	Experimental aircraft for wing pressure and aileron tests and operation from submarines.
K1230-1240	11	Avro 621 Tutor	Mongoose IIIC uncowled engines.
K1241	1	D.H.60 Gipsy Moth	Also reported as an Avro Tutor.
K1242-1253	12	Avro 504N	K1250-1251 became G-ACPV and G-ADBS.
K1254-1309	56	Westland Wapiti IIA	Built for Army co-operation squadrons in India.
K1310-1315	6	Vickers Victoria V	K1315 converted to Mk. VI. K1311-1314 converted to Valentia.
K1316-1415	100	Westland Wapiti IIA	30 renumbered after conversion of airframes to Wallace. K1318, 1322, 1324-1330, 1336, 1342, 1366, 1378 sold to Canada.
K1416-1447	32	Hawker Hart I	K1438 became the Audax prototype.
K1448-1453	6	Hawker Tomtit I	K1451 became G-AEVO.
K1454-1602	149	Armstrong Whitworth Atlas (TM/AC)	First 53 built as trainers (TM), remainder as army co-op (AC). K1573 rebuilt as KR1573.
K1603-1694	92	Bristol Bulldog IIA	Bristol Nos. 7459-7550. 10 became instructional airframes.

Serial Nos.	*Qty.*	*Aircraft Type*	*Remarks*
K1695	1	Fairey B.19/27 Hendon	Prototype modified to Air Ministry Specification 20/34. Rolls-Royce Kestrel III, then VI, engines, later Bristol Pegasus.
K1696	1	Cierva C.19/II and Avro 620	G-AAYO built by A. V. Roe at Hamble, purchased September 1930.
K1697-1720	24	Fairey IIIF Mk. IVB (G.P.)	Fairey Nos. F.1396-1419. K1697 was built as a Gordon and K1699, 1700, 1702, 1703, 1713, 1715 were converted to Gordons.
K1721-1728	8	Fairey IIIF Mk. IVB	Fairey Nos. F.1420-1427 converted on production line to Gordons, K1726 had trial installation of a Junkers Jumo V (205C) engine December 1936.
K1729-1748	20	Fairey Gordon	Fairey Nos. F.1428-1447. K1729-1730 fitted with dual control.
K1749-1778	30	Fairey IIIF Mk. IVB	Fairey Nos. F.1448-1477. K1756-1758, 1762-1778 were converted to Gordon.
K1779-1786	8	Hawker Tomtit	K1781-1786 became G-AFIB/EES/GEF/FVV/FKB/FTA.
K1787-1797	11	Avro 621 Tutor	Mongoose IIIC engines fitted except for K1797 which had a Lynx IV. K1791 became G-ACOV.
K1798-1823	26	Avro 504N	K1802, 1808, 1810, 1823 became G-ACRS/CNV/DDA/EDD.
K1824	1	D.H.80A Puss Moth	De Havilland No. 2044. Used by Air Officer Commanding Inland Area for communications, 1932.
K1825-1907	83	D.H.60M Gipsy Moth	First five built as trainers, remainder for communications.
K1908	1	Handley Page H.P.39 " Gugnunc "	G-AACN acquired n December 1930.
K1909-1925	17	Handley Page H.P.36 Hinaidi	Used mainly by No. 10 Squadron.
K1926-1946	21	Hawker Fury I	K1926, prototype Mk. I; K1935, prototype Mk. II; K1927, propeller trials.
K1947	1	Westland Pterodactyl IV	Third Pterodactyl type of the series built.
K1948	1	Cierva C.19/III and Avro 620	Built by A. V. Roe at Hamble as No. 5142. Registered G-ABCM and acquired by R.A.F. in December 1930.
K1949	1	Saro F.20/27	Accepted in 1933.
K1950-1955	6	Hawker Hart (F)	Forerunners of Demon. All tc No. 23 Squadron.

K1956-1990	35	Avro 504N	Ten to "M" series. K1962 and K1964 became G-ADGM and G-AFRM.
K1991	1	Fairey Long Range Monoplane	Fairey No. F.1671. Lion XIA engine for record flights. Planned as test-bed for Junkers Jumo IV engine.
K1992-1994	3	Boulton & Paul P.29 Sidestrand II	Replacement aircraft for No. 101 Squadron.
K1995-2034	40	Hawker Audax	K1996 completed as Hart Trainer, K1999 and 2020 converted to Hart (Special).
K2035-2082	48	Hawker Fury I	18 became instructional airframes in the "M" series.
K2083-2132	50	Hawker Hart (India)	K2105 was fitted with dual control. K2114 was converted to a Demon at Risalpur.
K2133	1	Vickers 173 Vellore IV	Mailplane. Formerly G-ABKC. To R.A.F. in August 1931.
K2134	1	Short S.8/8 Rangoon	Trials aircraft, then to Nos. 203 and 210 Squadrons.
K2135-2234	100	Bristol 105 Bulldog IIA	Bristol Nos. 7590-7689. K2188 built as a two-seat trainer, Bristol Type 124.
K2235	1	D.H.60M Moth	Built from standard parts at Farnborough and used for float experiments.
K2236-2320	85	Westland Wapiti	K2236-2251, Mk. VI; K2252-2288, Mk. IIA (Home Service); K2289-2305, Mk. IIA (Indian service). K2306-2320 renumbered K4337-4348 and K5071-5073 on conversion to Wallace. K2257, 2262, 2265, 2268, 2286, 2287 to the Royal Australian Air Force.
K2321-2339	19	Vickers Virginia X	K2327 was modified for parachute training.
K2340-2345	6	Vickers Victoria V	All but K2343 rebuilt as Valentias. K2340 was prototype Victoria VI.
K2346-2423	78	Avro 504N	Final production of 504 series. 23 to "M" series. Three to Civil Register.
K2424-2473	50	Hawker Hart I	K2434, Napier engine test-bed; K2455, fitted for special communications role; K2459, converted to trainer. K2439, 2446, 2462, 2463, 2465, 2469, 2471, 2472, 2473 were sold to the South African Air Force.
K2474-2475	2	Hawker Hart I (D.C.)	Became known later as Hart Trainer (Interim).
K2476-2495	20	Bristol Bulldog IIA	Bristol Nos. 7691-7710. K2478 and 2481 became 714M and 900M.
K2496-2513	18	Avro 621 Tutor	Lynx IV uncowled engines. Six to "M" series.
K2514-2566	53	Armstrong Whitworth Atlas I	Atlas trainers.

Serial Nos.	*Qty.*	*Aircraft Type*	*Remarks*
K2567-2601	35	D.H. 60T Tiger Moth I	De Havilland Nos. 1739-1773. Gipsy III engines. To Air Ministry Specification 23/31. K2586-2587 rigged for inverted flying. K2588-2592 were built as floatplanes for the Far East.
K2602	1	Gloster A.S.31 Survey	First Gloster twin-engined aircraft.
K2603-2649	47	Fairey Gordon	K2603, 2608, 2613, 2637, 2641 were rebuilt in service. K2620 and K2636 went to the Royal New Zealand Air Force.
K2650-2680	31	Vickers Virginia X	Final Virginia production.
K2681	1	Saro A.19 Cloud	Prototype flying-boat trainer to Air Ministry Specification 15/32.
K2682	1	Avro 618 Ten	For evaluation.
K2683-2769	87	Fairey Gordon I	Eleven to R.N.Z.A.F., three to Royal Egyptian Air Force, two to "M" series.
K2770	1	Westland Pterodactyl V	Fourth and final machine of the Westland-Hill Pterodactyl series to be built.
K2771	1	Vickers Type 253	Prototype to Air Ministry Specification G.4/31.
K2772	1	Parnall G.4/31	Prototype to Air Ministry Specification G.4/31.
K2773	1	Handley Page H.P.47	Prototype to Air Ministry Specification G.4/31.
K2774-2790	17	Hawker Osprey I	Floatplane/landplane versions.
K2791-2808	18	Vickers Victoria V	All but K2791 and 2801 converted to Valentia. K2808 used for experiments.
K2809	1	Short S.8/8 Rangoon	Used by Nos. 203 and 210 Squadrons.
K2810-2822	13	Vickers Vildebeest I	K2816, modified to long-range floatplane; K2818, converted to Mk. II; K2819 Pegasus IIM3 engine and Curtiss v.p. airscrew. K2821, converted to Mk. III went to R.N.Z.A.F. as NZ135.
K2823-2841	19	Hawker Nimrod I	K2823 became Mk. II prototype; K2840 was converted to Mk. II.
K2842-2858	17	Hawker Demon I	Seven became instructional airframes in the "M" series.
K2859-2872	14	Bristol Bulldog IIA	Bristol Nos. 7713-7726. Replacement order.
K2873	1	Bristol Type 118	Bristol No. 7561. Ex-G-ABEZ (R-3), to the R.A.F. in March 1932.
K2874-2883	10	Hawker Fury I	Replacement order. To Nos. 1, 25 and 43 Squadrons.
K2884-2887	4	Blackburn Baffin	Originally built as Ripons.
K2888-2889	2	Supermarine Southampton II	K2888 was ex-N253.

K2890	1	Supermarine Day & Night Fighter	Prototype to Air Ministry Specification F.7/30.
K2891	1	Westland F.7/30	Prototype to Air Ministry Specification F.7/30.
K2892	1	Blackburn F.7/30	Prototype to Air Ministry Specification F.7/30.
K2893	1	Avro 626 Sea Tutor	Trials aircraft, later to the Seaplane Training Squadron.
K2894-2898	5	Saro A.19 Cloud	Flying boat training aircraft.
K2899-2904	6	Hawker Fury I	Service replacement aircraft for No. 1 Squadron.
K2905-2908	4	Hawker Demon I	Service replacement aircraft for Nos. 41 and 64 Squadrons.
K2909-2914	6	Hawker Nimrod II	K2909-2911 built of stainless steel.
K2915	1	Hawker Hart	Experimental aircraft in 1933; to Hind standard, January 1935.
K2916-2924	9	Vickers Vildebeest II	K2916 floatplane used for tests for Latvian Government model.
K2925-2926	2	Hawker Nimrod II	Originally planned for stainless steel construction.
K2927-2945	19	Vickers Vildebeest II	K2929, 2934 and 2936 were modified as target tugs. K2940 was converted to Mk. III.
K2946-2963	18	Bristol Bulldog IIA	Bristol Nos. 7746-7763.
K2964-2965	2	Supermarine Southampton	K2964, Mk. III; K2965, Mk. II.
K2966-3030	65	Hawker Hart I	Built by Vickers Ltd. K3013, Hardy prototype. K3012 loaned to Canada. K3020, Bristol engine test-bed; K2966, 2970, 2975, 2976, 2978, 2987, 2993, 2997, 3004, 3011, 3014-3016, 3021, 3026, 3029 sold to S.A.A.F. K2986 sold to Southern Rhodesian Air Force.
K3031-3054	24	Hawker Hart I	Built by Armstrong Whitworth. K3031 converted to Hart (Intermediate) in 1938; K3033 used for Youngman dinghy experiments; K3036, Rolls-Royce engine test-bed.
K3055-3145	91	Hawker Audax	K3072, 3128-3138, 3140-3144 were converted to Hart (Special).
K3146-3158	13	Hawker Hart (T)	First production batch of Hart Trainers.
K3159-3169	11	Vickers Victoria VI	All converted to Valentia. K3169 sold to India.
K3170-3186	17	Bristol 124 Bulldog (TM)	Bristol Nos. 7727-7743. K3183 used as test-bed for Alvis engines.
K3187-3188	2	—	Not used.
K3189-3476	288	Avro 621 Tutor	K3372-3380 and K3475-3476 were produced as Avro 646 Sea Tutors.

Serial Nos.	*Qty.*	*Aircraft Type*	*Remarks*
K3477-3487	11	Fairey Seal	Fairey Nos. F. 1843-1853. K3485 was non-standard and fitted for dual control.
K3488	1	Westland P.V.6	Prototype Wallace, ex-Wapiti V G-AAWA and G-ACBR.
K3489-3503	15	Handley Page H.P.50 Heyford I	K3503 became the prototype Mk. II. K3492 was built to Mk. II standard.
K3504-3513	10	Bristol Bulldog IIA	Bristol 105 Nos. 7764-7773.
K3514-3545	32	Fairey Seal I	Fairey Nos. F. 1854-1885. K3519 became a trainer to Air Ministry Specification 24/32.
K3546-3559	14	Blackburn Baffin	K3546 retained for trials, remainder packed for shipment to Malta.
K3560	1	Saro A.27 London	Prototype to Air Ministry Specification R.24/31. Con verted to Mk. II.
K3561	1	Vought V-66E Corsair	Purchased from the U.S.A. for evaluation.
K3562-3573	12	Westland Wallace I	Rebuilt Wapiti airframes K1346, 1345, 1332, 1333, 1347, 1331, 1345, 1348-150, 1352, 1353.
K3574	1	Short R.24/31	Experimental aircraft known as Short " Knuckleduster ". Became 1154M.
K3575-3579	5	Fairey Seal	Fairey Nos. F.1908-1912. Landplane/floatplane version.
K3580-3582	3	Blackburn Perth I	K3580 crashed off Stornoway in 1935.
K3583	1	Bristol 130 Bombay	Bristol No. 7809. Prototype to Air Ministry Specification C.26/31.
K3584	1	D.H.82B Queen Bee	Prototype. De Havilland No. 5027. Tiger Moth conversions.
K3585	1	Armstrong Whitworth A.W.23	Prototype to Air Ministry Specification C.26/31. To Flight Refuelling Ltd. in April 1939 as G-AFRX.
K3586	1	Hawker Fury II	Known as the " High Speed Fury ". Became Merlin engine test-bed.
K3587	1	Bristol 120	Experimental general purpose aircraft. Ex-R.6.
K3588	1	Vickers 210 Vespa I	Ex-G-EBLD, G-ABIL and 0-5, acquired by the R.A.F. in June 1933. Became 1051M.
K3589-3590	2	Blackburn Baffin	First production of type as Baffin.
K3591	1	Blackburn B.3	Experimental aircraft to Air Ministry Specification M.1/30A.
K3592-3595	4	Short S.19 Singapore III	All served in No. 210 Squadron.

K3596	1	Heinkel He 64	Ex-D-2305 and G-ACBS to Farnborough for flap research. Later VP-YBI.
K3597-3598	2	D.H.82B Queen Bee	De Havilland Nos. 5038-5039. Ex-D.H.60GIII. Trials aircraft and later service targets.
K3599-3614	16	Vickers Valentia	K3601 became a flying classroom for the Electrical and Wireless School, Cranwell.
K3615-3653	39	Hawker Osprey III	For Fleet Air Arm (except K3616-3619, equipped for communication work with No. 24 Squadron, R.A.F.).
K3654-3662	9	Hawker Nimrod II	Several used as trainers at No. 1 Flying Training School 1935-36.
K3663	1	Cierva C.29	Experimentally fitted with Armstrong Siddeley Panther II engine.
K3664-3677	14	Westland Wallace I	Rebuilt Wapiti airframes as follows: K3664-3675 (ex-K-1354-1365), K3676 (ex-J9864), K3677 (ex-J9605).
K3678	1	Short S.8/8 Rangoon	Served in Nos. 203 and 210 Squadrons.
K3679-3721	43	Hawker Audax	K3719 became the prototype Hector. K3680, 3697, 3702, 3705, 3707 to the South African Air Force.
K3722-3729	8	Saro A.19P Cloud	Delivered from November 1933.
K3730-3742	13	Hawker Fury I	Delivered complete to No. 43 Squadron, 1934.
K3743-3763	21	Hawker Hart (T)	K3752 fitted with night flying equipment, October 1935.
K3764-3807	44	Hawker Demon	11 renumbered in " M " series, *e.g.*, K3800/2 became 1532/1005M.
K3808-3854	47	Hawker Hart I	Built by Vickers Ltd.; K3844 was converted to Hart (Intermediate).
K3855-3904	50	Hawker Hart I	Built by Armstrong Whitworth; K3873-3874 were Hart (Comm.) and K3881 was converted to Hart (Intermediate).
K3905	1	Fairey G.4/31	Fairey No. F.1926. (*N.B. A Hawker Hart also had the number* K3905 *incorrectly allotted.*)
K3906-3913	8	Westland Wallace I	K3907 became 1813M.
K3914-3920	7	Hawker Osprey IIIL	Delivered as Fleet Spotter Reconnaissance landplanes.
K3921-3922	2	Hawker Hart (India)	Both served intially in No. 39 Squadron.
K3923-3953	31	Bristol Bulldog (T.M.)	K3923, 3932, 3934 became 912M, 1168M, 1167M.
K3954	1	Hawker Osprey IIIL	Special Osprey modified to Mk. IV.

Serial Nos.	*Qty.*	*Aircraft Type*	*Remarks*
K3955-3972	18	Hawker Hart I	Built by Armstrong Whitworth. Some conversions to trainers later in service.
K3973	1	Supermarine Stranraer	Prototype. Trials aircraft, then to No. 210 Squadron.
K3974-3985	12	Hawker Demon I	Rolls-Royce Kestrel II engines fitted. K3979 became 1655M.
K3986-4009	24	Fairey Gordon II	Fairey Nos. F.1941-1964, K3987, 3993, 3995, 4000-4009 to Royal New Zealand Air Force.
K4010	1	Westland Wallace	Wapiti K2245 rebuilt in February 1934.
K4011	1	Blackburn Perth I	Final Perth with modified fuel system.
K4012-4020	9	Westland Wallace	Converted from Wapiti airframes K1334, 1339, 1341, 1344, 1370, 1372-1375.
K4021-4043	23	Handley Page H.P.50 Heyford I/IA	K4021 was non-standard and converted to Mk. III; K4029 was Intermediate Mk. IA/II.
K4044-4046	3	D.H.82B Queen Bee	D.H. Nos. 5044-5046. K4044 crashed in sea, January 1935.
K4047	1	Airspeed A.S.5 Courier	Used at Farnborough for experiments and then communications work.
K4048	1	Westland P.V.3	Westland No. WA.2419. To R.A.F. (ex-Everest Expedition as G-ACAZ). Ex-P-3.
K4049	1	Vickers 271 Wellington	Prototype to Air Ministry Specification B.9/32. First flew 15.6.36.
K4050-4070	21	Hawker Hardy	Built by Gloster Aircraft. Rolls-Royce Kestrel 1B engines fitted. Shipped overseas to Middle East.
K4071-4080	10	Blackburn Baffin	Delivered to equip No. 810 Squadron.
K4081-4104	24	Gloster Gauntlet I	K4094 had trial Browning gun installation.
K4105-4188	84	Vickers Vildebeest/ Vincent	K4105-4130, Vildebeest II as ordered but most completed as Vincent. K4131-4155, Vincent; K4156-4188, Vildebeest III. K4164 was Mk. IV prototype. Five to Royal New Zealand Air Force.
K4189	1	Bristol Bulldog IIA	Stainless steel construction to Air Ministry Specification 11/31 for static test.
K4190	1	Fairey Swordfish	Fairey No. F.2038. Prototype to Air Ministry Specification S.15/33. Was Fairey T.S.R.II.
K4191-4200	10	Supermarine Scapa	Rolls-Royce Kestrel III engines installed.
K4201-4225	25	Fairey Seal	K4212 fitted with dual control sets ex-K3485.

K4226-4229	4	D.H.82B Queen Bee	De Havilland Nos. 5048-5051.
K4230-4239	10	Avro 671 Rota I	Cierva C.30A built by A. V. Roe. Delivered to School of Army Co-operation, Odiham.
K4240	1	Handley Page H.P.52 Hampden	Prototype. First flew 21.6.36.
K4241	1	Blackburn Monoplane	Blackburn No. 2780/1, G-ABKV. To R.A.F. for trials, March 1934.
K4242-4291	50	D.H.82A Tiger Moth II	K4282 became 5284M.
K4292	1	Bristol 105 Bulldog IV	Bristol No. 7745. Ex-Mk. IIIA G-ABZW (R-7).
K4293-4294	2	D.H.82B Queen Bee	De Havilland Nos. 5088-5089. Floatplane versions.
K4295	1	Blackburn Shark I/II	Prototype to Air Ministry Specification S.15/33. Converted to Mk. II. Was Blackburn B-6.
K4296	1	Avro 671 Rota	Seaplane version of Rota with twin floats.
K4297-4298	2	Hawker Hart (Comm.)	Built by Armstrong Whitworth. Rolls-Royce Kestrel 1B4 engines. For No. 24 Squadron.
K4299	1	Armstrong Whitworth Type 29	To Air Ministry Specification P.27/32.
K4300-4302	3	Saro A-19P Cloud	Armstrong Siddeley Serval engines.
K4303	1	Fairey Battle	Prototype. To A.M. Spec. P.27/32 and 23/35.
K4304-4305	2	Fairey Seafox	Prototype to Air Ministry Specification 11/32. K4304 floatplane, later 1463M; K4305 landplane.
K4306-4321	16	Hawker Hardy	Built by Gloster Aircraft. Rolls-Royce Kestrel 1B engines.
K4322-4336	15	Hawker Osprey III	K4336 cancelled.
K4337-4348	12	Westland Wallace I	Built from Wapiti airframes K2306-2317; K4344 was used as an experimental tanker; K4346-4348 built to Mk. II standard.
K4349-4364	16	Blackburn Shark I	Delivered to equip No. 820 Squadron.
K4365-4384	20	Hawker Audax/Hart Special	Built by Gloster Aircraft. Rolls-Royce Kestrel IB5 engines initially fitted. K4365-4380 Hart (Special); K4381-4406, Audax.
K4385-4406	22	Hawker Audax	Built by Gloster Aircraft. Rolls-Royce Kestrel X engines initially fitted. K4390 became Hart (Special), K4392 sold to S.A.A.F.
K4407-4436	30	Hawker Hart (Special)	Built by Gloster Aircraft. K4407, 4414, 4416, 4432 may have been standard aircraft.

Serial Nos.	*Qty.*	*Aircraft Type*	*Remarks*
K4437-4495	59	Hawker Hart (Standard)	Built by Armstrong Whitworth. K4439 and K4442 converted to Hart (Intermediate). K4442, 4443, 4481, 4483 sold to Royal Egyptian Air Force; K4444, 4447-4451, 4455-4458, 4460-4465, 4467-4472, 4474, 4476-4477, 4479-4480, 4484-4485, 4488-4492, 4495 sold to the South African Air Force.
K4496-4544	49	Hawker Demon	Rolls-Royce Kestrel V engines. K4496 fitted with Frazer-Nash turret.
K4545	1	D.H. 82B Queen Bee	De Havilland No. 5099.
K4546-4564	19	Boulton & Paul P.75 Overstrand	To A.M. Spec. 23/34. Served minaly in No. 101 Squadron.
K4565	1	Supermarine Scapa	Ordered 1933.
K4566-4576	11	Bristol Bulldog (TM)	Ordered July 1934. Sold 1937.
K4577-4585	9	Short S.19 Singapore III	K4577 was a trials aircraft.
K4586-4587	2	Armstrong Whitworth A.W.38 Whitley	Prototypes to Air Ministry Specifications B.3/34 and B.21/35. K4586 became 2070M.
K4588-4614	27	Vickers Vildebeest III	K4589, 4591-4593, 4595-4598, 4612-4613 to Royal New Zealand Air Force. K4599 had dual controls.
K4615-4619	5	Vickers Vincent	K4617 became NZ321 in the Royal New Zealand Air Force.
K4620-4629	10	Hawker Nimrod II	Fleet Air Arm aircraft.
K4630-4635	6	Vickers Valentia I	K4632 was fitted with loudspeaker apparatus.
K4636-4655	20	Hawker Hind	K4636, 4638, 4639, 4641, 4644, 4645, 4647, 4649, 4650 were converted to trainers by General Aircraft in 1938 K4640 and 4643 went to Kenya and K4642 and 4650 to New Zealand.
K4656-4750	95	Vickers Vincent	Deliveries from August 1935. 25 subsequently to the Royal New Zealand Air Force.
K4751-4770	20	Hawker Hart (T)	Rolls-Royce Kestrel 1B engines. K4770 modified for target towing in the Far East.
K4771	1	Avro 652A Anson	Prototype to Air Ministry Specification G.18/35.
K4772	1	D.H.89M Dragon Rapide	To Air Ministry Specification G.18/35. Used at Farn borough 1937-38.
K4773	1	Saro A.33	To Air Ministry Specification R.2/33.
K4774	1	Short S.25 Sunderland	Prototype to Air Ministry Specification R.2/33.

K4775	1	Avro 671 Rota	Experimentally fitted with Civet Major engine at Farnborough 1935.
K4776-4778	3	Blackburn Baffin	Delivered complete to No. 812 Squadron.
K4779-4796	18	Fairey Seal	Fairey Nos. F.2093-2110. K4796 believed not built.
K4797	1	Supermarine Seagull V	Prototype. Renamed Walrus by R.A.F. in 1935.
K4798-4837	40	Avro Tutor	Replacement aircraft for training units.
K4838-4862	25	Hawker Audax (India)	Built by Gloster Aircraft. Rolls-Royce Kestrel 1B engines fitted. Shipped to India.
K4863-4878	16	Handley Page H.P.50 Heyford II	All but last three delivered to No. 7 Squadron, R.A.F.
K4879	1	Bristol 138A	To Air Ministry Specification 2/34 for high altitude research. Became 2393M.
K4880-4882	3	Blackburn Shark II	K4882 was modified to the Mk. III prototype.
K4883-4885	3	Vickers Vincent	Delivered in June 1936. K4885 to the Royal New Zealand Air Force as NZ314.
K4886-5052	167	Hawker Hart (T)	Built by Armstrong Whitworth. Rolls-Royce Kestrel X engines. K5022 to South African Air Force. K4929 to Fleet Air Arm in 1941.
K5053	1	Northrop 2E	Acquired from U.S.A. for evaluation.
K5054	1	Supermarine Type 300 Spitfire	Prototype to Air Ministry Specification F.37/34.
K5055	1	D.H.82B Queen Bee	De Havilland No. 5116. Tiger Moth conversion.
K5056-5058	3	Hawker Nimrod II	For Fleet Air Arm.
K5059-5060	2	D.H.82B Queen Bee	De Havilland Nos. 5127-5128.
K5061-5062	2	—	Reservation.
K5063-5069	7	Avro 626 Prefect	K5066 and K5069 became G-AHVO/RZ. K5063 became 1594M.
K5070	1	D.H.89	De Havilland No. 6267. Purchased for Air Council use.
K5071-5082	12	Westland Wallace I	Built from Westland Wapiti airframes K2318-2320, 2379-2380, 2252, 2254, 2260, 2264, 2266, 1412-1413.
K5083	1	Hawker Hurricane	Prototype. First flew 6.11.35. Became 1211M.
K5084	1	D.H.88 Comet	De Havilland No. 1996. G-ACSS for evaluation 1936.
K5085-5098	14	Fairey Hendon	Fairey (Stockport) built. Delivered complete to No. 38 Squadron.
K5099	1	Fairey P.4/34	First prototype. Merlin "F" engine. Became 3665M.
K5100-5114	15	D.H.82B Queen Bee	De Havilland Nos. 5134-5137 and 5153-5163.

Serial Nos.	*Qty.*	*Aircraft Type*	*Remarks*
K5115	1	Hawker Henley	Prototype to P.4/34. Later test-bed for Rolls-Royce Vulture engine.
K5116	1	Westland Wallace	G-ACJU, acquired 22.6.35.
K5117	1	—	Reservation.
K5118	1	D.H.82B Queen Bee	—
K5119	1	Bristol Type 146	To Air Ministry Specification F.5/34. First flew 11.2.38.
K5120-5176	57	Hawker Audax	Built by A. V. Roe & Co. K5138, 5146, 5158, 5166, 5176 sold to the South African Air Force. K5141, 5142, 5145, 5147 transferred to Straits Settlements Volunteer Air Force.
K5177	1	—	Reservation.
K5178-5179	2	Blackburn Skua	Prototypes to Air Ministry Specification O.27/34.
K5180-5199	20	Handley Page H.P.50 Heyford III	K5184 modified by Flight Refuelling Ltd. K5180 originally built as Mk. II.
K5200	1	Gloster G.37 Gladiator	Prototype to Air Ministry Specification F.7/30.
K5201-5256	56	Hawker Audax	Built by Bristol Aeroplane Co.
K5257-5263	7	Saro A.27 London I	First three delivered initially with Bristol Pegasus III engines; later all had Pegasus X engines installed. All conv. to Mk. II in 1937.
K5264-5367	104	Gloster Gauntlet II	39 became instructional airframes. 14 others sold to Finland in 1940 as follows: K5267, 5270, 5271, 5288, 5293, 5313, 5324, 5326, 5338, 5341, 5252, 5358, 5364, 5365.
K5368-5560	193	Hawker Hind	Built and issued as light bombers. K5373, 5377, 5379, 5384, 5397, 5408, 5410, 5423, 5427, 5436, 5439, 5440, 5446, 5447, 5449, 5450, 5460, 5465-5469, 5473, 5485, 5486, 5488, 5495, 5500, 5502-5509, 5511-5513, 5515, 5517, 5518, 5521, 5523, 5550, 5553, 5559 were converted to trainers by General Aircraft Ltd. in 1938. Both types were variously disposed to R.N.Z.A.F., S.A.A.F., Iran and as instructional airframes.
K5561-5585	25	Hawker Audax (India)	Built by A. V. Roe Ltd.
K5586-5603	18	Hawker Audax	A. V. Roe built ex-Westland contract.
K5604	1	Gloster F.5/34	Prototype to A.M. Spec. F.5/34. Became 2232M.
K5605	1	Vickers Valentia	Served in Middle East.
K5606	1	Armstrong Whitworth 19	Allotted A-3 for tests to A.M. Spec. G.4/31.

K5607-5659	53	Blackburn Shark II	Landplane/floatplane versions.
K5660-5662	3	Fairey Swordfish	Fairey Nos. F.2142-2144. K5662 completed as floatplane to Air Ministry Specification S.38/34.
K5663-5682	20	Hawker Fury	Rolls-Royce Kestrel IIS.
K5683-5741	59	Hawker Demon	Built by Boulton Paul. Kestrel VDR engines. K5694-5695, 5698-5699, 5705-5706, 5710-5712, 5718-5719, 5725-5727, 5729-5741 fitted with Frazer Nash turrets.
K5742-5767	26	Hawker Osprey IV	Several modified as trainers and target-tugs.
K5768-5771	4	Fairey Hendon	Order cancelled.
K5772-5783	12	Supermarine Walrus I	Initial R.A.F. Walrus production to Air Ministry Specification 2/35. K5774 and K5783 to New Zealand.
K5784-5897	114	Hawker Hart (T)	Built by Vickers. Rolls-Royce Kestrel X engines. K5784 to South African Air Force. K5869, 5874, 5895 to Fleet Air Arm in 1941.
K5898-5907	10	Hawker Demon	Built by Boulton & Paul. Turreted version except last two.
K5908-5913	6	Saro London I/II	K5908-5910, Mk. I, later conv. Mk. II; K5911-5913, Mk. II.
K5914-5923	10	Hawker Hardy	Built by Gloster Aircraft.
K5924	1	Miles M.3 Falcon	Acquired for evaluation.
K5925	1	Miles M.6 Hawcon	Acquired for evaluation.
K5926-6011	86	Fairey Swordfish I	Initial Swordfish production.
K6012-6086	75	Westland Wallace II	K6012, 6057, 6066, 6075, 6082 became 943/1560/1633/1562/1542M.
K6087-6126	40	Avro 621 Tutor	K6105 became G-AKFJ; K6098 became 3352M.
K6127-6128	2	Westland Lysander	Prototypes to Air Ministry Specification A.39/34. K6127 had various modifications.
K6129-6151	23	Gloster Gladiator	K6135 to Royal Hellenic Air Force.
K6152-6325	174	Avro 652A Anson I	K6212-6223 went direct to the Royal Australian Air Force as A4-1 to -12.
K6326-6368	43	Vickers Vincent	All except last eight delivered for No. 55 Squadron. 27 to the Royal New Zealand Air Force.
K6369-6414	46	Vickers Vildebeest IV	K6395, 6396, 6401, 6409, 6410, 6413, 6414 to R.N.Z.A.F.
K6415-6550	146	Hawker Hart (T)	Built by Armstrong Whitworth. Rolls-Royce Kestrel X engines. First 12 tropicalised. K6433 to Fleet Air Arm in 1941.
K6551-6552	2	Bristol 148	To Air Ministry Specification A.39/34. K6552 used as engine test bed.

Serial Nos.	*Qty.*	*Aircraft Type*	*Remarks*
K6553-6554	2	Cierva Gyroplane	Cancelled order.
K6555-6612	58	Fairey Hendon II	Cancelled order.
K6613-6856	244	Hawker Hind	Built as light bombers. K6621, 6640, 6657, 6658, 6671, 6673, 6683, 6685, 6687, 6688, 6690, 6703, 6712, 6714-6716, 6722, 6724, 6729, 6739, 6741, 6743, 6756-6760, 6775, 6776, 6793, 6805, 6810, 6811, 6813, 6818, 6820, 6821, 6823, 6827, 6829, 6831, 6834-6837, 6840, 6841 converted to Hind Trainers by General Aircraft Ltd.
K6857-6906	50	Handley Page H.P.50 Heyford III	Service version for Nos. 7, 97, 99, 148 Squadrons.
K6907-6922	16	Short Singapore III	K6912, 6917-6919 to Royal New Zealand Air Force.
K6923-6925	3	Avro 646 Sea Tutor	K6924 was converted to a landplane.
K6926	1	Hawker 1PV-4	Private venture aircraft. Serial allotted for trials.
K6927-6932	6	Saro London I/II	Deliveries from June 1937.
K6933-7032	100	Handley Page H.P.54 Harrow I/II	From K6971, built as Mk. II; many Mk. I's converted later to Mk. II. K6933 became G-AFRG and R.C.A.F. No. 794.
K7033-7182	150	Bristol 142M Blenheim I	K7034-7036, 7041-7042 and 7167 fitted with dual control. K7072 variously modified.
K7183-7262	80	Armstrong Whitworth A.W.38 Whitley I/II	K7183-7216, Mk. I; K7217-7262, Mk. II; K7248, engine test-bed.
K7263-7285	23	Hawker Fury II	First 19 to No. 25 Squadron.
K7287-7303	17	Supermarine Stranraer	Ordered 29.8.35. Service in Nos. 209, 228 and 240 Squadrons.
K7304-7306	3	Supermarine Scapa	Used by Nos. 202 and 228 Squadrons.
K7307-7468	162	Hawker Audax	Built by A. V. Roe Ltd.
K7469-7553	85	Hawker Audax	Built by The Bristol Aeroplane Company.
K7554	1	Hawker Henley	2nd prototype. Became 3674M.
K7555	1	Fairey P.4/34.	Second prototype. Fairey No. F.2266. Merlin I engine.
K7556	1	Vickers Wellesley	Prototype. Used later for Rotol airscrew testing.
K7557	1	Bristol 142	G-ADCZ(R-12) presented to the nation as " Britain First". Became 2211M.
K7558-7712	155	Fairey Battle	Built at Stockport. 136 fitted with Merlin I engines and 19 with Merlin II engines.
K7713-7791	79	Vickers Wellesley	K7717 and K7772 were Bristol engine test-beds.

K7792-7891	100	Gloster Gauntlet II	K7813, 7826, 7837, 7839, 7857, 7858, 7865, 7867, 7869 sold to Finland in 1940. K7831, 7833 disposed to South Africa.
K7892-8077	186	Gloster Gladiator	K8005-8007 to Iraq and K8056-8077 cancelled. K7939 was first with Browning guns. K7892, 7923, 7966, 7971, 7973, 8013, 8017-8019, 8031, 8047, 8054 to Royal Hellenic Air Force. K7907, 7928, 7989 to Iraqi Air Force in 1942. K8032 see L8032.
K8078-8087	10	Vickers Vildebeest IV	To No. 42 Squadron. Later all except K8082 to the Royal New Zealand Air Force.
K8088	1	Bristol 146	Construction not completed.
K8089	1	Gloster F.5/34	Second of experimental type. First flew March 1938. Became 2231M.
K8090-8167	78	Hawker Hector	Built by Westland Aircraft. K8098, 8102, 8105, 8114, 8115, 8117, 8130, 8148, 8159 to Irish Air Corps.
K8168-8172	5	Avro 621 Tutor	K8169 became 3353M.
K8173-8177	5	Boulton Paul P.75 Overstrand 1	Final delivery of type in 1937.
K8178	1	Vickers Warwick	Prototype. First flew 13.8.39. Used by Rolls-Royce for trials.
K8179-8180	2	*See Remarks*	Allotted to Handley Page and Armstrong Whitworth for Spec. B.1/35 projects.
K8181-8217	37	Hawker Demon	Boulton Paul built. Kestrel VDR. K8181-8189, 8194-8204, 8214-8217 fitted with turrets.
K8218-8306	89	Hawker Fury	Built by General Aircraft.
K8307-8308	2	General Aircraft Monospar S.T.25 Jubilee	K8308 became G-AHBK which crashed near Cirencester 2.6.47.
K8309	1	Hawker Hotspur	Prototype to Air Ministry Specification F.9/35.
K8310	1	Boulton Paul P.82 Defiant	Prototype to Air Ministry Specification F.9/35.
K8311-8335	25	Hawker Audax	Westland contract, sub-let to A. V. Roe Aircraft. K8313 and K8318 to South African Air Force.
K8336-8337	2	D.H. 82 Tiger Moth	Floatplane version.
K8338-8345	8	Supermarine Walrus	Service in No. 711 Sqn.
K8346-8449	104	Fairey Swordfish I	Floatplane/landplane versions.
K8450-8519	70	Blackburn Shark II	K8575 became 1127M.
K8520-8536	17	Vickers Wellesley	Vickers (Weybridge) built. Service in Nos. 35, 76 and 77 Squadrons.
K8537-8564	28	Supermarine Walrus	K8556 used at Farnborough. K8558 to Royal New Zealand Air Force.

Serial Nos.	*Qty.*	*Aircraft Type*	*Remarks*
K8565-8568	4	Short Singapore III	K8565 and K 8567 used by No. 4 Operational Training Unit in 1941.
K8569-8617	49	Fairey Seafox	For Fleet Air Arm catapult flights.
K8618-8619	2	D.H.91 Albatross	Provisionally registered E.2 and E.5, later became G-AEVV-VW and impressed as AX903-904.
K8620	1	Boulton Paul P.82 Defiant	Second prototype.
K8621	1	Hawker Hotspur	Second prototype. Cancelled.
K8622-8623	2	Fairey	Reserved for Fairey project to Specification F.9/35.
K8624	1	Armstrong Whitworth A.W.30	Project to Air Ministry Specification F.9/35.
K8625	1	Gloster	Project to Air Ministry Specification F.34/35.
K8626	1	Miles Hawk Major	Became 1081M.
K8627-8631	5	Hawker Hart (India)	Used by No. 39 Squadron in India. Kestrel IB. engines.
K8632-8673	42	D.H.82B Queen Bee	De Havilland Nos. 5165-5206.
K8674-8702	29	Westland Wallace II	K8696 became 3625M and K8701 became 2537M.
K8703-8845	143	Avro 652A Anson I	K8738-8741, 8792-8812 and 8840-8844 diverted from R.A.F. K8830-8837 fitted with dual control.
K8846-8847	2	Airspeed A.S.27 Irving	Defence biplane. Cancelled.
K8848-8852	5	Vickers Valentia I	K8850, radio trainer at Cranwell; remainder, No. 70 Sqn. transports.
K8853	1	Hendy Heck IIC	Used for gun-sight experiments at Farnborough. Later 3125M.
K8854-8855	2	Supermarine Sea Otter	Prototypes. K8855 destroyed at works by enemy action 26.9.40.
K8856-8859	4	Short S.19 Singapore III	K8856, No. 210 Sqn.; K8858-8859, No. 203 Sqn.
K8860-8886	27	Fairey Swordfish I	Landplane/floatplane versions.
K8887-8888	2	Airspeed A.S.30 Queen Wasp	Prototypes to Air Ministry Specification Q.32/35. K8888 modified to floatplane.
K8889-8890	2	Percival P.8	Prototype to Air Ministry Specification Q.32/35. Construction cancelled.
K8891-8935	45	Blackburn Shark III	K8906 became 1867M, K8929 became 3490M.
K8936-9175	240	Armstrong Whitworth A.W.38 Whitley	K8936-9015 Mk. III, K9016-9055 Mk. IV. K9056-9175 cancelled.
K9176-9675	500	Fairey Battle I	K9176-9486 (311) built at Stockport. Rolls-Royce Merlin II standard power unit. K9222 Exe, K9240 Dagger, K9331 Taurus II, test-beds.

			K9370 P.24 test-bed, shipped to U.S.A. in December 1941. K9487-9675 cancelled on introduction of "shadow factory" production scheme.
K9676-9681	6	Supermarine Stranraer	Ordered May 1936.
K9682-9686	5	Saro A.27 London II	Delivered from September 1937.
K9687-9786	100	Hawker Hector	Built by Westland Aircraft. K9697, 9715, 9725, 9761 to Irish Air Corps.
K9787-9999	213	Supermarine Spitfire I	First production order. Remainder numbered in "L" series, L1000-1096. First 174, Merlin II engines; remainder, Merlin III. K9788 and K9830 were converted to Mk. II standard. K9825, 9871 were later converted to Mk. VA. K9834 was converted for P.R. work in 1940.

BLACKOUT BLOCKS INTRODUCED

L1000–9999

"L" followed on alphabetically from "K", and the actual carry-over came in the middle of the initial production order for Spitfires.

A major change occurred after L7272. Hitherto, numbers had been allotted in direct numerical sequence, but from there onwards allocations for production orders were broken down into batches of between 10 and 50 numbers in runs, with unused numbers, known as "blackout blocks", in between. This system continued throughout the war and afterwards. L6591-6593, and L7269 may be taken as cancelled orders, and all other ranges of numbers not included as "blackout blocks".

From L7272 onwards the "Serial Nos." column will refer to the range of numbers allotted and the "Remarks" column will detail those batches of numbers within the range taken up. The "Quantity" column will give the total for the *allotted* numbers, not the *range* of numbers.

L1000-1096	97	Supermarine Spitfire I	Carried over from "K" series. L1028, 1031, 1096, converted in service to Mk. VA. L1004 was converted to P.R. XIII.
L1097-1546	450	Bristol 142M Blenheim I	L1483, 1485, 1488, 1489, 1497 sold to Turkey in 1939. L1424 was prototype Mk. IF.
L1547-2146	600	Hawker Hurricane I	Various diversions and modifications, *e.g.*, L1695 armament development, L1702 first with Merlin III engine, L1980 first with variable pitch airscrew.

Serial Nos.	Qty.	Aircraft Type	Remarks
			Diversions to Belgium, Yugoslavia, Rumania and Turkey. One to Iran. L1606 became G-AFKX. L1663, 1895, 2014, 2039, 2086 converted to Sea Hurricane. Renumbering on conversion to Mk. IIA and shipment to Russia: L1562 (to DR344), L1596 (to DG)618, L1658 (to DG622), L1684 (to DR354), L1769 (to DR359), L1807 (to DG628), L1824 (to DG625), L1831 (to DG642), L1836 (to DG636), L2099 (to DG637). L1708, 1710, 1711, 1874-1876 were sold to the S.A.A.F. L1751-1752, 1837-1840, 1858-1863 (12) were offset from production to become Yugoslav Air Force Nos. 205-206, 291-294, 312-317. L1759-1763, 1878-1888, 1890, 2021-2023(20) became Royal Canadian Air Force Nos. 310-329 of which 321 (L1884) became the Hillson F.H.40 Slip-wing Hurricane. L1918-1920, 1993-1997, 2040-2044, 2105-2111 were offset to Belgian Air Force. L2024-2025, 2027-2033, 2125-2139 were offset to the Turkish Air Force. L2077-2078, 2085, 2093-2097, 2104, 2112-2114 were offset to the Rumanian Air Force. L2079 offset to Iranian Air Force.
L2147-2157	11	Saunders-Roe	Saro A-33 development project to A.M. Spec. 21/36. Cancelled.
L2158-2168	11	Short S.25 Sunderland I	L2162 later became L2162/G.
L2169-2336	168	Supermarine Walrus	Mainly for Fleet Air Arm. L2301-2303 to Eire, L2222, 2236, 2285 to New Zealand.
L2337-2386	50	Blackburn Shark II	L2374 became 1752M.
L2387-2636	250	D.H.93 Don	L2387-2436 (50) only built, of which only 28 were delivered complete. All were grounded in March 1939.
L2637-2716	80	Vickers Wellesley I	Main deliveries to Middle East units.
L2717-2866	150	Fairey Swordfish I	Fairey Nos. F.2659-2808. L2840 used for rocket projectile tests, November 1943.

L2867-3056	190	Blackburn Skua	Sole production to Air Ministry Specification 25/36. L2870 crashed on trials and became 1201M. Several converted to target tugs following initial conversion of L3006.
L3057-3192	136	Blackburn Roc	Built by Boulton & Paul. Several built as float-planes. L3084 engine test-bed.
L3193-3242	50	Hawker Hart (T)	Cancelled A. V. Roe order.
L3243-3642	400	Hawker Henley	200 only built by Gloster Aircraft; L3243-3442. First 100 with Merlin II and second 100 with Merlin III engines. L3302, Vulture and L3414, Griffon engine test beds. L3441 was the only Henley to be tropicalised.
L3643-4031	389	Hawker Hotspur	Cancelled order placed with A. V. Roe.
L4032-4211	180	Handley Page H.P.52 Hampden I	First production order. L4032 had Wright Cyclone engines experimentally installed. L4038, 4041, 4075, 4076, 4086, 4091, 4105, 4115, 4118, 4141, 4144, 4150, 4170, 4196, 4201, 4204 were converted to Hampden T.B. (Torpedo Bomber).
L4212-4391	180	Vickers Wellington I	L4250, Prototype Mk. II (Vickers 298) later fitted for 40 m.m. Vickers cannon in dorsal position; after initial flight in this configuration, modified with twin fins. L4251, Prototype Mk. III (Vickers 299). L4212, 4221, 4227, 4356, 4358, 4374 converted to D.W.1; L4255 converted to an ambulance; L4244 converted to transport for Royal Navy. L4312-4316 were not delivered.
L4392-4436	45	Miles M.16 Mentor	Military communication version of Miles Nighthawk.
L4437-4440	4	—	Not allotted.
L4441-4518	78	Bristol 152 Beaufort I	First five non-standard. 71st and 72nd completed as Beaufighters; L4444 fitted with dual control; L4448 to Australia as pattern aircraft; L4456 experimental transport version, but not completed.
L4519-4533	15	Fairey Seafox	Second, and last, production batch.
L4534-4669	136	Airspeed A.S.10 Oxford I	L4538 used as civil transport. L4539 had experimental McLaren undercarriage. L4556, 4557, 4592, 4593 not delivered to R.A.F.

Serial Nos.	*Qty.*	*Aircraft Type*	*Remarks*
L4670	1	Dewoitine 510	Purchased from French, June 1937; scrapped March 1941.
L4671-4672	2	General Aircraft Monospar	L4671 was at the A. & A.E.E., Boscombe Down, in June 1939.
L4673-4816	144	Westland Lysander I/II	To L4738, Mk. I; from L4739, Mk. II. L4673 had twin cannon fitted; L4798 transferred to Free French Forces; L4732 converted to T.T.I.
L4817-4934	118	Bristol 142M/L Blenheim I/IV	L4823-4906, Mk. IV; remainder, Mk. I. L4822 had dual control; L4821, 4824, 4826, 4828 sold to Turkey in 1939.
L4935-5797	863	Fairey Battle I	Built by The Austin Motor Company. L4935-4937 non-standard. L4935-4993, Merlin II; L4994 *et seq*, Merlin III; L5286, Sabre test-bed. L5598-5797 were produced as T.T.I.
L5798-5807	10	Short S.25 Sunderland I	Delivered from September to December 1938.
L5808-5887	80	Bristol 130 Bombay	L5808-5857 (50) only built by Short & Harland. L5810, 5811, 5815, 5816, 5825 had dual control.
L5888-5911	24	D.H.82B Queen Bee	All delivered to store at Cardington in 1937.
L5912-6001	90	Miles M.14 Magister	R.A.F. trainer. L5952 and L5961 to Fleet Air Arm.
L6002-6101	100	Handley Page H.P.53 Hereford	Built by Short & Harland. L6011, 6018-6020, 6055, 6076, 6048, 6080, 6096 converted to Hampdens.
L6102	1	Vickers Viastra X	G-ACCC for radio and icing tests.
L6103	1	De Bruyne D.B.2 Snark	Built by Aero Research, Duxford as G-ADDL.
L6104-6345	242	Blackburn Botha I	Built at Brough. L6104-6105 were prototypes.
L6346	1	Miles M.8 Peregrine	Used for boundary layer con trol research.
L6347-6590	244	Blackburn Botha I	Built at Dumbarton. L6347-6546 (200) only completed.
L6594-6843	250	Bristol 142M Blenheim I	Built by A. V. Roe. L6696-6708, 6713-6718 to Rumania; L6813-6814, 6817-6834 to Yugoslavia. L6764-6773 to Finland.
L6844-6845	2	Westland Whirlwind	Prototypes to Air Ministry Specification F.37/35.
L6846	1	Miles M.7 Nighthawk	Four-seat instrument trainer for evaluation. Became 1587M.
L6847-6888	42	Westland Lysander II	L6867 modified to T.T.II; L6869 transferred to Free French Forces.
L6889-6890	2	Supermarine B.12/36	Prototypes destroyed by enemy action before completion.

L6891-6893	3	Blackburn B.2	Became 3158M, 3159M, 3877.M
L6894-6919	24	Miles M.14 Magister	L6914 & 6917 not built. L6909-6913 non-standard (M.14B) with Cirrus Major engines.
L6920-6949	30	D.H.82 Tiger Moth	Civil type purchased on production line.
L6950-7036	87	Boulton Paul P.82 Defiant I	First production. L6967 converted to T.T.III by Reid and Sigrist Ltd., November 1943. L6968, army co-operation trials at Odiham, 1940.
L7037	1	Bristol 138B	Became 2339M before being flown. Rolls-Royce Merlin.
L7038-7043	6	Saro A.27 London	Delivered January-April 1938.
L7044	1	Fairchild 24	Purchased in U.S.A., February 1937, for British Air Attaché, Washington.
L7045	1	Fairey Fantome	Evaluated for service February 1938 to June 1939.
L7046-7073	28	Avro 652M Anson I	Replacement order for offsets from earlier orders.
L7074-7173	100	Fairey Albacore	Fairey Nos. F.3274-3373. L7074, Prototype landplane; L7075, trials as floatplane.
L7174-7223	50	Hawker Hind (L.B.)	Built as light bombers. L7182, 7184, 7188, 7193, 7195-7198, 7202-7214, 7216, 7219-7220, 7223 converted to trainers by General Aircraft in 1938.
L7224-7243	20	Hawker Hind (T)	Built as trainers.
L7244-7245	2	Handley Page H.P.56/57 Halifax	Prototypes to Air Ministry Specification P.13/36. Became 3299M and 3474M.
L7246-7247	2	Avro 679 Manchester	Prototypes to Air Ministry Specification P.13/36. Became 3422M and 2738M.
L7248-7268	21	Saro A.36 Lerwick	Only production batch. L7248-7250 prototypes to Air Ministry Specification R.1/36.
L7270	1	Airspeed A.S.6J Envoy III	Ex-Royal Household G-AEXX. To Sweden June 1946 as SE-ASN.
L7271	1	Handley Page H.P.53 Hereford	Hereford prototype. Became 2057M.
L7272	1	Percival P-10C Vega Gull III	Became G-AFWG for Air Attaché Buenos Aires.
L7276-7584	200	Avro 679 Manchester I/683 Lancaster I	L7276-7325, 7373-7402, 7415-7434, 7453-7497, L7515-7526 (157) were Manchester I, of which L7517 was destroyed before delivery; L7527-7549 & 7565-7584 (43) completed as Lancasters.
L7589-7595	5	Cierva C.40 Rota II	L7589-7591 and L7594-7595 ordered to Air Ministry Specification 2/36.
L7596	1	D.H.86A	De Havilland No. 2348, G-ADYJ purchased as a " Flying Classroom ".

Serial Nos.	*Qty.*	*Aircraft Type*	*Remarks*
L7600 & 7605	2	Short S.29 Stirling	Prototypes to Air Ministry Specification B.12/36. L7600 crashed on first flight 14.5.39; L7605 became 3443M.
L7608-7623	16	Gloster Gladiator	L7609, L7611, L7620, L7621 and L7623 disposed to Royal Hellenic Air Force.
L7632-7701	62	Fairey Swordfish I	L7632-7661 & L7670-7701.
L7706-7707	2	Heston T.1/37	Trainer prototypes. L7706 became 2371M.
L7714	1	Miles M.15	Prototype to Air Ministry Specification T.1/37.
L7720-7764	30	D.H.82B Queen Bee	L7720-7729 & L7745-7764.
L7770-7899	100	Vickers Wellington I	Vickers (Chester) built. L7770-7772, Mk. I; L7773-7789, Mk. IA; L7790-7819, L7840-7874, L7885-7899, Mk. IC. L7771 converted to D.W.1; L7776 converted to Mk. XV.
L7903-7994	67	Avro 652A Anson I	L7903-7912, 7913-7922 to R.A.A.F., 7923-7932, 7945-7977, 7991-7994.
L7999 & 8002	2	Gloster F.9/37	Prototypes. L7999, Bristol Taurus T.E.1M, later Taurus III engine; L8002, Rolls-Royce Peregrine engine.
L8005-8032	28	Gloster Gladiator	L8005-8007 to Iran, L8011 to Royal Hellenic Air Force, L8008-8025 shipped to Middle East in 1939. Parts of L8032 became G-AMRK and was flown marked K8032.
L8037 & 8040	2	D.H.86B	De Havilland Nos. 2340-2341 (G-ADYC/D) acquired for W/T training.
L8051-8359	214	Miles M.14A Magister	L8051-8095, 8127-8176, 8200. 8237, 8249-8295, 8326-8359-L8204 to Fleet Air Arm.
L8362-9044	380	Bristol 142M/L Blenheim I/IV	Built by Rootes Securities. L8362-8407, 8433-8482, 8500-8549, 8597-8632, 8652-8701, 8714-8731, Mk. I; L8732-8761, 8776-8800, 8827-8876, 9020-9044, Mk. IV. L8384-8385 to Royal Hellenic Air Force; L8603-8608, 8619-8620, 8622-8630, 8632, 8652-8654 to Rumanian Air Force; L9025, 9026, 9028 sold to Finland in 1940.
L9145-9165	21	Avro 652A Anson I	L9161-9163 despatched direct to Australia.
L9166	1	Avro 642	VT-AFM 'Star of India' temporarily in R.A.F. service.
L9170-9482	220	Bristol 142M/L Blenheim IV	Built by Rootes Securities. L9170-9218, 9237-9273, 9294-9342, 9375-9422, 9446-9482.

			Up to L9273 were built as Mk. I and then modified to Mk. IV standard. L9195-9203 were sold direct to Finland in January 1940. L9309, 9311, 9312, 9376, 9377, 9380, 9384 were sold to the R.C.A.F. in February 1940.
L9485-9624	100	Handley Page H.P.54 Halifax I/II	L9485-9534, 9560-9584, 9600 9608 (84), Mk. I (of which L9534 became Mk. II prototype); L9609-9624 (16), Mk. II
L9635-9703	50	Airspeed A.S.10 Oxford I	L9635-9650, L9692-9703, intermediate version; L9651-9660, L9680-9691, advanced trainers.
L9704	1	Vickers Warwick	Bristol Centaurus engines initially fitted, Pratt & Whitney Double Wasps later.
L9705	1	Miles M.3B Falcon Six	Known as " Gillette Falcon " in 1944 with experimental "knife edge" wings.
L9706	1	Miles M.13 Hobby	G-AFAW for wind tunnel tests.
L9714-9785	60	Fairey Swordfish I	L9714-9743 and L9756-9785.
L9786	1	Short S.22 Scion Senior Floatplane	G-AETH acquired for evaluation. Sank at sea, 1944.
L9790-9999	137	Bristol 152 Beaufort I	L9790-9838, 9851-9897, 9932-9972. Continued in " N " (Second) Series (*q.v.*). L9940-9941, 9954, 9956, 9957, 9960, 9967, 9968 shipped direct overseas.

" M " AS A SUFFIX

THE letter " M " was not used in the normal way as a prefix to a numerical series, because it was already in use for a non-flying series of airframes. After its flying days were over, an aircraft was often relegated for ground instructional use. Up until 1921 such aircraft had retained their original service number, but from 1921 such airframes were allotted an R.A.F number in numerical sequence with the letter " M " as a suffix to denote the " Maintenance " series.

No full documentation for this series exists, and the earliest recording is 540M for a Bristol Fighter at No. 1 School of Technical Training pre-war, and 565M (ex-J9170, Fairey IIIF) is the earliest recorded re-numbering into the series. Since the series consists mainly of aircraft re-numbered from the normal aircraft series throughout the book, known airframes are not recorded here.

Acquisitions in the " M " series were recorded in numerical/chronological sequence, but not necessarily in batches of types, *e.g.*,

747M (ex-K2504) Avro Tutor
748M (ex-K3100) Hawker Audax
749M (ex-K1942) Hawker Fury
750M (ex-J9673) Fairey IIIF

On the other hand, when a particular type was withdrawn from service, batches did occur, *e.g.*,

679M (ex-K1233) Avro Tutor
680M (ex-K1790) Avro Tutor
681M (ex-K1792) Avro Tutor
682M (ex-K1793) Avro Tutor
683M (ex-K1794) Avro Tutor

When war came in 1939 the series had reached 1600M, and some 4,500 aircraft became instructional airframes during the war. Some impressed civil aircraft, unfit for flying, came direct into the " M " series, *e.g.*, 2080M (ex-G-AABX Avian) and similarly some U.S.A.A.F. aircraft came direct into the series without having a normal serial allotted. The series still continues and is now subscribed to over the 8000M mark.

NAVAL INDEPENDENCE 1916-1930

ONLY one major allocation of numbers occurs outside the alphabetical/chronological sequence of identity letter/numbers of British military aircraft, and this concerns the aircraft used by the Royal Naval Air Service up to 1918, followed by aircraft intended for fleet or coastal work ordered up to 1930. The R.F.C. and R.N.A.S. having jointly reached 10,000 in 1915, the R.F.C. started all over again from No. 1 with an alphabetical prefix, starting with " A " as already shown, while the Navy moved exactly half-way through the alphabet and started a new series with " N " as their prefix. It was pure coincidence that " N " stood for Navy but some contractors and units, observing aircraft with N prefixes, assumed that it was applicable to all Naval aircraft and applied it to some aircraft already under construction or in service. This caused some confusion in accounting, but an R.N.A.S. General Memorandum on the subject made the position clear.

The Navy did not intend to work through their numbers in sequence, but to allot blocks of numbers. Numbers under 1,000 were reserved for experimental aircraft, and 1,000 and over to production aircraft; these were further subdivided. Divisions were influenced by the class of aircraft, the Admiralty classifications being as follows: N.1a, Ships' Aeroplanes; N.1b, Single-seat Fighter Seaplanes; N.1c, Reconnaissance Fighter Seaplanes; N.2a, Light Boat or Seaplane; N.2b, Medium boat or Seaplane; N.3, Large Flying Boat.

EXPERIMENTAL SEAPLANES

N1–499 STARTING at No. 1 with the new " N " prefix, the R.N.A.S. allotted numbers to all their seaplanes ordered on contracts for experimental aircraft and the initial allocation, extending up to N300, was used until 1928 when up to N255 had been taken up. Missing numbers may be taken in general as allotted for aircraft ordered but not built, but official records do give Nos. 3, 6-7, 11-13 and 99 as blank numbers. Allocations for 196 and 244 cannot be ascertained.

In 1916 the number N300 was taken up for the first Sopwith Baby Seaplane built by Blackburn, but apart from this the system was discontinued at N255.

(N.B.—" P.V.", standing for " Private Venture " in other sections of the book, stands for " Port Victoria " in this section.)

N1	1	Port Victoria P.V.2	Built by R.N.A.S. using a Sopwith Baby fuselage. Modified to P.V.2*bis*.
N2	1	Whitehead Seaplane	Cancelled. 150 h.p. Smith engine envisaged.
N4	1	Sopwith Baby	130 h.p. Clerget.
N5	1	Sopwith 2F.1 Camel	Prototype. Crashed on take-off on second flight, 27.3.17.
N8	1	Port Victoria P.V.4	Built by R.N.A.S. Two-seat floatplane. Proved unsatisfactory.
N9	1	Fairey III	Fairey No. F.127, used in catapult experiments. Later K-103, then G-EAAJ.
N10	1	Fairey III/IIIA	Fairey No. F.128. Variously modified and later became G-EALQ.
N14	1	Wight N.1b Triplane	Wight Type 4. 130 h.p. Clerget. Not accepted after maker's trial.
N15	1	Nieuport As.14 Seaplane	Cancelled.
N16-17	2	Westland N.1b Scout Seaplane	N16 experimental floats, N17 standard floats.
N18-19	2	Norman Thompson Cruiser Flying Boat	Norman Thompson flying boat with two 320 h.p. Sunbeam engines.
N20-25	6	Submarine Patrol Aircraft (Pusher Type)	Ordered from Shorts (N20-21), Phoenix (N22-23) and Supermarine (N24-25) but later cancelled.
N26	1	Norman Thompson Flying Boat	Norman Thompson flying boat with one 140 h.p. Hispano engine.
N27-32	6	Handley Page N.2a (H.P. R/200)	N27-28 with float, and N29 with wheeled, undercarriage were built. N30 landplane & N31-32 floatplanes were cancelled.
N33-35	3	Robey Seaplane	Presumed allocation for cancellation of Robey Seaplane order concerning three aircraft.
N36	1	Short 200 Seaplane	200 h.p. engine replaced by 260 h.p. Sunbeam. Flown 21.8.17.
N37	1	Norman Thompson N.2a Tandem-seater	Flying boat fighter. 150 h.p., later 200 h.p., Hispano engine.
N38-40	3	Beardmore W.B.4 (N.1a)	N38 tested 20.5.18. N39-40 not completed.
N41-43	3	Beardmore W.B.5 (N.1a)	N41-42 only built. N43 not completed.
N44-49	6	Mann Egerton H.1/2 N.1a Seaboat Scout	N44, H.1; N45, H.2; N46-49, not completed.
N50	1	Grain Griffin	Converted Sopwith B.1. Allotted to Mediterranean Area, 31.12.18.

Serial Nos.	*Qty.*	*Aircraft Type*	*Remarks*
N51-52	2	Kingsbury-Davis	Gun machine project. Cancelled. One fuselage completed.
N53-54	2	Port Victoria P.V.5/5a	Built by R.N.A.S. N53, P.V.5; N54, P.V.5A.
N55	1	Port Victoria P.V.9	Built by R.N.A.S. First flown December 1917.
N56-58	3	Blackburn N.1b "Nib"	Hull only of N56 built by November 1918. Completed as Pellet G-EBHF. N57-58 were cancelled in 1917 before completion.
N59-61	3	Supermarine N.1b Baby	N59 used for extensive tests, first with 200 h.p. Hispano, then with a 200 h.p. Sunbeam Arab; N60 to Grain as spare. N61 was cancelled.
N62-63	2	Handley Page Type T	Experimental folding wings for Felixstowe F.3. Project cancelled before completion.
N64	1	Felixstowe F.3	Prototype used operationally. Written off 15.5.18.
N65	1	Felixstowe F.2c	Experimental F.2 used operationally from Felixstowe.
N66-73	8	Short N.2b	N66-7 only built. N66 was flown from December 1917.
N74	1	Sopwith T.1 Cuckoo	200 h.p. Hispano engine until January 1918 when fitted with Sunbeam Arab engine.
N75	1	Kingsbury Davis Triplane	Gun machine project cancelled due to other commitments by firm.
N76-81	6	Fairey N.2a Folding Aeroplane	2-seat tractor biplane project with 200 h.p. Sunbeam. Not built.
N82-83	2	Norman Thompson N.2c	N82 first flew October 1918. N83 constructed, but not erected.
N84-85	2	Tellier Flying Boat	200 h.p. Hispano. Gun trials at Grain.
N86-87	2	Phoenix P.5 Cork I/II	Hulls built by May, Harden and May. N86, Mk. I; N87, Mk. II.
N88-89	2	Fairey N.3	Cancelled, presumably in favour of N118-119.
N90	1	Felixstowe F.5	Prototype. Used for hydrophone trials from Grain, May 1918.
N91-96	6	Parnall Panther	N91 type tests, N92 fleet trials, N93 floating trials, N94 proof loading tests.
N97-98	2	Short School Seaplane	Trainer seaplane project. Cancelled. Numbers re-allotted.
N97-98	2	C.E.1 (Coastal Experimental No. 1)	Built by the Royal Aircraft Factory. N97, R.A.F. 3a engine; N98, Sunbeam Maori engine.

N100-106	7	Grain Griffin	R.N.A.S. built. N100 and N102, Sunbeam Arab engines; N101, N103-106, B.R.2 engines.
N107-109	3	Norman Thompson School	Project for flying boat trainers. Cancelled.
N110-112	3	Short Shirl	N110, Vee type undercarriage; N111, divided undercarriage; N112 was converted to a 2-seater.
N113-115	3	Blackburn Blackburd	N113 and N115 shipped to Mediterranean, 1919.
N116-117	2	Sage School N.4a/b/c	N116, N.4a converted to N.4b; N117, N.4c, crashed at New haven.
N118-119	2	Fairey Atalanta	N118, hull only built by The Phoenix Dynamo Co.; N119 built by Dick Kerr Ltd.
N120-122	3	Short Cromarty	N120 only completed. N121 partly built.
N123	1	Felixstowe Fury	Crashed on tests at Felixstowe and written off.
N124-126	3	Vickers Valentia	Built by Vickers (Barrow). Hulls built at Cowes.
N127	1	Felixstowe F.5	Cancelled. Ordered from May, Harden & May Ltd. and Vickers Ltd.
N128	1	Felixstowe F.5L	Ordered from America.
N129	1	Fairey Titania	Fairey No. F.337. Hull built by Fyfes at Hamble. Erected by The Phoenix Dynamo Co. Ltd.
N130	1	Felixstowe Fury	Construction abandoned September 1919 following crash of N123.
N131-132	2	Vickers Vigilant	Project with 8 Rolls-Royce Condor engines.
N133-135	3	Fairey Pintail I-III	Fairey Nos. F. 339-341. Delivery: N133 (Mk. I), 7.7.20, N134 (Mk. II), 25.5.21, N135 (Mk. III), 8.11.21.
N136-138	3	Parnall Puffin	Experimental aircraft contract.
N139	1	Blackburn Swift	Civil demonstration aircraft, G-EAVN, purchased in January 1921.
N140-142	3	Blackburn Dart	Experimental aircraft contract.
N143-145	3	Handley Page H.P.19 Hanley	To Air Ministry Specification 3/20. N143, Mk. I; N144, Mk. II; N145, Mk. III.
N146	1	Supermarine Seal	Basically Seagull type with tractor airscrew.
N147	1	Vickers Viking III	G-EAUK, acquired January 1921 for trials.
N148-149	2	English Electric M.3 Ayr	450 h.p. Lion IIB engines.
N150-152	3	Blackburn Blackburn	Blackburn Fleet Spotter to Air Ministry Specification 11/23.
N153-155	3	Avro Bison I/II	N154 had raised top wing to Mk. II standard.
N156-157	2	Vickers Viking V	Delivered 1922.

Serial Nos.	Qty.	Aircraft Type	Remarks
N158	1	Supermarine Seagull II	Improved Seagull I with revised tankage arrangement.
N159	1	Supermarine Seal	Experimental aircraft.
N160-162	3	Parnall Plover	N160, Bristol Jupiter engine; N161, amphibian version; N162, Armstrong Siddeley Jaguar engine.
N163-165	3	Fairey Flycatcher I	Fairey Nos. F.406-408. Deck-landing fighter to Air Ministry Specification 6/22. N163, initially Jaguar, later Jupiter, engine; N164, ship-plane with float or ski undercarriage, Jaguar engine; N165, amphibian, Jupiter engine.
N166-167	2	Blackburn Cubaroo	Experimental aircraft.
N168	1	English Electric P.6 Kingston.	Wooden construction.
N169	1	Vickers 83 Viking VII	Later named Vanellus.
N170	1	Supermarine Sea Lion II	Rebuilt Sea Lion II, G-EBAH, acquired in December 1923.
N171-172	2	Avro Ava I/II	N171, Mk. I; N172, Mk. II.
N173	1	Fairey Fremantle	Fairey No. F.420. G-EBLZ temporarily flown as N173.
N174-175	2	Supermarine Swan	To Air Ministry Specification 21/22. N175 became G-EBJY in 1924.
N176	1	Dornier Dolphin III	Acquired for evaluation.
N177-178	2	Felixstowe F.5 (Basic)	N177, metal hull (Short S.2); N178, hollow bottom hull (Saunders).
N179	1	Short Singapore I	Short No. S.677. Loaned to Sir Alan Cobham as G-EBUP, returned to R.A.F.
N180	1	Supermarine Sheldrake	Experimental development of Seagull in 1927.
N181-182	2	Parnall Peto	N181, Armstrong Siddeley Mongoose; N182, Bristol Lucifer IV.
N183-184	2	Beardmore Inverness	Rohrbach design.
N185	1	Blackburn Iris I/II/IV	Ordered January 1925 to Air Ministry Specification R.14/24. Variously modified.
N186	1	Saro A.3 Valkyrie	Three Rolls-Royce Condor IIIa engines. Ordered February 1925.
N187	1	Hawker Hedgehog	G-EBJN reserved for use as civil demonstration aircraft.
N188-189	2	Blackburn Airedale	First post-war monoplane for naval use as fleet spotter.
N190-192	3	Fairey Ferret I-III	Fairey Nos. F.538-40. To Air Ministry Specification 37/22. Mks. I-III respectively.
N193	1	Short S.1 Cockle	Short No. S.638, G-EBKA, acquired in July 1925.
N194-195	2	Gloster III/IIIA/IIIB	Schneider Trophy aircraft. N194 became IIIA, N195 IIIB was registered G-EBLJ.

N196	1	Supermarine S.4	Presumed Schneider Trophy aircraft G-EBLP.
N197	1	Saunders Medina	Presumed ex-G-EBMG.
N198	1	Fairey IIIF	Fairey No. F.574. To Air Ministry Specification 19/24. Tested both as landplane and seaplane.
N199-200	2	Short S.6 Sturgeon	To Air Ministry Specification 1/24. Convertible wheel/float undercarriage.
N201-202	2	Parnall Pike	Fleet fighter to Air Ministry Specification 1/24.
N203-204	2	Blackburn Ripon I/II	Landplane/seaplane versions. N203, Mk. I; N204, Mk. II.
N205-206	2	H.P.31 Harrow T.B.	First flown 24.4.26. To Air Ministry Specification 21/23. Used as test bed.
N207	1	Blackburn Sprat	Designed as convertible wheel/float trainer to Air Ministry Specification 5/24.
N208	1	Vickers Vendace	Ordered September 1925 to Air Ministry Specification 5/24 for a floatplane trainer.
N209-210	2	Avro Avocet	To Air Ministry Specification 17/25. N209, wheeled undercarriage; N210, floatplane of High Speed Flight in 1929.
N211	1	Vickers Vireo	To Air Ministry Specification 17/25.
N212-213	2	Supermarine Seamew	Scaled-down version of Southampton to Air Ministry Specification 31/24.
N214	1	Saunders A.4 Medina	Presumed allocation for G-EBMG during tests.
N215	1	Gloster Gnatsnapper I	Ordered May 1929 to Air Ministry Specification 21/26.
N216	1	Fairey Flycatcher II	Fairey No. F.873 to Air Ministry Specification 33/26. Mercury or Jaguar engines.
N217	1	Parnall Perch	Deck-landing trainer to Air Ministry Specification 5/24.
N218	1	Supermarine Southampton II	Metal-hull version of Southampton with Lion engines.
N219-221	3	Supermarine S.5	To Air Ministry Specification S.6/26 for Schneider Trophy.
N222-224	3	Gloster-Napier IV	To Air Ministry Specification 5/26. N222 converted to IVA, N223-224 to IVB.
N225	1	Fairey IIIF	Fairey No. F.890, 2nd IIIF Prototype.
N226	1	Short Crusader	Designed for 1927 Schneider Trophy Race.
N227	1	Gloster S.S.35 Gnatsnapper	Mks. I, II, III in succession, with Mercury, Jaguar, Kestrel engines.
N228-229	2	Short S.10 Gurnard	N228, Bristol Jupiter X engine; N229, Rolls-Royce F.XII engine. Wheel/float undercarriages.

Serial Nos.	*Qty.*	*Aircraft Type*	*Remarks*
N230	1	Vickers Vildebeest	Prototype. Vickers Types 132, 192, 194 Srs. I to III. Became G-ABGE and further modified.
N231	1	Blackburn Ripon II	Experimental.
N232-233	2	Parnall Pipit	Ordered July 1927 to Air Ministry Specification 21/26.
N234	1	Blackburn Nautilus	Ordered June 1928 to Air Ministry Specification 22/26.
N235	1	Fairey Fleetwing	Fairey No. F.1132. To Air Ministry Specification 22/26. Wheel/float undercarriage.
N236	1	Blackburn Beagle	Ordered December 1926 to Air Ministry Specification 24/25.
N237	1	Hawker Hoopoe	To Air Ministry Specification 21/26. Wheel/float undercarriage. Mercury, Jaguar and Panther engines fitted in succession.
N238	1	Blackburn Iris III	Prototype Mk. III. Delivered November 1929.
N239	1	Avro Buffalo II	Avro 571 (G-EBNW) rebuilt as Avro 572.
N240	1	Saro A.7 Severn	Flown to Aden for trials. Sunk in Channel 13.7.32.
N241	1	Blackburn Sydney	General Reconnaissance flying boat to A.M. Spec. R.5/27.
N242	1	Short S.11 Valetta	Became G-AAJY.
N243	1	Short Singapore II	Experimental.
N245	1	Saro Severn	Experimental.
N246	1	Short Singapore II	Flown to Aden for tropical trials.
N247-248	2	Supermarine S.6	Built for 1929 Schneider Trophy Contest. Modified to S.6A.
N249-250	2	Gloster-Napier VI	Built for 1929 Schneider Trophy Contest.
N251-253	3	Supermarine Southampton	N251, A14 hull; N252, Bristol Jupiter X engines; N253, Rolls-Royce Kestrel IV engines, became K2888.
N254	1	Gloster Gnatsnapper	Modified design of Gnatsnapper to Air Ministry Specification 16/30.
N255	1	Parnall Peto	First of six ordered.
N300	1	Sopwith Baby	Built by the Blackburn Aeroplane Co.

EXPERIMENTAL NAVAL AEROPLANES

N500–999

ONLY 47 numbers were taken up in this allocation, all during the period 1916-1917. It is doubtful if any of these experimental aircraft survived to 1919.

N500	1	Sopwith Triplane	Prototype with 110 h.p. Clerget engine.
N501	1	Wight Landplane	225 h.p. Rolls-Royce engine. Scrapped 15.9.16.
N502	1	Blackburn Triplane	Accepted at Eastchurch 20.2.17.
N503	1	Sopwith Pup	Admiralty Type 9901.
N504	1	Sopwith Triplane	2nd prototype with 130 h.p. Clerget engine.
N505-506	2	Parnall Zepp Strafer	N505, Sunbeam Maori engine; N506 not built (190 h.p. Rolls-Royce engine projected).
N507-508	2	Short Day Bomber	Project cancelled. Two 200 h.p. Sunbeams planned.
N509-510	2	Sopwith Triplane	N509, 150 h.p. Hispano; N510, 200 h.p. Hispano engine.
N511-514	4	Armstrong Whitworth F.K.10 Quadruplane	N511 (Fighter); N512 (Bomber) and N514 (Fighter) built by The Phoenix Dynamo Company as F.K.10s. N513 was not accepted.
N515-516	2	Sunbeam Bomber	Record of N515 (Sunbeam No. 171) only built.
N517-518	2	Sopwith 1F.1 Fighter	Camel prototypes. N517 to test at Brooklands 26.2.17.
N519-520	2	Handley Page Triplane Raider N.1a	Not built. 320 h.p. Sunbeam engine planned.
N521-522	2	Nieuport Triplane	130 h.p. Clerget. N521 only purchased. Transferred to R.F.C.
N523	1	Avro 523 Pike	Known as Avro Fighter. Built at Hamble.
N524	1	Sopwith Triplane	Loaned to French and returned to R.N.A.S.
N525	1	Beardmore W.B.1 Bomber	Delivered to Cranwell 8.6.17.
N526-531	6	Caproni Ca 42	Bomber triplanes acquired from Italy and returned to Italian Forces in 1918.
N532	1	Nieuport Triplane	110 h.p. Clerget. Transferred from R.F.C.
N533-538	6	Sopwith Triplane	Built by Clayton & Shuttleworth. 130 h.p. Clerget engines. 2 Vickers guns.
N539-540	2	Port Victoria P.V.7/P.V.8	N539, P.V.7 Grain Kitten; N540, P.V.8E astchurch Kitten.
N541-543	3	Sopwith Triplane	130 h.p. Clerget. Loaned to French Government. Returned.
N544-545	2	Voisin Gun Machine	French Voisin (200 h.p. Hispano) loaned for gun trials.
N546	1	Wight Quadruplane	110 h.p. Clerget. To Martlesham Heath 1.2.16.

PRODUCTION NAVAL CLASS N.1 AND N.2 SEAPLANES

N1000–2999 THIS range of numbers was reserved by the Admiralty's Air Department for production floatplanes and light flying boats. Documentation on allocations is 100 per cent complete and numbers and ranges of numbers omitted may all be taken as not allotted.

Serial Nos.	*Qty.*	*Aircraft Type*	*Remarks*
N1000-1009	10	Fairey Campania	Fairey Aviation Nos. F.16-25. Engines installed were as follows: N1000-1005, Rolls-Royce Eagle V; N1006, Sunbeam Maori II; N1007-1009, Rolls-Royce Eagle VII.
N1010-1039	30	Sopwith Baby	First production batch by the Blackburn Aeroplane & Motor Co. Ltd., with altered wing section from the Sopwith standard.
N1040-1059	20	F.B.A. (Franco-British Aviation) Flying Boat	Erected by Norman Thompson. Hulls built in France.
N1060-1069	10	Sopwith Baby	Second production batch by the Blackburn Aeroplane & Motor Co. Ltd.
N1070-1074	5	Admiralty A.D. Naviplane	Cancelled. Ordered from Supermarine Aviation with 140 h.p Smith engines.
N1075-1078	4	F.B.A. (Franco-British Aviation) Flying Boat	Italian-built with 160 h.p. Isotta-Fraschini engines fitted. Presented to R.N.A.S. at Otranto, June 1917.
N1079	1	—	Not allotted.
N1080-1089	10	Short 184 (Improved)	Built by Short Bros. with 240 h.p. Renault engines. N1081 had Linton-Hope floats fitted.
N1090-1099	10	Short 184 (Original)	Built by Short Bros. with 240 h.p. Renault engines, except N1098 which had a 260 h.p. Sunbeam engine.
N1100-1129	30	Sopwith Baby	Built by the Blackburn Aeroplane & Motor Co. Ltd. with 130 h.p. Clergets, except N1124 which had a 110 h.p. Clerget. N1121 was presented to the French.
N1130-1139	10	Short 184	Built by Frederick Sage & Co., Peterborough, with 240 h.p. Renault engines. N1130-1134 were of the Improved Type and N1135-1139 were of the Original Type.
N1140-1149	10	Short 184 (Improved)	Built by S. E. Saunders & Co. with 240 h.p. Renault engines.
N1150-1159	10	Short 320	Initial production batch by Short Bros. 320 h.p. Sunbeam Cossack engines fitted.

N1160-1179	20	Curtiss H.12	Cancelled. Two 250 h.p. Sunbeam engines planned.
N1180-1189	10	White & Thompson Flying Boat	Built by Norman Thompson. N1180-1185 had 120 h.p. Beardmore engines and N1186-1189 had 150 h.p. Hispano engines.
N1190-1219	30	Fairey Hamble Baby	Built by Parnall & Sons with 130 h.p. Clerget engines fitted.
N1220-1229	10	Short 184	Built by Robey & Co. Ltd., Lincoln, with 220 h.p. Renault engines.
N1230-1239	10	Short 184	Built by Frederick Sage & Co. Ltd., Peterborough.
N1240-1259	20	Short 184 (Intermediate)	Built by J. S. White & Co. Initial fit: N1240-1249 225 h.p. Sunbeam, N1250-1255 240 h.p. Renault, N1256-1259 260 h.p. Sunbeam.
N1260-1279	20	Short 184	Built by Robey & Co. Ltd. with Sunbeam engines of 225 or 240 h.p., except N1260 which had a 260 h.p. engine. N1260-1269 were of the Intermediate Type and N1270-1271 of the Original Type.
N1280-1289	10	Wight Converted Seaplane	Built by J. S. White & Co. with 260 h.p. Sunbeam engines, except N1280 which had 240 h.p. Renault engines.
N1290-1299	10	Admiralty A.D. Flying Boat	N1290 only completed, by Supermarine Aviation. N1291-1299 cancelled in March 1918.
N1300-1319	20	Short 320	N1312, 1313, 1315, 1316-1319 were delivered to Otranto and N1304 to Malta.
N1320-1339	20	Fairey Hamble Baby	Fairey Aviation Nos. F.129-148. 110 h.p. Clerget engines for first 10, remainder 130 h.p. Clergets.
N1340-1359	20	Sopwith 'Daily Mail'	Cancelled. Pre-war competition aircraft type.
N1360-1389	30	Short 320	Built by the Sunbeam Motor Car Co. Ltd. Deliveries mainly to home stations.
N1390-1409	20	Short 320	Built by Short Bros. Deliveries mainly to Mediterranean Areas.
N1410-1449	40	Sopwith Baby	Built by the Blackburn Aeroplane & Motor Co. Ltd., with 130 h.p. Clerget engines. N1430-1431 delivered to the French with 110 h.p. engines. This batch were fitted for firing Rankin Darts in place of initial machine-gun armament.

N1450–1779 (First Series)

Serial Nos.	*Qty.*	*Aircraft Type*	*Remarks*
N1450-1479	30	Fairey Hamble Baby	Fairey Aviation Nos. F.149-178. 130 h.p. Clerget engines.
N1480-1504	25	Short 320	Built by Short Bros. N1485 to Japanese Government.
N1505-1509	5	—	Not allotted.
N1510-1519	10	" Large America " Type	Cancelled. Ordered from the Aircraft Manufacturing Co. with two 250 or 310 h.p. Rolls-Royce engines.
N1520-1529	10	Admiralty A.D. Flying Boat	Built by Supermarine Aviation. N1526, N1528 and N1529 became Channel Mk. Is G-EAEM/L/D. In service 200 h.p. Hispano engines were standard, but N1525 had a Wolseley Viper temporarily fitted.
N1530-1579	50	Maurice Farman Seaplane	Ordered from the Aircraft Manufacturing Company with 140 h.p. Hispano engines. Record of N1530 only.
N1580-1589	10	Short 184	Built by Short Bros. with 240 h.p. Renault engines fitted.
N1590-1599	10	Short 184	Built by Frederick Sage & Co., Peterborough, with 240 h.p. Sunbeam engines in first 3 and 260 h.p. Sunbeams in rest.
N1600-1624	25	Short 184	Built by S. E. Saunders & Co. with 240 h.p. Renault engines, except for last four which had 260 h.p. Sunbeam engines.
N1625-1629	5	—	Not allotted.
N1630-1659	30	Short 184	Built by The Phoenix Dynamo Co. with 240 h.p. Renault engines except last 7 with 260 h.p. Sunbeams.
N1660-1689	30	Short 184	Built by The Brush Electrical Engineering Co. Ltd., Loughborough, with 240 h.p. Renault engines in first 12 and 260 h.p. Sunbeams in remainder.
N1690-1709	20	Short 320	Built by The Sunbeam Motor Car Co. Ltd.
N1710-1719	10	Admiralty A.D. Flying Boat	Built by Supermarine Aviation. N1710, 1711, 1714, 1715, 1716 became Channel Is G-EAEE/K/J/I/H on the Civil Register.
N1720-1739	20	Blackburn Kangaroo	Re-numbered B9970-9989 in the R.F.C. series.
N1740-1759	20	Short 184	Built by the Phoenix Dynamo Co. with 260 h.p. Sunbeam engines initially fitted.
N1760-1774	15	Short 184	Built by S. E. Saunders Ltd., 260 h.p. Sunbeams fitted.
N1775-1779	5	—	Not allotted.

N1780-1799	20	Short 184	Built by Frederick Sage & Co. Ltd., with 260 h.p. Sunbeam engines.
N1800-1819	20	—	Cancelled order.
N1820-1839	20	Short 184	Built by Robey & Co., Lincoln. N1820-1826 had 240 h.p. Renault engines initially fitted and N1827-1839 had 260 h.p. Sunbeams.
N1840-1889	50	Fairey Campania	Ordered from Barclay Curle & Co. Order cut to 12 and N1852-1889 not delivered.
N1890-1959	70	Fairey Campania	Cancelled. Presumed reserved for part of 100 order for Campanias placed with Frederick Sage & Co. and The Sunbeam Motor Car Company.
N1960-2059	100	Hamble Baby	Built by Parnall & Sons with 130 h.p. Clerget engines. N1960-1985 were produced as floatplanes and N1986-2059 as landplanes; the latter were known as Hamble Baby Converts.
N2060-2134	75	Sopwith Baby	Built by the Blackburn Aircraft & Motor Co. with 130 h.p. Clerget engines. N2121 went to U.S.A. in Feb. 1918.
N2135-2139	5	—	Not allotted.
N2140-2159	20	Norman Thompson N.T.4A " Small America "	Built by Norman Thompson with 200 h.p. Hispano engines. N2155 became G-EAOY on the Civil Register.
N2160-2179	20	—	Not allotted.
N2180-2199	20	Wight Seaplane	Built by J. S. White & Co. with 260 h.p. Sunbeam engines. N2195-2199 not delivered.
N2200-2229	30	Wight Converted Seaplane	Cancelled.
N2230-2259	30	Fairey IIIB	Fairey Aviation Nos. F277-306. N2246, N2255-2259 were built as IIIC. N2255 became IIIC G-EAPV.
N2260-2359	100	Norman Thompson N.T.2B	Norman Thompson built with Sunbeam Arab engines. Up to N2294 delivered. N2284 was exhibited at the 1919 Atlantic City Exposition. N2290 became G-EAQO.
N2360-2399	40	Fairey Campania	Built by Fairey Aviation. N2360-2374 had Rolls-Royce Eagle engines and N2375-2399 Sunbeam Maori II engines.
N2400-2429	30	Norman Thompson N.T.2B	Built by Norman Thompson. Majority held in store (less engines) until scrapped.
N2430-2449	20	—	Reservation.

Serial Nos.	*Qty.*	*Aircraft Type*	*Remarks*
N2450-2499	50	Admiralty A.D. Flying Boat	N2450-2455 (6) built by Supermarine Aviation, of which N2451-2452 became Channels G-EAEG/F on the Civil Register. N2462-2499 cancelled followed by further cancellation of N2456-2461.
N2500-2523	24	Norman Thompson N.T.2B	At least 14 built by S. E. Saunders & Co. and fitted with Sunbeam Arab engines.
N2524-2554	31	—	Not allotted.
N2555-2579	25	Norman Thompson N.T.2B	Delivered from mid-December 1917 by Norman Thompson with 150 or 200 h.p. Hispano engines.
N2580-2599	20	—	Cancelled order.
N2600-2659	60	Short 184	N2630-2659 only built by The Brush Electrical Engineering Co. Ltd. and delivered mainly to Mediterranean Areas with 260 h.p. Sunbeams.
N2660-2679	20	—	Cancelled order.
N2680-2739	60	F.B.A. (Franco-British Aviation) Flying Boat	Built by The Gosport Aviation Co. with 100 h.p. Gnôme Monosoupape engines.
N2740-2759	20	Norman Thompson N.T.4A	Ordered from Norman Thompson with 200 h.p. Hispano engines. No delivery record.
N2760-2789	30	Norman Thompson N.T.2B	Built by Norman Thompson. Held in store with Hispano engines installed. N2785-2789 believed not completed.
N2790-2819	30	Short 184	Built by The Brush Electrical Engineering Co. Ltd., Loughborough, with 260 h.p. Sunbeam engines fitted.
N2820-2849	30	Short 184	Built by Robey & Co., Lincoln, with 260 h.p. Sunbeam engines fitted.
N2850-2899	50	Fairey IIIA	Fairey Aviation Nos. F220-269. N2850-2852 and N2889-2899 produced with wheeled undercarriage: remainder built with skid type undercarriage. N2876 became G-EADZ.
N2900-2949	50	Short 184	Built by Robey & Co., Lincoln, with 260 h.p. Sunbeam engines.
N2950-2999	50	Short 184	Built by J. S. White & Co. with 260 h.p. Sunbeam engines. N2986, 2996, 2998 became G-EAJT/BGP/ALC on the Civil Register.

FRENCH AIRCRAFT TYPES

N3000–3999 THE initial purpose of this block allocation was for French aircraft, but the system lapsed after N3299 and was then discontinued.

N3000-3049	50	Henry Farman F.27	Tropical version built in France. 160 h.p. Canton-Unné engines fitted. N3001-3021 delivered to Mudros, of which N3018 was converted to a floatplane. N3025-3049 transferred to the R.F.C.; N3004, 3007 and 3008 presented to the Rumanian Government.
N3050-3099	50	Caudron G.III	French-built with 100 h.p. Anzani engines. Purchased and delivered mainly to equip Royal Naval Air Station Vendome.
N3100-3104	5	Nieuport Scout	French built with 130 h.p. engines.
N3105-3169	65	—	Cancelled order.
N3170-3209	40	Nieuport	French-built. N3170-3173, two-seaters with 110 h.p. Clerget engines; N3174-3183, two-seaters with 130 h.p. Clerget engines; N3184-3197, Nieuport Scout; N3198, Nieuport 12; N3199-3209, Nieuport Scout.
N3210-3239	30	Farman F.40	French-built with 160 h.p. Renault engines installed.
N3240-3299	60	Caudron G.III	50 French-built with 90 h.p. Anzani engines installed. N3270-3279 cancelled.
N3300-3374	75	Norman Thompson N.T.2B	Ordered from Supermarine Aircraft but cancelled before construction.
N3375-3999	—	—	Reserved. Taken up only by SPAD N3399.

LARGE FLYING BOATS

N4000–4999 A range of 1000 numbers was considered sufficient for large flying boats in 1916, but by 1918 it was almost completely subscribed, although many of the orders were cancelled later in that year. Orders for F.2A and F.3 flying boats were changed to F.5 boats and this is reflected in the remarks column.

N4000-4049	50	Felixstowe F.3/F.5	Built by Short Bros. N4000-4035, F.3; N4036-4049, F.5; N4019 became G-EAQT on the Civil Register.
N4050-4059	10	—	Not allotted.

N4060–4729 (First Series)

Serial Nos.	*Qty.*	*Aircraft Type*	*Remarks*
N4060-4074	15	Curtiss H.16	American-built, delivered from March 1918 and fitted with Rolls-Royce Eagle VIII engines in Britain.
N4075-4079	5	—	Not allotted.
N4080-4099	20	Felixstowe F.2A	Built by S. E. Saunders & Co., delivered from late July 1918.
N4100-4149	50	Felixstowe F.3	N4100-4117 (18) built by Dick Kerr Ltd.; N4118-4149 ordered as F.5, of which only N4128 is recorded as delivered.
N4150-4159	10	—	Not allotted.
N4160-4229	70	Felixstowe F.3/F.5	Built by The Phoenix Dynamo Co.; from N4184 completed as F.5s. N4177 became G-EBDQ. No record of delivery beyond N4193.
N4230-4279	50	Felixstowe F.3	Built by Dick Kerr Ltd., delivered before the N4100-49 batch recorded above.
N4280-4309	30	Felixstowe F.2A	Built by S. E. Saunders & Co. Delivered from mid-Nov. 17.
N4310-4321	12	Felixstowe F.3	Built in Malta Dockyard. Deliveries from March 1918.
N4322-4329	8	—	Not allotted.
N4330-4353	24	Curtiss H.12B	American-built. Erected in U.K. with Rolls-Royce Eagle engines fitted. Delivered from late January 1918. N4351-4353 cancelled.
N4354-4359	6	—	Not allotted.
N4360-4397	38	Felixstowe F.3	Built by Malta Dockyard from early September 1918. Quantity ordered reduced to 28.
N4398-4399	2	—	Not allotted.
N4400-4429	30	Felixstowe F.3	Built by The Phoenix Dynamo Company prior to N4160-4229 batch above.
N4430-4479	50	Felixstowe F.2A	Built by S. E. Saunders & Co. Delivered from mid-October 1918.
N4480-4579	100	Felixstowe F.2A/F.5	Quantity reduced to 80. N4505-4509, 4520-4529 and 4555-4559 were cancelled. Hulls were built by May, Harden & May and erection was by the Aircraft Manufacturing Company. Late deliveries were as F.5.
N4580-4629	50	Felixstowe F.2A/F.5	Built by S. E. Saunders & Co.
N4630-4679	50	Felixstowe F.5	Built by the Gosport Aviation Company. N4634 became G-EAIK.
N4680-4729	50	Felixstowe F.5	Cancelled. To have been built by May, Harden and May.

N4730-4779	50	Felixstowe F.5L	Cancelled. To have been built by Dick Kerr Ltd. with Liberty engines.
N4780-4829	50	Felixstowe F.5	Cancelled. To have been built by The Phoenix Dynamo Company.
N4830-4879	50	Felixstowe F.5	Built by Short Bros. Deliveries to N4839 confirmed.
N4880-4889	10	—	Not allotted.
N4890-4999	110	Curtiss H.16	Ordered from U.S.A. N4890-4899 erected in the U.K. with Rolls-Royce Eagle engines. Deliveries from N4900 in 1919 went straight to store without engines and were later scrapped except N4902 and N4905 to Canada. N4950-4999 cancelled.

NAVAL AEROPLANES

N5000–8999

FROM N5000 numbers were reserved for naval aeroplanes, but the system lapsed after Contract A.S. 37750 taking up to N8229, when seaplanes were included.

N5000-5029	30	Maurice Farman S.7 Longhorn	Built by Robey & Co. with 75 h.p. Rolls-Royce Hawk engines. N5010-5016 were transferred to the R.F.C.; N5017-5029 were cancelled.
N5030-5059	30	Maurice Farman S.7 Longhorn	Built by The Brush Electrical Engineering Co. Ltd., Loughborough. 80 h.p. Renault engines installed.
N5060-5079	20	Maurice Farman S.11 Shorthorn	Built by the Eastbourne Aviation Company. 80 h.p. Renault engines.
N5080-5119	40	Sopwith 1½-Strutter (Type 9400 2-seat fighter and Type 9700 1-seat bomber)	Type 9700 except N5080-5087, 5090, 5093, 5096, 5099, 5102, 5105, 5108, 5111, 5114, 5117, 5119 Type 9400. N5088, 5091-5092, 5094-5095, 5097-5098, 5100-5101, 5104, 5113, 5115-5116, 5118 to French.
N5120-5169	50	Sopwith 1½-Strutter (Type 9700 1-seat bomber)	Built by Westland Aircraft. N5122-5123, 5125-5127, 5129-5149 to French.
N5170-5179	10	Sopwith 1½-Strutter (Type 9400 2-seat fighter)	Built by Sopwith Aviation. N5176 to Greek Air Force.
N5180-5199	20	Sopwith Pup	Sopwith Aviation-built with 80 h.p. Le Rhône engines.
N5200-5249	50	Sopwith 1½-Strutter	Built by Mann, Egerton. N5200-5219, Type 9700, of which N5204 and N5213 were

N5200–5769 (First Series)

Serial Nos.	*Qty.*	*Aircraft Type*	*Remarks*
			converted to Type 9400. N5220-5249, Type 9400, of which N5235-5242 (less engines) were transferred to the Belgian Government.
N5250-5279	30	Avro 504B	Built by The Sunbeam Motor Car Co. Ltd. N5261, 5269, 5270 became 504H.
N5280-5309	30	Sage N.3	N5280 only built by Frederick Sage & Co., Peterborough. Remainder cancelled.
N5310-5329	20	Avro 504B	Built by British Caudron Co.
N5330-5349	20	Maurice Farman S.7 Longhorn	Built by The Phoenix Dynamo Company. 75 h.p. Rolls-Royce Hawk engines fitted.
N5350-5389	40	Sopwith Triplane	Built by Clayton & Shuttleworth Ltd., Lincoln, and delivered from early December 1916. N5385 and N5388 were presented to the French.
N5390-5419	30	Bristol Scout " D "	Built by the British & Colonial Aeroplane Co. Ltd. N5390-5399 fitted with 100 h.p. Gnôme Monosoupape engines, N5400-5419 with 80 h.p. Gnôme engines.
N5420-5494	75	Sopwith Triplane	Sopwith Aviation-built. N5430 to R.F.C. N5486 presented to Russia.
N5495-5499	5	—	Not allotted.
N5500-5549	50	Sopwith 1½-Strutter	Type 9700, built by Sopwith Aviation. N5506, 5515, 5527 were converted to Type 9400. N5504 became G-EAVB. N5538-5549 cancelled.
N5550-5559	10	—	Not allotted.
N5560-5599	40	Nieuport XV	Cancelled. 230 h.p. Renault engines planned.
N5600-5624	25	Sopwith 1½-Strutter	Built by the Westland Aircraft Works, N5600-5604 as Type 9700 and N5605-5624 as 9400.
N5625-5629	5	—	Not allotted.
N5630-5654	25	Sopwith 1½-Strutter	Built by Mann, Egerton & Co. Ltd. as Type 9400.
N5655-5659	5	—	Not allotted.
N5660-5709	50	Curtiss JN-4	Order reported as cancelled, but N5670-5673 recorded.
N5710-5719	10	—	Not allotted.
N5720-5749	30	Maurice Farman S.7 Longhorn	Built by the Brush Electrical Engineering Co. Ltd., Loughborough. 70-80 h.p. Renault engines fitted.
N5750-5759	10	Maurice Farman S.7 Longhorn	Built by the Phoenix Dynamo Co. Ltd. 75 h.p. Rolls-Royce Hawk engines fitted.
N5760-5769	10	—	Not allotted.

N5770-5794	25	B.E.2c	Cancelled. To have been built by Robey & Co. with 150 h.p. Hispano engines.
N5795-5799	5	—	Not allotted.
N5800-5829	30	Avro 504B	Built by Parnall & Sons. Ordered late July 1917.
N5830-5859	30	—	Not allotted.
N5860-5909	50	Nieuport Type 24	Built by British Nieuport. 130 h.p. Clerget engines fitted. N5906 went to the U.S.A.
N5910-5934	25	Sopwith Triplane	Ordered from Oakley & Co. First 3 only completed. N5912 extant.
N5935-5939	5	—	Not allotted.
N5940-5954	15	Sopwith 1½-Strutter	Cancelled.
N5955-5959	5	—	Not allotted.
N5960-6009	50	Airco D.H.4	Built by the Westland Aircraft Works with Rolls-Royce Eagle engines. N5995 *et seq* had higher undercarriage. N5970, 5980, 5986, 5987, 5990, 5991, 5994, 5995, 5998, 5999, 6002-6003, 6006, 6007 transferred to the R.F.C. as B3955-3968.
N6010-6029	20	Avro 504B	Built by Parnall & Sons, Bristol. 80 h.p. Gnôme engines fitted. N6015-6029 were transferred to the R.F.C.
N6030-6079	50	SPAD S.7/Nieuport	Cancelled. Re-allotted to Nieuports (130 h.p. Clerget) which were also cancelled.
N6080-6099	20	—	Not allotted.
N6100-6129	30	Beardmore W.B.III	Built by Wm. Beardmore & Co. Ltd. N6100-6112 were Type S.B.3F (Ship-board Type 3) with folding undercarriage, and N6113-6129 were Type S.B.3D (Ship-board Type 3) with dropping undercarriages.
N6130-6159	30	Avro 504B	Built by The Sunbeam Motor Car Co. Ltd. Armed version with gun interrupter and bomb gear.
N6160-6209	50	Sopwith Pup	Sopwith Aviation-built with 80 h.p. Le Rhône engines. N6204 presented to Russia.
N6210-6285	76	SPAD S.7	Ordered from Mann, Egerton, April 1917. N6210 only built.
N6286-6289	4	—	Not allotted.
N6290-6309	20	Sopwith Triplane	Final production of Triplanes by Sopwith Aviation.
N6310-6329	20	Maurice Farman S.11 Shorthorn	Built by the Eastbourne Aviation Company.
N6330-6379	50	Sopwith 1F.1 Camel	First production Camels by Sopwith Aviation. 130 h.p. Clerget engines. N6332 to the R.F.C.

N6380–7199 (First Series)

Serial Nos.	*Qty.*	*Aircraft Type*	*Remarks*
N6380-6429	50	Airco D.H.4	Built by the Aircraft Manufacturing Co. Ltd., Hendon, with R.A.F.3a or B.H.P. engines. N6380, 6382-6387, 6390, 6393, 6397, 6401, 6405, 6409 transferred to the R.F.C.
N6430-6459	30	Sopwith Pup	Built by Wm. Beardmore & Co. as Admiralty Type 9901A with skid under carriage.
N6460-6529	70	Sopwith Pup	N6460-6479 (20) only built by Sopwith Aviation as Admiralty Type 9901. N6480-6529 cancelled.
N6530-6579	50	Nieuport Scout	Cancelled. To have been built by British Nieuport.
N6580-6599	20	SPAD S.7	Built by Mann, Egerton & Co. Ltd. Re-numbered in "A" series.
N6600-6649	50	Sopwith 2F.1 Camel	Sopwith Aviation-built. N6610-6649 originally allotted to Bristol Scout "D".
N6650-6679	30	Avro 504B	Armament trainers, built by A. V. Roe & Co. with 80 h.p. Gnôme engines. N6650-6656 transferred to R.F.C.
N6680-6749	70	Beardmore W.B.III	Built by Wm. Beardmore & Co. as S.B.3D type. Last 30 built were stored without engines.
N6750-6849	100	Sopwith 2F.1 Camel	Built by Beardmore with 150 h.p. B.R.1 engines. Many allotted to warships.
N6850-6899	50	—	Not allotted.
N6900-6929	30	Sopwith T.1 Cuckoo	Built by the Blackburn Ae o-plane Co. Ltd. Sunbeam Arab engines fitted except for N6910, 6926, 6929, which had Wolseley Vipers.
N6930-6949	20	Sopwith T.1 Cuckoo	Ordered from Pegler Ltd. in 1917, delivered in 1919 with Arab engines.
N6950-6999	50	Sopwith T.1 Cuckoo	Built by the Blackburn Aeroplane & Motor Co. Ltd. with Sunbeam Arab engines, except N6971, 6997, 6999 which had Wolseley Vipers.
N7000-7099	100	Sopwith T.1 Cuckoo	Ordered from Fairfield Engineering Co. with Sunbeam Arab engines. Delivery of 31 only confirmed.
N7100-7149	50	Sopwith 2F.1 Camel	Ordered from Wm. Beardmore & Co. Ltd., but N7140-7149 were sub-contracted to Arrol Johnson Ltd.
N7150-7199	50	Sopwith T.1 Cuckoo	Built by the Blackburn Aeroplane & Motor Co. Ltd. with

			Sunbeam Arab engines, except N7151-7155 which had Wolseley Vipers fitted.
N7200-7299	100	Sopwith 2F.1 Camel	Ordered from Fairey Aviation. Cancelled.
N7300-7349	50	Sopwith 2F.1 Camel	Ordered from Pegler Ltd. Cancelled.
N7350-7389	40	Sopwith 2F.1 Camel	Ordered from Arrol Johnson Ltd. Up to N7369 only confirmed as delivered.
N7390-7399	10	—	Believed not allotted.
N7400-7549	150	Parnall Panther	Built by the British & Colonial Aeroplane Co. Ltd. N7530 became G-EBCM.
N7550-7649	100	Short Shirl	Ordered from the Blackburn Aeroplane & Motor Co. Ltd. Cancelled before end of war.
N7650-7679	30	Sopwith 2F.1 Camel	Ordered from Wm. Beardmore & Co. Ltd. Cancelled.
N7680-7841	162	Parnall Panther	Ordered from the British & Colonial Aeroplane Co. Ltd. Cancelled.
N7842-7849	8	—	Not allotted.
N7850-7979	130	Sopwith 2F.1 Camel	Ordered from Frederick Sage & Co. Cancelled.
N7980-8079	100	Sopwith T.1 Cuckoo	Built by the Blackburn Aeroplane & Motor Co. Ltd. Up to N8011 only confirmed delivered. Sunbeam Arab or Wolseley Viper engines fitted, except for N7990 with experimental fitting of Rolls-Royce Falcon.
N8080-8129	50	—	No record.
N8130-8179	50	Sopwith 2F.1 Camel	Built by Hooper & Co. Delivery up to N8159 confirmed.
N8180-8229	50	Sopwith 2F.1 Camel	Built by Clayton & Shuttleworth Ltd. Delivery up to N8204 confirmed.
N8230-8999	—	—	Not taken up.

SEAPLANES AGAIN

N9000–9999

WHEN the N1000-2999 allocation to floatplanes and light flying boats was fully taken up in 1918, a further allocation was made from 9000 upwards, but in 1919 it became a general policy to number all production marine aircraft in this range and it was completed in the mid-'twenties. N9000 was delivered on July 25th, 1918; N9450 marked the end of 1914-1918 War orders and the start of post-war fleet aircraft orders.

N9000–9607 (First Series)

Serial Nos.	*Qty.*	*Aircraft Type*	*Remarks*
N9000-9059	60	Short 184	Built by Robey & Co. 260 h.p. Sunbeam Maori enines fitted.
N9060-9099	40	Short 184	Built by the Brush Electrical Engineering Co. Ltd. 260 h.p. Sunbeam Maori engines fitted. N9096 became G-EBBM.
N9100-9139	40	Short 184	Built by J. S. White & Co. Sunbeam Maori engines fitted, except N9135 which had a Manitou.
N9140-9169	30	Short 184	Built by Robey & Co. with 260 h.p. Sunbeam Maori engines, except N9152 which had a 275 h.p. Maori III.
N9170-9199	30	Short 184	Ordered from Supermarine Aviation with 260 h.p. Sunbeam Maori engines. 15 only confirmed as delivered.
N9200-9229	30	—	Reservation.
N9230-9259	30	Fairey IIIB/C	Built by Fairey Aviation as IIIB and converted to IIIC in 1919 for the North Russian Expedition.
N9260-9289	30	Short 184	Built by The Brush Electrical Engineering Co. Ltd. 275 h.p. Sunbeam Maori III engines.
N9290-9349	60	Short 184	Ordered from Robey & Co., Lincoln. Up to N9317 only confirmed as delivered.
N9350-9399	50	Short 184	Cancelled order with The Brush Electrical Engineering Co.
N9400-9449	50	Short 184	Cancelled order with J. S. White & Co., East Cowes.
N9450-9499	50	Fairey IIID	Fairey Aviation Nos. F.344-393. Rolls-Royce Eagle engines. N9467, 9478, 9479, 9485, 9491, 9497, 9498 fitted with dual control.
N9500-9535	36	Westland Walrus	Development of D.H.9A basic design for fleet work, using D.H.9/D.H.9A parts.
N9536-9561	26	Blackburn Dart	First post-war torpedo bomber to go into production.
N9562-9566	5	Supermarine Seagull II	First post-war flying boat in R.A.F. service.
N9567-9578	12	Fairey IIID	Napier Lion engines fitted.
N9579-9590	12	Blackburn Blackburn	Known as Blackburn T.S.R. N9589 fitted with dual control.
N9591-9602	12	Avro Bison I/IA	N9594 converted to amphibian.
N9603-9607	5	Supermarine Seagull	N9604, Mk. I; N9605, Mk. IV (became G-AAIZ); N9603 and N9606-9607 not confirmed.

N9608-9610	3	Parnall Plover	N9608 and N9609 landplane, N9610 floatplane, version.
N9611-9619	9	Fairey Flycatcher	Fairey Aviation Nos. F430-438.
N9620-9629	10	Blackburn Dart	Second production batch, ordered in 1923.
N9630-9641	12	Fairey IIID	Fairey Aviation Nos. F.445-56. N9630-9635 fitted with Rolls-Royce Eagle engines and N9636-9641 with Napier Lion II engines.
N9642-9654	13	Supermarine Seagull III	N9653 and N9654 became G-EBXH and G-EBXI on the Civil Register.
N9655-9680	26	Fairey Flycatcher	N9672 was first of type for overseas.
N9681-9686	6	Blackburn Blackburn	Known as Blackburn T.S.R.
N9687-9696	10	Blackburn Dart	Ordered in 1923.
N9697	1	Fairey Flycatcher	Collided in mid-air with S1273, 25.2.32.
N9698-9701	4	—	Allocation not ascertained.
N9702-9708	7	Parnall Plover	N9705 became G-EBON in July 1926.
N9709-9713	5	English Electric P.5 Kingston	N9709, Mk. I; N9712, Mk. II; N9713, Mk. III; N9710 became Cork I.
N9714-9723	10	Blackburn Dart	Ordered in 1924.
N9724-9729	6	Handley Page Hanley/Hendon	To Air Ministry Specification 3/20. Built as H.P.19 Hanley and converted to H.P.25 Hendon.
N9730-9791	62	Fairey IIID	Fitted with Napier Lion engines.
N9792-9823	32	Blackburn Dart	Ordered for Fleet Air Arm in August 1924.
N9824-9835	12	Blackburn Blackburn	N9832 was reconstructed in January 1927 and again in September 1929.
N9836-9853	18	Avro 555A Bison II	Ordered in July 1924.
N9854-9895	42	Fairey Flycatcher	Ordered in August 1924.
N9896-9901	6	Supermarine Southampton I	N9896 converted to become the Mk. III prototype.
N9902-9965	64	Fairey Flycatcher	N9906 Southampton Mk. I/III compromised this number.
N9966-9977	12	Avro Bison II	Ordered December 1924.
N9978-9989	12	Blackburn Blackburn II	N9989 fitted with dual control.
N9990-9999	10	Blackburn Dart	Ordered in January 1925.

"N" IS USED AGAIN

N1000–9999

IN spite of the fact that the R.N.A.S. had used the "N" series, which continued for Fleet Air Arm aircraft up to 1926, this series was used again in 1937 as a follow-up to the "L" series. It was the first series to have "blackout blocks" throughout, but an exception was made for purchases of aircraft in America.

N1000–2016 (Second Series)

Serial Nos.	*Qty.*	*Aircraft Type*	*Remarks*
N1000-1186	135	Bristol 152 Beaufort I	N1000-1047, 1074-1118, 1145-1186. Batch continued from "L" series. N1183 was not delivered, being destroyed in the factory by enemy action. N1110 became Mk. II prototype. N1005-1007, 1021, 1027, 1029, 1030, 1045, 1078, 1107 were shipped direct to Canada. N1004, 1008, 1076, 1145 transferred to the South African Air Force.
N1190-1194	5	Airspeed A.S.10 Oxford	Advanced trainer version.
N1200-1320	97	Westland Lysander II	N1200-1227, N1240-1276, N1289-1320. N1289 and N1320 were converted to Mk. III. N1208, 1245, 1300 were transferred to Free French Forces.
N1323-1324	2	Airspeed A.S.39	Fleet Shadower prototypes to Air Ministry Specification S.23/37. N1324 was not completed.
N1330-1339	10	Avro 652A Anson I	N1330-1336 delivered direct to Australia.
N1345-1528	148	Armstrong Whitworth A.W.38 Whitley V	N1345-1394, N1405-1444, N1459-1508, N1521-1528.
N1531	1	Monospar Tricycle	Served in Nos. 92 and 93 Squadrons.
N1535-1812	202	Boulton Paul P.82 Defiant I	N1535-1582, N1610-1653, N1671-1706, N1725-1773, N1788-1812. N1550 and N1551 were converted to Mk. II. Conversions to T.T.III included: N1538, 1541, 1542, 1544, 1545, 1548, 1549, 1553, 1558, 1559, 1562, 1563, 1571, 1577, 1579, 1610, 1614, 1622, 1624, 1631-1634, 1639, 1640, 1642, 1643, 1648, 1672, 1674, 1683, 1689, 1691, 1693, 1696, 1697, 1699, 1700, 1701, 1726, 1728, 1730, 1733, 1736, 1742, 1744, 1747, 1751, 1756, 1764, 1771, 1772, 1789, 1796, 1807, 1812.
N1818-1847	30	D.H.82B Queen Bee	First delivery to "U" Flight, A.A.C.U.
N1854-2016	127	Fairey Fulmar I	N1854-1893, N1910-1959, N1980-2016. N1856-7 were planned as floatplanes. N1854 became G-AIBE. Main deliveries to Royal Navy, but N1883, 1931, 1957, 1987, 1993, 1999, 2004 were used by R.A.F.

N2020-2258	189	Fairey Battle I	Built at Stockport and Ringway. N2020-2066, N2082-2131, N2147-2190, N2211-2258. Several conversions to trainers. N2219 to Poland. N2111-2117, 2120-2123, 2130-2131, 2149, 2153-2155, 2211-2218, 2220-2222, 2224 (29) sold to Turkish Air Force in mid-1939.
N2259	1	Miles M.14A Magister	Replacement for L6917.
N2265-2314	50	Gloster Gladiator II	N2265-2302 were temporarily fitted with arrester hooks. N2278, 2280, 2283, 2285-2290, 2292, 2294 (11) to South African Air Force in 1941. N2307 was converted for meteorological work and N2308-2313 were tropicalised.
N2318-2729	300	Hawker Hurricane I	N2318-2367, 2380-2409, 2422-2441, 2453-2502, 2520-2559, 2582-2631, 2645-2674, 2700-2729. Up to N2422 had fabric-covered wings and from N2423 metal-covered wings. N2351, 2352, 2367, 2399, 2409, 2429, 2433, 2467-2469, 2488, 2489, 2590, 2591, 2618, 2630, 2631, 2648, 2660, 2671, 2706 were converted to Sea Hurricane. Renumbering on conversion to Mk. II for Russia concerned N2465 (to BV162), N2479 (to BV168), N2544 (to DG616), N2602 (to BV172), N2607 (to DG633), N2665 (to DR367).
N2735-2859	100	Vickers Wellington IC	Built by Vickers at Chester. N2735-2784, 2800-2829, 2840-2859. N2755, 2801, 2856, 2857 were converted to Mk. XVI.
N2865-3019	120	Vickers Wellington IA	Built by Vickers at Weybridge. N2865-2914, N2935-2964, N2980-3019. N2875 and N2990 were converted to Mk. XVI; N2871, 2877, 2880, 2886, 2887, 2909, 2944, 2947, 2954, 2955, 2958 were converted to Mk. XV.
N3023-3299	200	Supermarine Spitfire I	N3023-3072, 3091-3130, 3160-3203, 3221-3250, 3264-3299. N3297 was Mk. III prototype. Conversions to Mk. VA in service were: N3044, 3053, 3059, 3098, 3111, 3121, 3124, 3241, 3270, 3281, 3292.
N3300	1	Miles M.9 Kestrel Trainer	Prototype Master trainer.

Serial Nos.	Qty.	Aircraft Type	Remarks
N3306-3520	161	Boulton Paul P.82 Defiant I	N3306-3340, N3364-3405, N3421-3460, N3477-3520. N3488 converted to Mk. III. N3514 had the turret removed as a flying test-bed. N3380, 3386, 3457, 3504 transferred to Fleet Air Arm. Conversions to T.T.III were: N3312, 3321-3324, 3326, 3329, 3335, 3338, 3367, 3370, 3372, 3379, 3384, 3396, 3397, 3421, 3423, 3427, 3430, 3431, 3433-3436, 3438, 3440, 3441, 3450, 3454, 3456, 3480, 3487, 3489, 3491, 3497, 3498, 3502, 3505, 3507, 3508, 3511, 3517, 3519.
N3522-3631	100	Bristol 142L Blenheim IV	Built by A. V. Roe. N3522-3545, 3551-3575, 3578-3604, 3608-3631. N3544 and 3600 sold to Portuguese Air Froce in 1943.
N3635-3769	100	Short S.29 Stirling I	N3635-3684, 3700-3729, 3750-3769 (100), of which N3645, 3647-3651 (6) were destroyed at the Rochester works by enemy action. N3640, 3657 and 3711 became Mk. II and were re-converted to Mk. I or III. N3669-3670 were non-standard with dorsal turrets.
N3773-3991	204	Miles M.14A Magister	Miles Nos. 821-1024. N3773-3817, 3820-3869, 3875-3914, 3918-3945, 3951-3991. Off-set to Royal Egyptian Air Force requirements were N3862-3866, 3875-3879, 3885-3889, 3912-3914.
N3994-4147	123	Fairey Fulmar I/II	N3994-4016, Mk. I; N4017-4043, 4060-4100, 4116-4147, Mk. II. Delivered in main to Royal Navy, but N3995, 3996, 3997, 3999, 4009, 4014, 4041, 4087 also served for a period in R.A.F.
N4152-4425	200	Fairey Albacore	Fairey Nos. F3518-3706 and 3957-3967. N4152-4200, 4219-4268, 4281-4330, 4347-4391, 4420-4425.
N4557	1	Miles M.14A Magister	Taken on charge in June 1938. Replacement for L6914.
N4560-4853	200	Airspeed AS-10 Oxford	Built by de Havilland Aircraft. N4560-4609, 4630-4659, 4681-4700 (100), Mk. I; N4720-4739, 4754-4803, 4824-4853 (100), Mk. II. N4655 converted to Mk. V.

N4856-5385	500	Avro 652A Anson I	N4856-4899, 4901-4948, 4953-4989, 4995-5044, 5047-5094, 5096-5125, 5130-5178, 5182-5220, 5225-5274, 5279-5318, 5320-5359, 5361-5364, 5366-5385. Off-set from R.A.F. deliveries were: N4863-4867 (5) for Irish Air Corps; N4868, 4870, 4873, 4876, 4879, 4883, 4887, 4891, 4895, 4899, 4904, 4908, 4912, 4916, 4918, 4920, 4921, 4926, 4931, 4936, 4941, 4946, 4955, 4960, 4965, 4970, 4977, 4984, 4996, 5003, (30) for Royal Australian Air Force; N5150, 5155, 5160, 5165, 5170, 5175, 5185, 5190, 5200, 5205, 5210, 5215 (12) for Royal Hellenic Air Force. Others later shipped to Canada under Empire Air Training Scheme.
N5389-5438	50	Miles M.14A Magister I	Miles Nos. 1025-1074. N5389-5393, 5401-5404 to Irish Air Corps, March 1938.
N5444-5493	50	D.H.82 Tiger Moth II	De Havilland Nos. 3707-3720, 3726-3745, 3751-3765, 3777. Delivered in 1938.
N5500-5574	60	Gloster Sea Gladiator	N5500-5549, N5565-5574. N5513 became Gladiator II.
N5575-5930	240	Gloster Gladiator II	N5575-5594, 5620-5649, 5680-5729, 5750-5789, 5810-5859, 5875-5924. N5835-5849 to Portuguese Air Force; N5875-5892 direct to the Royal Egyptian Air Force as L9030-9047, and N5755, 5758, 5760, 5762, 5767, 5771 were delivered later. N5825, 5828, 5830, 5857 to Iraq, March 1944; 40 to Finland.
N6000-6129	100	Short S.29 Stirling I	Built by Short & Harland: N6000-6049, 6085-6104, 6120-6129 at Belfast, and N6065-6084 at Aldergrove. N6025-6028 and N6031 were destroyed by enemy action at the factory.
N6133-6138	4	Short S.25 Sunderland	N6133-6135 and N6138.
N6140-6242	100	Bristol Blenheim IV	N6140-6174, 6176-6220, 6223-6242.
N6246	1	D.H.86B	D.H. No. 2343. Special V.I.P. aircraft held by No. 24 Squadron. Ex-G-ADYG.
N6250-6439	140	Airspeed A.S.10 Oxford I/II	N6250-6270, Mk. I (less turrets); N6271-6299, 6320-6340, Mk. I (standard); N6341-6349, 6365-6384, 6400-6439, Mk. II. N6327 had twin fins fitted experimentally.

N6443–9999(Second Series)

Serial Nos.	*Qty.*	*Aircraft Type*	*Remarks*
N6443-6988	400	D.H.82A Tiger Moth	N6443-6490, 6519-6556, 6576-6625, 6630-6674, 6706-6755, 6770-6812, 6834-6882, 6900-6949, 6962-6988. N6604-6605 sold to South Africa; N6722 converted to Queen Bee; N6962-6963 sold to Burma.
N7000-7199	200	North American NA-16 Harvard I	Purchased from U.S.A. 123 re-shipped to Southern Rhodesia under the E.A.T.S.
N7205-7404	200	Lockheed Hudson I	N7344-7350, 7352, 7354-7356, 7360, 7370-7371, 7373, 7375, 7380-7391 delivered to the Royal Canadian Air Force. N7364 became G-AGAR. N7220 converted to a transport.
N7408-9017	500	Miles M.9A Master I	N7408-7457, 7470-7515, 7534-7582, 7597-7641, 7672-7721, 7748-7782, Mk. I; N7801-7822, special 6-gun fighter version; N7823-7846, 7867-7902, 7921-7969, 7985-8022, 8041-8081, Mk. I; N9003-9017 (15), Mk. I for Royal Navy. N7408 crashed before acceptance; N7412, prototype fighter conversion; N7422, prototype Mk. II; N7447 converted to Mk. II; N7994, prototype Mk. III. N7547 and N7548 to R.N.
N9020-9050	18	Short S.25 Sunderland I	N9020-9030, 9044-9050. Deliveries from mid-February 1939.
N9055-9106	50	Handley Page H.P.53 Hereford/H.P.52 Hampden	Built by Short & Harland. N9055-9081, 9084-9106 of which N9062, 9064, 9065, 9070, 9080, 9086, 9090, 9096, 9101, 9105 were converted to Hampden I. N9106 converted to Hampden I (T.B.).
N9107-9108	2	Airspeed A.S.6 Envoy	G-AFJD/E obtained for Communications Flight, Delhi.
N9114-9525	300	D.H.82 Tiger Moth	N9114-9163, 9172-9215, 9238-9279, 9300-9349, 9367-9410, 9427-9464, 9492-9523.
N9526-9999	350	Avro 652A Anson I	N9526-9575, 9587-9621, 9640-9689, 9713-9752, 9765-9790, 9815-9858, 9870-9919, 9930-9956, 9972-9999, of which N9648, 9657, 9666 were sold to Egypt and N9947-9952 were sold to Turkey before delivery to the R.A.F.

THE "P" SERIES

P1000–9999 THE letter " O " was not used, and P1000 followed on from N9999 in 1938. An exception to the " blackout blocks " was made for allocations for Hudsons and Harvards purchased from the U.S.A.

P1005-1139	100	Airspeed A.S.10 Oxford II	25 only built by Percival Aircraft as P1070-1094. Cancelled Nos. P1005-1054, 1095-1099, 1120-1139.
P1145-1356	200	Handley Page H.P.52 Hampden I	P1145-1189, 1194-1230, 1233-1261, 1265-1305, 1309-1356. Conversions to T.B. (Torpedo Bombers) were: P1145, 1147, 1150, 1151, 1157, 1158, 1160, 1164, 1166, 1169, 1177, 1188, 1189, 1207, 1208, 1214, 1215, 1219, 1229, 1236-1238, 1243, 1245, 1246, 1249, 1250, 1257, 1258, 1273, 1282, 1284, 1286, 1296, 1312-1314, 1335, 1344-1346, 1352, 1356. P1350 was re-equipped for speed increase investigation.
P1360-1659	200	Armstrong Whitworth A.W.41 Albemarle	P1360-1361 Prototypes to Air Ministry Specification B.18/38 built by Armstrong Whitworth Aircraft, remainder built by A. W. Hawkesley Ltd. P1362-1401, Mk. I; P1402-1409, 1430-1478, G.T.1; 1479, 1500-1510, S.T.1; 1511-1529, 1550-1553, G.T.1; P1554-1569, 1590-1609, 1630-1659, S.T.1. P1406 was the Mk. IV prototype. P1477, 1590, 1595, 1636, 1637, 1638, 1640, 1642, 1645, 1647 were flown to Russia.
P1665-1745	70	Westland Lysander I/II	P1665-1699, Mk. I; P1711-1745, Mk. II. P1666, 1668, 1680, 1681, 1683, 1715, converted to T.T.III. P1713, 1735, 1736, 1738, transferred to Free French Forces. P1723 had mock up of B.P. 'A' Mk. III turret.
P1749-1754	6	Percival Vega Gull III	All to No. 24 Squadron, November 1938.
P1758-1759	2	General Aircraft G.A.L.38	P1758 only completed to Air Ministry Specification S.23/37 for a " fleet shadower ".
P1764-1765	2	D.H.89 Rapide	D.H. Nos. 6421-6422. Gipsy VI engines. To No. 24 Squadron, November 1938.
P1767 & 1770	2	Fairey Barracuda	Fairey Nos. F. 4468-4469. Prototypes to Air Ministry Specification S.24/37.

Serial Nos.	*Qty.*	*Aircraft Type*	*Remarks*
P1774-1785	12	Folland 43/37	Special engine test-bed batch to Air Ministry Specification 43/37. Known installations are: P1774, Sabre I, Sabre II, Centaurus; P1775, Hercules VIII, Centaurus; P1776, Centaurus IV, Sabre I; P1777, Sabre I, Centaurus IV; P1778, Centaurus I and D.H. propeller tests; P1779, Hercules XI, various Sabre engines; P1780, Hercules XI and various Napier engines; P1781, Centaurus IV; P1782-1785, Hercules XI and various Bristol engines.
P1800-2059	200	Airspeed A.S.10/46 Oxford I/II/V	P1800-1849, 1860-1864, Mk. II; P1865-1899, 1920-1969, 1980-2009, 2030-2044, Mk. I; P2045-2059, Mk. II. P1864-1866 converted to Mk. V; P1864, Mk. III prototype. Transfers to Iranian Air Force were P1984, 1993, 2002 as 801-803. Transfers to R.N.Z.A.F. from production were: P1945 (as NZ255), P1953 (as NZ256), P1963 (as NZ257), P1983 (as NZ258), P1989-1992 (as NZ261-264), P1996-1999 (as NZ265-268), P2004-2009 (as NZ271-276), P2030-2044 (as NZ277-291), P2045-2059 (as NZ1201-1215).
P2062-2145	75	Handley Page H.P.52 Hampden I	Built by English Electric Co. P2062-2100, P2110-2145. Conversions to T.B. (Torpedo Bomber): P2064, 2065, 2067, 2078, 2080, 2084, 2095, 2113, 2119, 2126.
P2150	1	Miles M.14A Magister I	Replacement. Served No. 4 E.R.F.T.S.
P2155-2369	150	Fairey Battle	P2155-2204, 2233-2278, 2300-2336, 2353-2369.
P2374-2510	100	Miles M.14A Magister I	Miles No. 1611-1710. P2374-2410, 2426-2470, 2493-2510.
P2515-2532	18	Vickers Wellington IA	P2518, D.W.I; P2522, D.W.I (then Mk. IX); P2519, 2521, 2528 converted to Mk. XV.
P2535-3264	500	Hawker Hurricane I	Built by Gloster Aircraft. 2-blade Watts propeller fitted up to P2681, 3-blade Rotol airscrews fitted from P2682. P2535-2584, 2614-2653, 2672-2701, 2713-2732, 2751-2770, 2792-2836, 2854-2888, 2900-2924, 2946-2995, 3020-3069,

			3080-3124, 3140-3179, 3200-3234, 3250-3264, of which P2717, 2731, 2826, 2878, 2886, 2921, 2948, 2953, 2963, 2972, 2986, 2994, 3020, 3036, 3056, 3090, 3092, 3104, 3111, 3114, 3152, 3165, 3168, 3206, 3229 were converted to Sea Hurricane. Conversions and renumbering as Mk. II were: P2674 (to BV171), P2682 (to DG641), P2823 (to BV161), P2829 (to DR355), P2835 (to DR353), P2863 (to DR368), P2904 (to DR357), P2908 (to DR369), P2975 (to DR372), P3023 (to DR342), P3057 (to BV169), P3068 (to DG615), P3103 (to DR340), P3106 (to DR370), P3121 (to DR350), P3207 (to DG631), P3223 (to DG614), P3256 (to DR365).
P3265-3984	500	Hawker Hurricane I	*B = Built at Brooklands, L = Built at Langley.* P3265-3279, 3300-3324, 3345-3364, 3380-3399, B; 3400-3419, L; 3420-3429, 3448-3487, B; 3488-3492, 3515-3554, 3574-3578, L; 3579-3619, B; 3620-3623, L; 3640-3644, B; 3645-3684, 3700-3709, L; 3710-3739, 3755-3774, B; 3775-3789, 3802-3836, L; 3854-3903, B; 3920-3944, 3960-3984, L. P3714-3717, 3737-3739, 3757-3761, 3767-3768, 3770-3774, 3858-3869, 3872-3875, 3882-3889, 3897-3903 initially fitted with fabric-covered wings, remainder metal-covered. P3301, 3320, 3362, 3394, 3398, 3460, 3466, 3467, 3530, 3544, 3597, 3620, 3706, 3710, 3719, 3773, 3776, 3784, 3805, 3814, 3829, 3870, 3877, 3883, 3924-3926, 3934, 3975, 3979 converted to Sea Hurricane. Conversions and renumbering as Mk. II were: P3307 (to DR364), P3351 (to DR393), P3402 (to BV160), P3412 (to DG613), P3449 (to DR362), P3521 (to BV167), P3539 (to DG634), P3551 (to DR343), P3670 (to DG646), P3714 (to DR341), P3717 (to DR348), P3756 (to DG612), P3759 (to DR349), P3811 (to DG644), P3928 (to DR363).

Serial Nos.	*Qty.*	*Aircraft Type*	*Remarks*
P3991-4279	200	Fairey Swordfish	P3991-4039, 4061-4095, 4123-4169, 4191-4232, 4253-4279.
P4285-4418	120	Handley Page H.P.52 Hampden I	P4285-4324, 4335-4384, 4389-4418. Conversions to T.B. (Torpedo Bomber): P4304, 4306, 4312, 4315, 4347, 4369, 4373, 4395, 4401, 4418. P4335 was first Hampden with balloon cutters.
P4420-4673	200	Avro 652A Anson	Cancelled. P4420-4469, 4478-4500, 4521-4561, 4575-4613, 4627-4673.
P4677-4822	110	D.H.82B Queen Bee	D.H. Nos. 5291-5400. P4677-4716, 4747-4781, 4788-4822.
P4825-4927	70	Bristol 142L Blenheim IV	P4825-4864, 4898-4927. Diversions from R.A.F. service were: P4910, 4911, 4915, 4916, 4921, 4922 (6), to Royal Hellenic Air Force.
P4930-5112	164	Armstrong Whitworth A.W.38 Whitley V	P4930-4974, P4980-5029, P5040-5065, P5070-5112.
P5116-5165	50	Lockheed Hudson I	P5163-5164 sold to South African Government.
P5170-5209	40	Hawker Hurricane I	Canadian-built. Redesignated Mk. X. P5178 to Eire; P5195 to Russia; P5180, 5182, 5187, 5203, 5206, 5209 converted to Sea Hurricane. P5175, P5190, P5195, P5199, and P5204 converted to Mk. II and renumbered BV159, DG623, DG620, DG632 and BV170.
P5212 & 5216	2	Hawker Typhoon IA/IB	Prototypes to Air Ministry Specification F.18/37.
P5219 & 5224	2	Hawker Tornado	Prototypes to Air Ministry Specification F.18/37.
P5228-5294	50	Fairey Battle	P5228-5252 and P5270-5294.
P5298-5436	80	Handley Page H.P.52 Hampden I	Canadian-built. P5298-5337 by Quebec Group; P5338-5346, P5386-5400, P5421-5436 by Ontario Group. P5301, 5302, 5304, 5309, 5315, 5320, 5327, 5331, 5335, 5341, 5343, 5387, 5389 were converted to T.B. (Torpedo Bomber).
P5441-5564	65	Airspeed A.S.30 Queen Wasp	P5441-5445 (5) only completed. P5446-5450 partly built. P5451-5455, 5496-5525, 5546-5565 cancelled.
P5571-5620	50	Lockheed 14	Cancelled order.
P5625-5629	5	Airspeed A.S.6J Envoy III	P5626 became G-AHAC post-war.
P5634-5641	8	Percival Q.6 (P.16E)	P5634 and P5637 became G-AHTB/OM.
P5646-5720	50	Supermarine Walrus I	P5646-5670, P5696-5720. Mainly for Royal Navy.

P5723-5726	4	Curtiss Condor	G-AEWD/ZE/WE/WF taken over by R.A.F. Scrapped December 1939.
P5731-5775	28	D.H.82B Queen Bee	De Havilland Nos. 5401-5428. P5731-5749 and P5767-5775.
P5778	1	Airspeed A.S.6 Envoy	Works No. 33. G-ADBA, taken on charge.
P5783-5982	200	North American NA-16 Harvard I	P5783-5915 direct to Britain; P5916-5927 direct to Southern Rhodesia for Empire Air Training Scheme.
P5986-5993	8	Percival Vega Gull III	P5992 was registered G-AFVI for Air Attaché, Lisbon.
P5998-6322	222	Percival P.28 Proctor I	P5998, Mk. I; P5999-6037, 6050-6079, 6101-6113, Mk. IA; P6114-6130, Mk. I; P6131-6145, 6166-6167, Mk. IA; P6168-6200, 6226-6275, 6301-6322, Mk. I. Built as radio trainers. P5998 became P.29 light bomber (anti-invasion). P5999-6037, 6050-6061, 6063-6079, 6101-6113, 6131-6145, 6166-6167 for Fleet Air Arm, remainder for R.A.F. P6256 crashed on delivery flight.
P6326	1	Miles M.15 Trainer	To A.M.Spec. T.1/37. Was registered U-0234.
P6330	1	Waco ZVN	Acquired for tricycle undercarriage tests.
P6343-6466	100	Miles M.14A Magister	Miles Nos. 1711-1810. P6343-6382, 6396-6424, 6436-6466. P6418 to Royal Egyptian Air Force.
P6480-6769	200	Fairey Battle I	P6480-6509, 6523-6572, 6596-6645, 6663-6692, 6718-6737, 6750-6769. From P6616 (100) built as trainers.
P6785-6788	4	D.H.87B Hornet Moth	D.H. Nos. 8126, 8135, 8134, 8061. Floatplanes, used at Lee-on-Solent.
P6795-6880	75	Airspeed A.S.10 Oxford II	Built by de Havilland. Intermediate Type. P6795-6819, 6831-6880.
P6885-6961	62	Bristol 142L Blenheim IV	P6885-6934, 6950-6961. P6891, 6892, 6897, 6898, 6903, 6904 (6) to Royal Hellenic Air Force.
P6966-7269	200	Westland Whirlwind I	P6966-7015, 7035-7064, 7089-7122 (114) built. P7048 became G-AGOI. P7123-7128, 7158-7177, 7192-7221, 7240-7269 cancelled.
P7280-8799	1000	Supermarine Spitfire II (750 IIA, 170 IIB, 80 VA/B)	Vickers-Armstrongs (Castle Bromwich) built. P7280-7329, 7350-7389, 7420-7449, 7490-7509, 7520-7569, 7590-7629, 7660-7699, 7730-7759, 7770-7789, 7810-7859, 7880-

Serial Nos.	*Qty.*	*Aircraft Type*	*Remarks*
			7929, 7960-7999, 8010-8049, 8070-8099, 8130-8149, 8160-8209, 8230-8279, 8310-8349, 8360-8399, 8420-8449, 8460-8479, 8500-8549, 8560-8609, 8640-8679, 8690-8698—up to this point all were produced as Mk. IIA/IIB except for P8532, 8537-8539, 8542, 8560, 8564, 8578, 8581, 8585, 8600, 8603, 8604, 8606, 8607, 8609, 8640, which were built as Mk. V. Later, P7287, 7297, 7299, 7308, 7316, 7324, 7447, 7498, 7532, 7619, 7629, 7672, 7686, 7692, 7789, 7846, 7906, 7910, 7920, 7964, 7965, 7973, 7986, 8017, 8036, 8086, 8095, 8099, 8167, 8195, 8236, 8237, 8239, 8246, 8259, 8262, 8436, 8438, 8549, 8563, 8595 were converted to Mk. V. The remainder were built as follows: P8699-8703, Mk. V except P8701-8702, Mk. II; P8704-8706, Mk. II; P8707-8724, Mk. V; P8725-8729, Mk. II; P8740-8759, 8780-8799, Mk. V. P7505 and P8784 were converted to P.R.XIII. 52 Mk. IIs were conv. to A.S.R. IIc.
P8809-8818	10	Hawker Hurricane I	Hawker (Brooklands)-built. P8809, 8810, 8816, 8817, 8818 had fabric-covered wings.
P8822-9046	150	Airspeed A.S.10 Oxford I/II	P8822-8830, Mk. I; P8831-8854, Mk. II; P8855-8868, 8891-8916, Mk. I; P8917-8931, 8964-8994, Mk. II; P8995-8998, 9020-9046, Mk. I. 50 to R.N.Z.A.F. P8832-8833 fitted as ambulances.
P9051-9199	100	Westland Lysander II	P9051-9080, 9095-9140, 9176-9199. P9099 was converted to T.T.II. P9105 had Blackburn-Steiger high-lift wing fitted. P9109-9119, 9122-9123, 9125, 9126, 9128-9130, 9133, 9136 were converted to Mk. III. P9059, 9078, 9102, 9103, 9134, 9181, 9184 transferred to Free French Forces.
P9205-9300	82	Vickers Wellington IA/C	Vickers (Weybridge)-built. P9205-9236, Mk. IA; P9237-9250, 9265-9300, Mk. IC; P9223 produced as D.W.I. and P9238 as Mk. III proto-

			type; P9209, 9222, converted to Mk. XV; P9289, converted to Mk. XVI.
P9305-9584	200	Supermarine Spitfire I	P9305-9339, 9360-9399, 9420-9469, 9490-9519, 9540-9567 (183) built, of which P9566-9567 went to Turkey. P9307, 9308, 9309, 9315, 9384, 9551, 9552 were converted ior photographic reconnaissance. P9568-9584 cancelled. Later conversions to Mk. VA in service concerned P9367, 9448, 9540, 9550, 9556, 9563.
P9588-9589	2	D.H.89A Dominie	De Havilland Nos. 6455-6. Used by No. 2 Electrical and Wireless School.
P9594	1	Martin Baker M.B.2	Private Venture fighter. G-AEZD, to R.A.F. in March 1939.
P9600-9624	12	Short S.25 Sunderland I	P9600-9606, 9620-9624. P9601-9605 direct to No. 10 Sqn., R.A.A.F.
P9630	1	Consolidated 28-5	Taken on charge in January 1939. Sunk off Dumbarton 10.2.40.
P9639	1	Cierva C.40A	Served in No. 1447 Flight and No. 529 Squadron.
P9642-9986	250	Fairey Barracuda I/II	Fairey (Heaton Chapel)-built. P9642-9666 (25), Mk. I, of which P9647 was Mk. II prototype and P9642 was converted to Mk. II. P9667-9691, 9709-9748, 9787-9836, 9847-9891, 9909-9943, 9957-9986 (225), built as Mk. II. P9976 modified to Mk. V standard with trial installation of Griffon 7 engine.

THE START OF 1939-1945 WAR ORDERS

R1000–9999

"Q" was not used, because it was not a letter easily distinguished from the letter "O" or figure "0"; R1000 therefore followed on from P9999. It was during allocations in this series that war was declared.

R1000-1806	550	Vickers Wellington IC	Vickers (Chester)-built. R1000-1049, 1060-1099, 1135-1184, 1210-1254, 1265-1299, 1320-1349, 1265-1414, 1435-1474, 1490-1539, 1585-1629, 1640-1669, 1695-1729, 1757-1806, Mk. IC—but R1220, 1390, 1490, 1510, 1515, 1520, 1525,

Serial Nos.	*Qty.*	*Aircraft Type*	*Remarks*
			1530, 1535, 1585, 1590, 1610, 1615, 1620, 1625, 1650, 1655, 1695, 1705, 1715, 1725, 1765, 1775, 1785, 1795, were produced as Mk. IV. R1032, 1144, 1172, 1409, 1452, 1521, 1531, 1600, 1605, 1649, 1659, 1700, 1710, 1711, 1720, were converted to Mk. XVI. R1381-1389 were tropicalised.
R1810 & 1815	2	Supermarine 322 "Dumbo"	Air Ministry Specification S.24/37. Compromised numbers below. R1810, Merlin 30 engine; R1815, Merlin 32 engine.
R1810-1984	145	Miles M.14A Magister	Miles Nos. 1811-1955. R1810-1859, 1875-1924, 1940-1984. R1907 to Turkish Air Force.
R1987-2047	47	Westland Lysander II	R1987-2010, 2025-2047. R1998 converted to T.T.II; R2047 to Canada, 1940; R2036, 2039, 2040, 2043, 2045, 2046 to Free French Forces.
R2052-2479	300	Bristol 156 Beaufighter I/II	R2052-2055 prototypes. R2056-2057, Mk. IF; R2058, Mk. II prototype: R2059-2060, Mk. IF; R2061-2062, further Mk. II prototypes with modified fins; R2063-2101, 2120-2159, 2180-2209, 2240-2269, Mk. IF; R2270-2284, 2300-2349, 2370-2404, 2430-2479, Mk. IIF; R2274 converted to Mk. V.
R2485-2487	3	D.H.89 Rapide	De Havilland Nos. 6446-6448. Gipsy VI engines. Acquired to Air Ministry Specification T.29/38.
R2492 & 2496	2	Martin-Baker M.B.3/5	R2492 (M.B.3) first flew 3.8.42, crashed 13.9.42. R2496 (M.B.5) first flew 23.5.44.
R2510-2560	41	D.H.95 Hertfordshire	R2510 (de Havilland No. 95006), prototype only built. R2511-2529, 2550-2560 cancelled.
R2572-2652	72	Westland Lysander I	Westland (Yeovil)-built. R2572-2600, R2612-2652. R2573-2574 cancelled. R2650 delivered to Egyptian Air Force.R2572, 2575, 2578, 2581, 2587, 2588, 2589, 2591, 2593, 2594, 2597, 2598, 2632, 2638 converted to T.T.I; R2651-2652 converted to T.T.III.
R2676	1	Stearmond Hammond Model Y	Purchased for evaluation from K.L.M. Scrapped February 1942.

R2680-2689	10	Hawker Hurricane I	R2680-2681, Hawker (Brooklands)-built with fabric-covered wings; R2682-2689, Hawker (Langley)-built with metal-covered wings. R2683 was converted to Mk. II and renumbered BV163.
R2699-2703	5	Vickers Wellington I	R2701 was converted to D.W.1.
R2764-2766	3	D.H.95 Flamingo	De Havilland Nos. 95003/4/8. Impressed for No. 24 Squadron. R2766, ex-G-AGCC.
R2770-2799	30	Bristol 142L Blenheim IV	Avro-built. R2775, 2781, 2799 to Portuguese Air Force, September 1943.
R2800-3144	200	Bristol Blenheim	Cancelled. Numbers were allotted in error to Rootes. R2800-2805, 2825-2864, 2877-2926, 2939-2963, 2995-3040, 3096-3123, 3140-3144.
R3150-3299	100	Vickers Wellington IC	Vickers (Weybridge) - built. R3150-3179, 3195-3239, 3275-3299. R3298, Mk. V prototype with Bristol Hercules III (Type 421), later Hercules XI (Type 436). R3299, Mk. V 2nd prototype with Hercules VIII (Type 407), later Hercules XI. Conversions were R3217, 3225, 234, 32373 to Mk. XVI, R3221 to Mk. II.
R3303-3587	200	Avro 652A Anson I	R3303-3351, 3368-3413, 3429-3476, 3512-3561, 3581-3587. Majority shipped direct from production to Empire Air Training Scheme (Canada, South Africa, Australia).
R3590-3919	250	Bristol 142L Blenheim IV	Built by Rootes Securities. R3590-3639, 3660-3709, 3730-3779, 3800-3849, 3870-3919. R3623, 3830 to Portuguese Air Force, September 1943; R3877 to Free French Forces, August 1940.
R3922-4054	100	Fairey Battle	Built by The Austin Motor Co. R3922-3971, 3990-4019, 4035-4054. Mostly for Empire Air Training Scheme.
R4059	1	Lockheed Hudson I	Supplied in lieu of N7260, which crashed before delivery.
R4062-4067	6	Airspeed A.S.10 Oxford I	R4062-4065 to New Zealand; R4066-4067 to Rhodesia.
R4071	1	Miles M.3 Falcon	Used at Farnborough for spoler tests. Ex-PH-EAD became G-AGZX, later OO-FLY.
R4074-4232	100	Hawker Hurricane I	Built by Gloster Aircraft. R4074-4123, 4171-4200, 4213-4232, of which R4103-4104 went to S.A.A.F. Conversions

Serial Nos.	*Qty.*	*Aircraft Type*	*Remarks*
			and re-numberings as Mk. II: R4081 became DR358, R4091 became DR373, R4218 became BV155. Conversions to Sea Hurricane were: R4077, 4078, 4089, 4095, 4105, 4177, 4178, 4214, 4226.
R4236-4237	2	Vickers 432	Ordered to Air Ministry Specification F.22/39. Not built. Replaced by DZ217 & DZ223.
R4243-4521	200	Westland Whirlwind	Cancelled. R4243-4283, 4296-4325, 4345-4384, 4400-4445, 4460-4479, 4499-4521.
R4525-4744	150	Avro 679 Manchester	Cancelled order placed with Fairey Aviation. R4525-4554, 4572-4611, 4630-4649, 4670-4694, 4710-4744.
R4748-5265	400	D.H.82A Tiger Moth II	R4748-4797, 4810-4859, 4875-4924, 4940-4989, 5005-5044, 5057-5086, 5100-5149, 5170-5219, 5236-5265. R5106 and R5147 converted to Queen Bee. Direct deliveries to E.A.T.S. were: R4781, 4786-4797, 4810-4829, Southern Rhodesia; R5005-5011, R5067 5077, New Zealand; R4835-4844, 4879-4893, 5181-5186, 5256-5265, Australia.
R5269	1	Weir W-6 Helicopter	Built by G. and J. Weir. Broken up in 1941.
R5273-5477	150	Avro 679 Manchester	Cancelled order placed with Armstrong Whitworth. R5273-5320, 5339-5380, 5397-5426, 5448-5477.
R5482-5763	200	Avro 683 Lancaster I	R5482-5517, 5537-5576, 5603-5640, 5658-5703, 5724-5763. Merlin 20 engines initially.
R5768-5917	100	Avro 679 Manchester I/683 Lancaster I	Built by Metropolitan-Vickers. R5768-5797, R5829-5841, Manchester I; R5842-5868, R5888-5917, Lancaster I.
R5921-5934	14	D.H.89 Dominie	De Havilland Nos. 6457-6461, 6463-6471 to No. 2 Electrical & Wireless School.
R5938-6403	350	Airspeed AS-10 Oxford I/II	R5938-5979, 5991-6038, 6050-6059, 6070-6114, 6129-6163, 6177-6196 (200), Airspeed-built. R6211-6235, Mk. II; R6236-6248, 6263-6299, 6317-6341, Mk. I; R6342-6358, 6371-6403 (150), Mk. II, de Havilland (Hatfield)-built. R5938-5941 shipped direct to Southern Rhodesia and R6211-6225 direct to New Zealand.

R6416-6539	100	Airspeed A.S.10 Oxford	Cancelled order placed with Phillips & Powis. R6416-6439, 6453-6478, 6490-6539.
R6543-6591	25	Supermarine Walrus	R6543-6557, Vickers Armstrongs (Supermarine)-built. R6582-6591, Saunders-Roe-built.
R6595-7350	450	Supermarine Spitfire I/V	Vickers Armstrongs (Supermarine)-built. R6595-6644, 6683-6722, 6751-6780, 6799-6818, 6829-6840, 6879-6928, 6957-6996, 7015-7044, 7055 7074, 7114-7163, 7192-7218, built as Mk. I, of which R6602, 6620, 6720, 6722, 6759, 6761, 6770, 6776, 6801, 6809, 6817, 6882, 6888-6890, 6897, 6908, 6911-6913, 6919, 6923-6924, 6957, 6960, 6992, 7022, 7060, 7127, 7158, 7161, 7192, 7194-7196, 7205, 7207-7210, 7213, 7217-7218 were converted to Mk. V. R7219-7231, 7250-7279, 7290-7309, 7333-7350 were built as Mk. V, excluding R7250-7252 and 7257, completed as Mk. I. Conversions for P.R. use were: R7029-7034 (P.R. Type C); R7035-7044, 7055-7056 (P.R. Type D); R7130, 7308 (P.R. VII); R7335 (P.R. XIII). R6684 and R6924 conv. to Mk. II.
R7356-7480	100	Fairey Battle (T)	Built as trainers. R7356-7385 7399-7448, 7461-7480. Mostly delivered direct to Canada.
R7485-7573	50	Percival P.28/34 Proctor I/III	Built by F. Hills & Sons, R7485-7499, 7520-7529 (25). Mk. I; R7530-7539, 7559-7573 (25), Mk. III.
R7576-7923	250	Hawker Typhoon IA/IB	Built by Gloster Aircraft. R7576-7599, 7613-7655, 7672-7721, 7738-7775, 7792-7829, 7845-7890, 7913-7923. R7625 crashed before delivery.
R7936-7938	3	Hawker Tornado	Prototypes for R.A.F., Hawker and Rolls-Royce evaluation. R7936 only built by A. V. Roe at Manchester.
R7939-8197	198	Hawker Tornado	Cancelled. R7939-7975, 7992-8036, 8048-8091, 8105-8150, 8172-8197.
R8198-8231	15	Hawker Typhoon IA/IB	Hawker (Langley)-built. R8198-8200, R8220-8221, Mk. IA; R8222-8231, Mk. IB.
R8630-8981	250	Hawker Typhoon IA/IB	Built by Gloster Aircraft. R8630-8663, 8680-8722, 8737-8781, 8799-8845, 8861-8900,

Serial Nos.	*Qty.*	*Aircraft Type*	*Remarks*
			8923-8947, 8966-8981, IB except R8640, 8652, 8709, 8720, 8746 IA. R8891 was tropicalised.
R8987	1	Lockheed 12A	Lockheed No. 1206. G-AEMZ, impressed September 1939.
R8991-9135	100	Westland Lysander III	R8991-9030, 9056-9079, 9100-9135. Diversions from production were: R8991-8999 to Finland, and R9000 to Egypt.
R9138	1	Parnall 382 Heck III	G-AFKF impressed. Used by No. 24 Squadron, June 1941.
R9141-9358	150	Short S.29 Stirling I (Series I/II)	R9141-9170, 9184-9203, 9241-9290, 9295-9334, 9349-9358. Series II from R9295. R9188 and R9309 were converted to Mk. III.
R9363-9540	100	Handley Page H.P.59 Halifax II	R9363-9392, 9418-9457, 9482-9498, 9528-9540. R9534 became Mk. III prototype.
R9545-9564	20	D.H.89 Dominie	De Havilland Nos. 6473-6492. R9563 to Royal Navy.
R9567-9969	300	Avro 652A Anson I	R9567-9611, 9627-9670, 9685-9725, 9739-9781, 9798-9846, 9864-9899, 9928-9969. Many delivered for Empire Air Training Scheme.
R9974-9988	15	Airspeed A.S.10 Oxford I	Batches continue in "T" series.

THE "S" SERIES

S1000–1865

BY 1925 the first "N" series had reached its maximum of 9999 and a new series, the "S" series, was started which followed on at S1000 directly from N9999. The choice of "S" was due to two reasons; firstly, it stood for "Sea" and the series was primarily for aircraft equipped for flying over the sea; secondly, it was way ahead of the main series, which then had just started at K1000 and was not likely to reach R9999 for several years.

S1000-1035	36	Fairey IIID Mk. II	Ordered in March 1925. Float/wheel undercarriages interchangeable
S1036-1045	10	Supermarine Southampton I	Ordered in July 1925.
S1046-1057	12	Blackburn Blackburn I	Known as Blackburn T.S.R. (Torpedo - Spotter - Reconnaissance).
S1058-1059	2	Supermarine Southampton III	Ordered in July 1925.
S1060-1073	14	Fairey Flycatcher	Ordered in August 1925.

S1074-1108	35	Fairey IIID Mk. II	S1076 loaned to a company as G-EBPZ and converted to a 4-seater.
S1109-1114	6	Avro Bison II	Ordered in late 1926.
S1115-1120	6	Blackburn Dart	S1115 only confirmed.
S1121-1128	8	Supermarine Southampton II	Napier Lion engines. N1124 was non-standard with Rolls-Royce Kestrel engines.
S1129-1138	10	Blackburn Dart	Ordered November 1926. Convertible wheel/float undercarriages.
S1139-1148	10	Fairey IIIF Mk. I	Fairey Aviation Nos. F880-889. S1147 had undercarriage exchanged with K1731. S1140, 1143, 1144, 1146 were rebuilt.
S1149-1153	5	Supermarine Southampton	All used by No. 205 Squadron, R.A.F.
S1154-1158	5	Blackburn Mk. II	Ordered December 1926. Known as Blackburn Spotter.
S1159-1162	4	Supermarine Southampton	S1160 was Mk. III version.
S1163-1167	5	Avro Bison	Ordered in February 1927.
S1168-1207	40	Fairey IIIF Mk. I	Wood/metal construction with Napier Lion VA engines. S1189 sold to Greeks; S1171, 1174, 1179, 1181 were rebuilt; S1178, 1197, 1199, 1203 were rebuilt as Gordons. S1169, 1178, 1184, 1189, 1196 conv. to Mk. III and S1205 to Mk. IVA.
S1208-1227	20	Fairey IIIF Mk. II	All-metal version with Napier Lion XI engines. S1211, 1217 conv. to Mk. III.
S1228-1235	8	Supermarine Southampton II	Production aircraft.
S1236-1247	12	Hawker Horsley	Ordered September 1927.
S1248-1249	2	Supermarine Southampton	Numbers also issued to Hawker Horsley.
S1250-1262	13	Fairey IIIF Mk. II	All-metal version, ordered October 1927.
S1263-1264	2	Blackburn Iris III	S1263 had three Rolls-Royce Buzzard IIMS engines. S1264 with three Rolls-Royce Condor IIIB engines became Mk. V.
S1265	1	Blackburn Perth	Compromised number below.
S1265-1272	8	Blackburn Ripon II	S1268, Ripon IIA; S1266 converted later to Baffin and sold to New Zealand.
S1273-1297	25	Fairey Flycatcher	S1288 attached to High Speed Flight, 1929.
S1298-1302	5	Supermarine Southampton	S1302, Mk. II. Service with Nos. 201 and 203 Squadrons.
S1303-1356	54	Fairey IIIF Mk. III	Napier Lion engines, except S1325 with Armstrong Siddeley Panther. S1311 and S1343 were specially strengthened for catapulting. S1317 used in swept wing experiment.

Serial Nos.	Qty.	Aircraft Type	Remarks
S1357-1369	13	Blackburn Ripon IIA	S1358, S1359, S1364, S1366 and S1368 were converted to Baffins.
S1370-1408	39	Fairey IIIF Mk. IIIM	Ordered September 1929. S1377 sold to Greek Government.
S1409-1419	11	Fairey Flycatcher	Ordered March 1930.
S1420-1423	4	Supermarine Southampton	S1420 used by No. 205 Squadron 1930-33.
S1424-1432	9	Blackburn Ripon II	S1426, 1428, 1430-1432 were converted to Baffins; S1428 and S1431 were sold to New Zealand.
S1433-1435	3	Short S.8/8 Rangoon	S1433 (Short No. S.757) became G-AEIM.
S1436-1453	18	Hawker Horsley	S1436 did trials with Rolls-Royce Merlin C, and S1452 trials with Rolls-Royce Condor III.
S1454-1463	10	Fairey IIIF (D.C.)	All-metal version, ordered September 1929.
S1464	1	Supermarine Southampton	Mk. II. Used by No. 201 Squadron.
S1465-1473	9	Blackburn Ripon II	S1470 and S1473 converted to Baffins.
S1474-1552	79	Fairey IIIF Mk. IIIB	Fairey Nos. F.1317-1395. S1536 became "Fairy Queen" radio-controlled aircraft.
S1553-1574	22	Blackburn Ripon II	All converted to Baffins. S1553 and S1573 sold to New Zealand.
S1575	1	Saro Cutty Sark	Used by Seaplane Training Flight, Calshot.
S1576	1	Parnall Prawn	Used at Felixstowe.
S1577-1588	12	Hawker Nimrod I	Interchangeable wheel/float undercarriage.
S1589	1	Short Sarafand	Prototype to Air Ministry Specification R.6/28.
S1590	1	Fairey Flycatcher	Used by No. 404 Flight. Collided with S1067.
S1591	1	Armstrong Whitworth XVI	Trials at A. & A.E.E., then to No. 402 Flight in 1932.
S1592	1	Fairey Firefly III	Fairey No. F.1137. Was G-ABFH and Schneider Trophy team trainer.
S1593	1	Blackburn Iris II/VI	This Iris had a 37 mm. C.O.W. gun installed in enlarged bows.
S1594	1	—	Allocation not known.
S1595-1596	2	Supermarine S.6B	Both extant; S1595 at Science Museum, S1596 owned by Southampton Corporation.
S1597-1613	17	Hawker Horsley	Mainly to Far East for Nos. 36 and 100 Squadrons.
S1614-1639	26	Hawker Nimrod I	Interchangeable wheel/float undercarriage.

S1638	1	Supermarine Southampton	Compromised number above.
S1640	1	Blackburn M.1/30	To Air Ministry Specification M.1/30.
S1641	1	Vickers Type 207	To Air Ministry Specification M.1/30.
S1642	1	Handley Page H.P.46	To Air Ministry Specification M.1/30.
S1643-1647	5	Supermarine Southampton	All served in No. 201 Squadron, R.A.F.
S1648	1	Supermarine Scapa	Prototype to Air Ministry Specification R.20/31. Originally Southampton IV.
S1649-1674	26	Blackburn Ripon II	All converted to Baffin. S1649, S1654, S1655, S1657, S1670, S1674 sold to New Zealand.
S1675-1676	2	D.H.82 Tiger Moth	Floatplane version, to Air Ministry Specification T 6/33.
S1677-1704	28	Hawker Osprey I/III	S1699-1701, Mk. III built of stainless steel; S1702-1704, standard Mk. III; remainder, Mk. I.
S1705	1	Gloster T.S.R.38	To Air Ministry Specification S.15/33.
S1706	1	Fairey S.9/30	Fairey IIIF with single pontoon float.
S1707-1715	9	Vickers Vildebeest I	S1713 converted to Mk. III; S1714 and S1715 converted to Vincent standard; S1715 used for experiments.
S1716-1778	63	—	Reservation.
S1779-1865	87	Fairey IIIF Mk. III	Fairey Nos. F. 1526-1612. S1779-1836, Mk. IIIB; S1837-1844, Mk. III; S1845-1851, Mk. III (D.C.); S1852-1865 Mk. IIIB. S1835 used in centre-float trials. S1801 and S1805 to R.N.Z.A.F.; S1786 and S1817 to Royal Hellenic Air Force; S1789 converted to a catapult dummy.

"T" FOR TRAINERS?

T1000–9999

" S " having been used earlier for naval aircraft (albeit only to S1865), the series was overlooked in 1939 when R9999 was reached, and the follow-on came as T1000. These allocations reflect early wartime planning by placing large orders for training aircraft.

T1001-1404	285	Airspeed A.S.10 Oxford I/II (Continued from "R" Series)	Airspeed (Portsmouth)-built. T1001-1028, 1041-1047, Mk. I; T1048-1082, 1097-1111, Mk. II; T1112-1141, 1167-1180, Mk. I; T1181-1215, 1243-1263, Mk. II; T1264-1288,

Serial Nos.	*Qty.*	*Aircraft Type*	*Remarks*
			1308-1332, Mk. I; T1333-1348, 1371-1404, Mk. II; T1373, converted to Mk. V. T1265, 1269, 1270, 1272 to the R.N.Z.A.F.
T1419	1	Cierva C.40	Used for autogyro training from December 1939.
T1422-1771	250	Westland Lysander III	T1422-1470, 1501-1535, 1548-1590, 1610-1655, 1670-1709, 1735-1771. Among conversions to T.T.III were: T1445, 1450, 1453, 1456, 1458, 1461, 1532, 1534, 1571, 1583, 1616, 1623, 1626, 1633, 1642, 1674-1679, 1688, 1692, 1699, 1746, 1750, 1752, 1763. T1570, converted to T.T.III, was the only Lysander to be operated by the Royal Navy.
T1775-1776	2	D.H.85 Leopard Moth	VP-AEP/JC impressed in India
T1777-1783	5	D.H.82 Tiger Moth	Impressed in India. T1777-1779, 1782-1783.
T1788	1	Fane F.1/40	Fane No. 1 Two-seat air observation post, registered G-AGDJ.
T1793-2444	400	Bristol Blenheim IV	Built by Rootes Securities. T1793-1832, 1848-1897, 1921-1960, 1985-2004, 2031-2080, 2112-2141, 2161-2190, 2216-2255, 2273-2292, 2318-2357, 2381-2400, 2425-2444. T1855, 1857, 1867, 1875, 1935, 2077, 2079 were transferred to the Free French Forces; T1996 was transferred to the Turkish Air Force; T2431, 2434 were released to the Portuguese Air Force in 1943.
T2449 & 2453	2	Airspeed A.S.-45	Trainer prototypes to Air Ministry Specification T.4/39.
T2458-3000	300	Vickers Wellington IC	T2458-2477, 2501-2520, 2541-2580, 2606-2625, 2701-2750, 2801-2850, 2873-2922, 2951-3000. T2919, 2977, 2979, 2982, 2988, converted to Mk. VIII; T2850, 2920, 2969, converted to Mk. XVI. T2545 conv. to Mk. II and later used as engine test bed.
T3009-3447	300	Bristol 156 Beaufighter I/II	T3009-3055, 3070-3107, 3137-3183, 3210-3227, Mk. IIF (T3177 tested with Griffon engines); T3228-3250, 3270-3272, 3290-3333, 3348-3355, Mk. IC; T3356-3389, 3410-3447, Mk. IIF.

T3450-3907	300	Bristol 156 Beaufighter	Cancelled order placed with Vickers Armstrongs. T3450-3493, 3510-3550, 3583-3622, 3639-3685, 3701-3733, 3767-3799, 3822-3866, 3891-3907.
T3911-4121	150	Boulton Paul P.82 Defiant I	T3911-3960, T3980-4010, T4030-4076, T4100-4121. T4106 shipped to America. Conversion for Target towing as T.T. III concerned: T3919-3920, 3923, 3925, 3928, 3935, 3942, 3947-3948, 3950-3951, 3982-3984, 3986-3990, 3992, 3994, 4000-4002, 4004-4007, 4009, 4033, 4035-4036, 4043, 4046, 4047, 4050, 4060, 4062, 4064-4066, 4068, 4072, 4076, 4103, 4109, 4111-4112, 4114, 4120-4121.
T4130-4339	150	Armstrong Whitworth A.W.38 Whitley V	T4130-4179, 4200-4239, 4260-4299, 4320-4339.
T4623-5352	500	Bristol 156 Beaufighter I/VI	Built by Fairey Aviation at Stockport. Aircraft offset from production for the Royal Australian Air Force are indicated by their renumbering in the R.A.A.F's A19 series. T4623-4647 (25), Mk. IF; T4648-4670, 4700-4734, 4751-4800, 4823-4846, 4862-4899, 4915-4919, 4920-4931 became A19-1 to A19-12; T4932-4942, 4943-4947 became A19-13 to A19-17; T4970-4978 became A19-18 to A19-26; T4979-4990, 4991-5004 became A19-27 to A19-40; T5005-5007, 5027-5046, 5047-5055 became A19-41 to A19-49; T5070-5074 became A19-50 to A19-54; T5075 became A19-63; T5076 became A19-55; T5077 became A19-61; T5078-5080, 5081 became A19-56; T5082 became A19-64; T5083-5084 became A19-57 to A19-58; T5085, 5086 became A19-71; T5087-5088, 5089 became A19-62; T5090 became A19-59; T5091 became A19-60; T5092 became A19-72; T5093 became A19-66; T5094 became A19-65; T5095 became A19-67; T5096, 5097 became A19-68; T5098 became A19-70; T5099 became A19-69 (300), Mk. IC. T5100-5114, 5130-5175, 5195-5199, 5200-

Serial Nos.	*Qty.*	*Aircraft Type*	*Remarks*
			5201, became A19-73 to A19-74; T5202 became A19-77; T5203 became A19-76; T5204 became A19-78; T5205 became A19-75; T5206-5220, 5250-5253, 5254 became A19-86; T5255 became A19-88; T5256, 5257 became A19-89; T5258-5261, 5262 became A19-85; T5263 became A19-97; T5264 became A19-87; T5265-5269, 5270 became A19-90; T5271-5294, 5295-5296 became A19-98 to A19-99; T5297-5299, 5315-5326, 5327, became A19-111; T5328 became A19-110; T5329 became A19-115; T5330 became A19-112; T5331 became A19-114; T5332-5335, 5336 became A19-119; T5337 became A19-124; T5338 became A19-126; T5339 became A19-125; T5340 became A19-128; T5341 became A19-127; T5342 became A19-129; T5343-5344 became A19-135 to A19-136; T5345-5352 (175), Mk. VIC.
T5357	**1**	**D.H.95 Flamingo**	De Havilland No. 95001. Ex-G-AFUE, to No. 24 Squadron mid-1940.
T5360-8264	**2000**	**D.H.82 Tiger Moth II**	Built by Morris Motors. T5360-5384, 5409-5433, 5454-5503, 5520-5564, 5595-5639, 5669-5718, 5749-5788, 5807-5856, 5877-5921, 5952-5986, 6020-6069, 6094-6138, 6158-6202, 6225-6274, 6286-6320, 6362-6406, 6427-6471, 6485-6534, 6547-6596, 6612-6656, 6671-6720, 6734-6778, 6797-6831, 6854-6878, 6897-6921, 6942-6991, 7011-7055, 7085-7129, 7142-7191, 7208-7247, 7259-7308, 7325-7369, 7384-7418, 7436-7485, 7509-7553, 7583-7627, 7651-7700, 7723-7757, 7777-7821, 7840-7884, 7899-7948, 7960-8009, 8022-8066 8096-8145, 8166-8210, 8230-8264. Numbers were offset direct from production for Empire Air Training Scheme and for Commonwealth Air Forces. T5911-5920 (destined for Kenya), T6449-6454 (destined for South Africa) and

			T8030-8052 (shipped direct from production for No. 4 Elementary Flying Training School, South Africa) were all lost at sea. T6104, 6863, 6867, 7239 were converted to Queen Bee. T6099 became XL714, T7363 became XL716, T7291 became XL717 of the Royal Navy.
T8268-9037	500	Miles M.9/19 Master I/II	T8268-8292, 8317-8351, 8364-8412, 8429-8469, 8482-8507, 8538-8581, 8600-8640, 8656-8694, 8736-8784, 8815-8855, 8876-8885 (400), Mk. I. T8886, Mk. IV, uncompleted; T8887-8923, 8948-8967, 8996-9037, Mk. II; output from T8914 to T8999 was shipped direct to South Africa.
T9040-9078	20	Short S.25 Sunderland I	T9040-9050, 9070-9078. T9042, Mk. III prototype.
T9083-9115	15	Short S.25 Sunderland II	Built by Blackburn. T9083-9090, 9109-9115.
T9120	1	Taylorcraft Plus D	Acquired in 1939. Served at School of Army Co-operation, No. 651 Squadron and No. 1424 Flight. Became G-AHAF.
T9131-9260	100	Fairey Albacore	Fairey Nos. F4920-5019. T9131-9175, 9191-9215, 9231-9260.
T9264	1	General Aircraft Monospar ST-25 Universal	F-AQOM (ex-G-AEPG), impressed for the R.A.F. Was originally W7977.
T9266-9465	200	Lockheed Hudson I/II/III	T9266-9365, Mk. I; T9366-9385, Mk. II; T9386-9465, Mk. III. T9367 loaned to R.C.A.F.; T9305-9307 sunk en route; T9465 presented by Lockheed employees.
T9519-9538	20	Hawker Hurricane I	Built by the Canadian Car & Foundry Corporation. T9526 converted to Sea Hurricane.
T9540-9657	100	Bristol 152 Beaufort V	Australian-built. Seven only produced for R.A.F. and off-set to R.A.A.F. T9540-9569, 9583-9618, 9624-9657. Re-numbered in R.A.A.F. A9 series.
T9669-9982	220	Miles M.14A Magister	Miles Nos. 1956-2175. T9669-9708, 9729-9768, 9799-9848, 9869-9918, 9943-9982. T9899, 9900, 9903 to Turkish Air Force. Continued in "V" series.

"V" FOR VICTORY

V1000–9999

"U" was not used, since it could easily have been confused with "V" in manuscript records, and "V" therefore followed "T" in an allocation which sowed some of the seeds of victory.

Large blanks in this series suggest changed policies owing to the war emergency. Although this series was subscribed in late 1939 to early 1940, some of the aircraft did not emerge until 1942, by which time role prefixes had been introduced to Mark numbers.

Serial Nos.	*Qty.*	*Aircraft Type*	*Remarks*
V1003-1102	80	Miles M.14A Magister 1	Miles Nos. 2176-2255. V1003-1042, 1063-1102. Continued from "T" series. V1025 crashed on delivery.
V1106-1183	50	Boulton Paul P.82 Defiant I	V1106-1141, 1170-1183. Conversion to T.T.III for target towing included: V1106-1108, 1110-1112, 1114-1115, 1119-1120, 1123-1124, 1126-1127, 1132-1133, 1135, 1139, 1170, 1181.
V1186-1187	2	Cierva C.30A	Works Nos. 717 and 731. Ex-G-ACWR/O. Impressed December 1939.
V1201-1594	300	Fairey Battle T.T.I	V1201-1250, 1265-1280 (66) only built by The Austin Motor Co. V1281-1294, 1305-1354, 1375-1394, 1407-1456, 1470-1499, 1511-1560, 1575-1594 cancelled.
V1598-2831	780	Armstrong Whitworth A.W.41 Albemarle	302 built by A. W. Hawksley Ltd. V1598-1599, Mk.I; V1600, G.T.II; V1601-1647, 1694-1723, 1738-1759, S.T.II; V1760, Mk. IV; V1761-1787, 1809-1828, 1841-1842, S.T.V; V1843-1885, 1917-1941, 1962-2011, 2025-2039, S.T.VI; V2040-2054, 2067-2068, G.T.VI. Numbers V2069-2116, 2155-2179, 2193-2242, 2271-2300, 2314-2353, 2377-2436, 2440-2464, 2503-2542, 2573-2622, 2636-2665, 2681-2720, 2749-2798, 2812-2831 cancelled.
V3137-3138	2	Short S.30M Empire ("C" Class)	Short Nos. S880-881, ex-G-AFCU/V *Cabot* and *Caribou*, impressed in October 1939.
V3142	1	Boulton Paul P.92/2	Half-scale model for Air Ministry Specification F.11/37 project, built by Heston Aircraft.
V3145-3862	500	Airspeed A.S.10 Oxford I/II	Built by de Havilland. V3145-3194, 3208-3247, 3267-3296, 3310-3359, 3375-3404, 3418-

			3442, 3456-3480 (250), Mk. I; V3501-3540, 3555-3604, 3623-3647, 3665-3694, 3719-3748, 3768-3792, 3813-3862 (250), Mk. II. Numbers were shipped direct from production for Commonwealth countries, *e.g.*, V3153-3188 to Southern Rhodesia and V3269-3287 to South Africa.
V3865-4283	300	Airspeed A.S.10 Oxford I	Built by Standard Motors. V3865-3914, 3933-3957, 3972-3996, 4016-4065, 4079-4103, 4124-4173, 4192-4241, 4259-4283.
V4288-4719	300	Fairey Swordfish	Built by Blackburn Aircraft. V4288-4337, 4360-4399, V4411-4455, 4481-4525, 4551-4600, 4621-4655, 4685-4719.
V4724-4725	2	D.H.89 Rapide	G-AFNC/D, impressed for No. 24 Squadron, September 1939.
V4730	1	D.H.60 Gipsy Moth	VT-ACM impressed in India.
V4731	1	D.H.87 Hornet Moth	VT-AIT impressed in India.
V4732	1	Lockheed 12A	VT-AJS, impressed in India January 1940.
V4733	1	D.H.82 Tiger Moth	VT-ALF, impressed in India January 1940.
V4734	1	D.H.90 Dragonfly	VT-AHY, impressed in India January 1940.
V4738	1	D.H.60A Moth	G-AABH, impressed in 1940.
V4739	1	Miles Whitney Straight	G-AFCN, impressed in 1940.
V4742-5000	175	D.H.82B Queen Bee	V4742-4772, 4787-4805 (50) only built as D.H. Nos. 5429-5478. V4806-4827, 4852-4876, 4889-4909, 4926-4966, 4993-5006 cancelled.
V5010-5361	258	Airspeed A.S.30 Queen Wasp	Cancelled. V5010-5057, 5073-5112, 5131-5180, 5206-5240, 5262-5306, 5322-5361.
V5370-6529	800	Bristol 142L Blenheim IV	Built by Rootes Securities. V5370-5399, 5420-5469, 5490-5539, 5560-5599, 5620-5659, 5680-5699, 5720-5769, 5790-5829, 5850-5899, 5920-5969, 5990-6039, 6060-6099, 6120-6149, 6170-6199, 6220-6269, 6290 6339, 6360-6399. 6420-6469, 6490-6529. Released to the Portuguese Air Force in 1943 were: V5429, 5434, 5501, 5729, 5883, 6395.
V6533-7195	500	Hawker Hurricane I	Built by Gloster Aircraft. V6533-6582, 6600-6649, 6665-6704, 6722-6761, 6776-6825, 6840-6889, 6913-6962, 6979-7028, 7042-7081, 7099-7138, 7156-7195. Renumbering on conversion to Mk. II concerned: V6536 (to DG630),

Serial Nos.	*Qty.*	*Aircraft Type*	*Remarks*
			V6538 (to DR371), V6546 (to DR374), V6582 (to DG639), V6602 (to DG638), V6739 (to DR352), V6757 (to DG619), V6785 (to BV158), V6790 (to BV156), V6853 (to DG643), V6861 (to DG650), V6914 (to BV165), V6915 (to DR351), V6929 (to DG647), V6934 (to DG629), V6936 (to DR360), V6942 (to DR391), V6950 (to DG624), V6959 (to DG627), V6999 (to DG648), V7006 (to DR347), V7018 (to DR392), V7021 (to DR394), V7054 (to DR361), V7061 (to DG626), V7169 (to DR339). V6576, 6613, 7158, 7173 went to the Irish Air Corps. Conversions to Sea Hurricane concerned: V6536, 6537, 6541, 6545, 6555, 6556, 6564, 6577, 6610, 6649, 6697, 6700, 6723, 6727, 6731, 6751, 6756, 6759, 6760, 6779, 6794, 6799, 6801, 6802, 6815, 6817, 6843, 6854, 6858, 6867, 6881, 6886, 6923, 6924, 6933, 6944, 6952, 6957, 7001, 7005, 7027, 7043, 7046, 7049, 7050, 7063, 7070, 7071, 7077, 7100, 7113, 7125, 7129, 7130, 7133, 7135, 7157, 7161, 7162, 7170, 7172, 7182, 7189, 7191, 7194, 7195.
V7200-8127	691	Hawker Hurricane I	496 Hawker (Langley and Brooklands)-built. V7200-7209, 7221-7235 fabric-covered wings; remainder, metal-covered. V7236-7260, 7276-7318, 7337-7386, 7400-7446, 7461-7510, 7533-7572, 7588-7627, 7644-7690, 7705-7737, 7741-7780, 7795-7838, 7851-7862. Conversions to Sea Hurricane concerned: V7207, 7208, 7229, 7241, 7244, 7246, 7252, 7253, 7301, 7311, 7359, 7349, 7352, 7379, 7386, 7402, 7416, 7421, 7433, 7438, 7439, 7465, 7498, 7501-7506, 7588, 7600, 7623, 7646, 7647, 7650, 7665, 7675, 7681, 7685, 7745, 7824. Renumbering on conversion to Mk. II concerned: V7234 (to DG617), V7258 (to DG621), V7286 (to DR346), V7302 (to BV164), V7351 (to

			BV173), V7657 (to DG651), V7684 (to DG645). V7411, 7435, 7463, 7540 went to the Irish Air Corps. V7863-7900, 7917-7956, 7970-8000, 8023-8068, 8088-8127 cancelled.
V8131-8901	600	Bristol 156 Beaufighter	V8131-8170, 8184-8218 (75), Mk. IIF; 8219-8233, 8246-8289, 8307-8356, 8370-8385 (125), Mk. IF; V8386-8419, 8433-8472, 8489-8528, 8545-8594, 8608-8657, 8671-8720, 8733-8778, 8799-8848, 8862-8901 (400), Mk. VIF.
V8914	1	Blackburn B.20	Experimental retractable hull flying boat to Air Ministry Specification R.1/36.
V8920-8969	50	Westland Lysander	Cancelled. Project for Westland-assembled, Canadian-built aircraft.
V8975-9254	200	Lockheed Hudson III	V8975-8999, 9020-9065, short range version; V9066-9069, V9090-9129, 9150-9199, long range version; 9220-9254, short range version. V9235-9252, off-set to New Zealand.
V9280-9974	500	Westland Lysander IIIA	Westland (Yeovil)-built. V9280-9329, 9347-9386, 9401-9450, 9472-9521, 9538-9557, 9570-9619, 9642-9681, 9704-9750 (347), built as Mk. IIIA; V9751-9753, 9775-9824, 9844-9868, 9885-9906 (100), built as T.T.IIIA. V9907-9914, 9930-9974 cancelled. V9506, 9583, 9741 to U.S.A.A.F.; V9614 to Free French Forces. At least 86 were shipped to Canada. Eight IIIAs were shipped to Portugal. V9372, 9579, 9679, 9726 converted for glider towing.
V9976-9994	19	Handley Page H.P.59 Halifax II	Built by English Electric. Continued in " W " series.

THE "W" SERIES

W1000–9999

" W " followed " V " in April 1940, and with the tempo of operations increasing to all-out war, all available civil aircraft were impressed into service.

W1002-1276	181	Handley Page H.P.59 Halifax II	Built by the English Electric Co. Continued from " V " series. W1002-1021, 1035-1067, 1090-1117, 1141-1190, 1211-1253, 1270-1276.

Serial Nos.	*Qty.*	*Aircraft Type*	*Remarks*
W1280-1498	150	Avro 679 Manchester	Cancelled order placed with Armstrong Whitworth. W1280-1299, 1319-1350, 1374-1410, 1426-1475, 1488-1498.
W1505-2665	1000	Avro 652A Anson I	W1505-1524, 1529-1540, 1544-1570, 1576-1618, 1627-1676, 1690-1736, 1751-1800, 1814-1863, 1875-1924, 1932-1971, 1986-2025, 2031-2072, 2078-2099, 2109-2158, 2163-2212, 2216-2245, 2252-2291, 2298-2347, 2355-2398, 2403-2452, 2457-2496, 2499-2548, 2554-2592, 2598-2646, 2651-2665. Mainly delivered direct to Canada or Australia for Empire Air Training Scheme; only 155 retained in the U.K. W2656 to U.S.A.A.F.
W2670-3101	200	Supermarine Walrus I/II	Built by Saunders-Roe. W2670-2689, 2700-2729, 2731-2760, 2766-2798, 3005-3051, 3062-3101, Mk. I (except for W3010, 3047, 3051, 3076, 3078, Mk. II); built for Fleet Air Arm. W3007-3008 were transferred to the R.A.F. W2700, 2707, 2724, 2740, 3021 went to the Royal New Zealand Air Force.
W3109-3970	450	Supermarine Spitfire VA/VB	W3109-3138, 3168-3187, 3207-3216, 3226-3265, 3305-3334, 3364-3383, 3403-3412, 3422-3461, 3501-3530, 3560-3579, 3599-3608, 3618-3657, 3697-3726, 3756-3775, 3795-3804, 3814-3853, 3893-3902, 3931-3970. W3237 converted to Mk. III; W3112, 3135, 3831 converted to P.R.XIII. W3760 became an experimental floatplane version. Renumbering on conversion to Seafire IB concerned: W3212 (to NX883), W3371 (to PA119), W3372 (to NX980). The allotment of NX965 to W3646 was cancelled.
W3976-4037	50	Short S.25 Sunderland II/III	Short (Rochester)-built. W3976-3998, Mk. II; W3999-4004, W4017-4037, Mk. III.
W4041 & 4046	2	Gloster E.28/39 " Weaver "	W4041/G was first British jet. First flew 15.5.41.
W4050-4099	50	D.H.98 Mosquito	W4050 (ex-E-0234), 1st prototype. W4051, P.R.I; W4052, F.II prototype;

			W4053, F.II converted to T.III; W4054-4063, P.R.I; W4064-4072, B.IV/P.R.IV Ser. I; W4073-4099, F.II, of which W4073, 4075, 4077 were converted to T.III.
W4102-4700	454	Avro 683 Lancaster B.I	Avro (Manchester)-built. W4102-4140, 4154-4201, 4230-4279, 4301-4340, 4355-4384. W4114 became the Mk. III prototype. W4385-3300, 4414-4463, 4481-4524, 4537-4585, 4600-4641, 4655-4700 cancelled.
W4761-5012	200	Avro 683 Lancaster B.I/III	Built by Metropolitan-Vickers Ltd. W4761-4800, 4815-4864, 4879-4905, 4918-4967, 4980-4982 (170), Mk. I with Merlin 20 engines; W4983-5012 (30), Mk. III with Merlin 28 engines. W4783 became A66-2.
W5014-5015	2	D.H.82 Tiger Moth	G-AFZF and G-ADJE, impressed.
W5017-5315	270	Blackburn Botha I	Built at Brough. W5017-5056, 5065-5114, 5118-5157, 5162-5169 (138) only built. W5170-5211, 5216-5235, 5239-5288 5296-5315 cancelled.
W5352-5735	300	Vickers Wellington II/IC	W5352-5401, 5414-5463, 5476-5500, 5513-5537, 5550-5598, 5611 (200), Mk. II; W5612-5631, 5644-5690, 5703-5735 (100), Mk. Ic. W5686 and 5709 converted to Mk. XVI. Conversions to Mk. VIII were: W5615, 5619, 5623, 5631, 5645, 5647, 5649, 5653, 5655, 5657, 5659, 5661, 5662, 5671, 5672, 5674, 5676, 5678, 5725, 5728, 5730, 5735. W5389/G special mods including W2B jet in tail and W5518/G had W2/700 jet in tail.
W5740-5741	2	Taylorcraft Plus D	G-AFZH and G-AFZI, impressed.
W5746-5782	23	D.H.87 Hornet Moth	Impressed. W5746-5755, ex-G-ADKE /KH /KJ /KK/KL/KM/KR/EKS/DKW/DMM; W5770-5782, ex-G-ADMN/DMS/DNB /DNC /EPV /ESE/ETC/EWY/EZT /FDT /FDY/FEE/FMP.
W5783	1	D.H.85 Leopard Moth	G-AFDV, impressed from the Yorkshire Aero Club.
W5784	1	D.H.87 Hornet Moth	G-AFRE, impressed.
W5791	1	Stinson SR-9D Reliant	Works No. 5400, G-AFBI impressed.

Serial Nos.	*Qty.*	*Aircraft Type*	*Remarks*
W5795-5824	30	Vickers Wellington	W5795, Mk. VI prototype; W5796, Mk. V; W5797, Rolls-Royce test-bed; W 5798-5815, Mk. VIA. W5816-5824 (Mk. V) cancelled.
W5830	1	D.H.87 Hornet Moth	G-ADKE, impressed.
W5836-5995	100	Fairey Swordfish II	Built by Blackburn. W5836-5865, 5886-5925, 5966-5995.
W6000-6080	50	Short S.25 Sunderland II/III	W6000-6004, Mk. II; W6005-6016, 6026-6033, Mk. III(25), built by Blackburn at Dumbarton. W6050-6064, Mk. II (15), W6065-6068, 6075-6080, Mk. III (10), built by Short & Harland.
W6085	1	Percival Q.6	G-AFKC, impressed in Middle East.
W6089-6410	250	Bristol 156 Beaufighter	Cancelled order placed with Boulton Paul, W6089-6126, 6140-6185, 6200-6249, 6265-6300, 6316-6360, 6376-6410.
W6415	1	D.H.60G Gipsy Moth	G-ABOU impressed.
W6416	1	D.H.80A Puss Moth	G-ABKG, impressed.
W6417-6420	4	D.H. 82 Tiger Moth	G-AFWC to G-AFWF, impressed.
W6421-6422	2	D.H.87 Hornet Moth	G-ADKB and G-ADKN, impressed.
W6423-6425	3	D.H.89 Dragon Rapide	G-ADNH/EAM/EAJ, impressed.
W6455-6457	3	D.H.89 Dragon Rapide	G-AENN/EOV/FSO, impressed.
W6458-6460	3	D.H.94 Moth Minor	G-AFPC/D/S, impressed.
W6461-6463	3	Miles M.17 Monarch	G-AFCR/JZ/RZ, impressed.
W6464	1	Percival Vega Gull	G-AEYC, impressed.
W6467-6543	66	Bristol 152 Beaufort 1	W6467-6506, W6518-6543. Deliveries mainly to Operational Training Units. W6473 and W6484 were shipped to Canada.
W6546-6657	100	Airspeed A.S.10 Oxford II	Built by Percival Aircraft, W6546-6595, W6608-6657. Mainly to home units.
W6667-6670	4	Hawker Hurricane	Hawker (Langley)-built. Delivered July 1940.
W6675-7241	500	Westland Lysander III	17 Westland (Doncaster)-built as W6939-6945, 6951-6960. Cancelled numbers: W6675-6724, 6733-6782, 6788-6817, 6824-6863, 6869-6888, 6896-6938, 6961-6990, 6999-7048, 7053-7082, 7091-7140, 7145-7184, 7192-7241.
W7247-7409	150	Blackburn Botha	Cancelled. W7247-7296, 7300-7339, 7343-7362, 7368-7379, 7382-7409.

W7419	1	Short S.16 Scion	Short No. S.778, G-ACUZ, impressed.
W7422	1	Miles Whitney Straight	G-AEUY, impressed for Air Attaché, Paris.
W7426-7639	150	Short S.29 Stirling I	Built by the Austin Motor Co. W7426-7475, 7500-7539, 7560-7589, 7610-7639.
W7646	1	General Aircraft G.A.L.33 Cagnet	Ex-T.46. At School of Army Co-operation, June 1940.
W7650-7939	200	Handley Page H.P.59 Halifax II	Handley Page-built. W7650-7679, 7695-7720, 7745-7784, 7801-7826, 7844-7887, 7906-7939.
W7945-7949	5	D.H.60 Gipsy Moth	Impressed. Ex-G-AAPW/BER/AJP/BAI/CRR.
W7950-7956	7	D.H.82 Tiger Moth	Impressed. Ex-G-AFSL/SP/NR/SR/SG/GT/ST.
W7970	1	D.H.82 Tiger Moth	G-AFSU, impressed.
W7971-7975	5	D.H.94 Moth Minor	Impressed. Ex-G-AFPB/NI/OX/OY/OZ.
W7976	1	D.H. 60GIII Moth Major	G-ADAN, impressed.
W7977	1	General Aircraft Monospar	Re-numbered T9264.
W7978-7984	7	Stinson SR7-10 Reliant	Impressed. Ex-G-AFRS/EFY/EVX/FHB/EXW/FTM/EVY.
W7990-8129	100	Westland Lysander	Cancelled. W7990-7999, 8020-8069, 8090-8129. To have been built in Canada.
W8131-8250	120	Brewster 339 Buffalo	Mainly shipped direct from the U.S.A. to Singapore. W8131, ex-U.S. NX147B.
W8252-8401	150	Douglas Boston III	W8256, 8262, 8264, 8266, 8268, 8278, 8281, 8283, 8284, 8290, 8292 converted to Intruder version; W8257, 8265, 8275, 8276, 8300 fitted with Turbinlites; W8401 converted to trainer; W8274, 8277, 8317, 8328, 8341, 8352, 8366, 8369, 8393, 8396 converted to Havoc N.F.II.
W8405-8434	30	Consolidated Catalina I	W8431-8432 to Royal Canadian Air Force.
W8437-9099	500	Miles Master III/II	Built by Phillips & Powis Ltd. at South Marston. W8437-8486, 8500-8539, 8560-8599, 8620-8699, 8690-8739, 8760-8799, 8815-8864, 8880-8909, 8925-8974, 8980-9003 (414), Mk. III; W9004-9039, 9050-9099 (86), Mk. II.
W9104-9106	3	Lockheed 10A Electra	Impressed. Ex-G-AFEB/EPN/EPO.
W9110-9359	200	Hawker Hurricane I	Built by Gloster Aircraft. W9110-9159, 9170-9209, 9215-9244, 9260-9279, 9290-9329, 9340-9359. W9181 became

Serial Nos.	Qty.	Aircraft Type	Remarks
			DG635, and W9265 became DR356 on conversion to Mk. II. W9124, 9128, 9174, 9182, 9188, 9209, 9215, 9216, 9218, 9220-9224, 9237, 9272, 9276, 9277, 9279, 9311-9313, 9315, 9316, 9318, 9319 converted to Sea Hurricane; W9191 re-numbered DR345 on conversion to Mk. IIA.
W9365	1	D.H.89 Dragon Rapide	G-ADNI, impressed for the Royal Navy.
W9367-9368	2	D.H.60 Gipsy Moth	G-ABBD and G-AFWJ, impressed for the Royal Navy.
W9369	1	D.H.80A Puss Moth	G-ABIZ, impressed for the Royal Navy.
W9370-9371	2	D.H.85 Leopard Moth	G-ACLK and G-ADHB, impressed for the Royal Navy.
W9372	1	D.H.87 Hornet Moth	G-ADKV, impressed for the Royal Navy.
W9373	1	Miles M.3 Falcon	G-AEKK, impressed for the Royal Navy.
W9374	1	Percival Q.6	G-AFFE, impressed for the Royal Navy.
W9375-9378	4	Percival P.10 Vega Gull	Royal Navy impressments. Ex-G-AFIT/ELS/FBW/ETF.
W9379-9391	13	D.H.87 Hornet Moth	R.A.F. impressments. Ex-G-AFDU/FDW/EZH/FDF/EKY/EZY/DND/DKU/DIR/DLY/DMJ/FDG/DIS.
W9396-9975	350	Blackburn Botha	Cancelled. W9396-9415, 9434-9463, 9496-9545, 9558-9597, 9646-9665, 9702-9741, 9748-9772, 9821-9855, 9880-9899, 9936-9975, with X1000-1029 to complete 350 as contracted.

THE LICENSED SERIES

X1–25 IN 1917 it was made unlawful, under the Defence Regulations, to construct an aeroplane without official authority. This measure was intended to avoid wasting valuable material on building aircraft that stood no chance of official acceptance. The present policy, for the Service to notify industry of their operational requirements and to invite tenders, was then introduced. If a firm wished to venture privately on a project outside official requirements, but which showed promise, licence to construct was granted and such aircraft were numbered in a special " X " series. Full documentation for this series cannot be traced, but it is evident that the series was discontinued in 1918 and all such experimental aircraft were then re-numbered in the main series.

X1	1	Glendower	Not confirmed. Glendower Company applied for licence.
X2-5	4	Sopwith 2F.R.2 Bulldog	X2, single bay wings; X3, Mk. I; X4, Mk. II. X5, not confirmed. X3-4 became H4422-4423.
X7-8	2	Sopwith 2B.2 Rhino	Licence No. 14.
X10-11	2	Sopwith 3F.2 Hippo	X10 not confirmed. Licence No. 16. X11 became H4420.
X12-13	2	Nieuport Fighter	B.R.2 engine. Not adopted.
X14	1	Saunders T.1	"T.1" for H. H. Thomas (designer). Licence No. 13.
X15-17	3	Austin A.F.T.3 Osprey	Licence No. 17, X15 built. Work abandoned on X16-17 March 1918.
X18	1	Sopwith 3F.2 Hippo	Licence withdrawn early 1918. Became H4421.
X19-20	2	Armstrong Whitworth F.M.4 Armadillo	Licence No. 18. "F.M." for designer, F. Murphy.
X21-24	4	Armstrong Siddeley Sinaia	X21-2 completed as J6858-6859, X23-4 cancelled.
X25	1	Boulton & Paul P.6	Used by Boulton & Paul sales department in 1919.

THE "X" SERIES

X1000–9999

"X" had only been used briefly for a special series of licensed aircraft, and then only up to X26, so that X1000 was a logical follow-on from W9999 in 1940.

X1000-1029	30	Blackburn Botha	Cancelled. See remarks for W9396-9975.
X1032-1034	3	Percival P.10 Vega Gull	Impressed for service in Middle East. Ex-G-AEXU/ERL/FAV.
X1038-1040	3	Airspeed A.S.-10 Oxford I	Shipped to Southern Rhodesia as replacements for P1984, 1993, 2002.
X1045-1046	2	Supermarine Walrus	Built on contract for experimental aircraft by Saunders Roe.
X1050	1	Stinson 105 Voyager	Stinson No. 7504, on loan. Became G-AGZW and SE-BYI.
X1085-1086	2	Percival Vega Gull	Impressed. Became SE-ALA and SE-ALZ.
X2865-2867	3	D.H.83 Fox Moth	Impressed. Ex-G-ACDZ/CEX/BVK.
X2891	1	Heston 1 Phoenix	Heston No. 1/5. Series II model, ex-G-AESV.
X2893-3154	150	H.P.52 Hampden I	Built by the English Electric Co. X2893-2922, 2959-3008, 3021-3030, 3047-3066, 3115-3154. X2976, 3022, 3131 converted to T.B. (Torpedo Bomber) and left in Russian

Serial Nos.	*Qty.*	*Aircraft Type*	*Remarks*
			hands ex-No. 455 Squadron. X3115 was Mk. II prototype.
X3160-4003	500	Vickers Wellington IC/III	Vickers (Blackpool)-built. X3160-3179, 3192-3221 (50), Mk. IC; X3222-3226, 3275-3289, 3299-3313, 3330-3374, 3387-3426, 3445-3489, 3538-3567, 3584-3608, 3633-3677, 3694-3728, 3741-3765, 3784-3823, 3866-3890, 3923-3967, 3984-4003 (450), Mk. III. X3193 and X3935 converted to Mk. XVI. X3374 and X3595 Mk. X prototypes.
X4009-4997	500	Supermarine Spitfire I	X4009-4038, 4051-4070, 4101-4110, 4159-4188, 4231-4280, 4317-4331, Mk. I; X4332-4335, Mk. I P.R. Type C; X4336-4356, 4381, Mk. I; X4382-4386, Mk. I P.R. Type C; X4387-4390, 4409-4428, 4471-4490, Mk. I; X4491-4497, Mk. I P.R. Type C; X4498-4505, 4538, Mk. V P.R. Type C; X4539-4562, 4585-4624, 4641-4685, 4708-4722, 4765-4789, 4815-4859, 4896-4945, 4988-4997, Mk. I. X4708 & 4780 crashed before delivery. Completed or converted to Mk. V in service were: X4062, 4106, 4257, 4258, 4272, 4280, 4555, 4604-4606, 4620-4624, 4663-4671, 4902, 4922, 4997. X4942 was converted to Mk. VI. Conversions to P.R.XIII in 1943 concerned X4021, 4615, 4660, 4766. Other Spitfires in this range were variously modified for photographic reconnaissance work. X4717, 4989 were converted to Seafire IB. X4067, 4622, 4776 conv. to Mk. II.
X5000	1	Ford 5AT Trimotor	Ford No. 5AT-107 G-ACAE (ex-NC440H), impressed.
X5006-5007	2	British Aircraft Swallow II	G-AEIH and G-AEHK, impressed.
X5008	1	British Klemm Swallow	G-ACWA, impressed.
X5009	1	Klemm L.25 Salmson	G-AAZH, impressed.
X5010-5011	2	British Klemm Swallow	G-ACOW and G-ACRD, impressed.
X5017-5043	28	D.H.60 Gipsy Moth	X5017-5019, D.H.60A (ex-G-ABOE/AMS/AAO); X5020, D.H.60X (ex-G-AAPH); X5021-5027, D.H.60A (ex-

			G-AAEX/ BOY/ AVY/ BDU/ AEH/BPJ/ALW), X5028, D.H.60G (ex-G-AADH); X5029, D.H.60A (ex-G-ABUB); X5030, DH.60 (ex-G-AAIW); X5031-5037, D.H.60A (ex-G-AABK/ALV/ BDK/ABJ/ AKO/ BJI/ AIA); X5038, D.H.60X (ex-G-AAAA); X5039-5041, D.H. 60G (ex-G-ABCS/AJW/ALN) X5042, D.H.60A (ex-G-AFKY); X5043, D.H.60G (ex-G-AASZ).
X5044	1	D.H.80A Puss Moth	G-ABVX impressed.
X5045	1	D.H.82 Tiger Moth	G-ADJH, impressed.
X5046-5104	12	D.H.60 Gipsy Moth	Impressments. X5046-5048, D.H.60G (ex-G-AARA/AKU/ BCT); X5049, D.H.60A (ex-G-AFPY); X5050, D.H. 60G (ex-G-ADIL); X5051, D.H.60M (ex-G-AFMY); X5052-5055, D.H.60G (ex-G-ABXZ/ AFO/ FTG/AJS); X5056, D.H.60 (ex-G-AFDZ); X5104, D.H.60G (ex-G-AALG).
X5105-5110	6	D.H.82 Tiger Moth	G-AEWG/FSH/FSI/FSJ/FSM/ FSN, impressed.
X5111-5114	4	D.H.60 Gipsy Moth	G-ABJH/BGM/BLT/CCW, impressed.
X5115-5117	3	D.H.94 Moth Minor	G-AFOC/PI/OB, impressed.
X5118-5119	2	D.H.60 Gipsy Moth	G-ABAL/ARU, impressed.
X5120-5123	4	D.H.94 Moth Minor	G-AFOD/FOE/FPR/FRY, impressed.
X5124	1	D.H.60G III	G-ADAT, impressed.
X5125	1	Miles M.2H Hawk Major	G-ADIT, impressed; became 3017M.
X5126-5132	7	D.H.60 Gipsy Moth	Impressments. X5126-5127, D.H.60M (ex-AAYG/SL); X5128, D.H.60X (ex-G-EBRI); X5129, D.H.60G (ex-G-ABRO); X5130, D.H. 60M (ex-G-ABHN); X5131-5132, D.H.60GIII (ex-G-ACGX/BX).
X5133	1	D.H.94 Moth Minor	G-AFPH, impressed.
X5139-5319	140	Short S.29 Stirling II	Cancelled order placed in Canada. X5139-5183, 5200-5249, 5275-5319.
X5324	1	Stinson 105 Voyager	Imported from U.S.A.
X5330-6517	750	Vickers Wellington	Cancelled. X5330-5359, 5372-5421, 5446-5490, 5523-5547, 5596-5630, 5657-5701, 5726-5775, 5810-5844, 5859-5903, 5920-5964, 5985-6004, 6023-6062, 6079-6128, 6153-6202, 6245-6294, 6311-6355, 6380-6419, 6468-6517.

Serial Nos.	Qty.	Aircraft Type	Remarks
X6520-7317	500	Airspeed A.S.10 Oxford I/II	X6520-6564, 6589-6623, 6643-6692, 6726-6750, 6764-6813, 6835-6879 (250), Mk. I; X6880-6884, 6932-6981, 7031-7075, 7107-7156, 7176-7200, 7231-7265, 7278-7317 (250), Mk. II.
X7320-7525	150	D.H.89A Dominie	D.H. Nos. 6493-6583, 6585-6642. X7320-7354, 7368-7417, 7437-7456, 7482-7525. Deliveries X7332, 7341, 7348, 7350, 7394, 7397, 7400, 7414, 7437, 7448, 7452, 7453, 7482, 7486-7488, 7494, 7497-7499, 7506-7508 to the Royal Navy, remainder to the Royal Air Force, except for X7524-7525 (direct from contract for Misr Airways, lost at sea en route for Egypt, and replaced by X7384 and X7391). First ten had Gipsy VI engines, remainder Gipsy III.
X7533-7534	2	Taylorcraft Plus D	G-AGBF/AFWO, impressed.
X7540-8269	500	Bristol 156 Beaufighter I/VIC/IVF	Built at Old Mixon Shadow Factory, Weston-super-Mare. X7540-7541, Mk. IF; X7542 7543, Mk. VIF/C prototypes; X7544-7589, 7610-7649, 7670-7719, 7740-7779, 7800-7849, 7870-7879, Mk. I; X7880-7899, 7920-7924, Mk. VIF; X7925, Mk. VIC; X7926-7936, Mk. VIF; X7937-7939, Mk. VIC; X7940-7969, 8000-8029, Mk. VIF; X8030-8039, 8060-8099, Mk. VIC (X8095 Mk.X prototype); X8100-8109, 8130-8169, 8190-8229, 8250-8269, Mk. VIF.
X8273-8275	3	Short S.26 "G" Class	G-AFCK/J/1, *Golden Horn*, *Golden Fleece* and *Golden Hind*, impressed.
X8505-8511	7	D.H.89 Rapide	Impressed. Ex-G-AEXP/FEO/EXO/FAH/CTT/EPW/DBV.
X8518-8519	2	Stinson SR-5 Reliant	G-ACSV/ADDG, impressed.
X8520	1	Stinson SR-8 Reliant	G-AEJI, impressed.
X8521	1	Stinson SR-9 Reliant	G-AEYZ, impressed.
X8522	1	Stinson Junior Reliant	G-AFUW, impressed.
X8525-8817	200	Fairey Fulmar II	X8525-8574, 8611-8655, 8680-8714, 8729-8778, 8798-8817. First 22 (X8525-8546) delivered packed for shipping. Delivered to R.N., but X8693, 8701, 8743, 8773 used for a period by R.A.F.
X8825-8912	50	Percival P.30 Proctor IIA	X8825-8859, 8898-8912 cancelled. Intended for R.N.

X8916-8939	24	Bristol 152 Beaufort I	Bristol Nos. 9538-9561. Delivery during 1941. X8931 had D.C. set fitted.
X8940-9290	250	Fairey Albacore	Fairey Nos. F.5220-469. X8940-8984, 9010-9059, 9073-9117, 9137-9186, 9214-9233, 9251-9290.
X9294-9295	2	D.H.85 Leopard Moth	G-ACKR and G-ACUK, impressed.
X9296	1	D.H.60M Moth	G-ABNR, impressed.
X9297-9298	2	D.H.94 Moth Minor	G-AFPN and G-AFOU, impressed.
X9299	1	D.H.83 Fox Moth	G-ACIG, impressed.
X9300-9301	2	Miles M.3 Falcon Major	G-ADHI and G-AEFB, impressed.
X9302-9303	2	D.H.60G Gipsy Moth	G-ACMB and G-ABBJ, impressed.
X9304-9305	2	D.H.83 Fox Moth	G-ABUT and G-ACFF, impressed.
X9306	1	Miles M.17 Monarch	G-AFJU, impressed.
X9310	1	D.H.87 Hornet Moth	G-ADMR, impressed.
X9315	1	Percival Vega Gull	G-AFEH, impressed.
X9316	1	Lockheed 12A	G-AEOI, impressed.
X9317	1	D.H.95 Flamingo	G-AFUF, impressed.
X9318	1	D.H.82 Tiger Moth	G-AFSS, impressed.
X9319	1	D.H.87 Hornet Moth	G-AEET, impressed.
X9320	1	D.H.89 Rapide	G-ACYM, impressed.
X9321-9326	6	D.H.87 Hornet Moth	G-ADKD/DKP/DML/FBH/DNE/DOT, impressed.
X9327	1	D.H.90 Dragonfly	G-ADXM, impressed.
X9328-9329	2	Percival Q.6	G-AEYE and G-AFHG, impressed.
X9330-9331	2	General Aircraft ST-25 Monospar	Universal type G-AFSB and G-AFSA, impressed.
X9332	1	Percival Vega Gull II	G-AFAU, impressed.
X9333-9335	3	General Aircraft ST-25 Monospar	Universal type: G-AFIP, G-AFIV, G-AFWP, impressed.
X9336	1	Percival Q.6	G-AFGX, impressed.
X9337	1	D.H.90 Dragonfly	G-AFVJ, impressed.
X9338	1	Heston Phoenix Series II	G-AEYX, impressed.
X9339-9340	2	Percival Vega Gull	G-AEZK and G-AFBC, impressed.
X9341	1	General Aircraft ST-12 Monospar	G-ADLL, impressed.
X9342-9343	2	Airspeed A.S.5 Courier	G-ACLF and G-ADAY impressed.
X9344-9347	4	Airspeed A.S.5 Courier	G-ACLR-/ZL/NZ/VF, impressed.
X9348	1	General Aircraft ST-25 Monospar	Jubilee Type: G-ADPK, impressed. Later became DR848.
X9349	1	Percival Vega Gull	G-AELW, impressed.
X9363	1	Percival Q.6	G-AFKG, impressed.
X9364	1	Short S.16 Scion 2	G-ADDN, impressed.
X9365	1	General Aircraft ST-25 Monospar	Jubilee Type: G-ADVH, impressed.
X9366	1	Short S.16 Scion	Series 2: G-ADDR, impressed. Became 2724M.

Serial Nos.	Qty.	Aircraft Type	Remarks
X9367	1	General Aircraft ST-4 Monospar	G-ADJP impressed.
X9368	1	Percival Vega Gull	G-AFEM, impressed.
X9369	1	General Aircraft ST-25 Monospar	Jubilee Type: G-ADPL, impressed.
X9370	1	Airspeed Envoy III	VT-AIC, became G-AFWZ and impressed.
X9371	1	Percival Vega Gull	G-AEMB, impressed.
X9372-9373	2	General Aircraft ST-25 Monospar	Universal/Jubilee Type: G-AEPA and G-ADYN, impressed.
X9374-9375	2	Short S.16 Scion II/I	G-ADDP (Series II) and G-ACJI (Series I), impressed.
X9376	1	General Aircraft ST-4 Monospar	Mk. II version: G-ACCO, impressed. Became DR849.
X9377	1	General Aircraft ST-25 Monospar	Universal Type: G-AEGY, impressed.
X9378	1	D.H.80 Puss Moth	G-ABRR, impressed.
X9379	1	D.H.84 Dragon	G-ACHV. Became 2396M.
X9380-9385	6	D.H.85 Leopard Moth	G-ACLM/CMN/CPK/DCO/CSH/DWY, impressed.
X9386-9388	3	D.H.89 Rapide	G-ADDE/EMH, impressed for R.A.F.; G-AFEP, impressed for Royal Navy.
X9389-9390	2	D.H.90 Dragonfly	G-AEDV and G-AEFN, impressed.
X9391-9392	2	Percival Vega Gull	G-AEXV and G-AFEK, impressed.
X9393	1	Heston Phoenix Series II	G-AEMT, impressed.
X9394	1	Airspeed A.S.5 Courier	G-ACLT, impressed.
X9395-9399	5	D.H.84 Dragon	G-ACIU/CMJ/CLE/CAO/CPX, impressed.
X9400-9405	6	D.H.80 Puss Moth	G-ABLB/AZX/AZV/BKD/AXO/BHB, impressed.
X9406-9407	2	Percival Q.6	G-AFIX and G-AFFD, impressed.
X9430	1	Short S.16 Scion 2	G-ADDX, impressed.
X9431-9433	3	Spartan Cruiser II/III	X9431, II (ex-G-ACYL); X9432, III (ex-G-ADEL); X9433, II (ex-G-ACSM).
X9434	1	General Aircraft ST-4 Monospar	G-ABVP, impressed.
X9435-9436	2	Percival Vega Gull	G-AEWS and G-AEZL, impressed.
X9437	1	Airspeed A.S.5 Courier	G-ADAX, impressed.
X9438	1	D.H.60 Moth	G-AFZB, impressed.
X9439	1	D.H.80 Puss Moth	G-ABSO, impressed.
X9440	1	D.H.84 Dragon	G-ADCP, impressed.
X9441-9442	2	D.H.86B/D.H.86	G-AEJM and G-ADMY, impressed.
X9443-9447	5	D.H.87 Hornet Moth	G-ADJX/DJZ/DKC/FEC/FEF, impressed.

X9448-9451	4	D.H.89 Rapide	G-ADAL/DWZ/EML, impressed for R.A.F.; G-AFEZ, impressed for Royal Navy.
X9452	1	D.H.90 Dragonfly	G-ADNA, impressed.
X9453	1	General Aircraft ST-10 Monospar	G-ACTS, impressed.
X9454	1	Percival Q.6	G-AFMT, impressed.
X9455	1	Percival Vega Gull	G-AEJJ, impressed.
X9456	1	Short S.16 Scion	Series II: G-ADDV, impressed.
X9457	1	D.H.89 Rapide	G-ADFX, impressed.
X9458	1	D.H.87 Hornet Moth	G-ADKS, impressed.
X9460-9593	100	Supermarine Walrus I/II	Built by Saunders-Roe. X9460-9484, 9498-9532, 9554-9558, Mk. I; X9559-9593, Mk. II.
X9596	1	Stinson SR-8 Reliant	G-AELU, impressed in May 1940.
X9600-9993	270	Vickers Wellington IC	Vickers (Chester)-built. X9600-9644, 9658-9707, 9733-9767, 9785-9834, 9871-9890, 9905-9954, 9974-9993. Continued in " Z " series. X9663 and X9678 converted to Mk. XVI.

THE END OF A SYSTEM

Z1000–9999

" Y " was not used, to avoid confusion with " V ", and Z1000 followed on from X9999.

Z1040-1751	440	Vickers Wellington	Continued from " X " series. Vickers (Chester)-built. Z1040-1054, 1066-1115 (Z1071 converted to Mk. XVI), 1139-1181, Mk. IC (Z1150 converted to Mk. XVI); Z1182-1183, 1202-1221, 1243-1292, 1311-1345, 1375-1424, 1459-1496, Mk. IV; Z1562-1578, 1592-1626, 1648-1697, 1717-1751, Mk. III.
Z1755-1823	50	Supermarine Walrus II	Built by Saunders-Roe. Z1755-1784, 1804-1823.
Z1826-2126	200	Fairey Firefly I	Z1826-1829, prototypes; Z1830-1845, 1865-1914, 1942-1986, 2011-2060, 2092-2126, Mk. I; Z1831/G, Mk. II prototype; Z1835, converted to Mk. IV; Z1846, F.R.I. prototype; Z1855, Mk. III prototype; Z1875, N.F.II prototype; Z1901, converted to F.R.IA; Z2118, Mk. IV pro-

Serial Nos.	*Qty.*	*Aircraft Type*	*Remarks*
			totype; Z1893, 1909, 1953, 1980, 2020, 2021, 2025, 2027, 2054, 2058, 2108, 2111, 2119, converted to T.1.
Z2003	1	Aeronca Chief	VT-ALN, impressed in India for Bengal Communications Flight.
Z2134-2153	20	Consolidated 28 Catalina I	Z2134 and 2136-2140 to Royal Canadian Air Force; Z2152 to British Overseas Airways Corporation.
Z2155-2304	150	Douglas Boston III	Z2155 and Z2165 converted to Intruder version; Z2184, 2214, 2270 converted to Havoc N.F.II; Z2189 converted to a trainer. Z2200 transferred to U.S.A.A.F.
Z2308-4018	1000	Hawker Hurricane IIA/IIB/IIC	Hawker (Kingston, Brooklands and Langley)-built. Z2308-2357, 2382-2426, 2446-2465, 2479-2528, 2560-2594, 2624-2643, 2661-2705, 2741-2775, 2791-2840, 2882-2931, 2959-2993, 3017-3036, 3050-3099, 3143-3187, 3221-3270, 3310-3359, 3385-3404, 3421-3470, 3489-3523, 3554-3598, 3642-3691, 3740-3784, 3826-3845, 3885-3919, 3969-4018. Z2340 was broken up for spares before delivery. Z2320/G, 2326, 2885, 3092/G, 3564, 3919 used for various armament trials. Z3687 used for testing Armstrong Whitworth wing sections.
Z4022-4652	400	Hawker Hurricane I	Built by Gloster Aircraft. Z4022-4071, 4085-4119, 4161-4205, 4223-4272, 4308-4327, 4347-4391, 4415-4434,, 4482-4516, 4532-4581, 4603-4652. Z4489 converted to Mk. II. Z4039, 4051, 4053, 4055-4057, 4094, 4365, 4500, 4504, 4532, 4550, 4553, 4568, 4569, 4581, 4605, 4624, 4638, 4646, 4649, converted to Sea Hurricane.
Z4686-5693	600	Hawker Hurricane I/IIA/11B	Built by Gloster Aircraft. Z4686-4720, 4760-4809, 4832-4876, 4920-4939 (150), Mk. I —of which Z4686, 4778, 4835, 4846, 4847, 4849, 4851-4854, 4865-4867, 4873, 4874, 4876, 4920-4922, 4924-4926, 4929, 4933-4939 were converted to Sea Hurricane; Z4940-4969, 4987-4989 (33), Mk. IIA—

			of which Z4941 was converted to Mk. IIB; Z4990-5006, 5038-5087, 5117-5161, 5202-5236, 5252-5271, 5302-5351, 5376-5395, 5434-5483, 5529-5563, 5580-5629, 5649-5693 (417), Mk. IIB.
Z5721-6455	420	Bristol 142L Blenheim IV	Built by A. V. Roe. Z5721-5770, 5794-5818, 5860-5909, 5947-5991, 6021-6050, 6070-6104, 6144-6193, 6239-6283, 6333-6382, 6416-6455. Transfers after initial R.A.F. service included: Z5727, 5728, 5768, 5795 to Free French Forces. Z5736, 5760, 5762, 6030, 6035, 6341 to Portuguese Air Force in 1943.
Z6461-6980	300	Armstrong Whitworth A.W.38 Whitley V/VII	Z6461-6510, 6552-6586, 6624-6673, 6720-6764, 6793-6842, 6862-6881, 6931-6959 (279), Mk. V; Z6960-6969 (10) Mk. VII; Z6970-6980 (11), Mk. V. Z6660 was loaned to British Overseas Airways Corporation as G-AGDW.
Z6983-7162	100	Hawker Hurricane I	Built by the Canadian Car & Foundry Corporation. Z6983-7017, 7049-7093, 7143-7162. Conversions to Sea Hurricane I were; Z6987, 6995, 6997, 7008, 7015, 7016, 7050, 7055, 7057, 7061, 7065, 7067, 7069, 7071, 7073, 7078-7080, 7082-7091, 7093, 7144-7145, 7148, 7149, 7151-7155, 7160-7162.
Z7187	1	Short Scion Major	VQ-PAD ex-G-AEIL, impressed.
Z7188	1	D.H.89 Rapide	Reserved for VQ-PAC.
Z7189-7190	2	Short Scion Junior	VQ-PAA and VQ-PAB, impressed.
Z7193-7256	50	Percival P.30 Proctor II	Z7193-7222, 7237-7256, of which Z7253-7256 compromised numbers below and were renumbered BT278-281. Deliveries were to R.A.F. except for twelve (Z7239-7249 and Z7251) fitted out for the Fleet Air Arm. Z7198 was transferred to the U.S.A.A.F. The following were modified to Mk. III: Z7193-7194, 7196-7197, 7201, 7203, 7206, 7209, 7212-7214, 7216, 7218, 7222, 7237, 7238, 7248, 7252.
Z7253-7266	14	D.H.89 Rapide	Impressed, ex-G-AFLY/FLZ/FMA/FMF/FME/FMH/FMG/FMI/FMJ/DAI/DIM/

Serial Nos.	Qty.	Aircraft Type	Remarks
			DAG/DBW/CZE. Z7258 and 7261 were fitted out as ambulances.
Z7271-8323	600	Bristol 142L Blenheim IV	Built by Rootes Securities. Z7271-7320, 7340-7374, 7406-7455, 7483-7522, 7577-7596, 7610-7654, 7678-7712, 7754-7803, 7841-7860, 7879-7928, 7958-7992 (430), built; Z7993-8002, 8050-8099, 8143-8167, 8202-8236, 8274-8323, cancelled. Transfers after R.A.F. service were: Z7373, 7779, 7842, 7885 to Free French Forces; Z7492 to Portuguese Air Force and Z7986 to Turkish Air Force.
Z8328-9114	450	Vickers Wellington IC/II/VIII	Z8328-8377, 8397-8441, 8489-8538, 8567-8601, 8643-8662 (200), Mk. II; Z8702-8703; Mk. VIII; Z8704, Mk. IC; Z8705-8708, Mk. VIII; Z8709 Mk. IC; Z8710-8713, Mk. VIII; Z8714, Mk. IC; Z8715, Mk. VIII; Z8716, Mk. IC, Z8717, Mk. VIII; Z8718, Mk. IC; Z8719, Mk. VIII; Z8720, Mk. IC; Z8721, Mk. VIII; Z8722, Mk. IC; Z8723, Mk. VIII; Z8724, Mk. IC; Z8725, Mk. VIII; Z8726, Mk. IC; Z8727, Mk. VIII; Z8728-8736, 8761-8810, 8822-8871, 8891-8901, Mk. IC; Z8902, Mk. VIII; Z8903-8910, 8942-8991, 9016-9045, 9095-9114, Mk. IC. Z8709, 8831, 8850, converted to Mk. XVI; Z8570, experimentally fitted by Rolls-Royce with Rover-built W2B booster unit; Z8416, Vickers "S" gun tests.
Z9119-9529	250	Armstrong Whitworth A.W.38 Whitley	Z9119, Mk. V; Z9120-9124, Mk. VII; Z9125-9134, Mk. V; Z9135-9139, Mk. VII; Z9140-9168, 9188-9189, Mk. V; Z9190-9199, Mk. VII; Z9200-9232, 9274-9323, 9361-9363, Mk. V; Z9364-9383, Mk. VII; Z9384-9390, 9419-9443, 9461-9490, 9510-9515, Mk. V; Z9516-9529, Mk. VII. Z9208, 9216 loaned to British Overseas Airways Corporation as G-AGDU/V.

Z9533-9978	280	Bristol 142L Blenheim IV	Z9533-9552, 9572-9621, 9647-9681, 9706-9755, 9792-9836 (200), built by A. V. Roe; Z9886-9935, 9949-9978, cancelled.

COMMENCEMENT OF THE "DOUBLE-BARRELLED" SERIES

AA100–AE479

WHEN Z9999 was reached in 1940, the allocating authority in the newly-formed Ministry of Aircraft Production had the option of starting again at A1000 or using a new series as a follow-on; the latter course was chosen, and a system evolved using two initial letters in alphabetical sequence, AA, AB, AC *et seq* to AZ and then BA, BB, BC *et seq* to BZ. This was put into effect with the exception of certain letters, or combinations of letters, which for various reasons were not used. Since an additional letter was introduced, the number range was reduced from 1000-9999 to 100-999. Black-out blocks continued, with certain exceptions for which explanations are given under the appropriate headings. " AC " was not used to avoid confusion with " AG ".

Unlike the 1914-1918 War, when captured enemy aircraft had a separate series, airworthy captured German and Italian aircraft were allotted numbers in the normal sequence and the first of these occurs in this series.

AA100-AA273	120	Bristol 142L Blenheim IV	Cancelled. AA100-144, 178-202, 224-273. A. V. Roe order.
AA281-AA713	300	Boulton Paul P.82 Defiant I/II	AA281-330, 350-362, Mk. I—of which AA282-286, 288-292, 294-296, 298, 300-301, 306, 308, 310-311, 313-314, 316-317, 320-324, 326-330, 354, 358, 361, were converted to T.T.III; AA363-369, Mk. I converted to Mk. II on production line); AA370-384, 398-447, 469-513, 531-550, 566-595, 614-633, 651-670, Mk. II. AA671-673, 687-713 cancelled.
AA718-AB536	500	Supermarine Spitfire IV/V (Basically Mk. V standard)	AA718-767, Mk. VB (AA739 converted to P.R.XIII); AA 781-815, P.R.IV; AA833-882, 902-946, 963-982, Mk-VB (except AA874, 963, 968, 976, 977, 980, Mk. VC); AB118-132, P.R.IV (except AB124, Mk.VB, and AB130, Mk. VA); AB133-152, 167-216, 240-254, Mk. VB/C (AB176, 200, 211, converted to Mk. VI); AB255-284, Mk. VB; AB300-319, P.R.IV; AB320-349, Mk. VB

Serial Nos.	*Qty.*	*Aircraft Type*	*Remarks*
			(Tropicalised); AB363-382, 401-420, Mk. VB (except 365, 367, 368, 371, 372, 374, 377, 380, 381, 417, Mk. VC); AB421-430, P.R.IV; AB450, Mk. VII prototype; AB451, Mk. VB; AB452, 453, Mk. VC; AB454, Mk. VB; AB455, Mk. VC; AB456-460, converted to Mk. IX; AB461-469, Mk. VC; AB487-536, Mk. VB/C (except AB498, 506, 513, 516, 523, 527-530, 533-534, Mk. VI). AB499 converted to a floatplane; several re-numbered in MB, NX, PA series on conversion to Seafires.
AB639-AB773	100	Airspeed A.S.10 Oxford II	Built by Percival Aircraft. AB639-668, 685-729, 749-773. AB650 transferred to U.S.A.A.F.
AB779-AD584	500	Supermarine Spitfire VB	Vickers-Armstrongs (Castle Bromwich)—built. AB779-828, 841-875, 892-941, 960-994, AD111-140, 176-210, 225-274, 288-332, 348-397, 411-430, 449-478, 498-517, 535-584—of which AD354 and AD501 were converted to P·R.XIII and AD366 to Mk. IX. Several re-numbered in NX, PA series on conversion to Seafires.
AD589-AD653	50	Vickers Wellington III	AD589-608, 624-653—of which AD602, 608, 640 were lost in transit to the Middle East. AD646 first torpedo-bomber version conversion.
AD657 & AD661	2	Bristol 149 Bisley	Prototypes. Renamed Blenheim Mk. V.
AD665-AD714	50	Armstrong Whitworth A.W.38 Whitley V	Delivered January to February 1942.
AD719-AE442	425	Handley Page H.P.52 Hampden I	Built by the English Electric Co. AD719-768, 782-806, 824-873, 895-939, 959-988, AE115-159, 184-203, 218-267, 286-320, 352-401, 418-442. AD743, 908, 977 and AE194, 231, 307, 310, 363, were converted to T.B. (Torpedo Bomber) and transferred to the U.S.S.R.
AE444	1	D.H.95 Flamingo	D.H. No. 95005; G-AGAZ.
AE449-AE453	5	Bristol Blenheim IV	Replacement aircraft by A. V. Roe.

AE457-AE472	16	Douglas Boston I	Ex-Belgian contract. Conversions to Havoc and trainer version.
AE479	1	Messerschmitt Bf 109E	Captured by French. To Farnborough May 1940. To U.S.A. May 1942.

THE BRITISH PURCHASING MISSION

AE485–AP384 WITH the fall of France and the almost desperate situation of the United Kingdom, the British Purchasing Mission in the United States took immediate steps to place large orders and to take over aircraft contracts placed by the French. Since America was neutral, with a German Embassy functioning as in peacetime, there was little chance of keeping orders secret and therefore blackout blocks were dispensed with and the aircraft numbered consecutively.

This series, still in the initial " double-barrelled " letter allocation, set the style for subsequent series, the letters " I " and " O " not being used in case they should be confused with figures. Thus the sequence was: AE, AF, AG, AH, AJ, AK, AL, AM, AN, AP.

AE485-AE657	173	Lockheed Hudson III/IV/V	AE485-608, Mk. III; AE609-638, Mk. IV; AE639-657, Mk. V (long range). AE490, 494-504, to R.N.Z.A.F. as NZ2025-2036. AE581 was temporarily G-AGDU.
AE658-AE957	300	Lockheed Ventura I/II	Lockheed Nos. 4001-4300. AE 658-845, Mk. 1; AE846-957, Mk. II. AE658-AE687 were held in Canada; AE690, 694, 727, 752, 754, 765, transferred to South African Air Force. AE711 crashed at Quebec, AE740 crashed in Iceland and AE747 in Greenland before reaching the U.K.
AE958-AE977	20	Hawker Hurricane I (Re-designated Mk. X)	Built by the Canadian Car & Foundry Corporation. AE971-974 sunk en route to the U.K. AE963 was converted to Mk. II and renumbered DR366. All but AE970 and AE976 of remainder were converted to Sea Hurricane IB.
AE978-AF744	667	Lockheed 322 Lightning I/II	AE978-AF220, Mk.I ; AF221-744, Mk. II. Only a few Mk. I delivered, remainder reverted to U.S.A.A.C.

Serial Nos.	Qty.	Aircraft Type	Remarks
AF745-AF944	200	Vultee V-72 Vengeance II	Built by Northrop Aircraft. AF745-746 were non-standard. AF758, 778, 797, 800, 814, 820, 828, 840, 849, 859, 860, 862, 869, 874, 878, 888, 912, 918, 931, shipped direct to Australia.
AF945-AG344	300	Hawker Hurricane I (Re-designated Mk. X)	Built by the Canadian Car & Foundry Corporation. AF945-947, 949-955, 962, 963, 965-967, 969, 971, 973, 974, 976, 981, 982, converted to Sea Hurricane IB; AG122, 292, 341, converted to Mk. II. 24 renumbered to the R.C.A.F.; four lost en route to U.K.
AG345-AG664	320	North American NA-73 Mustang I	Twenty lost at sea in transit to Britain. AG357 experimentally fitted with rocket installations. Ten re-shipped to Russia.
AG665-AG684	20	Hawker Hurricane IIB	Built by the Canadian Car & Foundry Corporation. AG666-667 converted to Mk. IIC. AG672-679, 682-684 shipped to Russia. AG668 and AG681 lost at sea in transit.
AG685-AH184	400	Martin Baltimore I/II/III	Martin Nos. 1427-1836. AG685-734, Mk. I; AG735-834, Mk. II; AG835-AH184, Mk. III; 41 lost at sea in transit; two crashed before delivery.
AH185-AH204	20	North American NA-66 Harvard II	U.S.A.A.C. AT-6. Delivered to Southern Rhodesia.
AH205-AH429	225	Martin 167 Maryland I/II	AH205-279, Mk. I; AH280-429 (Martin Nos. 1827-1976), Mk. II. AH301-311, 313-331, 371, 373-380, 386-395, 406-426, 428-429 renumbered in South African Air Force 1600-1699 allocation.
AH430-AH529	100	Douglas Boston II	AH430 crashed in U.S.A. before delivery. AH431, 432, 434, 436, 437, 445-447, 450-453, 455, 458, 460, 462, 470-473, 478-479, 481, 483, 487, 490, 491, 497, 500, 502, 503, 505, 509, 510, 512, 518, 520, 523-525, 528-529 converted to Havoc II. AH431-432, 434, 436, 444-447, 450-451, 453, 460, 468, 470, 472-473, 478-479, 481, 483-484, 491, 497, 503 fitted with Turbinlite. AH438, 451, 454 transferred to U.S.A.A.F.

AH530-AH569	40	Consolidated 28 Catalina I	AH534 to Royal Australian Force. AH543 interned in Portugal; AH563 became G-AGDA.
AH570-AH739	170	Bell 14 Airacobra I	U.S.A.A.C. P-39D. Approximately 80 to R.A.F. and AH574 to the Royal Navy; remainder to Russia and U.S.A.A.F.
AH740	1	Douglas Boston III	Did not arrive in U.K. until June, 1945.
AH741-AH999	259	Curtiss Tomahawk I/IIA/IIB	AH741-880, Mk. I; AH881-990, Mk. 11A; AH991-999, Mk. IIB, AH936, 952, 965-971, 974-985, 987, 989-990 shipped to Russia.
AJ100-AJ153	54	Grumman Martlet II	Main deliveries direct to India. AJ107, 109-111 lost at sea.
AJ154-AJ162	9	Consolidated 28 Catalina I	AJ155 modified by Saunders-Roe.
AJ163-AJ537	375	Lockheed Ventura II	Lockheed Nos. 4301-4675. AJ235-442 to U.S.A.A.F.; AJ511-537 to U.S. Navy.
AJ538-AJ987	450	North American NA-66 Harvard II	AJ602-642, 663-682, 703-722, 738-752 shipped direct to Southern Rhodesia. AJ855-892 became NZ968-1005 of Royal New Zealand Air Force. AJ955-987 delivered to Canada.
AJ988-AJ999	12	Handley Page H.P.52 Hampden I	Built by Canadian Association Aircraft. Main deliveries to No. 32 O.T.U.
AK100-AK570	471	Curtiss Tomahawk IIB	AK210-224, 226-241 lost at sea in transit. Some deliveries offset to American Volunteer Group. AK254, 434, 440, 448, 470, 561 transferred from R.A.F. to Royal Egyptian Air Force.
AK571-AL230	560	Curtiss Kittyhawk I	24 diverted to Royal Canadian Air Force. AK601, 636, 680, 726, 778, 882, 931, 939, 960, 971, 992, 995, AL102, 178, 186, 188, 203 transferred to Turkish Air Force.
AL231-AL262	30	Grumman Martlet I	AL231-235 to Canada. Deliveries mainly to Donibristle.
AL263-AL502	240	Douglas Boston III	Bomber version in main. 28 shipped direct from U.S.A. to U.S.S.R.
AL503-AL667	165	Consolidated 32 Liberator II (B.II and C.II versions)	AL507, 512, 514, 516, 522, 524, 528, 529, 541, 547, 552, 557, 571, 592, 603, 619, used by B.O.A.C. as freighters G-AHYC/GEL/GJP/HZP/HYD/GTJ/GEM/HYE/GTI/GKU/HZR/GZI/GZH/HYF/

Serial Nos.	*Qty.*	*Aircraft Type*	*Remarks*
			HYG/GKT. AL604-609, 611-613, 615, 617-618, 621-623, 626, 628, 631-634, 637, 639-641 withheld from delivery for U.S.A.A.F. use. AL504 conv. to single-fin V.I.P. version for Prime Minister.
AL668-AL907	240	Douglas Boston III	Built by Boeing Aircraft. AL750, 774, 778, 780 converted to Havoc II with Turbinlite.
AL908-AL957	50	Vought Sikorsky V-156-B1 Chesapeake I	Main deliveries to Lee-on-Solent for Royal Navy.
AL958-AM257	200	North American NA-83 Mustang I	AL975/G, Mk. III prototype; AM106/G, armament experiments with rockets and two 40 mm. Vickers " S " guns. AL963 and AM121, 203, 208 Mk. X experimental aircraft.
AM258	1	Consolidated 28 Catalina	Ex-NC-777 Guba. Number allocated in error. Became SM706.
AM258-AM263	6	Consolidated 32 Liberator	Type LB-30A. AM259, 262, 263 were temporarily G-AGCD/HG/DS.
AM264-AM269	6	Consolidated 28 Catalina II	AM264 became instructional airframe 3435M.
AM270-AM369	100	Hawker Hurricane X	Built by the Canadian Car & Foundry Corporation. Deliveries mainly to U.S.S.R. AM288 converted to Mk. IIC.
AM370-AM519	150	Curtiss Tomahawk IIB	Considerable quantity diverted to American Volunteer Group in China.
AM518-AM537	20	Boeing Fortress I	Marked in error initially on AN518-537.
AM520-AM909	390	Lockheed Hudson V	AM703 *et seq*, long range version. AM589-594 shipped direct from Los Angeles to Auckland. AM707 loaned to British Overseas Airways Corporation as G-AGCE. AM759, 849, 897, 900 crashed in transit, and AM682 and AM691 were lost at sea in transit.
AM910-AM929	20	Consolidated 32 Liberator I	Ex-B-24A. AM918 and AM 920 loaned to British Overseas Airways Corporation as G-AGDR/HYB.
AM930-AM953	24	Lockheed Hudson III	Mainly delivered to Far East. AM951 crashed in transit.
AM954-AM999	46	Grumman Martlet II	AM954-963 delivered non-standard with fixed wings which were replaced with standard wings later except for AM954 lost in transit.

AN100-AN167	68	Handley Page H.P.52 Hampden I	Built by Canadian Associated Aircraft. AN123, 125, 127, 137, 146, 148, 149, 151-161, 163-164, 166-167 converted to T.B. (Torpedo Bomber).
AN168-AN217	50	Brewster 339 Buffalo I	Mainly delivered to Singapore.
AN218-AN517	300	Curtiss Tomahawk IIB	AN469-517 delivered direct to the U.S.S.R. Others were transferred to the Turkish and Royal Egyptian Air Forces.
AN518-AN537	20	Boeing Fortress I	B-17C. Delivered to No. 90 Squadron. Initially numbered AM518-537.
AN538-AP137	500	Vultee V-72 Vengeance I/II	AN538-837, Mk. II; AN838-AP137, Mk. I. AN838 and AN993 retained by U.S.A. AN670 crashed in U.S.A. before delivery. AN869, 870, 871, 873, 877, 879, 971, 973 sunk en route to India. 15 were diverted to Australia, as follows: AN853-857, 872, 874-876, 878, 892, 894, 896-898.
AP138-AP163	26	Hawker Hurricane X	Canadian-built.
AP164-AP263	100	North American NA-73 Mustang I	For R.A.F. Army Co-operation Command.
AP264-AP384	121	Bell 14 Airacobra I	Most of these taken over by U.S.A.A.F. Some despatched to U.S.S.R. Twelve were lost at sea in transit.

A 1940 "MEDLEY"

AP387–AZ999

THE upheaval of events in 1940 is reflected in this allocation, which follows the large block issued to the Purchasing Mission in America. Into this series, which includes normal production orders, come aircraft hastily impressed, escapees from countries overrun by the Nazis enrolled into R.A.F. service, captured enemy aircraft, and aircraft in transit to France and Belgium being diverted to the R.A.F.

Letter combinations not used in the AP-AZ range were AQ, AU and AY.

AP387-AP500	100	Airspeed A.S.10 Oxford II	Built by Percival Aircraft. AP387-436, 451-500. AP474 used for British Overseas Airways Corporation crew training.
AP506-AP510	5	Cierva C.30A	Ex-civil aircraft G-ACWM, G-ACWP, PH-HHH, G-ACWS, G-ACYE.
AP516-AP648	105	Hawker Hurricane IIB	Built by The Austin Motor Co. AP516-550, 564-613, 629-648. All except AP516 shipped to the U.S.S.R.

Serial Nos.	*Qty.*	*Aircraft Type*	*Remarks*
AP654-AP657	4	Airspeed A.S.10 Oxford	All delivered to Blind Approach Training Flights.
AP670-AR207	295	Hawker Hurricane IIB	Built by The Austin Motor Co. AP670-714, 732-781, 801-825, 849-898, 912-936 (195) built; AP937-956, AR113-162, 178-207 cancelled. Up to AP879 shipped to the U.S.S.R.
AR212-AR621	300	Supermarine Spitfire I/V	Built by Westland Aircraft, AR212-261 built as Mk. IA. but some converted later to Mk. IV and V; AR274-298, 318-347 (AR319 converted to P.R.XIII), 362-406, 422-461, Mk. VB—of which AR384, 442-448, 457-461 were converted to Seafire IB; AR462-471, 488-532, 546-570, 592-621, Mk. VC.
AR625	1	Fairey Battle	Rebuilt fuselage of K9192 with parts of K9437 and N2026.
AR630-AR694	65	Curtiss Mohawk III/IV	Ex-French order. After receipt, AR642, 643, 652, 664, 666, 668, 671, 673, 679, 680 were transferred to the Portuguese Air Force, and AR648, 657, 659, 660, 683, 684, 686, 688-689, 692-694 were transferred to the South African Air Force.
AR702-AR751	50	Martin 167 Maryland I	AR702-736 were accepted to American standards. AR720, 736, 740 were transferred to the Fleet Air Arm.
AR756-AS396	350	Airspeed A.S.10 Oxford I/II	Built by de Havilland. AR756-790, 804-853, 870-889, 909-953, 968-982, AS144-153 (175) Mk. I; AS154-188, 201-230, 254-278, 297-331, 347-396 (175), Mk. II, except AR930 & AS376 as Mk. V.
AS410-AS437	28	Brewster 339 Buffalo I	Ex-Belgian contract. Deliveries mainly to Fleet Air Arm.
AS440-AS462	23	Northrop 8-A5 Nomad I	Surplus U.S.A.A.C. A-17A, shipped to South Africa.
AS467-AS471	5	Curtiss Cleveland I	Surplus U.S. Navy SBC-4 Helldivers.
AS474-AS942	350	Airspeed A.S.10 Oxford I/II	AS474-523, 537-571, 591-640-665-704 (175), Mk. I; AS705-709, 726-745, 764-813, 828, 877, 893-942 (175), Mk. II. AS592 was Mk. V prototype. AS732 was transferred to the U.S.A.A.F.

AS958-AS976	19	Northrop 8-A5 Nomad I	Surplus U.S.A.A.C. A-17A, delivered to South Africa, except for AS967 and AS971 which crashed in the U.K. and AS958, which went there via the U.K.
AS981-AS983	3	Handley Page H.P. 42	G-AAUC/UE/XF impressed. *Horsa, Hadrian, Helena.*
AS987-AS990	4	Hawker Hurricane I	Replacement order.
AT109-AT260	250	Handley Page H.P.52 Hampden I	Built by the English Electric Co. AT109-158, 172-196, 216-260—of which AT109, 114, 117, 125, 135, 145, 150, 184, 193, 195, 232, 241, 243, 244, 251, 253, 256-259 were converted to T.B. (Torpedo Bomber). 130 cancelled.
AT439-AV502	950	Airspeed A.S.10 Oxford I	Built by de Havilland. 475 Mk. I and 475 Mk. II of original order reduced to 415 Mk. I, 175 Mk. II. and eventually only AT439-488, 502-536, 576-625, 641-685, 723-742, 760-799 (238) were built—as Mk. I. AT800-809, 845-889, 909-928, 962-996, AV118-167, 199-218, 242-276, 306-355, 381-425, 453-502 cancelled.
AV508-AV944	298	Boulton Paul P.82 Defiant II	Cancelled. AV508-557, 571-605, 633-682, 698-742, 768-787, 805-839, 863-892, 910-944.
AV951-AV952	2	D.H.87 Hornet Moth	G-ADKI and G-ADSK, impressed.
AV958-AV965	8	Fokker T-8W	Dutch Navy R-1, R-3, R-6, R-7, R-8, R-9, R-10, R-11 escapees to U.K. in May 1940.
AV968	1	Airspeed AS-4 Ferry	G-ABSI, impressed.
AV969	1	D.H.87 Hornet Moth	G-ADMO, impressed.
AV970-AV971	2	Miles M.11A Whitney Straight	G-AEWK and G-AERC, impressed.
AV972	1	D.H.87 Hornet Moth	G-AEKP, impressed.
AV973	1	Miles M.3B Falcon Six	G-AFBF impressed.
AV974	1	Short S.16 Scion	Series I. G-ACUY, impressed.
AV975	1	D.H.85 Leopard Moth	G-ACKN, impressed.
AV976	1	D.H.90 Dragonfly	G-AESW, impressed.
AV977	1	D.H.94 Moth Minor	G-AFOT, impressed.
AV978	1	Miles Hawk Trainer	Mk. III: G-AFET, impressed.
AV979	1	General Aircraft ST-6 Monospar	G-ACGI, impressed.
AV980	1	Avro Tutor	G-AFZW (ex-K3237), impressed.
AV981	1	Short S.16 Scion	Series 1. G-ACUW, impressed.
AV982	1	D.H.84 Dragon	G-AECZ, impressed.
AV983-AV986	4	D.H.85 Leopard Moth	G-ADBH/CSU/EFR/CRV, impressed.
AV987	1	D.H.90 Dragonfly	G-AEDH, impressed.

Serial Nos.	Qty.	Aircraft Type	Remarks
AV988-AV989	2	D.H.85 Leopard Moth	G-ACPG and G-ADAP, impressed.
AV990	1	Short S.16/1 Scion	Series 2. G-AEJN, impressed. Became 2722M.
AV991	1	D.H.60 Gipsy Moth	G-AACY, impressed.
AV992-AV994	3	D.H.90 Dragonfly	G-AEDJ/FRF/FRI, impressed
AV995-AV997	3	D.H.60M/60/60M Moth	G-AACU/PG/RH, impressed.
AW110-AW111	2	D.H.60M/60 Moth	G-AASR and G-ABXR, impressed.
AW112-AW113	2	D.H.94 Moth Minor	G-AFNG and G-AFNJ, impressed.
AW114	1	D.H.87 Hornet Moth	G-AEIY, impressed.
AW115-AW116	2	D.H.89 Rapide	G-ACTU and G-ADDD, impressed.
AW117	1	D.H.85 Leopard Moth	G-ACSJ, impressed.
AW118	1	D.H.87 Hornet Moth	G-AELO, impressed in Royal Navy.
AW119	1	D.H.60 Moth	G-ABJN, impressed.
AW120-AW123	4	D.H.85 Leopard Moth	G-ACKS/CLZ/EZI/CPF, impressed.
AW124	1	D.H.83 Fox Moth	G-ACEA, impressed.
AW125	1	D.H.85 Leopard Moth	G-ACTL, impressed.
AW126-AW136	11	D.H.60 Moth	G-AAET/AIV/ASY/BAE/BBA/BBX/BJT/BPD/BRD/BTS/CJG.
AW143	1	British Aircraft Eagle	Impressed in India.
AW144	1	D.H.60 Moth	Impressed in India.
AW145	1	D.H.60G Gipsy Moth	G-AFLV, impressed.
AW146	1	D.H.60 Moth	G-EBTZ, impressed. Became 2833M.
AW147	1	D.H.60 Cirrus Moth	G-EBRY, impressed.
AW148-AW149	2	D.H.60G Gipsy Moth	G-AAKP and G-ABOG, impressed.
AW150	2	Miles M.2 Hawk	G-ADGI, impressed.
AW151	1	D.H.94 Moth Minor	G-AFMZ, impressed.
AW152	1	Miles M.2 Hawk	G-ACTO, impressed.
AW153	1	D.H.60 Moth	G-EBTD, impressed.
AW154	1	D.H.84 Dragon	G-ACCZ, impressed.
AW155	1	D.H.89 Rapide	G-ADAK, impressed.
AW156	1	D.H.85 Leopard Moth	G-AFZG, impressed.
AW157-AW160	4	D.H.60G Gipsy Moth	G-EBXT/EBZC/EBZL/AAIE impressed.
AW161	1	D.H.60 Moth	G-ACPT, impressed.
AW162	1	D.H.60GIII Moth Major	G-ADFK, impressed.
AW163	1	D.H.84 Dragon	G-AEKZ, impressed.
AW164	1	D.H.90 Dragonfly	G-AEDK, impressed.
AW165-AW166	2	D.H.85 Leopard Moth	G-ACLL and G-ACLY, impressed.
AW167	1	Messerschmitt Bf 108	Taifun D-IJHW, impressed.
AW168-AW169	2	D.H.85 Leopard Moth	G-ACRC and G-ACKM, impressed.
AW170-AW173	4	D.H.84 Dragon	G-ACDN/CET/CKU/EMI, impressed.

AW177	1	Heinkel He 111H	Nr. 6353, shot down at Dalkeith and repaired.
AW180-AW181	2	D.H.60 Gipsy Moth	VT-AFP/L impressed.
AW183	1	British Aircraft Eagle	VT-AHP impressed in Far East.
AW187-AW384	150	Bristol 152 Beaufort I/II	Bristol (Filton)-built. AW187-221, 234-243 (45), Mk. I; AW244-253, 271-315, 335-384 (105) Mk. II.
AW392-AW414	23	Douglas Havoc I Boston II	Ex-French or Belgian contract. AW392-393, 400, 401, 404, 406, 411, 412 fitted with Turbinlites. AW394, 400, 403, transferred to U.S.A.A.F.
AW420-AW438	19	Northrop 8-A5 Nomad I	Surplus U.S.A.A.C. A-17.
AW443-AX656	750	Avro 652A Anson I/IV (533 Mk. I) (217 Mk. IV)	A. V. Roe (Newton Heath)-built. AW443-454, Mk. I; AW455-482, Mk. IV; AW483-488, Mk. I; AW489-492, 506-515, Mk. IV; AW516-521, Mk. I; AW522-540, 586, Mk. IV; AW587, Mk. I; AW588, Mk. IV; AW589-594, Mk. I; AW595-613, Mk. IV; AW614, Mk. I; AW615-616, Mk. IV; AW617-621, Mk. I; AW622-635, 653-657, Mk. IV; AW658-683, Mk. I; AW684-697, 739-750, Mk. IV; AW751, Mk. I; AW752-758, 778-795, Mk. IV; AW796-801, Mk. I; AW802-812, 833-843, Mk. IV; AW844-882, 897-918, Mk. I; AW919, Mk. IV; AW920, Mk. I; AW921-923, Mk. IV; AW924, Mk. I; AW925-927, Mk. IV; AW928, Mk. I; AW929-938, Mk. IV; AW939-941, 963-968, Mk. I; AW969, Mk. IV; AW970, Mk. I; AW971-972, Mk. IV; AW973-974, Mk. I; AW975-977, Mk. IV; AW978, Mk. I; AW979-981, Mk. IV; AW982, Mk. I; AX100-104, Mk. IV; AX105, Mk. I; AX106, Mk. IV; AX107-127, Mk. I; AX128-136, Mk. IV; AX137-149, 163-187, 218-267, 280-324, 343-372, 396-445, 466-515, 535-584, 607-656, Mk. I.
AX659-AX660	2	Short S.23 Empire " C "	Short Nos. S.841/846, G-AETY/UD, impressed. *Clio* and *Cordelia*.
AX666	1	Spartan 7W Executive	Impressed civil aircraft, YI-SOF.

Serial Nos.	*Qty.*	*Aircraft Type*	*Remarks*
AX672-AX673	2	Potez 63/11	French Nos. 670 and 699. Escaped from French territory after France surrendered and taken on R.A.F. charge in the Middle East.
AX674-AX675	2	Morane 406	French Nos. 826 and 827.
AX676	1	Caudron Simoun	
AX677	1	Marcel Bloch 81	French No. 4.
AX678-AX679	2	Potez 29	French Nos. 54 and 99.
AX680	1	Potez 63/11	French No. 395
AX681-AX682	2	Lockheed Type 14	Lockheed Nos. 1417 and 1496 ex-NC2333 and NC17398 acquired in Middle East.
AX683	1	Bristol Blenheim I	Ex-L1431 from South African Air Force.
AX684	1	Morane 406	Morane No. 819 French Air Force escapee.
AX685-AX687	3	Lockheed 18	Acquired in Middle East. Ex-South African Air Force as Nos. 231-233.
AX688	1	Lockheed 14	Acquired in Middle East.
AX689-AX690	2	Martin 167 Maryland	Presumed escapees from French Air Force.
AX691	1	Potez 63	Presumed escapee from French Air Force.
AX692-AX693	2	Martin 167 Maryland	Presumed escapees from French Air Force.
AX694	1	Loire N.30	Presumed escapee from French Air Force.
AX695	1	Waco ZGC-7	Bought in Egypt by Army for use of Long Range Desert Group.
AX696	1	Martin 167 Maryland	Presumed escapee. To S.A.A.F.
AX697	1	Waco YKC	As AX695 above.
AX698	1	Percival Gull Six	G-ADKX, impressed.
AX699-AX701	3	Lockheed 10A Electra	Taken on charge in M.E. Ex-YU-SAV/DA/BB.
AX702-AX705	4	Savoia S.M.79K	Yugoslav escapees to Middle East. Ex-YU-3712-3714 and 3702.
AX706-AX707	2	Dornier Do 17Ka	Yugoslav escapees to M.E. AX707 was ex-YU-3348.
AX708-AX715	8	Dornier Do 22 Kj	Yugoslav escapees to Middle East. Ex-YU-302, 306-309, 311-313
AX716	1	Rogojarski Sim XIV-H Srs. 1	Yugoslav escapee to M.E.
AX717-AX723	7	Lockheed 18-08 Lodestar	Purchased from U.S.A. for use in the Middle East. Registered G-AGCV/R/W/U/P/T/S for B.O.A.C.
AX725-AX747	23	Grumman Martlet I	Delivery to Middle East.
AX748-AX752	5	Avro 652A Anson I	Ex-Greek Air Force.
AX753-AX754	2	Grumman Martlet I	No delivery record. Probably lost at sea.
AX755	1	Douglas DC-2	Acquired in Middle East.
AX756-AX759	4	Lockheed 18-08 Lodestar	AX756 (ex-NC25630 and G-AGCN).

AX760	1	D.H.86A	G-ADFF impressed.
AX761	1	Grumman Martlet	Fleet Air Arm.
AX762	1	D.H.86	G-ADUE impressed.
AX763-AX765	3	Lockheed 18-08 Lodestar	Impressed in Middle East.
AX766	1	Lockheed 10 Electra	Acquired in Middle East.
AX767-AX769	3	Douglas DC-2	Taken on charge in Middle East. AX767 ex-VT-ARA.
AX772 & AX774	2	Messerschmitt Bf 110C-5	Captured German aircraft.
AX775-AX776	2	Caudron Goeland	Escapees from French Air Force to Britain.
AX777	1	Caudron Simoun	Escapee from French Air Force to Britain.
AX781-AX783	3	D.H.82 Tiger Moth	G-AELB/ELC/FMC impressed.
AX784	1	D.H.60 Moth	G-ABPC, impressed.
AX785-AX788	4	D.H.82 Tiger Moth	G-AFMD/EXG/FJG/FJH, impressed.
AX789	1	D.H.60G Gipsy Moth	G-AAKI, impressed.
AX790	1	D.H.94 Moth Minor	G-AFPK, impressed.
AX791	1	D.H.82 Tiger Moth	G-AFGJ, impressed.
AX792-AX794	3	D.H.60 Moth	G-ABES/EBST/ADEZ impressed.
AX795	1	D.H.86B (ex-D.H.86A)	G-ADYI, impressed.
AX797	1	D.H.90 Dragonfly	VT-AHW, impressed in India.
AX798	1	D.H.82 Tiger Moth	VT-AIF, impressed.
AX799	1	Curtiss Hawk	Taken on charge in India.
AX800	1	D.H.86	VT-AKZ, impressed in India.
AX801	1	D.H.85 Leopard Moth	Impressed in India.
AX803	1	Lockheed 12A	VT-AJS ex-G-AFCO, impressed in India.
AX804-AX805	2	D.H.85 Leopard Moth	Impressed for A.H.Q., India.
AX806	1	D.H.89 Rapide	VT-AIZ, impressed.
AX811-AX820	10	Brewster 339 Buffalo I	Mainly for Fleet Air Arm.
AX824-AX829	6	Grumman Martlet I	Assembled by Scottish Aviation.
AX834	1	Miles M.20	12-gun fighter prototype utilising standard Master parts. Ex-U-9.
AX840-AX844	5	D.H.86	G-ACYG, ACZO, AENR, ACZP, ACZR, impressed to Royal Navy.
AX848-AX851	4	Douglas Boston I	Ex-French aircraft. AX848 & 851 were converted to Havoc I.
AX854	1	Avro 504N	G-ACZC, impressed.
AX855	1	D.H.90 Dragonfly	G-AECX, impressed.
AX856	1	D.H.82 Tiger Moth	G-AFSX, impressed.
AX857	1	D.H.87 Hornet Moth	G-ADJV, impressed.
AX858	1	D.H.85 Leopard Moth	G-ACGS, impressed.
AX859	1	D.H.83 Fox Moth	G-ACFC, impressed.
AX860	1	Percival Q.6	G-AFVC (ex-F-AQOK), impressed.
AX861-AX862	2	D.H.85 Leopard Moth	G-ACNN and G-ACLW, impressed.
AX863	1	D.H.84 Dragon	G-ACKB, impressed.
AX864	1	Short S.16 Scion	Series 2. G-ADDO, impressed.
AX865	1	D.H.85 Leopard Moth	G-ACUO, impressed.

Serial Nos.	Qty.	Aircraft Type	Remarks
AX866	1	Percival P.3 Gull Six	G-ADPR, impressed.
AX867	1	D.H.84 Dragon	G-ACEK, impressed.
AX868-AX870	3	D.H.80A Puss Moth	G-ACTV/BDG/AZO, impressed.
AX871	1	Avro 504N	G-ADBM, impressed.
AX872	1	D.H.80A Puss Moth	G-ABGS, impressed.
AX873	1	D.H.85 Leopard Moth	G-ACRW, impressed.
AX874-AX875	2	Avro 504N	G-ADBP and G-ADET, impressed.
AX880-AX898	19	Curtiss Mohawk	Ex-French contract, Shipped to India, Portugal or South Africa.
AX900	1	Lockheed 10A	Impressed in Middle East. Also reported as Curtiss Tomahawk at Boscombe Down.
AX903-AX904	2	D.H.91 Albatross	K8618-8619 originally allotted. Both served with No. 271 Squadron. Ex-G-AEVV/W
AX910-AX918	9	Douglas Boston I	Ex-French order. All converted to Havoc I. AX913 fitted with Turbinlite and Long Aerial Mine and was later transferred to the U.S.A.A.F.
AX919	1	Junkers Ju 88A-1	Captured enemy aircraft. Believed Dessau-built Nr. 7036.
AX920-AX975	56	Douglas Boston I	AX921, 923, 924, 930, 936, 974, 975 converted to Havoc I. AX922 transferred to the U.S.A.A.F. as trainer. AX924 and 930 were fitted with Turbinlites.
AZ104-AZ856	525	Miles M.19 Master II	AZ104-143, 156-185, 202-226, 245-289, 306-340, 359-383, 408-457, 470-504, 519-563, 582-621, 638-672, 693-742, 773-817, 832-856. Many shipped direct to South Africa. AZ672 transferred to the U.S.A.A.F.
AZ861-AZ999	—	Bristol Blenheim V	*See next section.*

BRITISH AND AMERICAN PRODUCTION GEARED

BA100–BZ999 ORDERS at this critical stage continued to be placed with British and American firms for training and operational aircraft needed in the years ahead for which Winston Churchill had offered no prospect but blood, toil, tears and sweat. Into this section came more orders diverted from the French and Belgians and further impressments of civil aircraft. For the first time gliders appear in the system, whereas hitherto the serialling system had been confined to powered aircraft only.

Orders placed in America were again serial numbered consecutively. The sequences had already been set by the AA100 to AZ999 series, *i.e.*, 100 to 999 using BA, BB, BD, BE, BF, BG, BH, BJ, BK, BL, BM, BN, BP, BR, BS, BT, BV, BW and BZ as prefixes.

BA100-BB184	780	Bristol Blenheim V	Built by Rootes Securities at Blythe Bridge, Staffs. AZ861-905, 922-971, 984-999 from previous AZ series included in batch. BA100-118, 133-172, 191-215, 228-262, 287-336, 365-409, 424-458, 471-505, 522-546, 575-624, 647-691, 708-757, 780-829, 844-888, 907-951, 978-999, BB100-102, 135-184. Transfers to other Services concerned: BA137, 292, 395, 495, 591, 613, 614, 713, 854, 855, 887, 910, 922, 925 to Turkish Air Force; BA306, 394, 525, 596, 849 to Free French Forces; AZ986, 987, BA826 to Portuguese Air Force.
BB189-BB446	200	Handley Page H.P.59 Halifax II	Built by the London Aircraft Production Group. BB189-223, 236-285, 300-344, 357-391, 412-446.
BB450	1	Brewster Buffalo	Delivered to the Royal Navy, September 1940.
BB455-BB656	150	Vickers Wellington IC/VIII	50 only built by Vickers at Weybridge. BB455-484, 497-516, as Mk. I (except for BB461, 466, 471, 476, 481, 503, 513 as Mk. VIII). BB517-541, 566-600, 617-656 were cancelled in July 1941.
BB661-BB671	11	Miles M.14 Hawk Trainer	Impressments. BB661-662, Mk. III (ex-G-AFBS/DB); BB663-664, Mk. II (ex-G-AFTR/S); BB665-667, Mk. III (ex-G-AFWY/XA/XB). BB668-671 reserved for G-AFYV-Y but not taken up.
BB672-BB868	123	D.H.82 Tiger Moth	Impressment of aircraft at civil-operated Elementary Flying Training Schools in 1940. Previous identities as follows: BB672-BB674, G-ADOF/G/H; BB675-682, G-ADOI-P; BB683-690, G-ADOR/VN/VP/XK/XN/XO/XP/XR; BB691-692, G-AEEA/UV; BB693-BB701, G-ADGU/GV/GG/GH/GT/GX/GY/GZ/II; BB702-706, G-AEBY/EBZ/DGF/DGS/DGW; BB723, G-ABRC; BB724-730, G-ACDA/B/C/E/

Serial Nos.	Qty.	Aircraft Type	Remarks
			G/J/K; BB731-760, G-ADCG/DCH/DHT/DHU/DHV/DXB/DXD/DXJ/EVB/FGY/CDF/CDI/DHR/DHS/DHY/DHZ/DIA/DIB/DKG/DLV/DLW/DLZ/DMA/DSH/DXE/DXI/ELP/EMF/FGZ/FJK; BB788-812, G-ADIJ/DIH/CEZ/DJF/BUL/DHX/DWC/VY/VZ/WA/WB/VX/WE/WF/WK/WJ/WL/WM/WP/WO/WN/YB/YA/HN/UC; BB813-814, G-AFFA/WI; BB815-819, G-ADJC/JD/JG/JI/JJ; BB851-863, G-ADPA/PC/PF/PG/PH/OW/OX/OY/OZ/XT/XU/XV/XX; BB864-868, G-AECH/ECI/ECJ/FAR/FAS.
BB890-BB912	23	Douglas Boston I	BB891-895, 896-904, 907-909, 911-912 converted to Havoc; BB897, 899, 907-909 fitted with Turbinlites. BB891 and 896 transferred to the U.S.A.A.F. BB902, trainer version; BB903, Mk. II.
BB918-BB979	26	Curtiss Mohawk IV	BB918-937, 974-979. Shipped to India, South Africa or Portugal.
BD110-BD127	18	Douglas Boston I	All converted to Havoc; BD110, 111, 120 fitted with Turbinlites. BD115-116 were converted to trainers. BD121-122 transferred to Fleet Air Arm.
BD130-BD137	8	North American NA-66 Harvard II	BD130 to U.K.; BD131-134 to Southern Rhodesia; BD135-137 transferred to the U.S.A.A.F.
BD140	1	D.H.85 Leopard Moth	G-ACTG, impressed.
BD141	1	Miles Hawk Major	G-ADCY surveyed, but not taken on charge.
BD142	1	D.H.82 Tiger Moth	G-AFHT, impressed.
BD143	1	D.H.89 Rapide	G-AEPE, impressed.
BD144	1	D.H.85 Leopard Moth	G-ACHB, impressed.
BD145	1	Miles Whitney Straight	G-AFAB, impressed.
BD146-BD148	3	D.H.85 Leopard Moth	G-ACTJ/SF/MA, impressed.
BD149	1	D.H.90 Dragonfly	G-AFTF (ex-VH-UXA), impressed.
BD150	1	General Aircraft ST-12 Monospar	G-ADBN, impressed.
BD151-BD156	6	D.H.82 Tiger Moth	G-AFHI/EZC/BTB/FCA/DNV/ESD, impressed.
BD161	1	D.H.82 Tiger Moth	G-AESA, impressed.
BD162-BD164	3	D.H.60 Moth	G-ABLZ/BAO/AJJ, impressed.
BD165	1	Percival P.3 Gull Six	G-ADSM surveyed but not taken on charge.
BD166	1	D.H.60 Moth	G-AAWR, impressed.

BD167	1	D.H.85 Leopard Moth	G-ACHC, impressed.
BD168	1	Miles Whitney Straight	G-AFJJ, impressed.
BD169	1	D.H.85 Leopard Moth	G-ACKL, impressed.
BD170-BD171	2	D.H.82 Tiger Moth	G-AFJM/N, impressed.
BD172-BD173	2	D.H.85 Leopard Moth	G-ACOO/XH, impressed.
BD174-BD179	6	D.H.60 Moth	G-ACDV/CIB/CJB/BZS/BZU/BZV, impressed.
BD180	1	Miles M.2P Hawk Major	G-ADDK, impressed.
BD181	1	D.H.80A Puss Moth	G-ABDL, impressed.
BD182	1	D.H.94 Moth Minor	G-AFPG, impressed.
BD183	1	Miles Whitney Straight	G-AFJX, impressed.
BD189-BD693	300	Armstrong Whitworth A.W.38 Whitley V/VII	BD189-238, 252-296, 346-395, 411-422, Mk. V (BD360-362, 382-390 loaned to B.O.A.C. as G-AGCF-K, G-AGDX-Z, G-AGEA-C); BD423-434, Mk. VII; BD435-445, 493-512, 530-560, Mk. V; BD561-574, 620-625, Mk. VII; BD626-639, 659-674, Mk. V; BD675-693, Mk. VII.
BD696-BE716	600	Hawker Hurricane IIB/C	Built by Hawker Aircraft at Brooklands and Langley as follows: BD696-745, 759-786, Brooklands; BD787-793, 818-837, 855-899, 914-963, Langley; BD980-986, BE105-117, 130-149, Brooklands; BE150-174, 193-227, Langley; BE228-242, 274-308, 323-352, Brooklands; BE353-372, 394-428, 468-517, 546-560, Langley; BE561-590, 632-641, Brooklands; BE642-651, 667-716, Langley.
BE720-BF303	375	Bristol Blenheim	Ordered from A. V. Roe. Cancelled. BE720-769, 782-816, 834-883, 897-941, 955-994, BF109-138, 152-186, 199-248, 264-303.
BF274	1	Supermarine Spitfire IX	Prototype Mk. IX. Compromised number above.
BF309-BF580	200	Short S.29 Stirling I/III/IV	BF309-358, 372-416, 434-454 (116), Mk. I; BF455-483, 500-534, 561-580 (84), Mk. III; BF464, 468, 532, 575, 580 were converted to Mk. IV.
BF584-BF777	150	Fairey Albacore I	Fairey Nos. F5670-819. BF584-618, 631-680, 695-739, 758-777.
BF782-BG668	600	Airspeed A.S.10 Oxford I/II	BF782-831, 845-889, 904-953, 967-999, BG100-101, BG113-132, 149-183, 196-245, 260-274 (300), Mk. I; BG275-304, 318-337, 349-398, 415-459, 473-522, 541-545 (200), Mk. II; BG546-575, 588-637, 649-668 (100), Mk. I. BF807, 825, 858, 859, 861, 967;

Serial Nos.	Qty.	Aircraft Type	Remarks
			BG100, 115, 118, 171, 213, 263, 301, 423, 444, 445, 509, 521, 610 converted to Mk. V.
BG674-BH723	720	Hawker Hurricane IIB	450 only built by Gloster Aircraft as follows: BG674-723, 737-771, 783-832, 844-888, 901-920, 933-977, 990-999, BH115-154, 167-201, 215-264, 277-296, 312-361. Cancelled Nos.: 374-408, 422-471, 489-508, 524-568, 575-614, 630-664, 679-723.
BH727	1	D.H.60 Gipsy Moth	Ordered 1940.
BH732-BJ408	440	Hawker Hurricane I	Ordered from the Canadian Car & Foundry Co. as BH732-781, 797-841, 855-904, 921-955, 968-997, BJ112-136, 150-199, 213-257, 274-323, 332-351, 369-408. Re-allotted numbers in allocation to British Purchasing Commission in North America as follows: AE958-977, AF945-999, AG100-344, AG665-684, AM270-369.
BJ410-BJ419	10	North American NA-66 Harvard II	Record of BJ410, 412, 415 only. To Rhodesia in 1940.
BJ421-BJ428	8	Martin 167 Maryland I	Ex-French contract. Delivered to Middle East, January 1941.
BJ434-BJ453	20	Curtiss Mohawk IV	Ex-French contract. Mainly to India and South Africa.
BJ458-BJ501	37	Douglas Havoc I	Ex-French contract. BJ458-477, 485-501. BJ474 was converted to Mk. II; several were converted to trainers, of which BJ464 was the prototype; BJ460, 461, 467, 469, 470 were fitted with Turbinlites. BJ461, 466, 473, 488, 499 transferred to U.S.A.A.F.
BJ507-BJ527	21	Grumman Martlet I	Ex-U.S. Navy F4F.
BJ531-BJ550	20	Curtiss Mohawk IV	Mainly shipped to Portugal, India or South Africa.
BJ554-BJ570	17	Grumman Martlet I	Delivered to Royal Navy.
BJ574-BJ588	15	Curtiss Mohawk IV	BJ574, 575, 577, 581, 582, 583, 587, 588 only confirmed. Compromised numbers below.
BJ575	1	British Aircraft Swallow II	G-AFCB, impressed. Compromised Mohawk number above.
BJ581-BK564	600	Vickers Wellington III	Vickers (Chester)-built. BJ581-625, 642-675, 688-730, 753-801, 818-847, 876-922, 958-991, BK123-166, 179-214, 234-281, 295-315, 330-368, 385-408, 426-471, 489-517, 534-564.

BK569-BK588	20	Curtiss Mohawk III	Ex-French order. Mainly shipped to India and South Africa.
BK592-BK818	150	Short S.29 Stirling I/III	Built by The Austin Motor Co. BK592-628, 644-647 (41), Mk. I; BK648-667, 686-727, 759-784, 798-818 (109), Mk. III.
BK822	1	D.H.95 Flamingo	G-AGBY, impressed. Flown to Middle East.
BK826-BK829	4	D.H.60 Moth	G-AAAV/AHU/BEO/BTF, impressed.
BK830	1	D.H.87B Hornet Moth	G-AEZG, impressed.
BK831-BK832	2	D.H.94 Moth Minor	G-AFPT and G-AFPU, impressed.
BK833	1	D.H.60GIII Moth Major	G-ACRI, impressed.
BK834-BK836	3	D.H.60 Moth	G-AAGA/AYL/BFT, impressed.
BK837	1	D.H.87 Hornet Moth	G-ADMP, impressed.
BK838-BK840	3	D.H.94 Moth Minor	G-AFNF/NH/PM, impressed.
BK841-BK845	5	D.H.60 Gipsy Moth	G-ABHM/BJJ/AZE/AMV/BFD, impressed.
BK846	1	D.H.80 Puss Moth	G-ABEI, impressed.
BK847	1	D.H.94 Moth Minor	G-AFNK, impressed.
BK848	1	D.H.60 Gipsy Moth	G-ABXB, impressed.
BK852-BK853	2	Curtiss Tomahawk	Believed ex-American Volunteer Group aircraft.
BK867	1	D.H.85 Leopard Moth	G-ACKP, impressed.
BK868	1	Fairchild 24-C8E	Fairchild No. 2817: G-AFKW, impressed in October 1940.
BK869	1	Fairchild 24C	Fairchild No. 2718: G-AECO, impressed in October 1940.
BK870-BK871	2	D.H.80A Puss Moth	G-ABYP and G-ABLR, impressed.
BK872	1	Percival P.10 Vega Gull	VP-KCH, impressed.
BK876-BK879	4	Curtiss Mohawk	BK876 and 878 shipped to South Africa and BK879 to India.
BK882-BK883	2	Douglas Havoc I	BK882 had Turbinlite fitted; BK883 was Intruder version with Long Aerial Mine fitted.
BK891	1	British Aircraft Swallow	Impressed.
BK892	1	Avro 504N	G-ADEV, impressed November 1940. Became 3118M.
BK893-BK897	5	British Aircraft Swallow 2	G-AFGC/FGE/EHL/ELH/FGD, impressed—of which BK897 was converted to a glider for towed flight experiments.
BL112-BL216	90	Supermarine Sea Otter	Cancelled order with Blackburn Aircraft. BL112-151, 167-216.
BL220-BL223	4	Curtiss Mohawk	BL220 shipped to Portugal and BL221-223 to South Africa.
BL227-BL228	2	Douglas Havoc I	BL227 delivered to Fleet Air Arm. BL228 converted to trainer.

Serial Nos.	Qty.	Aircraft Type	Remarks
BL231-BM653	1000	Supermarine Spitfire VB	Vickers Armstrongs (Castle Bromwich)-built. BL231-267, 285-304, 311-356, 365-391, 403-450, 461-500, 509-551, 562-600, 613-647, 655-699, 707-736, 748-789, 801-833, 846-864, 887-909, 918-941, 956-998, BM113-162, 176-211, 227-274, 289-329, 343-386, 402-430, 447-493, 508-543, 556-597, 624-653—of which BL526, BM447 and BM591 were converted to Mk. XIII and others to Seafire IB.
BM671-BM877	150	Airspeed A.S.10 Oxford II	Built by Percival Aircraft. BM671-720, 737-785, 801-844, 871-877 for R.A.F., except BM825 to Fleet Air Arm. BM713, 830 conv. Mk. V.
BM898-BP772	1250	Hawker Hurricane IIB/IIC/IID and " Hurribomber "	Built by Hawker Aircraft at Brooklands or Langley as follows: BM898-936, 947-996, BN103-104, Brooklands; BN105-142, 155-170, Langley; BN171-189, 203-237, Brooklands; BN238-242, 265-298, 311-337, 346-380, Langley; BN381-389, 399-435, 449-497, 512-522, Brooklands; BN523-547, 559-603, 624-653, Langley; BN654, 667-680, Brooklands; BN681-682, Langley; BN683-693, Brooklands; BN694, Langley; BN695-698, Brooklands; BN699, Langley; BN700-701, Brooklands; BN702, Langley; BN703-705, 719-758, Brooklands; BN759, 773-802, 818-846, 859-882, 896-911, Langley; BN912-935, Brooklands; BN936-940, 953-992, BP109-141, 154-200, 217-239, Langley; BP240-245, 259-302, Brooklands; BP316-362, Brooklands and Langley; BP378-416, Langley; BP430-479, mainly at Langley; BP493-526, mainly at Brooklands; BP538-566, Brooklands; BP579-614, 628-675, 692-711, 734-772, Langley and Brooklands. Deliveries to R.A.F. Middle East and India, and to Soviet Air Force; some transferred to Turkish Air Force. BP297,

			299, 301, 318, 320, 322, 324, 326, 437-446, 606, 608, 653' 662, 667, 669-672, 692-697' 701, 705, 709, 710, 737, 742, 746, 750, 754, 758, 763, 768 were converted to "Hurri-bomber." BN795-797, 840-846, 859-863, 866, 961, 963, 965, 967, 969, 971, 973, 975, 977, 979, BP126, 131, 136, 141, 158, 163, 168, 173, 178, 183, 188, 193, 550-557, produced as IID and the remainder as IIB or IIC. BN114/G, 526/G, 571/G used for armament trials; BP 173 converted to Mk. IV.
BP775-BP839	50	Fairey Fulmar II	BP775-796, 812-839 to Royal Navy. BP777 transferred to No. 273 Squadron, R.A.F.
BP844-BS152	800	Supermarine Spitfire IV/VB/VC/VI/IX	BP844-892, 904-937, 950-993, BR106-143, 159-205, 226-256, 282-330, 344-393, 410-435, 459-499, 515-549, 562-605, 621-670, 977-987, BS104-152 (608) built as Mks. IV/V/VI/IX. BR683-721, 745-772, 799-831, 849-877, 890-929, 954-976 cancelled.
BS157-BS559	300	Supermarine Spitfire VC/VI/VII/IX	BS157-202, 218-255, 271-319, 335-367, 383-411, 427-474, 489-515, 530-559.
BS573-BS724	120	Supermarine Spitfire III	Cancelled. BS573-618, 634-659, 677-724.
BS730-BS747	13	Curtiss Mohawk IV	BS730-738, 744-747. Delivered mainly to India and South Africa.
BS755	1	Miles M.11A Whitney Straight	G-AECT, impresseed but not flown.
BS760-BS777	18	Martin 167 Maryland I	Ex-French order. BS777 to Free French Forces, July 1941. BS770, 777 converted for target towing.
BS784-BS798	15	Curtiss Mohawk IV	Eight to South Africa, six to India, one to Portugal.
BS803	1	Stinson SR-10C Reliant	Stinson No. 5902: NC21133, impressed. Later VP-KDV.
BS808	1	North American NA-66 Harvard II	Origin unknown. Shipped to Southern Rhodesia in December 1940.
BS814-BS815	2	Miles M.11A Whitney Straight	Impressed. Previously G-AEVF/VM.
BS816	1	D.H.84 Dragon	G-ACBW, impressed. To No. 6 A.A.C.U., November, 1940.
BS817	1	Fairchild 24-C8F	Fairchild No. 3126: G-AEOU, impressed. Became 2759M.
BS818	1	Miles Whitney Straight	G-AEXJ, impressed.
BS900-BT272	200	D.H.82 Tiger Moth	Allotted for trainers assembled in Bombay. BS900-936, 949-997, BT111-136, 153-183, 197-241, 261-272.

Serial Nos.	*Qty.*	*Aircraft Type*	*Remarks*
BT278-BT281	4	Percival P.30 Proctor III	Renumbered from Z7253-7256.
BT286-BT303	18	Bristol 156 Beaufighter VIF	Bristol (Filton)-built. All shipped overseas. BT292, 300 to U.S.A.A.F.
BT308/G	1	Avro Manchester III	Lancaster prototype. F2/1 jet fitted in tail in 1943.
BT312	1	D.H.95 Flamingo	De Havilland No. 95011: G-AFYH, impressed. Scrapped May 1954.
BT316-BT437	100	Supermarine Sea Otter	Cancelled order with Blackburn Aircraft. BT316-347, 357-401, 415-437.
BT440-BT442	3	Piper J-4A Cub Coupé	G-AFSZ/VL/WR, impressed.
BT447-BT456	10	Grumman Martlet	All lost at sea.
BT460-BT465	6	Douglas Havoc I	BT465 was fitted with Long Aerial Mine. BT464 was transferred to the U.S.A.A.F.
BT470-BT472	3	Curtiss Mohawk IV	Presumed ex-French order. All three shipped to India.
BT474	1	Fiat C.R.42	Brought down in Suffolk in November 1940 and reconditioned.
BT479-BV129	390	General Aircraft G.A.L.48 Hotspur II	Built by Harris Lebus. BT479-513, 534-557, 561-579, 594-640, 658-693, 715-755, 769-799, 813-861, 877-903, 916-948, 961-990, BV112-129. The following were converted to Mk. III: BT540, 566, 602, 632, 663, 735, 747, 751, 777, 784, 823, 895, 917, 946.
BV134-BV151	13	General Aircraft G.A.L.48 Hotspur I	Built by Slingsby. BV134-140, 146-151.
BV155-BV174	20	Hawker Hurricane IIA	Converted from Hurricane I.
BV180-BV181	2	Piper J-4A Cub Coupé	Piper Nos. 4-558-559: G-AFWA/B, impressed.
BV185-BV187	3	Heinkel He 115	Royal Norwegian Air Force Nos. 58/?/64. Escaped to U.K. from Nazis in 1940.
BV190-BV199	10	General Aircraft G.A.L.48 Hotspur I	Built by General Aircraft. BV199 converted to Mk. II prototype.
BV200	1	General Aircraft G.A.L.48 Hotspur II	Built by Airspeed.
BV203	1	Douglas Havoc I	Origin unknown. To No. 85 Squadron, May 1941.
BV207	1	Gotha Go 145	Argus-engined. Became 2682M.
BV208-BV209	2	Avro 504N	G-AEMP/CPV, impressed.
BV214-BV531	250	Vickers Warwick I	Vickers (Weybridge)-built. BV214-242, Mk. I except BV 216, Mk. II; 243-256, used by B.O.A.C. as G-AGEX-FK and returned to R.A.F. as C.I; BV269-316, 332-370, 384-421, 436-484, 499-531, planned as

			B.I of which the majority were converted to, and all from BV 352 delivered as, A.S.R.1.
BV535-BV658	100	Percival P.30 Proctor II	Built by F. Hills & Son. BV535-573, 586-612, 625-658. BV655 became a Mk.III. Main deliveries to Fleet Air Arm.
BV660-BV981	250	Fairey Barracuda II	Built by Blackburn. BV660-707, 721-766, 788-834, 847-885, 898-922, 937-981.
BV984-BV991	8	Piper J-4A Club Coupé	G-AFXU/XX/XV/VG/VM/TB/TC/VF, impressed.
BV999	1	Cierva C-30A	G-ACXW, impressed in January 1941.
BW100-BW183	84	Bell 14 Airacobra I	British Direct Purchase Contract. Delivered, but many handed back to U.S.A.A.F. in U.K. and others shipped to U.S.S.R.
BW184-BW207	24	North American NA-66 Harvard II	British Direct Purchase Contract.
BW208-BW307	100	Vultee 48C Vanguard	U.S.A.A.F. P-66, offered as advanced trainers but eventually diverted to China.
BW361-BW777	417	Lockheed Hudson IIIA	Ordered by direct purchase, but supplied under Lend/Lease. BW361-380 diverted to U.S. Navy, BW386-398 diverted to China, others up to BW460 held in Canada or shipped to Australia. BW461-613 taken over by U.S.A.A.F.; BW661-681, 736-755 shipped to Australia and BW756-767 to New Zealand.
BW778-BW827	50	Grumman Goose IA	Serials re-allotted to FP475-524 in Lend/Lease series (*q.v.*).
BW828-BW834	7	Pitcairn PA-39	Direct Purchase in U.S.A. BW828-830 lost at sea in January 1942.
BW835-BX134	200	Hawker Hurricane XA/XIB	Built by the Canadian Car & Foundry Corporation. BW835-884 produced as Sea Hurricane, except for BW841 and BW880 as Mk. X; BW885-999, BX100-134, Mk. XIB—of which BW886, 900, 921 were converted to Mk. XIC. Some fitted with 12 guns for Soviet Air Force.
BX135-BX434	300	Bell 14 Airacobra I	Many taken over by U.S.A.A.F. in U.K., others shipped to U.S.S.R. BX179, 188, 190, 191, 222, 232, 239, 241, 263, 264, 290, 296, 298, 319, 340, 371, and 427 were lost at sea.
BZ100-BZ154	55	Vultee Vigilant I	Ex-U.S.A.A.F. L-1A 41-18943 to 18997. Delivery of 13 only confirmed.

Serial Nos.	*Qty.*	*Aircraft Type*	*Remarks*
BZ155-BZ195	41	Vultee Vigilant IA	Delivery not confirmed.
BZ196-BZ669	461	Douglas Boston IIIA/IV/V	Supplied under) Lend/Lease. BZ196-352, 355-399, Mk. IIIA (ex-A-20C; BZ400-568, Mk. IV (ex-A-20C); BZ580-669, Mk. V (ex-A-20K). BZ647 crashed in the U.S.A. before delivery.
BZ711-BZ999	289	Consolidated 32 Liberator III/V/VI	Ordered on direct purchase, but delivered under Lend/Lease arrangements. BZ711-832 mainly delivered as G.R.V., of which BZ723, 743, 744, 760-762, 769, 773, 781, 783, 786, 792, 793, 804, 806 were converted to C.V; BZ833-860, Mk. III; BZ861-889, G.R.V—of which BZ869 and BZ871 were converted to C.V; BZ890-909, Mk. III; BZ910-921, G.R.V; BZ922-929, Mk. III; BZ930, G.R.V; BZ931, G.R.V (converted to C.V); BZ932-936, Mk. III; BZ937-945, G.R.V—of which BZ941 was converted to C.V; BZ946-959, Mk. III; BZ960, G.R.VI (converted to B.VI); BZ961, G.R.VI; BZ962, B.VI; BZ963-964, Mk. VI; BZ965, B.VI; BZ966-967, G.R.VI; BZ968, G.R.VI (converted to C.VI); BZ969, G.R.VI; BZ970 reported as C.IV; BZ971-972, C.VI; BZ973-974, B.VI; BZ975, G.R.VI; BZ976-978, B.VI; BZ979, G.R.VI (converted to C.VI); BZ980, Mk. VI; BZ981, C.VI; BZ982-983, B.VI; BZ984, G.R.VI; BZ985, G.R.VI (converted to C.VI); BZ986, C.VI; BZ987-988, G.R.VI; BZ989-990, B.VI; BZ991, G.R.VI; BZ992-993, B.VI; BZ994-995, G.R.VI; BZ996-998, B.VI; BZ999, G.R.VI.

THE "DOUBLE Ds"

DA100–DZ999

THE possibility of Lend/Lease caused direct purchase orders to be terminated abruptly by the British Purchasing Commission in America and this is reflected by the fact that the allocation from DA100 to DD599 was not taken up. The combination " DH " was not used, as it was too familiar as the abbreviation for " de Havilland ".

DD600-DD800	150	D.H.98 Mosquito II	De Havilland (Hatfield)-built. DD600-644, 659-691, 712-759, 777-800—of which DD715 was converted to Mk. XII. DD664 went to the R.A.A.F. as A52-1001. DD723 was a special version with Merlin 23 engines.
DD804-DD815	3	Blackburn Firebrand	Prototypes DD804, DD810, DD815 to Air Ministry Specification N.11/40. DD810 was rebuilt as NV636.
DD818	1	D.H.85 Leopard Moth	VT-AJP, impressed. Served at No. 1 Flying Training School, India.
DD820-DD821	2	D.H.80A Puss Moth	G-ABCR/UX, impressed. DD 820 served with Eighth U.S.A.A.F.
DD828-DD867	40	Short S.25 Sunderland III	Built by Blackburn. DD860 became G-AHEP.
DD870-DE126	120	Bristol 152 Beaufort	DD870-911, 927-944 (60), Mk. II; DD945-959, 974-999, DE 108-126 (60), Mk. I.
DE131-DF214	750	D.H.82A Tiger Moth II	Built by Morris Motors, DE 131-178, 192-224, 236-284, 297-323, 336-379, 394-432, 445-490, 507-535, 549-589, 603-640, 654-697, 709-747, 764-791, 808-856, 870-904, 919-957, 969-999, DF111-159, 173-214. DE395 became XL715.
DF220-DF536	250	Airspeed A.S.10 Oxford I	Built by Standard Motors. DF220-264, 276-314, 327-367, 390-433, 445-489, 501-536.
DF542-DG197	400	Vickers Wellington III	Vickers (Blackpool)-built. DF 542-579, 594-642, 664-709, 727-743 Mk. III; 150 only completed—of which DF609, 686, 701, 730, 740 were built as Mk. X and DF614 was converted to Mk. X, DF744-776, 794-832, 857-900, 921-956, 975-999, DG112-134, 148-197, cancelled.
DG200	1	Messerschmitt Bf 109E	Captured enemy aircraft.
DG202-DG213	12	Gloster F.9/40 " Rampage "	Jet-engined prototypes with engines as follows: DG202/G, Rover W2B; DG203/G, Power Jets W2/500; DG204/G, Metrovick F.2; DG205/G, Rover W2B/23; DG206-7/G, Halford H.1; DG208/G, W2B/23; DG209/G, W2B/27. DG210-213 cancelled.
DG219-DG424	150	Handley Page Halifax II/V	Built by Rootes Securities. DG219-230 (12) Mk. II; DG231-253, 270-317, 338-363,

Serial Nos.	*Qty.*	*Aircraft Type*	*Remarks*
			384-424 (138), Mk. V. DG223 crashed on test and was not delivered.
DG430-DG439	10	North American NA-66 Harvard II	DG430-439, of which DG432-439 were lost at sea.
DG442-DG447	6	Westland Lysander	Canadian built ex-R.C.A.F.
DG450-DG454	5	Armstrong Whitworth A.W.15 Atalanta	G-ABTL, G-ABTI, G-ABTJ, G-ABPI, G-ABTM, impressed in India.
DG455-DG464	6	D.H.82 Tiger Moth	DG455, 456, 457, 461, 462, 464, impressed in India.
DG468-DG479	12	Douglas DC-2	VT-AOU/Q/R/S/T/V/W/X/Y/Z and VT-APA/B, impressed in India.
DG483-DG529	39	D.H.82 Tiger Moth	DG483-487, 490-491, 493-503, 505-506, 508-513, 515-524, 527-529.
DG531 & DG534	2	D.H.60 Moth Major	Impressed in India.
DG536-DG548	9	D.H.82 Tiger Moth	DG536, 538-540, 544-548, impressed in India.
DG554-DG555	2	Douglas Havoc I	Origin unknown. DG554 Intruder version with Long Aerial Mine.
DG558 & DG562	2	Westland P.14 Welkin	Prototypes to Air Ministry Specification F.4/40.
DG566	1	General Aircraft G.A.L.42 Cygnet II	G-AGAL, impressed. Served in No. 24 Squadron.
DG570-DG573	4	Slingsby Hengist	Prototypes to Air Ministry Specification X.25/40. DG571 crashed on test at Dishforth, 1943.
DG576	1	Miles M.3 Falcon Six	Miles No. 280: G-AECC, impressed.
DG577	1	Miles Hawk Major	Miles No. 118: G-ACXT, impressed in January 1941. Became 4020M.
DG578	1	Miles M.2 Hawk	G-ACNX, impressed. Became 2617M.
DG579-DG589	11	D.H.60 Moth	G-AAFI/AHG/AVV/FKA/BDA/ARC/BZE/AJZ/AAC/BAT/AFS, impressed.
DG590	1	Miles Hawk Major	Miles M2H version: G-ADMW, impressed.
DG595	1	Avro 683 Lancaster	Second prototype. First flew 13.5.41.
DG597-DG609	3	Airspeed A.S.51 Horsa	DG597, 603, 609, prototypes to Air Ministry Specification X.26/40.
DG612-DG651	40	Hawker Hurricane IIA	Converted from Mk. I by Rolls-Royce and renumbered.
DG655-DG656	2	Avro 652 Avalon	Avro Nos. 698-699: G-ACRM-N, impressed in Februray 1941 and handed over to Royal Navy.
DG657-DG660	4	D.H.60 Gipsy Moth	G-AAJL/ABI/BBK/BTP, impressed.
DG661-DG662	2	D.H.80A Puss Moth	G-AAXR and G-ABLG, impressed early in 1941.

DG663	1	Airspeed A.S.6 Envoy III	Airspeed No. 32: G-ADAZ impressed.
DG664	1	Miles M.2R Hawk Major	Miles No. 211: G-ADLN, impressed.
DG665-DG666	2	Miles M.2X Hawk Trainer I	G-ADZA/EAX/ impressed. DG665 became 3015M.
DG667	1	Piper J-4A Cub Coupé	Piper No. 4-647; G-AFXS, impressed.
DG670	1	Hafner A.R.III Gyroplane	G-ADMV, used at Farnborough.
DG673-DG686	14	Slingsby Hengist I	Placed in store at Rawcliffe Paper Mills. All scrapped in October 1946.
DG689-DJ700	700	Avro 652A Anson I/IV	A. V. Roe (Newton Heath)-built except for DG689-727, A. V. Roe (Yeadon)-built. DG689-737, 750-787, 799-844, 857-880, 893-942, 956-987, DJ103-127, Mk. I; DJ128-133, Mk. IV; DJ134-149, 162-190, 205-248, 263-298, 314-361, 375-417, 430-478, 492-529, 545-589, 603-639, 656-700, Mk. I. Main deliveries to Empire Training Scheme.
DJ702 & DJ707	2	Bristol 160HA Blenheim V	Prototypes to Air Ministry Specification B.6/40. Originally named Bisley.
DJ710	1	Avro 641 Commodore	Avro No. 722: G-ACUG, impressed.
DJ711-DJ712	2	D.H.80 Puss Moth	G-AAXY and G-ABIN, impressed.
DJ713-DJ714	2	Miles M.11A Whitney Straight	G-AEUX and G-AEWA, impressed.
DJ715	1	Airspeed A.S.4 Ferry	G-ACFB, impressed.
DJ716	1	D.H.90 Dragonfly	G-AEWZ, impressed.
DJ972-DJ977	6	Short S.29 Stirling I	Replacement order for Stirlings destroyed by bombing.
DJ980-DK271	150	Handley Page Halifax V	Built by Fairey Aviation. DJ980-999, DK114-151, 165-207, 223-271.
DK274-DK277	4	Douglas Boston I	Arrived in damaged condition and struck off strength.
DK280	1	Messerschmitt Bf 108	G-AFRN, impressed.
DK284-DK339	50	D.H.98 Mosquito IV	DK284-303, 308-333, 336-339, of which DK297 went to Canada and DK296 to Russia. DK290/G had cutaway bomb bay. A few were delivered as P.R.IV; DK324 was a P.R.VIII.
DK346-DK358	4	Airspeed A.S.51 Horsa	Prototypes. DK346, DK349, DK353, DK358.
DK363-DK412	50	Blackburn Firebrand I/III	DK363-371, Mk. I; DK372-373, Mk. III prototypes; DK374-385, Mk. II; DK386-412, Mk. III.

Serial Nos.	*Qty.*	*Aircraft Type*	*Remarks*
DK414-DK667	200	Fairey Firefly I	Built by General Aircraft Limited. DK414-462, 476-513, 526-570 (132) built. DK426, 428, 429, 448, 453, 478, 489, 495, 499, 531, 540, 543, 550, converted to T.1; DK462, 513, 527, 567, converted to T.2.; DK566, converted to T.3 DK588-619, 633-667 cancelled.
DK670-DK792	100	Fairey Swordfish II	Built by Blackburn Aircraft. DK670-719, 743-792.
DK800-DL546	500	Miles M.19 Master II	Phillips & Powis (Reading)-built. DK800-843, 856-894, 909-957, 963-994, DL111-155, 169-204, 216-256, 271-301, T.II; DL302-309, 324-325, G.T.II; DL326-373, 395-435, 448-493, 509-546, T.II; some conversions to G.T.II. DL131-155 delivered to South Africa; DL251, 252, 271, 272, 275, 276, 278-280, sold to Royal Egyptian Air Force, and DK891 to Portugal.
DL552-DM196	400	Miles M.19/27 Master II/III	Phillips & Powis (South Marston)-built. DL552-585, 599-648, 666-713, 725-753, 767-793 (188), Mk. III; DL794-803, 821-866, 878-909, 935-983, DM108-140, 155-196 (212), Mk. II. DL863, 891, 902, 937, 840, DM113, 174, to Turkish Air Force; DL976-979, 983, DM166-168, 170, 173, 179, 180, to Royal Egyptian Air Force. DL852/G rocket experiments.
DM200-DM581	300	Miles M.19 Master II	Phillips & Powis (Doncaster and Sheffield)-built. DM200-245, 258-295, 312-361, 374-407, 423-454 only (200) built. DM455-464, 478-526, 541-581 (100) cancelled. DM227, 232-235, to Royal Egyptian Air Force; DM231, 273, 276, 335, 346, 351, 376, 454, to Turkish Air Force.
DM594-DN232	395	Hawker Tornado	A. V. Roe order cancelled. DM594-642, 664-709, 727-776, 794-842, 857-900, 921-957, 975-999; DN112-134, 148-197, 210-232.
DN241-DN623	300	Hawker Typhoon IB	Built by Gloster Aircraft, DN241-278, 293-341, 356-389, 404-453, 467-513, 529-562, 576-623—of which DN323 was tropicalised.

DN625-DN998	250	Fairey Barracuda I/II	18 only built by Westland Aircraft as DN625-629 (Mk. I) and DN630-642 (Mk. II). Cancelled Nos. were: DN643-669, 693-730, 756-805, 839-874, 897-935, 957-998.
DP176-DP200	25	Short S.25 Sunderland III	Short (Windermere)-built. DP191, 195, 198-200, converted to Mk. V.
DP206 & DP210	2	General Aircraft G.A.L.49 Hamilcar	Prototypes to Air Ministry Specification X.27/40.
DP226	1	General Aircraft G.A.L.50	Half-scale model of G.A.L.49 registered T-0227.
DP237	1	Miles M.11A Whitney Straight	G-AEYA, impressed in April 1941.
DP240	1	General Aircraft G.A.L.45 Owlet	G.A.L. No. 134: G-AGBK, impressed in July 1941.
DP244	1	D.H.60GIII Moth Major	Impressed in India in 1941.
DP245-DP266	22	D.H.82 Tiger Moth	Impressed in India. No record of DP248 and DP259.
DP279-DP713	300	Airspeed A.S.51 Horsa 1	Built by Harris Lebus and group factories. DP279-294, 303-315, 329-353; 368-399, 412-440, 484-506, 513-562, 567-575, 592-631, 644-681, 689-713. DP593-598, 614, 617, 701 to U.S.A.A.F.
DP714-DP841	100	Airspeed A.S.51 Horsa 1	Built by The Austin Motor Co. DP714-726, 739-777, 794-841. DP725 to U.S.A.A.F.
DP843	1	D.H.80A Puss Moth	Reported as impressment.
DP845	1	Supermarine Spitfire III/IV/XX (in succession)	Prototype to Air Ministry Specification F.4/40.
DP845	1	Miles Whitney Straight	G-AEVG, impressed. Compromised number above.
DP846	1	D.H.80A Puss Moth	G-ABTV, impressed.
DP847	1	British Aircraft Eagle	G-ADVT, impressed. Originally owned by Marquess of Donegal.
DP848	1	Miles M.2H Hawk Major	G-AENS, impressed.
DP849	1	D.H.80 Puss Moth	G-ABMC impressed.
DP850	1	D.H.80A Puss Moth	G-ABMP, impressed.
DP851	1	Supermarine Spitfire	Protoyype F.21 after modification successively from Mk. IV Mk. XX.
DP851	1	Miles M.2H Hawk Major	G-AEGP, impressed. Became 3016M. Compromised number above.
DP852	1	Piper J4B Cub Coupé	Piper No. 4-653: G-AFXT, impressed in March 1941.
DP853-DP854	2	D.H.80A Puss Moth	G-AEIV and G-ABMS, impressed.
DP855	1	Miles Whitney Straight	G-AEVL, impressed. Compromised number below and renumbered NF751.

Serial Nos.	Qty.	Aircraft Type	Remarks
DP855-DR335	300	Fairey Barracuda II	Built by Boulton Paul. DP 855-902, 917-955, 967-999, DR113-162, 179-224, 237-275, 291-335.
DR339-DR394	40	Hawker Hurricane IIA	DR339-374, 391-394. Mk. Is renumbered on conversion for shipment to the U.S.S.R.
DR423-DR427	5	Harlow PJC-5	Assembled in India. DR425 to No. 22 A.A.C.U.
DR471-DR600	100	Vickers Wellington VI	Vickers (Weybridge) built. DR 471-484, Mk. VI; DR485-504, 519-527, Mk. VIA; DR528 Mk. VI; DR529-549, 566-600, cancelled. DR484 had its rear turret deleted.
DR606	1	D.H.60 Moth	G-AAYT, impressed.
DR607-DR608	2	D.H.80A Puss Moth	G-ABKZ and G-ABIU, impressed.
DR609-DR610	2	British Aircraft Eagle	G-ACPU/DJS, impressed. DR610 became 2680M.
DR611	1	Miles M.11A Whitney Straight	G-AETS, impressed. (See DR617).
DR612	1	Miles M.11A Whitney Straight	G-AEVA impressed.
DR613	1	Wicko G.M.I Warferry	G-AFJB, impressed.
DR616	1	Miles M.20	Naval prototype to Specification N.1/41, Ex-U-0228.
DR617	1	Miles M.11A Whitney Straight	Number applied incorrectly to DR611.
DR622-DR624	3	Cierva C.30A	Impressed autogyros, G-ACYH /WH/WF.
DR626	1	Bucker Jungmann	Requisition of ex-enemy aircraft.
DR628	1	Beech C-17R	Ex-U.S. 39-139. Allotted for personal use of Prince Bernhardt.
DR629	1	Consolidated BT-7	Allocation cancelled.
DR630	1	D.H.80 Puss Moth	Re-allotted HM534.
DR633-DR749	100	Fairey Fulmar II	Final Fulmar production. DR 633-682, 700-749.
DR755	1	D.H.80 Puss Moth	G-AAVB, impressed.
DR761	1	D.H.75 Hawk Moth	Impressed in Middle East.
DR808	1	Percival Vega Gull	Impressed.
DR848-DR849	2	General Aircraft ST-4 and ST-25 Monospar	Ex-X9348 and X9376. Types ST-25 Jubilee & ST-4 Mk. II.
DR851-DR860	10	General Aircraft G.A.L.49 Hamilcar	Experimental batch. DR852 and DR855 became 4311M/4457M.
DR863-DS169	150	Boulton Paul P.82 Defiant T.T.1	DR863-896, 914-949, 961-991, DS121-159 (140) built. DR 944, ejection-seat experiments. DS160-169 cancelled.
DS173-DS175	3	Bell 14 Airacobra	For evaluation from July 1942.
DS180	1	Beechcraft C-17R	Beechcraft No. 118: G-AESJ, impressed in May 1941.

DS183-DS598	—	—	Cancelled order.
DS601-DS852	200	Avro 683 Lancaster II	Built by Armstrong Whitworth Aircraft. DS601-635, DS647-692, 704-741, 757-797, 813-852. Up to DS627 were fitted with Bristol Hercules VI engines, remainder with Hercules XVI engines. DS 708 tested servo-spring tabs for the Brabazon.
DS858-DT479	400	Airspeed A.S.10 Oxford I/II	Cancelled order with de Havilland for 200 Mk. I and 200 Mk. II. DS858-897, 915-950, 962-989, DT108-146, 161-210, 224-265, 279-313, 325-374, 387-418, 432-479.
DT481-DT808	250	Handley Page H.P.59 Halifax II	Built by the English Electric Company. DT481-526, 539-588, 612-649, 665-705, 720-752, 767-808.
DT810 & DT812	2	Avro 683 Lancaster II	Prototype Mk. II. DT810 only built.
DT813-DT887	50	Fairey Barracuda II	Fairey (Heaton Chapel)-built. DT813-831, 845-865, 878-887. DT845 was Mk. V prototype.
DT926-DV150	100	Fairey Firefly I	DT926-961, 974-998, DV112-150 produced as F.I; DT974 and DV132 converted to T.I; DT976 converted to T.3; DV119, 127 converted to F.R.I; DV121 converted to T.T.1.
DV155-DV407	200	Avro 683 Lancaster III/I	Built by Metropolitan-Vickers. DV155-202, 217-247, 263-276, Mk. III; DV277-282, Mk. I; DV283-290, Mk. III; DV291-297, Mk. I; DV298, Mk. III; DV299-309, Mk. I; DV310, Mk. III; DV311-312, 324-345, 359-382, Mk. I; DV383-384, Mk. III; DV385-394, Mk. I; DV395, Mk. III; DV396-407, Mk. I; DV379 became B.O.A.C. test-bed G-AGJI. DV170,199 became Mk. VI.
DV411-DV953	415	Vickers Wellington IC	Vickers (Chester)-built. DV 411-458, 473-522, 536-579, 593-624, 638-678, 694-740. 757-786, 799-846, 864-898, 914-953, Mk. IC—of which DV491, 594, 617, 704, 738, 761, 762, 822, 886, 920, 921, 924, 942 were converted to Mk. XVI.
DV956-DW113	45	Short S.25 Sunderland III	DV956-980 (25) built by Short Bros; DV985-994, DW104-113 (20) built by Short & Harland.
DW115-DW502	250	Vickers Warwick	Cancelled.

Serial Nos.	*Qty.*	*Aircraft Type*	*Remarks*
DW506 & DW512	2	Vickers Windsor	Prototypes. DW506, Vickers 447 (Merlin 65); DW512, Vickers 457 (Merlin 82).
DW515-DW796	—	—	Cancelled order.
DW802-DX157	200	Bristol 152 Beaufort I	DW802-836, 851-898, 913-962, 977-999, DX114-157. The following were transferred to the Turkish Air Force: DW 930, DX125, 144, 147, 149, 153.
DX160	1	Folland E.28/40	Torpedo-bomber project. Not built.
DX161	1	Percival P.33	Fighter project. Not built.
DX166&DX171	2	Short S.35 Shetland	Prototypes to Air Ministry Specification R.14/40. DX171 became G-AGVD on completion.
DX177	1	Focke-Wulf Fw 200B	Condor (ex-OY-DAM), impressed as G-AGAY in May 1941.
DX181-DX243	50	Percival P.34 Proctor III	Built by F. Hills & Sons. DX181-201, 215-243.
DX249-DX266	4	Bristol 163 Buckingham	Prototypes. DX249, 255, 259, 266. Named Beaumont at project stages.
DX278-DX420	100	Westland Welkin I	DX278-295, 308-349, 364-389, 407-420. Not issued to service and not all late deliveries were flown. DX340 used as engine test-bed.
DX437-DX835	420	D.H.82 Tiger Moth II	De Havillland (Australia)-built. DX437-461, 474-512, 526-557, 569-612, 627-723 and others not known. 120 shipped to South Africa and 94 to Southern Rhodesia.
DX840-DZ202	—	—	Not allotted.
DZ203	1	Boeing 247D	Boeing No. 1726; NC13344, impressed.
DZ209	1	Bellanca Pacemaker	G-ABNW (ex-I-AAPI), impressed for Fleet communication duties.
DZ213	1	D.H.83 Fox Moth	G-ACIY, impressed for Royal Navy.
DZ217 & DZ223	2	Vickers 432	Prorotypes to A.M. Spec. F.7/41. DX223 not completed.
DZ228-DZ761	400	D.H. 98 Mosquito II/IV	DZ228-272, 286-310 (70), N.F. II; DZ311-320, 340-388, 404-442, 458-497, 515-559, 575-618, 630-652 (250), B.IV except for the following as P.R.IV: DZ419, 431, 438, 459, 466, 473, 480, 487, 494, 517, 523, 527, 532, 538, 544, 549, 553, 557, 576, 580, 584, 588, 592, 596, 600, 604;

			DZ653-661, 680-727, 739-761 N.F.II; DZ342, 364, 404, 424, P.R. VIII; DZ411 loaned to B.O.A.C. as G-AGFV; DZ 540, B.XVI prototype; DZ 594/G had bulged bomb bay; DZ714 had a special H2S scanner installed; DZ630-652 with 40 others specially modified for Operation Highball.
DZ779-DZ986	250	Handley Page Halifax	Cancelled order. DZ779-819, 837-877, 893-924, 937-986, EA104-147, 160-201.

LEND/LEASE INTRODUCED

EA100–EZ999

ON 11th March, 1941, the Lend/Lease Act was passed and an Aircraft Allocation Committee decided the priorities of issue to the nations deemed " vital to the defence of the United States ". A large block of numbers, starting at ET100, was reserved for Lend/Lease requirements approved by the U.S. authorities. Germans could travel freely, since America was not yet at war, and there was little point in using black-out blocks; Lend/Lease aircraft were therefore numbered consecutively. Since these concerned the allocation of United States Army Air Force, United States Navy and Marine Corps aircraft, the designation of the American service concerned is given, where appropriate.

Up to ET were normal orders placed by the Ministry of Aircraft Production. The Series carried over an order for Halifax bombers from the end of the DZ-prefixed numbers to begin an EA series, but since EA was often used as an abbreviation for " Enemy Aircraft ", this series was not used further and the main numbering sequence began with EB.

EB127-EB276	100	Handley Page Halifax V	Built by Rootes Securities. EB127-160, 178-220, 239-258, 274-276.
EB282-EB410	100	Armstrong Whitworth A.W.38 Whitley V/VII	EB282, Mk. VII; EB283-313, Mk. V; EB327-336, Mk. VII; EB337-367, 384-391, Mk. V; EB392-401, Mk. VII; EB402-410, Mk. V.
EB414-EB975	400	Airspeed A.S.10 Oxford I/V	Airspeed-built. EB414-423, Mk. I (all to South Africa); EB424, Mk. V (to Southern Rhodesia); EB425-461, 483-518, 535-584, 599-640, 654-677, Mk. V—of which all but two went to Canada as airframes; EB689-703, 717-761, 777-826, 838-870, 884-930, 946-975, Mk. I. EB849, 884, 888, 894, 915, 924, 953, 962-966, 968 converted to Mk. V.

Serial Nos.	*Qty.*	*Aircraft Type*	*Remarks*
EB978-ED300	180	Airspeed A.S.10 Oxford II/I	Built by Percival Aircraft EB978-999, ED108-157, 169-196 (100), Mk. II; ED197-204, 215-236, 251-300 (80), Mk. I.
ED303-EE202	620	Avro 683 Lancaster	Avro (Manchester)-built. ED 303-334, 347-396, Mk. I—except for ED362, 371/G (with Lincoln type nose), 378, 383, 387, 388, 390, 393, 395, 396, Mk. III; ED408-453, 467-504, 520-569, 583-631, 645-668, 688-737, 749-786, 799-842, 856-888, 904-953, 967-999, EE105-150, 166-202, Mk. III—except for ED409, 411, 412, 414, 418, 420, 422, 425, 430, 436, 439, 443, 446, 447, 451, 498, 521, 522, 525, 528, 533, 537, 548, 550, 552, 554, 567, 569, 586, 588, 591, 594, 600, 601, 604, 610, 615, 622, 631, 650, 661, 692, 703, 715, 732, 735, 749, 751, 754, 755, 757, 758, 761-763, 766, 769, 770, 773, 774, 777, 778, 780-782, Mk. I. Of these, 23 B.IIIs were modified in early 1943 for the famous Dam-Busting operation of 17th May 1943. These were: ED765/G, ED817/G, ED825/G, ED864/G, ED865/G, ED886/G, ED887/G, ED906/G, ED909/G, ED910/G, ED 915/G, ED918/G, ED921/G, ED924/G, ED925/G, ED927/G, ED929/G, ED932/G, ED 934/G, ED936/G, ED937/G.
EE205	1	Junkers Ju 88A-6	Captured German aircraft.
EE210-EE599	300	Gloster G.41 Meteor I/III/IV (which became F.1/F.3/F.4 in service)	EE210-229, F.1; EE230-254, 269-318, 331-369, 384-429, 444-453, F.3 (Derwent engines, except EE230-244 with Wellands); EE454-493, 517-554, 568-599, F.4. EE240/G to U.S.A.; EE221/G had W2/700 jets installed; EE212/G, non-standard empennage; EE215 had re-heat on Wellands; EE227, Trent turbo-props; EE249/G, W2/700 jets, pressure cabin and other modifications; EE337, Royal Navy deck landing trials; EE360/G, F.4 prototype; EE 338 and 416, ejection seat trials; EE397, flight refuell-

			ing trials; EE530, Mk. VII prototype; EE531, wing-folding tests; EE454-455 modified for World Speed Record. EE521 and EE524 conv. to U.15. Disposals to Argentina and Australia.
EE600-EE867	200	Supermarine Spitfire VC	Built by Westland Aircraft. EE600-644, 657-690, 713-753, 766-811, 834-867.
EE871-EF323	260	Short S.29 Stirling III/IV	Built by Short & Harland. EE871-918, 937-975, EF114-163, 177-217, 231-277, 289-316, Mk. III; EF317-323, Mk. IV. EE889, 900, 960, 962, 966, EF141, 213, 214, 234, 237, 241-244, 248, 256, 260, 261, 263-265, 267-270, 272-277, 292, 293, 295-298, 303, 305-306, 309, 311, 314, 316 converted to Mk. IV.
EF327-EF518	150	Short S.29 Stirling I/III/IV	Built by Short Bros. EF327-369, 384-400, Mk. I; EF401-412, Mk. III; EF413, Mk. I; EF425-470, 488-518, Mk. III. EF404, 429, 435, 446, 470, 506 converted to Mk. IV.
EF523	1	Fairchild 24C8-F	G-AFFK, impressed.
EF526-EF753	185	Supermarine Spitfire VC	Built by Westland Aircraft. EF526-570, 584-616, 629-656, 671-710, 715-753.
EF805-EG704	600	Avro 652A Anson I	A. V. Roe (Yeadon)-built. EF805-839, 858-890, 903-941, 952-993, EG104-148, 165-195, 208-246, 251-280, 293-335, 350-396, 412-447, 460-507, 524-561, 583-616, 629-655, 672-704.
EH310-EH872	415	Bristol 160 Blenheim V	Built by Rootes Securities. EH310-355, 371-420, 438-474, 491-517 (160) only completed. EH518-533, 550-581, 599-634, 651-700, 718-749, 763-796, 802-831, 848-872 cancelled.
EH875-EJ127	120	Short S.29 Stirling III	Built by The Austin Motor Co EH875-909, 921-961, 977-996, EJ104-127, Mk. III—of which EH897, EH950 and EJ106 were converted to Mk.IV.
EJ131-EJ172	35	Short S.25 Sunderland III	EJ131-145 built at Rochester, EJ149-158 built at Windermere and EJ163-172 built at Belfast. EJ152, 153, 155, 167, 171, 172, converted to Mk. V.
EJ175-EJ454	270	Hawker Typhoon IB	Cancelled order. EJ175-222, 234-283, 296-334, 347-392, 405-454, 467-503.

Serial Nos.	Qty.	Aircraft Type	Remarks
EJ504-EJ896	300	Hawker Tempest V	EJ504, EJ518-560, 577-611, 626-672, 685-723, 739-788, 800-846, 859-896. EJ518, annular cooling trials. Conversions to T.T.5 post-war were as follows: EJ580, 585, 599, 643, 660, 663, 667, 669, 740, 744, 753, 758, 786, 801, 805, 807, 839, 846, 862, 875, 879, 880. EJ841 was converted to Mk. VI.
EJ900-EK543	400	Hawker Typhoon IB	Built by Gloster Aircraft. EJ900-934, 946-995, EK112-154, 167-197, 208-252, 266-301, 321-348, 364-413, 425-456, 472-512, 535-543. EJ906 was tropicalised.
EK572-EK596	25	Short S.25 Sunderland III	Built by Blackburn Aircraft.
EK601-EK967	250	Blackburn Firebrand IV/V	EK601-638, 653-694, 719-740 (102), Mk. IV; EK741-748, 764-799, 827-850 (68), Mk. V. EK851-867, 885-913, 934-967 (80), cancelled. EK630 was non-standard.
EK969-EL141	50	Bristol 152 Beaufort I	Bristol (Filton)-built. EK969-999, EL123-141. Main delivery to training units.
EL145-EL534	300	Bristol 156 Beaufighter VI	Bristol (Weston)-built. EL145-192, 213-218, Mk. VIF; EL 219-246, 259-305, 321-370, 385-418, 431-479, 497-534, Mk. VIC. 19 re-numbered in the R.A.A.F. EL393, Mk. X prototype.
EM258-EM716	300	Miles Master II/ Martinet I	Phillips and Powis (Reading)-built. EM258-304, 317-355, 371-409 (125), Master II—of which EM381, 385, 405 went to the Turkish Air Force; EM410-420, 434-481, 496-532, 545-593, 613-662, 677-716 (235), Martinet I.
EM720-EM989	222	D.H.82 Tiger Moth II	Built by Morris Motors. EM 720-756, 771-819, 835-884, 893-931, 943-989. Numbers shipped direct to India.
EM995 & EM996	2	D.H.80A Puss Moth	G-ABLP and G-ABLX, impressed.
EM999	1	Miles M.11A Whitney Straight	G-AERV, impressed.
EN112-EN759	500	Supermarine Spitfire VII/IX/XI/XII	EN112-156, 171-207, F.IX (except for EN178 and 192, H.F.VII); EN221-238, F.XII EN239-270, F.IX; EN285, H.F.VII; EN286-296, F.IX; EN297, H.F.VII; EN298-

			309, F.IX; EN310, H.F.VII; EN311-315, 329-340, F.IX; EN341-343, P.R. XI; EN344-370, 385-430, 444-456, F.IX; EN457, H.F.VII; EN458-464, F.IX; EN465, H.F.VII; EN466-469, F.IX; EN470, H.F.VII; EN471-473, F.IX; EN474, H.F.VII; EN475-476, F.IX; EN477, H.F.VII; EN 478-483, 490-493, F.IX; EN 494-497, H.F.VII; EN498, F.IX; EN499, H.F.VII; EN 500-504, F.IX; EN505-506, H.F.VII; EN507-508, PR.XI; EN509, H.F.VII; EN510, F.IX; EN511-512, H.F.VII; EN513-534, 551-571, F.IX; EN572-583, L.F.IX; EN601-627, F.XII; EN628-637, L.F. IX; EN652-685, P.R.XI. EN686-695, 710-759 cancelled.
EN763-ER200	905	Supermarine Spitfire VB/C	Built at Castle Bromwich. EN763-800, 821-867, 887-932, 944-981, EP107-152, 164- 213, 226-260, 275-316, 327-366, 380-417, 431-473, 485-523, 536-579, 594-624, 636-669, 682-729, 747-795, 812-847, 869-915, 951-990, ER114-146, 159-200. EN830 fitted with DB605A engine by Germans. Some converted to Seafire IB.
ER206-ES369	750	Supermarine Spitfire VB/C	Built at Castle Bromwich. ER206-229, 245-283, 299-345, 461-510, 524-571, 583-626, 634-679, 695-744, 758-791, 804-834, 846-894, 913-948, 960-998, ES105-154, 168-214, 227-264, 276-318, 335-369. Main deliveries to North Africa and Middle East. Some conversions to Mk. IX.
ES372-ES902	400	Airspeed Horsa	Cancelled order placed with Tata Industries, India.
ES906	1	Messerschmitt Bf 109F	Captured enemy aircraft.
ES913	1	Wicko G.M.1 Warferry	Wicko No. 8: G-AFKK, im pressed in May 1941.
ES914-ES915	2	General Aircraft G.A.L.42 Cygnet II	G-AGAU and G-AGBN, impressed.
ES916-ES921	6	D.H.80A Puss Moth	G-AAZW/BIA/BJU/BLY/ CYT/EOA, impressed.
ES922	1	Miles M.11A Whitney Straight	G-AERS, impressed in May 1941.
ES923	1	Piper J-4A Cub Coupé	Piper No. 4-612: G-AFWS, impressed.

Serial Nos.	*Qty.*	*Aircraft Type*	*Remarks*
ES924 & ES943	2	Wicko G.M.1 Warferry	Wicko Nos. 4/2- G-AFAZ/EZZ impressed.
ES944	1	British Aircraft Eagle	Works No. 133: G-AEFZ, impressed.
ES945	1	D.H.85 Leopard Moth	Ex-Belgian to Royal Navy.
ES946	1	Desoutter I	G-AAPS, impressed.
ES947	1	Wicko G.M.1 Warferry	Works No. 7: G-AFKU, im pressed.
ES948-ES950	3	British Aircraft Eagle	ES948, Eagle II (ex-G-AEKI); ES949-950, Double Eagle (ex-G-ADVV/EIN).
ES952	1	British Aircraft Swallow II	G-AEDX, impressed. Became 2786M.
ES953-ES954	2	D.H.80A Puss Moth	G-ABDM and G-ACIV, impressed.
ES955	1	Messerschmitt Bf 108	G-AFZO (ex-D-IDBT), impressed. See ES995.
ES956-ES960	5	Taylorcraft Plus C & C/2 conversions	G-AFNW/UY/WK/WM/UZ, impressed. ES956, 958, 959 Model C/2.
ES980-ES995	16	Vickers Wellington IC/VIII	Vickers (Weybridge)-built. All flown to Middle East. Mk. IC except for ES986,Mk. VIII.
ES995	1	Messerschmitt Bf 108	ES995 was painted in error on ES955.
ET100-EV699	1500	Curtiss Kittyhawk 1/1A (P-40D/E)	Many diversions by shipments to Australia and New Zealand and by rail consignments to Canada.
EV700-EV724	25	Fairchild Argus I	Not delivered. Replaced by HM164-188.
EV725-EV811	87	Fairchild Argus I/II	EV725-768, Mk. I; EV769-811, Mk. II. EV755, 756, 758, 760, 761, 766, were lost at sea in transit to Britain.
EV812-EW322	411	Consolidated 32 Liberator B.VI/G.R. VI (B-24)	EV812-817, B.VI; EV818, G.R. VI; EV819, G.R.VI; EV820, B.VI; EV821, G.R.VI; EV 822, B.VI; EV823-824, G.R. VI; EV825-826, B.VI; EV 827, G.R.VI; EV828, B.VI converted to G.R.VI and later to C.VI; EV829-837, G.R.VI; EV838-839, B.VI; EV840, G.R.VI; EV841, B. VI; EV842, G.R.VI; EV843-847, B.VI; EV848, G.R.VI; EV849-852, B.VI; EV853, G.R.VI; EV854-855, B.VI; EV856, G.R.VI; EV857, B. VI; EV858, G.R.VI; EV 859-860, B.VI; EV861, G.R. VI; EV862, B.VI; EV863, G.R.VI; EV864, Mk. VI; EV865, B.VI; EV866, G.R. VI; EV867-868, B.VI; EV 869, G.R.VI; EV870, B.VI;

			EV871-874, G.R.VI; EV875-876, B.VI; EV877-899, G.R. VI—of which EV879, 880, 886, 888, 890, 896, 898 were converted to C.VI; EV900-918, B.VI; EV919, G.R.VI; EV920-932, B.VI—of which EV929 was converted to C.VI; EV933, G.R.VI; EV 934, B.VI; EV935-936, G.R. VI—of which EV936 was lost on delivery flight; EV937-938, B.VI; EV939, G.R.VI; EV940-941, B.VI; EV942, G.R.VI; EV943, G.R.VI converted to C.VI; EV944, B.VI converted to C.VI; EV945, G.R.VI; EV946, B.VI; EV 947, G.R.VI; EV948, G.R.VI converted to C.VI; EV949, B.VI; EV950, G.R.VI; EV 951-952, B.VI; EV953-956, G.R.VI; EV957-971, B.VI of which EV962 was converted to C.VI; EV972, G.R.VI; EV973-984, B.VI—of which EV980 was lost on delivery flight; EV985, G.R.VI; EV 986-988, G.R.VI converted to C.VI; EV989-991, B.VI; EV992, G.R.VI converted to C.VI; EV993, B.VI; EV994-EV998, G.R.VI—of which EV995, 997, 998 were converted to C.VI; EV999, B.VI; EW100, G.R.VI converted to C.VI; EW101-126, B.VI; EW127-137, delivery cancelled; EW138-207, B.VI—of which EW147 was converted to C.VI and EW148 was lost on delivery flight; EW208-218, Mk. VI (role not known except for EW215, B.VI); EW219-250, B.VI—of which EW249 was converted to C.VI; EW251-252, Mk. VI role not known); EW253-287, B.VI—of which EW276 was converted to C.VI; EW 288-322, G.R.VI—of which EW290, 297, 310 were converted to C.VI.
EW341-EW610	270	Fairchild Cornell I (PT-26-FA)	Ex-U.S.A.A.F. 44-19288 to 19557. Deliveries mainly to South Africa and Canada.
EW611-EW634	24	Consolidated Liberator VII (C-87)	EW611, ex-U.S.A.A.F. 44-39219, became G-AKAG.

Serial Nos.	Qty.	Aircraft Type	Remarks
EW873-EW972	100	Lockheed Hudson VI (A-28A)	EW949, 950, 952, 953, diverted to Royal New Zealand Air Force. EW892 & 898 crashed in U.S.A. before delivery.
EW973-EW997	25	Lockheed Lodestar IA/II	EW973-982, Mk. IA; EW983-997, Mk. II.
EW998	1	North American NA-97 Mustang	U.S.A.A.F. A-36 42-83685 for evaluation.
EW999	1	Douglas DC-4 Skymaster I (C-54B)	U.S.A.A.F. 43-17126 for personal use of the Prime Minister.
EX100-EZ799	1600	North American Harvard IIA (AT-6G) and III (AT-6D)	EX100-846, Mk. IIA; EX847-EZ258, Mk. III; EZ259-458, Mk. IIA; EZ459-799, Mk. III cancelled. Batches to Fleet Air Arm (*e.g.*, EZ364-383 and 399-425) and to Commonwealth Air Forces.
EZ800-EZ999	200	Vultee Vengeance I/IA (A-31)	Built by Northrop Aircraft. EZ800-818, Mk. I; EZ819-999, Mk. IA. Main deliveries direct to India. No record of EZ880-888 and 906-974 being delivered.

LEND/LEASE

FA100–HD776

THE FA-FZ series was devoted solely to Lend/Lease allocations; GA100-GZ999 was not used, and since HA was an abbreviation for " Hostile Aircraft ", this was not used as a serial prefix. HB100 therefore followed on from FZ999, and Lend/Lease allocations continued up to HD776.

Where appropriate the previous American Service designation is given in brackets in the " Aircraft Type " column.

FA100-FA674	575	Martin Baltimore IIIA (A-30) IV (A-30A)	FA100-380, Mk. IIIA (ex-U.S.A.A.F. 41-27682 to 27962); FA381-674, Mk. IV (ex-U.S.A.A.F. 41-27963 to 28256). Some to Fleet Air Arm (*e.g.*, FA466) as Target Tugs. FA187 to R.C.A.F.
FA695-FA713	19	Boeing 299P Fortress II (B-17F)	FA700 and FA711, ex-U.S.A.A.F. 41-24599 and 42-5238.
FB100-FB399	300	North American NA-104/111 Mustang III (P-51 B/C)	FB100-124, Mk. III (P-51B); FB125-399, Mk. IIIB (P-51C).
FB400-FB522	123	Martin Marauder II (B-26C-MO)	Martin (Omaha)-built. Deliveries mainly to Middle East.

FB523-FB845	323	Stinson V-77 Reliant I (AT-19)	Initial deliveries mainly to the to the Fleet Air Arm.
FB918-FD417	400	Vultee Vengeance III (A-31)/IV (A-35)	FB918-FD117, Mk. III; FD 118-221, Mk. IV Srs.I; FD 222-417, Mk. IV Srs.II. FD 122-124, 126, 128-130, 134, 137, 159, 180, 184, 187, 188, 190, 194-196, 200-201, diverted to U.S.A.A.F. FD288, 307, 339, 381 and 415 crashed in the U.S.A. before delivery.
FD418-FD567	150	North American NA-91 Mustang IA (P-51)	FD418-437, 450-464, 466-469, 510-527, not delivered.
FD568-FD767	200	Lockheed Ventura IIA(B-34)	Lockheed Nos. 4676-4875 (ex-U.S.A.A.F. 41-38020 to 38219. Many diversions.
FD768-FD967	200	Douglas DC-3 Dakota I (C-47)/III (C-47A)	FD768-818, Mk. I—of which six were diverted to British Overseas Airways Corporation. FD819-967, Mk. III (C-47A)—of which FD906-908 and FD956-958 were diverted to the South African Air Force. FD879 was fitted out to V.I.P. standard.
FD968-FD999	32	Boeing PT-27	For use at Flying Training Schools in U.S.A. and Canada.
FE100-FE266	167	D.H.82C Tiger Moth (PT-24)	Canadian-built. To U.S.A.A.F. as 42-964 to 1130.
FE267-FE999	733	North American Harvard IIB (AT-16)	FE882-883 given incorrectly to FR882-883 Expeditor.
FF406-FF412	7	Fairey Swordfish III	—
FF419-FG268	750	Brewster Bermuda I (A-34/SB2A-1)	FF419-868, ex-U.S.A.A.F. A-34; FF869-999, FG100-268, ex-U.S.N. SB2A-1. Many conversions to T.T.I, of which FF557 was the prototype.
FG857	1	Douglas Dakota I	No record.
FH100-FH166	67	North American Harvard IIB(AT-16)	Mainly diverted to Royal Australian Air Force. FH107-116 only to R.A.F.
FH167-FH466	300	Lockheed Hudson IIIA (A-29A)	FH169-174, 176-214, to Commonwealth; FH215-226, 320-328, 434-441, to Royal New Zealand Air Force; FH387, 409, 450, to Chinese Air Force; FH416 to Canada.
FH618-FH650	33	D.H.82C Tiger Moth (PT-24)	Canadian-built. To U.S.A.A.F. as Nos. 42-1131 to 1163.
FH651-FH999	349	Fairchild Cornell I (PT-26)	FH651-850, ex-U.S.A.A.F. 42-14299 to 14498; FH851-999, ex-42-15330 to 15478. All but FH651, 681, 710-714 to Canada, except FH681, 779, 984 which crashed before delivery in the U.S.A.

Serial Nos.	*Qty.*	*Aircraft Type*	*Remarks*
FJ100-FJ649	550	Cessna Crane IA (AT-17A)	For Empire Air Training Scheme. Re-numbered on delivery to Royal Canadian Air Force.
FJ650-FJ700	51	Fairchild Cornell I (PT-26)	Ex-U.S.A.A.F. 42-15479 to 15529. All delivered to Canada for Empire Air Training Scheme.
FJ741-FK108	268	Boeing PT-27	Used in America and Canada.
FK109-FK160	52	Martin Marauder I (B-26A)	FK109 delivered to Britain, November 1942. From FK112 delivered to Middle East direct from U S.A.
FK161-FK183	23	North American NA-62B Mitchell I (B-25B)	FK161 only to U.K.; remainder direct to 111 O.T.U., Nassau.
FK184-FK213	30	Boeing 299-O Fortress IIA (B-17E)	Delivered from March 1942. FK192 retained for use in Canada.
FK214-FK245	32	Consolidated 32 Liberator III (B-24D-CO)	FK216 delivered to Canada. FK243 crashed in Canada before delivery to R.A.F.
FK246-FK312	67	*Reserved*	FK246 only taken up, for Lockheed Lodestar IA (C-60).
FK313-FK361	49	Fairchild 24W Argus I (C-61)	Fairchild Nos. 322-370: ex-U.S.A.A.F. 42-32117 to 32165.
FK362-FK380	19	Martin Marauder IA (B-26B-MA)	FK372 and FK380 crashed in the U.S.A. before delivery.
FK381-FK813	433	Lockheed Hudson VI/IIIA	FK381-730, Mk. VI (ex-U.S.A.A.F. A-28A); FK731-813, Mk. IIIA (ex-U.S.A.A.F. A-29). FK496, returned to U.S.A.A.F.; FK714, to Portuguese Air Force.
FK814-FL163	250	Stinson V-77 Reliant I	Main deliveries to Royal Navy—of which first four went direct to Fleet Air Arm at Trinidad.
FL164-FL218	55	North American NA-82 Mitchell II (B-25C)	FL209 crashed in transit.
FL219-FL448	230	Curtiss Kittyhawk IIA (P-40F)	Offset from U.S.A.A.F. allocation 41-13697 to 14599. FL273 and FL369-448, returned to U.S.A.A.F.; FL230-232, 235-236, 239-240, were lost at sea before reaching R.A.F. service; FL263, 270, 276, 280, 282, 305, 307, were handed over to Free French Forces.
FL449-FL464	16	Boeing 299-O Fortress IIA (B-17E)	Delivered April to July 1942. FL461 not received.
FL503-FL652	150	Douglas DC-3 Dakota III (C-47A)	FL521-523 to South African Air Force. Main deliveries to R.A.F. in India.

FL653-FL670	18	Beech Traveller I (UC-43)	Delivered from March 1943 to Middle East (Suez). FL659-670 lost at sea in S.S. *Agurmonte* 10.6.43.
FL671-FL709	39	North American NA-8 Mitchell II (B-25C)	Deliveries June/July 1942.
FL710-FL730	21	Curtiss Kittyhawk III (P-40M)	Offset from U.S.A.A.F. allocation 43-5403 to 6002. Delivered to Middle East, September/October 1942.
FL731-FL850	120	Republic Thunderbolt I (P-47D)	FL738 crashed in U.S.A. Deliveries mostly to Far East (India).
FL851-FL874	24	North American NA-82 Mitchell II (B-25C)	Delivery of FL859 only confirmed.
FL875-FL905	31	Curtiss Kittyhawk III (P-40M)	Delivered to Middle East late 1942.
FL906-FL995	90	Consolidated 32 Liberator III/V (B-24D)	FL906-936, Mk. III—of which FL909, 915, 917, 918, 920, were temporarily registered G-AGFN/O/P/R/S, and FL927/G was finished to G.R.V standard. FL937-938, G.R.V; FL939-940, Mk. III; FL941, G.R.V converted to C.V; FL942, G.R.V; FL943, Mk. IIIA; FL944, G.R.V; FL945, Mk. III; FL946-991, G.R.V.—of which FL970 and FL979 were converted to C.V; FL992, C.III; FL993-995, Mk. III.
FM100-FM299	200	Avro 683 Lancaster B.X	Built by Victory Aircraft, Canada. FM100-229 only completed, of which a number were modified post-war in Royal Canadian Air Force service.
FM230-FM999	—	*Reserved*	Reserved allocation for Canadian-built aircraft. FM300 (Lincoln XV) and FM400 (York) only built.
FN100-FN319	220	Grumman Wildcat IV (F4F-4B)	Martlet IV, renamed. FN172-188, delivered direct to Mombasa; FN109-111, 205-207, lost at sea in transit.
FN320-FN449	130	Grumman Hellcat I (F6F-3)	Originally named Gannet for Fleet Air Arm.
FN450-FN649	200	Curtiss Seamew I (SO3C-2C)	Record of FN453, 463-467, 472-475, 483, 489, 573, 608, 622, 631 only delivered.
FN650-FN749	100	Vought-Sikorsky Kingfisher I (OS2U-3)	Mainly delivered direct to Middle East and West Africa, except for last 14 to Jamaica.
FN750-FN949	200	Grumman Avenger I (TBF-1B/1C)	Originally named Tarpon I.
FN956-FN999	44	Lockheed Ventura V (PV-1)	Built by Vega Aircraft Corporation. FN965 and 991 not

Serial Nos.	Qty.	Aircraft Type	Remarks
			delivered; FN967, 972, 973, 974, 979, were held in Canada.
FP100-FP324	225	Consolidated 28 Catalina IB (PBY-5B)	Delivered to Scottish Aviation, Prestwick and to Saunders-Roe, Beaumaris for processing for R.A.F. FP221, 224, became G-AGFL/FM. FP290-297 were delivered to Dartmouth, Canada, under the Empire Air Training Scheme.
FP325-FP454	130	Avro 652A Anson	Canadian-built. Diverted to Royal Canadian Air Force.
FP455-FP469	15	Grumman Gosling I (J4F-2)	Originally named Widgeon. Delivered to Royal Navy in West Indies area.
FP470-FP524	55	Grumman Goose (JRF-5/6B)	FP470-474, Mk. I (ex-U.S. Navy JRF-5); FP475-524, Mk. IA (ex-U.S. Navy JFR-6B). Delivered to Piarco.
FP525-FP536	12	Consolidated Catalina IIIA (PBY-5A)	FP534 was retained by U.S. Navy.
FP537-FP684	148	Lockheed Ventura V (PV-1)	FP642, 643, 644, 648, 649, were not delivered; FP645 and FP647 crashed before delivery.
FP685	1	Consolidated 32 Liberator II	Ex-U.S.A.A.F., handed over from service for R.A.F. use.
FP686	1	Vultee Vengeance I	Delivered to India.
FP687-FP736	50	Avro 652A Anson II	Canadian-built for Empire Air Training Scheme in Canada.
FP738-FP747	10	Grumman Goose	Record of FP740 and FP742 only delivered. Used at Miami.
FP748-FP997	250	Avro 652A Anson II	Order turned over to Royal Canadian Air Force. Some numbers re-allotted.
FR111-FR140	30	Curtiss Kittyhawk III (P-40M)	Delivered to Middle East, November 1942 to February 1943.
FR141-FR209	69	North American NA-82/96 Mitchell II (B-25C/G)	B-25C (except for FR208-209, B-25G). Allotments to Dutch forces as follows: FR141-151, 156-157, 159-161, 163, 168-171, 190-200, but FR148 was lost in transit.
FR210-FR361	152	Curtiss Kittyhawk III (P-40M)	Main deliveries to the Middle East.
FR362-FR384	23	North American NA-82 Mitchell II (B-25C)	North American (Inglewood)-built. FR368 lost in transit before delivery.
FR385-FR392	8	Curtiss Kittyhawk III (P-40M)	Deliveries from November 1942 to August 1943.
FR393-FR397	5	North American NA-82 Mitchell II (B-25C)	North American (Inglewood)-built. 1942/43 deliveries.
FR401-FR404	4	Vultee V-74 Vigilant I (L-1)	Ex-U.S.A.A.F. 40-262 to 265.

FR405-FR406	2	Noorduyn Norseman	Canadian aircraft for R.A.F. evaluation.
FR408	1	Bell Kingcobra I (P-63A)	U.S.A.A.F. 42-68937, to Royal Aircraft Establishment for evaluation.
FR409-FR411	3	North American Mustang V/IV/III (P-51F/G/B)	FR409, Mk. V (ex-U.S.A.A.F. XP-51F); FR410, Mk. IV (ex-U.S.A.A.F. XP-51G); FR411, Mk. III (ex-U.S.A.A.F. P-51B).
FR412-FR521	110	Curtiss Kittyhawk III (P-40M)	Main deliveries late 1942. FR460-471 diverted from delivery to R.A.F.
FR556-FR778	223	Waco Hadrian I/II (CG-4A)	FR556-580, Mk. I; FR581-778, Mk. II. FR580 to Canada.
FR779-FR872	94	Curtiss Kittyhawk III (P-40M)	Delivered to Middle East.
FR879-FR883	5	Beechcraft Navigator (AT-7B)	FR880 renumbered PB2 (Prince Bernhardt No. 1); FR881-882 to India. See FE882-883.
FR884-FR885	2	Curtiss Kittyhawk IV (P-40N)	Delivered October 1943.
FR886-FR889	4	Piper Cub (L-4B)	No record of R.A.F. or F.A.A. service.
FR890-FR939	50	North American NA-99 Mustang II (P-51A)	FR901 had special long range ferry tanks fitted.
FR940-FR948	9	Beechcraft Expeditor I (C-45B)	All to No. 32 Operational Training Unit in Canada.
FS100-FS499	400	Curtiss Kittyhawk III/IV/II (P-40)	FS100-269, Mk. III (to Russia); FS270-399, Mk. IV; FS400-499, Mk. II.
FS500-FS660	161	Fairchild 24W Argus II (UC-61A)	Fairchild Nos. 381-541: ex-U.S.A.A.F. 43-14417 to 14577. FS513 to Yugoslav Air Force.
FS661-FT460	700	North American Harvard IIB (AT-16)	Diversions to Royal Indian Air Force, etc.
FT461-FT535	75	Beechcraft Traveller (GB-2/C-43)	Ex-U.S. Navy GB-2 and U.S.A.A.F. UC-43. All to Royal Navy.
FT542-FT831	290	Fairchild M-62A-3 Cornell II (PT-26A-FE)	Fleet (Canadian)-built in exchange for 286 PT-27 returned U.S.A. Originally U.S.A.A.F. Nos. 42-70957 to 71246.
FT833-FT839	7	Sikorsky Hoverfly I (YR-4/YR-4B)	FT833-834, YR-4; FT835-839, YR-4B. All for Fleet Air Arm.
FT849-FT954	106	Curtiss Kittyhawk IV (P-40N)	FT898-904 were lost at sea in transit.
FT955-FT974	20	North American Harvard III (AT-6D)	All to Fleet Air Arm. Ex-U.S. 42-44538 to 44557.
FT975-FT996	22	Beechcraft Expeditor I (C-45B) II (C-45F)	FT975-979, Mk. I; FT980-996, Mk. II. All delivered to the Royal Navy.
FT998-FT999	2	Consolidated Canso	Built in Canada by Boeing Aircraft.

Serial Nos.	*Qty.*	*Aircraft Type*	*Remarks*
FV100-FV899	800	Fairchild Cornell II (PT-26A)	Deliveries mainly to Canada and India. FV661-734 to Royal Canadian Air Force.
FV900-FW280	281	North American NA-82/87 Mitchell II (B-25D/C)	FV900-939, ex-U.S.A.A.F. B-25D-15-NA; FV940-FW280, ex-U.S.A.A.F. B-25C. FW220, 237, 246, 251, 259, 260, 272, 274, 278-280, were held in Canada for the Royal Canadian Air Force.
FW281-FW880	600	Martin Baltimore V (A-30A)	Ex-U.S.A.A.F. as follows: FW281-405, A30A-10-MA (43-8438 to 8562); FW406-505, A30A-15AMA (43-8563 to 8662); FW506-605, A30A-20-MA (43-8663 to 8762); FW606-705, A30A-25-MA (43-8763 to 8862); FW706-880, A30A-30-MA (43-8863 to 9037). FW288, 323, 511, crashed before delivery. All to R.A.F., except FW356, 384, 456, 527, 746 to Royal Navy. Transfers post-war were FW392, 422, 470, 514, 570, 572, 624, 703, 705, 869, to French Air Force early in 1946; and FW419, 439, 584, 592, 649, 660, to Italian Air Force mid-1946.
FW881-FX197	217	Fairchild Cornell II (PT-26A)	Deliveries mainly to Canada and India.
FX198-FX497	300	North American Harvard IIB (AT-16)	Delivered from April 1944 mainly to U.K.
FX498-FX847	350	Curtiss Kittyhawk IV (P-40N)	FX670, ex-U.S.A.A.F. 43-23166.
FX848-FZ197	250	North American Mustang III (P-51B/C)	FX893, armament tests. FX848, 849, 907, 909, 910, 911, 913, 914, 915, 916, 918, 927, 928, 932, 948 were handed back to U.S.A.A.F. on arrival in Britain.
FZ198-FZ427	230	Fairchild Cornell II (PT-26B-FE)	Ex-U.S.A.A.F. 43-36248 to 36477. Mainly delivered to India.
FZ428-FZ439	12	Beech Traveller I (C-43)	Delivered from October 1943. FZ429 crashed in the U.S.A. before delivery.
FZ440	1	Bell Kingcobra (P-63A-9-BE)	U.S.A.A.F. 42-69423 for evaluation at R.A.E. Farnborough.
FZ441-FZ442	2	Noorduyn Norseman	Canadian-built.
FZ443	1	Beechcraft Traveller 1	Ex-U.S.A.A.F. 43-10875.
FZ548-FZ698	151	Douglas DC-3 Dakota III (C-47A)	Douglas (Oklahoma and Long Beach)-built. FZ603-606 to South African Air Force. FZ676 not received, having been lost after leaving

			Reykjavik en route for Britain. FZ613 became V.I.P. Mk. III; FZ602 became VP913 of the Royal Indian Air Force.
FZ699-FZ718	20	Fairchild Cornell II (PT-26B-FE)	Ex-U.S.A.A.F. 43-36478 to 36497.
FZ719-FZ828	110	Fairchild 24W Argus II (UC-61A)	Ex-U.S.A.A.F. 43-14695 to 14804, delivered mainly to Middle East and India.
HB100-HB299	200	Beechcraft Expeditor I/II (C-45)	HB100-206, Mk. I (C-45B-BH); HB207-299, Mk. II (C-45F-BH). Some converted to Mk. III for the Royal Canadian Air Force.
HB300-HB550	251	Vultee Vengeance II (A-35B-VN)	Series II. Some conversions to T.T.IV.
HB551-HB758	208	Fairchild Argus II (UC-61A)/ III (UC-61K)	HB551-643, Mk. II (ex-U.S.A.A.F. 43-14824 to 14916); HB644-758, Mk. III ex-U.S.A.A.F. 43-14918 to 15032).
HB759	1	Beechcraft Expeditor	No delivery record.
HB760	1	Fairchild Argus III (UC-61K)	Ex-U.S. 43-14917.
HB761-HB820	60	Boeing 299 Fortress III (B-17G)	HB761-790, B-17G-BO; HB791-820, B-17G-VE. HB794, 797-798, 804, 806-814 diverted to U.S.A.A.F. HB778/G and HB796/G were specially equipped.
HB821-HB961	141	North American NA-104 Mustang III (P-51C)	Deliveries from April 1944.
HB962-HD301	240	Republic Thunderbolt I/II (P-47)	HB962-HD181, Mk. I (P-47D); HD182-301, Mk. II (P-47D-25).
HD302-HD400	99	North American NA-87/108 Mitchell II/III (B-25D/J)	HD302-345, Mk. II (B-25D); HD346-400, Mk. III (B-25J). HD310-315, 317-320, 322-326, 331-335, 337-345, were retained in Canada.
HD402-HD751	350	Martin M-179 Marauder III (B-26F/G)	HB402-601, B-26F (ex-42-96329 to 96528); HD602-751, B-26G.
HD752-HD776	25	Beechcraft Expeditor II (C-45F-BH)	Main deliveries to the Royal Navy.

MID-WAR HOME PRODUCTION

HD804–JR999

RUNNING concurrently with the Lend/Lease allocation from ET100 was the allocation of numbers as each order was placed by the Ministry of Aircraft Production, from HD821 onwards. When HZ999 was reached the follow-on was made with JA, omitting IA100-IZ999 completely. The usual letter combination prefixes were used, with the exception of JE, JH and JJ.

Serial Nos.	*Qty.*	*Aircraft Type*	*Remarks*
HD804-HD936	100	Supermarine Walrus II	Built by Saunders-Roe for the Royal Navy. 34 later transferred to the R.A.F. HD804-837, 851-878, 899-936. HD909 to Canada.
HD942-HF606	1100	Vickers Wellington IC/III/X/XII/XIV	Vickers (Chester)-built. HD942-991, HE101-134, 146 (85), Mk. IC; HE147-184, 197-244, 258-306, 318-353, 365-398, 410-447, 459-508; 513-556, 568-615, 627-667, 679-715, 727-772, 784-833, 845-873, 898-931, 946-995, Mk. X; HF112, Mk. III, HF113-120, Mk. XII; HF121-155, 167-208, 220-252, 264-312, 329-363, 381-422, 446-451, Mk. XIV; HF452-495, 513-545, 564-606, Mk. X. The Mk. Xs were produced as B.X, but post-war HE214 and HE910 converted to T.10.
HF609-HF816	153	Vickers Wellington III/X/XI	Vickers (Blackpool)-built. HF609-650, 666-703, 718-764, 791-816, Mk. III (except HF614, 622, 626, 630, 634, 638, 642, 646, 650, 669, 723, 726, 729, 732, 735, 739, 743, 747, 751, 755, 759, 763, 793, 797, 808, 811, Mk. X; and HF720, 803, 804, Mk. XI).
HF828-HF922	84	Vickers Wellington IC/VIII	Vickers (Weybridge)-built. HF828-869, 881-922, Mk. IC (except HF828, 838, 850, 854, 857, 860, 863, 866, 869, 883, 886, 889, 892, 895, 901, 904, 907, 910, 913, 916, 919, 922, Mk. VIII). Variously fitted with Leigh Lights or for torpedo bombing.
HF938-HG633	440	Vickers Warwick I/II/III	Vickers (Weybridge)-built. HF938-987, HG114-156, 169-193, 207-214 (126), A.S.R. I; HG215-256, 271-307, 320-340 (100), C. III; HG341-365, 384-414, 435-459, 476-525, 538-539 (133), G.R.II. HG517-525 equipped for meteorological role. HG540-585, 599-633 cancelled. HG 141, 341, 345, Centaurus engine test-beds.
HG641	1	Hawker Tornado	Prototype. Tested with Bristol Centaurus IV and V engines.
HG644-HG732	75	D.H.89 Dominie	Built by Brush Coachmakers Ltd., Loughborough. HG644-674, 689-732—of which

			HG644-647 were offset to the Turkish Air Force; HG707, 710, 711, were sold to Iran; HG648, 649, 654-656, 663, 665, 669, 674, became NZ523-529, 531, 530 of the Royal New Zealand Air Force. HG694,697, 700, 706, 708-709, 713-714, 716-717, 725-727, were delivered to R.N.
HG736-HG989	200	Airspeed A.S.51 Horsa 1	Built by The Austin Motor Co. HG736-770, 784-819, 831-880, 897-944, 959-989.
HH109-HH919	600	General Aircraft G.A.L.48 Hotspur II	Built by Harris Lebus, assisted by Wm. Lawrence & Co., Mulliners, and Waring & Gillow. HH109-153, 167-198, 223-268, 284-333, 346-388, 401-431, 445-493, 517-566, 579-623, 636-674, 688-732, 751-800, 821-853, 878-919. The following were converted to Mk. III; HH143, 175, 180, 190, 228, 231, 261, 294, 323, 326, 330, 373, 518, 526, 529, 536, 555, 565, 610, 691, 694, 698, 704, 723, 724, 754, 767, 774-776, 781, 783, 784, 786, 789, 835, 838, 889. Diversions to R.C.A.F. were: HH418-419, 421, 425, 427, 521, 551-553, 557-562, 564, 579, 580, 646-647, 654, 667.
HH921-HH975	34	General Aircraft G.A.L.49 Hamilcar I	HH921-930 built by General Aircraft Ltd. HH931-935, 957-975 built by group factories consisting of the Birmingham Railway Carriage & Wagon Co. Ltd., Co-operative Wholesale Society and A.C. Motors Ltd.
HH979	1	Avro 641 Commodore	G-ACZB, impressed Aug. 1941.
HH980	1	Desoutter I	G-AATK, impressed Aug. 1941.
HH981	1	D.H.80A Puss Moth	G-ABEH, impressed.
HH982-HH988	7	Taylorcraft Plus C/2	G-AFVA/VZ/VY/VB/UD/TZ/UX, impressed. HH983 C/1.
HJ108-HJ628	390	D.H.98 Mosquito	Allocation for orders in Canada. Numbers re-allotted. HJ108-149, 164-201, 222-270, 284-317, 333-378, 391-422, 447-491, 510-557, 573-628.
HJ642-HJ833	150	D.H.98 Mosquito II/VI	De Havilland (Hatfield)-built. HJ642-661, N.F.II; HJ662/G, F.B.VI prototype; HJ663-682, F.B.VI; HJ699-715, N.F.II; HJ716-743, 755-792, 808-833, F.B.VI and HJ732, F.B.XVIII. HJ667, 680, 681, 718, 720,721,723, 792 tempor-

Serial Nos.	Qty.	Aircraft Type	Remarks
			arily registered G-AGKO/GC/GD/GE/GF/GG/GH/KR. HJ-732/G 6 pdr. gun experiments.
HJ851-HK536	450	D.H.98 Mosquito II/III/XIII/XVII	De Havilland (Leavesden)-built. HJ851-899, T.III; HJ911-944, N.F.II; HJ945-946, N.F.12; HJ958-999, T.III; HK107-141, 159-204, 222-236, built as N.F.II but delivered to Marshall's, Cambridge, for conversion to N.F.XII; HK237-265, 278-327, 344-362, N.F.XVII; HK363-382, 396-437, 453-481, 499-536, N.F.XIII. HK535-536 renumbered SM700-701.
HK535-HK806	200	Avro 683 Lancaster I	Vickers-Armstrongs (Castle Bromwich)-built. HK535-579, 593-628, 644-664, 679-710, 728-773, 787-806. HK541 was fitted with long range saddle tank.
HK811-HK817	7	D.H.82 Tiger Moth	Impressed in India.
HK818	1	D.H.60 Gipsy Moth	Impressed in India.
HK820-HK821	2	Douglas DC-2	Impressed in Middle East.
HK822	1	Grumman Goose	Served with R.A.A.F.
HK823	1	Curtiss Mohawk	Possibly ex-French.
HK827	1	Junkers Ju 87B	Captured enemy " Stuka " in Middle East.
HK828-HK831	4	D.H.86	Impressed in M.E. Ex-SU-ACR, G-ACWD/DUI/DUG.
HK832	1	Fairchild 91	Impressed.
HK833-HK835	3	Avro Tutor	Impressed in Middle East.
HK837	1	Douglas DC-2	Acquired from U.S.A.
HK838	1	Percival Q.6	G-AFMV, impressed.
HK839	1	D.H.60 Moth Major	Impressed in Middle East.
HK843-HK844	2	D.H.86B/D.H.86	G-AEAP/CPL, impressed in Middle East.
HK845	1	Martin 167	Ex-Vichy aircraft.
HK846	1	Messerschmitt	Type unknown.
HK847	1	Douglas DC-2	Ex-NC14280.
HK848	1	Savoia S.79	—
HK849	1	Messerschmitt	Type unknown.
HK851-HK852	2	Lockheed Lodestar	HK851, ex-41-29635.
HK853	1	Avro Tutor	Impressed.
HK855	1	Lockheed 18-07 Lodestar	G-AGIL, impressed.
HK859	1	Caproni Ca101	Captured Italian aircraft.
HK860	1	Saiman C202	Impressed Italian aircraft.
HK861	1	D.H.80A Puss Moth	G-ABTD, impressed in M E
HK862	1	D.H.89 Rapide	G-AFFC, impressed.
HK863	1	Miles Hawk	SU-AAP, impressed.
HK864	1	D.H.89 Rapide	G-AFEN, impressed.
HK866	1	D.H.80 Puss Moth	G-AARF, purchased by A.H.Q., Iraq.
HK867	1	Douglas DC-2	Impressed in Middle East.
HK868	1	Short S.22 Scion Senior	G-AECU, impressed.

HK869-HK903	35	Douglas Boston III	Non-standard aircraft, released by Russia Commission at Abadan for use in Western Desert (50 Spitfires later were given in lieu).
HK904-HK911	6	D.H.60M Moth	Taken over from Iraqi Air Force in 1943.
HK912	1	Douglas Boston III	As per remarks for HK869-903.
HK913	1	Percival Q.6	Ex-Iraqi YI-ROI.
HK914	1	Caproni	Presumed captured
HK918	1	Douglas Boston III	To Royal Navy.
HK919-HK920	2	Junkers 52/3m	Ex-enemy aircraft.
HK921-HK924	4	Douglas Boston III	Ex-Russian allocation.
HK926-HK930	5	Vultee Vigilant	Ex-U.S.A.A.F.
HK931	1	Fairey Battle	Believed ex-Greek.
HK934-HK935	2	Douglas Boston III	Presumed ex-Russia Commission.
HK936-HK939	4	Piper Cub	Ex-U.S.A.A.F.
HK940	1	Fiat G.12	Captured Italian aircraft.
HK944-HK956	6	North American Mustang	Ex-Twelfth U.S.A.A.F. HK944-947, 955-956.
HK959	1	Junkers Ju 88	Acquired in Cyprus.
HK960-HK972	13	Douglas Boston III	Ex-Russian allocation.
HK973-HK975	3	Lockheed Lodestar	G-AGBO/CT/CW, impressed.
HK976	1	Cant Z.501	Ex-Italian Air Force No. 147/11.
HK977-HK979	3	Cant Z.506B	Ex-Italian aircraft.
HK980-HK981	2	Lockheed Lodestar	G-AGBP/CX, impressed.
HK982	1	Lockheed 14	G-AFKE, impressed.
HK983	1	Douglas DC-2	Made up from spares. Allotted for personal use of Air Marshal Sir Keith Park.
HK984	1	Lockheed 14	G-AFMR, impressed.
HK986-HK987	2	Fieseler Fi 156 Storch	—
HK990	1	Lockheed 18	Impressed.
HK993	1	Douglas DC-2	Ex-VT-CLE.
HL340-HL432	7	Vultee Vigilant	HL340-342, 429-432.
HL530-HL531	2	Piper Cub	EI-ABZ and G-AFTD, impressed.
HL532-HL536	5	Taylorcraft Plus C/2	G-AFVW/TO/UB/TN/TY, impressed.
HL537	1	D.H.80A Puss Moth	G-AAZP, impressed.
HL538	1	Miles Hawk Major	G-AEGE, impressed.
HL539	1	General Aircraft G.A.L. 42 Cygnet II	G-AFVR, impressed.
HL544-HM157	388	Hawker Hurricane IIB/C	HL544-591, 603-634, 654-683, 698-747, 767-809, 828-867, 879-913, 925-941, 953-997, HM110-157. HL673 was converted to a Sea Hurricane.
HM159-HM160	2	Fokker F.XXII	G-AFXR and G-AFZP, impressed.
HM161	1	Fokker XXXVI	G-AFZR, impressed.
HM164-HM188	25	Fairchild 24W Argus I (C-61)	Fairchild Nos. 208-232: ex-U.S.A.A.F. 41-38764 to 38788. For Royal Air Force and Air Transport Auxiliary use.
HM279-HM485	162	Percival P.34 Proctor III	Built by F. Hills & Son. HM279-324, 337-373, 390-433, 451-485.

Serial Nos.	Qty.	Aircraft Type	Remarks
HM494	1	Tipsy B-2	Ex-G-AGBM, ex-F-0222, impressed.
HM495	1	General Aircraft G.A.L. 42 Cygnet II	G-AGBA, impressed.
HM496	1	Miles M.3 Falcon Major	G-ADFH, impressed.
HM497	1	Wicko Warferry	Impressed.
HM498	1	D.H.87 Hornet Moth	OY-DOK, escaped from Denmark.
HM499	1	Wicko G.M.1 Warferry	G-AFVK, impressed.
HM500	1	British Klemm Eagle	G-ADID, impressed.
HM501	1	Taylorcraft Plus C/2	G-AFVX, impressed.
HM502	1	Cessna C.34 Airmaster	G-AEAI, impressed.
HM503	1	Miles M.12 Mohawk	G-AEKW, impressed.
HM504-HM505	2	Avro 621 Tutor	G-ABIR and G-ABIS, impressed.
HM506	1	British Aircraft Eagle II	G-AEGO, impressed.
HM507-HM508	2	Desoutter Mk. II/I	G-AAZI (Mk. II) and G-AANB (Mk. I), impressed.
HM509	1	Junkers Ju 88A-5	M2+MK Nr. 6073 of *Luftwaffe* which landed in error at Chivenor.
HM510	1	Slingsby T.8 Kirby Tutor	Glider, impressed for the Air Training Corps.
HM511	1	Scott Primary	Glider, impressed for the Air Training Corps.
HM512	1	Slingsby T.2 Primary	Glider, impressed for the Air Training Corps.
HM513	1	Dagling Primary	Glider, built by R. F. Dagnell, impressed for the Air Training Corps.
HM514-HM515	2	Slingsby T.2 Primary	Gliders, impressed for the Air Training Corps.
HM516	1	Scott Nacelled Primary	Glider, impressed for the Air Training Corps.
HM517	1	Slingsby T.2 Nacelled Primary	Glider, impressed for the Air Training Corps.
HM518	1	Zander & Scott Nacelled Primary	Glider, impressed for the Air Training Corps.
HM519-HM520	2	Slingsby T.2 Primary	Glider, impressed for the Air Training Corps.
HM522-HM524	3	Slingsby T.7 Kirby Cadet	Gliders, impressed for the Air Training Corps.
HM525-HM526	2	Slingsby T.8 Kirby Tutor	Glider, impressed for the Air Training Corps.
HM527	1	Slingsby T.7 Kirby Cadet	Glider, impressed for the Air Training Corps.
HM528-HM533	4	Slingsby T.2 Primary	Gliders, impressed for the Air Training Corps.
HM534	1	D.H.80A Puss Moth	U.S. Navy 8877 (used by U.S. Naval Attaché, London), impressed. Became G-AHLO.
HM535	1	Zander & Scott Nacelled Primary	Glider, impressed for the Air Training Corps.
HM536	1	Kassel Zogling	Glider, impressed for the Air Training Corps.

HM537	1	Nacelled Primary	Glider, type not known.
HM538	1	Kassel Prufling	Glider, impressed for the Air Training Corps.
HM539	1	Slingsby T.7 Kirby Cadet	Glider, impressed for the Air Training Corps.
HM540-HM541	2	Primary glider	Gliders, impressed for the Air Training Corps. Type not known.
HM542	1	Slingsby T.8 Kirby Tutor	Glider BGA294, impressed for the Air Training Corps.
HM543	1	Slingsby T.7 Kirby Cadet	Glider, impressed for the Air Training Corps.
HM544	1	D.H.94 Moth Minor	G-AFPO, impressed.
HM545	1	Miles M.18 Mk. II	Ex-U-8 and U-0224, acquired by R.A.F., became G-AHKY.
HM546-HM547	2	Slingsby T.2 Primary	Glider, impressed for the Air Training Corps.
HM548	1	Slingsby T.2 Nacelled Primary	Glider, impressed for the Air Training Corps.
HM549	1	Slingsby T.2 Primary	Glider, impressed for the Air Training Corps.
HM550	1	Slingsby T.7 Kirby Cadet	Glider, impressed for the Air Training Corps.
HM551	1	Slingsby T.2 Primary	Glider, impressed for the Air Training Corps.
HM552	1	Slinsgby T.7 Kirby Cadet	Glider, impressed for the Air Training Corps.
HM553	1	Slingsby T.2 Primary	Glider, impressed for the Air Training Corps.
HM554	1	Slingsby T.2 Nacelled Primary	Glider, impressed for the Air Training Corps.
HM555-HM557	3	Slingsby T.2 Primary	Gliders, impressed for the A.T.C.—of which HM555 and HM557 were modified.
HM558	1	Slingsby T.8 Kirby Tutor	Glider, impressed for the Air Training Corps.
HM559	1	Slingsby T.2 Primary	Glider, impressed for the Air Training Corps.
HM560	1	Desoutter Mk. I	G-ABMW, impressed.
HM561-HM564	4	Slingsby T.2 Primary	Glider, impressed for the Air Training Corps.
HM565	1	Piper J-4A Cub Coupé	G-AFSY, impressed.
HM566-HM568	3	Slingsby T.4 Falcon III	Glider, impressed for the Air Training Corps.
HM569	1	D.H.84 Dragon	G-ADOS, imprsesed.
HM570	1	Avro 638 Club Cadet	G-ACHP, impressed.
HM571	1	Tandem type glider	Glider, impressed for the Air Training Corps.
HM572	1	Weltensegler Hols-der-Teufel	Glider, impressed for the Air Training Corps.
HM573	1	Lockheed 12A	G-AGDT, impressed.
HM574	1	Wicko G.M.1 Warferry	G-AFKS, impressed.
HM575	1	Slingsby T.7 Kirby Cadet	Glider, impressed for the Air Training Corps.
HM576	1	Slingsby T.1 Falcon I	Glider, impressed for the Air Training Corps.
HM577	1	Weltensegler Hols-der-Teufel	Glider, impressed for the Air Training Corps.

Serial Nos.	*Qty.*	*Aircraft Type*	*Remarks*
HM578	1	Slingsby T.1 Falcon	Glider, impressed for the Air Training Corps.
HM579	1	D.H.94 Moth Minor	G-AFRR, impressed.
HM580-HM581	2	Cierva C.30A	G-ACUU/I, impressed.
HM582	1	D.H. 60 Moth	G-ACXF, impressed.
HM583	1	Miles M.28/1	Ex-U-0237, became G-AJVX.
HM584-HM585	2	D.H.94 Moth Minor	G-AFPL and G-AFTH, impressed.
HM586	1	Kassel Sailplane	Glider, impressed for A.T.C.
HM587	1	Schneider Grunau Baby	Glider, impressed for A.T.C.
HM588-HM589	2	Primary glider	Gliders, impressed for A.T.C.
HM590	1	Secondary glider	Glider, impressed for A.T.C.
HM591	1	Slingsby T.12 Gull I	Glider, impressed for A.T.C.
HM592	1	Slingsby T.14 Gull II	Glider, impressed for A.T.C.
HM593	1	Stinson SR-8 Reliant	G-AEOR, impressed.
HM595 & HM599	2	Hawker Tempest	Prototypes to Air Ministry Specification F.10/41. HM595, Mk. V-VI; HM599, Mk. I.
HM603-HN212	375	Airspeed A.S.10 Oxford I	Built by Percival Aircraft. HM603-650, 666-700, 721-767, 783-813, 827-875, 889-918, 945-990, HN111-149, 163-212.
HN217-HN855	450	Airspeed A.S.-10 Oxford I	Airspeed (Portsmouth)-built. HN217-239, 254-284, 298-346, 363-386, 405-441, 467-495, 513-554, 576-614, 631-671, 689-738, 754-790, 808-855. HN217, 235-237, 280, 306, 340, 341, 343, 346, 367, 533, 542, 549, 551, 602, 605, 790 converted to Mk. V.
HN861-HP528	400	Miles M.25 Martinet T.T.I	Phillips & Powis (Woodley)-built. HN861-894, 907-916, 938-984, HP114-149, 163-183, 199-227, 241-288, 303-335, 348-393, 405-448, 464-496, 510-528—of which HN909, 945, HP222, 272, 310 were converted to Queen Martinet.
HP848-HR648	500	D.H.98 Mosquito F.B.VI	Built by Standard Motors. HP848-888, 904-942, 967-989, HR113-162, 175-220, 236-262, 279-312, 331-375, 387-415, 432-465, 485-527, 539-580, 603-648.
HR654-HR988	250	Handley Page H.P.59 Halifax II	HR654-699, 711-758, 773-819, 832-880, 905-952, 977-988. HR758 was used for engine experiments; HR845 and HR909 had experimental turrets.
HS101-HS150	50	Airspeed A.S.51 Horsa I	HS110, 119, 138, 139, 147, shipped to New York in 1943.
HS154-HS678	400	Fairey Swordfish II	Built by Blackburn Aircraft. HS154-196, 208-231, 254-299, 312-346, 361-410, 424-471, 484-519, 533-561, 579-625, 637-678.

HT525-HV162	400	Airspeed Horsa	Cancelled. HT525-562, 577-621, 645-694, 712-748, 769-812, 830-878, 896-933, 948-996, HV113-162.
HV266 & HV270	2	Hawker P.1005	Not built. Twin-engined bomber to Air Ministry Specification B.11/41.
HV275-HW881	1000	Hawker Hurricane IIB/IIC/IID	HV275-317, 333-370, 396-445, 468-516, 534-560, 577-612, 634-674, 696-745, 768-799, 815-858, 873-921, 943-989, HW115-146, 167-207, 229-278, 291-323, 345-373, 399-444, 467-501, 533-572, 596-624, 651-686, 713-757, 779-808, 834-881. Several were off-set to the Soviet and Turkish Air Forces; HV892-893 were delivered to the South African Air Forcè. HW182/G and HW187/G were used for armament trials.
HX147-HX357	150	Handley Page Halifax II/III	HX147-191, 222-225, Mk. II; HX226-247, 265-296, 311-357, Mk. III.
HX360	1	Junkers Ju 88	Ex-enemy aircraft, used at Air Fighting Development Unit.
HX364-HX786	300	Vickers Wellington IC/VIII	Vickers (Weybridge)-built. HX364-403, 417-452, 466-489, 504-538, 558-606, 625-656, 670-690, 709-751, 767-786. Mk. VIII except Mk. Ic as follows: HX364-371, 373-375, 377-378, 380, 382, 384-385, 387, 389-390, 392-393, 395, 397, 399-400, 402, 417, 421, 423, 425, 429, 431, 433, 435, 438, 440, 442, 445-447, 449, 451, 468, 470, 472, 475, 478, 480, 483-484, 486, 488, 506, 508, 510, 514, 516, 518, 521, 523, 525, 527, 529, 533, 536, 558, 560, 564, 567, 569, 571, 573, 577, 580, 583, 585, 589, 591, 594, 597, 601, 603, 606, 627, 631, 633, 635, 637, 639, 643, 645, 648, 651, 655, 670, 673, 676, 680, 682, 685, 688, 710, 712, 714, 716, 718, 722, 724, 727, 730, 734, 736, 739, 742, 746, 748, 750. 767, 769, 773, 775, 778, 781, 785. Deliveries to Middle East. Some fitted with Leigh Lights and others produced as torpedo bombers.
HX789	1	D.H.86	VT-AKM, impressed in India.

Serial Nos.	Qty.	Aircraft Type	Remarks
HX790-HX791	2	D.H.89A Rapide	VT-AJB/LO, impressed in India.
HX792	1	D.H.90 Dragonfly	VT-AIE, loaned by H.E.H. The Nizam of Hyderabad.
HX793	1	Lockheed 18	VT-AAM, impressed in India.
HX794	1	Percival P.3 Gull Six	Impressed in India. Ex-VT-AGY and G-ACYS.
HX795-HX797	3	D.H.94 Moth Minor	VT-ALI, VT-AMD, VT-AME, impressed in India.
HX798	1	Lockheed 12A	VT-AMB (ex-G-AFXP), loaned by the Maharajah of Jaipur.
HX802-HX984	130	D.H.98 Mosquito F.B.VI	De Havilland (Hatfield)-built. HX802-835, 849-869, 896-922, 937-984 F.B.VI, except HX902-904 F.B.XVIII. HX849-850 not delivered
HZ102-JA645	850	Vickers Wellington III/X/XI/XIII	Vickers (Blackpool)-built. HZ102-150, 173-209, 242-250 produced as Mks. III/X/XI; HZ251-284, 299-315, 351-378, 394-439, 467-489, 513-550 produced as Mks. X/XI; HZ 551 Mk. XIII; HZ552-554, 570-572, Mk. X; HZ573-578, Mk. XIII; HZ579-582, Mk. X; HZ583-604, 633-660, 689-712, Mk. XIII; HZ713-720, Mk. X; HZ721-727, 752-770, 793-808, Mk. XIII; HZ809-818, Mk. X; HZ819-820, 862-897, 937-940, Mk. XIII; HZ941-950, Mk. X; HZ951-981, JA104-110, Mk. XIII; JA111-140, Mk. X; JA141-151, 176-184, Mk. XIII; 185-194, Mk. X; JA195-210, Mk. XIII; JA256-260, Mk. X; JA261-273, 295-318, 337-340, Mk. XIII; JA341-352, Mk. X; JA353-363, 378-426, 442-447, Mk. XIII; JA448-481, 497-513, Mk. X; JA514-518, Mk. XIII; 519-534, Mk. X; JA535-539, 561-585, 618-645, Mk. XIII. The Mk. Xs were produced as B.X but post-war HZ 472 and JA532 conv. to T.10.
JA672-JB748	550	Avro 683 Lancaster III	A. V. Roe (Manchester)-built. JA672-718, 843-876, 892-941, 957-981, JB113-155, 174-191, 216-243, 275-320, 344-376, 398-424, 453-488, 526-567, 592-614, 637-684, 699-748. Merlin 28 engines were installed in early production, Merlin 28s or 38s at mid-production and Merlin 38s on

			late production. JB127 converted to Mk. I, JB675 and JB713 converted to Mk. VI. JB240 crashed on delivery flight from 32 M.U. and did not enter service. Two with special electrical equipment were JB683/G and JB720/G.
JB781-JD476	350	Handley Page H.P. 59 Halifax II	Built by the English Electric Co. JB781-806, 834-875, 892-931, 956-974, JD105-128, 143-180, 198-218, 244-278, 296-333, 361-386, 405-421, 453-476. JD212 was used in rocket projectile experiments and JD300 was fitted with a .5 in. ventral gun position.
JF274-JG695	800	Supermarine Spitfire F.VIII/L.F.VIII/ H.F.VIII	Vickers-Armstrongs (Supermarine)-built. JF274-300, F.VIII; JF316-321, Mk. VIII converted to Mk. XIV; JF322-327, F.VIII; JF328, H.F. VIII; JF329-364, 392-427, 443-461, F.VIII; JF462, L.F.VIII; JF463-485, 501-502, F.VIII; JF503-504, L.F.VIII; JF505-513, F.VIII; JF514-515, L.F.VIII; JF516-528, 557-592, 613-630, 658-676, 692-716, F.VIII; JF740-789, 805-850, 869-893, L.F.VIII; JF894-899, F.VIII; JF900-902, 926-967, JG104-124, 157-159, L.F.VIII; JG160, F.VIII; JG161, L.F.VIII; JG162, F.VIII; JG163-165, L.F.VIII; JG166, F.VIII; JG167-204, 239-275, 312-356, 371-387, 404-432, 465-500, 527-568, 603-624, 646-695, L.F.VIII. JF477 crashed on test flight and was not delivered. Many deliveries went direct to India and Australia, and 135 were renumbered in the R.A.A.F. from A58-300 onwards. JF299 was the first Spitfire with rear-view fuselage. JG204 was experimentally fitted with Mk. 23 wing section.
JG713-JL395	989	Supermarine Spitfire VC (with conversions to Mk. IX)	Vickers-Armstrongs (Castle Bromwich)-built. JG713-752, 769-810, 835-852, 864-899, 912-960, JK101-145, 159-195, 214-236, 249-285, 303-346, 359-408, 425-472, 506-551, 600-620, 637-678, 705-742, 756-796, 803-842, 860-892,

Serial Nos.	Qty.	Aircraft Type	Remarks
			922-950, 967-992, JL104-140, 159-188, 208-256, 301-338, 346-395. Deliveries were to Gibraltar and North West Africa. Conversions to F.IX/L.F.IX on production or in service were JG722, 739, JK429, 463, 535, 611, 620, 641, 659, 668, 762, 769, 770, 795, 796, 840, 860, 880-884, 979, 980; JL106-111, 134-138, 159, 163, 165, 172, 177-180, 217, 223, 226-230, 239, 252-256, 347, 349, 351, 353, 354, 356, 359, 361, 364, 366, 369, 370, 372, 373, 375-377, 383-385, 395.
JL421-JM417	546	Bristol 156 Beaufighter VIC/X/XI (including VIC Interim Torpedo Fighter version)	Bristol (Weston)-built. JL421-454, 502-549, 565-582, Mk. VIC; JL583, Mk. VIC (Interim T.F.); JL584-592, Mk. VIC; JL593, 610-618, Mk. VIC (Interim T.F.); JL619-628, Mk. VIC; JL629-638, Mk. VIC (Interim T.F.); JL639-648, Mk. VIC; JL649-658, Mk. VIC (Interim T.F.); JL659, 704-712, Mk. VIC; JL713-722, Mk. VIC (Interim T.F.); JL723-735, 756-779, 812-826, Mk. VIC; JL827-835, Mk. VIC (Interim T.F.); JL836-855, 869-875, Mk. VIC of which 15 were re-numbered in the A19 R.A.A.F. series; JL876-915, 937-948, Mk. XI—of which JL946 became R.A.A.F. A19-148; JL949-957, JM104, Mk. VIC (Interim T.F.); JM105-136, 158-185, 206-250, 262-267, Mk. XI—of which 20 were transferred to the R.A.A.F.; JM268-291, 315-356, 379-417, Mk. X—of which 7 were transferred to the R.A.A.F.
JM431-JM593	111	Bristol 152 Beaufort I	JM431-470, 496-517, 545-593.
JM659-JM722	50	Short S.25 Sunderland III	Short (Rochester)-built. JM659-689, 704-722. JM667 and 714-720 were converted to Mk. V. JM681, 715, 716, 719 were converted to Sandringhams. JM660-665 and JM722 were loaned to B.O.A.C.

JM738-JN257	250	Supermarine Sea Otter I	JM738-773, 796-837, 861-885, 905-922, 943-989, JN104-142, 179-205, 242-257.
JN273-JN683	200	Miles M.25 Martinet T.T.I.	Phillips & Powis (Woodley)-built. JN273-309, 416-460, 485-513, 538-555, 580-601, 634-682. JN275, trainer prototype. JN668, trainer conversion (became G-AKOS). JN588-589 were delivered to the Fleet Air Arm. JN290 was converted to Queen Martinet.
JN703	1	Miles M.18	Prototype. Ex-U-0236.
JN729-JN877	100	Hawker Tempest V Series I	Hawker (Langley)-built. JN729-773, 792-822, 854-877. JN807 and JN871 were converted to T.T.5 post-war. JN750 was converted to Mk. VI.
JN882-JP338	250	Handley Page H.P.59 Halifax II	Built by the London Aircraft Production Group. JN882-926, 941-978, JP107-137, 159-207, 220-259, 275-301, 319-338.
JP361-JR535	600	Hawker Typhoon IB	Built by Gloster Aircraft. JP361-408, 425-447, 480-516, 532-552, 576-614, 648-689, 723-756, 784-802, 836-861, 897-941, 961-976, JR125-152, 183-223, 237-266, 289-338, 360-392, 426-449, 492-535. JR210 had TR210 painted on in error.

THE SECOND LEND/LEASE ALLOCATION

JS100–KV300

WITH subsequent appropriations by Congress of Lend/Lease Aid, a further allocation of numbers was allotted to Britain, JS100-KT100, of which up to KP311 were taken up. The allocation included the reservation KA100-KB999 for aircraft built in Canada. Previous United States service designations are given in the " Aircraft Type " column.

JS101-JS218	118	Avro 652A Anson	Built in the Amherst Plant of the Canadian Car & Foundry Corporation.
JS219-JS468	248	Hawker Hurricane XII	Built by the Canadian Car & Foundry Corporation. JS372-373 were blank numbers.

Serial Nos.	Qty.	Aircraft Type	Remarks
			Produced as 63 Mk. XIIC, 185 Mk. XIIB. Main shipments to Russia and the Far East. Some conversions to Sea Hurricane, *e.g.*, JS253, 328, 334, 336.
JS469-JS888	420	Chance Vought Corsair II (F3A-1)	Built by Brewster Aircraft.
JS889-JS984	96	Lockheed Ventura V (PV-1)	Diversions to the South African Air Force.
JS996	1	Grumman Gosling I (J4F-2)	Used at Miami by various commissions.
JS997-JS999	3	Douglas Dauntless I (SBD-5)	Designated D.B. Mk. I. JS998 to Royal Air Force, JS997 and JS999 to Royal Navy.
JT100-JT704	605	Chance Vought Corsair I (F4U-1)/II (F4U-1D)	JT100-194, Mk. I (F4U-1); JT195-704, Mk. II (F4U-1D). Main deliveries to Blackburn Aircraft for modifications for Royal Navy. JT100-554 could take only a single 142 gallon drop tank under fuselage; JT555-634 could take in addition a 137 gallon drop tank under starboard wing and JT635-704 could take 137 gallon drop tanks under both wings.
JT773	1	Grumman Avenger I (TBF-1)	Originally named Tarpon I.
JT800-JT898	99	Lockheed Ventura V (PV-1)	General reconnaissance version. Some diversions to the South African Air Force.
JT923-JT928	6	Douglas Dauntless I (SBD-5)	JT923-926 to Royal Air Force, JT927-928 to Royal Navy.
JT963-JT972	10	Chance Vought Corsair III (F3A-1)	Built by Brewster Aircraft.
JT973-JT999	27	Consolidated Liberator C.IX (RY-3)	First deliveries delayed until February 1945.
JV100-JV324	225	Grumman Hellcat I (F6F-3)/II (F6F-5)	JV100-221, Mk. I; JV222-324, Mk. II.
JV325-JV924	600	Grumman Wildcat V (F4F-4)/VI (FM-2)	JV325-636, Mk. V (built by Grumman); JV637-924, Mk. VI (built by General Morors). Offset from U.S. Navy Nos. 14992-16791.
JV925-JV935	11	Consolidated Catalina IVA (PBY-5A)	Delivered September to October 1943.
JV936-JV999	64	Consolidated Liberator IX (RY-3)	Record of JV936 only delivered.
JW100-JW125	26	Curtiss Helldiver (SBW-1B)	Delivered to Inskip, Lancashire for R.N. but JW119 to R.A.F.
JW550-JW669	120	Curtiss Seamew I (SO3C-2C)	Full delivery not completed.
JW700-JW784	85	Grumman Hellcat II (F6F-5)	—

JW785-JW836	52	Grumman Wildcat VI (FM-2)	Built by General Motors.
JW857-JW899	43	Grumman Hellcat II (F6F-5)	—
JX100-JX131	32	Martin Mariner I (PBM-3B)	JX121, 122, 125, 127, 129, 131, returned to the U.S. Navy in 1944.
JX200-JX437	238	Consolidated 28 Catalina IVA (PBY-5A)/ IVB (PB2B-1)	JX200-269, Mk. IVA built by Consolidated—of which JX228, 230-232, 234-237 were diverted to New Zealand. JX270-437, Mk. IVB built by Boeing (Canada).
JX470-JX501	32	Consolidated Coronado I (PB2Y-3B)	Record of JX470-472, 486, 490, 494, 495, 496, 498, 501 only delivered.
JX570-JX662	93	Consolidated Catalina IVA (PBY-5A)/ IVB (PB2B-1)/ VI (PB2B-2)	JX570-585, Mk. IVA—of which JX575 and JX577 became G-AGID/E; JX586-610, Mk. IVB—of which all but JX586, 588, 593, 595, 598-600 were retained in Canada; JX611-662, Mk. VI, delivered to the Royal Australian Air Force.
JX663-JX669	7	Curtiss Queen Seamew (SO3C)	Radio-controlled target drone for the Royal Navy.
JX670-JX999	330	Grumman Hellcat II (F6F-5/F6F-5N)	JX965-967 delivered as N.F.II.
JZ100-JZ746	647	Grumman Avenger I (TBF-1B)/ II (TBF-1C)/ III (TBM-3)	JZ100-300, Mk. I (TBF-1B); JZ301-634, Mk. II (TBM-1C) built by Grumman; JZ635-746, Mk. III (TBM-3) built by General Motors.
JZ771-JZ774	4	Curtiss Queen Seamew (SO3C)	Radio-controlled target drone for the Royal Navy.
JZ775-JZ827	53	Grumman Hellcat II (F6F-5)	Production aircraft.
JZ828-JZ859	32	Consolidated Catalina VI	11 diverted to R.A.A.F.
JZ860-JZ889	30	Grumman Wildcat VI (FM-2)	Built by General Motors. Main deliveries to Far East and Australia.
JZ890-JZ999	110	Grumman Hellcat II (F6F-5)	JZ890-911, 947-959, 965-967, 995-999, produced as N.F.II (F6F-5N).
KA100-KA102	3	D.H.98 Mosquito F.B.21	Canadian - built. KA100 crashed in transit.
KA103-KA773	671	D.H.98 Mosquito F.B.26/T.29	Canadian-built. F.B.26 except for: KA117, 120-122, 137-139, 141, 149-150, 158, 166-167, 172-174, 202-203, 206-207, 221. 232-234, 242-243, 280-281, 290, 297-301, 312-314, delivered as T.29. KA153, 197, 237, 259, 260, 316, 317 were lost in transit before reaching service. KA451-773 cancelled.

Serial Nos.	Qty.	Aircraft Type	Remarks
KA873-KA929	58	D.H.98 Mosquito T.22/F.B.24/T.27	Canadian-built. KA873-876 T.22, KA877-KA895, T.27; KA896-897, T.22; KA898-927, T.27 and KA928-929, F.B.24 cancelled.
KA930-KA999	70	D.H.98 Mosquito B.25	Canadian-built. Deliveries to R.A.F. and Royal Navy. KA968 was lost in transit to service.
KB100-KB299	200	D.H.98 Mosquito B.20	Canadian-built. Up to KB179, Merlin 31 engines installed initially and Merlin 33 engines in all subsequent. KB113, 119, 196, 216, 220, 230, 296, crashed on test or delivery flight. KB130-131, 139, 141, 152, 159, 171, 183, 187 were off-set to the U.S.A.A.F.
KB300-KB324	25	D.H.98 Mosquito B.7	First Canadian-built Mosquitos. Several retained in Canada. KB306, 312-313, 315-317 off-set to U.S.A.A.F.
KB325-KB369	45	D.H.98 Mosquito B.20	Canadian-built. KB326 off-set to the U.S.A.A.F. KB340 crashed in transit.
KB370-KB699	330	D.H.98 Mosquito B.25	Canadian-built. KB370, 381, 398, 475, 479, 489, 503, 504, 505, 525, 526, 540, 562, 563, 575, 589, 591, 593, 626 were written off before reaching service.
KB700-KB999	300	Avro Lancaster B.X	Built by Victory Aircraft, Canada. Various post-war conversions by Royal Canadian Air Force.
KD100-KD107	8	Spartan 7-W Executive	Used in Canada.
KD108-KD160	53	Grumman Hellcat II (F6F-5)	KD108-117, 153-157, produced as N.F.II (F6F-5N).
KD161-KE117	857	Chance Vought Corsair IV (FG-1D)	Built by Goodyear. Main deliveries to British Pacific Fleet.
KE118-KE265	148	Grumman Hellcat II (F6F-5)	KE160-169, 215-219, produced as N.F.II (F6F-5N).
KE266-KE285	20	Consolidated Liberator C.IX (RY-3)	No delivery record.
KE286-KE304	19	Curtiss Queen Seamew I (SO3C)	No delivery record.
KE305-KE309	6	North American Harvard III (SNJ-4)	—
KE310-KE429	120	Chance Vought Corsair IV (FG-1)	Built by Goodyear.
KE430-KE609	180	Grumman Avenger III III (TBM-2)/ IV (TBM-4/3E)	Built by General Motors. KE430-539, Mk. III; KE540-609, Mk. IV, not delivered.
KF100-KG309	1110	North American Harvard IIB (AT-16)	Mainly for Royal Air Force, but a few to the Royal Navy. KF758-900 not delivered; KF901-999 delivered as Tar-

			get Tugs and converted for flying training. KG100-309 not delivered. Diversions to Royal Indian and New Zealand Air Forces.
KG310-KG809	500	Douglas Dakota III (C-47A)	KG483-484 to the South African Air Force. KG507, KG542, KG723, KG765 were fitted to V.I.P. standard. KG508 crashed off Brazilian coast before delivery. Many offset to R.C.A.F. & R.I.A.F.
KG810-KG820	11	Vultee Vengeance IV Series II (A-35B)	For R.A.F., except KG812 and KG818 to the R.N.
KG821-KH420	500	Consolidated 32 Liberator VI/VIII (B-24J)	KG821-822, G.R.VI; KG823-846, B.VI—of which KG827 was converted to C.VI; KG847, G.R.VI; KG848, B.VIII converted to C.VIII; KG849-870, G.R.VI—of which KG863-866, 868, were converted to C.VI; KG871-894, B.VI—of which KG880, 886, 888, 891, 892, 894, were held in Canada; KG895-918, G.R.VI—of which KG899-902, 905-906, 908, 914-916, 918, were converted to C.VI; KG919-931, B.VI—of which KG920, 922-924, 929-931, were retained in Canada; KG932, no record; KG933-934, B.VI; KG935, no record; KG936, G.R.VI converted to C.VI; KG937-942, B.VI; KG943-958, B.VIII—of which KG950 was converted to C.VIII; KG959, G.R.VIII converted to C.VIII; KG960, B.VIII converted to C.VIII; KG961-966, G.R.VIII; KG967-978, B.VI—of which KG978 was retained in Canada; KG979-984, G.R. VIII—of which KG980, 983, 984, were converted to C.VIII; KG985-986, G.R.VI — of which KG985 was converted to C.VI; KG987-989, G.R. VIII converted to C.VIII; KG990-992, G.R.VI; KG993-999, KH100-122, B.VI—of which KH105-110 were retained in Canada; KH123-124, G.R.VI; KH125-126, G.R.VIII converted to C.VIII; KH127, G.R.VI; KH128-133, G.R.VIII—of which all but KH129 was

Serial Nos.	Qty.	Aircraft Type	Remarks
			converted to C.VIII; KH134, G.R.VI; KH135-136, G.R.VIII; KH137-142, no record; KH143, G.R.VIII; KH144-145, no record; KH146, G.R.VIII converted to C.VII; KH147-151, B.VI; KH152-154, no record; KH155-176, B.VI—of which KH171-176 were retained in Canada; KH177-184, G.R. VIII—of which KH177, 179, 181, 182, 184, were converted to C.VIII; KH185-197, no record except of KH189, G.R.VIII; KH198-200, G.R.VI converted to C.VI; KH201-202, no record; KH203-218, B.VI—of which KH208 was converted to C.VIII; KH219-220, no record; KH221, G.R.VIII; KH222-226, G.R.VIII converted to C.VIII; KH227-238, B.VIII; KH239-258, B.VI; KH259-268, G.R.VIII —of which KH259-260, 265-266, were converted to C.VIII; KH269-284, B.VI—of which KH279 was converted to C.VI; KH285-289, no record; KH290, G.R.VIII; KH291-294, G.R.VIII converted to C.VIII; KH295-297, no record except of KH296 as Mk. VI; KH298, G.R.VIII converted to C.VIII; KH299-304, no record except of KH302, G.R.VIII; KH305, G.R.VI converted to C.VI; KH306, G.R.VIII; KH307, no record; KH308, G.R.VIII converted to C.VIII; KH309-320, B.VI; KH321-324, no record except of KH322, G.R.VIII converted to C.VIII and KH323, B.VI; KH325-328, B.VI; KH329-341, G.R.VIII—of which KH333, 334, 337, 340, were converted to C.VIII; KH342-343, no record; KH344, G.R.VI converted to C.VI; KH345, no record; KH346-347, G.R.VIII converted to C.VIII; KH348, G.R.VI converted to C.VI; KH349-

			368, B.VI; KH369-376, B.VIII; KH377-385, G.R.VI —of which KH377, 380, 381, were converted to C.VI; KH386, B.VI; KH387-388, G.R.VIII; KH389-408, B.VI; KH409, no record; KH410-418, G.R.VIII—of which KH411-412 were converted to C.VIII; KH419-420, G.R.VI converted to C.VI.
KH421-KH870	450	North American Mustang III (F-51B/C)/ IV (P-51D)/ IVA (P-51K)	KH421-640, Mk. III; KH641-670, Mk. IV; KH671-870, Mk. IVA. KH470 and KH687 crashed in the U.S.A. before delivery.
KH871-KH992	122	Waco Hadrian II (CG-4A)	Main deliveries to India; KH944-947 to Canada.
KH998-KJ127	30	Boeing 299 Fortress III (B-17G-VE)	Deliveries from October 1944.
KJ128-KJ367	240	Republic Thunderbolt II (P-47D-25)	Mainly delivered to India in late 1944.
KJ368-KJ467	100	Stinson Sentinel I (L-5)/II (L-5B)	KJ368-407, Mk. I; KJ408-467, Mk. II. Main deliveries to Far East.
KJ468-KJ560	93	Beechcraft Expeditor II (C-45F)	Deliveries to the Middle East.
KJ561-KJ800	240	North American NA-108 Mitchell III (B-25J)	KJ774, 777-783, 785, 787-792, 795-799, diverted to the U.S.A.A.F. KJ641 and KJ764 to R.C.A.F.
KJ801-KK220	320	Douglas DC-3 Dakota IV (C-47B)	Deliveries from August 1944. KK159 to the South African Air Force.
KK221-KK378	158	Consolidated Liberator VI/VIII (B-24J)	KK221-228, G.R.VI—of which KK221, 222, 224, 226, 228, were converted to C.VI; KK229-236, B.VI; KK237-242, Mk. VI (held in Canada); KK243-247, B.VI; KK248, B.VI converted to C.VI; KK249-250, G.R.VIII; KK251-258, G.R.VI—of which KK251, 252, 254, 255, 257, were converted to C.VI; KK259, G.R.VIII; KK260, G.R.VI converted to C.VI; KK261-264, G.R.VIII; KK265-267, G.R.VI converted to C.VI; KK268, G.R.VIII; KK269-288, B.VI; KK289-300, G.R.VIII—of which KK295 was lost before delivery; KK301-320, B.VI; KK321-336, G.R.VIII—of which KK322 was converted to C.VIII; KK337, G.R.VI converted to C.VI; KK338-339, G.R.VIII; KK340-342,

Serial Nos.	*Qty.*	*Aircraft Type*	*Remarks*
			G.R.VI converted to C.VI; KK343-362, B.VI; KK363-367, G.R.VIII; KK368, G.R.VI converted to C.VI; KK369-370, G.R.VIII; KK371-378, G.R.VI converted to C.VI.
KK379-KK568	190	Fairchild 24W Argus III (UC-61K)	KK522-567 to Canada. Main deliveries to India and Middle East.
KK569-KK968	400	Waco Hadrian II (CG-4A)	Main deliveries to India. CG-4A except KK790-791, CG-13A.
KK969-KL113	45	Sikorsky Hoverfly I (R-4B)	KL110 to Canada. Main deliveries to Royal Navy. KK990 became ground-running rig for Percival P.74 project.
KL133-KL161	29	North American NA-87 Mitchell II (B-25D)	All delivered to No. 5 Operational Training Unit, R.C.A.F. Boundary Bay.
KL162-KL167	6	Waco CG-13A-FO	Gliders for evaluation. KL162-163 to U.K.; KL164-167 to India.
KL168-KL347	180	Republic Thunderbolt II (P-47D-25)	Main deliveries to the Far East in 1945.
KL348-KL689	342	Consolidated 32 Liberator VI (B-24J)	KL348-351, G.R.VI converted to C.VI; KL352-388, B.VI—of which KL371 and 386 were lost before reaching the R.A.F.; KL389, no delivery record; KL390, G.R.VIII; KL391-393, B.VI—of which KL392 was lost in transit; KL394, G.R.VIII lost in the U.S.A.; KL395-470, no record of delivery; KL471-472, G.R.VIII; KL473, B.VI; KL474, G.R.VIII; KL475-476, B.VI—of which KL476 crashed in the U.S.A. before delivery; KL477, G.R.VIII; KL478-479, B.VI; KL480/G, G.R.VIII; KL481-489, B.VI—of which KL486 was converted to C.VI; KL490, G.R.VIII; KL491-492, B.VI; KL493, G.R.VIII; KL494-495, B.VI—of which KL494 was converted to C.VI; KL496-498, G.R.VIII—of which KL496 was converted to C.VIII; KL499, B.VI converted to C.VI; KL500, G.R.VIII; KL501, B.VI; KL502, G.R.VIII; KL503, B.VI converted to C.VI;

			KL504, B.VI; KL505, G.R.VIII; KL506, no record; KL507-508, B.VI; KL509, G.R.VIII; KL510, B.VI; KL511, G.R.VIII; KL512-513, B.VI; KL514, G.R.VIII, KL515-516, B.VI; KL517, G.R.VIII; KL518-519, no record; KL520, G.R.VIII; KL521, B.VI; KL522, G.R.VIII; KL523-531, B.VI —of which KL529 was converted to C.VI; KL532, G.R.VIII; KL533/G, G.R. VIII; KL534, B.VI; KL535, no record; KL536-538, B.VI; KL539, no record; KL540-541, B.VI; KL542, G.R.VIII; KL543, B.VI; KL544, G.R.VIII; KL545-549, B.VI —of which KL548 was converted to C.VI; KL550-551, G.R.VIII; KL552, B.VI; KL553-554, G.R.VIII; KL555, no record; KL556-557, B.VI; KL558-559, G.R.VIII; KL560, B.VI; KL561-562, G.R.VIII; KL563-564, B.VI; KL565-568, G.R.VIII; KL569, B.VI; KL570, G.R.VIII; KL571 601, B.VI—of which KL576, 578, 593-595 were converted to C.VI; KL602-606, no record of delivery; KL607, B.VI; KL608, B.VIII converted to C.VIII; KL609-610, B.VIII; KL611-617, B.VI—of which KL613, 617 were converted to C.VI; KL618, B.VIII; KL619-630, B.VI—of which KL619-623, 625, 627-628, 630, were converted to C.VI; KL631, B.VIII converted to C.VIII; KL632-633, B.VI; KL634, B.VIII converted to C.VIII; KL635-639, B.VI—of which KL637, 639, were converted to C.VI; KL640, B.VIII converted to C.VIII; KL641-642, B.VI converted to C.VI; KL643, B.VIII converted to C.VIII; KL644-652, B.VI—of which KL645-647, 650-652, were converted to C.VI; KL653, B.VIII; KL654-655, B.VI; KL656, B.VIII; KL657-658, B.VI converted to C.VI;

Serial Nos.	Qty.	Aircraft Type	Remarks
			KL659-662, B.VIII; KL663-667, B.VI converted to C.VI; KL668, B.VIII; KL669-670, B.VI converted to C.VI; KL671, B.VIII; KL672-673, B.VI converted to C.VI; KL674-675, B.VIII; KL676, B.VI converted to C.VI; KL677-678, B.VIII; KL679, B.VI converted to C.VI; KL680, B.VIII; KL681-683, B.VI converted to C.VI; KL684, B.VIII; KL685-689, B.VI converted to C.VI.
KL690-KL829	140	Douglas Invader I (A-26)	KL690-691 only delivered for evaluation. Bulk delivery cancelled in June 1945.
KL830-KL837	8	Boeing Fortress III	Some off-set to Royal Canadian Air Force.
KL838-KL976	139	Republic Thunderbolt II (P-47D-25)	KL838-887 only delivered, to complete quota of 558.
KL977-KL999	22	Douglas DC-4 Skymaster (C-54D)	KL977-986, 988-999.
KM100-KM799	700	North American Mustang IV (P-51K/D)	KM100-492, ex-U.S.A.A.F. P-51K; KM493-743, ex-U.S.A.A.F. P-51D; KM744-799 not delivered.
KN100-KN149	50	Beechcraft Expeditor II (C-45F-BH)	Delivered to India for the R.A.F. February-July 1945.
KN200-KN701	502	Douglas DC-3 Dakota IV (C-47B)	Diversions to Royal Canadian Air Force, mainly from KN610. KN327 to the South African Air Force. All to C.IV standard except KN628 and KN647, V.I.P.IV. KN437, 465-467, 501-505, 523-527, 537, 539-544, 548-555, 557, 559, 585-587 fitted with glider pick-up winch.
KN702-KN836	135	Consolidated 32 Liberator VI/VIII (B-24J-FO)	KN702-707, B.VI converted to C.VI; KN708-718, no delivery record; KN719-743, G.R.VIII —of which KN719, 720, 727, 734, 737, 739, 743, were converted to C.VIII and KN723 was converted to C(VIP).VIII; KN744-752, B.VI—of which KN747-750 were converted to C.VI; KN753-758, G.R.VIII of which KN754, 756-758, were converted to C.VIII; KN759-760, B.VIII; KN761, G.R.VIII converted to C.VIII; KN762, B.VIII; KN763, G.R.VIII converted to C.VIII; KN764, B.VIII; KN765, G.R.VIII converted to

			C(VIP).VIII for Mr. Jinnah; KN766, B.VIII; KN767, G.R.VIII; KN768, B.VIII (crashed before delivery); KN769, G.R.VIII; KN770, G.R.VIII converted to C.VIII; KN771-772, B.VIII; KN773, G.R.VIII converted to C.VIII; KN774, B.VIII; KN775 G.R.VIII converted to C.VIII; KN776, G.R.VIII; KN777-779, G.R.VIII; KN780-784, B.VIII; KN785-789, G.R.VIII —of which KN786 was converted to C.VIII; KN790-791, B.VIII; KN792, G.R.VIII converted to C.VIII; KN793-794, B.VIII; KN795, G.R.VIII converted to C.VIII; KN796, B.VIII; KN797, G.R.VIII; KN798, B.VIII; KN799-800, G.R.VIII; KN801-802, B.VIII; KN803-805, G.R.VIII; KN806-808, B.VIII; KN809-811, G.R.VIII—of which KN810 was converted to C.VIII; KN812, B.VIII; KN813, G.R.VIII converted to C.VIII; KN814-816, B.VIII. From then to KN836 odd numbers G.R.VIII and even numbers B.VIII, of which KN825, 828, 829, 831, 833, 835 were converted to C.VIII and KN826 burnt out at Lydda on its delivery flight.
KN837-KN986	150	Sikorsky Hoverfly II (R-6A)	Built by the Nash-Kelvinator Corporation. First 40 only delivered, mainly to R.A.F. but KN855 and KN879 went to the Royal Navy.
KN987	1	North American Mustang IV (P-51H)	To Boscombe Down for evaluation.
KP100-KP124	25	Beechcraft Expeditor II (UC-45F-BH)	For Fleet Air Arm communications.
KP125-KP196	72	Consolidated Liberator VIII (B-24LJ-FO)	KP125-140 delivered as G.R.VIII (odd numbers) and B.VIII (even numbers), and KP141-146 as G.R.VIII, of which KP128, 129, 146 were converted to C.VIII. KP147-196 were not delivered.
KP208-KP279	72	Douglas Dakota IV (C-47B)	Main deliveries to India and Middle East, 1945.
KP308-KP328	21	North American NA-108 Mitchell III (B-25J)	1945 Lend/Lease delivery. All returned to U.S.A.A.F.
KP329-KV300	—	—	Reserved for Lend/Lease deliveries. Not taken up.

QUANTITY AND QUALITY

KV301–PZ999 QUANTITIES ordered became larger as the war progressed, and the order for 2,190 Spitfires numbered between MH298 and ML428 was the largest single order ever placed. At the same time attempts were made to introduce new types, and experimentation and research resulted in prototypes and special modifications.

The serialling system continued on the general lines set by precedent from AA100 to AZ999, but there were a few anomalies. The combination NC was used, the first time that C had been used in the double-barrelled prefix allocation, but on the other hand NZ was not used in order to avoid confusion with aircraft of the Royal New Zealand Air Force which used NZ as the prefix to their numerical serialling system.

To set the scene in time, KV100-999 serials were allotted to orders placed in February 1942.

Serial Nos.	*Qty.*	*Aircraft Type*	*Remarks*
KV301-KV893	400	Bristol Buckingham B.I (Later T.I/C.I conversions)	KV301-346, 358-372, 402-450, 471-479 only built as B.I up to KV337, then as C.I. KV322 had experimental central dorsal fin. KV480-500, 518-535, 549-581, 600-641, 656-692, 723-756, 769-786, 801-845, 861-893 cancelled.
KV896-KW673	500	Bristol 156 Beaufighter VIF/X	Built by Rootes Securities. KV896-944, 960-981, KW101-133, 147-171, 183-203, (150), Mk. VIF; KW204, KW216-250, 263-276 (50), Mk. X cancelled; KW277-298, 315-355, 370-416 (110), Mk. X; KW-431-478, 491-536, 549-576, 586-633, 654-673, cancelled. KV923, 938, 941, 961 and KW130 to U.S.A.A.F. in Middle East.
KW969-LA144	1500	Hawker Hurricane IIB/IIC/IID/IV/V	KW696, Mk. IID, KW697-698, Mk. IIC (Bomber), KW699, Mk. IIB; KW700, Mk. IID; KW701-703, Mk. IIB; KW704, Mk. IID; KW705-706, Mk. IIB; KW707, Mk. IIC; KW708, Mk. IID; KW709-710, Mk. IIB; KW711, Mk. IIC; KW712, Mk. IID; KW713-714, Mk. IIB; KW715, Mk. IIC; KW716, Mk. IID; KW717-718, Mk. IIC; KW719, Mk. IIC (Bomber); KW720, Mk. IID; KW721-722, Mk. IIC; KW723, Mk. IIC (Bomber); KW724, Mk. IID; KW725-727, Mk. IIC (Bomber);

			KW728, Mk. IID; KW729-731, Mk. IIC (Bomber); KW745-747, Mk. IIC; KW748, Mk. IIB; KW749, Mk. IID; KW750-752, Mk. IIC (Bomber); KW753, Mk. IID; KW754-756, Mk. IIC (Bomber); KW757, Mk. IID; KW758-760, Mk. IIC (Bomber); KW761, Mk. IID; KW762-764, Mk. IIC; KW765, Mk. IID; KW766-768, Mk. IIC; KW769, Mk. IID; KW770, Mk. IIC (Bomber); KW771-772, Mk. IIB; KW773, Mk. IID; KW774, Mk. IIC (Bomber); KW775, Mk. IIB (Bomber); KW776, Mk. IIC (Bomber); KW777, Mk. IID; KW791, Mk. IIC (Bomber); KW792, Mk. IV; KW793, Mk. IIB; KW794, Mk. IID; KW795, Mk. IIC; KW796-797, Mk. IIC (Bomber); KW798, Mk. IID; KW799-800, Mk. IV; KW801, Mk. IIC (Bomber); KW802, Mk. IID; KW803, Mk. IIC (Bomber); KW804, Mk. IV; KW805, Mk. IIC (Bomber); KW806, Mk. IID; KW807-810, Mk. IV; KW811-815, Mks. IIC, IIB, IIC, IIB, IIC respectively, all Bomber versions; KW816-817, Mk. IV; KW818-832, 846-847, Mk. IIC (Bomber); KW848, Mk. IIB (Bomber); KW849-858, Mk. IIC (Bomber); KW859-881, odd numbers Mk. IID, even numbers Mk. IIC (Bomber) except KW872, Mk. IIB; KW893, Mk. IIC (Bomber); KW894, Mk. IID; KW895, Mk. IIC (Bomber); KW896, Mk. IID; KW897, Mk. IV; KW898, Mk. IID; KW899, Mk. IV; KW900-907, even numbers Mk. IID, odd numbers Mk. IIC (Bomber); KW908-911, Mk. IV; KW912-917, Mk. IIC all bomber versions except KW914; KW918-921 Mk. IV; KW922-924, Mk. IIC (Bomber); KW925, Mk. IIC; KW926-936, 949-982, KX101, Mk. IIC (Bomber); KX102-105, Mk. IIC of which KX104 was

Serial Nos.	*Qty.*	*Aircraft Type*	*Remarks*
			bomber version; KX106-118, Mk. IIC (Bomber); KX119, Mk. IIC; KX120-122, Mk. IID; KX123, Mk. IIC; KX124, Mk. IID; KX125-133, Mk. IIC (Bomber); KX134-137, Mk. IIC; KX138-139, Mk. IIC (Bomber); KX140-141, Mk. IIC; KX142, Mk. IID; KX143-146, 161-164, Mk. IIC (Bomber); KX165-172, odd numbers Mk. IID, even numbers Mk. IIC (Bomber); KX173-177, Mk. IID; KX178-180, Mk. IV; KX181, Mk. IID; KX182-187, Mk. IIC (Bomber);-KX188-190, Mk. IV; KX191-197, Mk. IIC (Bomber) KX198-200, Mk. IV; KX201-202, 220-224 Mk. IIC (Bomber); KX225-234, Mk. IID; KX235-240, Mk. IIC (Bomber); KX241-250, Mk. IID; KX251-261, 280-292, Mk. IIC (Bomber); KX293-305, Mk. IID; KX306-307, 321-369, 382-404, Mk. IIC all Bomber versions except KX367. KX405 Mk. V later Mk. IV; KW406-414, Mk. IV; KX415-424, Mk. IID; KX425, 452-460, Mk. IIC (Bomber); KX461-470, Mk. IID; KX471-491, 521-535, Mk. IIC (Bomber); KX536-545, Mk. IV; KX546-564, Mk. IIC (Bomber); KX565-567, 579-585, Mk. IV; KX586-621, 691-696, Mk. IIC (Bomber); KX697-705, Mk. IV; KX706-736, 749-784, 796-799, Mk. IIC (Bomber); KX800-809, Mk. IV; KX810-819, Mk. IIC (Bomber); KX820-829, Mk. IV; KX830-838, 851-861, Mk. IIC (Bomber); KX862 Mk. IV; KX863, Mk. IIC (Bomber); KX864-866, Mk. IID; KX867-875, Mk. IIC (Bomber); KX876-885, Mk. IV; KX886-892, 922-967, KZ111-156, 169-184, Mk. IIC (Bomber) of which KZ134 was converted to Mk. IIB; KZ185-192, Mk. IV; KZ193. Mk. V; KZ194, Mk.

			IV; KZ195-201, 216-218, Mk. IIC (Bomber); KZ219-228, Mk. IV; KZ229-238, Mk. IIC (Bomber); KZ239-248, Mk. IV; KZ249-250, 266-299, Mk. IIC (Bomber); KZ300-301, 319-326, Mk. IV; KZ327-356, 370-373, Mk. IIC (Bomber); KZ374-383, Mk. IV; KZ384-393, Mk. IIC (Bomber); KZ394-404, Mk. IV; KZ405 Mk. IIC (Bomber); KZ406-407, Mk. IV; KZ408-412, 424-470, 483-526, 540-549, Mk. IIC (Bomber); KZ550-559, Mk. IV; KZ560-569, Mk. IIC (Bomber); KZ570-579, Mk. IV; KZ580-582, 597-603, Mk. IIC (Bomber); KZ604-613, Mk. IV; KZ614-619, Mk. IIC (Bomber); KZ620-621, Mk. IV; KZ622-632, 646-653, Mk. IIC (Bomber); KZ654-663, Mk. IV; KZ664-673, Mk. IIC (Bomber); KZ674-683, Mk. IV; KZ684-689, 702-705, Mk. IIC (Bomber); KZ706-715, Mk. IV, KZ716-721, Mk. IIC (Bomber); KZ722-723, Mk. IV; KZ724, Mk. IIC (Bomber); KZ725 Mk. IIC, KZ726 Mk. IV; KZ727-750, 766-801, 817-862, 877-903, Mk. IIC all Bomber version, except KZ858; KZ904-916 Mk. IV; KZ917-920, 933-949, LA101-144, Mk. IIC (Bomber). Main deliveries to Russia, India and Middle East.
LA157-LA165	5	Curtiss Mohawk	LA157-158 and 163-165, assembled in India.
LA157-LA582	300	Supermarine Spitfire F.21	120 Vickers-Armstrongs (Castle Bromwich)-built. LA187-236, 249-284, 299-332. LA188 was modified for high-speed tests. LA333-346, 368-395, 417-457, 480-519, 536-582, cancelled; some completed as Seafires as below.
LA428-LA564	92	Supermarine Seafire F.45/F.46	LA428-462, 481-495 (50), F.45 built by Vickers-Armstrongs (Castle Bromwich); LA541-564 (24), assembled as F.46 at South Marston. LA565-582 cancelled.
LA586 & LA589	2	Percival P.31 Proctor IV	Prototypes. Originally named Preceptor.

Serial Nos.	Qty.	Aircraft Type	Remarks
LA594	1	Hawker Typhoon	Centaurus-engine prototype, not completed.
LA602-LA610	3	Hawker Tempest II	Prototypes LA602, 607, 610. LA610, ex-Tempest III completed as Fury prototype.
LA619-LA623	5	Lockheed 12A	Ex-U.S.A.A.F.
LA632-LA750	114	General Aircraft G.A.L.49 Hamilcar I	Group-built. LA632-655, 669-691, 704-750. LA728, second Mk. X prototype. LA704 converted to Mk. X.
LA763-LA951	150	Armstrong Whitworth A.W.38 Whitley V	LA763-793 (31) Mk. V; LA794-798, 813-817 (10), Mk. VII; LA818-856, 868-899, 914-951 (109), Mk. V.
LA964-LB251	150	Vickers Wellington IC/IC(T.B.)/VIII	Vickers (Weybridge)-built. LA964 Mk. VIII, LA965 Mk, IC, LA966-967 Mk. VIII. LA968 Mk. IC, LA969-972 Mk. VIII, LA973 Mk. IC, LA974-977 Mk. VIII, LA978 Mk. IC, LA979-983 Mk. VIII, LA984 Mk. IC, LA985-987 Mk. VIII, LA988 Mk. IC, LA989-993 Mk. VIII, LA994 Mk. IC, LA995-998 Mk. VIII, LB110 Mk. IC, LB111-115 Mk. VIII, LB116 Mk. IC, LB117-119 Mk. VIII, LB120 Mk. IC, LB121-125 Mk. VIII, LB126 Mk. IC, LB127-130 Mk. VIII, LB131 Mk. IC, LB132-140 Mk. VIII, LB141 Mk. IC, LB142-147 Mk. VIII, LB148 Mk. IC, LB149-151 Mk. VIII, LB152 Mk. IC; LB153-156, 169-173 Mk. VIII; LB174 Mk. IC; LB175-197, 213-251 Mk. VIII. N.B. All Mk. IC were completed as torpedo bombers except LA973 which was standard. Of the Mk. VIII, the following were fitted with Leigh Lights: LA966, 971, 976, 982, 987, 992, 998, LB114, 124, 129, 135, 140, 145, 150, 153, 156, 178, 186, 194, 216, 220, 224, 231, 236.
LB263-LB385	100 +1	Taylorcraft Auster I	LB263-299, 311-352, 365-385. LB295 built additional to contract.
LB401-LB538	100	Airspeed A.S.-10 Oxford I	LB401-429, 442-462 (50), Standard Motors-built; LB469-492, 513-538 (50), Airspeed-(Christchurch) built.

LB542-LF956	1961	Hawker Hurricane IIB (Bomber)/ IIC (Bomber)/ IV	Hawker (Langley)-built. LB542-575, 588-624, 639-687, 707-744, 769-801, 827-862, 873-913, 927-973, 986-999, LD100-131, 157-185, 199-219, 232-266, 287-315, 334-351, 369-416, 435-470, 487-508, 524-539, 557-580, 594-632, 651-695, 723-749, 772-809, 827-866, 885-905, 931-979, 993-999, LE121-146, 163-183, 201-214, 247-273, 291-309, 334-368, 387-405, 432-449, 456-484, 499-535, 552-593, 617-665, 679-713, 737-769, 784-816, 829-867, 885-925, 938-966, 979-999, LF101-135, 153-184, 197-237, 256-298, 313-346, 359-405, 418-435, 451-482, 494-516, 529-542, 559-601, 620-660, 674-721, 737-774, produced as Mk. IIC (Bomber version)—except for LB643-652, 682-687, 707-710, 743-744, 769-776, 849-853, 993-999. LD100-102, 160-169, 216-219, 232-237, 290-294, 442-451, 465-470, 487-490, 563-572, 605-609, 788-797, 862-866, 885-889, 969-979, LE132-136, 268-273, 291-294, 393-402, 505-512, 514, 567-571, 653-661, 748-757, 834-843, 921-925, LF106-115, 430-435, 451-474, 481-482, 494-510, 592-596, produced as Mk. IV and LE737, 745, 785, 794, 805, 852, produced as Mk. IIB (Bomber version).
LF779-LF882	75	D.H.82B Queen Bee	Built by Scottish Aviation. LF779-803, 816-839, 857-867 (60), completed. LF868-882 cancelled.
LF886-LF963	65	Airspeed A.S.58 Horsa II	Built by The Austin Motor Co. LF886-923, 937-963. Twenty transferred to the U.S.A.A.F.
LG511-LH601	750	Airspeed A.S.51 Horsa I	Built by Harris Lebus. LG511-534, 547-593, 616-658 cancelled except for LG550. LG662-699, 713-749, 761-798, 814-856, 868-896, 911-952, 966-999, LH113-154, 167-189, 202-249, 263-301, 316-359, 373-415, 429-476, 490-536, 549-583, 597-601.
LH942-LJ334	220	Airspeed A.S.-51 Horsa I	LH942-976, LJ101-144, 157-193, 206-241, 256-291, 303-334. LJ271 was converted to Mk. II.

Serial Nos.	Qty.	Aircraft Type	Remarks
LJ440-LJ670	175	Short S.29 Stirling III/IV	Built by Short Bros. LJ440-483, 501-544, 557-596, 611-653, 667-670, Mk. III/IV. LJ512, Mk. IV prototype; LJ530, Mk. V prototype.
LJ810-LK370	360	Short S.29 Stirling IV	Built by Short & Harland Ltd. LJ810-851, 864-899, 913-956, 969-999, LK114-156, 169-211, 226-257, 270-313, 326-370.
LK375-LK624	200	Short S.29 Stirling III/IV	Built by The Austin Motor Co. LK375-411, 425-466, 479-521, 535-576, 589-624, Mk. III—of which LK405, 428, 431, 432, 433, 439, 440, 498, 505, 509, 510, 512, 513, 542-545, 548, 549, 551, 553-560, 562, 566, 567, 573, 589, 606, were converted to Mk. IV.
LK626-LK887	200	Handley Page Halifax V/III	Built by Fairey Aviation. LK626-667, 680-711, 725-746, Mk. V; LK747-766, 779-812, 826-850, 863-887, Mk. III.
LK890-LL615	480	Handley Page Halifax V/III	Built by Rootes Securities. LK890-932, 945-976, 988-999, LL112-153, 167-198, 213-258, 270-312, 325-367, 380-423, 437-469, 481-521, 534-542, Mk. V; LL543-559, 573-615, Mk. III.
LL617-LM296	450	Avro 683 Lancaster II/I	Built by Armstrong Whitworth Aircraft. LL617-653, 666-704, 716-739 (100), Mk. II; LL740-758, 771-813, 826-867, 880-923, 935-977, LM100-142, 156-192, 205-243, 257-296 (350), Mk. I. LL735 had experimental jet engines installed. LL780/G, armament experiments; LL948, converted to Mk. III.
LM301-LM756	350	Avro 683 Lancaster I/III	A. V. Roe (Yeadon)-built. LM301-310 built as Mk. I, but LM306 and LM308 were converted to Mk. III. Rest built as Mk. III as follows: LM311-346, 359-395, 417-448, 450-493, 508-552, 569-599, 615-658, 671-697, 713-756, built as Mk. III but LM448, 485, 489, 492, 695 were converted in service to Mk. I.
LM769-LN153	225	Vickers Warwick V	Vickers (Weybridge)-built. LM769-776 cancelled. LM777-803, 817-858, 870-909 built. LM910-913, 927-968, 980-997, LN110-153, cancelled.

LN157-LR210	1382	Vickers Wellington X	Vickers (Chester)-built. LN157-189, 221-248, 261-303, 317-353, 369-409, 423-468, 481-516, 529-571, 583-622, 635-676, 689-723, 736-778, 791-823, 836-879, 893-936, 948-989, LP113-156, 169-213, 226-268, 281-314, 328-369, 381-415, 428-469, 483-526, 539-581, 595-628, 640-686, 699-733, 748-788, 802-849 863-889, 901-930, 943-986, LR110-142, 156-164, 168-183, 195-210, B.X—of which LN376, 608, 657, 756, 819, 865, 988, LP256, 361, 431, 596, 597, 705, 804, 806, 846, 916-918, 926, 959, 968, LR112, 158, 204, were converted to T.10 post-war. LN715 and LN718 used as flying test-beds; LP523, 11-seat transport.
LR227	1	D.H.87 Hornet Moth	VT-AKE, impressed in India.
LR228-LR229	2	D.H.82 Tiger Moth	VT-AKW/JV impressed in India.
LR230-LR235	6	Douglas DC-3	Ex-U.S.A. civil aircraft pur chased and flown to India.
LR236	1	D.H.82 Tiger Moth	VT-AQE impressed in India.
LR241 & LR244	2	Miles M.25 Martinet	Prototypes.
LR248-LR513	202	D.H.98 Mosquito	De Havilland (Hatfield)-built. LR248-276, 289-313, 327-340, 343-389, 402-404, F.B.VI; LR405-446, 459-481, P.R.IX except LR475-477 B.IX; LR495-513, B.IX. LR387 conv. to Mk. 33.
LR516-LR585	59	D.H.98 Mosquito III	De Havilland (Leavesden)-built. LR516-541, 553-585.
LR631-LR881	213	Supermarine Seafire IIC/III	Built by Westland Aircraft. LR631-667, 680-712, 725-764, Mk. IIC; LR765-820, 835-881, Mk. III.
LR885-LS149	129	Bristol 152 Beaufort I/II	LR885-908, 920-963, 976-999, LS113-128, Mk. I; LS129-149, T.II.
LS151-LS461	250	Fairey Swordfish II	Built by Blackburn Aircraft. LS151-193. 214-248, 261-299, 315-358, 362-403, 415-461.
LS464-LS974	400	Fairey Barracuda II	Fairey (Heaton Chapel)-built. LS464-506, 519-556, 568-595, 608-653, 668-713, 726-763, 778-820, 833-878, 891-936, 949-974.
LS978-LV332	750	Avro 652A Anson I	A. V. Roe (Yeadon)-built. LS978-999, LT112-160, 175-210, 231-258, 271-307, 334-378, 410-459, 472-503, 521-549, 575-610, 641-682, 701-745, 764-797, 823-849, 872-

Serial Nos.	*Qty.*	*Aircraft Type*	*Remarks*
			899, 921-961, 978-999, LV122-167, 199-230, 252-300, 313-332. Main deliveries to South Africa and Australia. LT209-210 were lost at sea on delivery to South Africa. Transfers to the South African Air Force (with S.A.A.F. Nos.) were: LT337 (4347), LT341 (4349), LT345 (4346), LT351 (4351), LT352 (4394), LT353 (4388), LT475 (4383), LT477 (4379), LT481 (4386), LT482 (4387), LT484 (4392), LT874 (4475).
LV336-LV346	11	Consolidated 32 Liberator III	Special 1942 delivery for Battle of Atlantic. Ex-U.S.A.A.F. 41-1107, 1087, 1127, 1096, 1122, 1097, 1114, 1111, 1093, 1124, 1108.
LV482-LV623	100	Armstrong Whitworth A.W.41 Albemarle G.T.VI Series II	Built by A. W. Hawkesley Ltd. LV482-501, 532-577, 590-623.
LV626-LV639	4	Avro 685 York	Prototypes LV626 (Mk. I-II prototype), LV629, LV633 (C(V.I.P.)I), LV639.
LV643-LV756	70	Supermarine Spitfire L.F.VIII	LV643-681, 726-756, shipped in main to India.
LV760-LV762	3	Lockheed 12A	EX-Dutch aircraft L2-32, L2-30 and L201.
LV763	1	D.H.87 Hornet Moth	VT-AIU impressed.
LV764	1	D.H.82A Tiger Moth	Impressed.
LV765-LV767	3	D.H.80A Puss Moth	VT-ABG/ABZ/ABW, impressed in India.
LV768	1	Miles Hawk	VT-AIR impressed.
LV769	1	Piper Cub Cruiser	VT-AKT, impressed.
LV771-LW210	240	Handley Page H.P.61 Halifax B.III/A.VII	LV771-799, 813-842, 857-883, 898-923, 935-973, 985-999, LW113-143, 157-179, 191-195, B.III; LW196-210, B.VII.
LW223-LW724	360	Handley Page H.P.61 Halifax B.II/B.III	Built by The English Electric Co. LW223-246, 259-301, 313-345 (100) B.II; 346-348, 361-397, 412-446, 459-481, 495-522, 537-559, 572-598, 613-658, 671-696, 713-724.
LW727-LX152	240	Airspeed A.S.10 Oxford I/A.S.46 Oxford V	Built by Percival Aircraft. LW727-759, 772-799, 813-835, 848-879, 891-927, Mk. I; LW928-930, 945-947, Mk. V; LW948-973, 985-999, LX113-152, Mk. I.
LX156-LX777	450	Airspeed A.S.-10 Oxford I	LX156-199, 213-245, 258-289, 301-333, 347-369, 382-401, 415-448, 462-489, 502-541, 555-582, 595-617, 629-648, 661-699, 714-746, 759-777—of which LX366-369, 382-401,

			415-416, 467-470, 510-512, 561-565 were delivered direct to the Middle East for the Turkish Air Force. LX417-422 were delivered to Portuguese Air Force in September 1943 and LX423-426 were delivered direct to Takoradi for the Free French Forces.
LX779-LZ544	480	Bristol 156 Beaufighter T.F.X	Bristol (Weston)-built. LX779-827, 845-887, 898-914, 926-959, 972-999, LZ113-158, 172-201, 215-247, 260-297, 314-346, 359-384, 397-419, 432-465, 479-495, 515-544. LX880 became prototype Mk. XI. Transfers to R.A.A.F.: LX988-995, as A19-164 to 171; LZ321-328, as A19-180 to 187; LZ195-201 and LZ215 as A19-172 to 179.
LZ548 & LZ551	2	D.H.100 Vampire	Prototypes built by English Electric to Air Ministry Specification E.6/41. LZ551/G was hooked for deck trials.
LZ556-LZ804	200	Percival P.34 Proctor III	Built by F. Hills & Sons. LZ556-603, 621-663, 672-717, 730-771, 784-804. Several were delivered direct to India.
LZ807-MA906	680	Supermarine Spitfire	Vickers-Armstrongs (Castle Bromwich)-built. LZ807-815, Mk. VC; LZ816, L.F.IXB; LZ817-830, Mk. VC; LZ831-833, Mk. IX; LZ834-835, Mk. VC; LZ836-843, Mk. IX; LZ844-848, 861-899, Mk. VC; LZ915-925, Mk. IX; LZ926-956, 969-988, Mk. VC; LZ989-998, MA221-260, Mk. IX; MA261-266, Mk. VC tropicalised; MA279-315, Mk. VC (except for MA298, L.F.IX); MA328-368, Mk. VC—of which MA329 and MA357 were converted to L.F.IX; MA369, Mk. IX; MA383-397, Mk. VC; MA398-428, 443-487, 501-546, 559-601, 615-643, Mk. IX; MA644-657, Mk. VC —of which MA645, 646, 648, 651, 655, 657, were converted to Mk. IX; MA670-704, Mk. VC—of which MA687, 690, were converted to Mk. IX; MA705-713, 726-767, 790-819, 831-849, Mk. IX; MA850-863, 877, Mk. VC—of which MA860 was converted to Mk. IX; MA878-879, Mk. IX; MA880-906, Mk. VC.

Serial Nos.	*Qty.*	*Aircraft Type*	*Remarks*
MA919	1	D.H.60 Moth	Impressed in India, ex-VT-AET.
MA920	1	Taylorcraft BL-2	Impressed in India. Ex-VT-ALW.
MA921	1	Piper Club Cruiser	Impressed in India.
MA922	1	D.H.85 Leopard Moth	Ex-Madras Flying Club.
MA923	1	Piper Cub	VT-AKV, impressed in India.
MA924	1	Taylorcraft	VT-ALX impressed in India.
MA925	1	Douglas DC-3	Impressed in India.
MA926	1	Zlin 212 Tourist	VT-ALU, impressed in India.
MA927	1	Percival Vega Gull	VT-ALT, impressed in India.
MA928-MA929	2	Douglas DC-3	Impressed in India.
MA930	1	Tipsy Trainer	VT-AKQ, impressed in India.
MA931	1	D.H.60 Gipsy Moth	VT-ANR, impressed in India.
MA932-MA937	6	D.H.82 Tiger Moth	VT-AMS/OF/PW/PX/OM/LM, impressed in India.
MA938	1	D.H.60 Moth	VP-CAB impressed in India.
MA939	1	D.H.60 Gipsy Moth	VP-CAC, impressed in India.
MA940	1	D.H.82 Tiger Moth	VP-CAE, impressed in India.
MA941	1	D.H.60 Gipsy Moth	VT-AAB, impressed in India.
MA942	1	Percival Vega Gull	VT-AIV, impressed in India.
MA943	1	Douglas DC-3	Impressed in India.
MA944	1	Miles Whitney Straight	VT-AKF, impressed in India.
MA945	1	British Aircraft Eagle	VT-AKO, impressed in India.
MA946	1	D.H.80A Puss Moth	VT-ACH, impressed in India.
MA947-MA948	2	D.H.82 Tiger Moth	Impressed in India.
MA949-MA950	2	D.H.60 Gipsy Moth	VT-ACW and VT-AEI, im pressed in India.
MA951-MA952	2	D.H.82 Tiger Moth	Impressed in India.
MA953	1	D.H.60 Moth	Impressed in India.
MA954-MA955	2	D.H.83 Fox Moth	Impressed in India.
MA956-MA957	2	North American Mitchell II (B-25C)	Possibly ex-Dutch. Both to No. 681 (P.R.) Squadron.
MA958	1	Piper Cub	Impressed in India.
MA960	1	Stinson Reliant	Impressed in India.
MA961	1	D.H.89 Rapide	Impressed in India.
MA962	1	Percival Gull	Impressed in India.
MA963-MA968	6	D.H.89 Rapide	Impressed in India. MA963-965, 966, 968 only confirmed.
MA970-MB327	200	Supermarine Seafire IIC	MA970, converted to become Mk. III prototype. MA971-999, MB113-123, Mk. IIC. Further details not known.
MB328-MB375	48	Supermarine Seafire IB	Air Service Training Ltd. conversion and re-numbering of Spitfire VB as follows: Ex-BL676, BL687, BL678, BL694, AB416, AB410, AB413, AB408, AB376, AB261, AB415, BL679 BL689, AB414, AB379, AB409, AR344, AR445-446, AR443, AR459, AR442, AB404-407, AB492, AB408, EP148, AR457-458, EP141, AR460-461, EP142, EP144, EP146-147, EP291, EP293-

			296, EP299, EP301-302, EP304, EP308.
MB378-MB758	300	Fairey Firefly I	MB378-419, 433-479, 492-536, 549-593, 613-649, 662-703, 717-758, F.I various modifications to T.1, T.2 and T.3 post-war.
MB761-MD403	426	Supermarine Spitfire	MB761-769, F.VII; MB770-793, P.R.XI; MB794-805, F.XII; MB806, F.VII; MB807, F.IX; MB808, 820-828, F.VII; MB829-863, 875-882, F. or L.F.XII; MB883-887, F.VII; MB888-911, P.R.XI; MB912-916, 929-935, F.VII; MB936-958, P.R.XI; MB959-976, L.F.VIII; MD100-146, 159-190, F.VII; MD191-199, 213, P.R.X; MD214-256, 269-303, 315-356, 369-403, L.F.VIII.
MD612-MD807	150	Fairey Barracuda II	Built by Blackburn Aircraft. MD612-656, 674-723, 736-778, 792-807.
MD811-ME293	300	Fairey Barracuda III	Built by Boulton Paul. MD811-859, 876-924, 945-992, ME104-152, 166-210, 223-270, 282-293.
ME295-ME551	200	Avro 683 Lancaster III/I	A. V. Roe (Yeadon)-built: ME295-337, 350-395, 417-458, 470-503, 517-551, Mk. III except for 44 Mk. I as follows: ME328, 330, 350, 352, 371-375, 383-384, 419-421, 431-440, 445-451, 455-458, 470, 475-477, 479-480, 482, 490, 495.
ME554-ME868	250	Avro 683 Lancaster I/III	Built by Metropolitan-Vickers. ME554-596, 613-650, 663-704, 717-759, 773-814, 827-868 produced as Mk. I but ME567, 590, 620-623, 625 were converted to Mk. III in service.
ME870-MF742	600	Vickers Wellington X/XIII/XIV	Vickers (Blackpool)-built. ME870-883, Mk. X; ME884-914, 926-950, Mk. XIII; ME951-960, 972-999, MF113-124, Mk. X; MF125-130, Mk. XIII; MF131-144, Mk. X; MF145-156, 170-192, Mk. XIII; MF 193-203, Mk. X; MF204-213, 226-235, Mk. XIII; MF236-249, Mk. X; MF250-267, 279-280, Mk. XIII; MF281-288, Mk. X; MF289-310, Mk. XIII; MF311-316, Mk. X; MF317-320, 335-345, Mk. XIII; MF346-351, Mk. X; MF352-

Serial Nos.	*Qty.*	*Aircraft Type*	*Remarks*
			366, Mk. XIII; MF367-372, Mk. X; MF373-377, 389-398, Mk. XIII; MF399-404, Mk. X; MF405-419, Mk. XIII; MF420-424, 439-441, Mk. X; MF442-449, Mk. XIII; MF450-451, Mk. XIV; MF452-459, Mk. X; MF460-467, Mk. XIII; MF468-479, Mk. X; MF480, 493-499, Mk. XIII; MF500-538, 550-572, Mk. X; MF573-582, Mk. XIII; MF583-596, 614-615, Mk. X; MF616-623, Mk. XIII; MF624, Mk. X; MF625, Mk. XIII; MF626-635, Mk. X; MF636-643, Mk. XIII; MF644-655, Mk. X; MF656-659, 672-675, Mk. XIII; MF676-687, Mk. X; MF688-694, Mk. XIII; MF695-706, Mk. X; MF707-713, 725, Mk. XIII; MF726-727, Mk. XIV; MF728-739, Mk. X; MF740-742, Mk. XIII. ME890, 907, 940, MF190, 466, 643, to Royal Hellenic Air Force, April 1946. The Mk. Xs were completed as B.X, but ME954, 972, 979, 997, MF313, 523, 535, 564, 567, 626-628, 633-634, 695, were converted to T.10 post-war. ME905 crashed on test.
MG102-MH237	800	Avro 652A Anson I	A. V. Roe (Yeadon)-built. MG102-147, 159-199, 214-256, 270-314, 327-368, 381-423, 436-478, 490-536, 549-596, 613-656, 669-701, 714-757, 770-813, 826-874, 888-928, 962-999, MH103-135, 149-196, 210-237. Conversions included: MG159, to Mk. 19; MG198, 220, 289, 366, 415, 500, 517, 684, to Mk. 13.
MH298-ML428	2190	Supermarine Spitfire V/IX	Vickers-Armstrongs (Castle Bromwich)-built. MH298-311, Mk. VC; MH312-336, 349-390, Mk. IX; MH413-456, 470-496, L.F.IX; MH497, F.IX; MH498-512, 526-563, L.F.IX; MH564-568, 581-596, Mk. VC; MH597-599, Mk. IX; MH600, Mk. VC; MH601-604, Mk. IX; MH605, Mk. VC; MH606-626, 635-636, Mk. IX; MH637-646, Mk. VC; MH647-

			678, 691-740, 750-800, 813-856, 869-912, 924-958, 970-999, MJ114-156, 169-203, 215-258, 271-314, 328-369, 382-428, 441-485, 498-536, 549-589, 602-646, 659-698, 712-756, 769-801, 814-858, 870-913, 926-967, 979-999, MK112-158, 171-213, 226-268, 280-326, 339-379, 392-428, 440-486, 499-534, 547-590, 602-646, 659-699, 713-756, 769-812, 826-868, 881-926, 939-969, 981-999, ML112-156, 169-216, 229-277, 291-323, 339-381, 396-428, L.F./F./H.F.IX.
ML430-ML722	229	Bristol 152 Beaufort T.II	ML430-476, 489-524, 540-586, 599-635, 649-692, 705-722.
ML725-ML884	150	Short S.25 Sunderland III	ML725-774, 777-801 (75), Short-built; ML807-831 (25), Short & Harland-built; ML835-884 (50), Blackburn-built. ML739, 741, 745, 747, 757, 758, 765, 779, 780, 784, 785, 796-798, 801, 807, 809, 818-821, 824, 839, converted to Mk. V; ML783, 784, 788, 818, 828, 838, 840, 843, converted to Sandringham.
ML896-MM431	350	D.H.98 Mosquito	De Havilland (Hatfield)-built. ML896-924, B.IX; ML925-942, 956-999, MM112-156, 169-205, 219-226, B.XVI—of which ML926/G had experimental radar bomb sights and ML980, 995, MM117, 193, were converted to T.T.39; MM227-257, P.R.IX; MM258, P.R.XVI prototype; MM271-314, 327-371, 384-397, P.R.XVI—of which several were transferred to the U.S.A.A.F.; MM398-423, F.B.VI; MM424-425, F.B.XVIII; MM426-431, F.B.VI.
MM436-MM822	300	D.H.98 Mosquito	De Havilland (Leavesden)-built. MM436-479, 491-534, 547-590, 615-623, N.F.XIII; MM624-656, 669-685, N.F. XIX; MM686-710, 726-769, 783-822, N.F.30.
MM838-MM948	100	Bristol 156 Beaufighter VIF	Bristol (Filton)-built MM838-887, 899-948 Delivered from May 1943.
MM951-MP203	800	Hawker Typhoon IB	Built by Gloster Aircraft. MM951-995, MN113-156, 169-213, 229-269, 282-325, 339-381, 396-436, 449-496, 513-

Serial Nos.	Qty.	Aircraft Type	Remarks
			556, 569-608, 623-667, 680-720, 735-779, 791-823, 851-896, 912-956, 968-999, MP113-158, 172-203. MN290 tropicalised. MN235 to U.S.A. in March 1944.
MP275-MP474	150	Airspeed A.S.10 Oxford I	Built by The Standard Motor Co. MP275-314, 338-376, 391-430, 444-474.
MP469	1	D.H.98 Mosquito XV (H.A.)	Special high altitude prototype. Compromised numbers above.
MP486	1	General Aircraft G.A.L.48 Twin Hotspur	Prototype.
MP496	1	Airspeed A.S.10 Oxford	Originally numbered MP469. See above.
MP499	1	Focke-Wulf Fw 190A-3	Captured enemy aircraft.
MP502-MP825	250	Vickers Wellington XI/XII/XIII/XIV	Vickers (Weybridge)-built. MP502, Mk. XI; MP503, Mk. XII; MP504, Mk. XI; MP505-515, Mk. XII; MP516-535, Mk. XI, of which MP518, 520, 522, 526, 531, 533-534 were conv. to Mk. XVII; MP536-542, Mk. XII; MP543-549, 562-601, 615-656, 679-703, Mk. XI except for MP575, 578, 581, 584, 587, 590, 593, 596, 599, 615, 618, 620, 622, 624, 626, 628, 630, 632, 634, 636, 638, 650, 652, 654, 656, 680, 682, 684, 686, 688, 690 were completed as Mk. XII and MP548 was conv. to Mk. XVII; MP704-724, 738-774, Mk. XIII except MP710, 712, 714, 716, 718, 720, 722, 724, 739, 741, 750, 752, 754, 756, 758, 760, 763, 766, 769, 772, 774, Mk. XIV; MP789-825 Mk. XIV except MP790, 793, 796, 800, Mk. XIII.
MP829 & MP832	2	Vickers Windsor	Sixth and seventh prototypes. Order cancelled before completion.
MP838/G	1	D.H.100 Vampire	First armed Vampire. Originally named Spider Crab.
MS470-MS496	27	Vickers Wellington X	Vickers (Blackpool)-built.
MS499-MS931	355	Miles M.25 Martinet T.T.I	MS499-535, 547-590, 602-647, 659-705, 717-759, 771-820, 832-876, 889-931—of which MS515, 723, 730, 741, 847, were converted to Queen Martinet.

MS934-MT454	330	Taylorcraft Auster A.O.P.IV/A.O.P.V/ A.O.P.III	MS934-981, MT100-145, 158-199, 213-256, 269-314, 328-355, A.O.P.IV; MT356, A.O.P.V prototype; MT357-367, A.O.P.V; MT368-369, 382-419, 431-453, A.O.P.III; MT454, Mk. III converted to Mk. IV. MT393, 407, 408, 432, 445, 450 were transferred to the Royal Australian Air Force, 1944-45; MT387, 391, 442, sold to the Dutch Air Force, 1946-47; MT405-406, to the Royal Hellenic Air Force.
MT456-MT500	45	D.H.98 Mosquito N.F.30	De Havilland (Leavesden)-built. MT466 converted to N.F.36. MT462 and 464, 465, 479 went to the U.S.A.A.F.
MT502-MV514	700	Supermarine Spitfire VIII/XIV	MT502-527, 539-581, 593-635, 648-689, 703-748, 761-802, 815-846, Mk. VIII; MT847-858, F.R.XIV; MT872-915, 925-969, 981-999, MV112-156, 169-208, 231-245, Mk. VIII; MV246-273, 286-320, Mk. XIV; MV321-329, 342-346, Mk. VIII; MV347-386, Mk. XIV; MV398-441, 456-487, 498-514, Mk. VIII.
MV521-MV570	50	D.H.98 Mosquito N.F.30	De Havilland (Leavesden)-built. MV538, 548, 562, 568, to the French Air Force.
MV660-MV990	260	Supermarine Seafire	Cancelled. MV660-707, 720-761, 774-823, 846-885, 899-941, 954-990.
MV989 & MV993	2	Grumman Goose	Lend/Lease allocation.
MW100-MW333	200	Avro 685 York C.1	MW100-149, 161-210, 223-272, 284-333—of which MW100-102 were V.I.P. versions; MW104, 106, 109-112, 114-120, 122-128, passenger versions; MW105, 130-139, 141-149, 161-168, freighters; and the remainder passenger-cum-freighter versions. MW103, 108, 113, 121, 129 went to, British Overseas Airways Corporation as G-AGJA-E. MW107 became S.A.A.F. 4999.
MW335-MW373	39	Hawker Hurricane IIC	Bomber version. MW352, 353, 373 sold to Portugal.
MW375-MW732	300	Hawker Tempest II	Ordered from Bristol Aircraft at Filton and Banbury. MW375-423 and 435 (50) only built of which MW376-383, 385-393 and 395-404 went to the Indian Air Force. MW436-

Serial Nos.	Qty.	Aircraft Type	Remarks
			478, 491-536, 548-589, 591-633, 645-686, 699-732, cancelled.
MW735-MW856	100	Hawker Tempest II	Hawker (Langley)-built. MW735-778, 790-835, 847-856—of which 54 were sold to the Indian Air Force.
MX450-MX455	6	Percival P.31A-C Proctor IV	Development aircraft delivered from April 1943.
MX457	1	Stampe S.V.4B	Ex-OO-ATD aircraft. Used by No. 24 Squadron.
MX459	1	Koolhoven F.K.43	Ex-Dutch Army No. 965 flown to Britain. Was PH-ASN, became PH-NAU.
MX463	1	D.H.60 Moth	Belgian Air Attaché's aircraft, taken on strength.
MX535-MX983	365	Fairey Barracuda II	Built by Blackburn Aircraft. MX535-576, 591-638, 652-696, 709-753, 767-808, 820-864, 877-907(300) built; MX908-923, 935-983 cancelled.
MX988-MX997	4	Bristol 164 Brigand	Prototypes to Air Ministry Specification H.7/42. MX988, 991, 994, and 997. MX997 was replaced by TX374.
MZ100-MZ255	132	Taylorcraft Auster A.O.P.III	MZ100-145, 157-198, 212-255—of which MZ105 and MZ110 were temporarily converted to Mk. II. Transfers and sales to other air forces were: MZ105, 122, 123, 134, 135, 137, 144, 158, 162, 174, 181, 182, 183, 188, 195, 197, 212, 213, 218, 220, 228, 230, 247, 249, 251, 252 to the Royal Australian Air Force 1944/45; MZ133, 160, 169, 187, 221, 227, 233, 244, 248 to the Royal Hellenic Air Force; MZ110, 125, 126, 136, 138, 140, 141, 143, 145, 164, 167, 170, 178, 179, 189, 192, 194, 196, 214, 216, 219, 223, 224, 229, 231, 236, 239, 250, 253 shipped to the Dutch Air Force from Dagenham late 1945/early 1946. MZ232, 235 to the Czech Air Force 1945.
MZ260-MZ264	5	Short S.29 Stirling III	Replacement aircraft for N6025-6028 and N6031 built by Short & Harland.
MZ269 & MZ271	2	Short S.45 Seaford	Prototypes, used for armament and hydrodynamic research.
MZ282-MZ495	180	Handley Page H.P.61 Halifax B.III	Built by London Aircraft Production Group. MZ282-321, 334-378, 390-435, 447-495.

MZ500-MZ939	360	Handley Page H.P.61 Halifax B.III	Built by The English Electric Co. MZ500-544, 556-604, 617-660, 672-717, 730-775, 787-831, 844-883, 895-939.
MZ945-NA488	360	Handley Page H.P.61 Halifax B.III/A.VII	Built by Rootes Securities. MZ945-989, NA102-150, 162-205, 218-263, 275-309, B.III; NA310-320, 336-380, 392-431, 444-468, A.VII. NA469-488, cancelled.
NA492-NA704	180	Handley Page H.P.61 Halifax B.III	Built by Fairey. NA492-531, 543-587, 599-644, 656-704.
NA710-NB766	762	Vickers Wellington X	263 Vickers (Chester)-built. NA710-754, NA766-811, 823-870, 893-937, 949-997, NB110-139, B.X. Batches NB140-155, 167-213, 225-269, 282-329, 341-385, 398-443, 456-502, 514-556, 569-613, 625-670, 684-714, 739-766 cancelled. NA714, 752, 780, 781, 786, 788, 793, 830, 831, 834-836, 841, 843, 846, 848, 849, 852-854, 859, 868, 897, 904-907, 915-916, 918-921, 924, 928, 955, 958, 964, 967, 971, 975, 979, 987, 989, NB110, 113, 115-119 converted post-war to T.10.
NB767-NC408	441	Vickers Wellington XIV	300 Vickers (Chester)-built. NB767-783, 796-841, 853-896, 908-952, 964-999, NC112-160, 164-209, 222-234. NC235-268, 280-327, 339-387, 399-408 cancelled.
NC414-ND133	500	Vickers Wellington X/XIII/XIV/XVIII	Vickers (Blackpool)-built. NC414-418, Mk. XIII; NC419, Mk. XIV; NC420, Mk. XIII; NC421-432, Mk. X; NC433-440, Mk. XIII; NC441-442, Mk. XIV; NC443-452, Mk. X; NC453-459, 471, Mk. XIII; NC472-480, Mk. X; NC481-489, Mk. XIII; NC490-493, Mk. XIV; NC494-502, Mk. X; NC503-510, Mk. XIII; NC511-513, Mk. XIV; NC514-517; Mk. X; NC518-519, unconfirmed; NC529-533, Mk. X, NC534-541, Mk. XIII; NC542-544, Mk. XIV; NC545-554, Mk. X; NC555-562, Mk. XIII; NC563-571, Mk. X; NC572-576, 588-589, Mk. XIII; NC590-591, Mk. XIV; NC592-601. Mk. X; NC602-609, Mk. XIII; NC610-613, Mk. XIV; NC614-621, Mk. X; NC622-625, Mk. XIV; NC626-

Serial Nos.	*Qty.*	*Aircraft Type*	*Remarks*
			631, Mk. XIII; NC632, 644-647, Mk. XIV; NC648-655, Mk. X; NC656-663, Mk. XIII; NC664-671, Mk. X; NC672-677, Mk. XIV; NC678-692, 706-724, Mk. X; NC725, unconfirmed; NC726-740, Mk. X; NC741-747, Mk. XIII; NC748-750, 766-770, Mk. X; NC771-776, Mk. XIV; NC777-784, Mk. X; NC785-788, Mk. XIV; NC789-796, Mk. X; NC797-800, Mk. XIV; NC801-813, 825-827, Mk. X; NC828-835, Mk. XIV; NC836-847, Mk. X; NC848-855, Mk. XIV; NC856-867, Mk. X; NC868-869, Mk. XVIII; NC870, 883-889, Mk. XIV; NC890-901, Mk. X; NC902-907, Mk. XIV; NC908-925, Mk. X; NC926-928, Mk. XVIII; NC929, 942-990, Mk. X; ND104-128, Mk. XVIII; ND129-133, Mk. XIV. Post-war NC426, 430, 497, 498, 500, 502, 515, 546, 615, 648, 719, 720, 790, 793, 811, 812, 836, 839, 845, 856, 892, 898, 916, 918, 920, 925, 929, 958, 963, 968, 981, 987 were converted to T.10.
ND139-ND322	150	Bristol 156 Beaufighter VIF	Bristol (Filton)-built. ND139-186, 198-243, 255-299, 312-322. ND282, 291, 296, 321 to U.S.A.A.F.
ND324-NE181	600	Avro 683 Lancaster III	A. V. Roe (Manchester)-built. ND324-368, 380-425, 438-479, 492-538, 551-597, 613-658, 671-715, 727-768, 781-826, 839-882, 895-936, 948-996, NE112-151, 163-181—of which ND418, 479, 558, 673, 784, were converted to Mk. VI. NE147 was modified for flight refuelling.
NE193-NE832	500	Bristol 156 Beaufighter T.F.X	Bristol (Weston)-built. NE193-232, 272-260, 282-326, 339-386, 338-446, 459-502, 515-559, 572-615, 627-669, 682-724, 738-779, 792-832. 30 offset to the R.A.A.F.
NE858-NF414	350	Fairey Swordfish II/III	Built by Blackburn Aircraft. NE858-906, 920-957, 970-999, NF113-161, 175-217, 230-250 (230), Mk. II; NF251-274, 298-347, 369-414 (120), Mk. III.

NF418-NF665	200	Supermarine Seafire L.III	Built by Westland Aircraft. NF418-455, 480-526, 531-570, 575-607, 624-665. 26 of these with fixed wings were L.IIC (hybrid).
NF668-NF739	60	Hawker Sea Hurricane IIC	Hawker (Langley)-built. NF668-703, 716-739.
NF744	1	Slingsby T.4 Falcon III	Glider, impressed.
NF745	1	D.F.S./49 Grunau Baby	Glider BGA148, impressed.
NF746	1	B.A.C. Primary	Glider, impressed.
NF747	1	Miles Whitney Straight	G-AFZY, impressed.
NF748	1	Miles M.2F Hawk Major	G-ACWY, impressed.
NF749	1	Parnall Heck II	G-AEGH, impressed.
NF750	1	Miles M.2W Hawk Trainer	G-ADWT, impressed.
NF751	1	Miles Whitney Straight	G-AEVL, impressed (see DP855).
NF752	1	Miles M.2F Hawk Major	G-ACYO, impressed.
NF753	1	Lockheed 12A	Bought in U.S.A.
NF754-NF755	2	Focke-Wulf Fw 190	Enemy aircraft captured in Middle East.
NF756	1	Henschel Hs 129	Enemy aircraft captured in Middle East.
NF847-NF896	50	D.H.89A Dominie	Deliveries to the Royal Air Force except for NF850, 854, 855, 864, 866, 867, 871-873, 879-881, to the Royal Navy.
NF900	1	Miles M.33 Monitor	Prototype to Air Ministry Specification Q.9/42.
NF906-NG503	400	Avro 683 Lancaster I	Built by Armstrong Whitworth Aircraft. NF906-939, 952-999, NG113-149, 162-206, 218-259, 263-308, 321-367, 379-421, 434-469, 482-503. NG234 converted to Mk. III; NG465 converted to Mk. VI.
NG757-NH611	600	Supermarine Spitfire L.F.IX/H.F.IX	Ordered from Vickers-Armstrongs (Castle Bromwich). NG757-798, 813-856, 868-913, 929-968, 979-999, NH112-147, cancelled. NH148-158, 171-218, 230-276, 289-326, 339-381, 393-438, 450-496, 513-558, 570-611 (368), built as L.F.IX (except for NH148, 153, 181, 190, 194, 236, 250, 256, 262, 267, 271, 275, 293, 297, 310, 313, 360, 362, 418, 420, 422, 433, 437, 450, 459, 478, 482, 486, 488, 513, 518, 528, 534, 536, 539, 542, 545, 547, 572, 577, 578, 582, 587, 611, H.F.IX).
NH614-NH929	225	Supermarine Spitfire VIII/XIV	NH614, H.F.VIII; NH615-636, L.F.VIII; NH637-661, 685-720, 741-759, 775-813, 831-875, 892-929, Mk. XIV.

Serial Nos.	Qty.	Aircraft Type	Remarks
NJ170-NJ194	25	Short S.25 Sunderland III	Built by Blackburn Aircraft. NJ170-172, 176-177, 179, 180, 182, 187-188, 190-194, converted to Mk. V; NJ171 and NJ188 converted to Sandringham V.
NJ200-NJ239	40	Short Seaford/Solent	Built by Short Bros. NJ200-207 converted to Solents G-ALIJ/GWU/KNO/KNP/KNR/KNS/KNT/KNU. NJ208-239 cancelled.
NJ253-NJ277	25	Short S.25 Sunderland III/V	Built by Short & Harland. NJ253-258 built as Mk. III—of which all but NJ256 were converted to Mk. V. NJ253, 255, 257, converted to Sandringham. NJ259-277, Mk. V.
NJ280-NJ607	250	Airspeed A.S.10 Oxford I	Built by Percival Aircraft. NJ280-322, 345-382, 397-400 (85) only completed. Cancelled Nos.: NJ401-443, 459-494, 510-558, 571-607. NJ318 was re-numbered VX587.
NJ609-NK132	338	Taylorcraft Auster A.O.P.III/V	NJ609-651, 664-703, 716-746 (114), A.O.P.V; NJ747-758, 771-818, 830-876, 889-935, 947-995, NK112-132 (224), A.O.P.III. Transfers to other air forces were: NJ749, 771, 783, 785, 797, 800, 832, 834, 838, 859, 861, 890, 910, NK113, 123, 126, to the Royal Australian Air Force; NJ780, 786, 790, 796, 811, 836, 894, 975, NK125, to the Royal Hellenic Air Force; NJ756, 776, 779, 799, 801, 808, 809, 818, 870, 871, 896, 897, 916, 918, 934, 952, 957, 961, 971, 972, to the Dutch Air Force. NK129 to the Czech Air Force.
NK136 & NK138	2	Vickers 480 Windsor	Prototypes. NK136 became 6222M. NK138 not completed.
NK139-NL251	800	Avro 652A Anson	A. V. Roe (Yeadon)-built. NK139-187, 199-244, 260-303, 314-351, Mk. I; NK352-356, 368-369, Mk. X; NK370-406, 419-451, Mk. I, NK452-462, converted to Mk. III/IV; NK475-516, 528-568, 581-623, 636-679, 692-738, 750-793, 806-848, 861-906, 919-958, 970-999, NL112-155, Mk. I (except for NK426-428, 431-433, 439, 443, 446-449, 487-493, 528-534, 657-662, 664-

			668, 695-696, 699, 702, 710, 722, 725, 733, 737, 753, 766-772, 775, 778, 781, 784, 786-787, 789, 791, 793, 819-820, 827-828, 831-832, 835, 838, 841, 844, 847, 862, 920, 921, 924-925, 930-935, NL112-116, Mk. X; NK790, 870-875, 919-920, 986-999, NL125, 128-129, 132-133, 136-137, 140-141, 144-145, 148-149, Mk. XI; NL152, V.I.P.XIX, NL153, Mk. XII); NL169-170, Mk. I; NL171-172, Mk. XII; NL173-174, Mk. I; NL175-176, Mk. XII; NL177-178, Mk. I; NL179-180, Mk. XII; NL181-208, 220-246, Mk. XI; NL247-251, Mk. XII. NK666 and NK668 were fitted out as ambulances.
NL255	1	Hawker Hurricane V	Prototype.
NL690-NM214	350	D.H.82A Tiger Moth II/I	Built by Morris Motor Co. NL690-735, 748-789, 802-847, 859-899 (175), Mk. II; NL903-948, 960-999, NM112-158, 171-214, Mk. I. NL785-789 and 802-805 were diverted to Portugal in 1943.
NM217-NM810	450	Airspeed A.S.10 Oxford I	Airspeed (Portsmouth)-built. NM217-254, 270-314, 329-370, 385-429, 444-488, 509-550, 571-615, 629-676, 681-720, 736-760, 776-810. NM532-533 were destroyed by fire before delivery.
NM814-NM906	70	Supermarine Spitfire F.R.XIV	NM814-823 (10) only built by Vickers-Armstrongs (Chattis Hill). NM824-855, 879-906, cancelled.
NM910-NM982	60	Supermarine Seafire L.II	NM910-949, 963-982, produced in lieu of Spitfires EN686-695, 710-759.
NM984-NN330	200	Supermarine Seafire L.III/L.IIC	Built by Westland Aircraft. NM984-999, NN112-157, 169-214, 227-270, 283-330. A few with fixed wings delivered as L.IIC.
NN333-NN641	250	Supermarine Seafire III	Built by Cunliffe-Owen. NN333-367, 379-418, 431-476, 488-528, 542-586, 599-641.
NN644	1	Messerschmitt Bf 109F	Captured enemy aircraft.
NN660-NN667	3	Supermarine Spiteful	Prototypes NN660, 664, 667 to A.M. Spec. F.1/43.
NN670 & NN673	2	Vickers 480 Windsor	Fourth and fifth prototypes, not completed. Plans for NN673 with turboprops.
NN694-NN816	100	Avro 683 Lancaster I	Built by The Austin Motor Co. NN694-726, 739-786, 798-816. NN801 Mk. VII prototype.

Serial Nos.	Qty.	Aircraft Type	Remarks
NP156-NP403	200	Percival P.31 Proctor IV	Built by F. Hills & Son. NP156-198, 210-254, 267-309, 323-369, 382-403.
NP406-NP533	100	Miles Monitor T.T.II	NP406-425 only built. NP426-448, 461-506, 523-533, cancelled.
NP490	1	D.H.94 Moth Minor	VP-CAG, purchased in Ceylon for naval C.-in-C.
NP491	1	British Aircraft Swallow	VP-CAF, purchased in Ceylon for R.N. communications.
NP664	1	Waco CG-4A Hadrian	American-built glider.
NP671 & NP674	2	General Aircraft G.A.L.55	Training glider prototypes to A.M.Spec. TX.3/43.
NP681-NP927	200	Handley Page Halifax A.VII/B.VI	NP681-723, 736-781, 793-821 (118), A.VII except for NP715, 752, 753, B.VI; NP822-836, 849-895, 908-927 (82), B.VI.
NP930-NR290	200	Handley Page Halifax B.III	Built by the English Electric Co. NP930-976, 988-999, NR113-156, 169-211, 225-258, 271-290.
NR293-NR666	300	Miles M.25 Martinet T.T.1	NR293-336, 349-390, 405-446, 460-503, 516-556, 569-616, 628-666. NR542 was not delivered. NR387 and NR599 were converted to Queen Martinet.
NR669-NR853	150	D.H.89A Dominie I	Built by Brush Coachworks Ltd. De Havilland Nos. 6768-6917. NR669-701, 713-756, 769-815, 828-853. NR748 and NR788 produced as Mk. II. NR745-746 to Rhodesia.
NR857-NS204	200	Fairey Swordfish III	Built by Blackburn Aircraft. NR857-898, 913-958, 970-999, NS112-156, 168-204.
NS487-NS493	3	Supermarine Seafire XV	Prototypes: NS487, 490, 493, of which NS493 was modified to Mk. XVII standard.
NS496-NS816	250	D.H.98 Mosquito XVI	De Havilland (Hatfield)-built. NS496-538, 551-585 P.R.XVI; NS586-589 P.R.32; NS590-596, 619-660, 673-712, 725-758, 772-816 P.R.XVI.
NS819-NT238	250	D.H.98 Mosquito F.B.VI/XVIII	De Havilland (Hatfield)-built. NS819-859, 873-914, 926-965, 977-999, NT112-156, 169-207, 219-238, F.B.VI (except for NT200, 224, 225, F.B.XVIII.
NT241-NT621	300	D.H.98 Mosquito N.F.30	De Havilland (Leavesden)-built. NT241-283, 295-336, 349-393, 415-458, 471-513, 526-568, 582-621.
NT623-NT872	200	Westland Welkin	NT623 only built. NT623-666, 680-725, 738-779, 793-823, 836-872 cancelled.

NT888-NV632	500	Bristol 156 Beaufighter T.F.X	Bristol (Weston)-built. NT888-929, 942-971, 983-999, NV113-158, 171-218, 233-276, 289-333, 347-390, 413-457, 470-513, 526-572, 585-632.
NV636	1	Blackburn Firebrand	T.F.2 prototype, built from airframe of DD810.
NV639-NV793	130	Hawker Tempest V Series II	NV639-682, 695-735, 749-793. NV768 used for annular cooling experiments by Napier. Post-war conversions to T.T.5 were NV645, 661, 664, 665, 669, 671, 699, 704, 711, 723, 725, 762, 778, 780, 781, 793.
NV917-NX482	369	Hawker Tempest V/VI	Hawker (Langley)-built. NV917-948, 960-996 (69), Mk. V—of which NV917, 922-923, 928, 937, 940, 960, 962, 965, 974-975, 978, 992, 994-996 were converted post-war to T.T.5; NV997-999, NX113-156, 169-209, 223-268, 281-288 (142), Mk. VI. NX289-325, 338-381, 394-435, 448-482 cancelled.
NX484-NX545	50	Taylorcraft Auster III	NX484-509, 522-545. Transfers to other air forces were: NX494, 498, 500, 501, 528, 533, 535, to the Royal Australian Air Force; NX486, 534, 537, 545 to the Dutch Air Force.
NX548-NX794	200	Avro 683 Lancaster I/VII	Built by The Austin Motor Co. NX548-589, 603-610 (50), B.I; NX611-648, 661-703, 715-758, 770-794 (150), B.VII.
NX798 & NX802	2	Hawker Fury	Prototypes to Air Ministry Specification F.2/43. Sold to Egypt and Pakistan respectively.
NX805-NX876	60	General Aircraft G.A.L. 49 Hamilcar I	Group built. NX805-838, 851-876.
NX879-PA129	118	Supermarine Seafire IB	Spitfire VB converted by Air Service Training and renumbered NX879-928, 940-967, 980-989, PA100-129.
PA143 & PA147	2	Supermarine Seagull	Prototypes to Air Ministry Specification S.14/44.
PA158-PA835	500	Avro 683 Lancaster I	Ordered from Vickers-Armstrongs at Chester. 235 only built. PA158-198, 214-239, 252-288, 303-351, 365-396, 410-452, 473-478, 509, built as B.I. PA479-508, 510-512, 526-563, 579-625, 646-687, 701-737, 752-799, 816-835, cancelled.

Serial Nos.	Qty.	Aircraft Type	Remarks
PA838-PA961	100	Supermarine Spitfire P.R.XI	PA838-871, 884-913, 926-961. Some transferred to the U.S.A.A.F.
PA964-PD196	800	Avro 683 Lancaster III/I and Lancastrian	A. V. Roe (Manchester)-built PA964-999, PB112-158, 171-213, 226-267, 280-308, 341-385, 397-438, 450-490, 504-542, 554-596, 609-653, 666-708, 721-768, 780-823, 836-881, 893-936, 949-994, Mk. III; PB995-998, PD112-139, Mk. I (Special); PD140-146, 159-171, 174-196, were reserved for Lancastrians—of which PD193-194 were built and renumbered VH737 and VH742. Others were registered as civil aircraft as follows: PD140, G-AGLF; PD141-146, G-AGLS-X; PD159-168, G-AGLY-MH; PD169-182, G-AGMJ-X. Remainder cancelled.
PD198-PD444	200	Avro 683 Lancaster I	Built by Metropolitan-Vickers. PD198-239, 252-296, 309-349, 361-404, 417-444.
PD446-PD623	145	Hawker Typhoon IB	PD446-480, 492-536, 548-577, 589-623 built by Gloster.
PD625-PD692	43	Gliders—type as per remarks column	Built up by Air Training Corps cadets from spares and acquisitions. PD625-635, 637-639, 641, 643-647, 650-652, 656, 659-662, 665-666, 679, 682, 685-686, 690-692 reported as Kirby Cadet; PD654-655, 658, 664, 680-681 reported as Dagling.
PE101-PE248	100	Avro 685 York C.I	PE101-108 (8) only built. PE109-129, 146-191, 224-248, cancelled.
PE510-PE878	300	Vickers Windsor 1	Order reduced to 100, then 40, and finally cancelled. PE510-553, 565-606, 618-658, 671-715, 727-769, 782-826, 839-878.
PE882	1	Focke-Wulf Fw 190A-4	Captured when landed at West Malling in error.
PE885-PF367	300	Hawker Tempest II	Ordered from The Bristol Aeroplane Co. Cancelled. PE885-927, 939-966, 978-999, PF112-158, 171-213, 225-266, 280-319, 333-367.
PF370	1	Westland Welkin II	Prototype to Air Ministry Specification F.9/43. Later became P-17 and then WE997.
PF379-PF680	245	D.H.98 Mosquito B.XVI/P.R.34	Built by Percival Aircraft. PF379-415, 428-469, 481-526,

			538-579, 592-619 (195), B.XVI; PF620-635, 647-680 (50), P.R.34. PF673, 678-680, converted to P.R.34A. PF445, 452, 481-483, 560, 562, 568-570, 576, 599, 604-606, 609, 658, 666, converted to T.T.39.
PF690-PF817	100	Airspeed A.S.-51 Horsa I	PF690-725, 739-770, 786-817.
PF820-PG442	400	Vickers Wellington X/XIV/XVIII	Vickers (Blackpool)-built. PF820-822, Mk. XIV; PF823-830, Mk. X; PF831-838, Mk. XIV; PF839-846, Mk. X; PF847-854, Mk. XIV; PF855-862, Mk. X; PF863-866, 879-882, Mk. XIV; PF883-888, Mk. X; PF889-893, Mk. XIV; PF894-901, Mk. X; PF902-911, Mk. XIV; PF912-915, 927-930, Mk. X; PF931-940, Mk. XIV; PF941-948, Mk. X; PF949-958, Mk. XIV; PF959-966, Mk. X; PF967-968, 979-986, Mk. XIV; PF987-994, Mk. X; PF995-999, PG112-116, Mk. XIV; PG117-124, Mk. X; PG125-134, Mk. XIV; PG135-138, Mk. X; PG139-148, Mk. XIV; PG149-152, Mk. X; PG153-157, 170-174, Mk. XIV; PG175-182, Mk. X; PG183-192, Mk. XIV; PG193-196, Mk. X; PG197-206, Mk. XIV; PG207-210, Mk. X; PG211-215, 227-231, Mk. XIV; PG232-235, Mk. X; PG236-239, Mk. XVIII; PG240-245, Mk. XIV; PG246-249, Mk. XVIII; PG250-253, Mk. X; PG254-257, Mk. XVIII; PG268-265, Mk. X; PG266-269, 282-285, Mk. XIV; PG286-297, Mk. X; PG298-303, Mk. XIV; PG304-326, 338-348, Mk. X; PG349-356, Mk. XVIII; PG357-366, Mk. X; PG367-370, Mk. XVIII; PG371-379, 392-394, Mk. X; PG395-400, Mk. XVIII; PG401-422, Mk. X. The Mk. Xs were produced as B.X, but post-war PF989-991, PG136-137, 152, 176, 233, 262, 265, 287, 292-296, 312, 314-315, 317-318, 341-342, 357, 359, 372-373, 379, 414, 416, 419-420 converted to T.10.

Serial Nos.	*Qty.*	*Aircraft Type*	*Remarks*
PG425-PG610	150	Hawker Hurricane IIB/C	Bomber variant. PG425-456, 469-499, 512-554, 567-610.
PG614-PG922	270	D.H.82A Tiger Moth	PG614-658, 671-716, 728-746 (110) only, built by Morris Motors. PG747-769, 782-824, 837-871, 884-922, cancelled.
PG925-PH535	400	Airspeed A.S.-10 Oxford I	PG925-956, 968-999, PH112-157, 169-215, 227-268, 281-327, 339-379, 391-425, 447-489, 502-535. PH528-535 were renumbered VB861-868 in February 1945.
PH528-PH865	264	Avro 652A Anson C.XII/XIX	A. V. Roe (Yeadon)-built. PH528-569, 582-626, 638-679, 691-735, 747-789, 803-840, Mk. XII; PH841-845, 858-865, Mk. XIX.
PJ660-PJ872	150	Hawker Hurricane XIIA	Built by the Canadian Car & Foundry Corporation. PJ660-695, 711-758, 779-813, 842-872. All were to basic Mk. IIB or IIC standard.
PJ876	1	Junkers Ju 88C-6	Surrendered enemy aircraft. Werke Nr. 360043.
PJ878-PK237	175	Short S.29 Stirling V/IV	PJ878-923, 935-959, 971-999, PK113-158, 171-186, Mk. V; PK225-237, Mk. IV. Built by Short & Harland.
PK240-PK245	3	Supermarine Seafire XV	Prototypes PK240, 243, 245. Ordered as Griffon-engined Seafires.
PK248-PK309	50	Airspeed A.S.-10 Oxford I	PK248-269, 282-309. Many converted post-war to Consuls.
PK312-PL499	800	Supermarine Spitfire IX/22/24	Vickers-Armstrongs (Castle Bromwich)-built. 571 only built. PK312-356, 369-412, 426-435, F.22; PK436-468, cancelled; PK481-525, 539-582, 594-635, 648-677, F.22; PK678-689, 712-726, F.24; PK727-754, 769-811, 828-868, 883-926, 949-990, cancelled; PK991-998, PL123-169, 185-227, 246-288, 313-356, 369-408, 423-466, 488-499, Mk. IX.
PL758-PM676	600	Supermarine Spitfire XI/XIX	351 only built by Vickers-Armstrongs (Chattis Hill and Aldermaston). PL758-799, 823-866, 881-925, 949-998, PM123-168, P.R.XI; PM184-228, 245-288, 302-347, 367-404, 419-461, cancelled; PM462, P.R.XIX; PM478-495, cancelled; PM496-519, 536-581, 596-637, 651-661, P.R.XIX; PM662-676, cancelled.

PM679	1	Focke-Wulf Fw 190A-4	Captured when landed at Manston in error.
PM682-PN164	300	Fairey Barracuda III	Fairey (Heaton Chapel)-built. PM682-723, 738-780, 796-838, 852-897, 913-958, 970-999, PN115-164. PM940, 941, 944 were converted to Mk. V prototypes.
PN167-PN362	150	Handley Page Halifax B.III/A.VII/B.VII	Built by Fairey Aviation. PN167-208, B.III; PN223-267, 285-327, 343-344, as 69 A.VII and 21 B.VII. PN345-362 not completed.
PN365-PN619	200	Handley Page Halifax B.III	Built by the London Aircraft Production Group. PN365-406, 423-460 (80), B.III; PN461-470, 485-527, 540-566, 581-619, cancelled.
PN623-PN996	300	Vickers Warwick V/I	Vickers (Weybridge)-built. PN623-667, 681-696, cancelled; PN697-725, 739-782, 796-825, G.R. V; PN826-839, 853-862, A.S.R. I; PN863-898, 910-952, 964-996, cancelled.
PN999	1	Focke-Wulf Fw 190A-3	Captured enemy aircraft. Served in No. 1426 Flight.
PP103-PP132	30	Short S.25 Sunderland V	Built by Short Bros. PP110, 124, 129, 143 became NZ4105, 4113, 4110, 4119 of the R.N.Z.A.F.
PP135-PP164	30	Short S.25 Sunderland III/V	Built by Blackburn Aircraft. PP135-144, Mk. III—of which PP137, 141, 143-144 were converted to Mk. V; PP145-164 were built as Mk. V.
PP139	1	Supermarine Spitfire F.21	Prototype. Compromised number above.
PP142-PP389	200	Handley Page Halifax VI/VII/VIII	PP142-164 (compromised Sunderland serials above and were re-numbered TW774-796), PP165-187, 203-216, B.VI; PP217-243, C.VIII; PP244-247, A.VII; PP259-296, 308-338, C.VIII; PP339-350, 362-389, A.VII. Many to Civil Register, including conversions to Halton as follows: PP224, 228, 234, 236, 268, 269, 277, 308, 310, 314, 315, 316, 336.
PP391-PP660	200	Fairey Firefly I	PP391-437, 456-497, 523-567, 580-623, 639-660. PP485, 523, 657, to T.3 were among post-war conversions.
PP663-PP918	200	Avro 683 Lancaster I	Vickers-Armstrongs (Castle Bromwich)-built. PP663-695, 713-758, 772-792 (100) only built. PP793-806, 820-866, 880-918, cancelled.

Serial Nos.	Qty.	Aircraft Type	Remarks
PP921-PR334	250	Supermarine Seafire L.III	Built by Westland Aircraft. PP921-957, 969-999, PR115-156, 170-215, 228-271, 285-334.
PR338-PR506	134	Supermarine Seafire F.XV	Built by Cunliffe-Owen. PR338-379, 391-436, 449-479, 492-506.
PR525-PS681	800	Hawker Tempest II	Hawker (Langley)-built. PR525-567, 581-623, 645-689, 713-758, 771-815, 830-876, 889-921 (332) only completed. PR922-928, 941-967, 979-999, PS115-157, 173-215, 229-273, 287-329, 342-387, 408-449, 463-507, 520-563, 579-625, 637-681, cancelled.
PS684-PS935	200	Supermarine Spitfire XIX (Spiteful)	PS684-725, 739-781, 795-830, ordered as Spitefuls, were cancelled. PS831-836, 849-893, 908-935 (79) were built as Spitfire P.R.XIX.
PS936-PW250	1500	Supermarine Spitfire/ Seafire (Original order for Spitfire F.21)	693 Vickers-Armstrongs (Castle Bromwich)-built. Contract had various amendments and cancellations. PS936-943 cancelled; PS944-957, Seafire F.47; PS958-987, PT163-203, 220-229, cancelled; PT335-380, 395-436, 451-498, 523-567, 582-627, 639-683, 697-738, 752-795, 818-859, 873-915, 929-970, 986-999, PV115-160, 174-215, 229-270, 283-327, 341-359, Spitfire L.F.IX (except for PT398, 432, 434, 455, 460, 462-463, 465-466, 470, 473-474, 480-481, 486, 488, 493, 601, 605, 608, 612, 614, 619, 627, 640, 650, 657, 714, 733, 753, 756, 760-761, 764-766, 768, 781, 787, 818, 835, 847, 876, 888, 903-905, 907, 910, 913, 915, 929, 931-932, 941, PV229, 232, 238, 259 (subsequently conv. to L.F.IX), 261, 264, 269, 283-284, 286, 290, 296, 299, 303-304, 308, 312, 318, 321, 324, 343,-344 346, as H.F.IX); PV360-385, and batches between PV399 and PV733, cancelled Spitfires; PV734-739, 752-797, 820-865, 879-919, 934-984, PW112-122, cancelled Seafires; PW134-158, 173-196, 221-250, cancelled Spitfires.

PW255-PW633	224	Short S.29 Stirling IV	PW255-266 (12) built by Short Bros.; PW384-435, 438-465 (80) built by Short & Harland; PW466-479, 493-525, 539-580, 593-599 (Mk. IV), and PW600-633 (Mk. V), cancelled.
PW637-PW897	200	Airspeed Horsa II	Built by Harris Lebus. PW637-678, 693-735, 742-790, 812-847, 862-897.
PW925-PW932	3	Avro 694 Lincoln	Prototypes. PW925, 929, 932.
PW937	1	Miles M.28 Mk. III	Miles No. 4684. Was registered U-0242, and G-AISH was reserved but not taken up.
PW943	1	Handley Page H.P.74 Hermes	Flew as G-AGUB. Later became VX234.
PW947-PX198	125	Miles Martinet T.T.I	PW947-988, PX101-147, 163-198. PW979 was converted to a Queen Martinet.
PX203	1	Cierva W.9	Experimental helicopter to A.M. Specification E.16/43.
PX210-PX446	179	D.H.103 Hornet F.I/III	145 built. PX210-253, 273-288 (60), F.I; PX289-315, 328-369, 383-398 (85), F.III. PX399-425, 440-446, cancelled. PX212 and PX214 were Sea Hornet F.20 prototypes; PX216, F.II prototype; PX230-232, N.F.21 prototypes; PX239, converted to F.20 and then F.21; PX249, modified to P.R.II; PX290, modified to F.IV.
PZ161-PZ476	250	D.H.98 Mosquito F.B.VI	De Havilland (Hatfield)-built. PZ161-203, 217-259, 273-316, 330-358, 371-419, 435-476, F.B.VI—of which PZ251-252, 300-301, 346, 467-470 were converted to F.B.XVIII.
PZ479-PZ727	200	Bristol Beaufighter T.F.X	Cancelled. PZ479-515, 528-569, 583-626, 638-680, 694-727.
PZ730-PZ865	112	Hawker Hurricane IIC (Bomber)	Final Hurricane production. PZ730-778, 791-835, 848-865. PZ865 became G-AMAU.

VICTORY

RA100–VN999

THE character of this series reflects the course of the war in the final years. From RA100, allotted from July 1943 when the Second Front was still nearly a year ahead, there were large orders placed, but by the time production was effected events had overtaken policies and some contracts were modified, cancelled or cut.

SA to SK was reserved for further Lend/Lease deliveries which were, in the event, not necessary. Victory is emphasized by the numbers of captured enemy aircraft taken on charge for evaluation or temporarily utilised as transports.

Serial Nos.	*Qty.*	*Aircraft Type*	*Remarks*
RA356-RA363	3	Fairey Spearfish	Prototypes. RA356, 360, 363, to Air Ministry Specification O.5/43.
RA365-RA493	100	Gloster Meteor F.IV	RA365-398, 413-457, 473-493. RA382 had lengthened nose; RA418 and RA430 had F.R. type nose; RA435 had after-burners; RA490 had F.8 tail and Metrovick F.2/4 Beryl engines; RA491 had Avon and later Atar 101 turbines. RA367, 371, 373, 375, 397, 398, 415, 417, 421, 430, 432, 433, 438, 439, 441, 442, 454, 457, 473, 479 were converted to U.15.
RA500-RA806	250	Avro 683 Lancaster/ 694 Lincoln	201 built by Metropolitan-Vickers. RA500-547, 560-607, 623-627, Lancaster I; RA628-655, Lincoln I; RA656-658, 661-693, 709-724, Lincoln II; RA725-749, 763-786, cancelled Lincolns; RA787-806, Lancaster I.
RA809	1	Baynes Carrier Wing Bat	Experimental aircraft built by Slingsby.
RA812-RB140	200	Slingsby T.7 Cadet TX.I	RA812-841 built by S. Fox & Son and A. Davies Ltd.; RA843-872 built by Otley Motors; RA875-924 built by Slingsby Sailplanes; RA928-968, 980-999, RB112-140, built by Papworth Industries, Cambridgeshire (except for RA939, 941, 943, 945, 947, 949, 957, 995, 997, 999, RB113, 115, 117, 119, 121, 123, 125, 127, by Enham Industries).
RB140-RB189	50	Supermarine Spitfire F.XIV	Ordered in August 1943. RB140 compromised number above.
RB192-RB512	255	Hawker Typhoon IB	RB192-235, 248-289, 303-347, 361-408, 423-459, 474-512. RB379 was the only Typhoon shipped to Russia.
RB515-BR987	373	Supermarine Spitfire/ Spiteful	RB515-525, 527-531, 535 (17) built as Spiteful F.14; RB526, cancelled Spiteful; RB532-534, 536-557, 571-615, 628-669, 683-725, 738-783, 796-843, 857-898, 912-953, 965-987, cancelled Spitfires.
RD130-RD867	500	Bristol 156 Beaufighter T.F.X	Bristol (Weston)-built. RD130-176, 189-225, 239-285, 298-335, 348-396, 420-468, 483-525, 538-580, 685-728, 742-

			789, 801-836, 849-867. Conversions to T.T.10 post-war were: RD515, 545, 546, 548, 564, 566, 573, 577, 688, 693, 694, 708, 710, 747, 751, 752, 754, 758, 759, 761, 763, 764, 767, 771, 778-781, 783 788 802, 806, 807, 809, 811, 812, 814, 815, 821, 828, 831, 832, 849, 850, 851, 854, 855, 859, 860, 862, 864, 867.
RD869-RD998	40	Supermarine Sea Otter A.S.R.II	RD869-898, RD913-922.
RE100-RF119	700	Avro 683 Lancaster/ 694 Lincoln	A. V. Roe-built. RE100-114, cancelled; RE115-140, 153-188, 200-222, 225-226, Lancaster B.III (built at Yeadon); RE227-257, Lincoln I (built at Chadderton); RE258-268, 281-288, Lincoln I (built at Yeadon); RE289-325, 338-380, 393-424, Lincoln B.2 (built at Chadderton). RE290, converted to Mk. I; RE339/418, Theseus test-beds. RE425-435, 449-493, 518-561, 575-605, 621-670, 683-726, 740-785, 798-839, 853-895, 918-955, 967-999, RF111-119, cancelled Lincolns.
RF120-RF577	370	Avro 683 Lancaster/ 694 Lincoln	Ordered from Armstrong Whitworth Aircraft. RF120-161, 175-197, Lancaster B.I; RF198-216, 229-273, 286-326, Lancaster B.III; RF329-332, Lincoln B.II; RF333-334, Lincoln B.I; RF335-370, 383-427, 440-485, 498-539, 553-577, Lincoln B.II.
RF580-RF966	300	D.H.98 Mosquito F.B.VI	Built by Standard Motors. RF580-625, 639-681, 695-736, 749-793, 818-859, 873-915, 928-966.
RF969-RG318	200	D.H.98 Mosquito P.R.XVI/34	De Havilland (Hatfield)-built. RF969-999, RG113-158, 171-175 (82), P.R.XVI; RG176-215, 228-269, 283-318 (118), P.R.34—of which RG176-178, 181, 189, 194, 195, 198, 201, 202, 240, 259, 265, 268, were converted to P.R.34A. RG171-173 were hooked for the Royal Navy. RF996, off-set to the U.S.A.A.F.; RF991, RG129, 134, 143, 150, to the South African Air Force.
RG324	1	Armstrong Whitworth A.W.52G	Prototype flying-wing glider.
RG327 & RG333	2	Miles M.38 Messenger	Prototypes built at Woodley.

Serial Nos.	Qty.	Aircraft Type	Remarks
RG345-RG879	400	Handley Page Halifax B.III/A.VII/B.VII	Built by the English Electric Co. RG345-390, 413-446 (80), B.III; RG447-458, 472-479 (20), A/B.VII; RG480-513, 527-568, 583-625, 639-679, 693-736, 749-790, 813-853, 867-879 (300), B.VI.
RG882-RH365	300	Miles M.25 Martinet/ M.50 Queen Martinet	RG882-929, 948-997, Martinet for the Royal Air Force; RH113-121, Martinet for the Royal Navy; RH122-148, 162-192, Queen Martinet for the Royal Air Force (except RH169, 182, 185, 186 for the Royal Navy); RH193-205, 218-259, 273-315, 329-365, cancelled.
RH368-RH680	250	Miles M.38 Messenger	21 only built for R.A.F. RH368-378, built at Reading; RH379-409, cancelled; RH420-429, built at Newtownards, Northern Ireland; RH430-468, 483-525, 539-580, 595-635, 648-680, cancelled in January 1944.
RH742-RH851	80	Bristol 164 Brigand 1	RH742-754, T.F.1/F.1—of which RH745 was non-standard with triple fins; RH755, T.F.1 converted to B.1; RH756, B.1; RH757-758, B.1 converted to T.4 then T.5; RH759, B.1; RH760, B.1 converted to T.4; RH761, B.1; RH762, B.1 converted to T.4 then T.5; RH763, B.1 converted to MET.3; RH764, B.1; RH765-769, B.1 converted to T.4; RH770, B.1; RH771, B.1 converted to T.4; RH772, B.1; RH773, T.F.1; RH774, B.1 converted to T.4 then T.5; RH775, B.1 converted to T.4; RH776-777, 792-793, B.1; RH794, B.1 converted to T.4; RH795, B.1; RH796, T.F.1 modified to B.1; RH797, B.1, prototype conversion to T.4 then T.5; RH798, B.1; RH799, B.1 converted to T.4; RH800, B.1 converted to T.4 then T.5; RH801, B.1 converted to T.4; RH802 B.1, converted to T.4 then T.5; RH803, B.1; RH804, B.1 converted to T.4 then T.5; RH805-808, B.1 converted to T.4; RH809-812,

			B.1; RH813, B.1 converted to T.4 then T.5; RH814-819, B.1; RH820-821, B.1 to Pakistan Air Force as N-1125-1126; RH822-825, B.1; RH826, B.1 converted to T.4 then T.5; RH827-828, B.1; RH829, B.1 converted to T.4 then T.5; RH830, B.1; RH831-832, B.1 converted to T.4 then T.5; RH850-851, B.1.
RJ111-RJ231	100	Airspeed A.S.51 Horsa I	Airspeed (Christchurch)-built. RJ111-143, 150-196, 212-231.
RJ245-RJ359	100	Airspeed A.S.51 Horsa I	Built by Harris Lebus. RJ245-287, 290-316, 330-359.
RJ362/G	1	Bell 27 Airacomet	U.S.A.A.F. YP-59A.
RJ759-RK323	300	Fairey Barracuda III	RJ759-799, 902-948, 963-966 (92) built by Boulton Paul. RJ967-999, RK111-158, 172-215, 228-269, 283-323 cancelled.
RK328-RK784	300	Fairey Barracuda III/V	Fairey (Heaton Chapel)-built. RK328-369, 382-428, 441-485, 498-523 (160), Mk. III; RK530-542, 558-574 (30), Mk. V. Nos. to RK784 cancelled.
RK787 & RK791	2	Short Sturgeon I	Prototypes to A.M. Spec. S.11/43, built by S. & H.
RK798-RK926	100	Supermarine Spitfire IX	Vickers-Armstrongs (Castle Bromwich)-built. RK798-819, 835-868, 883-926, L.F.IX (except RK798, 860, 901, 908, 911-912, 916-917, 924, H.F.IX).
RK929-RL390	282	D.H.98 Mosquito N.F.30/36	De Havilland (Leavesden)-built. RK929-954, N.F.30; RK955-960, 972-999, RL113-158, 173-215, 229-268, N.F.36. RL248 was N.F.38 prototype. RL269-273, 288-329, 345-390, cancelled. RL248 N.F.38 prototype.
RL936-RL986	40	D.H.89A Dominie I/II	Built by Brush Coachworks Ltd. D.H. Nos. 6918-6957, RL936-946, Mk. I; RL947-968, 980-986, Mk. II.
RM160-RM230	100	Percival Proctor IV	Built by F. Hills & Son. RM160-197, 219-230 (50) only produced. RM231-257, 273-295 (50), cancelled.
RM298-RM612	250	D.H.82A Tiger Moth	Cancelled. RM298-335, 348-389, 405-448, 463-507, 520-566. 579-612.
RM615-RN221	406	Supermarine Spitfire XIV/XIX	RM615-625, F.XIV; RM626-647, P.R.XIX; RM648-656, 670-713, 726-770, 783-825, 839-887, 901-943, 957-999, RN113-160, 173-221, Mk. XIV or XIVE produced as F.XIV/XIVE except RM786, RN204, 217-221 F.R.XIV.

Serial Nos.	Qty.	Aircraft Type	Remarks
RN228	1	Messerschmitt Bf 109G-6	Captured German aircraft.
RN236	1	Macchi C.202	Captured Italian aircraft.
RN241 & RN244	2	Fairey Spearfish	To Air Ministry Specification O.5/43. RN244 was not flown.
RN264-RN306	40	Short S.25 Sunderland V	RN264-273 (10) built by Short Bros.; RN277-306 (30) built by Blackburn Aircraft.
RN309-RN520	175	Airspeed A.S.58 Horsa II	Airspeed (Christchurch)-built. RN309-349, 362-405, 418-459, 473-520.
RN523-RN941	325	Airspeed A.S.51 Horsa I	Built by Harris Lebus. RN523-568, 583-625, 638-679, 693-738, 752-795, 809-850, 865-902, 918-941.
RN959-RP299	167	Bristol Buckingham/ Buckmaster	Ordered as Buckingham. RN959-999, RP113-121, cancelled; RP122-156, 170-215, 228-246 (100), built as Buckmaster I; RP283-299, cancelled.
RP312-RR178	600	Vickers Wellington X/XVIII	226 Vickers (Blackpool)-built. RP312-358, 373-415, 428-469, 483-526, 538-561, 565-590, Mk. X (except RP330-335, 348-351, 392-395, 412-415, 428-429, Mk. XVIII); RP591-606, 619-663, 677-718, 735-778, 791-835, 848-889, 903-947, 959-999, RR113-156, 169-178 (374), cancelled. The Mk. Xs were produced as B.X, but post-war RP312, 314, 316, 317, 319-323, 325, 328, 329, 341, 352, 353, 355, 375, 377, 382-389, 391, 587, were converted to T.10. RP468 had tail boom radar and became G-ALUH.
RR181-RR265	73	Supermarine Spitfire IX/XVI	Vickers-Armstrongs (Castle Bromwich)-built. RR181-205, L.F.IX; RR206 H.F.IX; RR207-208, L.F.IX; RR209, H.F.IX; RR210-211, L.F.IX; RR212-213, 226-227, L.F. XVI; RR228, H.F.IX; RR229-230, L.F.XVI; RR231-232, H.F.IX; RR233, cancelled; RR234, L.F.XVI; RR235, H.F.IX; RR236, L.F.XVI; RR237, L.F.IX; RR238-239, H.F.IX; RR240, L.F.XVI; RR241, H.F.IX; RR242-243, L.F.XVI; RR244 H.F.IX; RR245, L.F.XVI; RR246, H.F.IX; RR247-250, L.F.XVI; RR251-252,

			H.F.IX; RR253, L.F.IX; RR254, H.F.IX; RR255-257, L.F.XVI; RR258-260, H.F.IX; RR261, L.F.XVI; RR262, H.F.IX; RR263, L.F.XVI; RR264, H.F.IX; RR265, L.F.XVI.
RR270-RR319	50	D.H.98 Mosquito T.III	De Havilland (Leavesden)-built.
RR321-RR906	450	Airspeed A.S.10 Oxford I	RR321-367, 380-382 (50) only built by Airspeed. RR383-425, 438-480, 495-536, 549-590, 613-656, 666-708, 723-766, 779-819, 835-880, 892-906, cancelled.
RR915 & RR919	2	D.H.103 Hornet	Prototypes to Air Ministry Specification F.12/43.
RR923-RR995	60	General Aircraft G.A.L.49 Hamilcar I	Group built. RR923-959, 973-995. RR925, 926, 929, 935, 936, 943, 944, 948, 949, 953, 956, 973, 978, converted to Mk. X. Delivered from December 1944.
RR997-RR998	2	Lockheed Lodestar II	Ex-U.S.A.A.F. 42-56018 and 56019. Originally allotted FS737-738.
RS102-RS225	100	Avro 694 Lancaster B.IV/V (Lincoln)	Cancelled order with Vickers-Armstrongs (Castle Bromwich). RS102-147, 159-189, 203-225.
RS227-RS497	200	Handley Page Halifax	Cancelled order with Fairey Aviation. RS227-258, 273-305, 318-358, 375-418, 433-459, 475-497.
RS501-RS633	109	D.H.98 Mosquito F.B.VI	De Havilland (Hatfield)-built. RS501-535, 548-580, 593-633.
RS637-RT123	300	D.H.98 Mosquito VI/35	75 built by Airspeed. RS637-680, 693-698 (50), F.B.VI; RS699-723 (25), B.35—of which RS701, 702, 704, 706-710, 712, 713, 715-720, 722 were converted to T.T.35. Cancelled numbers were RS724-725, 739-779, 795-836, 849-893, 913-948, 960-999. RT105-123.
RT140-RT456	240	Avro 683 Lancaster I	Cancelled order with Vickers-Armstrongs (Chester). RT140-183, 197-228, 245-290, 315-350, 362-403, 417-456.
RT458-RT644	150	Taylorcraft Auster V	RT458-499, 513-540, 553-582, 595-644.
RT646	1	Supermarine Seafang 32	Prototype. Cancelled.
RT651 & RT656	2	Blackburn YA-1 Firecrest	Prototypes to Air Ministry Specification S.28/43. RT656 not completed.
RT665 & RT668	2	Airspeed A.S.57 Ambassador	Prototypes. Nos. allotted for G-AGUA/KRD but not used.

Serial Nos.	*Qty.*	*Aircraft Type*	*Remarks*
RT670-RT750	70	Avro 683 Lancaster B.VII	30 built by Austin Motors as RT670-699; RT700-701, 713-750 cancelled.
RT753-RT999	200	Handley Page H.P.71 Halifax A.VII/A.IX	150 built by Handley Page. RT753-757 (5), A.VII; RT758-799, 814-856, 868-908, 920-938 (145), A.IX. RT939-958, 970-999 cancelled. RT793, 846, 852, 888, 901, 907, 938, became 1156, 1155, 1159, 1157, 1160, 1162, 1161 of the Royal Egyptian Air Force.
RV104-RV290	150	Handley Page H.P.61 Halifax B.III	Cancelled order with the London Aircraft Production Group. RV104-145, 158-198. 213-248, 260-290.
RV295-RV367	60	D.H.98 Mosquito B.XVI/B.35	De Havilland (Hatfield)-built, RV295-326, 340-363 (56), B.XVI; RV364-367 (4), B.35—of which RV348-350, 365, 366, 367 were conv. to T.T.35.
RV370-RX151	1500	Supermarine Spitfire	Vickers-Armstrongs (Castle Bromwich) order considerably amended. RV370-445 and allocations to RV895 cancelled; RV896-905, 918-959, 971-999, RW113-156, 168-209, 225-258, 273-315, 328-343, cancelled August 1944. 40 only built: RW344-359, 373-396, as L.F.XVI. Allocations to RX151 cancelled.
RX156-RX530	300	Supermarine Seafire L.III	160 built by Westland Aircraft. RX156-194, 210-256, 268-313, 326-353. Numbers to RX530, including RX428-469, cancelled.
RX534-RX583	50	Airspeed A.S.58 Horsa II	Airspeed (Christchurch)-built. Delivered from March 1945.
RX595-RZ408	550	Airspeed A.S.51/58 Horsa I/II	Built by Harris Lebus. RX595-634, 647-688, 700-717 (100), Mk. I; RX718-735, 749-779, 792-835, 848-889, 902-937, 949-998, RZ112-156, 170-203, 215-259, 280-325, 338-380, 393-408 (450), Mk. II.
RZ410-RZ581	100	General Aircraft G.A.L. Hamilcar I	RZ410-431 only built. RZ413, 430, 431, converted to Mk. X. Numbers to RZ581 cancelled.
SL541-SL798	263	Supermarine Spitfire L.F.IX/L.F.XVI	131 Vickers-Armstrongs (Castle Bromwich)-built. SL541-579, 593-624, L.F.XVI; SL625-635, 648-665, L.F.IX—of which 24 went to Czechoslovakia; SL666-690, 713-745, L.F.XVI. SL572, 593, 667,

			677, 682-684, 686, 714, 716, 722-723, 726, 729-732, 734-744, 746-747, 759-798, 812-857, 873-889, cancelled.
SL890-SM698	537	Supermarine Spitfire L.F.IX/L.F.XVI	400 Vickers-Armstrongs (Castle Bromwich)-built. SL890-915, 928-959, 971-999, SM112-134, cancelled; SM135-150, 170-177, L.F.IX; SM178-213, 226-258, 273-316, 329-369, 383-427, L.F.XVI; SM441-463, L.F.IX; SM464-488, 503-516, L.F.XVI; 517-548, 563-597, 610-645, L.F.IX (except SM567, L.F.XVI); SM646-648, 663-671, L.F.-XVI; SM672-698 cancelled.
SM700-SM701	2	D.H.98 Mosquito N.F.XIII	HK535 and HK536 renumbered.
SM706	1	Consolidated Catalina	" Guba " (ex-NC777) renumbered from AM256 (ex-G-AGBJ).
SM801-SM809	3	Gloster G.A.1/2	Prototypes SM801, SM805, SM809 to Air Ministry Specification E.1/44. SM801 (G.A.1) and SM805 (G.A.1) not built. SM809 (G.A.2) built but damaged in transit by road to Boscombe Down for test and was not flown.
SM812-SM997	150	Supermarine Spitfire XIV/XVIII	132 built. SM812-842, F.XIV; SM843-845, F.R.XVIII; SM858-875, cancelled; SM876-899, 913-938, F.R.XIV; SM939-956, 968-997, F.XVIII. SM990-991 to Royal Indian Air Force.
SN102-SN416	250	Hawker Tempest F.V Series II (Conversions later to T.T.5)	SN102-146, 159-190, 205-238, 253-296, 310-355 (201) built. SN368-416 cancelled. Conversions to T.T.5 were: SN127, 146, 209, 215, 219, 227, 232, 259-261, 271, 273-276, 293, 317, 321, 326, 329 (prototype conversion), 331-333, 340, 342, 346, 354. SN354 was fitted with two 40 mm. cannon.
SP136-SP355	70	Supermarine Seafire	Built by Cunliffe-Owen. SP136-168, 181-197, F.XV; SP323-327, 341-355, F.XVII.
SR376-SR389	14	Boeing Fortress II	Lend/Lease: ex-U.S.A.A.F., supplied for No. 214 Squadron early in 1944.
SR392	1	Miles M.39B " Libellula "	Tandem wing research aircraft, ex-U-0244.
SR395-SR400	6	Supermarine Spitfire P.R.X	Ordered in February 1944 and delivered from April 1944.

Serial Nos.	Qty.	Aircraft Type	Remarks
SR406-SR440	34	North American NA-104/111 Mustang III (P-51B/C)	SR406-438, 440 to R.A.F. from the U.S.A.A.F. Respective U.S. Nos:— 43-12162, 12407, 12412, 12473, 12484, 12427, 70114, 12189, 12177, 7039, 6831, 12155, 12188, 12456, 12480, 12399; 42-10663 106683, 106630; 106687; 43-7071, 7144, 5595, 7171, 6829, 12420, 7152, 7135; 42-103209, 106478, 106431; 43-7007, 12420, 7159.
SR446-SR645	140	Supermarine Seafire XV	Built by Westland Aircraft. SR446-493, 516-547, 568-611, 630-645, as F.XV. SR451, 462, 470, 471, 534, 642, became UB401, 414, 417, 405, 407, 403 with the Burmese Air Force.
SR661 & SR666	2	Hawker Sea Fury X	Prototypes, ordered 22.3.44.
SR707-SR907	150	Avro 694 Lancaster B.IV/V (Lincoln)	Cancelled order to Vickers-Armstrongs (Castle Bromwich). SR707-749, 766-790, 814-851, 864-907.
SR910-SS338	250	Bristol 156 Beaufighter T.F.X	10 only built: SR910-919, of which seven were converted to T.T.10 as follows: SR911-914, 916, 917, 919. Numbers to SS338 cancelled.
SS341-ST475	800	Avro 694 Lincoln B.I/II (ordered as Lancaster B.IV/B.V	A. V. Roe (Yeadon). SS341-386, 399-435, 449-480, 493-535, 549-589, 603-650, 664-698, cancelled. SS713-714, B.I; SS715-718, B.II (6) only built by A. V. Roe at Yeadon. SS719-758, 773-815, 828-869, 882-925, 937-968, 980-999, ST113-157, 171-215, 228-269, 283-327, 339-369, 381-425, 438-475, cancelled.
ST477-ST790	250	Avro Lancaster/ Lincoln	Cancelled order with Metropolitan-Vickers. ST477-513, 528-569, 583-627, 641-680, 693-735, 748-790.
ST794-SV341	350	Handley Page Halifax B.VI	ST794-818 (25) only built by English Electric as B.VI or G.R.VI, but ST794, 796, 798, 801-804, 807, 809-813, 815, 817, 818 were converted to Met.VI. ST795, 797, 799, 800 went to the French Air Force. Cancelled numbers were ST819-835, 848-890, 905-946, 958-999, SV113-158, 173-215, 228-269, 280-315, 328-341.
SV344-SV736	300	Handley Page Halifax A.VII	Cancelled order with Rootes Securities. SV344-388, 401-

			435, 448-479, 493-535, 548-583, 595-638, 653-695, 715-736.
SV739-SW240	300	Miles Monitor	Cancelled. SV739-768, 783-815, 828-869, 881-923, 935-973, 985-999, SW113-158, 173-198, 215-240.
SW243-SW279	37	Avro 683 Lancaster B.I	Built by Metropolitan-Vickers but assembled by A. V. Roe at Woodford. SW244 had saddle tank fitted.
SW283-SW316	34	Avro 683 Lancaster B.III/I	Built by Armstrong Whitworth Aircraft. SW283-295, B.III—of which all were converted to A.S.R.III and all except SW290-292 were subsequently converted to G.R.III; SW296-297, B.I; SW298-316, B.I (F.E.).
SW319-SW377	47	Avro 683 Lancaster B.III	A. V. Roe (Yeadon)-built. SW319-345, 358-377. SW342, 6-engined experimental with Armstrong Siddeley Mamba and Adder in nose and tail. SW319-320, 324-327, 329-330, 334, 336-338, 344, 361-377 were converted to A.S.R.III and the majority of these later became G.R.III.
SW386-SW772	300	Hawker Typhoon IB	Built by Gloster Aircraft. SW386-428, 443-478, 493-537, 551-596, 620-668, 681-716, 728-772. Deliveries from January 1945, except for SW408, deleted from contract.
SW777	1	Supermarine Spitfire	Prototype, completed to P.R.XIX standard.
SW781-SX546	500	Supermarine Seafire F.15/F.17	322 built by Westland Aircraft. SW781-828, 844-875, F.XV (standard fuselage); SW876-879, 896-921, F.XV (rear-view fuselage); SW922-939, 951-985, cancelled; SW986-993, SX111-139, 152-201, 220-256, 271-316, 332-370, 386-389, F.XVII; SX390-432, 451-490, 503-546, cancelled. SW799, 817, 863, 899 became UB402, 412, 404, 420 of the Burmese Air Force.
SX549	1	Supermarine Spitfire F.21	Prototype. Ordered 27.4.44 from Cunliffe-Owen Aircraft Ltd. Delivered in November, 1944.
SX558-SX921	280	Avro 683 Lancaster	Cancelled. Vickers-Armstrongs (Chester) order. SX558-589, 605-648, 663-698, 713-759, 772-813, 828-863, 879-921.

Serial Nos.	Qty.	Aircraft Type	Remarks
SX923-SZ493	350	Avro 694 Lincoln B.2	60 built by Armstrong Whit-worth Aircraft. SX923-958, 970-993. SX971 had Derwent under belly, SX973 had Proteus installed, SX974 Nomad installed and cut-away bomb bay. SX994-999, SZ113-158, 172-215, 228-259, 275-306, 319-363, 380-415, 429-471, 488-493, cancelled.
SZ559-SZ611	40	Short S.25 Sunderland G.R.V	28 built by Short & Harland a SZ559-584, 598-599; SZ600 611, cancelled. SZ561 and SZ584 became NZ4114-411 of R.N.Z.A.F.
SZ958-TA724	500	D.H.98 Mosquito F.B.VI/N.F.XIX/ B.35	De Havilland (Hatfield)-built SZ958-999, TA113-122 (52) F.B.VI; TA123-156, 169-198 215-249, 263-308, 323-35 (180), N.F.XIX; TA369-38 (20), F.B.VI; TA389-413 425-449 (50), N.F.XIX TA469-508, 523-560, 575-60 (107), F.B.VI; TA604-611 cancelled; TA614-616 (3) P.R.XVI; TA617-618, 633 670, 685-724 (80), B.35—o which TA633, 634, 637, 639 641, 642, 647, 651, 660, 662 664, 669, 685, 699, 703, 71 718, 719, 720, 722, 724 wer converted to T.T.35. TA65 converted to P.R.35.
TA738-TE578	1884	Supermarine Spitfire H.F.IX/L.F.IX/ L.F.XVI (*N.B. Basically the Mk. XVI was the Mk. IX with American-built Merlin* 266 *in place of the British Merlin* 66 *of the Mk. IX*)	1,492 Vickers-Armstrong (Castle Bromwich)-built TA738-780, 793-840, 854-888 905-948, 960-999, TB115-150 TB168-197 (TB194 cancelled) 213-256, 269-308, 326-34 352-396, 413-450, 464-50 515-549, 563-598, 613-65 674-718, 733-759, 771-80 824-868, 883-925, 938-95 971-999, TD113-158, 175-21 229-267, 280-325, 338-37 395-408; batches TD409-95 cancelled; TD952-958, 97 999, TE115-158, 174-215, 228 259, 273-315, 328-359, 375 408 (TE386 cancelled), 434 480 (TE472 cancelled), 49 535, 549-578.
TE580 & TE583	2	Handley Page H.P.67 Hastings	Prototypes to Air Ministr Specification C.3/44.
TE587-TE999	370	D.H.98 Mosquito F.B.VI	Built by Standard Motor TE587-628, 640-669, 683-70 708-725 to Royal Nav

			TE738-780, 793-830, 848-889, 905-932, F.B.VI. TE933-944, 958-999, cancelled.
TF209	1	Messerschmitt Me 410A-3	Captured in Italy. Damaged in June 1944.
TF895-TG129	100	Hawker Sea Fury F.B.10/11	TF895-928, 940-955 (50), F.B.10; TF956-973, 985-999, TG113-129 (50), F.B.11.
TG263-TG271	3	Saro SR/A1	Prototypes TG263, 267, 271 to Air Ministry Specification E.6/44. TG263 flew as G-12-1.
TG274-TG448	120	D.H.100 Vampire F.1	Built by the English Electric Co. to an order placed in May 1944. TG274-315, 328-355, 370-389, 419-448. TG274/G, trials; TG275, F.3 prototype; TG276, modified to F.2; TG278, Ghost engine; TG280, second F.2 prototype; TG281, variously modified; TG283 and TG306, converted to DH108; TG286, F.21 prototype; TG328, converted to F.20. 23 off-set to French Air Force.
TG499-TG624	100	Handley Page H.P.67 Hastings C.I	TG499-537, 551-587, 601-624. TG517, 565-567, 616, 620-624 converted to MET.1—of which TG517 was later modified to T.5.
TG758-TG945	150	Avro 694 Lincoln	Cancelled order with Austin Motors Ltd. TG758-799, 813-856, 870-908, 921-945.
TH186-TH446	200	Handley Page H.P.61 Halifax B.VI	Cancelled. TH186-227, 241-287, 302-338, 351-392, 415-446.
TH450-TH974	376	Vickers Wellington X	Cancelled order with Vickers (Blackpool). TH450-496, 521-560, 574-598, 612-647, 661-686, 719-757, 777-815, 829-869, 883-927, 937-974.
TH977-TJ158	69	D.H.98 Mosquito B.35	De Havilland (Hatfield)-built. TH977-999, TJ113-158, B.35—of which TH977, 978, 980, 981, 987, 989-992, 996, 997, TJ113, 114, 116-119, 120, 122, 125-127, 131, 135, 136, 138, 140, 147-149, 154-155, 157, were converted to T.T.35. TH985, 989, TJ124, 145 conv. to P.R 35.
TJ167 & TJ170	2	Douglas Dakota C.2	TJ167 (ex-U.S.A.A.F. 42-6478) became 6252M. TJ170 allotted to Lord Tedder.
TJ187-TJ707	400	Taylorcraft Auster A.O.P.V	TJ187-228, 241-276, 290-325, 338-380, 394-438, 451-487, 504-546, 563-607, 621-657, 672-707. TJ707 became Mk.

Serial Nos.	*Qty.*	*Aircraft Type*	*Remarks*
			VI prototype. TJ207 with Queen Bee floats was first Auster floatplane.
TJ714 & TJ717	2	Bristol 166 Buckmaster	Prototypes. Bristol Nos. 12024-12025.
TJ720-TJ909	150	Avro 685 York C.I	Cancelled. TJ720-762, 777-807, 820-866, 881-909.
TK580	1	Saro A.37 Shrimp	G-AFZS, scaled research aircraft. Tested Shetland tail.
TK586 & TK589	2	North American Mustang F.4	TK589 (ex-P-51K 44-13332), for trials 1945.
TK591-TK707	94	D.H.98 Mosquito B.35	TK591-635, 648-656, B.35—of which TK591-594, 596, 599, 603, 604, 605-610, 612, 614, 616, conv. to T.T.35 and TK615, 632, 650 to P.R.35. TK657-679, 691-707 cancelled.
TK714-TK826	90	General Aircraft G.A.L.59 Hamilcar I	TK714-750, 763-791 built. TK792-798, 810-826, cancelled. TK722, 726, 735-738, 741-744, 746-747, to Mk. 10.
TK828-TL735	600	Airspeed A.S.58 Horsa II	Built by Harris Lebus. TK828-869, 882-913, 927-963, 978-999, TL114-157, 173-215, 229-261, 274-312, 328-369, 384-427, 440-481, 495-536, 549-587, 602-643, 659-691, 712-735.
TL773-TM136	199	Supermarine Spitfire IX	Cancelled order with Vickers-Armstrongs (Castle Bromwich). TL773-815, 829-870, 884-916, 930-967, 979-999, TM115-136.
TM163-TM251	77	Supermarine Spitfire	Cancelled order with Vickers-Armstrongs (Castle Bromwich). TM163-205, 218-251.
TM379 & TM383	2	Supermarine Seafire	Prototypes: TM379, F.45; TM383, F.46.
TM944-TN247	150	Handley Page Halifax	Cancelled order with Fairey Aviation. TM944-983, TN101-115, 130-153, 166-213, 225-247.
TN250-TN462	150	Vickers Wellington XIV	Cancelled order with Vickers-Armstrongs (Blackpool). TN250-289, 310-324, 340-363, 380-427, 440-462.
TN466-TN864	300	D.H.98 Mosquito	Cancelled order with Leavesden plant. TN466-497, 510-530, 542-590, 608-640, 652-674, 690-736, 750-789, 802-838, 850-864.
TP181 & TP187	2	Douglas Dakota C.IV	TP187, ex-U.S.A.A.F. C-47A 42-92771 glider pick-up aircraft.
TP190	1	Junkers Ju 88G	Captured. Werke Nr. 712273.
TP195-TP456	300	Supermarine Spitfire XIV/XVIII	206 built. TP195-235, F.R.XVIII; TP236-240, 256, F/F.R.XIV; TP257-298, 313-350, 363-408, 423-456, F.R.XVIII.

TP814	1	Messerschmitt Bf 109G-6/U-2	Captured when landed at Manston in error 21.7.44.
TP819	1	Miles M.17 Monarch	Temporary number for U-0226, later G-AGFW.
TR210	1	Hawker Typhoon IB	Number painted on in error for JR210.
TS261-TS266	4	Short S.29 Stirling IV	Re-numbered on conversion. TS261 was EF454, TS262 was LK562, TS264 was LK512, TS266 was LJ575.
TS291-TS358	50	Slingsby T.7 Cadet TX.1	Gliders: TS291-311, 330-358.
TS363 & TS368	2	Armstrong Whitworth A.W.52	Prototypes.
TS371-TS387	6	Westland Wyvern I	Prototypes/pre-production. TS371, 375, 378, 380, 384, 387, to A.M. Spec. N.11/44.
TS409-TS416	3	Supermarine Attacker	Prototypes. TS409, 413, 416, to Air Ministry Specification E.10/44.
TS422-TS436	12	Douglas Dakota C.III	Ex-U.S.A.A.F. TS422-427, 431-436. TS422, ex-42-100882; TS423, ex-42-100884.
TS439	1	Heinkel He 177A-5	Captured enemy aircraft.
TS444 & TS449	2	D.H.98 Mosquito T.R.33	Prototypes, built at Leavesden for handling trials.
TS459 & TS463	2	Slingsby T.7 Cadet TX.1	Glider.
TS467	1	R.F.D. Dagling	Glider.
TS472	1	Junkers Ju 88S-1	Ex-enemy aircraft.
TS475-TS497	23	Short Sturgeon T.T.2	Short & Harland built. TS475, 479-482 converted to T.T.3.
TS507-TS513	3	General Aircraft G.A.L.56	Tailless research. TS507, 510, 513, had various wing plan forms.
TS515	1	General Aircraft G.A.L.61	Prototype.
TS519-TS539	21	Convair Liberator IV	Converted as follows: TS519-520, B.IV; TS521-523, C.IV; TS524-526, B.IV; TS527, C.IV; TS528, B.IV; TS529-530, C.IV; TS531-532, B.IV; TS533-534, C.IV; TS535, B.IV; TS536, C.IV; TS537, no record; TS538-539, C.IV.
TS543-TS672	100	Short S.29 Stirling V	Cancelled. TS543-592, 605-620, 639-672.
TS789-TS813	60	Avro 685 York C.1	TS789-813 to British Overseas Airways Corporation. TS814-822, 838-863, cancelled.
TS866-TS912	40	Avro Tudor I/II/V	TS866-875, Mk. I (except TS868-869, Mk. IVB); TS883-892, Mk. II (except TS883, Mk. VII); TS893-902, Mk. II (G-AJJS-KB); TS903-908, Mk. V (G-AKBY-CD); TS909-912, Mk. II (G-AKTH-K).
TS915-TT110	50	Fairey Spearfish	TS915-935, 963-990, TT110, cancelled.

Serial Nos.	Qty.	Aircraft Type	Remarks
TT176 & TT181	2	Avro Tudor 1/4C	Ex-G-AGPF/ST. TT176 became VX192. TT181 rebuilt as VX195.
TT186-TT248	30	D.H.103 Sea Hornet	TT186-213, 217-218, F.20/F.R.20; TT187 P.R.22 prototype.
TT191-TT197	3	Vickers Viking	Prototypes to Air Ministry Specification 17/44. Numbers TT191, 194, 197 re-allotted.
TT336-TT343	3	Convair Liberator VI (B-24H)	TT336 (ex-44-10597), converted to B.IV; TT340 (ex-42-94797), converted to B.IV; TT343 (ex-42-51350), converted to C.IV.
TT346 & TT349	2	Grumman Tigercat	U.S. Navy F7F-2N.
TT353-TT974	400	Airspeed A.S.58 Horsa II	15 only, built by Harris Lebus as TT353-367. TT368-393 424-469, 487-536, 568-616, 638-669, 682-707, 747-794, 834-872, 895-940, 952-974, cancelled.
TV100-TV160	50	General Aircraft G.A.L.49 Hamilcar	Cancelled. TV100-112, 124-160.
TV163-TV177	5	Percival P.40 Prentice	Prototypes TV163, 166, 168, 172, 177, to Air Ministry Specification T.23/43.
TV954-TW119	50	D.H.98 Mosquito T.III	De Havilland(Leavesden)-built, TV954-984, TW101-119.
TW227-TW295	50	D.H.98 Sea Mosquito T.R.33	De Havilland (Leavesden)-built. TW227-257, 277-295. TW240, T.R.37 prototype. TW230/G for Highball trials.
TW362-TW642	200	Taylorcraft Auster A.O.P.V/VI	TW362-402, 433-478, 496-520, A.O.P.V; TW521-522, A.O.P.V Seaplane; TW523-540, 561-598, 613-642, A.O.P.VI.
TW647-TW671	25	Avro 683 Lancaster B.I(F.E.)	Built by A.W.A. Delivered June/July 1945.
TW677-TW754	56	Fairey Firefly I/IV	TW677-679, F.I; TW687-699, 715-754, F.R.IV. TW695, experimental contra-prop version.
TW758-TW769	12	Convair Liberator B.VI	Delivered to Middle East, January 1945.
TW774-TW796	23	Handley Page Halifax A.VII	PP142-164 renumbered. Delivered early 1945.
TW806-TW857	50	Fairey Barracuda	Cancelled order placed with Boulton Paul. TW806-837, 840-857.
TW858-TW911	50	Avro 683 Lancaster B.I	Built by A.W.A. TW858-873, 878-911, mostly to Far East standard.
TW915-TW929	15	Avro 683 Lancaster B.I	Built by Metropolitan-Vickers but to Vickers-Armstrongs (Chester) for assembly.

TX145-TX150	3	Gloster G.A.2/3	Prototypes TX145 (G.A.2), TX148 (G.A.2), TX150 (G.A.3).
TX154-TX257	100	Avro 652A Anson C.XIX	A. V. Roe (Yeadon)-built. TX154-197, 201-235, 237-257—of which 13 were diverted to civil use as follows: TX201-202, 240-245, 247, 250-252, 255. Deliveries as Series 1 except TX223, 253-254, 256-257 Series 2.
TX263-TX273	11	Avro 683 Lancaster III	A. V. Roe (Manchester)-built.
TX274-TX290	14	Avro 691 Lancastrian IV	A. V. Roe (Manchester)-built. TX274-276, 280-282 became G-AGWG-L.
TX293	1	Short S.25 Sunderland G.R.V	Used at M.A.E.E., Felixstowe.
TX300-TX319	20	D.H.89A Dominie II	All sold back to de Havilland.
TX374	1	Bristol 164 Brigand T.F.1	Fourth prototype in lieu of MX997.
TX386-TX804	300	Gloster Meteor III	Cancelled. TX386-428, 531-567, 572-614, 618-645, 649-688, 693-737, 739-776, 779-804.
TX807	1	D.H.100 Vampire F.II	Sent to Australia.
TX974-TZ240	157	Supermarine Spitfire XIV/XVIII	TX974-998, F.XIV; TZ102-149, 152-176, 178-199, F.R.XIV; TZ200-205, 210-240, F.R.XVIII.
TZ483-TZ569	72	Avro 685 York 1	Cancelled. TZ483-531, 547-569.
TZ598-TZ738	100	Supermarine Spitfire P.R.XIX	Cancelled. TZ598-637, 658-692, 714-738.
TZ747-VA195	178	Supermarine Spitfire L.F.XVI	Cancelled. Vickers-Armstrongs (Castle Bromwich). TZ747-791, 815-843, 866-898, 921-957, 969-998, VA192-195.
VA201-VA250	50	Supermarine Spitfire	Cancelled. L.F./F.22 ordered from Vickers-Armstrongs (Castle Bromwich).
VA278-VA336	30	Percival Proctor	Cancelled. VA278-291, 321-336. To have been built by F. Hills & Son.
VA359-VA368	10	Bristol 166 Buckmaster T.1	Main delivery to Far East, April 1946.
VA386-VA436	30	Hawker Tempest F.II	Ordered from the Bristol Aeroplane Co. as VA386-395, 417-436. Cancelled.
VA701-VA750	50	Convair Catalina G.R.IIA	Canadian-Vickers-built. 36 produced. R.C.A.F. Nos. 9701-9736.
VA871-VA948	50	D.H.98 Mosquito T.III	De Havilland (Leavesden)-built. VA871-876 to R.A.F.; VA877-881 to Royal Navy; VA882-894, 923-928 to R.A.F. VA929-948 cancelled.
VA962-VB849	500	D.H.103 Hornet F.1/P.R.II	Five only built as P.R.II: VA962-966; remainder cancelled: VA967-997; VB108-135, 154-196, 213-257, 280-299, 324-358, 379-394, 409-

Serial Nos.	*Qty.*	*Aircraft Type*	*Remarks*
			436, 452-497, 525-558, 584-596, 621-653, 682-699, 716-748, 764-793, 808-849.
VB673	1	Avro 691 Lancastrian	Prototype conversion of Lancaster airframe. Became G-AGLF. Compromised above.
VB852	1	Convair Liberator VI	U.S.A.A.F. 42-50744, converted to C.IV in January 1945.
VB857	1	Hawker Fury X	Third prototype, built by Boulton Paul and assembled by Hawker.
VB861-VB869	9	Airspeed A.S.10 Oxford T.II	Airspeed-built. VB861-868, ex-PH528-535. VB862-869 sold to makers before delivery.
VB880-VB889	10	Short S.25 Sunderland G.R.V	Built by Blackburn at Dumbarton. VB880, 881, 883 became NZ4111, 4112, 4107 of R.N.Z.A.F.
VB893 & VB895	2	Supermarine Seafang F.32	Prototypes to Air Ministry Specification N.5/45.
VB904	1	Convair Liberator C.IV	U.S.A.A.F. 42-52766, handed over in U.K. Conv. to Mk. VI.
VD120	1	Slingsby Falcon	Glider for Air Training Corps.
VD121	1	Slingsby T.8 Kirby Tutor	Glider for Air Training Corps.
VD122	1	Schneider Grunau Baby	Glider for Air Training Corps.
VD123-VD124	2	Slingsby T.7 Kirby Cadet	Glider for Air Training Corps.
VD125	1	Slingsby Falcon	Glider for Air Training Corps.
VD126	1	Slingsby T.6 Kite 1	Glider for Air Training Corps.
VD127	1	Slingsby T.8 Kirby Tutor	Glider for Air Training Corps.
VD128	1	Schneider Grunau Baby	Glider for Air Training Corps.
VD129	1	Slingsby T.7 Kirby Cadet	Glider for Air Training Corps.
VD160-VD162	3	Slingsby T.4 Falcon III	Gliders for Air Training Corps.
VD163	1	Primary Nacelle	Glider for Air Training Corps.
VD164	1	R.F.D. Dagling	Glider for Air Training Corps.
VD165	1	Slingsby T.6 Kite 1	Glider for Air Training Corps.
VD166	1	Slingsby T.7 Kirby Cadet	Glider for Air Training Corps.
VD167	1	Slingsby T.8 Kirby Tutor	Glider for Air Training Corps.
VD168	1	Schneider Grunau Baby	Glider for Air Training Corps.
VD169	1	Slingsby T.8 Kirby Tutor	Glider for Air Training Corps.
VD170	1	Slingsby Falcon	Glider for Air Training Corps.
VD171	1	Slingsby T.7 Kirby Cadet	Glider for Air Training Corps.
VD172	1	Schneider Grunau Baby	Glider for Air Training Corps.
VD173-VD174	2	Slingsby T.7 Kirby Cadet	Glider for Air Training Corps.
VD175	1	Slingsby Falcon	Glider for Air Training Corps.

VD176	1	Slingsby T.6 Kite 1	Glider for Air Training Corps.
VD177	1	Slingsby T.7 Kirby Cadet	Glider for Air Training Corps.
VD178	1	Slingsby T.8 Kirby Tutor	Glider for Air Training Corps.
VD179	1	Kirby T.7 Kirby Cadet	Glider for Air Training Corps.
VD180	1	—	Believed glider for A.T.C.
VD181	1	Slingsby T.8 Kirby Cadet	Glider for Air Training Corps.
VD182	1	Schneider Grunau Baby	Glider for Air Training Corps.
VD199	1	Dart Totternhoe	Glider for Air Training Corps.
VD200	1	Slingsby T.6 Kite I	Glider for Air Training Corps.
VD201-VD202	2	Slingsby T.4 Falcon III	Glider for Air Training Corps.
VD203	1	Slingsby T.12 Gull I	Glider for Air Training Corps.
VD204	1	Schneider Grunau Baby IIB	Glider for Air Training Corps.
VD205	1	Slingsby Falcon	Glider for Air Training Corps.
VD206	1	Slingsby T.8 Kirby Tutor	Glider for Air Training Corps.
VD207	1	Slingsby T.9 King Kite	Glider for Air Training Corps.
VD208	1	Slingsby T.8 Kirby Tutor	Glider for Air Training Corps.
VD209	1	Schneider Grunau Baby	Glider for Air Training Corps.
VD210-VD211	2	Slingsby T.7 Kirby Cadet	Gliders for Air Training Corps.
VD212	1	Slingsby T.7 Kirby Cadet	Glider for Air Training Corps. Converted to T.8 standard.
VD213	1	Slingsby T.6 Kite I	Glider for Air Training Corps.
VD214	1	Slingsby T.7 Kirby Cadet	Glider for Air Training Corps.
VD215	1	Schneider Grunau Baby	Glider for Air Training Corps.
VD216	1	Schleicher Rhonbussard	Glider for Air Training Corps.
VD217	1	Slingsby T.8 Kirby Tutor	Glider for Air Training Corps. Ex-BGA368.
VD218	1	Slingsby T.8 Kirby Tutor	Glider for Air Training Corps.
VD219	1	Slingsby Falcon	Glider for Air Training Corps.
VD220	1	—	Believed glider for A.T.C.
VD221	1	Slingsby T.7 Kirby Cadet	Glider for Air Training Corps.
VD222	1	Schneider Grunau Baby	Glider for Air Training Corps; previously PD351.
VD223	1	—	Believed glider for A.T.C.
VD224	1	D.F.S./30 Kranich 2	Glider for Air Training Corps.
VD226	1	Slingsby T.6 Kite II	Glider.
VD238-VD253	16	Avro Lancastrian I	VD238, 241, 253 only built.
VD249	1	Convair Liberator C.IV	Ex-U.S.A.A.F. 44-10533, handed over in U.K.
VD258	1	Messerschmitt Bf 109G	Ex-German aircraft.
VD281-VD299	19	Avro 691 Lancastrian IV	Not built.
VD358 & VD364	2	Messerschmitt Bf 109G	Captured enemy aircraft.
VD490-VE593	600	Supermarine Seafire F.45/F.46/F.47	Cancelled. VD490-499, 521-568, 582-597, 618-653, 679-

Serial Nos.	Qty.	Aircraft Type	Remarks
			696, 714-748, 763-792, 809-856, 869-893, 925-961, 984-999, VE135-162, 176-193. 233-259, 274-296, 328-362, 379-391, 406-447, 462-498, 516-542, 563-593.
VF100-VF110	11	Miles M.50 Queen Martinet	Acquired in 1946. Scrapped in 1947.
VF137-VF167	28	Avro 671 Lancastrian I	VF137-156, 160-167.
VF172	1	Blackburn YA-1 Firecrest	To Air Ministry Specification S.28/43.
VF176-VF200	25	Slingsby T.7 Cadet TX.I	Gliders for Air Training Corps.
VF204	1	Fiat G.55	Captured Italian Aircraft.
VF241	1	Messerschmitt Me 163B	For evaluation.
VF247 & VF251	2	Lockheed Type 14	Served in Middle East.
VF265-VF283	19	D.H.100 Vampire F.1	Built by the English Electric Co. VF268-269 to the F.A.A.
VF300-VF348	49	D.H.100 Vampire F.1/F.III	Built by the English Electric Co. From VF315 built as F.III; VF315 became F.20.
VF482-VF665	144	Taylorcraft Auster A.O.P.VI	VF482-530, 543-582, 600-648, 660-664; VF665, T.7 prototype, became Marshalls M.A.4; VF517, Floatplane; VF565, A.O.P.7; VF516, 543, 628, 635, 636 converted to T.10.
VG471-VG679	150	Supermarine Seafang F.31/32	VG471-478, F.31: VG479-505, not all completed but VG479-480 were built as F.31 and VG481, 482, 486, 488-490, were built as F.32; VG540-589, 602-650, 664-679 cancelled.
VG692-VG703	12	D.H.100 Vampire F.3	Built by the English Electric Co. VG701 became an F.20 of the Royal Navy.
VG919	1	Fieseler Fi 156 Storch	Ex-enemy aircraft.
VG957-VH144	67	Fairey Firefly F.R.4	VG957-999, VH121-144—of which VH959, 961, 962, 967, 974, 981, 993, VH127, 132, converted to T.T.4. Conversions to U.9 included VG964.
VH513	1	Heinkel He 162	Ex-AM65, Werke Nr. 120098.
VH519	1	Messerschmitt Me 262	Werke Nr. 500210. Ex-German aircraft. Air Min 81.
VH523	1	Heinkel He 162A-2	Was Air Min 59.
VH526	1	Heinkel He 162	Ex-AM58 Werke Nr. 120021.
VH530	1	Arado Ar 234	Ex-enemy aircraft.
VH534	1	Kirby T.7 Cadet	Glider.
VH610	1	Junkers Ju 188	Ex-German aircraft.
VH724-VH742	19	Avro 691 Lancastrian C.III	VH737, ex-PD193: VH742, ex-PD194. Remainder of the numbers not taken up.
VH751-VH756	6	Fieseler Fi 156 Storch	Impressed ex-enemy aircraft.
VH890	1	Messerschmitt Me 262	Enemy aircraft for evaluation.

VH901-VH977	50	Fairey Barracuda	Ordered from Boulton Paul. VH901-934, 962-977 cancelled
VH980-VJ118	33	Supermarine Attacker	Cancelled. To A.M.Spec. E.10/44 and E.1/45.
VJ120-VJ413	200	Waco Hadrian II (CG-4A)	Ex-U.S.A.A.F. VJ120-165, 198-222, 239-284, 313-349, 368-413.
VJ416 & VJ421	2	Lockheed Hudson C.III	Ex-British Overseas Airways Corporation G-AGDC/K.
VJ735-VK655	144	Waco Hadrian II (CG-4A)	Ex-U.S.A.A.F. VJ735-781, 821-847, VK573-609, 623-655.
VK874-VK880	3	Arado Ar 234B	VK874, VK877 (ex-AM26), VK880.
VK888	1	Junkers Ju88C-6	Werke No. 621642.
VK893	1	Messerschmitt Me 262A	Tested at Farnborough.
VK895	1	Blohm & Voss Bv 138B	Tested at Felixstowe in February 1946.
VK900 & VK903	2	Bristol Type 170	Prototypes, Ex-G-AGPV/VB.
VL226-VL233	16	Vickers Viking C.1/2	VL226-227 C.1A; VL228-233 C.2; VL237-244 cancelled.
VL245-VL248	4	Vickers Viking C.2	Royal Flight. VL245, Royal staff aircraft; VL246-247, V.V.I.P. standard for Royal Family; VL248, servicing aircraft. VL275 multi-wheel undercarriage experiments.
VL249-VL282	22	Vickers Valetta C.1	VL249, 262-282. VL249, Valetta C.1 prototype. Some conversions to C.2.
VL285-VL363	60	Avro Anson C.19 Series II	VL285-313, 333-363. Mainly for overseas. Last six (VL358-363) diverted for civil use.
VL515-VL516	2	Scottish Aviation A.4/45	VL516 became XE514 Pioneer.
VL522-VL523	2	Auster N	Prototypes for evaluation to A.M. Spec. A.2/45.
VL529-VL531	3	Heston J.C.6	To Air Ministry Specification A.2/45.
VL613-VL625	13	D.H.98 Mosquito P.R.34	De Havilland (Hatfield)-built in 1946. VL625 P.R.34A.
VL726-VL732	7	D.H.98 Mosquito F.B.VI	Airspeed-built. Delivery completed June 1946.
VL892-VL935	4	Boulton Paul P.108 Balliol T.1	Prototypes to Air Ministry Specification T.7/45. VL892, 917, 925, 935.
VL958 & VL963	2	Bristol Type 171 Mk. I	Sycamore prototypes to Air Ministry Specification E.20/45 VL963 was ex-G-ALOU.
VL967-VL986	20	Avro 691 Lancastrian C.2	A. V. Roe (Woodford)-built. Delivered January to March 1946. VL982-986 cancelled.
VL991	1	Junkers Ju 88G	Ex-AM9 Werke Nr. 621965, Scrapped March 1950.
VM109 & VM118	2	Slingsby Kirby Cadet 20	Prototype gliders to Air Ministry Specification TX.8/45.
VM125-VM132	3	Avro 701 Athena	Prototypes, powered as follows: VM125 (Mamba), VM129 (Dart), and VM132 (Mamba).

Serial Nos.	Qty.	Aircraft Type	Remarks
VM143-VM278	26	Bücker Bü 181	VM143, 148, 151, 157, 162, 169, 174, 179, 181, 188, 193, 199, 206, 213, 215, 220, 227, 231, 238, 243, 252, 259, 263, 269, 274, 278, All ex-*Luftwaffe*.
VM286	1	Piper Cub (L-4B)	Ex-U.S.A.A.F. 43-630 Grasshopper.
VM291-VM296	6	Fieseler Fi 156 Storch	Ex-*Luftwaffe* aircraft for No. 83 Group Communication Squadron. Werke Nr. 779, 1576, 2010, 1665, 5746, 2547.
VM305-VM418	95	Avro 652A Anson	VM305, T.20 prototype; VM306, T.22 prototype; VM307-342, VM351-394, VM406-409, C.19; VM410-418, T.20.
VM466	1	Siebel Si 204	Ex-*Luftwaffe* aircraft.
VM472	1	Fieseler Fi 156 Storch	Ex-*Luftwaffe* aircraft for use of G.O.C., 21st Army Group.
VM483	1	Dornier Do 24T	Ex-*Luftwaffe* aircraft for evaluation.
VM489	1	Fieseler Fi 156 Storch	Ex-*Luftwaffe* aircraft for use by No. 26 Squadron.
VM495-VM508	3	Messerschmitt Bf 108	Ex-*Luftwaffe* aircraft. VM495, VM502 and VM508.
VM515-VM696	105	Slingsby T.7 Cadet TX.1 and T.8 Cadet TX.2	Gliders for the Air Training Corps. VM515-559, 583-598, 630-633 (65), T.1; VM634-667, 681-696 (40), T.2.
VM701-738	18	Avro 691 Lancastrian II	VM701-704, 725-738. Deliveries from October 1945.
VM743	1	Blohm & Voss Bv 138	Ex-German aircraft for evaluation, 1946.
VM748 & VM761	2	Arado	Ex-German aircraft for evaluation.
VM768-VM796	29	Bücker Bü 181	Ex-German aircraft.
VM824-VM846	23	Fieseler Fi 156 Storch	Ex-German aircraft.
VM851-VM862	12	Messerschmitt Bf 108	Ex-German aircraft.
VM865-VM874	3	Junkers Ju 88	Ex-German aircraft. VM865, VM870 and VM874.
VM885-VM887	3	Siebel Si 204	Ex-German aircraft.
VM892	1	Junkers Ju 52/3m	Ex-German aircraft.
VM897-VM898	2	Fieseler Fi 156 Storch	Ex-German aircraft.
VM900-VM987	60	Junkers Ju 52/3m	Ex-German aircraft. VM900-932 and VM961-987.
VN101-VN140	40	Siebel Si 204	Ex-German aircraft.
VN143	1	Junkers Ju 188E	Ex-German aircraft.
VN148	1	Schneider Grunau Baby	Ex-German glider.
VN153	1	Heinkel He 162A-2	Ex-German aircraft Air Min 64.
VN158 & VN163	2	Savoia S.M.82	Ex-Italian aircraft.
VN169-VN175	7	Bücker Bü 181	Ex-German aircraft.
VN176-VN177	2	Junkers Ju 52/3m	Ex-German aircraft.
VN266-VN267	2	Fieseler Fi 156 Storch	Ex-German aircraft. Werke Nr. 5987 and 5388.

VN301-VN496	150	Supermarine Spitfire F.24	Originally ordered as F.22. VN301-334, 477-496 (54) only built. VN335-348, 364-397, 413-439, 456-476, cancelled.
VN501-VN673	135	Supermarine Seafire F.46/F.47	Cancelled. VN501-528, 542-563, 567-598, 614-645, 653-673.
VN684-VN702	6	Percival P.40 Prentice	Pre-production. VN684, 687, 691, 695, 700, 702.
VN709-VN756	40	Junkers Ju 52/3m	Ex-German aircraft. VN709-731 and VN740-756.
VN782-VN787	6	Bücker Bü 181	Ex-*Luftwaffe* aircraft. Werke Nr. 331303, 177, 6384, 120519, 258, 301659.
VN799-VN850	4	English Electric Canberra B.1	Prototypes to Air Ministry Specification B.3/45. VN799, 828, 850, Avon engines; VN813, Nene engines, later used as D.H. Spectre test-bed; VN828, modified by Boulton Paul to have B.8 type canopy.
VN865 & VN870	2	Dornier Do 24	Ex-*Luftwaffe* aircraft, held at Felixstowe.
VN874	1	Junkers Ju 88	Ex-*Luftwaffe* aircraft.
VN877	1	Fieseler Fi 156 Storch	Ex-*Luftwaffe* aircraft.
VN885	1	Siebel Si 204A	Ex-*Luftwaffe* aircraft.
VN887	1	Blohm & Voss Bv 138	Ex-*Luftwaffe* aircraft.
VN889	1	Avro 652A Anson C.XIX Series 1	Works No. 1285.
VN895-VN898	4	Percival P.44 Proctor C.5	For use of British Air Attachés.

POST-WAR POLICIES

VP100–XZ999

AFTER the war the serialling system continued in exactly the same way as hitherto except that orders were in far smaller quantities. During the period 1946 to date, Mark numbers changed from Roman numerals to Arabic figures, and role prefix letters were invariably used in the full official designation.

Apart from straightforward production, this section includes American aircraft supplied on loan under the Mutual Aid Defence Pact and various civil aircraft temporarily taken on charge for evaluation or trooping.

This section is, however, in the interests of security, by no means complete from WA onwards, and allocations for aircraft currently in service have not been included—with certain exceptions where security is in no way compromised.

The XA100-XZ999 series is currently in use; how far allocations have been taken up is not known. Into this series, hovercraft have been introduced.

Serial Nos.	Qty.	Aircraft Type	Remarks
VP109-VP120	3	Westland Wyvern T.F.2	Prototypes to Specification N.12/45. VP109 and VP113, Python engine; VP120, Clyde engine.
VP178-VP202	25	D.H.98 Mosquito B.35	Airspeed (Christchurch)-built. VP178, 181, 191, 197, conv. to T.T.35. VP183 to P.R.35.
VP207	1	Hawker Fury I	Third Fury prototype, built from stock items in 1947.
VP254-VP294	29	Avro 696 Shackleton G.R.1	VP254-268, 281-294. Initial production. VP258, 259, 293 mod. to T.4.
VP301 & VP312	2	Avro 688 Tudor 3	Temporary serials in 1948 for G-AIYA and G-AJKC.
VP320-VP339	20	Siebel Si 204	Ex-German aircraft.
VP342-VP355	14	D.H.98 Mosquito T.3	De Havilland (Hatfield)-built.
VP401-VP422	3	Hawker P.1040	Sea Hawk prototypes to Air Ministry Specification N.7/46. VP401 (P.1040, converted to P.1072), VP413 and VP422.
VP427-VP495	64	Supermarine Seafire F.47	VP427-465, 471-495. Ordered 8.4.46.
VP501	1	Blohm & Voss Bv 222	Ex-German for evaluation. Test-flown at Calshot.
VP509-VP538	30	Avro 652A Anson C.19 Series II	VP512 became G-AKFE.
VP543	1	Horten Ho IV	Acquisition of German glider.
VP546	1	Fieseler Fi 156 Storch	Ex-German aircraft. Air Min 101.
VP550	1	Junkers Ju 352	Ex-enemy aircraft. Air Min 109.
VP559-VP582	24	D.F.S./14 S.G.38	Schulgleiter gliders.
VP587	1	Schneider Grunau Baby 2	Glider.
VP591	1	D.F.S./30 Kranich 2	Glider.
VP952-VP981	30	D.H.104 Devon C.1	Original order for 50 cut back to 30. VP975 became G-AOIZ. Some to V.I.P. standard.
VR131-VR140	10	Westland Wyvern T.F.1	Pre-production to Specification 17/46P for R.N. evaluation.
VR189-VR324	124	Percival P.40 Prentice T.1	First production order. VR189-212, 218-253, 257-296, 301-324.
VR330-VR349	20	D.H.98 Mosquito T.3	De Havilland (Hatfield)-built. Mostly sold abroad.
VR363 & VR371	2	Short S.A.2 Sturgeon T.T.2	Prototypes to Air Ministry Specification Q.1/46.
VR380 & VR382	2	Bristol 170	To A.M.Spec. C.9/45. Ex-G-AGPV/UT. Used for air interceptor radar tests.
VR546-VR557	2	Fairey Gannet	Prototypes to Spec. GR.17/45.
VR566-VR582	17	Avro 701 Athena T.2	VR569 became G-ALWA; VR570 crashed on test; VR581-582, cancelled.
VR590-VR606	17	Boulton Paul P.108 Balliol T.2	VR596 and VR598 hooked for carrier trials. VR599 became Sea Balliol T.21.

VR792-VR806	15	D.H.98 Mosquito B.35	Built by Airspeed. VR793 and VR802 converted to T.T.35.
VR836-VR893	32	D.H.103 Sea Hornet F.20	VR836-864, 891-893.
VR918-VR952	35	Hawker Sea Fury F.B.11	VR918-919 to Royal Canadian Navy.
VR955	1	Lockheed 18-56 Lodestar	G-AGCM, acquired in October 1946.
VR961-VR972	12	Supermarine Seafire F.47	Supermarine (South Marston)-built. Last Seafires produced.
VS201	1	D.F.S./70 Meise	Glider.
VS208	1	D.F.S./Kranich	Glider.
VS213	1	Kranich I	Glider.
VS220	1	Schneider Grunau Baby	Glider.
VS241-VS486	180	Percival P.40 Prentice T.1	Built by Blackburn Aircraft. VS241-290, 316-338, 352-397, 409-414 (125) VS415-445, 463-486 cancelled.
VS491-VS603	90	Avro 652A Anson T.20/T.21/C.21/T.22	VS491-534, 558-561, T.20; VS562-591, T.21 (except 565-566, 568, 570-572, 574-575, 578, 584, 586, 588, 591 as C.21); VS592-603, T.22.
VS609-VS804	140	Percival P.40 Prentice T.1	VS609-654, 681-698, 723-758. VS759-767, 774-804 cancelled.
VS812-VS869	44	Bristol 164 Brigand B.1/MET.3	VS812-816, B.1—of which VS813-814 were converted to T.4 then T.5; VS817-VS832, MET.3; VS833-839, 854-869, B.1—of which VS833, 837, 855, 858, 865, 866, 867, were converted to T.4 and all these T.4s except VS858 were reconverted to T.5.
VS968-VS987	20	Gloster G.41M Meteor P.R.10	VS968 was prototype P.R.10.
VT102-VT347	198	Gloster G.41G Meteor F.4	VT102-150, 168-199, 213-247, 256-294, 303-347. VT150 became Mk. 8 (G.41K) prototype; VT347 became P.R.5 (G.41H) and crashed on first flight. VT104-107, 110, 112-113, 118, 130, 135, 139, 142, 168, 175, 177, 179, 184, 187, 191, 192, 196-197, 219-220, 222, 226, 230, 243, 256, 259, 262, 268, 260, 282, 286, 289, 291, 294, 310, 316, 319, 329-330, 332, 338, converted to U.15.
VT362-VT504	117	Fairey Firefly A.S.5	VT362-381, 392-441, 458-499; VT500-504 to the Royal Australian Navy. VT364, 370, 372, 403, 413, 419, 427, 429, 430, 461, 470, 485, 493-495, 497, converted to U.9; VT440 converted to T.5.

Serial Nos.	Qty.	Aircraft Type	Remarks
VT581-VT631	44	D.H.98 Mosquito T.3	De Havilland (Hatfield)-built. VT581-596, 604-631, for R.A.F. (except VT582, 583, 595, 596, 611, 615, 618, 619, 622-624, 626-631, to Royal Navy).
VT651-VT707	50	D.H.98 Mosquito N.F.38	VT651-683, 691-707. 21 to Yugoslav Air Force.
VT724-VT737	14	D.H.98 Mosquito T.R.37	De Havilland (Broughton)-built.
VT762	1	Schneider Grunau Baby	Glider.
VT789	1	Percival P.46	Test-bed for Youngman-Baynes high-lift flaps.
VT793-VT874	64	D.H.100 Vampire F.3	Built by the English Electric Co. VT793-835 and 854-874. VT795 and 802-805 became F.20. VT832-835 sold to Norway.
VT916-VT925	10	Schneider Grunau Baby 2	Disposed by sale.
VT935	1	Boulton Paul P.111/P.111A	High speed research aircraft to A.M.Spec. E.27/46.
VT951	1	Boulton Paul P.120	High speed research aircraft to A.M.Spec. E.27/49.
VT976-VT997	22	Auster A.O.P.6	Diverted to Belgian Air Force. Deliveries from July 1947.
VV106 & VV119	2	Supermarine 510/535	Research aircraft to Air Ministry Specification E.41/46. VV106, Type 510; VV119, Type 535.
VV136-VV232	76	D.H.100 Vampire F.3/F.B.5/F.20	Built by the English Electric Co. VV136-165 completed as F.20; VV187-213, F.3—of which VV209-211 were diverted to India; VV214-232, F.B.5.
VV239-VV381	91	Avro 652A Anson T.21/22	80 built. VV239-264, 293-333, T.21—of which VV244, 246, 253-254, 261, 263, were converted to C.21; VV358-370, T.22. VV371-381 (T.22), cancelled.
VV400-VV401	2	EoN Olympia	Sailplanes.
VV430-VV441	12	D.H.103 Sea Hornet N.F.21	For the Royal Navy.
VV443-VV736	200	D.H.100 Vampire F.B.5	Built by the English Electric Co. VV443-490, 525-569, 600-640—of which VV613 became Venom F.1 prototype, VV655-700, 717-736—of which VV718, 720-723, 725-736, went to the French Air Force and VV694 to Lebanese Air Force.

VV740-VW114	197	Avro 652A Anson T.20/21	VV740-789, 805-854, cancelled Mk. 19s; VV866-867, T.20; VV880-919 and 950-999, T.21, built. VW100-114, cancelled Mk. 22s.
VW120	1	D.H.108	Research aircraft.
VW126-VW135	3	Avro 696 Shackleton	Prototypes VW126, 131, 135, to A.M.Spec R.5/46.
VW140-VW206	53	Vickers Valetta C.1	VW140-165, 180-206, ordered November 1946. VW188 became an interim trainer.
VW209	1	Sikorsky S-51	Dragonfly prototype, G-AJOP, acquired in August 1947.
VW214-VW218	5	Vickers Viking IA	EX-G-AGON/GRM/GRN/HPA/HOX. VW214-216, Type 498; VW217-218, Type 614.
VW224-VW243	20	Hawker Sea Fury F.B.11	VW230-231 to Royal Canadian Navy.
VW255-VW315	58	Gloster G.41G Meteor F.4	VW255-304, 308-315. VW258, 266, 273, 275, 276, 280, 285, 293, 299, 303, 308 were converted to U.15. VW286, 288, to Royal Netherlands Air Force.
VW360-VW379	16	Gloster G-41L/M Meteor F.R.9/P.R.10	VW360, F.R.9 prototype used by Ferranti Ltd. for radar development work. VW361-371, F.R.9; VW376-379, P.R.10; VW364 used by Martin-Baker for Mk. 1E ejection-seat tests.
VW410-VW489	70	Gloster G.43 Meteor T.7	VW410-459, 470-489. VW415 became N.F.11 prototype; VW443, special modifications; VW413, N.F.11 nose fitted. VW447 to Royal Navy.
VW495-VW539	42	Slingsby T.7 Cadet TX.1 & T.8 Cadet TX.2	Gliders for the Air Training Corps. VW495-524, TX.1; VW528-539, TX.2.
VW541-VW718	128	Hawker Sea Fury F.B.11	VW541-590, 621-670, 691-718. VW563, 571 to R.C.N. VW554, 667 to Burmese Air Force as UB456, 462.
VW743	1	Schneider Grunau Baby	Glider for Air Training Corps.
VW780-VW791	12	Gloster G.41G Meteor F.4	VW781 and VW791 were converted to U.15.
VW802-VW864	60	Vickers Valetta C.1	VW802-851 and 855-864.
VW867-VW886	20	Westland Wyvern T.F.2/S.4	T.F.2 except VW880-886 completed as S.4 and VW868, 870-871, 873, converted to S.4.
VW890-VW893	4	Avro 701 Athena T.2	Prototypes to Air Ministry Specification T.14/17.
VW897-VW900	4	Boulton Paul P.108 Balliol T.2	Prototypes to Air Ministry Specification T.14/47.
VW905	1	Bristol Sycamore 2	Bristol No. 12869, ex-G-AJGU, for evaluation.
VW908	1	D.F.S. Grunau	Glider.
VW912	1	Slingsby T.12 Gull I	Glider BGA379. Ex-G-ALPA.

Serial Nos.	*Qty.*	*Aircraft Type*	*Remarks*
VW915	1	B.A.C.VII	Glider.
VW918	1	Dittmar Condor	Glider.
VW920	1	B.A.C.III	Secondary glider.
VW930-VW979	46	D.H.103 Sea Hornet N.F.21/22	VW930-939, N.F.22; VW945 980, N.F.21.
VW985-VX130	40	Auster A.O.P.6	VW985-999 and VX106-130. VX123 converted to T.10. VX126-127 Antarctic models.
VX101	1	Messerschmitt Bf 109G	Compromised number above.
VX133-VX138	3	Supermarine 508/525	Prototypes to Specification N.9/47. VX133, Type 508; VX136, Type 529; VX138, Type 525.
VX141	1	Vickers 496 Viking IA	G-AGOM of British European Airways, to M.O.S.
VX147	1	Ercoupe 415-CD	Works No. 4784: ex-NC7465H and G-AKFC, for evaluation.
VX154	1	Fieseler Fi 156 Storch	For evaluation and study by Ministry of Supply.
VX158 & 161	2	Short S.A.4 Sperrin	Prototypes to Air Ministry Specification B.14/46.
VX165-VX185	4	English Electric Canberra	Prototypes. VX165 and VX169, B.2; VX181, P.R.3 prototype converted to B.5. VX185, B.5 to B.8 prototype.
VX190	1	Brunswick Zaunkönig II	Built at Brunswick Technical College. Tested at Farnborough. Became G-ALUA.
VX192-VX202	4	Avro 688/689 Tudor	VX192, Mk. I (ex-TT176); VX195, Mk. I (TT181, rebuilt as Mk. 8); VX199 (ex-TS883, ex-G-AGRX), Mk. 7; VX202, Mk. 2 ex-G-AGRY.
VX206	1	Bristol 167 Brabazon 1 Mk. 1	Serial applied, but was registered G-AGPW for first flight.
VX211 & VX217	2	Vickers Viscount	VX211 (Type 630, G-AHRF); VX217 (Type 663, G-AHRG, test-bed for Tay engine).
VX220 & VX224	2	Armstrong Whitworth A.W.55 Apollo	Works Nos. 3137-3138: G-AIYN and G-AMCH, for Ministry of Supply research.
VX229 & VX231	2	Handley Page (Reading) H.P.R.1 Marathon	G-AILH and G-AHXU. VX231 had trial engine installations.
VX234	1	Handley Page H.P.74 Hermes 2	G-AGUB, to M.O.S. in October 1953. Ex-PW943.
VX238	1	Vickers 495 Viking IA	G-AGOL, to Ministry of Supply in February 1950.
VX245-VX252	8	D.H.103 Sea Hornet 21	For Royal Navy.
VX249	1	Handley Page (Reading) H.P.R.1 Marathon	Allotted G-ALVW. Number compromised above.
VX272 & VX279	2	Hawker P.1052	Research prototypes to A.M. Spec. E.38/46. VX279 became the P.1081.
VX275	1	Slingsby Sedbergh TX.1	Glider presented to No. 123 Gliding School.

VX280-VX310	27	Hawker Sea Fury T.20	VX280-292, 297-310. VX292 to Burmese Air Force as UB451.
VX330	1	Handley Page H.P.88	Supermarine 510 fuselage with scaled Victor wing and tail. Built by Blackburn.
VX343	1	Bristol 167 Brabazon I Mk. II	Allocation for G-AIML which was not completed.
VX350	1	Fairey F.D.1	Fairey No. F.8466. Research delta-wing aircraft.
VX371-VX436	50	Fairey Firefly A.S.5	VX371-396, 413-438. VX414, first with power-folding wings; VX373, T.5. Some conversions, *e.g.*, VX418, 421, 429, to U.9.
VX442-VX454	3	Bristol 175 Britannia 101	VX442, 447, 454, ordered July 1948. VX442, 447 became G-ALBO/RX.
VX461-VX476	10	D.H.100 Vampire F.B.5	Built by The English Electric Co. at Samlesbury. VX461-464, 471-476.
VX483-VX580	63	Vickers Valetta C.1/2	VX483-485, 490-499, 506-515, 521-530, 537-546, 555-565, C.1; VX564, T.3 prototype; VX571-580, C.2.
VX587	1	Airspeed A.S.65 Consul	Ex-G-AKCW, which was converted Oxford NJ318. Leonides test-bed.
VX591	1	Fairey Gyrodyne	Provisionally allotted to G-AIKF.
VX595-VX600	6	Westland WS-51 Dragonfly H.R.1	Initial production for Fleet Air Arm.
VX608-VX764	112	Hawker Sea Fury F.B.11	VX608-643, 650-696, 707-711, 724-730, 748-764—of which VX724-729, 749-752 and 755-764 went to R.A.N.
VX770 & VX777	2	Avro 698 Vulcan.	Prototypes.
VX784 & VX790	2	Avro 707A/B	Delta-wing research. VX784, 707A; VX790, 707B.
VX818	1	Hawker Fury Trainer	Iraqi order converted to Admiralty requirements.
VX828-VX838	3	Vickers 668 Varsity	Prototypes VX828, 835, 838.
VX856	1	Vickers 618 Viking	Nene engine test-bed (ex-G-AJPH), for M.O.S.
VX860-VX916	51	D.H.98 Mosquito N.F.38	De Havilland (Broughton)-built. VX860-879, 886-916. 33 sold to Yugoslavia.
VX922-VX942	12	Auster A.O.P.6/T.7	VX922-925, A.O.P.6; VX926-929, 934-936, T.7: VX942 A.O.P.6 converted to T.10.
VX950-VZ359	215	D.H.100 Vampire F.B.5	Built by the English Electric Co. at Samlesbury. VX950-990, VZ105-155, 161-197, 206-241, 251-290, 300-359 for R.A.F. except VX973, VW142-143, 145-146, 148 to R.N. Diversions to French Air Force: VX950-952, VZ120, 129, 132-141, 144, 152-

Serial Nos.	*Qty.*	*Aircraft Type*	*Remarks*
			153, 161-162, 164-169, 172, 176, 191, 196-197, 207, 209, 211, 215, 317-221, 223, 226, 257-258, 270, 284-285. VZ252-256 to Italian Air Force.
VZ345-VZ372	21	Hawker Sea Fury T.20	VZ345-355, 363-372. Compromised other numbers.
VZ366	1	Avro 689 Tudor 2	Avro No. 1263, G-AGRZ.
VZ386-VZ649	215	Gloster Meteor F.4/T.7/F.8/F.R.9/P.R.10/U.16	VZ386-419, R.A.F.; VZ420-426 diverted to Egyptian Air Force; VZ427-429, 436-437, R.A.F. (48) F.4 built by A.W.A. of which VZ386, 389, 401, 407, 414, 415, 417 were conv. to U.15. VZ438-485, 493-517 (73) F.8 built by Gloster; VZ518-532, 540-569 (45) F.8 built by A.W.A. of which VZ445, 485, 506, 513, 514, 520, 530, 554 were converted to U.16 and VZ455, 503 were converted to U.21; VZ577-611 (35), F.R.9; VZ620, P.R.10; VZ629-648 (20), T.7; VZ649, T.7 with P.R.10 type nose fitted. VZ438 was converted to T.T.8. All subsequent to VZ569 built by Gloster.
VZ655-VZ715	41	D.H.103 Sea Hornet	VZ655-664, P.R.22; VZ671-682, 690-699, N.F.21; VZ707-715, F.R.20.
VZ720	1	Avro 689 Tudor 2	G-AGSA, to service in 1949.
VZ724	1	Cierva W.11 Air Horse	Experimental helicopter to Spec. E.19/46 demonstrated temporarily as G-ALCV.
VZ728	1	Reid & Sigrist R.S.4 Bobsleigh	Ex-G-AGOS Desford trainer.
VZ739-VZ799	51	Westland Wyvern	VZ739, prototype T.3 to Specification T.12/48. VZ745-766, 772-799, S.4.
VZ808-VZ877	63	D.H.100 Vampire F.B.5	De Havilland-built, at Hatfield up to VZ840 and remainder at Broughton. VZ808-852, 860-877—of which VZ810, 814, 817, 820, were transferred to the French Air Force, VZ873 to the Lebanese Air Force and VZ843 to the R.N.Z.A.F.
VZ960-VZ966	7	Westland WS-51 Dragonfly H.R.1	For R.N. but VZ960 used by R.A.F. as H.C.2. VZ966 had experimental four-blade rotor.
WA101-WA460	319	D.H.100 Vampire F.B.5	Built by the English Electric Co. at Samlesbury. WA101-150, 159-208, 215-264, 271-

			320, 329-348, 355-403, 411-460. 11 disposed to R.N.Z.A.F. were WA305, 314, 317, 338, 342, 374-376, 379, 381, 388 and WA365 was sold to the Lebanese Air Force.
WA469-WA534	60	Supermarine Attacker F.1/F.B.1	WA469-498, 505-526, F.1; WA527-534, F.B.I.
WA546-WA547	2	Gloster Meteor N.F.11	Prototypes to Air Ministry Specification F.24/48.
WA555	1	Cierva W-11 Air Horse	G-ALCW, stored after crash of VZ724.
WA560-WA569	10	Bristol 164 Brigand B.1/T.4	Bristol Nos. 12876-85. WA560 built as B.1 and converted to T.4; WA561-569 built as T.4—of which WA561, 565, 566 were converted to T.5.
WA576-WA578	3	Bristol 171 Sycamore 3	Pre-production. Ex-G-ALSS-U. WA578 became H.C.10 prototype.
WA590-WB181	400	Gloster Meteor T.7/F.8/F.R.9/P.R.10	WA590-639, 649-698, 709-743, T.7; WA755-794, 808-857, 867-909, 920-971, 981-999, WB105-112, F.8—of which WA775,842, were converted to U.16; WB113-125, 133-143, F.R.9; WB153-181, P.R.10. Diversions to R.A.A.F. were WA694, 782, 783, 786, 907, 909, 934, 936-939, 941-942, 944-949, 951-952, 954, 956-958, 960-961, 998.
WB188-WB202	3	Hawker Hunter (P.1067)	Prototypes WB188, 195, 202, to A.M. Spec. F.3/48. WB188 and WB195 Avon engines; WB202 Sapphire engines and F.2 prototype.
WB210 & WB215	2	Vickers 660/671 Valiant	Prototypes to Air Ministry Specification B.9/48.
WB220	1	Westland WS-51	G-AJHW for Antarctic.
WB228 & WB236	2	Bristol 164 Brigand	Replacement aircraft for two off-set to Pakistan Air Force.
WB243-WB440	168	Fairey Firefly A.S.5/6	WB243-272, 282-316, 330-382, 391-424, A.S.5; WB425-440, A.S.6. WB246, 257, 307, 331, 341, 365, 373-374, 391-392, 402, 410, 414, 416, converted to U.9; WB406, to T.T.5.
WB446-WB465	20	Avro 652A Anson T.21	A. V. Roe (Woodford)-built.
WB470 & WB473	2	Bristol 175 Britannia	Allocations not taken up.
WB482-WB484	3	Bristol 170 Mk. 21E	Ex-G-AIMI/O/R, used by the R.A.A.F. as A84-1, 2, 4.
WB490-WB494	5	Avro 706 Ashton	WB490, Mk. 1; WB491, Mk. 2; WB492-493, Mk. 3; WB494, Mk. 4.
WB505-WB523	14	Fairey Firefly A.S.6	WB505-510, 516-523—of which WB509, 510, 518, 519, 523 went to the R.A.N.
WB530-WB535	6	D.H.104 Devon C.1	Delivered in 1949.

Serial Nos.	*Qty.*	*Aircraft Type*	*Remarks*
WB549-WB768	200	D.H.C.1 Chipmunk T.10	WB549-588, 600-635, 638-662, 665-706, 709-739, 743-768. WB554, 765, 767 to Ghana Air Force as G159, 155, 161. WB565, 615, 647, 693, 754 transferred to Army Aviation.
WB771 & WB775	2	H.P.80 Victor	Prototypes.
WB781-WB797	3	Blackburn B-54/B-54/B-88	Prototypes. WB781, 788, 797, types Y.A.7/Y.A.5/Y.B.1 to Spec. G.R. 17/45.
WB810	1	Westland WS-51 Dragonfly	G-ALIL, acquired in March 1949 for evaluation.
WB818-WB861	38	Avro 696 Shackleton M.R.1A	WB818-837, 844-861. WB833 was converted to M.R.2. WB819, 820, 822, 826, 831, 832, 837, 844, 847, 849, 858 conv. to T.4.
WB870-WB912	36	D.H.103 Hornet F.3	WB870-889, 897-912. Mainly delivered to Far East.
WB919-WB993	69	Slingsby T.21B Sedbergh TX.1	WB919-948, 955-993. Gliders, mainly for A.T.C. Built by Slingsby except for WB974-993, by Martin Hearn.
WD122-WD149	21	Avro 694 Lincoln B.2	Built by Armstrong Whitworth Aircraft. Final Lincoln production: WD122-133, 141-149. Modifications to B.2/4A.
WD157-WD171	15	Vickers Valetta C.1	WD168 became 7479M; WD162 became G-APIJ.
WD280	1	Avro 707A	Experimental delta-wing to Air Ministry Specification E.10/49.
WD282-WD397	100	D.H.C.1 Chipmunk T.10	WD282-310, 318-338, 344-365, 370-397. WD308, 329 to Ghana Air Force as G150, 158. WD325 transferred to Army Aviation.
WD402-WD458	47	Avro 652A Anson T.21/T.22	WD402-418, T.21; WD419-422, 433-436, T.22. WD437-458, cancelled.
WD475-WD500	26	Handley Page H.P.67 Hastings C.2	WD475-499, C.2; WD500, C.(V.I.P.)4.
WD585-WD800	200	Gloster Meteor N.F.11	Built by Armstrong Whitworth Aircraft. WD585-634, 640-689, 696-745, 751-800. WD592, 606, 610, 626, 629, 630, 641, 645-647, 649, 652, 657, 678, 679, 702, 706, 767, 780 etc. were converted to T.T.20.
WD804 & WD808	2	Gloster G.A.5 Javelin	Prototypes to Specification F.4/48. WD804 was built Hucclecote, but assembled at Bentham.
WD824-WD923	95	Fairey Firefly A.S.6	WD824-872, 878-923.
WD929-WE195	105	English Electric Canberra B.2/P.R.3/T.4	WD929-966, 980-999, WE111-122 (70) B.2; WE135-151 166-175 (27) P.R.3; WE188

			195 (8) T.4. WD963 and WE118 conv. to T.4. WD935, 939, 942, 983 to R.A.A.F. WD940 became 51-17352 of U.S.A.F. Engine test-beds were: WD930 Avon R.A.26 & 29, WD933 Sapphire Sa6/7, WD943 Avon R.A.7/14R, WD952 Olympus, WD959 Avon R.A.7R/14R/24R. Off-sets to R.A.A.F. WD935 (A84-1), WD939 (A84-307), WD942 (A84-2), WD983 (A84-125). WD955 conv. to T.17. WD993, WE171-172 to the Venezualan Air Force.
WE235-WE249	11	D.H.103 Sea Hornet	WE235-242, F.20; WE245-247, P.R.22.
WE255-WE483	200	D.H.112 Venom F.B.1	WE255-294, 303-332, 340-389, 399-438, 444-483. WE381 became F.B.4 prototype.
WE488	1	Fairey Gannet	Third prototype. Fairey F.8749.
WE496 & WE505	2	Handley Page (Reading) H.P.R.2	Prototypes to Air Ministry Specification T.16/48.
WE522 & WE530	2	Percival P.56 Provost	Prototypes to Air Ministry Specification T.16/48.
WE534-WE616	72	Auster T.7	WE534-572, 587-616. WE563 became NZ1707. WE552, 590 to Hong Kong Auxiliary Air Force.
WE670	1	Avro 706 Ashton Mk. 3	Variously modified, including Avon R.A.14 under fuselage.
WE673-WE826	104	Hawker Sea Fury F.B.11/T.20	WE673-694, 708-736, F.B.11; WE737-742, 767-784, modified for Iraq and off-set from R.N.; WE785-806, F.B.11; WE820-826, T.20. WE673-674, 676, 796 to R.A.N.
WE830-WE849	20	D.H.100 Vampire F.B.5	Built by the English Electric Co. at Samlesbury.
WE853-WE976	119	Gloster G.41K Meteor F.8	WE853-891, 895-939, 942-976 built by A.W.A. and Gloster. WE877, 880, 886, 890, 896, 898, 900, 903, 906, 908, 911, 918, 928, 971 diverted to R.A.A.F. WE867, 915, 934, 962, converted to U.16 and WE902, 960, 961 to U.21.
WE979-WE993	15	Slingsby T.30B Prefect TX.1	Gliders, mainly for the Air Training Corps.
WE997	1	Westland Welkin N.F.2	PF370 renumbered. Only Mk. 2 Welkin built.
WF112-WF114	3	Saro Skeeter 3/4	WF112-113, partly built by Cierva, completed by Saro as Mk. 3. Became Mk. 3B when modified for Bombardier engines. WF114, Mk. 4.

Serial Nos.	*Qty.*	*Aircraft Type*	*Remarks*
WF118-WF136	20	Percival P.57 Sea Prince 1	WF118-133, T.1; WF136-138, C.1.
WF143-WF303	151	Hawker Sea Hawk F.1/F.2/F.B.3	WF143-192, 196-235, F.1; WF240-279, F.2; WF280-289, 293-303, F.B.3. WF143-161, 167-177 were built by Hawker remainder by A.W.A.
WF308-WF315	3	Westland WS-51 Dragonfly H.C.2	Malayan trials aircraft: WF308, 311, 315. WF308 was ex-G-ALMC.
WF320	1	Blackburn G.A.L.60 Universal	Blackburn No. 1000 Universal Freighter. Beverley prototype, ex-G-AMUX.
WF324-WF429	60	Vickers Varsity T.1	WF324-335, 369-394, 408-429. WF416 became VK501 of Royal Jordanian Air Force.
WF434-WF574	70	Boeing 345 Washington B.1 (B-29 Superfortress)	Ex-U.S.A.A.F. aircraft, loaned under M.D.A.P. 1950-1954. WF434-448, 490-514, 545-574.
WF578-WF586	5	D.H.100 Vampire F.B.5	Built by the English Electric Co. at Samlesbury. WF578-579, 584-586.
WF590-WF627	24	Hawker Sea Fury F.B.11	WF590-595, 610-627.
WF632	1	Short S.B.3	Ex-Sturgeon T.T.2 airframe.
WF638-WF883	179	Gloster Meteor F.8/T.7	WF638-662, 677-716, 736-760 (90), F.8 of which WF681, 706, 716, 741, 743, 751, 755, 756 were converted to U.16 and WF659 to U.21. WF766-795, 813-862, 875-883, T.7. WF746, 750 to R.A.A.F. and WF696-699 and 701 to Royal Netherlands Air Force. Up to WF688 built by A.W.A., rest by Gloster.
WF886-WF928	25	English Electric Canberra B.2/P.R.3	WF886-892, 907-917, B.2; WF922-928, P.R.3. WF907 testbed for Avon development and Gyron Junior. WF915 to R.N.Z.A.F. WF916 conv. to T.17. WF914 to the Venezualan Air Force.
WF934 & WF949	2	Percival P.57 Sea Prince T.1	For the Royal Navy.
WF954-WF979	23	D.H.103 Hornet F.3/4	WF954-962, 966-967, F.3; WF968-979, F.4.
WF984	1	D.H.104 Devon	Acquired in June 1950. Used at Empire Test Pilots School.
WF989-WG230	100	Boulton Paul P.108 Balliol T.2	WF989-998, WG110-159, 173-187, 206-230. WG224, 226, 227, 230 became CA310, 301, 302, 311 of R.Cey.A.F.
WG236 & WG240	2	D.H.110	Sea Vixen prototypes to Air Ministry Specification F.4/48.
WG256-WG267	12	Vickers Valetta T.3	WG256 conv. to T.4.

WG271-WG491	150	D.H.C.1 ChipmunkT.10	WG271-289, 299-336, 348-364, 392-432, 457-491—of which the first 16 were shipped for the R.A.T.G. WG288 to Ghana Air Force as G151. WG323 and WG432 transferred to Army Aviation.
WG496-WG499	4	Slingsby T.21B Sedbergh TX.1	Gliders for the Air Training Corps.
WG503	1	Percival P.56	Prototype. Became 7159M.
WG507-WG558	20	Avro Shackleton M.R.1/2	WG507-511, 525-529 M.R.1. WG530-533, 553-558 M.R.2. WG511, 527 conv. to T.4.
WG564-WG656	42	Hawker Sea Fury F.B.11/T.20	WG564-575, 590-604, 621-630, F.B.11; WG652-656, T.20.
WG661-WG754	50	Westland WS-51 Dragonfly H.R.3	For the Royal Navy. WG661-670, 705-709, 718-726, 749-754. WG725 to R.A.F. as 7703M.
WG760 & WG763	2	English Electric P.1A	Lightning prototypes.
WG768	1	Short S.B.5	Experimental aircraft for English Electric P.1 data.
WG774 & WG777	2	Fairey F.D.2	High speed research. WG774 held World Speed Record; later remodelled to BAC-221.
WG783-WG784	2	Slingsby T.30A Prefect TX.1	Gliders.
WG788-WG789	2	English Electric Canberra B.2	Replacement aircraft for Canberras sold to other air forces.
WG793-WG931	79	D.H.100 Vampire F.B.5/F.R.9	WG793-807, 826-847, F.B.5; WG848-851, 865-892, 922-931, F.R.9. Up to WG831 built by de Havilland at Broughton and remainder by English Electric at Samlesbury. WG826, 846 to R.N.Z.A.F.
WG935-WH573	390	Gloster Meteor T.7/F.8/F.R.9/P.R.10	WG935-950, 961-999, WH112-136, 164-209, 215-248, T.7; WH249-263, 272-320, 342-386, 395-426, 442-484, 498-513, F.8 of which WH258, 284, 309, 315, 320, 344, 349, 359, 365, 369, 372, 373, 376, 381, 419, 420, 469, 499, 500, 505, 506, 509 were converted to U.16 and WH460 to U.21; WH533-557, F.R.9; WH569-573, P.R.10. WG974, 977, WH252, 254, 259, 414, 417, 475, 479, 481 to R.A.A.F.
WH575	1	Bristol Freighter Mk. 31	Ex-G-AINK. Acquired for winterisation trials in Canada. Became ZK-AYG.
WH581-WH623	26	Hawker Sea Fury F.B.11	VH581-594, 612-623. Ordered 18.8.50. WH619 to Burma.
WH627-WH632	6	Fairey Firefly A.S.6	WH630 became Admiralty instructional airframe A2385.
WH637-WH984	183	English Electric Canberra B.2/T.4/P.R.7	WH637-674, 695-742 (86) B.2 built by E.E. Co. WH853-887, 902-925, 944, 948-984

Serial Nos.	Qty.	Aircraft Type	Remarks
			(60) B.2 Short & Harland built. WH772, P.R. 3(1); WH838-850 (13) T.4 E.E.Co. built. WH773-780, 790-804 (23) P.R.7; WH793 P.R.9 proto. Conversions: WH637, 651, 658-659, 674, 706, 854, 861 to T.4; WH638, 652, 704, 720, 733, 860, 921, 945 to U.10; WH714, 903-904 to T.11; WH839 to T.13; WH704, 720, 876, 921 to D.14; WH946-948, 954-961, 963-974, 977, 981-984 to B.15; WH946, 948, 957, 964, 972, 981, 983 to E.15; WH646, 664, 665, 740, 863, 872, 874, 902 to T.17; WH718, 856, 876, 887 to T.T.18; WH714, 724, 903-904, 975 to T.19; WH780, 797, 801, 803 to T.22. WH792 composite P.R.7/9. WH664, 653, 658, 662, 672, 674, 707, 855, 867, 871, 883 to R.R.A.F.; WH647, 649, 712, 730, 732, 862, 877, 881 to Venezuela; WH659, 726, 868, to Peru; WH711, 905 to R.S.A.F. WH645, 666, 739, 878 to R.N.Z.A.F. WH838 to Qatar. WH699 was *Aries IV*.
WH989-WH992	4	Westland WS-51 Dragonfly H.R.3	Delivered to Royal Navy.
WJ104-WJ216	72	Fairey Firefly A.S.6/T.7/A.S.7	WJ104-121, A.S.6; WJ146-153, A.S.7; WJ154-174, 187-209, T.7; WJ215-216, A.S.7. WJ109, 112, 113, 121 to R.A.N. WJ149-153, 188 conv. U.8.
WJ221-WJ301	52	Hawker Sea Fury F.B.11	WJ221-248, 276-292, 294-297, 299-301. Offsets to R.A.N. & R.C.N. WJ232, 290 became UB467-468 of Burmese Air Force.
WJ306	1	Slingsby T.21B Sedbergh TX.1	Glider.
WJ310	1	D.H.104 Dove 1 (Prototype)	G-AGPJ for evaluation. Later CR-CAC.
WJ316	1	Auster 'S'	Prototype.
WJ320	1	Bristol 170 Mk. 31	Bristol No. 12827. Arctic trials aircraft ex-G-AINL.
WJ324-WJ343	20	Handley Page Hastings C.2/4	WJ324-326 (H.P.94), C(VIP)4; WJ327-343 (H.P.67), C.2.
WJ348-WJ350	3	Percival P.57 Sea Prince C.1/2	WJ348 C.1; WJ349 and WJ350, C.2.
WJ354-WJ408	36	Auster A.O.P.6	WJ354-378, 398-408. WJ363, 368, 401, 404 conv. to T.10.
WJ461-WJ504	37	Vickers Valetta C.1/C.2/T.3	WT461-487, T.3; WJ491-499, C.1; WJ504, C.2, WJ464,

			466, 469, 471, 473, 477, 482-483, 485-486 conv. to T.4.
WJ509-WJ561	28	Avro 652A Anson T.21/C.21	WJ509-519, 545-561, T.21 (except WJ512, 549, 552, C.21).
WJ564-WJ707	100	English Electric Canberra B.2	WJ564-582, 603-649, 674-682 (75) B.2 Handley Page built. WJ683-707 (25) cancelled. WJ622 crashed on delivery. Conversions: WJ567-568, 577, 613, 617, T.4; WJ621, 624, 638, U.10; WJ610 T.11 & T.19; WJ638 to D.14; WJ565, 576, 581, 605, 607, 625, 630, 633, 635 to T.17; WJ574, 614, 629, 632, 636, 639, 680, 682 to T.T.18. WJ571, 572, 578, 606, 612, 613, 644 to R.R.A.F. WJ570 to Venezuela. WJ605 to R.N.Z.A.F. WJ617 to S.A.A.F.
WJ712-WJ881	100	English Electric Canberra B.2/B.6/P.R.7/T.4	WJ712-734, 751-753 (26) B.2 but WJ715, 717-718, 721 conv. to T.T.18. WJ754-784 (31) B.6 but WJ761, 762 764, 766, 770, 771, 773, 774, 776-778, 781-783 conv. to B.16. WJ815-825 (11) P.R.7. WJ857-881 (25) T.4. Offsets: WJ784 France, WJ860 Peru, WJ868 Qatar.
WJ886-WJ950	50	Vickers Varsity T.1	WJ886-921, 937-950, WJ900 became 82001 of R.S.A.F.
WJ954	1	Vickers Valiant B.2	Prototype for low-level ops.
WJ960 & WJ965	2	Supermarine 541 Swift	Prototypes. WJ960 became F.4.
WJ971-WK190	100	English Electric Canberra B.2	A.V. Roe-built. WJ971-995, WK102-146, 161-165 (75) B.2. WK166-190 (25) cancelled. Test-beds: WK141 Sapphire 7, Viper 8 & 11; WK163 Scorpion. Conversions: WJ987, WK107, 165 to U.10; WJ975, WK106 to T.11 & T.19; WJ984 to B.15; WJ971, 977, 981, 986, 988, WK102, 111 to T.17; WK118, 122-124, 126-127, 142 to T.T.18. Disposals: WJ974, 976, WK112, Peru; WJ980 to Venezuela; WJ981, 988 R.N.Z.A.F. WK108 R.R.A.F.: WK130, 137-138 to Germany.
WK194-WK315	100	Supermarine 541/549 Swift F.1/F.2/F.3	Vickers Armstrong (South Marston) built. WK194-213, F.1 but WK195 conv. to F.3 and WK201 to F.2, WK198 to F.4. WK199 to R.A.A.F. WK214-221, 239-246, F.2; WK247-271, F.3, WK272-281, F.4; WK287-315, F.R.5;

Serial Nos.	Qty.	Aircraft Type	Remarks
			WK274, 276, 277, 278, 280, 281 conv. F.R.5.
WK319-WK342	24	Supermarine Attacker F.B.2	To Nos 800, 803, 890 Squadrons of the Fleet Air Arm.
WK348-WK373	26	Fairey Firefly T.7	Mainly used for training.
WK376-WK385	3	D.H.112 Sea Venom F.A.W.20	Prototypes. WK376, 379, 385. Folding wings WK385 only.
WK389-WK503	85	D.H.112 Venom F.B.1 (B = Brooklands-built C = Chester-built F = Fairey built H = Hatfield built M = Marshall's built)	WK389-390 (F), 391-392 (M), 393-394 (C), 395 (B), 396-410 (C): 411-417 (M), 418-422 (F), 423-425 (B), 426-428 (M); 429-437, 468-483 (C); 484-488 (M), 489-491 (C), 492-493 (F), 494-495 (C), 496 (F), 497-500 (C), 501-503 (M).
WK506-WK643	100	D.H.C.1 Chipmunk T.10	WK506-523, 547-591, 607-643. Offsets: WK612, 616, 637 as G156, 157, 160 Ghana Air Force; WK569 R. Jordanian A.F.; WK615 R. Malaysian A.F. WK511, 635 to R.N. and WK512, 515, 549, 559, 613, 620, 630, to Army Aviation. WK617 to Kenya.
WK647-WL488	510	Gloster Meteor F.8/F.R.9/T.7	WK647-696, 707-756, 783-827, 847-893, 906-955, 966-994, WL104-143, 158-191, F.8. Conversions: WK648, 675, 693, 709, 716-717, 721, 729, 731, 737, 738, 743-747, 783-784, 789-790, 793, 795, 799, 807, 812, 852, 855, 859, 870, 877, 883, 885, 890, 911, 925-926, 932, 942, 949, 971, 980, 989, 993, WL110, 124, 127, 134, 160, 162-163 to U.16; WK710, 797, 879, WL136 to U.21. WL192-207, 221-234 cancelled. WL255-265, F.R.9. WL332-381, 397-436, 453-488, T.7. WK935 long nose for prone pilot. WK375 had F.8 tail/F.R.9 nose. Gloster-built except WK707-756, 906-935 A.W.A. WL332-334, 336-337, 350-353 to R.N. WK650, 670, 674, 682-686, 688, 690, 715, 727-728, 735, 748, 791-792, 796, 798, 800, 821, 877, 907, 909-910, 912, 913, 931, 937-938, 944, 946, 973 to R.A.A.F. Plus various offsets.
WL493-WL616	82	D.H.100 Vampire F.B.9	WL493-518, 547-587, 602-616. WL493 to R.N.Z.A.F.
WL621-WL709	67	Vickers Varsity T.1	WL621-642, 665-692 (50) built. WL693-709 cancelled.
WL715-WL734	20	Boulton Paul P.108 Sea Balliol T.21	Production aircraft for the Royal Navy.
WL737-WL801	40	Avro 696	WL737-759, 785-801. WL741,

		Shackleton M.R.2	745, 757-758, 754, 756-757, 787, 790, 793, 795 conv. to A.E.W.2.
WL804-WL874	60	D.H.112 Venom N.F.2	WL804-810 Hatfield-built, WL811-833, 845-874 Chester-built.
WL876-WL888	13	Westland Wyvern S.4	Production for R.N.
WL892-WL999	90	D.H.112 Venom F.B.1	WL892-935, 954-999 cancelled Bristol order.
WM143-WM403	192	Gloster Meteor N.F.11	A.W.A.-built. WM143-192, 221-270, 292-307, N.F.11 except WM261 N.F.14 prototype. WM308-341, 362-367, N.F.13. WM368-403, N.F.11 conversions: WM148, 151, 158-160, 167, 223, 224, 230, 234, 242, 255, 270, 292-293 T.T.20. Diversions: WM296-307, 368-371, 375-383, France: WM309, 312, 320, 334, 335, 366 Israel; WM325-326, 328, 338, 340, 362 Egypt; WM330, 332, 333, 336, 337, 341, Syria; WM384-403, Denmark.
WM472-WM495	24	Hawker Sea Fury F.B.11	Exports: WM472-478, R.C.N.; WM483-486 Iraq, WM488 Burma.
WM500-WM577	60	D.H.112 Sea Venom F.A.W. 20/21	WM500-523, 542-567, F.A.W. 20; WM568-577, F.A.W. 21.
WM659-WM733	50	D.H.113 Vampire N.F.10	WM659-677, 703-733. Diversions: WM659-662, 664-667, 675-676, 707-710, 715, 717, 719-721, 723-725, 728, 731-732 to I.A.F.
WM735-WM756	9	Percival P.57 Sea Prince T.1/C.2	WM735-742, T.1; WM756, C.2.
WM759	1	Short S.45 Solent 3	G-AKNS (ex-NJ205) on loan.
WM761-WM899	100	Fairey Firefly T.7/U.8	WM761-779, 796-809, T.7; WM810-823, U.8; WM824-832, 855, T.7; WM856-863, U.8; WM864-879, T.7; WM880-899, U.8.
WM901-WN119	100	Hawker Sea Hawk F.1/F.B.3	WM901-905, F.1 (built by Hawker); WM906-945, 960-999, WN105-119, F.B.3 (built by A.W.A.)
WN124-WN127	4	Supermarine Swift F.R.5	Production aircraft delivered in 1956.
WN132-WN303	138	Boulton Paul P.108 Balliol T.2	WN132-171 (40) built. WN172-181, 196-234, 255-303, cancelled. WN132, 147, 148, 155-157, 164, 166 were off-set to Ceylon.
WN309-WN321	13	Gloster G.43 Meteor T.7	Standard production aircraft.
WN324-WN336	13	Westland Wyvern S.4	Standard production aircraft.
WN339-WN464	100	Fairey Gannet A.S.1	Fairey Nos. F.9111-9210. WN339-378, 390-429, 445-464. From WN339 built at Hayes and from WN370 at Stock-

Serial Nos.	*Qty.*	*Aircraft Type*	*Remarks*
			port. WN365, T.2 prototype; WN372, A.S.4 prototype. WN456-459 to R.A.N.
WN467	1	English Electric Canberra T.4	Prototype T.4, to Air Ministry Specification T.2/49.
WN470	1	Hawker P.1083	Cancelled at advanced stage.
WN474-WN487	10	Hawker Sea Fury F.B.11	WN474-479, 484-487 ordered in April 1951. WN474 and WN479 to R.C.N.
WN492-WN500	9	Westland WS-51 Dragonfly	Production aircraft.
WN506-WN674	120	Boulton Paul P.108 Valliol T.2	Built by Blackburn Aircraft. WN506-535 (30) only built. WN536-555, 573-601, 634-674 (90) cancelled.
WN888-WP194	150	Hawker Hunter F.2/F.5	Built by A.W.A. WN888-921, 943-953, F.2; WN954-992, WP101-150, 179-194, F.5.
WP199-WP223	25	Vickers Valiant B.1	WP199-203, pre-production Vickers Type 674; WP204 onwards, Vickers Type 706. WP199 converted as test-bed for Pegasus vectored-thrust turbofan; WP205, B(PR).1 trials aircraft and modified for Blue Streak trials. WP217, 219, 221, 223 to B(PR).1 standard.
WP227		D.H.112 Venom N.F.2	Prototype N.F.2. Ex-G-5-3, became 7098M.
WP232-WP256	25	D.H.113 Vampire N.F.10	WP246, 249, to Indian Air Force as ID1605-1606.
WP262-WP271	10	EoN Eton TX.1	Primary gliders.
WP275-WP304	30	Supermarine Attacker F.B.2	For Royal Navy.
WP307-WP321	15	Percival P.57 Sea Prince T.1	Works Nos. 57-71. For Royal Navy.
WP324-WP333	10	Boulton Paul P.108 Sea Balliol T.21	Production aircraft for the Royal Navy.
WP336-WP346	11	Westland Wyvern S.4	Production aircraft for the Royal Navy.
WP351-WP354	4	Fairey Firefly U.8	Final Firefly production. Last delivery in March 1956.
WP493-WP510	18	Westland WS-51 Dragonfly H.R.3	Last Dragonflies for Royal Navy. WP493-504 (12) built; remainder cancelled.
WP514-WP516	3	English Electric Canberra B.2	Replacement aircraft for diversions to other air forces.
WP772-WP988	145	D.H.C.1 Chipmunk T.10	WP772-811, 828-872, 898-930, 962-988. Several disposed to Civil Register. WP787, 802, 894 became G152-154 of Ghana Air Force and WP798, 987 became T200-201 of Royal Jordanian Air Force. WP772, 925, 928, 930, 964, 972, 983 transferred to Army Aviation.

WP990-WR269	150	D.H.100 Vampire F.B.9	WP990-999, WR102-111, 114-158, 171-204 by D. H., WR205-215, 230-269 by Fairey.
WR272-WR808	270	D.H.112 Venom F.B.1/F.B.4/N.F.2	WR272-321, 334-373 (90) F.B.1; WR374-383, 397-446, 460-509, 525-564 (150) F.B.4; WR565-574, 586-635, 650-699, 715-764, F.B.4 cancelled; WR779-808 (30) N.F.2. Assembled in various plants.
WR951-WR990	40	Avro Shackleton M.R.2/3	WR951-969 (19) M.R.2. Conversions: WR966, 969 to M.R.2(T); WR960, 963, 965 to A.E.W.2. WM970-990 (21) M.R.3. WR973 non-standard.
WS103-WS154	30	Gloster G.43 Meteor T.7	WS103-117, R.N.; WS140-141, to Belgium; WS142-151, Brazil; WS152-154, R.A.F. WS111, F.R.9 nose.
WS590-WS848	200	Gloster Meteor N.F.12/N.F.14	A.W.A. built. WS590-639, 658-700, 715-721, N.F.12; WS722-760, 774-812, 827-848, N.F.14.
WS960-WT122	50	English Electric Canberra B.2	WS960-999, WT113-122 cancelled Handley Page order.
WT097-WT121	3	Douglas Skyraider A.E.W.1	WT097, 112, 121 incorrectly applied to WT943, 982, 983.
WT140-WT189	50	English Electric Canberra B.2	Cancelled order placed with A. V. Roe.
WT205-WT542	195	English Electric Canberra B.6/P.R.7/B(I)8/T.4	WT205-213, B.6 Short-built. WT208-210, 213 conv. to B.15. WT301-305, B.6; WT306-325, B(I)6. WT326-342, 344-347, 362-368, B(I)8. WT369-374, B.6; WT375-387, 397-422, 440-469 cancelled. WT475-492, T.4. WT503-542, P.R.7. WT302-303, 324, 369, 372-374 conv. to B.16. WT510, 525, 535 conv. to T.22. WT340, 342, 364, 368 to Peru; WT491-492 to R.A.A.F. WT528 was *Aries V*.
WT555-WT811	200	Hawker Hunter F.1/4	WT555-595, 611-660, 679-700, F.1; WT701-723, 734-780, 795-811, F.4. WT702, 722, 745-746, 755, 772, 799 to T.8. WT711-713, 718, 721, 723, 744, 771, 804, 806, 808-810 to G.A.11. Disposals to Switzerland and Peru.
WT827-WT841	4	Gloster Javelin (prototypes)	WT827, 830, 836. WT841, T.3 proto. assembled by A.S.T.
WT845-WT846	2	Westland WS-51 Dragonfly H.C.4	WT845 was H.C.4 version prototype.

Serial Nos.	*Qty.*	*Aircraft Type*	*Remarks*
WT849	1	Douglas Skyraider A.E.W.1	Supplied under Mutual Defence Aid Pact.
WT851	1	Supermarine Attacker F.B.2	Replacement aircraft.
WT854 & WT859	2	Supermarine 544	Prototypes to A.M.Spec. N.113D.
WT865-WT919	40	Slingsby T.31B Cadet TX.3	WT865-877, 893-919. Gliders for the Air Training Corps.
WT923-WT926	4	Bristol 171 Sycamore H.C.11	For Army Communications. Ex-G-ALSV/SY/TA/TC.
WT933 & WT939	2	Bristol 171 Sycamore 3	WT933 (ex-G-ALSW) to Middle East for tropical tests; WT939 (ex-G-ALTB) to Canada for Arctic trials.
WT943-WV185	50	Douglas Skyraider A.E.W.1	M.D.A.P. WT943-969, 982-987, WV102-109, 177-185.
WV189-WV225	25	Sikorsky S-55 Whirlwind H.A.R.21/H.A.S.22	M.D.A.P. WV189-198, H.A.R.21 (ex-U.S. Navy 130182-130191); WV199-205, 218-225, H.A.S.22 (ex-U.S. Navy 133739-133753).
WV253-WV412	100	Hawker Hunter F.4	Hawker (Kingston)-built. WV253-281, 314-334, 363-412. WV272, 318, 383, converted to T.7 by Armstrong Whitworth Aircraft; WV276, Avon 121 trials; WV319, 322, 363, 396, converted to T.8. WV256, 257, 267, 374, 380-382 conv. to G.A.11.
WV418-WV686	200	Percival P.56 Provost T.1	WV418-448, 470-514, 532-580, 601-648, 660-686. WV533 offset to Sudan. WV645-648 became T.52 R.R.A.F. 136-139. WV501 & WV678 to Muscat & Oman Air Force.
WV689-WV691	3	D.H.113 Vampire N.F.10	To Indian Air Force as ID607, ID606, ID604.
WV695	1	Bristol 171 Mk. III	Ex-G-ALSZ; became A91-1 of the Royal Australian Air Force.
WV698-WV755	27	Percival P.66 Pembroke C.1	WV698-712, 729-753, C.1; WV754-755, C.(P.R.).1. WV707 & 711 to Southern Rhodesian Air Force.
WV781-WV784	4	Bristol 171 Sycamore H.R.12	Trials batch to Coastal Command early in 1952.
WV787	1	English Electric Canberra B.2	Experimental model with Sapphire engines.
WV792-WV922	85	Hawker Sea Hawk F.G.A.4	Built by Armstrong Whitworth Aircraft. WV792-807, 824-871, 902-922.
WV925	1	Slingsby T.21B Sedbergh TX.1	For evaluation. Acquired in 1952.
WV928	1	D.H.112 Venom N.F.3	Prototype. Became 7189M.
WV933-WV944	12	Westland WS-51 Dragonfly H.R.3	Cancelled order.

WW134	1	Supermarine Scimitar	Third prototype; first Scimitar with blown flap.
WW137-WW298	96	D.H.112 Sea Venom F.A.W.21	WW137-154, 186-225, 261-298.
WW339	1	Sikorsky S-55	Works No. 55016: G-AMHK, for evaluation. Sold to Norway as LN-ORK.
WW342-WW355	14	Boeing 345 Washington B.1 (B-29 Superfortress)	Ex-U.S.A.A.F. aircraft, supplied under Mutual Defence Aid Pact. Returned to U.S.A.
WW378	1	Bristol 170	Ex-G-AHJN. Became A81-4.
WW381-WW453	55	Percival P.56 Provost T.1	WW381-398, 417-453.
WW458 & WW461	2	D.H.115 Vampire T.11	Prototypes. WW461 became T.22.
WW465-WW586	29	Avro 685 York	Temporary trooping serials as follows: WW465-468 (G-AGNN/GNS/GSO/HFG); WW499-504 (G-AHFB/HFD/GOB/HFH/GJB/HFA); WW-506-512 (G-AHEY/HFC/GJA/GNP/GNY/GNM/MGK); WW514 (G-AGNT), WW540-542 (G-AGSM/JA/OA); WW-576-582 (G-AGNO/GOD/HFE/GOF/GJE/GNL/GNX); WW586 (G-AHFB).
WW589-WW598	10	Hawker Hunter F.4/F.6	Hawker (Kingston)-built. WW589-591, F.4; WW592-598, F.6—of which WW593-596 were converted to F.R.10.
WW599-WW665	46	Hawker Hunter F.1/F.4	Hawker (Blackpool)-built. WW599-610, 632-645, F.1; WW646-665, F.4. Conversions included WW659 to G.A.11 and WW661, 664 to T.8. WW662 conv. to F.52 for Peru.
WW669-WW710	42	D.H.112 Venom F.B.1	Cancelled order with Bristol Aeroplane Co. Ltd.
WW868	1	Avro 685 York	Temporary serial for G-AHFE. WW578 was also allotted.
WX200-WX266	50	D.H.100 Vampire F.B.9	Final F.B.9 production. WX200-241, 259-260. WX261-266 cancelled. WX212, 219, 228, 230-231 to S.R.A.F. as SR113, 115, 114, 108-109.
WX493-WX556	52	Lockheed Neptune M.R.1	Ex-U.S. Navy aircraft, supplied under M.D.A.P. WX493-529, 542-556.
WX785-WX949	123	D.H.112 Venom N.F.3	WX785-810, 837-886, 903-949. All disposed in 1958.
WX953	1	Westland WS-51 Dragonfly H.C.4	Used by R.A.F.
WX958	1	D.H.104 Dove	Ex-G-ALVT, sold to the Argentine Government.
WX962-WX981	20	Gloster G.41L Meteor F.R.9	Last F.R.9s produced. Delivered in 1952.

Serial Nos.	Qty.	Aircraft Type	Remarks
WZ273-WZ302	30	Supermarine Attacker F.B.2	Production aircraft for Royal Navy.
WZ306 & WZ311	2	Vickers Viking IB	Serials for trooping, allotted to G-AJFT and G-AJFR.
WZ315-WZ320	6	D.H.112 Venom N.F.3	Presumed larger order was cut.
WZ353-WZ357	5	Vickers Viking IB	Serials for trooping by civil Vikings G-AJFS/IXS/IXR/KTU/KTV.
WZ361-WZ405	41	Vickers Valiant I	WZ361-375, B.1; WZ376 B(PR)K.1; WZ377-379, B-(PR)1; WZ380, B(PR)K.1; WZ381, B(PR)1; WZ382 B(PR)K.1; WZ383-384, B(PR)1; WZ389-405 B(PR)-K.1.
WZ414-WZ620	143	D.H.115 Vampire T.11	WZ414-430, 446-478, 493-521, 544-593, 607-620.
WZ627-WZ656	30	Hawker Sea Fury F.B.11	Final Sea Fury production. Ordered in November 1951. WZ633-641 to R.C.N.
WZ662-WZ731	56	Auster A.O.P.9	WZ662-679, 694-731.
WZ736 & WZ744	2	Avro 707A/707C	Delta-wing experimentals. WZ736, 707A; WZ744, 707C.
WZ749	1	Westland WS-51 Dragonfly H.C.2	G-ALEG, intended for R.A.F. in 1951; cancelled.
WZ753-WZ832	62	Slingsby T.38 Grasshopper TX.1	Gliders for the Air Training Corps. WZ753-798, 817-832.
WZ838-WZ841	4	Handley Page H.P.81 Hermes 4	Temporary trooping serials for G-ALDA/B/C/F.
WZ845-WZ884	40	D.H.C.1 Chipmunk T.10	Final production Chipmunks for the R.A.F. WZ851 became T203 of Royal Jordanian Air Force. WZ882 was transferred to Army Aviation.
WZ889	1	Blackburn B.101 Universal Freighter 2	Blackburn No. 1001. Beverley prototype. Was registered G-AMVW.
WZ893-WZ946	39	D.H.112 Sea Venom F.53	WZ893-911, 927-946. All offset to R.A.N.
WZ966-WZ968	3	Boeing 345 Washington B.1 (B-29 Superfortress)	Ex-U.S.A.A.F. B-29 (44-62283, 62282, 62296), supplied under the Mutual Defence Aid Pact. All returned to U.S.A.
WZ972-WZ973	2	Vickers Viking	G-AHOP/N, issued with temporary trooping serials.
WZ984-WZ985	2	Douglas Dakota	G-AGWS/ZG, issued with temporary trooping serials.
XA100-XA172	53	D.H.115 Sea Vampire T.22	First production T.22. XA100-131, 152-172.
XA177	1	Auster B.4	G-AMKL, light general purpose aircraft for evaluation.
XA181	1	Supermarine 545	Not flown.
XA191-XA192	2	Avro 685 York	Temporary trooping serials for G-AMGK/GNM.
XA209 & XA213	2	Short Seamew A.S.1	Prototypes.
XA219-XA221	3	Bristol Sycamore H.R.50	Sycamore 3 for Royal Australian Navy.

XA225-XA244	20	Slingsby T.38 Grasshopper TX.1	Gliders for the Air Training Corps.
XA249-XA278	30	Handley Page (Reading) H.P.R.5 Marathon T.11	Ex-civil aircraft, taken over by R.A.F. in 1952 (except XA277-278, sold to Japan as JA-6009-6010).
XA282-XA313	32	Slingsby Cadet TX.3	Gliders for the A.T.C.
XA319-XA530	140	Fairey Gannet A.S.1/A.S.4/T.2	A.S.1s built as follows: XA319-335, 340-343, 349-351, 356-359, 387-389, 399-405, 434, 436 at Hayes; XA336-339, 344-348, 352-355, 360-364, 390-398 at Stockport; of these XA326-334, 343, 350-351, 356, 359, 389, 403, 434 were off-set to R.A.N. and XA349, 397-398, 409 to Indonesian Navy. A.S.4s built as follows: XA410-414, 419-420, 426-429, 435, 451-453, 460-464, 469-471 at Hayes; XA415-418, 421-425, 430-433, 454-459, 465-468, 472-473 at Stockport of which XA414, 459-460, 472 were conv. to A.S.6 and XA430, 454, 466, 471 to C.O.D.4. T.2s XA508-530 were built at Hayes of which XA514 and 517 went to R.A.N. and XA521 was conv. to T.5 for Indonesian Navy.
XA536	1	English Electric Canberra B.2	Converted to T.11 and T.19.
XA539	1	D.H.112 Venom	Trials in 1954.
XA544-XA836	200	Gloster Javelin F.(A.W.)1/2/4/5/6	XA544-572, 618-628, F(AW)1; XA629-640, F(AW)2; XA641-667, 690-719, F(AW(5; XA720-737, 749-767, F(AW)4; XA768-781, 799-814, F(AW)2; XA815-836, F(AW)6. XA522 development aircraft for D.H. Gyron Junior DGJ.10 engines.
XA842	1	Westland WS-55 Whirlwind	EX-WW339.
XA847-XA856	3	English Electric P.1B	Lightning prototypes. XA847, 853, 856.
XA862-XA871	10	Westland WS-55 Whirlwind H.A.R.1	XA862 (ex-G-AMJT) to R.A.F. in March 1953.
XA876	1	Slingsby T.34 Sky	Glider used at the Empire Test Pilots School.
XA879-XA880	2	D.H.104 Devon C.1	D.H. Nos. 04374 and 04433.
XA889-XA913	25	Avro 698 Vulcan B.1	First production Vulcans. XA903 Olympus 593 test-bed. Conversions to B.1A.
XA917-	—	Handley Page H.P.80 Victor B.1	First production Victors. Conversions to BK.1a and K.1.
XA952	1	Vickers Swallow	Flying scale model project.

Serial Nos.	Qty.	Aircraft Type	Remarks
XB246	1	Douglas DC-3 Dakota	Temporary trooping serial for G-AMBW.
XB251-XB256	6	Westland WS-51 Dragonfly H.R.4	Production for use in Malaya by R.A.F.
XB259-XB291	20	Blackburn B.101 Beverley C.1	Initial production. XB259-260 were temporarily G-AOAI/ED. XB259-269, 283-291.
XB296-XB449	100	Grumman Avenger A.S.4	Ex-U.S. Navy, supplied under M.D.A.P. to Royal Navy. XB296-332, 355-404, 437-449.
XB474-XB524	20	Hiller H.T.1 (HTE-2)	Helicopters supplied under M.D.A.P. to the Royal Navy. XB474-481, 513-524.
XB530-XD129	370	North American Sabre F.1/F.4 (N.B. F.1s were re-designated F.2s in May 1953)	Canadian-built, supplied under Mutual Defence Aid Pact. XB530-550, 575-603, 608-646, F.1; XB647-650, F.4; XB664-713, 726-769, F.1; XB770-775, F.4; XB790-839, F.1; XB851-855, F.4; XB856-900, F.1; XB901-905, F.4 (renumbered XB912-916); XB917-961, 973-977, 991-999, F.4; XD117-129, F.4 (renumbered XB978-990).
XD145 & XD151	2	Saunders-Roe SR.53	Britain's first mixed-power interceptor (rocket/turbojet).
XD158	1	Gloster Javelin F.2	Prototype with U.S. radar.
XD163-XD188	13	Westland WS-55 Whirlwind H.A.R.2/4	XD163-165, 179-188. Conversions to H.A.R.10 included XD165, 182, 186.
XD196-XD197	2	Bristol 171 Sycamore H.R.13	First search and rescue Sycamores for Fighter Command.
XD212-XD357	100	Supermarine Scimitar F.1	XD212-250, 264-282, 316-333 (76) built. XD334-357 cancelled.
XD363-XD364	2	Westland WS-55 Whirlwind	Renumbered XJ393-394.
XD366	1	Vickers Varsity T.1	Replacement for Varsity WJ900 to R.S.A.F. as 82001.
XD375-XD627	160	D.H.115 Vampire T.11	XD375-405, XD424-463, XD506-554, XD588-627.
XD632	1	Handley Page H.P.81 Hermes 5	Temporary trooping serial for G-AKFP *Hamilcar*.
XD635-XD637	3	Vickers Viking	Temporary trooping serials for G-AHOT/W/R.
XD649	1	Westland WS-51 Mk. IA.	G-AKTW, temporarily to R.A.F. Became Westland Widgeon.
XD653-XD656	4	Bristol 171 Sycamore H.R.51	Sycamore 4 for Royal Australian Navy.
XD667-XD670	4	Avro 685 York	Temporary trooping serials for G-AMUN/MUU/MUV/GNU.
XD674-XD694	10	Hunting Jet Provost T.1	Trials batch: XD674-680, 692-694. XD694 first T.2.
XD696	1	Avro 720	Not completed.
XD706-XD781	60	North American Sabre F.1	M.D.A.P. XD706-736, 753-781 (ex-R.C.A.F. Nos. 19707-

			19731, 19749-19773, 19793-19802).
XD759	1	Fairey Jet Gyrodyne	G-AJJP Gyrodyne converted. Compromised number above, later renumbered XJ389.
XD798-XD802	5	Westland WS-55 Whirlwind H.A.R.2	Production aircraft.
XD812-XD893	56	Vickers Valiant B.1	Included Vickers Type 758 B(K).1. XA812-830, 857-875 (38) built. XA876-893 cancelled.
XD898	1	Fairey Gannet A.S.4	Offset to R.A.N.
XD903-XD988	70	Supermarine Swift F.R.5	XD903-930, 948-977, F.R.5 built by Vickers Armstrong at South Marston and Swindon. XD919 crashed on delivery. XD943 P.R.6 not completed. XD978-988 cancelled.
XE169-XE277	60	Short Seamew A.S.1/M.R.2	XE169-186, 205-216 (30) M.R.2 built. XE173-176 conv. to A.S.1. XE217-231, 263-277, cancelled.
XE280	1	Douglas DC-3	Allocation for Trooping for G-AMRA.
XE286-XE288	3	Bristol 173	XE288 (ex-G-AMYH) for naval trials.
XE294-XE299	6	Vickers V.1000	Cancelled.
XE306-XE322	17	Bristol 171 Sycamore H.R.14	To equip No. 275 Squadron, R.A.F. initially. XE313-317 G-AMWK-O transferred to the R.A.F.
XE327-XE490	98	Hawker Sea Hawk F.G.A.4/6	Built by A.W.A. XE327-338, F.G.A.4; XE339-344, 362-411, 435-463, 490, F.G.A.6.
XE512-XE515	4	Scottish Aviation Prestwick Pioneer C.C.1	XE512 and XE514 (ex-G-AKBF/NAZ) to R.A.F. in September 1953.
XE506	1	Hunting Provost T.1	Replacement aircraft.
XE521	1	Fairey Rotodyne	Experimental VTOL transport. Project abandoned Feb. 1961.
XE526-XE656	100	Hawker Hunter F.6	Hawker (Kingston) - built. XE526-561, 579-628, 643-656. XE537-540, 547, 549, diverted to Indian Air Force as F.56 and XE526-529, 533, 536, 541-542, 545, 553-555 as F.58 to Swiss Air Force. Conversions included XE532, 544, 546, 550, 552, 581, 584, 594, 597, 599, 607, 609-611, 614-618, 620, 623-624, 627, 643, 646, 649-652, 654-655 to F.G.A.9 and XE556, 579-580, 585, 589, 596, 599, 614, 621, 625-626 to F.R.10. XE531 conv. to T.12. XE591 to Royal Saudi Air Force.
XE657-XE718	50	Hawker Hunter F.4	Hawker (Blackpool) - built. XE657-689, 709-718. Con-

Serial Nos.	Qty.	Aircraft Type	Remarks
			versions include XE664-665 to T.8; XE673, 674, 680, 682, 685, 689, 711, 712, 716, 717 to G.A.11.
XE727-XE	—	M.L. U.120D	Pilotless target.
XE758-XE812	34	Slingsby T.31B Cadet TX.3	Rebuilt TX.1 gliders. XE758-762, 784-812.
XE816-XE998	134	D.H.115 Vampire T.11	XE816-833, 849-897, 919-961, 975-998.
XF113-XF124	12	Supermarine Swift F.7	Production aircraft but this type did not enter service.
XF259-XF261	3	Westland WS-51 Dragonfly H.C.4	Production aircraft.
XF265-XF269	5	Bristol 171 Sycamore H.C.14	Second production batch for R.A.F.
XF273-XF279	7	Gloster G.43 Meteor T.7	Last production Meteors.
XF284-XF285	2	Avro 685 York	Temporary trooping serials for G-AMUL and G-AMUM.
XF289-XF370	50	Hawker Hunter F.4	Hawker (Blackpool) - built. XF289-324, 357-370. XF310 and XF321 were converted to T.7; XF289, 322, 357, 358 to T.8 and XF291, 296-297, 300, 301, 303, 368 to G.A.11.
XF373-XF527	100	Hawker Hunter F.6	Built by Armstrong Whitworth Aircraft. XF373-389, 414-463, 495-527. Conversions to F.G.A.9 included XF376, 378 388-389, 419-421, 424, 430 431, 435, 436, 442, 445-446, 456, 462, 508, 511, 519 and to F.R.10 XF422, 426, 428-429, 432, 436, 438, 441, 457-460. XF463, 497, 499-501, 503, 505 diverted to Indian Air Force.
XF537	1	Avro 689 Tudor 2	Temporary trooping serial for G-AGRY.
XF540-XF614	50	Percival P.56 Provost T.1	Production aircraft. XF540-565, 591-614.
XF619 & XF623	2	Douglas DC-3 Dakota	Temporary trooping serials for G-AMYX and G-AMYV.
XF629-XF633	5	Vickers Viking 1B	Temporary trooping serials for G-AJBO/IVO/HPO/HPM/JCD.
XF645-XF648	4	Douglas DC-3 Dakota	Temporary trooping serials for G-AMVC/SF/VB/SH.
XF650-XF663	14	Bristol 170 Freighter	XF650-655, Mk. 32; XF656-663, Mk. 21. Last two numbers of allocation only used for G-AIME/H. First 12 allocations were intended for G-AMWA/MWB/MWC/MWD/MWE/MWF/GVB/GVC/HJP/ICS/IFS/IFV.
XF667	1	Douglas DC-3 Dakota	Temporary trooping serial for G-AMSH.

XF672-XF673	2	Boulton Paul P.108 Balliol T.2	Replacements for diversions to Ceylon.
XF678-XF693	16	Percival P.56 Provost T.1	Replacements for offsets to Rhodesia. XF682, 683, 688 to Muscat & Oman Air Force.
XF700-XF730	13	Avro 716 Shackleton M.R.3	Production aircraft for Coastal Command. XF700-711, XF 730.
XF739	1	Avro 688 Tudor 1	Avro No. 1257 (G-AGRI), temporarily on charge, 1953.
XF746-XF757	5	Douglas DC-3 Dakota	XF746-748, 756, 757. Temporary trooping serials for G-AMVL/YJ/ZC/PP/JU.
XF774 & XF778	2	Supermarine Swift F.7	Prototype F.7s.
XF785	1	Bristol Type 173 Mk. 1	Bristol No. 12871 (G-ALBN), used for naval trials in 1953.
XF796-XF799	4	Percival Pembroke C(PR).1	Production aircraft.
XF828	1	D.H.110 Sea Vixen	Naval prototype, third D.H.110 prototype.
XF833	1	Hawker Hunter F.6	Type P.1099, utilising parts of P.1083 prototype.
XF836-XF914	66	Percival P.56 Provost T.1	XF836-854, 868-914. XF845, 847-848, 853-854 to R.M.A.F. XF849-852, 870-873, 878-881 to R.R.A.F.
XF919	1	Avro 685 York	Temporary trooping serial for G-AMUS.
XF923 & XF926	2	Bristol T.188	Stainless steel research aircraft.
XF929-XF931	3	Boulton Paul P.108 Balliol T.2	Replacement aircraft for diversions to Ceylon.
XF932-XF999	55	Hawker Hunter F.4	Hawker (Blackpool) - built. XF932-953, 967-999. Conversions include XF977 to G.A.11. XF942, 967, 977, 985 991, 994, 995 to T.8.
XG127-XG298	110	Hawker Hunter F.6	XG127-137, 169-172, 185-211, 225-239, 251-274, 289-298, Hawker (Kingston)-built; XG150-168, built by A.W.A. Conversions to F.G.A.9 included XG127, 130, 134-136, 151, 154-158, 164, 169, 194-195, 201, 205, 207, 228-229, 237, 251-254, 256, 260-262, 264-265, 273, 291, 292, 296, 298 and to F.R.10, XG127 and 168.
XG303	1	Saro Skeeter Mk. 5	G-AMTZ, for evaluation 1954.
XG307-XG337	20	English Electric Lightning F.1	Pre-production batch. XG307-313, 325-337. XG310 converted to prototype F.3.
XG341-XG342	2	Hawker Hunter F.4	Hawker (Blackpool)-built.
XG349-XG350	2	Vickers Viking	Temporary trooping serials for G-AHPM and G-AJCD.
XG354-XG441	28	Bristol 173	Cancelled. XG354-358, 419-441.
XG447-XG476	26	Bristol 192 Belvedere H.C.1	XG447-468, 473-476.

Serial Nos.	Qty.	Aircraft Type	Remarks
XG491	1	M.L.120	—
XG496	1	D.H.104 Dove 1B	Ex-G-ANDX.
XG500-XG549	36	Bristol 171 Sycamore H.C.14	Production aircraft. XG500-523, 538-549.
XG554	1	English Electric Canberra B.6	Replacement order.
XG558-XG563	6	Scottish Aviation Prestwick Pioneer C.C.1	Production aircraft.
XG567-XG568	2	Vickers Viking	Temporary trooping serials for G-AKBH & G-AIVO.
XG572-XG597	26	Westland WS-55 Whirlwind	H.A.R.3 from XG572, A.S.7 from XG589.
XG603	1	D.H.114 Heron Series 2	No. 14058 for British Joint Services Mission, Washington.
XG606-XG737	100	D.H.112 Sea Venom F.21/22	XG606-638, 653-680, F.21; XG681-702, 721-737, F.22.
XG742-XG777	20	D.H.115 Sea Vampire T.22	XG742-749, 766-777.
XG783-XG889	65	Fairey Gannet A.S.1/A.S.4/T.5/T.2	XG783-798, 825-855, 869-875, 880-890, of these XG784-785, 787, 789, 791-792, 795-796, 825-826 were A.S.1; XG783, 786, 788, 790, 793-794, 797-798, 827-855 were A.S.4; XG869-875, 880-881, 888 were T.2 and XG882-887, 889-890 were T.5. XG837-838, 841-842, 845, 847, 851, 854-855 were cancelled. Conversions included XG790 to C.O.D.4 and XG798 and XG831 to A.S.6. Transfers to R.A.N. included XG795, 825, 826, and 888 which returned to R.N. for conv. to T.5. XG829-830, 833-836, 839-840, 843-844, 846, 849-850, 852-853 to German Navy and XG874 to Indonesian Navy.
XG895-XG896	2	Vickers Viking	Temporary trooping serials for G-AJBO and G-AIVH.
XG897-XG898	2	Avro 685 York	Temporary trooping serials for G-AMRJ and G-ANRC.
XG900 & XG905	2	Short S.C.1	Experimental V.T.O.L.
XG929	1	Avro 685 York	Temporary trooping serial for G-ANSY.
XH116-XH124	9	Blackburn Beverley C.1	Production aircraft.
XH129-XH240	52	English Electric Canberra P.R.9/B.6	Ordered from S. & H. XH129-137, P.R.9 built; XH138-151, 158-163, B.6 cancelled; XH164-177, P.R.9 built; XH178-186, P.R.9 cancelled. XH203-244, B(1)8 built. XH203, 205, 227, 229-230, 232-233, 235-240 offset to I.A.F.

XH249	1	Fairey Rotodyne Z	Cancelled.
XH264-XH368	66	D.H.115 Vampire T.11	XH264-278, 292-330, 357-368. XH268-271 to Rhodesia.
XH375	1	D.H.114 Heron C.3	D.H.14059 ex-G-5-7 for the Queen's Flight.
XH379	1	Bristol 173 Mk. 2	Bristol No. 12872 (G-AMJI) 4-blade rotor naval trials.
XH385	1	Bristol 170 Mk. 31E	Ex-G-AMSA. Bristol No. 13142.
XH390-XH447	20	Gloster Javelin T.3	XH390-397, 432-438, 443-447.
XH455 & XH463	2	D.H.C.2 Beaver	G-AMVU (Srs. 1) & G-ANAR (Srs. 2) for "Battle Royal".
XH469	1	Scottish Aviation Prestwick Pioneer 2	G-ANRG for Exercise "Battle Royal", September 1954.
XH475-XH563	37	Avro 698 Vulcan B.1/B.2	XH475-483, 497-506, 532, B.1 all conv. to B.1A. XH533-539, 554-563, B.2. XH560, 563 conv. to S.R.2.
XH567-XH584	6	English Electric Canberra T.4/B.6	XH567-570(4) B.6. XH583-584 T.4. XH568 special nose probe. XH570 conv. B.16.
XH587-XH675	33	H.P.80 Victor B.1/B.2	XH587-594, 613-621, 645-651, 667, B.1; XH668-675, B.2. All B.1s except XH617 conv. to B.1A. Later XH615, 620, 646-648, 667 conv. to B.(K)1A and XH587-591, 614, 616, 618-619, 621, 645, 649-651 conv. to K.1A. B.2s XH669-671, 673, 675 conv. to K.2 and XH672, 674 to S.R.2.
XH682	1	Bristol 171 Mk. 3	Bristol No. 12886 (G-ALSR) used by Ministry of Supply.
XH687-XJ178	219	Gloster Javelin F.(A.W.)5/6/7/8/9	XH687-692, F.(A.W.)5; XH-693-703, F.(A.W.)6; XH704-725, 746-758, F.(A.W.)7 of which XH707-609, 711-713, 715-717, 719, 721-725, 747, 749, 751-753, 755-758 were conv. to F.(A.W.)9. XH759-772 built as F.(A.W.) 9. XH773-792, F.(A.W.)7 of which XH773-774, 776-780, 785, 787-788, 791-792 were conv. to F.(A.W.)9. XH793 built as F.(A.W.)9. XH794-795 F.(A.W.)7 of which XH794 was conv. to F.(A.W.)9. XH833-836, F.(A.W.)7 conv. to F.(A.W.)9. XH837-838, F.(A.W.)7. XH839-847, F.(A.W.)7 conv. to F.(A.W.)9. XH848-849, F.(A.W.)9. XH871-896, F.(A.W.)9, XH897-912, 955-964. F.(A.W.)7 of which XH897-899, 903-910, 955- 956, 961 conv. to F.(A.W.)9. XH965 F.(A.W.)9. XH966-993, XJ113-130, 165, F.(A.W.)8. XJ166-178 cancelled.

Serial Nos.	*Qty.*	*Aircraft Type*	*Remarks*
XJ249-XJ257	3	English Electric Canberra B.6	Cancelled order. XJ249, 254, 257.
XJ264	1	Avro 685 York	Trooping serial for G-ANVO.
XJ267-XJ309	5	Handley Page H.P.81 Hermes	Temporary trooping serials. XJ267, 269, 280, 281, 309 for G-ALDX/P/U/K/I.
XJ314	1	Thrust Measuring Rig	R-R "Flying Bedstead".
XJ319-XJ350	10	D.H.104 Sea Devon C.20	XJ319-324 ex-G-AMXP/NDY, XB-TAN, G-AMYP/XY/XZ; XJ347-349 ex-G-AMXT/X/W.
XJ355	1	Saro Skeeter Mk. 6 (A.O.P. prototype)	Wks No. SR905. G-ANMH acquired November 1955.
XJ361	1	Bristol 171 Mk. 4	Wks No. 13202 ex-G-AMWU.
XJ362-385	9	Bristol 171 Sycamore H.R.14	XJ362-364, 380-385.
XJ389	1	Fairey Jet Gyrodyne	Ex-G-AJJP, 2nd prototype renumbered from XD759.
XJ393-XJ437	30	Westland WS-55 Whirlwind H.A.R.1-5	XJ393-394 H.A.S. 3 ex-XD363-364. XJ395-402 H.A.S.3 of which XJ398 was prototype H.A.R.5. XJ407-414, H.A.S.4, XJ426, 428 H.A.R.4, XJ429-430 H.A.R.2. XJ431, H.A.R.1; XJ432-436, H.A.R.2; XJ437, H.A.R.4; Conversions to H.A.R.10: XJ398, 407, 409, 410, 411, 412, 414, 426, 428-430, 432-433, 435, 437.
XJ440	1	Fairey Gannet	Prototype. Fairey No. F9431. Crashed nr. Bristol 26.4.60.
XJ445	1	Westland WS-55 Whirlwind H.A.R.5	Used at Farnborough. Laid down as H.A.R.6.
XJ450-XJ466	4	Scottish Aviation Pioneer C.C.1	XJ450-451, 465-466.
XJ470	1	Bristol 170 Freighter 31	Used at A.A.E.E., Boscombe Down. Delivered Mar. 1955.
XJ474-XJ611	78	D.H.110 Sea Vixen F.(A.W.)1/2	D.H. Christchurch built. XJ474-494, 513-528, 556-586, 602-611. Conversions to F.(A.W.)2: XJ489-491, 494, 516-518, 521, 524, 526, 558-561, 564-565, 570-572, 575-576, 578-582, 584, 602, 604, 606-610.
XJ615 & XJ627	2	Hawker P1101 Hunter Trainer (T.7 two-seat) prototypes	XJ615 Avon RA21, XJ627 (Avon 204) later became T.72 J721 of Chilean Air Force.
XJ632-XJ718	45	Hawker Hunter F.6	Built at Kingston. XJ632-646, 673-695, 712-718. Conversions: XJ634, 637, 639, 676 to F.6A; XJ632, 635-636, 638, 640, 642-645, 673-674, 680, 683-691, 695, 713, 716-718 to F.G.A.9; XJ633, 694, 714 to F.R.10. XJ677-679, 681-682 to Iraqi A.F. and XJ712, 715 to R. Saudi A.F. after R.A.F. service XJ645,

			694 became F.56A A968-969 of Indian A.F; XJ713 became F.71 J722 of Chilean A.F., XJ645 became F.73A 831 of R. Jordanian A.F.; XJ632, 642-643, 680, 684, 685, 689 became F.74A 505, 518, 515, 511, 513, 502, 517 and XJ633, 714 became F.74B 534, 533 of Singapore Air Defence Command.
XJ723-XJ766	19	Westland WS-55 Whirlwind H.A.R.2	XJ723-724, H.A.R.4; XJ725-730, 756-760, H.A.R.2; XJ761, H.A.R.4; XJ762-766, H.A.R.2. Conversions to H.A.R.10 include XJ723-724, 726-727, 729, 757, 758, 760, 761, 763-764.
XJ771-XJ776	6	D.H.115 Vampire T.11	XJ773 to Swiss Air Force.
XJ780-XJ784	5	Avro Vulcan B.2	R.A.F.
XJ804	1	Vickers Viking 1B	Trooping serial for G-AJPH.
XJ823-XJ825	3	Avro Vulcan B.2	R.A.F.
XJ830-XJ831	2	Handley Page (Reading) H.P.R.5 Marathon	Ex-G-AMHS & G-AMHV for R.A.E. Farnborough. XJ830 reverted to G-AMHS.
XJ836-XJ887	18	Gloster Javelin (F.153D thin-wing series)	Cancelled. XJ836-842, 877-887.
XJ895-XJ919	9	Bristol 171 Sycamore H.R.14	XJ895-898, 915-919.
XJ924-XJ936	4	Fairey Ultra-light helicopter	XJ924, XJ928 ex-G-AOUJ, XJ930, XJ936 ex-G-AOUK.
XJ941	1	Auster J-5G Autocar	G-ANVN to Malaya 1956 for pest control trials. Became VR-TBR.
XJ945-XK111	50	Hawker Hunter F.6	Cancelled order with Hawker (Blackpool). XJ945-959, 971-997, XK103-111.
XK136-XK355	153	Hawker Hunter F.6	Built at Kingston. XK136-156 for R.A.F. less 10 to Iraqi A.F. XK157-176, 213-224 to Indian A.F. as BA201-232. XK225-241, 257-306, 323-355 cancelled. XK141, 149 conv. to F.6A. XK136-140, 150-151, 154 conv. to F.G.A.9. XK142 conv. to F.74B for Singapore Air Defence Command No. 522.
XK367-XK370	4	Scottish Aviation Prestwick Pioneer C.C.1	XK367 used as ambulance.
XK374-XK421	25	Auster A.O.P.9	XK374-382, 406-421.
XK426	1	Rolls-Royce Thrust Measuring Rig	Crashed at Hucknall 28.11.57.
XK429-XK436	3	Bristol T.188	XK429, 434, 436 cancelled.
XK440-XK473	11	English Electric Canberra P.R.9	XK440-443, 467-473 ordered from S & H. Cancelled.
XK479-XK482	4	Saro Skeeter A.O.P.11	XK479 conv. to T.11 and XK482 conv. to A.O.P.12 before delivery to Army.

Serial Nos.	Qty.	Aircraft Type	Remarks
XK486-XK536	20	Blackburn N.A.39 Buccaneer S.1	Pre-production. XK486-491, 523-536. XK527 became S.2.
XK577	1	Gloster Javelin T.3	R.A.F.
XK582-XK637	25	D.H.115 Vampire T.11	XK582-590, 623-637.
XK641-XK650	3	English Electric Canberra B.6/T.4	XK641 B.6; XK647 & 650, T.4 to I.A.F. as IQ994/995.
XK655-XK716	13	D.H.106 Comet C.2	XK655, 659, 663, 2R ex-G-AMXA/C/E: XK669-670, T.2 (ex-G-AMXB/F) *Taurus* and *Corvus*. XK671, 695-698, C.2 (ex-G-AMXG/H/I/J/L) *Aquila*, *Perseus*, *Orion*, *Cygnus* and *Pegasus*. XK699, 715, 716, C.2 *Sagittarius*, *Columba* and *Cepheus*. All built at Hatfield, except XK 716 at Chester.
XK724-XK768	6	Folland Gnat	XK724, 739-741, 767, 768. XK768 to I.A.F. as IE1059.
XK773	1	Saro Skeeter Mk. 6	Wks No. SR904. Ex-G-ANMG.
XK776-XK784	3	M.L. Utility Mk. 1	Inflatable wing aircraft, XK776, 781, 784.
XK788-XK824	10	Slingsby T.38 Grasshopper TX.1	XK788-791, 819-824 for A.T.C.
XK859-XK885	6	Percival Pembroke C.1	XK859-862, 884-885.
XK889	1	Percival P.74	Experimental helicopter for M.O.S. Not flown.
XK895-XK897	3	D.H.104 Sea Devon C.20	D.H. Nos. 04472-04474. XK897 became G-AROI.
XK902-XK903	2	Bristol 171 Sycamore H.R.51	For R.A.N. XK903 re-serialled XL507.
XK906-XK945	20	Westland WS-55 Whirlwind H.A.S.7	XK906-912, 933-945.
XK951-XK959	4	English Electric Canberra B(I)8	XK951-952 R.A.F. XK953, 959 to I.A.F. as IF895/898.
XK964	1	Saro Skeeter Mk. 6	Wks Nos. SR906.Ex-G-ANMI.
XK968-XL113	14	Westland S.55 Whirlwind H.A.R.2/4	XK968-970, 986-991, H.A.R.2; XL109-113, H.A.R.4. XK968-970, 986, 987-988, 990-991, XL109, 110-112 conv. to H.A.R.10.
XL117-XL152	8	Blackburn Beverley C.1	XL117-119 renumbered 130-132, 148-152.
XL158-XL233	18	Handley Page H.P.80 Victor B.2	XL158-165, 188-193, 230-233, XL162-164, 188, 231-233 conv. to B.2R. XL161, 165, 193, 230 conv. to S.R.2. Later XL158, 160-164, 188-192, 231-233 conv. to K.2.
XL237-XL314	22	Hawker Seahawk F.6 (becoming F.50)	XL237-241, 269-275, 305-314 to R. Ned. Navy.
XL317-XL446	24	Avro Vulcan B.2	XL317-321, 359-361, 384-392, 425-427, 443-446.
XL449-XL503	30	Fairey Gannet A.E.W.3	XL449-455, 471-482, 493-503 for Royal Navy.
XL507	1	Bristol 171 Sycamore H.R.51	For R.A.N. Was incorrectly marked XK903 for 2 days.

XL511-XL513	3	Handley Page H.P.80 Victor B.2/K.2	Converted to B.2R, then later to K.2.
XL517-XL588	10	Scottish Aviation Prestwick Pioneer C.C.1	XL517 ex-G-AOGK to R.A.F. in 1956. XL518-520, 553-558.
XL563-XL623	55	Hawker Hunter T.7/T.8	XL563-587, 591-605, 609-623 for R.A.F. as T.7. 10 (XL580-582, 584-585, 598-599, 602-604) T.8 for R.N. XL602-603 conv. to T.8M. XL605, 620 to R. Saudi A.F.
XL628-XL629	2	English Electric Lightning T.4	Prototypes of trainer version.
XL635-XL660	10	Bristol 253 Britannia C.1	XL635-640, *Bellatrix, Argo, Vega, Sirius, Atria, Antares.* XL657-660, *Rigel, Adhara, Polaris, Alphard.*
XL664-XL706	18	Scottish Aviation Prestwick Pioneer C.C.1	XL664-674, 700-706 of which XL668, 670-674 were offset to Royal Ceylonese Air Force.
XL710	1	D.H.C.3 Otter	For 1956 Commonwealth Trans-Antarctic Expedition. Became R.N.Z.A.F. NZ6081.
XL714-XL717	4	D.H.82A Tiger Moth	Reconditioned for Royal Navy. Ex-G-AOGR/IK/IL/XG (ex-T6099, T7373, DE395, T7291).
XL722	1	Sikorsky S-58 Wessex	Prototype. American-built.
XL727-XL729	3	Westland WS-58 Wessex H.A.S.1	R.N. pre-production. XL728 to H.C.2 standard for R.A.E.
XL734-XL814	27	Saro Skeeter A.O.P.12	XL734-740, 762-772, 806-814.
XL820-XL829	10	Bristol 171 Sycamore H.R.14	Production.
XL833-XL900	45	Westland WS-55 Whirlwind H.A.S.7	XL833-854, 867-884, 896-900. XL839, 843, 873, 875, 880, 896, 898, 900 conv. to H.A.S.9.
XL905-XL921	5	Saro S.R.177	XL905-907, 920-921 cancelled.
XL929-XL956	7	Percival P.66 Pembroke C.1	XL929-931, 953-956 for R.A.F.
XL961	1	D.H.114 Heron 2 Series 2	G-AMTS for Princess Margaret's East African Tour.
XL966-XL997	12	Scottish Aviation Twin Pioneer C.C.1	XL966-970, 991-997 for R.A.F.
XM103-XM112	10	Blackburn B.101 Beverley C.1	R.A.F.
XM117-XM126	10	Hawker Hunter T.7	To R. Ned. A.F. as N311-320.
XM134-XM218	48	English Electric Lightning F.1/F.1A	XM134-147, 163-167 F.1; XM168 not completed, parts used for static tests; XM169-192, 214-216 F.1A; XM217-218 not built.
XM223	1	D.H.104 Devon C.1	D.H. No. 04498, conv. to C.2.
XM244-XM279	23	English Electric Canberra B.(I)8	XM244-247, 261-279. XM273 to Peru as No. 253.
XM284-XM291	8	Scottish Aviation Twin Pioneer C.C.1	R.A.F.
XM295-XM296	2	D.H.114 Heron C.(VVIP)4	Built by D.H. at Chester for The Queen's Flight. XM296 to R.N. in 1972.
XM299-XM331	9	Westland WS-58	XM299-301, 326-331. XM299

Serial Nos.	*Qty.*	*Aircraft Type*	*Remarks*
		Wessex H.A.S.1	conv. to H.C.2 standard. XM327-328 conv. to H.A.S.3.
XM336	1	Gloster Javelin T.3	R.A.F.
XM346-XM480	100	Hunting Jet Provost T.3	XM346-387, 401-428, 451-80. Conversions to T.3A.
XM489-XM520	10	Bristol 253 Britannia C.1	XM489-491, *Denebola, Aldebaran* & *Procyon;* XM496-498, *Regulus, Schedar, Hadar;* XM517-520, *Avoir, Spica, Capella* & *Arcturus.*
XM524-XM565	20	Saro Skeeter A.O.P.12	XM524-530, 553-565.
XM569-XM657	40	Avro Vulcan B.2	XM569-576, 594-612, 645-657.
XM660-XM687	15	Westland WS-55 Whirlwind H.A.S.7	XM660-669, 683-687.
XM691-XM709	14	Folland Gnat T.1	XM691-698, 704-709.
XM714-XM794	27	Handley Page H.P.80 Victor B.2	XM714-718 (5 only) B.2 built. XM715, 716, 718 conv. to S.R.2. XM715 and XM717 to K.2. XM745-756, 785-794 cancelled.
XM797 & XM819	2	Edgar Percival E.P.9	Army evaluation. Later G-ARTU/V.
XM823 & XM829	2	D.H.106 Comet 1XB	Ex-IA G-ARTU/V.
XM832-XM931	39	Westland WS-58 Wessex H.A.S.1	XM832-845, 868-875, 915-931. XM833, 834, 836, 837, 838, 844, 870-872, 916, 918-920, 923, 927 conv. H.A.S.3. XM875 conv. A.S.R.
XM936	1	English Electric Canberra B.(I)8	Replacement aircraft. To Peruvian Air Force No. 254, 1975.
XM939-XM963	12	Scottish Aviation Twin Pioneer C.C.1	XM939-943, 957-963.
XM966-XN112	30	English Electric (later B.A.C.) Lightning T.4	XM966-974, 987-997. XM966-968 conv. to T.5. XM989, 992 to R. Saudi A.F. as T.54s. XN103-112 cancelled.
XN117	1	Hunting (later B.A.C.) Jet Provost T.3	Ex-G-23-1. To Aden for tropical trials 1958.
XN122	1	Folland Gnat	Trials at Aden. Later I.A.F.
XN126-XN127	2	Westland WS-55 Whirlwind H.C.C.8	Produced for The Queen's Flight, later became H.A.R.10.
XN132-XN133	2	Sud Alouette II	A.A.C trials 1958.
XN137	1	Hunting Percival Jet Provost T.3	—
XN142	1	D.H.C.2 Beaver Series 2	G-ANAR for Army, 1958.
XN146-XN189	19	Slingsby T.21B Sedbergh TX.1	XN146-157, 183-189 mainly for A.T.C.
XN194-XN253	24	Slingsby T.31B Kirby Cadet TX.3	XN194-199, 236-253 mainly for A.T.C.
XN258-XN314	25	Westland WS-55 Whirlwind H.A.S.7	XN258-264, 297-314. XN258, 309-311 conv. to H.A.S.9.
XN318-XN321	4	Scottish Aviation Twin Pioneer C.C.2	C/N 573-6. All delivered to Far East.
XN326	1	Folland Gnat F.1	For M.O.S. evaluation, 1959.
XN332-XN334	3	Westland P.531/0	Evaluation batch for Royal Navy. XN332 ex-G-APNV.

XN339-XN355	17	Saro Skeeter A.O.P.12	For Army Air Corps.
XN357-XN387	15	Westland WS-55 Whirlwind H.A.S.7	XN357-362, 379-387. XN359, 384, 386, 387 converted to H.A.S.9.
XN392-XN404	3	Bristol 252 Britannia C.2	XN392, 398, 404 named *Acrux*, *Altair*, *Canopus*.
XN407-XN443	15	Auster A.O.P.9	A.A.C. XN407-412, 435-443.
XN448-XN450	3	Bristol Sycamore H.R.51	For Royal Australian Navy.
XN453	1	D.H.106 Comet 2E	G-AMXD converted as flying radar research laboratory.
XN458-XN643	100	Hunting (later B.A.C.) Jet Provost T.3	XN458-473, 492-512, 547-559, 573-607, 629-643. XN467-468 became prototype T.4s.
XN635	1	Bristol Sycamore H.R.51	Incorrectly numbered. See XR592.
XN647-XN710	40	D.H.10 Sea Vixen F.(A.W.)1	XN647-658, 683-710. All but XN648, 695, 698, 701, 703, 708-710 conv. to F.(A.W.)2. XN657 to D.3.
XN714 & XN719	2	B.A.C. (Hunting) H.126	Jet flap research aircraft.
XN723-XN797	44	English Electric (later B.A.C.) Lightning F.2	XN723-735, 767-797. Most conv. to F.2A standard.
XN814-XN858	20	Armstrong Whitworth A.W.660 Argosy C.1	XN814-821, 847-858. XN814, 816, 855 conv. to E.1.
XN862-XN903	40	Northrop KD2R-5 Shelduck D.1	Targets for Royal Navy. XN862-876, 893-917.
XN922-XN983	50	Blackburn (later Hawker Siddeley) Buccaneer S.1/2	Produced for R.N. XN922-935, 948-973, S.1; XN974-983, S.2. Some S.2s to R.A.F.
XP103-XP160	40	Westland WS-58 Wessex H.A.S.1	XP103-118, 137-160. Conversions to H.A.S.3; XP104, 105, 110, 116, 118, 137-140, 142-143, 147, 150, 153, 156.
XP165-XP192	8	Westland Scout A.H.1	A.A.C. XP165-167, 188-192. XP166 had Wasp tail. XP189 Lynx rotor test.
XP197-XP229	9	Fairey Gannet A.E.W.3	For Royal Navy. XP197-199, 224-229.
XP232-XP286	33	Auster A.O.P.9	A.A.C. XP232-254, 277-286. XP254 prototype Beagle-Auster A.O.P.11.
XP293-XP295	3	Scottish Aviation Twin Pioneer C.C.2	Final production for R.A.F.
XP299-XP405	52	Westland WS-55 Whirlwind H.A.R.10	XP299-303, 327-333, 338-363, 392-405.
XP408-XP450	20	Armstrong Whitworth A.W.660 Argosy C.1	XP408-413, 437-450. XP413, 439, 448 conv. E.1. XP411, 417 were being conv. to T.2 when programme was abandoned.
XP454-XP495	20	Slingsby T.38 Grasshopper TX.1	XP454-464, 487-495 for Air Training Corps.
XP500-XP542	30	Folland Gnat T.1	XP500-516, 530-542.
XP547-XP688	100	B.A.C. Jet Provost T.4	XP547-589, 614-642, 661-688.
XP693-XP765	47	B.A.C. Lightning F.3	XP693-708, 735-765.
XP769-XP827	36	D.H.C.2 Beaver A.L.1	A.A.C. XP769-780, 804-827.
XP831 & XP836	2	Hawker P.1127	Kestrel prototypes.
XP841	1	Handley Page H.P.115	Research Aircraft.
XP846-XP910	40	Westland Scout A.H.1	A.A.C. XP846-857, 883-910.

Serial Nos.	*Qty.*	*Aircraft Type*	*Remarks*
XP915	1	D.H.106 Comet 3	Ex-G-ANLO for research.
XP918-XP959	15	D.H.110 Sea Vixen F.(A.W.)1/2	XP918 F.(A.W.)1 conv. to F.(A.W.)2. XP919-925, 953-959 built as F.(A.W.)2.
XP966-XP967	2	Sud SE3130 Alouette II	For evaluation by Army Air Corps.
XP972-XP984	4	Hawker P.1127 Kestrel	Development models XP972, 976, 980, 984.
XR105-XR143	16	Armstrong Whitworth A.W.660 Argosy C.1	XR105-109, 133-143. XR137, 140, 143 conv. to E.1; XR136 conv. to T.2.
XR148-XR209	40	Northrop KD2R-5 Shelduck D.1	Aerial targets for Royal Navy. XR148-162, 185-209.
XR213-XR216	4	D.H.C.2 Beaver A.L.1	For Muscat & Oman Air Force.
XR219-XR227	9	B.A.C. TSR-2	First 3 only completed.
XR232	1	Sud Alouette II	Purchased in France.
XR236-XR271	16	Auster A.O.P.9	A.A.C. XR236-246, 267-271.
XR290-XR351	44	Beech SD-1 Peeping Tom	Drone for Army. XR290-314, 333-351.
XR352-XR354	3	Northrop Shelduck D.1	Drone for Royal Navy.
XR362-XR371	10	Short & Harland Belfast C.1	For R.A.F. Named *Samson Goliath*, *Pallus*, *Hector*, *Atlas*, *Heracles*, *Theseus*, *Spartacus*, *Ajax*, *Enceladus*.
XR376-XR387	12	Sud SE3130 Alouette II	For Army Air Corps.
XR391	1	D.H.114 Heron C.4	For The Queen's Flight.
XR395-XR399	5	D.H.106 Comet C.4	Built by D.H. (Chester).
XR431-XR433	3	Fairey Gannet A.E.W.3	For Royal Navy.
XR436	1	Westland P.531	For Empire Test Pilots School.
XR441-XR445	5	D.H.114 Sea Heron C.20	Ex-civil G-AORG/H, VR-NAQ/NCE/NCF for R.N.
XR447-XR450	4	Northrop Shelduck D.1	Drone for Royal Navy.
XR452-XR487	18	Westland WS-55 Whirlwind H.A.R.10/ H.C.C.12	XR452-458, 477-485 H.A.R. 10. XR486-487 H.C.C.12 for The Queen's Flight.
XR493	1	Westland P.531	R.N. Wasp proto. Ex-G-APVM.
XR497-XR529	30	Westland WS-58 Wessex. H.C.2	XR497-511, 515-529.
XR534-XR574	20	Folland Gnat T.1	XR534-545, 567-574.
XR588	1	Westland WS-58 Wessex H.C.2	Prototype.
XR592	1	Bristol 171 Sycamore H.R.51	For Royal Australian Navy. Incorrectly numbered XN635.
XR595-XR640	24	Westland Scout A.H.1	XR595-604, 627-640.
XR643-XR707	50	B.A.C. Jet Provost T.4	XR643-681, 697-707.
XR711-XR773	45	B.A.C. Lightning F.3/F.6	XR711-722, F.3; XR723-728, 747, F.6; XR748-751, F.3; XR752-773, F.6.
XR801-XR802	2	Vickers 744/745 Viscount	Ex-civil air liners for Empire Test Pilots School.
XR806-XR810	5	Vickers 1106 (later B.A.C.) VC-10	Named *George Thompson V.C.*, *Donald Garland V.C. & Thomas Gray V.C.*, *Kenneth*

			Campbell V.C., *Hugh Malcolm V.C.* and *David Lord V.C.*
XR814	1	Cushioncraft C.C.2	Hovercraft for evaluation.
XR818-XR	—	Northrop Shelduck D.1	Drone for Royal Navy.
XR920-	—	Beech SD-1 Peeping Tom	Drone for Army.
XR937	1	Sud SE3130 Alouette II	For evaluation.
XR942-XR944	3	Beagle-Wallis WA-116	G-ARZA-C for evaluation.
XR948-XS111	41	Folland Gnat T.1	XR948-955, 976-987, 991-999 XS100-111.
XS115-XS154	20	Westland WS58 Wessex H.A.S.1	XS115-128, 149-154. XS119, 121-122, 149, 153 conv. to H.A.S.3.
XS159-XS172	14	Hiller H.T.2	Hiller for UH-12E R.N.
XS175-XS231	35	B.A.C. Jet Provost T.4	XS175-186, 209-231. XS231 became prototype T.5 and XS230 was converted to the same standard.
XS235	1	D.H.106 Comet 4C	Navigational Systems trials.
XS238	1	Auster A.O.P.9	
XS241	1	Westland WS-58 Wessex H.U.5	Prototype for R.N.
XS246-XS	—	Northrop Shelduck D.1	Drone for Royal Navy.
XS341	1	"Scott-Furlong Predator"	Fictitious. No given mock-up I.T.V. "The Plane Makers".
XS349	1	Hughes 269A	Helicopter for evaluation.
XS412	1	Westland WS-55 Whirlwind H.A.R. 10	For R.A.F.
XS416-XS460	20	B.A.C. Lightning T.5	XS416-423, 449-460. XS460 exported as T.55.
XS463 & XS476	2	Westland Wasp H.A.S.1	For development trials.
XS479-XS523	40	Westland WS-58 Wessex H.U.5	XS479-500, 506-523.
XS527-XS572	30	Westland Wasp H.A.S.1	XS527-545, 562-572 for R.N.
XS576-XS590	15	D.H.110 Sea Vixen F.(A.W.)2	Production for Royal Navy. XS577 conv. to D.3.
XS594-XS647	31	H.S.780 Andover C.1	XS594-613, 637-647. XS599, 600, 602, 604, 608, 611-613, 638, 645 to R.N.Z.A.F. as NZ7620-7629. XS603, 605, 610, 639-641 conv. E.3.
XS650-XS652	3	Slingsby 45 Swallow	Gliders for A.T.C.
XS655	1	Westland SRN-3	Hovercraft for evaluation.
XS660-XS670	11	B.A.C. T.S.R.2	Cancelled.
XS674-XS679	6	Westland WS-58 Wessex H.C.2	For R.A.F.
XS681-XS683	3	Brantly B.2	XS682 B.2A, XS683 B.2B.
XS684	1	Hughes 269A	G-ASBD evaluated.
XS688-XS696	9	H.S. Kestrel F.G.A.1	Tripartite evaluation as Nos 8, 9, 0, 1-6. XS688-694 became USAF 64-18262 to 18268.
XS700-XS706	7	Hiller H.T.2	Hiller UH-12E for R.N.
XS709-XS739	20	H.S.125 Dominie T.1	XS709-714, 726-739 for R.A.F.
XS742-XS784	22	Beagle B.206Z Basset C.C.1	XS742-743 B.206Z1/Z2 for evaluation. XS765-784 for

Serial Nos.	Qty.	Aircraft Type	Remarks
			R.A.F. XS770 used by The Queen's Flight.
XS789-XS794	6	H.S.748 Andover C.C.2	XS789-790 VIP standard for The Queen's Flight.
XS798	1	Vickers VA-1	Modified by A.T.C.
XS856	1	Vickers VA-3	Hovercraft for evaluation.
XS859	1	Slingsby T.45 Swallow	BGA1136 for evaluation.
XS862-XS889	28	Westland S-58 Wessex H.A.S.1	XS862, 873 converted to H.A.S.3.
XS893-XS938	33	B.A.C. Lightning F.6	XS893-904, 918-938.
XS941	1	Miles M.100 Student 2	G-APLK for evaluation.
XS944	—	B.A.C. T.S.R.2	Cancelled.
XT101-XT150	50	Agusta-Bell 47G3 Sioux A.H.1	Italian-built for Army Aviation.
XT151-XT250	100	Bell 47G3 Sioux A.H.1	Westland built.
XT255-XT257	3	Westland WS-58 Wessex H.A.S.3	For Royal Navy.
XT269-XT288	20	H.S. Buccaneer S.2A/C	Modified to S.2B/D.
XT305-XT	—	Northrop KD 2R-5 Shelduck D.1	Aerial targets for Royal Navy.
XT405-XT406	2	Bell 47G3 Sioux A.H.1	For Army Aviation.
XT414-XT443	30	Westland Wasp H.A.S.1	For Royal Navy.
XT448-XT487	40	Westland WS-58 Wessex H.U.5	For R.N. XT452, 478 given to Bangladesh.
XT492-XT493	2	Westland SRN-5	Hovercraft. XT493 conv. SRN-6 Mk.5.
XT498-XT570	50	Bell 47G3 Sioux A.H.1	XT498-516, 540-570.
XT575	1	Vickers Viscount 800	Ex-OE-LAG for R.R.E.
XT581	—	Northrop SD-1	Drone for Army.
XT592	1	Westland SRN-5	Hovercraft for evaluation.
XT595-XT598	4	McDonnell-Douglas Phantom F.G.1	Pre-delivery examples of F-4K for Royal Navy.
XT601-XT607	7	Westland WS-58 Wessex H.C.2	For R.A.F. XT601, 604 modified for rescue role.
XT610	1	Scottish Aviation Twin Pioneer	G-APRS acquired for Empire Test Pilots' School.
XT614-XT649	36	Westland Scout A.H.1	For Army Aviation.
XT653	1	Slingsby 45 Swallow	Glider.
XT657	1	Westland SRN-5	Hovercraft. Conv. to SRN-6 Mk.5.
XT661	1	Vickers Viscount 838	Ex-9G-AAV for M.O.A.
XT667-XT681	15	Westland WS-58 Wessex H.C.2	For R.A.F.
XT729-XT7	—	Northrop KD2R-5 Shelduck D.1	Aerial targets for Royal Navy.
XT752	1	Fairey Gannet T.5	Ex-WW365 & G-APYO.
XT755-XT774	20	Westland WS-58 Wessex H.U.5	For Royal Navy. XT770 & XT772 for V.I.P. use.
XT778-XT795	18	Westland Wasp H.A.S.1	For Royal Navy.
XT798-XT849	49	Bell 47G3 Sioux A.H.1	XT798-820, 824-849.
XT852-XT914	46	McDonnell-Douglas Phantom F.G.1/ F.G.R.2 (F-4K/M)	XT852-853 YF-4M pre-delivery. XT857-876, F.G.1; XT891-914, F.G.R.2.
XT965	1	Ventura	Drone for Royal Navy.
XV101-XV109	9	B.A.C. VC-10	Named *Lanoe Hawker V.C.*,

			Guy Gibson, V.C., Edward Mannock V.C., James McCudden V.C., Albert Ball V.C., Thomas Mottershead V.C., James Nicolson V.C., William Rhodes-Moorhouse V.C. and *Arthur Scarf V.C.* respectively.
XV118-XV141	24	Westland Scout A.H.1	For Army Aviation.
XV144	1	D.H.106 Comet 2E	Ex-G-AMXK for B.L.U.E.
XV147-XV148	2	H.S.801 Nimrod M.R.1	Protos. Ex-Comet airframes.
XV152-XV168	17	H.S. Buccaneer S.2A	Conversions to S.2B.
XV176-XV223	48	Lockheed Hercules C.1	XV208 conv. to W.2.
XV226-XV263	38	H.S.801 Nimrod M.R.1	Production for R.A.F.
XV268-XV273	6	D.H.C.2 Beaver A.L.1	For Army Aviation.
XV276-XV281	6	H.S. Harrier G.R.1	Pre-production.
XV290-XV307	18	Lockheed Hercules C.1	C-130Ks for R.A.F.
XV310-XV324	15	Bell 47G3 Sioux H.T.2	Westland-built for R.A.F.
XV328-XV329	2	B.A.C. Lightning T.5	For R.A.F.
XV332-XV361	30	H.S. Buccaneer S.2A/C	Conversions to S.2B/D.
XV370-XV373	4	Sikorsky WS-61 Sea King H.A.S.1	XV370 ex-G-ATYU American S-61. Rest Westland WS-61.
XV393-XV592	120	McDonnell-Douglas Phantom F.G.R.2/ F.G.1	XV393-442, 460-501 (92), F.G.R.2. XV565-592, F.G.1.
XV614 & XV617	2	British Hovercraft SRN-6 Wellington	Hovercraft to Army and Navy for evaluation.
XV622-XV639	18	Westland Wasp H.A.S.1	Production for R.N.
XV642-XV709	56	Westland WS-61 Sea King H.A.S.1	XV642-677, 695-714 for R.N. XV698 conv. to H.A.S.2.
XV719-XV733	15	Westland S-58 Wessex H.C.2/H.C.C.4	XV719-731, H.C.2; XV732-733 H.C.C.4 Queen's Flt.
XV738-XV810	60	H.S. Harrier G.R.1	XV738-762, 776-810. Majority conv. to G.R.1A, then G.R.3.
XV814	1	D.H. Comet 4	Ex-G-APDF.
XV821-XV8	—	Ventura	Drones for R.N.
XV859	1	Westland SRN-6	Hovercraft.
XV863-XV869	7	H.S. Buccaneer S.2A	Majority conv. to S.2D.
XV884-XV947	50	General Dynamics F/TF-111K	Cancelled. XV884-887, TF-111K; XV902-947, F-1111K.
XV951	1	Slingsby T. 53B	Glider for evaluation.
XV983	1	Slingsby T.61 Falke	Ex-G-AYUP.
XW10 -XW1	—	Northrop KD2R-5 Shelduck D.1	Drones.
XW174-XW175	2	H.S. Harrier T.2	Two-seat prototypes.
XW179-XW195	17	Bell 47G3 Sioux A.H.1	Westland-built for Army.
XW198-XW237	40	Sud SA330 Puma H.C.1	Westland-built for R.A.F.
XW241	1	Sud SA330E	F-ZJUX for evaluation.
XW246	1	British Hovercraft SRN-5	Hovercraft. SRN-5006.
XW249	1	Cushioncraft C.C.1	Hovercraft.
XW255	1	British Hovercraft BH-7	Hovercraft.
XW264-XW272	9	H.S. Harrier T.2	Majority conv. to T.2A/T.4.
XW276	1	Sud SA341 Gazelle	French prototype 03 for test.
XW280-XW284	5	Westland Scout A.H.1	For Army Aviation.
XW287-XW438	110	B.A.C. Jet Provost T.5	XW287-336, 351-375. 404-438.
XW4-XW5	—	Northrop KD2R-5 Shelduck D.1	Aerial targets for R.N.
XW525-XW550	26	H.S. Buccaneer S.2B	For R.A.F.

Serial Nos.	*Qty.*	*Aircraft Type*	*Remarks*
XW560-XW566	3	B.A.C./Breguet Jaguar	British-built prototypes SO6 SO7 and two-seat BO8. XW 560, 563, 566.
XW612-XW617	6	Westland Scout A.H.1	For Army.
XW626	1	D.H. Comet 4C	Ex-G-APDS.
XW630	1	H.S. Harrier G.R.1	Converted to G.R.3.
XW635	1	Beagle D.5/180 Husky	Named *Spirit of Butlin's*. Presented to A.T.C. by Butlin's and Hughie Green.
XW664-XW666	3	H.S. Nimrod R.1	R.A.F.
XW672-XW	—	Northrop KD2R-5 Shelduck D.1	Drones.
XW750	1	H.S.748 Srs 107	Ex-G-ASJT for R.A.E.
XW763-XW771	9	H.S. Harrier G.R.1	Majority to G.R.3 via G.R.1A.
XW778-XW780	3	H.S. Harrier T.2	Re-numbered XW925-927.
XW784	1	Mitchell Procter Kittiwake	Built by R.N. apprentices, Arbroath.
XW788-XW791	4	H.S. 125 C.C.1	R.N./R.A.F.
XW795-XW799	5	Westland Scout A.H.1	Final production.
XW8-XW8	—	Northrop KD2R-5 Shelduck D.1	Aerial targets for R.N.
XW835-XW839	5	Westland Lynx	Prototypes. Colour-coded yellow, light grey, red, turquoise and orange.
XW842-XW913	60	Sud 341 Gazelle A.H.1 (Army) H.T.2 (Navy) H.T.3 (R.A.F.)	XW842-844, A.H.1; XW845, H.T. 2; XW846-851, A.H.1; XW852, H.T.3; XW853-854, H.T.2; XW855, H.C.C.4; XW856-857, H.T.2; XW858, H.T.3; XW859-861, H.T.2; XW862, H.T.3; XW863-864, H.T.2; XW865, A.H.1; XW866, H.T.3; XW867-868, H.T.2; XW869, A.H.1; XW870, H.T.3; XW871, 884, H.T.2; XW885, A.H.1; XW886-887, H.T.2; XW888-889, A.H.1; XW890-891, H.T.2; XW892-893, A.H.1; XW894-895, H.T.2; XW896-897, A.H.1; XW898, H.T.3; XW899-901, A.H.1; XW902, H.T.3; XW903-905, A.H.1; XW906, H.T.3; XW907, H.T.2; XW908-909, A.H.1; XW910, H.T.3; XW911-913, A.H.1.
XW916-XW924	9	H.S. Harrier G.R.1	Majority conv. G.R.3 via G.R.1A.
XW925-XW927	3	H.S. Harrier T.2	Later conv. to T.4.
XW930	1	H.S.125 C.C.1	Ex-G-ATPC for R.A.F.
XW933-XW934	2	H.S. Harrier T.2/T.4	T.2 converted to T.4.
XW938	1	Piper Twin Commanche	PA-30 ex-G-ATMT.
XW983	1	Schiebe SF-25B Motorfalke	Powered glider evaluated for A.T.C. ex-G-AYUP.
XW986-XW988	3	H.S. Buccaneer S.2B	Delivered to R.A.E.
XW991-XW999	—	MQM-74A Chuka	Drones.
XX101	1	Cushioncraft C.C.1	Hovercraft. Army evaluation.

XX105	1	B.A.C. One-Eleven	Series 201. Ex-G-ASTD.
XX108-XX150	30	B.A.C./Breguet Jaguar G.R.1/T.2	XX108-122, G.R.1; XX136-150, T.2.
XX153	1	Westland Lynx	Army prototype.
XX154-XX353	126	Hawker Siddeley Hawk T.1	XX154, 156-205, 217-266, 278-327, 329-353.
XX367	1	Bristol Britannia	Series 312F. Ex-EC-BSY.
XX370-XX462	79	Sud 341 Gazelle A.H.1 (Army) H.T.2 (Navy) H.T.3 (R.A.F.)	XX370-373, A.H.1; XX374, H.T.3; XX375-381, A.H.1; XX382, H.T.3; XX383-390, A.H.1; XX391, H.T.2; XX392-395, A.H.1; XX396, H.T.3; XX397, H.T.2: XX398-405, A.H.1; XX406, H.T.3; XX407-409, A.H.1; XX410, H.T.2; XX411-414, A.H.1; XX415, H.T.2; XX416-418, A.H.1; XX419, 431, H.T.2; XX432-435, A.H.1; XX436, H.T.2; XX440, A.H.1 ex-G-BCHN. XX441, H.T.2; XX442-445, A.H.1; XX446, H.T.2; XX447-450, A.H.1; XX451, H.T.2; XX452-462, A.H.1.
XX466-XX467	2	Hawker Hunter T.7	Ex-Jordanian T.66.
XX469	1	Westland Lynx	1st naval prototype.
XX475-XX500	26	Scottish Aviation Jetstream T.1/2	T.1s for R.A.F. except XX476, 478-487, 489, T.2s for R.N.
XX505-XX508	4	H.S.125 C.C.2	R.A.F.
XX510	1	Westland Lynx	2nd naval prototype.
XX513-XX714	130	Scottish Aviation Bulldog T.1	XX513-562, 611-640, 653-672, 685-714 for R.A.F.
XX719-XX847	81	B.A.C./Breguet Jaguar G.R.1/T.2	XX719-768, 817-827, G.R.1; XX828-847, T.2.
XX885-XX901	17	H.S. Buccaneer S.2B	For R.A.F.
XX904-XX911	4	Westland Lynx	Prototypes. XX904, 907, 910, 911.
XX914	1	B.A.C. VC-10	Ex-G-ATDJ for R.A.E.
XX915-XX916	2	B.A.C./Breguet Jaguar T.2	For R.A.F.
XX919	1	B.A.C. One Eleven	Series 400.
XX946-XX950	5	Panavia Tornado	Prototypes.
XX955-XZ120	45	B.A.C./Breguet Jaguar G.R.1	XX955-979, XZ101-120.
XZ128-XZ	—	H.S. Harrier G.R.3/T.2	From XZ145 T.2.
XZ166-	—	Westland Lynx	From XA170 A.H.1.
XZ227-XZ2	—	Westland Lynx H.A.S.2/A.H.1	For R.N./Army and Aeronavale.
XZ280-XZ287	8	Hawker Siddeley Nimrod M.R.2	For R.A.F. Conversions to A.E.W.3s include XZ286.
XZ290-XZ3	—	Sud SA.341 Gazelle A.H.1	For Army.
XZ355-XZ4	—	B.A.C./Breguet Jaguar G.R.1	For R.A.F.
XZ430-XZ432	3	H.S. Buccaneer S.2	
XZ438-XZ	—	H.S. Harrier F.R.S.1	For R.N.
XZ550-XZ564	15	Schiebe SF-25B Venture T.2	Powered gliders for Air Training Corps.

Serial Nos.	*Qty.*	*Aircraft Type*	*Remarks*
XZ570-	—	Westland Sea King H.A.S.2/H.A.R.3	From XZ570 H.A.S.2 for R.N., from XZ585 H.A.R.3 for R.A.F.
XZ630	—	Panavia Tornado	For R.A.F.
XZ930-		Sud SA.341 Gazelle	
ZA101-		H.S. Hawk	ZA101 export model.
ZA140-ZA	—	B.A.C. VC-10 tanker conversions	Ex-civil aircraft.
ZA250		H.S. Harrier T.52	Also registered G-VTOL.

APPENDIX

INTELLIGENCE NUMBERING—AIR MIN SERIES

AT the end of the 1939-1945 War a large-scale evaluation of former enemy aircraft was embarked upon by British Air Intelligence. Aircraft brought to the United Kingdom for evaluation were numbered in a special series from No. 1 with the prefix AIR MIN for Air Ministry series. Such aircraft were normally for static evaluation or exhibition, but when required to fly a normal serial number was allotted. Details not known where numbers have been omitted.

Air Min No.	*Aircraft Type and Number (where known)*	*Remarks*
1	Junkers Ju88	Held by Central Fighter Establishment.
2	Junkers Ju88	Held by Radio Warfare Establishment.
3	Junkers Ju88G	
4	Siebel Si204D-1	German markinks BU+PP.
5	Siebel Si204D-1	Held by No. 6 Maintenance Unit.
6	Junkers Ju290	First example of type held.
8	Junkers Ju352A-1	First of type acquired.
9	Junkers Ju88G 621965	Serial VL991. Scrapped 1950.
10	Focke Wulf FW190A	Sent to South Africa.
11	Focke Wulf Ta152H-1 150168	Number also allotted to FW190.
12	Siebel Si204D	
13	Siebel Si204D	
14	Junkers Ju88G 620788	German marking NF+DW.
15	Messerschmitt Bf110G	
16	Junkers Ju88G	
17	Arado Ar232B	German marking R+A3.
18	Junkers Ju352	
19	Junkers Ju352	
20	Heinkel He219A-7	
21	Heinkel He219A-7	
22	Heinkel He219V11 310189	Sub-type prototype.
24	Arado Ar234B-2	Crashed ferrying 27.8.45.
25	Arado Ar234B	Held by No. 6 Maintenance Unit.
26	Arado Ar234B 140476	Serial VK877.
27	Focke Wulf FW189A-3	
28	Siebel Si204D-1	
29	Focke Wulf FW190A-8 584219	Held at Henlow.
30	Messerschmitt Bf110G-4	No. 730037.
31	Junkers Ju88G-6 623192	
32	Junkers Ju88G-6	Crashed 15.10.45.
33	Junkers Ju88G	At Fighter Interception Development Unit.
34	Messerschmitt Bf110G	
35	Junkers Ju188A	Shipped to U.S.A.
41	Junkers Ju88G	
42	Siebel Si204D	
43	Heinkel He219A-7	
44	Heinkel He219A-7	
45	Junkers Ju188A	
46	Siebel Si204D	
47	Junkers Ju88	

48	Junkers Ju88G-7 622838	German marking 3C.
49	Siebel Si204D	
50	Messerschmitt Me262 111980	Shipped to South Africa.
51	Messerschmitt Me262 112372	Serial VK893.
52	Blohm & Voss BV138B-1	Held at Felixstowe.
53	Bucker Bu180	Trainer type.
55	Siebel Si204D	
56	Siebel Si204D	German marking BU+AP.
57	Junkers Ju290A-3	German marking BK+.
58	Heinkel He162A 120021	Serial VH526.
59	Heinkel He162A 120076	Serial VH523. To Canada.
60	Heinkel He162 120074	
61	Heinkel He162A-2 120072	Crashed at Aldershot 9.11.45.
62	Heinkel He162A-2 120086	Shipped to Canada 1946.
63	Heinkel He162A	Held in Imperial War Museum.
64	Heinkel He162A	Serial VN153.
65	Heinkel He162A	Serial VH513.
66	Heinkel He162A	Found at Leck.
67	Heinkel He162A	Found at Leck.
68	Heinkel He162A	
70	Blohm & Voss BV138B	No. 310081.
72	Messerschmitt Me410A	Held at Cosford.
73	Messerschmitt Me410	
75	Focke Wulf FW190A-8 733682	At the Imperial War Museum.
76	Messerschmitt Bf108	
77	Junkers Ju88A	
79	Messerschmitt Me262	
80	Arado Ar234B	
81	Messerschmitt Me262A 500210	Serial VH519. Shipped to Australia.
83	Junkers Ju388K	German marking PE+IP.
84	Messerschmitt Bf108B	
85	Messerschmitt Bf110G	
87	Messerschmitt Bf108	
89	Messerschmitt Bf108	
90	Fieseler Fi156C Storch	
92	Arado Ar196	Serial VM748.
94	Focke Wulf FW200C	German marking GC+AF.
95	Focke Wulf FW200C	
96	Focke Wulf FW200C	
99	Fieseler Fi156C-3 Storch	Shipped to South Africa.
100	Fieseler Fi156C Storch	
101	Fieseler Fi156C Storch	Serial VP546. No. 475061.
102	Junkers Ju52/3M	Scrapped 1948.
103	Junkers Ju52/3M	Scrapped 1948.
104	Junkers Ju52/3M	Ex-D-AUAV.
106	Dornier Do217M 6577	German marking U5+HK.
107	Dornier Do217M 56158	Delivered to Stanmore.
108	Junkers Ju188A 230776	
109	Junkers Ju352A	Serial VP550
110	Junkers Ju352	
111	Focke Wulf FW190F-8	
112	Junkers Ju88A-6	
113	Junkers Ju188	Serial VN143. German marking IH..GT.
114	Dornier Do24T 1135	
117	Focke Wulf FW58	German marking TE+8K.
118	Dornier Do24T	
119	Siebel Si104A	
120	Arado Ar96B	Delivered to Woodley.

Air Min No.	*Aircraft Type and Number (where known)*	*Remarks*
121	Arado Ar96B	
122	Bucker Bu181C-3	
123	Arado Ar96B	Delivered to Woodley.
200-206	Messerschmitt Me163	
209	Messerschmitt Me163	
210	Messerschmitt Me163	To Deutsches Museum, Munich, 1964.
211-213	Messerschmitt Me163B	
214	Messerschmitt Me163B-1	
215	Messerschmitt Me163B	To Institute of Technology, Cranwell.
216	Messerschmitt Me163	
217	Messerschmitt Me163-1	Held at Colerne. No. 191904.
218-219	Messerschmitt Me163-1	
220-222	Messerschmitt Me163B	
223	Dornier Do335A	Crashed 18.1.46.
224	Savoia-Marchetti S.M.95	
225	Dornier Do335A-12	Crash at Cove, Hants.
226	Arado Ar234B	
227	Arado Ar234B	Held by No. 6 Maintenance Unit.
228	Arado Ar234B-2	Held by No. 6 Maintenance Unit.
229	Arado Ar234B	Held by No. 6 Maintenance Unit.
230	Focke Wulf FW190	
231	Junkers Ju88G-1 712273	Serial TP190. German marking 4R+UR.

ABBREVIATIONS

Abbreviation	*Explanation*
A.A.	Anti-aircraft gunfire
A.A.C.	Army Air Corps
A.A.C.U.	Anti-aircraft Co-operation Unit
A.A.E.E.	Aircraft & Armament Experimental Establishment
A.M.C.	Aircraft Manufacturing Company
A.M.Spec.	Air Ministry Specification
A.O.P.	Air Observation Post
A.S.	Armstrong Siddeley
A.T.C.	Air Training Corps
A.W.	Armstrong Whitworth
A.W.A.	Armstrong Whitworth Aircraft
B.A.C.	British Aircraft Corporation
B.O.A.C.	British Overseas Airways Corporation
B.P.	Boulton Paul
Conv.	Converted
C.O.W.	Coventry Ordnance Works
D.H.	de Havilland
E.A.T.S.	Empire Air Training Scheme
E.E.Co.	English Electric Company
H.F.	Henry Farman
H.S.	Hawker Siddeley
I.A.F.	Indian Air Force
M.A.E.E.	Marine Aircraft Experimental Establishment
M.E.	Middle East
M.F.	Maurice Farman
M.D.A.P.	Mutual Defence Aid Pact
M.O.A.	Ministry of Aviation
M.O.S.	Ministry of Supply
M.S.	Morane Saulnier
O.T.U.	Operational Training Unit
R.A.A.F.	Royal Australian Air Force
R.A.N.	Royal Australian Navy
R.A.T.G.	Rhodesian Air Training Group
R.C.A.F.	Royal Canadian Air Force
R.Cey.A.F.	Royal Ceylonese Air Force
R.C.N.	Royal Canadian Navy
R.F.C.	Royal Flying Corps
R.I.A.F.	Royal Indian Air Force
R.M.A.F.	Royal Malayan Air Force
R.N.A.S.	Royal Naval Air Service
R.Neth.A.F.	Royal Netherlands Air Force
R.N.Z.A.F.	Royal New Zealand Air Force
R.R.A.F.	Royal Rhodesian Air Force
R.R.E.	Royal Radar Establishment
R.S.A.F.	Royal Swedish Air Force
S.A.A.F.	South African Air Force
S. & H.	Short & Harland
S.R.A.F.	Southern Rhodesian Air Force
U.S.	United States
U S.M.C.	United States Marine Corps
V I.P.	Very Important Person standard